On stage

under the advisory editorship of J. Jeffery Auer

On Stage: *a history of theatre* second edition

Vera Mowry Roberts Hunter college of the city university of new york

Harper & Row, publishers New york, evanston, san francisco, london

Sponsoring Editor: Voras D. Meeks
Project Editor: Duncan R. Hazard
Designer: Gayle Jaeger
Production Supervisor: Stefania J. Taflinska

**On Stage: A History of Theatre,
Second Edition**

Library of Congress Cataloging in
Publication Data

Roberts, Vera Mowry.
    On stage: a history of theatre.

    Bibliography: p.
    1. Theatre—History. I. Title.
PN2101.R55 1974   792'.09   73-9285
ISBN 0-06-045499-7

STILL FOR CHRISTOPHER
Who by this time has discovered a wonderful
world of his own

Contents

Preface

It goes without saying that in the course of ten years' time much has happened to the world of theatre, to one's knowledge about that world, and to one's perspective on both world and knowledge. The end of a decade is as good a time as any to reassess and revise.

Accordingly, the original work which bears this title has undergone minute scrutiny and reconsideration. Some chapters have been rewritten; in others there are only minor changes. The chronicle, of course, has been brought up to date and new illustrations added. In a few instances, illustrations from the old edition have been dropped or changed, for what seem like good reasons, and some rearrangement has been made. The Play List and Study Problems have been expanded, and some new terms have been added to the Glossary.

As in the previous edition, no attempt has been made here to include exhaustive lists of plays and playwrights, or of theatres, designers, or actors. Concentration—then and now—has been on those materials and persons which marked a change in, or trend of, or significant contribution to the general stream of theatre history. Thus, there is little time or space expended on theatre in South America, in Africa, and in parts of Europe and Asia at times when theatre there had no influence on the general stream of theatre history.

During the past decade, many people have kindly told me that *On Stage* has been valuable to them. I trust that the new edition will prove more valuable, and that its clarifications will demonstrate even more strongly the seamless continuity of past and present, and the strength of theatre studies in helping to develop man's image of himself and of his world.

To the list of acknowledgments in the first edition and to those given with the illustrations, I would like to add the names of J. Christopher Roberts, Charles Gattnig, Fritz A. Kracht, Ellen Kaufman, Joel Zuker, and the host of students who have continually enlarged my perceptions and my understanding.

VERA MOWRY ROBERTS

Preface to the first edition

While this book was in the making, a scholarly acquaintance of mine expressed a polite interest.

"A book on theatre, eh? Garrick's perhaps?" (Garrick was an eighteenth-century actor and playright.) "Or is it on arena staging?" He knew that I had been one of a small group which, some years ago, founded Arena Stage in the nation's capital.

"No, the whole thing," I said.

"From the Greeks to Broadway?" He was incredulous.

"From before the Greeks," I replied firmly. But I was beginning to wonder. Was I about to produce another digest, another condensation—modern shortcuts which I abhor? "Read the play itself; read the whole book," I had always told my students who were given to plot outlines and condensed books. But my misgivings, fortunately, gave way to certainty. It is not reasonable to suppose that even the most devoted of college students would cover, for himself, all the original materials that went into the making of this book.

I am aware that specialists will deplore the necessary brevity of particular treatments, and I am aware that in trying to include all aspects of theatre I may be accused of superficiality in some. But I am convinced that any study of so significant a part of our cultural history must be placed in historical and social perspective if an initial understanding and appreciation is to be gained. The production of a play is not an isolated event. It grows out of the author's orientation to his world and is influenced by his potential audience and its tastes in subject matter and production styles. The author is bound by the theatrical means at his disposal. All of these aspects of theatre must be taken into account.

The plan of this book is the result of several years of study and teaching in the history of theatre. I know this plan will work. It allows for comparisons from period to period; it brings an almost incredible welter of information into comprehensible form. Each chapter considers the place of theatre in the social framework of its age, the producers, actors, and audience; the plays themselves; the location and design of the playhouse; the settings, including lighting and music; the costumes and makeup; and the actors and acting styles of the age. At the end of each chapter is a summary of the unique contributions to theatre in the period thus covered. However, the plan is predicated on the proposition that this presentation is a basic study guide for further exploration. It is assumed that the individual teacher, and the individual student, will find inspiration and the basic materials for additional study in the plays themselves and in other source works. No one can know theatre in any period without knowledge of the plays that were being performed, so appropriate lists are included. Neither can one's knowledge be adequate without some conception of how they were done and what it meant to the people who did them as well as to those who saw them. As a guide to further study, I have appended a play list and bibliography, as well as a suggested guide to further thought and inquiry.

Perhaps more than any other area of specialization, theatre avoids the worst connotations of the term and, by its very nature, takes the student into many areas of human knowledge—literature, art, music, politics, economics, philosophy, science, invention—exploring practically all of man's activities and ideas. The study of theatre can be and ideally *is* the most "liberalizing" of all the liberal arts. Certainly it is a most rewarding field of study for those insatiable people who desire to know "all about everything."

It would be a manifest error to contend that this is all that can be said about the history of theatre. Yet I submit that my experiences as both teacher and student, and my fairly extensive labors in many fields of theatrical activity, have convinced me that this is a workable presentation. I trust that those who use the book will likewise find it so.

Acknowledgments

No one writes of theatre history these days without being greatly indebted to the many scholars who have done significant research in the field, and I hereby make grateful acknowledgment to these many people. In the matter of illustrations, my debt is more specific. Some of the pictures I have used are from those I have collected through the years. The others come from sources which are acknowledged in their captions; each has my sincere thanks. For materials which have been published elsewhere, I am grateful to the following publishers for permission to use them in this book: Harvard University Press (Vitruvius, *The Ten Books of Architecture*, translated by Morris Hicky Freeman, 1914); The University of Chicago Press (Flickinger, *The Greek Theatre and Its Drama*, 1934); Coward-McCann, Inc. (Sayler, *Inside the Moscow Art Theatre*, 1925); David McKay Co., Inc. (Cheney, *The Theatre*, 1935), Edizione Radio Italiana, Torino (Bacchelli and Longhi, *Teatro e immagini del Settecento Italiano*, 1954); Harcourt, Brace & Company (Macgowan and Jones, *Continental Stagecraft*, 1922); and Skira International, Switzerland. Finally, I must mention the following persons as having been particularly helpful in the long and arduous task of finding the right illustrations: Helen D. Willard, Harvard Theatre Collection; Richard Leacroft, Leicester, England; Mary Isabel Fry, Henry E. Huntington Library and Art Gallery; Robert Treat Paine, Jr., Museum of Fine Arts, Boston; Prof. Dr. Jericke, Goethe-Nationalmuseum, Weimar, Germany; Dr. Vriesen, Theatermuseum, Munich, Germany; Prof. Alois Nagler, Yale University; Messrs. Tangen and Messing, Museum of Modern Art; George Freedley, Curator, Theatre Collection, New York Public Library; George M. Reid, Cleveland Museum of Art; Prof. Glenn Hughes, University of Washington; Prof. Paul Baker, Baylor University; Victor Jackson, New York City; Herbert B. Kennedy, Jr., Stanford University; and Mr. and Mrs. Warner Schreiner, New York City.

VERA MOWRY ROBERTS

1 The ever-present beginnings

Theatre as an art form—existing autonomously and for its own sake—is generally conceded in Western culture to have begun with the Greeks, as did so many other components of the Western tradition. A part of the reason for this generally accepted idea lies in the fact that it is from ancient Greece that we inherit the first written-down playscripts, whose influence on later theatre practice has been incalculable. But to accede entirely to this concept is to perpetuate a misconception that has for too long plagued the theatre historian: that the value (if not indeed the very existence) of theatre is dependent upon the plays themselves. Actually, in the complex art of theatre, the script is but one of the elements—albeit the most enduring in time. The fundamental act of theatre occurs whenever a player or impersonator communicates directly, by act and word, to an audience or observers, who are active participants in the communication. Various degrees of sophistication and various kinds of accoutrements may also be present in the theatrical experience: costumes for the players, comfortable accommodations for the audience, carefully formulated and unchanging scripts, specially designed settings, music, dance, unique lighting. But all of these are merely *additions* to the essential entity—that primal communion of player and audience.

It is for this reason that consideration of the history of theatre must start at a point in time long before the Greeks—in the primitive societies which pre-dated the splendor of Periclean Athens. It is in these societies that the theatrical elements were born and grew; the glory that was Greece had its antecedents in prehistory. It is perfectly true that theatre in human society has been a part of man's community existence since long before recorded history. From the dawn of time to the present moment, dramatic presentations have been concerned with inspiration. education, and entertainment—with the worship and propitiation of the gods, with the initiation and indoctrination of the young, and with thought-provoking or laughter-impelling ideas and situations. There is hardly a facet of man's existence which has not been touched by or absorbed in theatre.

Since its primitive beginnings, theatre has assumed many shapes and forms. Many people today are inclined to think of theatre in terms of Broadway openings and luxurious productions. But this narrow refinement is the end product of a long and complicated development. Just as all of man's other social institutions can be traced to primitive beginnings, so too can theatre. Even the very new technique of using psychodrama in the treatment of mental illness is but a highly sophisticated application of one principle of primitive dance-drama. To trace the development of theatre from root to flower can enrich our understanding and appreciation of what is perhaps the oldest art form. It can show us further that even today's* theatre permits no narrow definition, but has a breadth of influence and application which is truly astonishing.

Anyone who will observe a child's birth, growth, and development may see in the process a microcosm of the development of man. He may watch the slow process wherein the mind distinguishes between fact and fantasy, the flowering of imagination and its subsequent discipline, the dawn of social consciousness. If he is particularly interested in theatre, he sees its beginnings in the imitative propensity which is natural to all children, that faculty through which the child learns so much of the world around him. He watches the child assume myriad characters and act out innumerable life situations: the little girl plays mother, schoolteacher, nurse; the little boy plays father, doctor, cowboy. Upon occasion children even play dog, cat, tree, or bullfighter, creating situations and dialogue as the play progresses. Francis Fergusson, the twentieth-century critic, calls this propensity "the histrionic sensibility: the mimetic perception of action" and says that it is "a basic, or primary, or primitive virtue of the human mind."

It is easy, therefore, to see in the development of the child an analogy to the race of man, and to observe the beginnings of theatre in the imitative faculty of primitive man, who used his skill to show his fellow-tribesmen how he made the bow they so much admired, how he overcame the wily bear whose meat they enjoyed, how he obtained the scalp that dangled from his belt.

The theatre historian is fortunate in the uneven development of civilization, for he does not have to depend utterly upon speculation concerning prehistoric man. Within recorded history civilized man has come into contact with primitive man in practically all stages of development and has noted his characteristics and his activities. Human beings in remote areas of the world, who have long been the subject of study by ethnologists and anthropologists, have furnished us with some idea of the progressive growth of social institutions, including theatre. So we can imagine the steps which led in remote ages to the sudden flowering of the great age of classic Greek theatre, where, we generally contend, Western drama originated.

Necessity, magic, and pleasure

The rudiments of theatre seem to have developed in primitive society for three basic reasons: (1) the need to supplement the spoken language, (2) the need to insure and to increase food supply, and (3) the need to insure victory over human foes. The reasons could hardly be more fundamental. Other motivations for primitive drama were initiation rites and pleasure plays.

What chiefly distinguishes man from his fellow-animals is his power to articulate speech. In the very early eras of communication, however, even this power was not sufficiently developed to transmit from person to person all that was thought or desired. Even today, it has been observed that among the Arapaho Indians of the Plains and in some of the pygmy tribes of Africa language is in such a low state of development that talk is almost impossible in the dark, since communication relies so heavily on gesture. No doubt prehistoric man, impelled to explain or describe or warn his fellow-tribesmen, found the language at his command inadequate and supplemented the spoken word with appropriate gestures. Thus theatre, that unique combination of word and action, was born. Today, people who "talk with their hands" are harking back to these early beginnings.

One step beyond this basic use of the histrionic sensibility leads to the realm of magic, which Sir James Fraser (in his seminal study on magic and religion, *The Golden Bough*) defines as "direct control of natural phenomena by incantation and ritual." In all societies everywhere, he points out, magic seems to have preceded religion, which he defines as "a belief in powers higher than man and an attempt to propitiate or please them." Practical necessity tends always to precede abstraction.

In primitive tribes the chief activity is getting food. Most of the primitive theatricals, observed and supposed, are dedicated to this practical purpose. An example is the marathon Buffalo Dance of the Mandan Indians of North America, which may go on for weeks without stopping until a buffalo herd is sighted. Another example is the Sun

BUFFALO DANCE OF THE MANDAN INDIANS
Charles Bodmer's painting shows a dance designed to insure the food supply of a hunting tribe. The dancers wearing buffalo heads represent the quarry, others the hunters. As in all similar primitive rituals, the object of the performance is to insure a successful hunt. (The American Museum of National History)

Dance of the Plains Indians, which recognizes the importance of sunshine for plant growth. The Cherokees, too, observed a seasonal succession of dance-dramas celebrating the growth and maturation of corn, their staple food.

Sympathetic magic was also invoked in the activities of the primitive tribes other than food-getting.

Ritual dramas were presented as prelude or postlude to battles with other tribes. Much publicized by the movies and television, the typical firelit war dance has the dual purpose of securing the favor of the gods, and of exciting the warriors to a pitch of enthusiasm which might insure victory in the coming fight. Less publicized is another type of war dance, like that of the Sea Dyaks of Borneo. This dance is a very dramatic and elaborate presentation which enacts not only the motive for the coming battle, but also the departure of the warriors, the ambuscades, the surprise attack, the combat, the victory, the homecoming, the mourning of the dead, and the commemoration of their bravery. Here, indeed, is a complete and unified drama.

From the child's "Cowboy and Indians" to Amos 'n Andy's "Mystic Knights of the Sea" and the Ancient Order of the Scottish Rite, man creates drama. Circumcision, first communion, Bar Mitzvah, initiations of all sorts, have kinship with the various initiation exercises observed in primitive tribes. All imply a death to the old life, birth into a new life, education in its practices, and a pledge to follow them. All are accompanied by ceremonies which often involve special costumes, special settings, ritualized texts, prescribed actions, and sometimes music—in other words, the attributes of the drama. Practically everyone is acquainted with this manifestation of the drama, and to primitive man it was a most important function; by it the boys of the tribe were transformed into men, and the continuity of community life was insured.

Just as children seem often to "play pretend just for fun," so primitive man has been seen to engage in what seem to be purely pleasure plays. The Canoe Dance of the Australian natives seems to be a play of this nature, as does the Baboon Dance of the African Bushmen. And certainly among the Omaha Indians, in whose vocabulary the same word means "to love" and "to dance," the love dances seem to be engaged in for purely pleasurable purposes. It is true, of course, that pleasure plays are in the minority when counted with the plays of purpose, but this fact can be explained by the greater amount of time early man necessarily spent in purposeful activity.

Drama a community activity

In the drama of primitive peoples the production was a group effort. Depending upon the type and purpose of the play, the participants were the whole tribe (excepting, usually, the women, who were considered "unclean" and hence unfit to communicate with the gods), the warriors alone, the medicine man alone, a specially designated clan or clans, or various combinations of these. Where women participated, they most frequently supplied the musical accompaniment, though sometimes they were permitted to be actors (such as the Corn Maidens in the Great Serpent Play of the Hopi Indians of

northern Arizona), and there is at least one play on record, from Samoa, where women were the only participants.

Audiences generally included all those members of the tribe who were not participants in the play, but frequently the audience was limited to men, and sometimes to a very select group of the initiate. However the plays were produced, acted, or viewed in primitive society, they were an integral part of group activity, taken with great seriousness and sometimes with great enjoyment by every member of the social group.

Religious origins of dance-drama

Primitive magic rites were engaged in not only to relate what had passed, but to dominate what was to come. The observed order of nature, the round of the seasons, the battle between winter and summer, the necessity to perpetuate for coming generations whatever seeming controls had been developed, led to the rise of myths and thence to religious observances, that attempt to please and/or propitiate supernatural powers.

Religion has everywhere been the source of the drama, no less with primitive man than with the ancient Greeks or the medieval mystery players. It is not difficult for us to trace what must have happened. In very early times, when the social group was exceedingly small, the oldest and wisest of the group was looked upon with great reverence and respect by the other members, for he knew from experience the best hunting grounds, the deepest water holes, the driest caves. He was the helper and protector of the family group. When he died, the family group needed to feel that he was still watching over them and protecting them. They observed that death meant the cessation of movement, the passage of something invis-

APACHE CROWN DANCE
Allen Houser, Apache artist, paints the sacred Gan Dance in which masked dancers personify the Mountain Spirits as part of a ceremony to promote the welfare of girls who have just reached puberty and to pray for good crops for the whole community. (Courtesy of the Denver Art Museum, Denver, Colorado)

ible (for the body as they had known it was still there); therefore, they conceived an idea of spirit as movement. Everything that moved was given personality—animals, trees, and plants, though the latter two were moved only by the wind. Early man reasoned that if spirit was everywhere in the world about him, then the spirit of his deceased beloved kinsman must still be about as well. So arose ancestor worship, universally an early form of religion. So, too, nature worship began, i.e., the propitiation of the spirits of natural phenomena. Somewhere along the line, it was conceived that the spirits of men and of animals were interchangeable, and thus arose the gamut of totem cults.

NAVAJO MEDICINAL DRAMA AND INITIATION
In this detail from a Navajo group at The
American Museum of Natural History, a
masked man representing a god is exorcising
the evil spirits from a patient. To the right,
a boy is being initiated by a goddess who is
whipping him with yucca leaves. Close by
stands the masked figure of the Talking God
ready to sprinkle the youth with cornmeal to
signify his holy condition. (The American
Museum of Natural History)

AZTEC TEMPLE COMPLEX AT TENOCHTITLAN
This is a reconstruction by Ignacio Marquina
from descriptions by Spanish conquerors
and remaining Aztec monuments in Mexico.
Its grandeur and complexity are some indication of the degree of culture achieved by
the Aztecs. The decorated platform in the
center of the picture is such as might have
been used for dramatic presentations. (The
American Museum of Natural History)

Rites to solicit the aid of the great and
wise of past times, ceremonies to propitiate
natural forces, functions to honor the tribal
totem—each developed as the spirit world
grew. It has already been remarked that war
dances were performed at least partly to win
the favor of the spirits, and the various rain
dances and sun dances were aimed at controlling these natural elements through sympathetic magic. Rainmakers were important
members of aboriginal societies. The beating
together of stones to simulate thunder, the
waving of forked sticks to represent lightning, the scattering of quartz crystals to represent the desired rain—all have appeared in
the rain dances to show the spirits what the

supplicants desired and needed. The races of
men who cherished totems honored the symbol with ceremonies of propitiation so that
the totem animal, and hence the tribe, might
flourish, or so that, in cases where the totem
animal was the main food supply, there
might be plentiful numbers to fulfill the
tribal needs. Some of the primitive love
dances have the actors in animal or bird costume as an inducement to the animal or bird
so represented to propagate and flourish.

Nature-rites (aimed primarily at insuring
the food supply) seem everywhere of primal
importance in primitive societies. The extension of the spirit world and its inclusion of
the great and wise of past times, led to the

DAKOTA SUN DANCE
A painting by Short Bull, Chief of the Ogala Dakota Sioux tribe, illustrates the circular form maintained in the vegetation ritual performance depicted. Here the object is to call down the power of the sun to aid in making the crops grow and insuring the food supply. The circle in the center represents the windbreak made of fresh green cottonwood boughs forming a circular enclosure within which the ceremonies are held. The figures within the circle are represented as performing the famous torture feature of the sun dance in which devotees are suspended by cords passing through their skin. The camp of the assembled people is indicated by the tepees with their typical tribal decorations. (The American Museum of Natural History)

development of myth-cults. The change from nature-rite to myth-cult had significant reverberations for the future development of theatre, for it led to the portrayal by certain players of the individual king, hero, or god celebrated in the myth, and *impersonation* —the basic function of the actor as distinct from the ritual priest—was born.

Rituals sacred and inflexible

In all the early ceremonies, dance, music, and poetry were combined. The performance was generally called a dance even where there was a great deal of speaking. As rituals developed, their form became fixed, and not the slightest variation was permitted from

WAR DANCE OF THE APACHES
This drawing by George Catlin shows the
Apaches preparing for a war against the
Navajos. It is typical of the round dances
found in all primitive societies. The performers, armed with spear and shield, encircle the giant spear in the center to transfer its power to themselves. The audience
stands round about on all sides. Here is one
of the earliest forms of arena staging. (The
American Museum of Natural History)

performance to performance. Though there
was no written language, the spoken word
was sacred, and the plays were passed on
from generation to generation by word of
mouth. It is generally true that proficiency
in these ceremonies became a part of the initiation exercises of all primitive peoples.

The materials of the plays came from
the daily lives of the people, just as the "let's
pretend" games of modern children are derived from their experience. A ceremonial
war dance originated in a particular happening at a specific time; then, through repetition, was generalized to symbolize all experience of this type as universally as the tribe
could conceive. So meticulous was early man

in the observance of a fixed ceremony that the slightest deviation was thought to portend disaster, and the culprit was, at least reportedly, sometimes put to death. It is said that on the island of Gaua in the New Hebrides the old men used to stand by with bows and arrows to shoot at any performer who made a mistake.

Comic elements introduced

Since their plays were so intimately bound up with significant matters, primitive peoples had a drama which was almost always serious in tone and intent. Comic elements arrived late, but arrive they did. Animal impersonations are inherently comic, and the slightest exaggeration on the part of the impersonator would no doubt provoke laughter in the audience. We shall see that comedy was insinuated into the serious church drama of the Middle Ages; just so it must have entered the serious ceremonials of primitive man. The development of this tendency seems apparent in the burlesques of more serious hunting rites of some Australian natives, such as the Rock Wallaby Hunt where the hunter consistently misses his quarry and is roundly abused by his companions. The natives of the Philippines have such a comic play, in which a searcher for honey suffers various indignities that are comic in the extreme. And so it goes. Man laughs, and as he becomes more at ease in his environment—or as he needs to find relief from a harsh environment—he finds things at which to laugh. When the environment fails to provide material, man invents it. In addition, as religious ceremonies begin to lose their deep significance, they tend more and more to metamorphose into the comic. We know what happened to the Feast of Fools in the medieval church; primitive man no doubt had his own Feast of Fools.

Primitive man was thus both inventive and versatile in the creation of dramatic ceremonies. Transcriptions which have been made of some of the Polynesian songs and the Iroquois chants show a high order of poetic composition, and we can only suppose that the lack of a written language has prevented us in many instances from appreciating much of this creative ability. The following translation of a portion of a Navajo ceremony will illustrate the high poetic value of much of primitive dance-drama:

In Kininaekai
In the house made of dawn
Oh, Talking God!
His feet, my feet restore.
His limbs, my limbs restore.
His body, my body restore.
His mind, my mind restore.
His voice, my voice restore.
His plumes, my plumes restore.
With beauty before him, with beauty
   before me,
With beauty behind him, with beauty
   behind me,
With beauty around him, with beauty
   around me,
With pollen beautiful in his voice,
   with pollen beautiful in my voice,
It is finished in beauty.
It is finished in beauty.
WASHINGTON MATTHEWS, TRANS.
Navajo Myths, Prayers, and Songs

Playing areas improvised

It is obvious that with a nomadic tribe of hunters there could be no fixed and designated playhouse or even a playing area. The ceremonials were held wherever the tribe encamped. Often this playing space was no more than an open area in the center of the camp. Sometimes for special initiation rites,

a particular location was arranged outside the camp proper. The Hopi Indians, for instance, had an elaborate arrangement for their drama of the Great Serpent, held during the March moon. They erected six or seven *kivas* (ceremonial chambers), each identically arranged, and in each of which was given the entire drama of six acts, the actors moving from the first to the second, and so on, as they completed each act. This arrangement, of course, called for a company of players for each act.

The Aztecs were the first people known to have a rudimentary permanent theatre, but they could hardly be called primitive. They evidently set up permanent platforms in the town market place, sometimes of wood, sometimes of stone and variously decorated, upon which were presented their dramatic performances. These platforms were always of generous size, and the audience stood around them to watch the shows.

Rudimentary settings developed

Primitive dance-dramas were almost always presented in what we today call arena staging. The oldest form of dance-drama is the round. In times and places where the entire tribe participated in the performance, the form was that of the round. When only some participated while some watched, as in the

Dakota Sun Dance or the Apache War Dance, the form was still circular. Most often the center of the circle held either a person or an object—a setting in other words. A Paleolithic wall painting from Cogul in Spain shows a group of nine women dancing around the figure of a man. A fire in the center of the ring, a pit, or a post were customary props. The principle of these ceremonies was the same everywhere: the participants aimed to possess the qualities (usually life giving) of the person or thing encircled. Supposedly, purification comes from fire, the fertility of Mother Earth from the pit, and the strength of growing things from the post or its equivalent. A living tree, stacks of sugar cane, bunches of fruit, bags of rice, a stack of spears, even a beribboned maypole can be the central object. The dancers who revolve around the pole may carry flowers, fruit, branches of trees, spears, or colored ribbons to identify themselves with the object of the dance. Thus, almost universally, some idea of form and setting was apparent from the first.

Sometimes these rudimentary settings were complicated and fairly elaborate. In an initiation ceremony of New Guinea, the Duk-Duk and his wife first appear from the sea, dancing on a raft, then they land on the beach where they continue the ritual. In one of their hunting dances the Indians of New Spain choose a large, smooth stretch of ground for a stage, and erect poles with huge pieces of bark, usually painted with totemic designs, fastened between them. At the back and at each side of the stage huge fires serve as footlights. In a large semicircle in front sit the women, who pound upon rolled opossum rugs and beat boomerangs together to form the orchestral accompaniment.

In one of the Australian initiation dramas, a large piece of ground is cleared and laid out with banks of dirt and brakes of bushes to form acting areas in which the

PRIMITIVE MASKS
The mask shown above, made and worn by the Indians of the Northwest Coast, is intricately carved and articulated. When fully closed it represents a fish; with top and bottom flaps open, it becomes a bird; with all flaps open, it represents a human face. The masks opposite are worn by men of the Fly River tribes in Papua, who assume the character of oracles in their initiation ceremony, taboo to women. Each man makes his own mask of tapa cloth stretched over a frame. Its height indicates the tribal position of the man wearing it. (The American Museum of Natural History)

women dance, the men perform, and the novices participate. For the rain dance of the Dieri tribe a special lodge is built which, at the climax of the presentation, is destroyed by certain of the participants who knock it down with their heads to signify the piercing of the clouds by rain. In the drama of the Great Serpent, mentioned above, the Hopis light each *kiva* with a fire, at which is stationed a prop man who smothers the fire at appropriate intervals to cause a blackout while the scenes and actors shift. The prop men also use blocks of clay into which corn-

stalks are set and painted drops having circular holes through which are thrust representations of the serpents which dance by virtue of a behind-the-scenes operator. In some of the North American Indian ceremonials elaborate sand paintings are employed. These lend an effective picturesque quality to the performances.

Costumes universally in use

Though few of the primitive tribes had special theatres or settings, none ever lacked costume and makeup. Masks or their equivalent were universally used. Most interesting of these are the tortoiseshell masks of the Torres Straits and the immense basketwork headpieces of the Bismarck Archipelago. But whatever their materials, the masks almost without exception covered the entire head of the wearer and sometimes his shoulders and trunk as well. Sometimes the masks are recognizable abstractions of the animals or birds to be hunted, sometimes they are totemic symbols, and sometimes they seem to be no more than frightening caricatures. In all cases they function not only as a disguise, but also as an aid to the wearer in assuming the identity of the character he is impersonating.

In some hunting dramas, the participants don the heads and skins of animals, as do the Plains Crees, who entice a buffalo herd by assuming the disguises of a buffalo calf and of a wolf who pretends to attack the calf. Costume items frequently involve highly decorative use of feathers, quills, and the teeth and skins of animals. Performers may wear leg rattles of tortoiseshell, and use various hand props, such as spears, wands, and —in the Booger Dance of the Cherokees—a gourd representing a phallus. Body paint is often used; an interesting application of this technique has been observed among the Australian natives who memorialized their first contacts with white men in a dramatic play by simulating the appearance of the white men. They painted their faces a brownish white and their bodies red or blue, while they tied rushes onto their legs and covered their heads with imitation cabbage-tree hats.

Universally in these primitive dance-dramas, it is important that the performer lose his own identity and assume that of the character he is impersonating. Only thus can he project the qualities of his characterization to his audience. He must *be* what he is masked and costumed to represent. He is *possessed* by the spirit of the image. The Javanese dancer who puts on a horse effigy is fed with stalks of grain; the ancient Germanic tribesman assumes the spirit of an animal the moment he dons its skin.

Acting becomes an art

As the social organization of primitive tribes increased in complexity, the performance of ritual dramas ceased to be a function of the whole community and fell to the lot of special clans, a shaman, a medicine man, or a priest. These specialized performers were often highly trained and specially gifted. The Hopi Snake Dance, for instance, was performed by the Snake and Antelope clans, each consisting of ten highly trained men who performed for nine days.

Needless to say, the length of some of these performances made great demands on the actors, since stress was laid on correctness of action, speech, songs, and music. Endurance, if nothing else, was a prime requisite, and sometimes the participants had to undergo actual physical torture as part of the performance. Interestingly enough, among the Areoi of Polynesia and the natives of New Pomerania, groups of actors toured performances to other islands and villages. Such touring companies also existed among the Mayas of Yucatan, although here again, as with the Aztecs, their society could hardly be called primitive.

Summary

The beginnings of drama are everywhere in human activity. Primitive man dramatized, in deadly earnest, his major concerns—his success in his struggle to survive and his relationship to the spirit world. These concerns are still basic to drama, in highly diversified forms, no matter what the state of civilization. In acting out these concerns and thereby attempting to control his environment, primitive man assumed various characters with the help of costume and makeup, chiefly masks; he made use of special effects and settings of some sort; and he made music an almost universal accompaniment.

Comedy also appeared, though sparse and late. Man does not laugh at himself when he lives in fear. But as he becomes more at ease with his environment, he can—and does —laugh, a laughter which is the product of his developing objectivity about himself and his world.

In primitive drama, then, the serious mood predominates, but there are also some elements of comedy. There is also the religious emphasis which was to recur in succeeding periods, the costumes, and the special effects and settings which have almost universally been parts of theatrical production. Incantations and chants—the magic power of the spoken word—began in primitive times, and certainly the importance of The Word has had recurring emphasis through the ages. The assumption of a character other than his own by the primitive dancer-actor set him apart from his fellows and created the special art of the actor. Though the seamless and uncompartmentalized life of primitive man largely preceded the emergence of theatrical activities as a separate art form engaged in for its own sake (except perhaps for the few "pleasure plays" mentioned above), the essence of theatre evident in the communication between the actor and audience—their participation in a mutually rewarding experience—did exist in primitive dance-drama and many of the elements which would be important to theatre later were first made manifest.

The present age undoubtedly knows more now about pre-Greek societies than the Greeks themselves did, even though they were much nearer in time than we are to the great and ancient civilizations of Mesopotamia, Anatolia, Crete, and Egypt. Herodotus, the earliest of Greek historians whose work survives (it dates from about 434 B.C.), wrote primarily about the Persian Wars, but incidentally of the states which he presumably visited: Egypt, Scythia, Thrace, Lydia, Media, Assyria, Babylon—the principalities and powers of the lands surrounding the Nile, the Tigris and the Euphrates, and of Asia Minor. Much of his work is suspect by modern standards, but recent investigations have proved the existence of complex and unique civilizations in the Tigris-Euphrates Valley and in the Nile Valley prior to 3000 B.C. The Sumerian city-states of the former location were overwhelmed by successive waves of foreign conquest, each of which more or less effectively wiped out the preceding culture. But from the union of Upper and Lower Egypt in 3100 B.C., there existed in the Nile Valley a continuous and identifiable culture for more than 3000 years—the oldest continuous civilization in the Western world.

Poorly developed theatre

There exists no adequate explanation why some civilizations of an apparently high order do not develop a drama which combines great plays with great productions as the classic Greeks did. The ancient Hebrews, for instance, had no drama to speak of, though certainly dance was a part of their culture; some, however, have seen indications in the Song of Solomon and The Book of Job that these were intended for dramatic presentation. The ancient Peruvians and the Aztecs of Mexico, on the other hand, seem to have had a regular and impressive drama.

The Peruvians composed both tragedies and comedies to be played by noblemen and their sons before the court on festival occasions. The tragedies dealt with the splendor of former kings and heroes or commemorated military events of signal importance, while the comedies seem to have had for their subject matter things of domestic import or scenes of everyday life. The texts were evidently in blank verse. The Aztec scripts also seem to have been written in verse and comprise comedy as well as tragedy. As mentioned above, they were usually presented in a special kind of theatre, although sometimes they were given on the steps or terraces of temples by actors carefully trained by the priests.

What evidences of dramatic activity exist for the lands of Mesopotamia, Anatolia, and Crete seem to indicate semidramatic presentations firmly anchored to myth-cults or to fertility or seasonal themes. A New Year's Day play in Babylon is described as representing the suffering of the god Bel, who went to the underworld and returned after three days. Phrygia in Asia Minor celebrated the rites of Attis in pantomimic dances accompanied by recitative. And Theodore H. Gaster tells us, in his *Thespis: Ritual, Myth, and Drama in the Ancient Near East*, that similar presentations occurred among not only the Hittites, but also the Babylonians, the Hebrews, the Syrians, and the Egyptians.

Certainly the most germane consideration for our continuum is that of ancient Egypt, which is so intimately tied to the classic world from which we generally say our Western history began. It will be obvious, in the ensuing discussion, that at no time in ancient Egypt did dramatic activity divorce itself from myth-cult and religious observance. Nowhere and at no time did theatre become an autonomous art form.

EGYPTIAN TEMPLE
A model of the temple of Queen Hatshepsut, reconstructed as it was in 1480 B.C. In just such a temple as this it is believed that scenes of the Abydos Passion Play were presented in ancient Egypt. (The Metropolitan Museum of Art)

It is true, of course, that prehistoric Egyptians, as did all primitive people, danced. Among the earliest records of very ancient Egypt are ones which show dance-dramas similar to those of primitive societies. Women dancers accompanying a coffin, as depicted in an Old Kingdom tomb near Sakkara (2500 B.C.), throw their legs high in a step that might indicate life triumphing over death. A wall painting (1900 B.C.) from the Middle Kingdom shows three dancers doing a pantomime which is entitled "The Wind." Some Old Kingdom dance figures, adorned with grapevines, are swinging branches; others are shown with arms bent at the elbow, fingertips on shoulders, in representation of the cow-goddess with her horns. It may be supposed, then, that the early development of Egyptian dance-drama followed the same lines as elsewhere.

However, so far as Egyptologists can ascertain, the ancient Egyptians never developed a high order of drama and their only dramatic presentations were connected with religious observance. They were usually accompanied by grand processionals and festivals and often lasted several days. As in many later periods of the theatre, the pres-

EGYPTIAN DANCE AND MUSIC
This tomb-painting from Thebes shows musicians playing to accompany dancers. The musicians are the long-skirted figures, while the dancers wear short skirts.

entations were generally seasonal, following the inundation pattern of the Nile as did so many of the institutions of Egyptian life. Some presentations were evidently dependent upon the funeral rites of prominent citizens. At any rate, with one exception, there seem to have been no regulated, repeated performances of given plays such as we are accustomed to in many later periods of theatre.

First recorded drama

The oldest evidences of the drama in Egypt are the fifty-five so-called Pyramid Texts which date back to about 3000 B.C. These were written on the inside walls of tombs, mastabas, and pyramids and dealt with the resurrection of the entombed. They are supposed to be dramas because they incorporate stage directions and indications of characters

ANOTHER TOMB PAINTING OF DANCERS
From the Acropolis of Memphis at Sakkara, this painting depicts a group of professional dancers, hair weighted behind, performing to the clapping of two figures at the left.

speaking separate lines. It has been estimated that over a period of time about four thousand such texts were produced. They are presumed to be a development from even more ancient rites celebrating the return of spring as symbolic of the return of life after the winter solstice, a deeply rooted primitive nature rite.

Another type of ancient Egyptian drama was the Coronation Festival Play, which was evidently performed to celebrate the crowning of a new monarch. The earliest of these to be discovered is a Memphite drama of about 3100 B.C., which had the god Ptah as one of its characters and was performed in the capital of the First Dynasty. Another of these plays dates from the Middle Kingdom (about 2000 B.C.) and commemorates the coronation of Senroset I. If a ruler lived long enough to mark the thirtieth anniversary of his coronation, this jubilee occasion was marked by a special drama called a Heb Sed, which seems to have enacted the events of his long reign.

There is evidence that the priests occasionally presented a Medicinal Drama which celebrated their skill in the administration of medicine; it also memorialized the goddess Isis' cure of her child Horus from the bite of a scorpion by using herbs and magic. It is a pertinent speculation that these Medicinal Dramas were developments from the more primitive dances of the shaman or medicine man whose ritual was supposed to cure or prevent disease.

During the ascendency of the god Ptah, when Memphis was the leading city of ancient Egypt, a *Creation Drama* was evidently staged there periodically, from perhaps 3000 to 2000 B.C. But Memphis declined in importance, other gods gained stature over Ptah, and the Creation Drama disappeared.

The most interesting of these ancient plays is the Abydos Passion Play, which was evidently celebrated yearly from 2500 B.C. down to between 569 and 526 B.C. Our most accurate record of it comes from an actor, I-kher-nefert, who in 1868 B.C. wrote of his commission to produce the drama at Abydos and to play the leading role. The production involved a processional pageant, a series of dramatic scenes, and a triumphant festival. This elaborate production seems to have moved from place to place, culminating in the Temple of Osiris at Abydos. It detailed the suffering and death of Osiris, the passion of his sister-wife Isis, the birth of their son Horus, and the final resurrection of Osiris and his establishment as ruler of the Land of the Dead. It was essentially a fertility drama concerned with the annual inundation of the Nile.

All of these texts are serious in intent and presentation, and there is no evidence of any comical elements present in any of them. The ancient Egyptians took their drama seriously—of necessity, since it was so irrevocably linked to religious observance. The highly traditional and comparatively unchanging culture of the Egyptians precluded the development of theatre into a separate and identifiable art and pursuit.

Priesthood controls production

In ancient Egypt there seem to have been no playhouses or specialized playing areas. The Coronation Festival Plays, the Heb Seds, and the Pyramid Texts were played in the mortuary temples which accompanied the tombs of the kings. The Medicinal Dramas and the Passion Plays were done in the temples erected for the worship of the deities. All dramatic activities seem to have been under the direction of the priests, who were very powerful members of society. All presentations were evidently given by daylight. Characters were costumed in accordance with their roles, and where they were impersonating one of the animal-headed deities they wore head masks. Makeup was in an advanced stage of development in ancient Egypt, even for ordinary purposes, so it is reasonable to suppose that makeup was likewise used extensively in the dramatic presentations. Actors were generally recruited from the priesthood, though when large casts were needed, these were supplemented by chosen laymen.

Performances, even when dealing with mythological materials, tended to be as realistic as possible, and there is some evidence that in the long Abydos Passion Play the battle scenes were so realistic as to entail the actual combat and death-in-battle of some of the participants.

Although there is no actual evidence, it is supposed that all performances were in some

FUNERARY PAPYRUS
This papyrus from a tomb of the XXI Dynasty, Thebes, shows the costumes and the use of masks in ancient Egypt. (The Metropolitan Museum of Art, Rogers Fund, 1930)

way accompanied by music, for the ancient Egyptians were very fond of music and had a special deity, Bes, to preside over it.

Summary

Theatre in ancient Egypt, in common with many other institutions and practices of that society, was inextricably bound up with the cult of the dead. The Pyramid Texts bear a relationship to the more primitive cult of ancestor worship; the Medicinal Dramas are extensions of the feats of medicine men and shamans. Even the most truly dramatic presentation, the Abydos Passion Play, might be said to derive from plays of primitive nature worship. The most outstanding characteristic of Egyptian drama, the emphasis upon spectacle, derives from the primitive propensity for putting on a good show. This emphasis upon spectacle also indicates a characteristic which will continue for centuries to come.

If the drama of ancient Egypt marked any advance from the dance-drama of less civilized societies, it would seem to be on the basis of two characteristics. First, there seemed to be more dependence upon the spoken word, as evidenced by the Pyramid Texts and I-kher-nefert's record. And secondly, the extant references seem to indicate that myth-cults had almost completely supplanted sympathetic magic and nature-rites as the basis of dramatic activity.

The elements present in primitive dance-drama and in the drama of ancient Egypt recur again and again in later periods of theatre, most notably in the Greek period—our first acquaintance with real theatre.

It is obvious that the great triumvirate of Greek tragedy—Aeschylus, Sophocles, and Euripides—did not, like Minerva, spring full-armed from the head of Zeus, but were the end products of a long line of development. Several reputable scholars have pointed out that Egyptian culture was greatly admired by the Greeks, among other reasons for its religious development. Even Herodotus, a Greek historian living in the fifth century B.C., held that the Greek Dionysus was but a slightly disguised Egyptian Osiris, whose suffering, death, and resurrection made him the symbol of the renewal of life and the yearly round of the seasons. It has been suggested that the acceptance of the Egyptian deity and his "naturalization" in Greek legend brought ceremonies to Greece which, for the first time, can truly be called dramatic.

That is to say that in Greece alone, among all the preceding and contemporaneous cultures, ceremonies and rituals devised for nature-rites or myth-cults developed into the autonomous and unique art form of theatre. The Greeks produced dramatic literature which became the world's heritage, and created a store of criticism which influenced the course of theatre through successive ages. That this phenomenon occurred solely in Greece was due to the happy conjunction of social and intellectual forces that obtained in the Athenian city-state from just prior to the Persian War through the Macedonian conquest, or roughly from 550 to 300 B.C. The overriding ethos of that period is best expressed in the saying of Protagoras that "Man is the measure of all things." Every facet of human thought and expression, every area of natural phenomena, came under investigation and exploration—and that is why practically all areas of study in which we still engage originated with the Greeks. The investigative minds of the ancient Greeks discovered order in the universe, and traveled freely in many spheres of thought. This untrammeled exploration and experimentation—both abstract and concrete—led to a veritable explosion of knowledge and creative activity. In the area of our particular interest, what began as religious rite and ritual developed into a new thing under the sun—theatre *qua* theatre—although it never lost at least a nominal connection with religious festivals.

Festival origins of tragedy and comedy

Dionysus was the god of fertility whose powers applied especially to wine, the wealth of Greece. Four festivals were held in his honor during the year. The first of these was the Festival of Vintage, sometimes called the Country or Rural Dionysia; it was held in late December and early January. The second was the Festival of the Winepress, the Lenaea, held in late January and early February. The third was the Festival of Tasting, the Anthesteria, held in late February and early March. The fourth and last was the great Festival of Celebration, or the City Dionysia, held in late March and early April. Greek drama came to flower in this last festival.

The pattern of the Dionysiac feast is described by Aristophanes in *The Acharnians*; Aristophanes uses the peasant celebration as part of a comic action. He tells of a processional, led by the daughter of a peasant as a Canephorus bearing the sacrificial offering, followed by a slave bearing the phallus, symbol of fertility, who in turn is followed by the master of the house singing the usual spicy phallic song, while the mistress of the house watches from the rooftop. Here is the essence of all Dionysiac festivals—sacrifice, symbol, and song. Festivals involving more than one family were correspondingly elaborated, but these essentials were always present. In the earliest times the sacrifice was a human one; later a goat, an ox, or a bull, representative of the god, was substituted. This was a dedicated offering, without blemish, and the worshippers partook of the uncooked flesh to acquire the characteristics of the god. They pretended the animal was resurrected, sometimes immediately substituting the animal selected for the next festival's sacrifice, sometimes pretending that the sacrificed animal was actually drawing a plow. (In this latter case the sacrifice tended to be an ox, rather than a goat.) A statue of Dionysus was a part of the procession, or, later, a young man impersonated the god. Designated participants intoned a chant called a *dithyramb*, detailing the exploits of the god. In the god's honor, some of the participants were dressed as satyrs or goatmen, and some were attired to represent the dead, thus indicating that Dionysus was the lord of life and could resurrect the dead. After the sacrifice, there was dancing, singing, and much drinking of wine.

Aristotle tells us in his *Poetics* (360 B.C.):

Tragedy, indeed, originated from those
who led the dithyramb, but comedy
from those who sung the Phallic verses,
which even now in many cities remain
in use; and it gradually increased as
obvious improvements became known. And
tragedy, having experienced many changes,
rested when it had arrived at its proper
nature.

Sec. 1449a, ll. 10–15
THEODORE BUCKLEY TRANSLATION

Dithyramb and phallic song were at first extemporaneous, becoming conventional in the course of time. Participants at first were any who cared to join in the celebration, often the whole population of a village. Later, the performers were specialized, just as in the primitive dramas elsewhere. The cithara player, Arion, is credited with regularizing the dithyramb in song and dance. As time went on, its subject matter came to include not only the exploits of Dionysus, but those of other gods and heroes. Sometime near the middle of the sixth century B.C., a leader of a rural Icarian dithyrambic chorus, Thespis by name, is said to have instituted the revolutionary innovation of separating himself from the chorus by ascending the sacrificial table and posing questions which the chorus answered in song and dance. Thus dialogue was born, and from this early rite dramatic tragedy grew, though the dithyramb, in its purer form, also continued on a separate course. The innovation of dialogue was so popular that it developed despite the adverse criticism of many, including the lawgiver Solon who accused Thespis of telling lies.

Comedy, on the other hand, was the outgrowth of another part of the festival. At the time when specified participants were performing in the processional and sacrificial festivities, it became the custom for the young men about town to dress themselves in special costumes and to participate, quite unofficially, in the rites. The townspeople, who were spectators, engaged in badinage with these self-appointed performers, and the interchanges developed into a customary part of the celebration. This type of interchange grew from *komos* (a revel, or a band of revellers) into comedy, which originally used two choruses instead of the one used in tragedy; tragedy, in turn, is so named from *tragos* (goat) or *tragodia* (goat song), performed to honor the Dionysiac symbol.

The festival contests

In 534 B.C., the tyrant Pisistratus, whom the citizens of Athens had invested with power, brought the actor-director Thespis to Athens and instituted as a part of the City Dionysia the drama contests which remained a part of that celebration throughout the Golden Age of Greece. The play which Thespis presented won the first prize.

For more than two centuries the pattern of Attic drama remained fairly constant. Of the four great festivals of Dionysus, three included drama; only the Anthesteria had no plays. At the Country Dionysia in December and January, both tragedies and comedies were presented. In some cases the works of playwrights who later competed in the great City Dionysia were presented; in other cases these rural celebrations were graced with performances of plays and companies hitherto seen at the larger celebration. At the Lenaea both comedies and tragedies were presented, but the accent was on comedy; the attendant procession was not splendid but riotous. The Lenaea record for 419 and 418 B.C. at Athens shows that two trilogies of tragedies and five comedies were given. Earlier the comedies had numbered three.

The great festival of ancient Greece, the City Dionysia, took place in late March and early April, when Athens was crowded with foreign dignitaries, businessmen, and tourists. It lasted for five or six days, and even prisoners were released so that they might attend. It was the high point of the Attic year, the greatest of all the religious festivals. (It must be remembered that the production of plays in the Greek theatre remained a part of religious observance from first to last.) The festival began on the first day with a procession in which the figure of Dionysus was carried from his temple on the Acropolis to his grove where the sacrifice was offered. At nightfall, a procession returned the figure by torchlight to the theatre which was named in his honor, situated under the Acropolis. There it stood for the

succeeding days of the festival. The second day, and often the third, was taken up with a contest between dithyrambic choruses representing the various Attic tribes. On the third or fourth day the presentation of tragedies began. Three poets participated, each presenting three tragedies and a satyr play. These began at dawn and ended by noon on each of the three days. The afternoons were devoted to comedy; sometimes three were given at a festival, sometimes five. Some scholars have said that the six-day festival was characteristic of earlier times, with the third day devoted to five comedies and the last three to the tragedies and satyr plays. The five-day festival, pressured by the economies of the Peloponnesian War (431–404 B.C.), caused a change in schedule, with three tragedies, a satyr play, and a comedy being given on each of the last three days. At the end of the festival prizes were awarded to the best poet in each form—traditionally a goat for tragedy and a basket of figs and a bottle of wine for comedy, as well as varying sums of money appropriated by the state. It was for this theatre that Aeschylus, Sophocles, Euripides, and Aristophanes wrote.

Poets were permitted to compete as soon as they were citizens, at age twenty. Aeschylus presented his first play at twenty-five, Sophocles at twenty-eight, and Euripides at twenty-six. All poets submitted their plays to a public official (called the *archon*) who chose the plays to be presented and designated the leading actor for each. This actor was paid by the state, and in the days when the number of actors in each play rose to three, all three were paid by the state. All other expenses were borne by a citizen (called the *choregus*) who either volunteered or was drafted for the job. This first of all theatrical patrons was usually a wealthy resident who hired and paid the chorus and its leader, as well as any supporting actors necessary, and who bore all costs of production. Great competition arose among these citizen-patrons and it is reported that some of them were led into bankruptcy as a result of their prodigal spending. Often there were lavish productions which included not only refreshments for the entire audience of seventeen to twenty thousand people, but an extravagant party for the actors as well. As a reward for his participation, a winning patron had a tripod erected in his honor on the avenue leading to the theatre. Rivalry was destroyed about 308 B.C., when the functions of the patrons were designated to a public official known as the judge or *agonothetes*.

Provisions for awarding the prizes were elaborate. To select the judges one name from each of the ten Attic tribes was drawn from ten sealed jars. From the votes of these ten judges, five were drawn from a covered jar to decide the prize. Originally prizes were awarded only to participating poets and patrons, but by 446 B.C. prizes were also awarded to the outstanding tragic actors, and somewhat later to the outstanding comic actors. These prizes were always limited to the principal actor in each trilogy or comic play.

In the early days the playwright was frequently his own chief actor and director, as Aeschylus was. Sophocles is said to have refrained from taking leading male roles because of the lightness of his voice, although he won critical praise for his playing of women's parts, chiefly that of Nausicaa, and he always directed the plays that he had written. Euripides seems to have been content with the role of director and left acting chores to others. Playwrights not only directed their own plays, but composed the music which was always a part of the performance.

The audience was tremendous, and critical. Since the productions were part of a great religious festival, visitors and as many of the citizens of Athens as could crowd into the theatre were in attendance. In the early days admission was free, but when the state began to bear the costs of production as well as the chief actors' salaries, an admission fee was charged. Provision was made, however, for subsidizing admissions for those unable to pay; every citizen of Athens was entitled to his "theoric money." There were no reserved seats except for the priests of Dionysus, who sat in special chairs near the front, and for state guests. Tickets in the form of coins were issued, lead ones for general admission, ivory ones for reserved seats.

Performances began at dawn, and wealthy citizens often sent their slaves ahead of them to hold seats. The less wealthy members of the audience came, often in the hours of darkness before dawn, and milled about the entrances for vantage points from which to get the seats they wished when they were allowed to enter the theatre. Everyone was in a festive mood, and there was much quarreling over particularly advantageous locations. The spectators wore garlands on their heads, and brought lunch and sometimes sunhats and cushions, for it would be a long day. The audience was critical and was not slow in letting its opinion be known. Unpopular plays were often hooted from the theatre, and unpopular actors pelted with figs, olives, nuts, or even stones. The actor Aeschines nearly lost his life in such a stone barrage, it is said, and thereafter retired from the theatre permanently. Applause was as much in order then as now, and it is difficult to conceive that the judges were not influenced by the public reception of the various presentations.

All preparations for the productions were conducted in secret, and though the stories of the tragedies were generally well known to the audiences, being drawn largely from

the myths and legends of the House of Atreus and the Trojan Wars, the trappings of production and the interpretations of the individual poets were always eagerly anticipated. Sometimes the results were unexpected; it is said that children died and women miscarried when the horribly costumed Furies appeared in the last play of Aeschylus' *Oresteia* trilogy (458 B.C.). Public interest in the production had been aroused, as was usual, by the presentation a few days before the event of a preview, or *proagon*, in a place adjoining the theatre. This preview used the playwright and performers in an announcement of the forthcoming production, and is perhaps the earliest publicity device known. For such a preview, Sophocles is said to have startled his audience by dressing his chorus in mourning to mark the death of Euripides (406 B.C.).

The Attic citizen took his drama seriously, not only because it was a part of a great religious festival, but because he loved talk and display and the tales the poets told. This first great theatre audience was composed of spectators widely distributed in social station and in personal propensities, but united in their love of good theatre. It was an audience in many ways comparable to that of Shakespeare's day. In these two periods (as perhaps in no other) great and diverse audiences witnessed great plays combined with great productions and acting to make unsurpassed theatre.

Playwriting develops to admirable heights

In the dramatic presentations of the City Dionysia, there were three types of plays presented: tragedy, satyr play, and comedy. Presentations were governed by the rule that the tragic poets must present three tragedies plus a satyr play which treated the personages or the situations of the preceding trilogy in burlesque fashion. A chorus of satyrs was always present, and this comic afterpiece with its special style is thought to have been included in the festival primarily to perpetuate the satyrs who had traditionally been a part of the Dionysiac celebration. No doubt, also, its comic and lascivious complexion had tremendous popular appeal, being designed to relieve the heaviness of the tragedies. All three of the great classic dramatists wrote satyr plays. Aeschylus is said to have been a master in this type, but of the many which he must have written, only a few fragments survive. The not-very-entertaining fragment of *The Trackers* of Sophocles, which is all that we have of his satyr plays, is surely not representative of his skill. Our only adequate idea of the type comes from Euripides, whose *Cyclops* survives in its highly entertaining entirety.

There seems to have been a time when the three tragedies of the chosen playwright formed a trilogy; i.e., they were written on a single theme, like the *Oresteia* of Aeschylus. But since this is the only trilogy extant, and single, unified plays obviously not parts of a trilogy have survived from both before and after its date, the trilogy tradition is hard to specify. It does seem to be true, however, that three tragedies were presented on a single day of the festival, and that these three were the work of a single dramatist. After the fifth century, the satyr play was relegated to a comparatively unimportant place in the festival; only one seems to have been given from that time forward and that preceding the revival of an old tragedy.

Presumably it was Thespis who transformed the chorus leader into an actor, but in the early days of Aeschylus there was still only one actor. Aeschylus is credited with being the first, in his later plays, to add a second actor who was then called *hypokrites*, or "answerer." Sophocles added another to make three, all of whom eventually came to be called hypokrites. Throughout the entire period of Greek drama there were never more than three participants designated as "actors," although in addition to the chorus there seem to have been various nonspeaking extras. Needless to say, each of the actors was frequently called upon to play more than

one role in a given play, since the *dramatis personae* could number up to eleven, though six to eight were more usual.

In the early plays, the chorus was large and was an integral part of the drama. In *The Suppliants* (c. 467 B.C.) of Aeschylus, the chief characters are the fifty daughters of Danaus, who perform the "title role" as the chorus. They were, of course, played by fifty men since no women performers appeared in classic Greek theatres. Aeschylus is generally credited with reducing this unwieldy chorus

to twelve for each part of the trilogy; Sophocles raised it again to fifteen, a figure which seems to have remained fairly constant thereafter. In comedy, the traditional size of the chorus was twenty-four.

As playwrights discovered the advantages of enlarging the parts of the actors as opposed to that of the chorus, the function of the chorus became less important. In contrast to *The Suppliants*, which opens with the appearance of the chorus, *Agamemnon* (458 B.C.) opens with a single dramatic figure

PHYLAKES SCENE
From a vase painting, the scene (left) shows
the raised booth stage and the grotesque
padding of the actors, while the statuette
above, from Boetia c. 400 B.C., confirms the
painting. (Museum of Fine Arts, Boston)

and the effective monologue of the Watch-
man; the total number of lines are about
equally divided between chorus and characters. In Aeschylus' works, however, the chorus
is an essential part of the mood and the action of the plays. Sophocles' chorus plays a
lesser, though relevant, part in the action
and is more often than not employed to give
lyrical emphasis to a climax or to prepare
for a shift in mood. With Euripides, the
actors gain still more ground at the expense
of the chorus. The number of characters is
increased (in *The Phoenician Women* there
are eleven), and the lines of the chorus are
fewer in number and mostly explanatory of
the action. Aristotle comments that it was
the playwright Agathon, who won the first
of his two victories in 416 B.C., who first
wrote choral odes which were unconnected
with the plot and served only as interludes.
Though its function thus deteriorated, the
chorus seems always to have been a part of
tragedy; in the later comedies it disappeared
entirely.

From the first appearance of Thespis at
Athens to the first plays of Aeschylus, and
indeed contemporary with him, many poet-
playwrights were being produced at the Theatre of Dionysus. There are recorded the
names of some of these but not much more.
Of Pratinus (who flourished in 496 B.C.), the
record states simply that he was one of the
three competing poets when Aeschylus first
participated in the festival, and that he was
especially successful in his satyr plays. Of
Choerilus (523–482 B.C.), it says that he wrote
one hundred sixty plays and won thirteen
victories, but none of his plays are extant.
Of Phrynichus, who won his first poetic
victory in 511 B.C., a few scattered fragments
remain; it is recorded that he incurred a
fine for his *Capture of Miletus*, whose subject matter embarassed the government because of the many foreign guests in the

audience, and the play was never imitated. Our knowledge of Greek drama is based upon only thirty-two tragedies and twelve comedies, three sizable fragments, and one satyr play. This is all that has been preserved of the hundreds that must have been written. It can be assumed, with some reason, that Aeschylus, Sophocles, Euripides, and Aristophanes were the best of all those who wrote for the Greek theatre, both because these alone have survived, and because what can be garnered of the critical opinion of their contemporaries seems to verify such a judgment. In any event, it was not until Shakespeare that playwriting achieved so great a peak, and then it was considerably different in kind.

Aeschylus (525–456 B.C.), hero of Marathon and other battles of the Persian Wars and highly respected citizen of Athens, is the first of the three great tragedians. He is considered by some critics to be the greatest tragic poet of all time. Of the ninety plays for which there are titles, only seven are extant. He won the prize for tragedy at Athens thirteen times, taking his first award when he was forty-one years old. The most famous of his works is the *Oresteia* trilogy, in which is told the story of the House of Atreus; the three plays are entitled *Agamemnon, The Libation Bearers,* and *The Furies.* It opens with the return of Agamemnon from the Trojan Wars; he is murdered by his wife, Clytemnestra; she in turn perishes at the hands of Orestes, their son; Orestes is persecuted by the Furies, and is at the end pardoned by the goddess Athena. In addition to the play called *The Persians* (evidently not a part of a trilogy), there are three others generally supposed to be single plays of what were originally three trilogies: *The Suppliants, Prometheus Bound,* and *The Seven Against Thebes.* The subject matter of four more of his trilogies

GREEK COMEDY
A comic mask from Smyrna shows the typical grotesque features (above), while a vase painting (right) depicts the comic chorus of mounted knights in Aristophanes' play. (Museum of Fine Arts, Boston)

is recorded, but of the rest nothing beyond the titles is known.

Fortunately, the extant plays cover a large part of his career so that their progression forms an illustration of the development of dramatic art. The earliest have a close formal affinity with the narratives from which they are taken. The chorus of young women in *The Suppliants,* or the Elders in *The Persians,* really constitute chief characters, and the plays themselves are not so much representations of dramatic conflicts as delineations of the effects of past events on sympathetic onlookers. The single element of dramatic conflict acted out in view of the audience (the essence of drama today) is the attempt of the Herald in *The Suppliants* to drive the daughters of Danaus to the waiting ship of the sons of Aegyptus. The chorus has more than two-thirds of the

lines of the play. In each of these plays the hero and the antagonist are not developed as individuals; the emphasis is on the results of past actions. Aeschylus further develops this rudimentary dramatic form, however, in *The Seven Against Thebes;* Eteocles, the hero, holds the stage most of the time, though the antagonist Polynices is not represented, and the chorus is prominent and important. By the time Aeschylus arrived at his final great trilogy, the dramatic element—as opposed to the lyric, elegiac, or narrative—was paramount. Agamemnon and Clytemnestra are real, complex embodiments of hero and antagonist; interest lies in present action, in the represented dramatic conflict, rather than in past events. Dramatic art thus came of age.

Aeschylus grew to artistic maturity as the democracy of Athens was rising to the peak of its greatness, and he is a masterful interpreter of that society. The chief interest of his plays lies not primarily in the isolated, individual character, but in that character placed in the total scheme of things; he presents his central theme with piercing insight and great dramatic power. Yet—and here is the measure of his skill as a dramatist—his people are individually characterized to the degree that the audience becomes intensely interested in what happens to them. Aeschylus presupposed a superhuman factor in the universe; he believed in the fundamental dignity and worth of man, his possession of free will, and his responsibility in the exercise of that will. His poetry is often impassioned, full of images, irresistible in movement. That he was held in highest esteem by his contemporaries is witnessed by the well-known

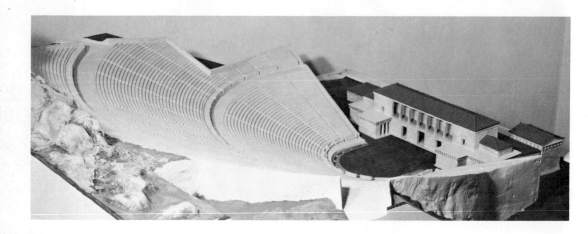

ANCIENT THEATRE OF DIONYSUS AT ATHENS
This model shows the theatre as it was in about 400 B.C. At this time, the orchestra was a full circle, with the skene on the perimeter opposite the seats. The altar in the center of the orchestra is not apparent in this model, but the paradoi, proskenion, and episkenion are clearly visible. Also apparent is the fact that the arrangement of the seats was dictated by topography. (Cleveland State University)

decree issued shortly after his death that anyone wishing to produce one of his plays should be "given a chorus," that is, be allowed to produce it at the City Dionysia.

Sophocles (496–406 B.C.) was but sixteen years older than Euripides (480–406 B.C.), and they died within a few months of each other. But the subject matter and the treatment in Sophocles' plays make him older in the art of the drama than Euripides. He was nearly ninety when he died, having served with distinction as a general in the army, and on several occasions as part of embassies to other powers. He had written about 125 plays; seven of these are extant. It is recorded that he won twenty-nine prizes, eighteen of them at the City Dionysia.

He used much of the same subject matter as Aeschylus, but was more interested than the older dramatist in the tragic interplay between characters and in the inner conflicts of an individual character. His three best-known plays are *Antigone*, *Electra*, and *Oedipus Rex;* the others still extant are *The Women of Trachis*, *Ajax*, *Philoctetes*, and *Oedipus at Colonus*. A comparison of his *Electra* with Aeschylus' *Libation Bearers* reveals that Sophocles used the legend of Electra to inquire into human character and its motivations, whereas the older dramatist was concerned with the rightness of the blood feud.

Building upon the advances in dramatic structure evident in the plays of Aeschylus,

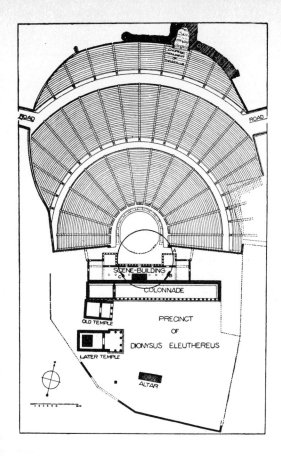

PLAN OF THE THEATRE OF DIONYSUS
This is the plan of the theatre as remodeled by Lycurgus in the fourth century B.C., when stone benches were installed for the audience, and the original skene transformed into a colonnade. The superimposed circle shows the position of the old orchestra which was used in the days when there was no scene building at all. (Flickinger, *The Greek Theatre and Its Drama*, University of Chicago Press, 1934)

Sophocles brought dramaturgy to a state of perfection. In *Antigone*, for instance, he opened immediately with a scene of conflict between two of the major characters, Ismene and Antigone, and continued with a series of incidents which form an effective plot with elements of suspense and alternating scenes of reassurance and despair. By the time he wrote *Oedipus Rex*, his tools had been perfected, and the balance between plot and character was firmly established. Though the essence of this play is the withdrawal of veils from the past, Sophocles unfolded his plot with a careful selection of scenes, each revelation being not merely exposition, but dramatic motivation for the next action of the hero. The characters are always present on stage when they are needed, and their delineation is unerring. The choral odes are germane and not mere interludes.

From *Oedipus Rex*, a play of faultless construction in which the leading character is driven to his doom by the ineluctable series of his own choices, Aristotle chiefly draws his definition of the tragic hero: "a man who is highly renowned and prosperous, but one who is not pre-eminently virtuous and just, whose misfortune, however, is not brought upon him by vice and depravity, but by some error of judgment or frailty." (*Poetics*, Sec. 1453a, ll. 5–10.) Edith Hamilton, the renowned Greek scholar, calls Sophocles "the quintessential Greek" (*The Greek Way*, 1930), a dramatist who displays an unerring skill in balanced construction, who handles complex dramatic situations with clarity and symmetry, who writes verse that is lucid, fluent, and grand. He is the essence of everything that we mean when we speak of the glory that was Greece, the consummate artist in everything that he did.

Although Euripides was a contemporary of Sophocles, Euripides is the much more modern of the two. Euripides never attained the artistic perfection of Sophocles, but he probed more deeply into the psychological motivations of his characters. He was a dramatist in conflict. He was at war with the accepted theology of his day, though he bowed to it in ritual observances; he inveighed against imperialism and military aggressions; he saw the legends of heroes as the glorification of tyrants,

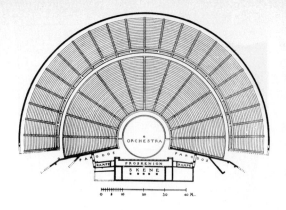

schemers, cowards; he was a passionate critic of his times, who fought against the passing of Periclean Athens through the long life-and-death struggle with militaristic Sparta when things intellectual were being smothered in things practical and freedom of speech and action was continually being curtailed. He died a short while before Athens fell to Sparta, a political and military event which rendered the resurrection of an Attic Golden Age impossible. He had been a friend of Protagoras, Socrates, and Alcibiades, and only the fact that his criticisms were never voiced directly, but through the characters in his plays, saved him from the unhappy fate that awaited the others. He did, however, become a voluntary exile from Athens in a kind of personal protest against the abuses he abhorred. He suffered the disapproval of his contemporaries in another way, for of the ninety-two plays which he wrote only five took the prize for tragedy. Interestingly enough, we have more plays of his than of any other classic dramatist; eighteen serious plays and a satyr play are extant.

His modernity is seen in his treatment of the Electra myth, for his title character is presented as a sexually frustrated, neurotic young woman, and her brother as a weak-willed boy motivated by his sister. His *Medea* shows a woman being driven mad by jealousy, and his Phaedra in *Hippolytus* is overpowered by a guilty passion. Euripides engaged in psychological analysis centuries before the term was invented; hence he is called by some the father of modern drama. He was highly critical of militarism, giving the world its greatest pacifist play, *The Trojan Women*, as well as the antiwar play, *Hecuba*. He was also constantly questioning the power and authority of the gods, as he does in *Heracles, Ion,* and *Iphigenia Among the Tauri*.

THE GREEK THEATRE AT EPIDAURUS
Above, a plan showing the perfectly symmetrical arrangement of the seating area, and the full orchestra circle of the Classic period (Dörpfeld and Reich, *Das Greichishe Theater*). Right, the present ruins, showing the lintel over the passageways which integrated skene and seats, the orchestra of hard-packed earth, and the altar in the center of the orchestra. (Theatre Collection, New York Public Library)

His dramatic skill was not so well balanced as that of Sophocles; his interest in character generally outweighed his attention to plot construction. His aim seems to have been the representation of complex characters in as many emotional and theatrical scenes as possible, and he allows the unity of his plays to depend largely on the revelation of character. He is credited with introducing the prologue as a means of explaining the complicated plot to follow, and of inventing the dramatic *deus ex machina* to untangle it. His plays contain a wealth of realistic detail and thus seem closer in time than do the more artistically balanced productions of Sophocles. Euripides also enlarged the types of possible plays by writing what might be called tragi-comedy or romantic drama (*Iphigenia Among the Tauri, Alcestis*), and a most delightful high comedy (*Helen*). These new genres pointed forward to the comedies of Menander. In point of view, Euripides was an iconoclast; in treatment, however, he often tried to adhere to the traditional and the accepted. He, like

many another dramatist after him, conformed to the extent that would gain him a hearing while he attempted to say that which was revolutionary.

Of tragic playwrights after Euripides there is little record and there are no literary remains. It is recorded that a play of Philocles actually defeated Sophocles' *Oedipus Rex* in the contest, and it is said that the playwright Agathon wrote plays for which he invented the characters instead of borrowing them from legend or history. Euphorion, son of Aeschylus, Iophon, son of Sophocles, and Euripides, nephew of his namesake, also wrote tragedies in addition to reviving the plays of their great ancestors. But no new names arose to rival their greatness.

Though the glory of Greek drama was tragedy, comedy had a parallel development, also growing out of the early festivals of Dionysus, though from the secular aspect. In one of his few references to it in the *Poetics*, Aristotle says that "there are no early records of comedy because it was not highly valued," and that "it was a long time before

comic dramas were licensed by the magistrate; the earlier comedies were produced by amateurs." Perhaps in addition to its roots in the *komos* of the Dionysiac festival, it had accretions from the *phylakes*, those topical, occasional, and often bawdy sketches performed by itinerant players on platform stages, to the delight of their audiences. These of course would be "not highly valued" by the literati, being "folk events," such as had existed before the regularized dramatic contests at Athens, and such as would exist for many centuries after. In any event, comedy was more improvisational than tragedy and dealt with current ideas of interest rather than with traditional materials. For these reasons it remained more episodic than tragedy. A multiplicity of characters developed with less and less emphasis upon the importance of the chorus as an integral part of the action. The traditional twenty-four members of the comic chorus were generally divided into two equal groups, one for each side of the argument comprising the central issue of the play. The functions of the chorus were gradually assumed by individual characters. There were supposedly some two hundred fifty-two writers of comic plays. These comedies used caricature, lampoon, invective, sarcasm, irony, parody, and satire to make their point. They were more important than tragedy at the Lenaea, and though less important at the City Dionysia, prizes were awarded the comic writers beginning in 449 B.C., although prizes for comic actors were not awarded at the City Dionysia until many years later. Perhaps the civic pride of Athens prevented the elevation of a form which made fun of it in view of visiting dignitaries.

The entire life of classic comedy is generally divided into three periods: Old, ending with the fifth century B.C.; Middle, to about 340 B.C.; and New, in which the best work dates from about 300 B.C. Aristophanes (448–380 B.C.) is the best representative of Old Comedy, and the only writer of that comedy whose plays are extant. Of his forty known plays, eleven texts have come down to us, some of which were first performed at the Lenaea and some at the City Dionysia. We know the names of some of his predecessors —Cratinus, Eupolis, Epicharmus—but only scattered fragments of their works remain.

If Sophocles "drew men as they ought to be and Euripides drew men as they are" (a statement ascribed to Sophocles by Aristotle), then Aristophanes drew them as they should not be. Aristotle said that "comedy tends to represent the agents as worse than the men of the present day" (*Poetics*, Sec. 1448a, 1. 20). The examples bear out this statement. In them public figures are rendered ridiculous—rulers, thinkers, warriors, lawyers, politicians, writers. Sharp wit and good conservative citizen that he was, Aristophanes seemed to enjoy exposing undemocratic motives, selfish or unwise decisions, ridiculous manias on the part of officials and

public alike. Each of his plays is a kind of dramatic cartoon, which makes fun of the serious pursuits of society by showing them to be *un*serious. Six of his plays are classed as political satires: *The Acharnians, The Knights, The Wasps, The Peace, Lysistrata,* and *The Women in Parliament.* Five are called philosophical and literary satires: *The Clouds, The Women at the Festival, The Frogs, The Birds,* and *Wealth,* his last play.

Tradition has it that in *The Knights* the playwright's attack on the militaristic demagogue, Cleon, who had succeeded Pericles, was so incisive that no actor would undertake the part and no mask maker would produce the character mask. Aristophanes himself is said to have played the part, smearing his face with winelees to indicate the alcoholic propensities of his model. Another tradition is that Socrates, impaled in *The Clouds,* was so diverted by his comic counterpart that he rose from his place in the audience so that the spectators might see and appreciate the cleverness of the dramatic takeoff. Euripides came in for his share of ridicule in *The Acharnians, The Women at the Festival,* and *The Frogs.* Aeschylus, as well, is a character in the last of these. Scholars are fond of pointing out the original of a famous college yell in the chorus of this play, when they simulate their namesakes with a "brekekekex, ko-ax, ko-ax." Situations as well as persons are satirized in the plays of Aristophanes. In *The Acharnians,* for instance, an Athenian citizen, tired of war, makes a private treaty with the enemy, and enjoys the advantage of trading with them. Aristophanes departs from topical satire in his later plays and becomes more diffuse. This tendency coincides with the decline of democracy in Athens and marks the death of Old Comedy.

There are only fragmentary remains of Middle Comedy, though thirty-seven names

RUINS OF THE THEATRE OF DIONYSUS AT ATHENS
The present ruins, of course, are of the theatre as it was remodeled by the Romans during the reign of Nero. The orchestra is reduced to a semicircle, paved, and surrounded by a wall. (Theatre Collection, New York Public Library)

are listed as its writers. Alexis and Antiphanes were evidently the most eminent in this period, although there now exists not a single play of either. Anaxandrides of Rhodes, who wrote sixty-five comedies in the fourth century B.C., is said to have destroyed or sold for waste paper his unsuccessful plays. From the extant fragments, scholars have deduced that Middle Comedy was less ribald, less personal, less fantastic than Old Comedy. Its plays had more plot, more dramatic illusion. The chorus decreased in dramatic importance and the material was more social than political.

New Comedy was new in ways other than being simply more recent. The Aristophanic rhetorical structure (*prologue, parados, agon, parabasis, episodes, stasimon,* and *exodus*) had entirely disappeared along with the chorus. There was no representation of actual persons in the comedies to be performed, such as had been the delight of Aristophanes' audiences. Times had changed and with them the form of comedy—that theatrical phenomenon most closely tied to the social whole, being absolutely dependent upon the value scheme of the society which produces it.

Menander (342-292 B.C.) is the outstanding representative of New Comedy; contemporary critical comment names him the most able of all his fellows. Certainly he was the most revived and most copied of them all. He is supposed to have written about one hundred five comedies of which only scattered fragments remained until four much more complete texts were recovered early in this century. They were found in an old Egyptian papyrus which had been torn up to protect various legal documents, and they were complete enough so that they could be more or less satisfactorily reconstructed. They are comedies of errors called *Hero, The Girl from Samos, The Shearing of Glycera* (sometimes translated as *The Rape of the Locks*), and *The Arbitration*. Within the last few years there was discovered in Switzerland another Menander play, *The Curmudgeon*, which is the only complete text of a Menander play now extant. It is a delightfully lively comedy which gives modern readers an insight into Menander's great comic genius. By this time (the second half of the fourth century) the disappearance of the chorus had allowed for the expansion of the possible cast of characters—none of them representations of actual persons, all of them representative types drawn from the social milieu of the times. There were evidently twenty-seven of these types, such as: irascible and good-natured old fathers, light-minded and honest sons, cunning servants, greedy parasites, swaggering soldiers, dishonest matchmakers, obliging companions, parasitic relatives, and impudent prostitutes. These types reappeared in later epochs of the theatre. Situations were domestic in character, and generally farcical in presentation. Plots usually turned on such things as an ill-used maiden or a foundling who turned out to be wellborn. The background was that of middle-class city life, and the drama-

A GREEK THEATRE IN HELLENISTIC TIMES
Right, present ruins of the theatre at Delphi. Above, detail of a model of Delphi in about 160 A.D., showing the theatre with the Temple of Apollo behind the scene-house. Note that the stage is raised and approached by an inclined plane; the skene, at stage level, is backed by panels which may, upon occasion, have been scenically painted. (The Metropolitan Museum of Art, Dodge Fund, 1930)

tist's observation of this milieu was exact. His graceful composition, urbanity, wit, and apt characterization caused his plays to be widely admired and mightily copied.

Presumably Menander's sixty or more fellow-writers of comedy, including Philemon and Apollodorus of Gela, followed the same pattern, writing of the same subjects in the same way. What plays there are by Plautus, the Roman comic writer, give an excellent sample of what late Greek comedy must have been. The plots and characters are stereotyped, yet in the best of the plays there is presented a vast panorama of human weakness and charm, an interplay of character upon character in basic relationships transcending time and place.

So, for more than two and one-half centuries the Greek drama developed into perhaps the greatest theatre the world has ever known, and then, first in tragedy and later in comedy, declined to ineffectualness. The course of the drama paralleled and reflected the rise and decline of the great Greek democratic society.

The theatre of Dionysus

There are no contemporary descriptions of the playhouse in which the great Attic plays were produced. Aristotle, writing in the fourth century, says little or nothing of the physical aspects of the drama. For many years all that was known of playing space and production in the ancient Greek theatre was derived from *The Ten Books on Architecture* of the Roman architect Vitruvius, which was written about 15 B.C., and from the *Onomastikon* of Pollux, which appeared in the second century A.D. Pollux's work was based, in part, upon the seventeen-book *Theatrike Historia* of King Juba II of Mauretania, who began his compilation at the time of Augustus, but whose total work was subsequently lost. Both Pollux and Vitruvius are obscure and contradictory, and their information obviously includes developments much later in point of time than the sixth and fifth centuries. More authoritative reconstructions have been possible through archaeological research, and through production indications in the plays themselves. In the former field, a great debt is owned to Wilhelm Dörpfeld, whose excavations in the late nineteenth century led to an interesting study published in 1896. So far as the plays themselves are concerned, the perspicacious reader may still today see rudimentary production guides in them. This discussion will not enter into the scholarly dispute which has raged and indeed still rages concerning the production aspects of the great plays, but will present in the following pages what seems a reasonable, and reasonably authenticated, exposition.

In the Golden Age of Greece, each major city erected a theatre as one of the edifices dedicated to religion. This theatre was an evolution from the circular dancing place of the early Dionysiac festivals around which the spectators sat or stood. There was an obvious advantage in having this dancing place, or *orchestra*, in a hollow since a large crowd of spectators could have vantage points on surrounding hillsides. The Theatre of Dionysus at Athens, the most famous of them all, began in just such a simple fashion, with the original *theatron*, or seeing-place, on the hillslope under the Acropolis, and the original orchestra at the foot of the hill. It was merely a circle of hard-stamped earth, and there were no seats for the spectators except perhaps some removable chairs near the circle for the dignitaries. The first plays of Aeschylus were evidently given in this spot, with no scenic background except the wide blue Grecian sky and the Attic countryside.

Various archaeological and literary researches have traced the evolution of this playhouse through the Classic era, the Hellenistic period, and the Roman Empire. The relation of audience to actors changed as the years passed. As the fifth century B.C. progressed, wooden benches were provided for the spectators. The increase in the number of speaking parts in the dramas dictated an arrangement for the expeditious entrances of the actors and a place for their changing of masks. About 465 B.C., nine years before the death of Aeschylus, and at the time when Sophocles was at the beginning of his career, the orchestra circle was moved closer to the hillside to allow for the construction of a long, wooden building between the orchestra circle and the old Temple of Dionysus. In this building, also, the wooden seats were stored when a production was not in progress. At the same time the hillside was somewhat hollowed out at the center and built up on the lower ends, so that the rows of seats in the bottom section could be carried around three-quarters of the orchestra circle. The second and third tiers of seats did not form complete semicircles, but were limited at the sides and top by topography and by other construction. The seats faced toward the circle where both actors and chorus performed. The wall of the scene building, or *skene*, served as the background for the plays, and at this time probably had a single door facing the orchestra circle. A massive, T-shaped stone foundation, extending beyond this single door, seems to have been the base for the erection of whatever temporary altar, temple, porch, or stairway was called for by a particular play.

Toward the end of the fifth century B.C., foundations were laid for a stone skene with projecting side wings to be erected in front of the old one. When this building was completed, the T-shaped foundation lay within it, and may have been used as a base for the erection of superstructures. The building had three doors, and was probably two stories high. It no doubt followed the basic plan which had proved practical in the temporary wooden structures used before this time.

In the fourth century the theatre was re-

MENANDER WITH MASKS
This bas-relief of Menander holding a comic mask shows the relative size of the mask as compared with the actual human head. The standing figure may represent an actor. The masks on the table are two of those common to New Comedy—the courtesan and the comic slave. (Lateran Museum)

modeled by Lycurgus, with fine stone benches for the audience, a throne in the center of the first row of seats for the priest of Dionysus, and other special seats of honor; a new skene was erected, and the original one was transformed into a colonnade. This was the final form of the Greek theatre.

The remains of the theatre at Epidaurus (c. 350 B.C.) give a good idea of the Classic Greek theatre. It is perfectly symmetrical, with twenty-two sections of seats in the outer circle, and twelve in the inner circle. This theatre, attributed by Pausanias to Polyclitus, had lintels over the passageways between theatron and skene, thus achieving a unity which most Greek theatres did not possess.

Playhouses change to suit the plays

The development of dramatic literature in the Hellenistic Age (330–30 B.C.), which succeeded the Classic period, deemphasized the importance of the chorus, and placed the burden of the performance on the actors; this change was reflected in the theatre proper by the development of a raised stage for the actors. Theatres built in this period, such as those at Priene, Assos, Ephesus, and Delos, among others, retained the theatron, orchestra, and skene, but the skene now encroached somewhat on the orchestra circle, and was different in construction from the Classic skene. It invariably had at least two stories, and the chief acting level was the *proskenion*, or roof of the first story. This acting area was approached on either side by ramps and was ten to twelve feet high. Theatres which had been built in Classic times, such as those at Athens, Eretria, and other places, were refurbished with the new Hellenistic stage building, just as in the time of the Roman Empire most Greek theatres were once more remodeled with the Roman stage design and semicircular orchestra. The present remains at Athens belong to the period of Nero.

Fundamental to the Greek idea of a theatre was the open-air playing space; Greek skies were almost always sunny and spectators could protect themselves from too much sun by wearing hats. Tiered seats, sectioned off by walkways (much in the manner of a modern football stadium) were standard, and these seats encircled the orchestra about three-quarters of the way around. Sight lines were generally good from every seat and, in spite of the fact that these theatres seated from fifteen to twenty thousand people, the acoustics were remarkable. All seats except those in the front row were backless benches, again like most football stadiums today. The front row held stone chairs with backs, the center one usually more ornate than the others and reserved for the priest of Dionysus. Often there was an open space behind this row where additional chairs could be placed if the list of dignitaries in attendance exceeded the special seating area. The orchestra circle was of packed earth; its size varied, but generally was quite large. The diameter of the circle at the Theatre of Dionysus at Athens was in its early days about eighty-five feet, and later about sixty-five. When the Roman engineers began remodeling Greek theatres, they paved the orchestra with stone, as they did at

Athens. In the center of the orchestra circle in the Classic theatre was an altar. In dramatic productions it was variously used: in *The Persians* it was a monument; in *Prometheus Bound*, the rock to which the god was lashed. In the theatre at Eretria in Magnesia, there was an underground passage leading from the altar to the interior of the skene, and scholars have speculated that these are the "Charon's steps" mentioned by Pollux.

As has been noted, the skene was originally made of wood, then of stone, and was over one hundred feet long, with wings projecting about fifteen feet to either side. It faced the tiers of seats on the opposite side of the orchestra. The front wall of the skene was pierced by doors—one, then three, then five. In the Classic period, the actors entered directly to the orchestra from the skene, although some scholars say that there was a slightly raised platform for the actors, with a step or two down to the orchestra, from the first skene onwards. In the Hellenistic period, the raised stage with the side ramps for access was called the proskenion, the chief acting area for plays from which the chorus had disappeared. The second story of the skene, even from pre-Hellenistic times, was called the *episkenion*. The passageways (*paradoi*) between the extending wings of the skene and the near row of seats were used sometimes for the entrances of actors, for chorus entrances, and for the entrance of the audiences. In performance, it was the convention, founded on fact in the theatre at Athens, that the right-hand passageway marked entrances from the city and places near at hand, the left those from the country and other places farther away.

This was the functional structure of the Greek theatre; it was sometimes elaborated, often decorated, but fairly constant in its basic design.

Greeks, too, knew the art of illusion

Knowing something of the basic design of the theatre, scholars long supposed that the scenic decoration of the Attic drama was austere in the extreme, and the productions eminently simple. But compilations of scattered references in recent years have revised this opinion: Greek dramatists were as interested as any in the long history of the theatre in the invention and use of whatever trappings would enhance the scenic illusion. There seems to be general agreement now about the nature of at least some of these.

Even in the days before any kind of skene was erected at Athens and the only background for a given play was the natural open topography, effective dramatic use was made of the retaining wall of the orchestra circle opposite the audience. It seems probable that the ghost of Darius in *The Persians*, for instance, would rise from below this six-foot wall—a theatrical effect if there ever was one—and that it could also be used for disappearances. It also seems likely that even at this early period necessary properties, like tombs and altars, were set up at the edge of the terrace formed by this wall.

With the coming of the skene as a regular part of the theatre, further developments were possible. One of the earliest and most universally used was the *mechane*, which was evidently a kind of crane affixed to the roof of the skene and equipped with pulleys and ropes. It was used for ascents and descents of various kinds, as in the *Orestes* of Euripides where Apollo soars with Helena in the air above the palace roof; as in *The Mad Hercules* where Iris and Lyssa appear and one descends while the other flies away (this would presuppose a double operation of some sort); as in *The Clouds* where Socrates is ridiculed by suspending him in a basket midway between heaven and earth; as in *The Peace*, where, parodying Pegasus, Trygaeus ascends to heaven on a beetle. The mechane was needed primarily for the appearance of a god in a play, who usually interfered to effect dramatic resolutions of one sort or another; the term *deus ex machina* (god from a machine) has come to stand for any contrivance which inorganically effects the resolution of a dramatic dilemma. The mechane seems to have raised actors from orchestra or stage level to the roof of the episkenion; this area, where action could also take place, is what is apparently meant by another often-mentioned contrivance of the Greek theatre—the *theologeion*, or speaking place of the gods.

Another mechanical aid to the dramatic illusion was a platform on wheels or rollers, the *eccyclema*, which could be shoved out from one of the doors of the skene as the action demanded, and pulled back in again. It was used for reveals, so that offstage action could be made visible to the spectators. The convention of Greek theatre disallowed murders on the stage itself, but it was often necessary or desirable that the audience see the results of such action. Creon's dead wife is wheeled out in *Antigone*, as are Medea's dead children, and for comic effect Euripides is wheeled round in *The Acharnians* because he is too busy to come out himself.

Several ancient writers speak of the thunder tub; its use is obvious. Some speak of hides filled with stones beaten against brass plates, others of the pouring of stones into brass tubs. In any event, this contrivance was the ancient ancestor of the present-day thunder sheet. Also mentioned

are traps of various kinds; perhaps the "Charon's steps" at Eretria are a form of these. A beacon tower is also mentioned, and some writers speculate that this may have been nothing more than a specialized use of the roof of the episkenion or, in the earlier days of temporary settings, a structure especially erected.

Aristotle credits Sophocles with the introduction of the art of painting or decorating the skene. The earlier wooden skene was very probably supplemented by additional front structures; slots in the wall of the skene have been interpreted as anchoring spots for such additional structures. Sophocles, in his role of producer-director, might well have embellished these temporary structures, as well as the walls of the permanent skene, with paintings. Pollux and Vitruvius both mention three-sided prisms, or *periaktoi*, rotating on beams set into holes near the extremities of the stage area, with each side painted differently. These may also go back to Classic times, and were certainly used in the Hellenistic period; it has been postulated that periaktoi painted on each side with the symbols of lightning and rapidly rotated constituted the "lightning machines" to which references are made.

There were also removable screens of wood or hide (*pinakes*) which, in the Hellenistic theatre, were placed between the columns fronting the skene. Cross-sections of several of these columns seem to verify, by their evident construction, that they were built to take screens which could be inserted between them. Whether these screens were painted abstractly or literally is not known, but the illusion they afforded must have been welcome to the dramatists. They were used both between the columns of the lower story and in the large openings (*thyromata*) on the second story, the stage level in Hellenistic times.

Vitruvius says that the Greek theatre had three types of painted scenes: tragic, comic, and satyric. He may have been simply conjecturing from the known types of plays, or he may have had reference to various styles of painting the screens and set pieces. Vitruvius even mentions by name a Greek scene painter—Agatharcus—who, he says, evolved a system of perspective painting for scenery. At any rate, the decoration of these movable pieces would be done in subject matter and style to suit the play being produced. We shall see later how this statement of Vitruvius affected scenic design in the Renaissance.

There is also mention of something called a semicircle, which is supposed to have been a painted set piece placed in the orchestra whenever sea battles and sea scenes were called for. There is no doubt, too, that actual chariots were used when demanded, being driven through passageways into the orchestra circle, and that other literal props were employed as needed. Attic dramatists were no less interested in scenic investiture than those of later periods. However, since the plays were always given by daylight, special lighting effects were nonexistent; night and storms were played in bright sunshine, being announced in the dialogue and aided only by such devices as the thunder tub and the lightning machine. Peter Arnott, a modern scholar of classic Greece, points out that in the later productions of tragedies, the presence of a lamp on stage indicated that the scene was taking place at night—a convention similar to that of the Elizabethan theatre. Audiences then, as now, accepted theatrical conventions readily.

All performances were enhanced, however, with musical accompaniment. Just as dance was an integral part of the drama, so too was music. Originally playwrights scored their own scripts and choreographed them as well. Both Aeschylus and Sophocles were proficient in these skills. Later the labor was divided, and separate artists supplied music and choreography. The chief musician was the flute player who preceded the entrance of the chorus, and who generally established himself on the altar for the duration of the play, accompanying both song and dance from that position. Every patron, or choregus, was anxious to secure the most accomplished flute player for his performances, and there was much competition to obtain the best. The competition was resolved when, in later times, the flutists were chosen by lot for the various performances. The flute was often accompanied by a harp, though we have little idea of what the melodies were like. We know only that Greek modes in music differed materially from our own, and that the ancients had little or no idea of polyphony. There is but one extant fragment of ancient Greek music written down; it is from Euripides' *Orestes*.

The scenic illusion was further enhanced by the appearance of the performers, which was in no way realistic, but highly conventional with different conventions for the three types of plays.

In the costuming for tragedy, the effect aimed for was that of figures larger than life-size, who would be impressive, dignified, and easily seen and heard in the very large theatres in which they played. In the earliest days of Greek theatre, actors in the tragedies were garbed in the long, rich, Asiatic robes of the priests of Dionysus and wore Asiatic leg boots. This style gradually gave way to highly decorated Ionian dress. Then, as the fifth century progressed, costumes for tragedy became standardized, with a traditional dress for each role.

While the Athenian citizen never covered his arms in the ordinary business of life, the tragic actor wore an ornamented dress with long sleeves. It was generally striped or embroidered perpendicularly, and an ornamented belt was worn not at the normal waistline, as the Greeks usually belted their clothes, but high up in the style we know as Empire. The colors of these robes were standardized for the various characters: olive green, for instance, signified mourning; queens wore white with purple borders. Additional barbaric jewelry was added for such a character as Medea. Overgarments, or mantles, of saffron, frog-green, gold, or purple were frequently added. No one wore hats except for travelers. Members of the chorus were uniformly dressed to represent the characters they were impersonating in that drama—old men, maidens, women of the city, and so forth. (Mention has already been made of the effect on the audience of a most special costuming of a chorus of Furies.) Because they had to dance, members of the chorus wore their ordinary footwear or went barefoot, whereas the tragic actor wore a thick-soled boot, the *kothurnos*, a development from the earlier Asiatic leg boot. These boots, with the long lines of his costume plus the mask and body padding to give horizontal compensation, made the tragic actor about seven-and-a-half feet tall, a truly awesome size. A probably apocryphal story is told of how an audience in Spain fled in fear and panic when a traveling company of Greek tragedians first appeared before them.

Much of the impressiveness of the Greek theatre lay in the masks of the performers, an interesting holdover from more primitive times. They were made of linen, cork, or wood, and fitted over the entire head, as primitive masks almost invariably do. The tragic mask was considerably larger than life-size, and typically rose in a dome-shaped fashion at the crown of the head. This protuberance, the *onkos*, effectively precluded the wearing of hats. Female characters some-

times drew their mantles over their heads, but as noted above, only travelers wore hats, and in these cases special masks or none at all were worn. Since no more than three actors appeared in the speaking roles of a given play, the masks, which could be changed as many times as necessary, made doubling possible. The actor simply retired within the skene, or to designated dressing room areas, and changed his mask. Sometimes more than one mask was provided for a single character, as was the case for Helen in Euripides' play of that name when she reappears pale and with her hair shorn, or for the Oedipus of Sophocles, who appears besmeared with blood after he has put out his eyes. Sometimes compensation is made in the script for the fact that the actor had no time to change a mask, as when Electra is bid make no sign of joy at her brother's return. In time the features of these masks became conventional; Pollux lists twenty-eight varieties of tragic masks: six old men, eight young men, eleven women, and three servants, in addition to necessary exceptions like Argus, the horned Acteon, the Gorgon, and so forth. The masks of tragedy and comedy which are so familiar to the modern world are two-dimensional representations of the old Greek masks. In every case, the mouth was opened wide to allow the voice of the actor to emerge, and a convincing case has been built up through investigation and experiment to prove that the mask included some sort of megaphonic arrangement to increase the carrying power of the wearer's voice.

Taken as a whole, the costume for tragedy was colorful and impressive. The weight and thickness of the actor's outfit forced him to move slowly, but he was trained to move gracefully. The result was well suited to the mood of the plays. And certainly the members of the audience had little difficulty

identifying the various characters immediately, even from the farthest seats.

The costume for comedy differed considerably. The tunic was short and worn over
long, tight undergarments. The body was gro-
tesquely padded before and behind, and
graced with a phallus made of red leather.
This phallus, a carryover from the Dionysiac
revels, served the double purpose of being a
charm against evil and a sign of fertility. The
wearing of the phallus disappeared during
the time of Middle Comedy in the fourth century. On his feet the comic actor wore short,
soft boots, *socci*, and on his head a mask.
These masks lacked the dome-like protuber-
ances of tragic masks; they tended to be
grotesque, and were made in a wide variety
of characters. Since satire and invective were
so much a part of Greek comedy, portrait
masks were common and, as mentioned,
both Socrates and Euripides were thus represented in the plays of Aristophanes. These
masks were an early manifestation of the
art we now call caricature.

The choruses of comedies were usually

in fantastic dress, intended to represent their
characters—wasps, Furies, birds. Many vase
paintings give us a good idea of the wide
variety that was achieved in these costumes.
Here, too, color was significant, no less than
in the tragedies, helping audiences to identify characters more easily.

In the satyr plays, the actors wore uniform masks and uniform costumes which included hip fur, a phallus, and a tail—the traditional satyr representation.

Acting highly specialized

As in that other great period of the theatre,
the Elizabethan, women were never seen on
the stage. Acting companies were made up
solely of men, and infrequently included a
boy or two. There may have been social or
religious reasons for this, but the chief consideration was a practical one: the light
voices of women could hardly carry in those
huge theatres, nor could women sustain the
weighty costumes and the arduous demands
of performance.

Members of the acting profession were
carefully selected and most arduously
trained. Demosthenes once remarked that
actors should be judged by their voices, politicians by their wisdom. Indeed, voice training formed a large part of the actor's education. There were specialized voice teachers,
and voice production was practiced in all
postures. Not only was the speaking voice
assiduously cultivated, but the Attic performer practiced proficiency in song as well.
In the ordinary course of a performance he
was called upon to use three types of voice
production: the iambic trimeter parts were
done in a declamatory style, with particular
emphasis upon enunciation; the recitative
was intoned to musical accompaniment; the
song proper was used for the lyrical pas-

sages. Songs were written for solo, duet, trio, or chorus, though never in harmony.

In addition to his vocal accomplishments, the actor was obliged to have at his command a whole catalogue of conventionalized gesture—a complete technical system of gesticulation. The styles differed for tragedy and for comedy; it is no wonder that actors specialized in one or the other of these two types, rarely performing in both.

Furthermore, the actor was a finished dancer, with complete command of the art of movement. Members of the chorus, no less than the actors, were accomplished dancers, singers, and speakers as well. Each type of play had its own dance movement. In tragedy it was the *emmeleia*, a slow and graceful movement which involved not just the feet, but the whole body. In comedy it was the *kordax*, a swift-moving and bawdy dance. The dance of the satyr play, the *sikinnis*, was a parody of the tragic dance in riotous and licentious form.

Those designated "actors" were highly specialized performers. The three actors of the theatre of Sophocles later came to be called the *protagonist*, the *deuteragonist*, and the *tritagonist*. They had special personal attributes and performed special functions in the plays. All were called hypokrites, in contradistinction to the *choreuti*, or members of the chorus, and the *choryphaeus*, or leader of the chorus. The protagonist was the chief actor; a play was said to be "done by" him. He played all the leading roles—Antigone, Electra, Medea, Oedipus, and so on. The deuteragonist was next in importance and played the chief supporting roles, such as Creon in *Antigone*. The tritagonist was the least important of the three. He played the passionate heralds, dignified kings, and so on. All three of these doubled in other roles where necessary.

There were other actors who, as today, assumed the nonspeaking roles to round out the performance. Needless to say, this area was a training ground for the higher ranks.

The chorus leader was frequently assigned lines in the play as were also individual members of the chorus. For example, the chorus of old men in *Oedipus Rex* speak singly as well as together, and the leader is a special part. Through the passageways, the chorus entered the orchestra circle where they remained throughout the performance, moving and speaking as the script demanded and the playwright directed. The actors evidently moved from orchestra to skene and back again as was necessary, now with and among the chorus, now apart from them. The whole effect was one of carefully synchro-

nized movement and utter discipline. There is no doubt that all performers were carefully trained, and well rehearsed for each production.

Acting was a highly esteemed profession in ancient Greece, and people from all walks of life joined its ranks. By Hellenistic times, its members had joined together in an actors' guild which they called the Artists of Dionysus, and on the basis of their fundamental religious employment (remember that the Attic theatre was a part of the worship of Dionysus), they were, by action of the Amphictyonic Council, exempted from military service. Earlier, of course, there had been no such exemption; Aeschylus did his military duty until he was sixty and was a widely renowned soldier as well as play-

wright, and Sophocles had held the military rank of general. The Artists of Dionysus set up a system of rules governing employment and working conditions, much in the manner of today's Actors' Equity, even extending their concern to traveling companies. Being, in a sense, priests, actors were sometimes used as emissaries of the government, and no doubt this increased their stature in the eyes of the ordinary citizens. Indeed, in Hellenistic times, when the actors had gained ascendency in importance over playwrights (since new, great playwrights did not exist), it is apparent that they sought such assignments in order to enhance their prestige. In succeeding centuries, actors never again enjoyed such prestige and social standing; not until nearly our own day would they overcome the disrepute in which they lived.

There was wide variation in the income of actors; leading members of the profession commanded very high salaries. There is a record which shows that Polus, a leading protagonist, received the equivalent of twelve hundred dollars for two days' performances —a sum which would be considered generous even today. Sometimes the protagonist served as a contractor, supplying all the parts and paying his company as he saw fit. Lesser actors received smaller sums, with the nonspeaking actors getting least of all. It is easy to imagine that the lesser members of provincial companies were likely to fare as poorly as similar actors do today.

The Greek theatre operated on the star system, that much abused attribute of the modern theatre. Particular performers were idolized in much the same way as they are today. There was Nicostratus, who is said to have been so perfect an actor that the highest praise a provincial performer could receive was to have it said, "He does it like Nicostratus!" Other players of note included Aristodemus, Neoptolemus, Athenodorus, and Phrynichus, for all of whom high praise is on record. It was the same Polus we have mentioned as being particularly well paid, who is said to have used an urn containing the ashes of his son to induce the proper emotion when he was playing Electra mourning over her supposedly dead brother's ashes. How modern in spirit that sounds!

At first, particular actors were associated with individual poets, as were Mynniscus and Cleander with Aeschylus, Tlepolemus and Cleidimides with Sophocles. Later, actors, like musicians, were assigned to the plays by lot—a practice which must have proved upsetting to the playwright-director.

As the art of playwriting declined, the prominence of the actors increased. As with all star systems, however, this one fell upon

COMIC ACTORS
Statuettes from the fourth century B.C., depicting comic actors—two men and a woman —although, of course, the female would have been played by a man. (The Metropolitan Museum of Art, Rogers Fund, 1913; Museum of Fine Arts, Boston)

evil days, and it is written that by Aristotle's time it had become vicious.

Summary

When we say that Western theatre as we know it began with the Greeks, we have perhaps said all. Our conception of that shining and miraculous age is largely derived from the great Greek dramatic literature. Never before or since has man achieved so perfect a balance between the visible and the invisible, the material and the spiritual, the image and the imageless. As Edith Hamilton has pointed out, this balance is possible only when the mind and spirit are in harmony as they were with the Greeks, the mind seeing everything as related to the whole, the spirit seeing everything as highly individual, and the combination of mind and spirit seeing beauty in everything. Thus the magnificent simplicity of the Parthenon is related to the Greek landscape, making both more beautiful by their juxtaposition; thus the figures of Greek tragedy, though highly individual, illuminate man in his human, material, and divine relationships. The complete individual seen at the same time as completely universal is the heritage and the greatness of Greek tragedy. The immense influence of the Greek dramatic concept is apparent through the ages to our own day.

Hardly less influential is the final form of Greek comedy, with its universal character types, whose voices reecho and whose images are seen in many times and places.

Not only were the dramatic forms of tragedy and comedy invented and developed by the ancient Greeks, but dramatic criticism also began with them—notably with Aristotle's *Poetics*, the influence of which has been almost incalculable through the ages. It is Aristotle who for all time pointed out the essence of the theatrical experience in his six elements: thought, plot, character, language, music or mood, and spectacle.

The productions of these plays, though they largely remained attached to religious observance, won a widespread following among many classes of society as a necessary and highly respected profession, requiring native talent and a long period of intensive training. Directors, choreographers, and composers reached specialization, as (from what we can discover) did scenographers. By the end of the Golden Age of Greece it is possible to define theatre as a separate and distinct art form: Theatre is that performing, or occurrent, art whose basis is the *act*, through which are perceived both the character and the range of human experience in the semblance of virtual life. It is, in other words, that art form which most vividly explores and represents what is meant by the state of being human. We have the Greeks to thank for that.

It is true that without the theatre of Greece there would undoubtedly be theatre of some sort today. But it is likewise certain that a theatre without the Greek tradition would be a very different one from that which we know and admire.

About fifteen years after the death of Aristophanes, and almost twenty-five years before the birth of Menander, the city of Rome evidently saw its first dramatic performance. The historian Livy (59 B.C.–17 A.D.) tells us that in 364 B.C., in order to "disarm the wrath of the gods" who had visited the city with a pestilence, the consuls "amongst other efforts . . . instituted scenic entertainments." How much like the reasons for drama among primitive men this is! The "scenic entertainments," Livy goes on to say, were mimetic dances by natives of Etruria "imported from abroad." The music, dance, and verse of these Etruscan players became very popular in Rome, and were much imitated by young Romans.

Though Livy is reported to have despised theatre, since by his time it had become a public nuisance, his mention of the above event, and his subsequent notations concerning the activities of Livius Andronicus and the popularity of the *atellanae* do point to the eclectic origins and the spotty development of theatrical activity in the Roman Republic and the early years of the Roman Empire. For Roman theatre was not a unified and generic art form as it had been earlier in Greece, but a series of graftings and imitations, with effective dramatic writing totally over before theatre architecture began. (The former belongs largely to the Republic, the latter to the Empire.)

The Etruscan dances of which Livy speaks were evidently those of just such rustic festivals as were prevalent throughout the archaic world, but the bawdy songs which accompanied them had their origins in Fascinum in South Etruria, and remained popular as "Fescennine Verses" in Rome for a very long time. The atellanae were short, improvised farces with stock characters wearing masks, which were so named because they had originally come from Atella in Campania—an area populated by the Greeks since the eighth century B.C. They were no doubt similar to the phylakes of Attica, and remained popular with the Romans from the early Republic to the late Empire. A third component of Roman theatricals was the mimes, a sub-literary species involving jugglers, acrobats, dancers, and mountebanks—both male and female of low social station—who set up their booth stages to perform without masks as they moved from festival to festival throughout the ancient world. They survived even the fall of Rome. The Livius to whom Livy refers is the true beginner of real theatre in Rome, and will be dealt with a little later. Before his advent about the middle of the third century B.C., the predominant entertainment in Rome was what Horace later called *satura* (literally a bowl of different kinds of fruit), which included music, dancing, and short, comic sketches. At the same time, as the Latin scholar W. Beare points out in *The Roman Stage*, the atellanae and Etruscan dances, gladiatorial combats, and equestrian performances were also popular. A mixed bag, indeed!

Roman theatre an instrument of government

Aside from the early effort of two frightened consuls to propitiate the gods, Roman drama —more accurately, theatricals—had no connection with religion. The Romans were not a philosophic people, but a practical one. They had many deities to whom they paid lip service, but true religious fervor was absent from their way of life. They were early and widely skeptical, and preferred to put their trust in arms, tools, and politics. Their political and military acumen is demonstrated by the fact that from the legendary founding of Rome in 753 B.C. the comparative handful of dedicated citizen-soldiers had survived a hundred years of Tarquin domination, and in the historically short space of about two hundred years from the founding had conquered the whole of the Italian peninsula, including the Etruscans and all the city-states of Magna Graecia. Thence they went on to absorb Sicily, Corsica, Sardinia, Spain, Carthage, and Macedonia. In 146 B.C. Corinth was destroyed by the Roman army, and in 86 B.C. Athens was sacked by Sulla. At the death of the first Roman Emperor, Augustus, in 14 A.D., the Empire had spread throughout the Mediterranean world, including all of what is now France and Asia Minor. It reached its outermost limits by 117 A.D. at the end of the reign of Trajan, stretching from the Irish Sea to the Caspian, and from the Tigris-Euphrates Valley to Tangier. It is no wonder that the Roman emphasis was upon the arts of war rather than those of peace, nor that the extremely heterogeneous population finally defeated any attempt at realizing a uniquely Roman image of that most man-centered of the arts—theatre.

One of the earliest entertainments offered the Roman public was the frequent Roman Games (*Ludi Romani*), the earliest of which was established in the sixth century B.C. to honor Jupiter. In the early days of the Republic the peoples of Rome were an abstemious, courageous race of citizen-soldiers who possessed, above all, personal integrity and love of the state. At the end of the second Punic War (201 B.C.) there were less than fifty holidays in the year. The austere senators looked down on the frivolity of dramatic performances, and permitted no permanent theatres to be built. The succeeding centuries of conquest and civil war which led to the establishment of the Empire in 31 B.C. saw a breakdown in the stern asceticism of the Roman populace, and the corresponding lengthening of the time devoted to entertainment; by the last days of the Republic there were seventy-six holidays in the year. The Empire committed itself to a policy of "bread and circuses" as a palliative for civic abuses, and by the fourth century the yearly calendar included one hundred seventy-five official holidays; more than one hundred of these were given over to plays and theatrical entertainments, sixty-four to chariot races, and ten to gladiatorial combats.

From first to last, the games retained their official air because they were in the magistrates' charge; expenses were paid by the state, by the magistrates themselves, or by some wealthy patrician. They were always free to the populace. In addition to the "official" holidays, times of special games were set on the occasions of the opening of public buildings, for triumphs, and for funerals. Always there were more kinds of events than plays: circus races, gladiatorial fights, beast-fights, boxing, rope-dancing, etc. The presentation of drama was merely one in a number of choices. Among his other duties, the magistrate in charge contracted with a theatrical producer like Ambivius Turpio for dramatic presentations. Turpio produced the plays of Terence, each of which in turn he had bought at his own expense from the playwright, on speculation; they remained his property and were preserved because of their commercial value. Though there were always some freemen who were actors—and a few of them attained distinction, fame, and wealth—the performers were more often slaves under control of a manager who literally had the power of life and death over his company. Since dramatic performances had no status except as an entertainment among many entertainments, acting was, by and large, considered "an extremely mean and trivial craft."

In an interesting contradistinction to the policy at Athens, the Senate early declared that no Roman citizen could be an actor; if he joined the abased profession, he summarily lost all his civil rights. This stand probably resulted from a combination of republican resistance to the theatre on the grounds that it did not contribute to the austere existence deemed best for the citizen-soldier, and the fact that, as the Roman conquests spread and many captives were brought home to Rome, many Greek or Greek-trained performers became Roman slaves. In any event, actors were *infami* in the later Roman Republic and the Empire—an onus that has attached to them through many centuries, in many ways, and which is not entirely dissipated even today.

Needless to say, the audiences for dramatic performances in Rome were invariably festive and gay. In the early days of the Republic when there were few holidays, they were looked forward to as a pleasant release from the workaday world; in the later Empire, when half the year was a holiday, theatre was a diversion consuming time which hung heavy. Simulated sea battles, wild animal fights, contests between man and beast and between man and man variously armed, as well as the spectacular chariot races, vied with tragic spectacle, comedy, mime, and pantomime for the attention of the populace. Lavish display was everywhere, subsidized by the wealthy to impress and divert the poor.

Though no permanent theatre buildings were constructed in Rome prior to 55 B.C., audiences seem always to have been assigned seating strictly according to social class on all occasions of "official" performances. In the permanent theatres of the Empire, there was a definite hierarchy of assignment. The emperor and the donor of the play occupied the special boxes on either side of the stage; the senators sat in the semicircular orchestra on special chairs brought in for them;

the first fourteen rows of seats were reserved for the knights; the rest of the seats were allotted to the various social classes, with the most unimportant and poorest citizens occupying the seats farthest from the stage. Each spectator entered the theatre with a ticket in the form of a coin, on which was a picture, a name, and a number to indicate the section of the house in which he was to sit. Here is the first recorded use of the reserved-seat house. At various spots throughout the house were persons paid by the donor, or the playwright, or one or more of the actors, to applaud vigorously; they were the theatre's first *claqueurs*. The rowdy audience was presumably kept in order by *conquistores* whose assignment in the theatre was to maintain order, by the *dissignators*, who showed people to their seats (our first instance of ushers), and by the *praeco* or crier, who called for silence.

From the earliest days of the Republic, it was necessary for theatrical producers to make special efforts to please the public, to attract and hold their attention. As the diversity of holidays and entertainments (and the consequent competition for audience attention) increased in the time of the Empire, this effort to please the public became more frantic. There was ever increasing need for more and more thrills to titillate the increasingly jaded public taste with spectacular productions which descended finally to vulgarity and licentiousness and led to the eclipse of the drama which had been the glory of Greece.

Use and abuse of the Greeks

There was no indigenous tragedy in the Roman theatre. Whatever tragedy existed was sparse and poor, copied or adapted from the Greeks. At best we know of but thirty-six authors of tragedy in Roman times, with a total output of about one hundred fifty plays—not many more than Sophocles alone wrote during his lifetime. There are extant only meager fragments except the plays of Seneca (4 B.C.–65 A.D.), preserved perhaps because of his great fame.

Tragedy was introduced to Roman audiences by Livius Andronicus in 240 B.C., when he was thirty years old. He is said to have been a manumitted Greek slave, largely responsible for bringing Greek literature to Rome. Until his death in 204 B.C., he continued to translate, adapt, and copy the Greek plays. He evidently did not specialize exclusively in tragedy, for although none of his plays are extant in their entirety, there are titles of eight tragedies and three comedies. The Latin scholar W. Beare lists the tragedies as: *Achilles, Aegisthus, Ajax, Andromeda, Danae, Equos Troianus, Hermione,* and *Tereus,* and says of their author that he was "respectable but colorless." That they were still known in the first century B.C. is evidenced by a remark of Cicero, who said that they were not worth reading. The remark is also, incidentally, some proof that the actual performance of literary drama was falling into disuse in Cicero's time. Naevius (c. 260–c. 199 B.C.) was also a writer of both tragedy and comedy, supposedly forty plays in thirty years. Most of them were translations from the Greek or written on Greek models. But he also evidently invented the Roman historical play, the *fabula praetexta,* named for the purple-bordered toga which Roman magistrates wore. One of these was cited by the Roman scholar Varro (116–27 B.C.) as being about the Roman victory at Clostidium; another told the legendary story of Romulus; and a third was *The Rape of the Sabine Women.* It is written that Naevius died in exile at Utica because his propensity for satire brought him into conflict with a wealthy and powerful family.

At any rate, after Naevius there are no more plays with characters named and identified as living persons.

Ennius (239–169 B.C.) was an influential dramatist whose tragedies Cicero loved, quoting him copiously. There are twenty titles extant, with about four hundred lines of verse. His material is from the Greek masters, chiefly Euripides, but it is obvious that his attitude is rhetorical rather than dramatic: a tendency for striving after effect, for overstatement. Among his plays is also a fabula praetexta called *Sabinae.* Perhaps most famous of the writers of tragedy was one who specialized in the form—Pacuvius (220–130 B.C.), son of Ennius' sister, and renowned for his learning. There are twelve titles extant, and about four hundred lines from which it is possible to derive the facts that he was fond of elaborate and surprising stage effects, including the appearance of ghosts. His plays were popular on the stage for more than a century. He also wrote at least one fabula praetexta, *Paulus Ambrasia.*

More prolific than Pacuvius was Lucius Accius (170–80 B.C.) for whom the titles of forty tragedies and two praetexta, and about seven hundred ninety lines are extant. They reveal a propensity to violent, melodramatic plots, flamboyant characters, and bombastic language. It is said that the great Latin poet, Virgil (70–19 B.C.) "studied" Accius. It is of a production of his *Clytemnestra* in an ampitheatre in 55 B.C. that Cicero complains in *The Golden Ass* of "the sight of six hundred mules." No wonder literary drama succumbed to spectacle, and that after the death of Strabo in 87 B.C., plays largely ceased to be written for performance.

Certainly by the time Seneca was alive (4 B.C.–65 A.D.) plays were being written only to be read, and not to be performed. There was an almost complete divorce between theatre and drama. The theatres themselves were occupied chiefly with mime and pantomime; the literati contented themselves with denigrating these "cheap" entertainments and composed pieces to read to one another. Thus were Seneca's nine plays written—our first examples of "closet drama." Beare (*The Roman Stage*, p. 236) states that the first actual production of a Seneca play was of his *Troades* at Trinity College, Cambridge, in 1551. His other titles are *Medea, Phaedra, Agamemnon, Oedipus, Thyestes, Hercules Furens, Phoenissae,* and *Hercules Oetaeus.*

It is difficult to conceive of these tedious, bombastic, and bloody plays as descendants of classic Greek tragedy. What the Roman author seems to have done is to take from the Greek stories all those instances which allowed him to write extended descriptions, high-flown oratory, and tedious debates, and which emphasized horror for its own sake. In the first act of *Hercules Oetaeus* the hero speaks a long passage describing his labors; Seneca's Medea pours forth her emotions in an avalanche of words; principal characters almost invariably speak one after the other in the oratorical style of debate rather than in conversation; Thyestes dines from the limbs of his children and recognizes their severed heads in full view of the audience. Seneca makes revenge the chief motive of many of his plays: *Agamemnon* opens with the ghost of Thyestes swearing vengeance on the House of Atreus. The revenge motive, the ghosts, the scenes of bloody horror, were adopted by Renaissance dramatists, who thus corrupted the Greek concern with fate, the death of heroes, and the emotional impact of rash deeds. Seneca emphasized all the wrong things in his adaptation of the Greeks, making melodrama rather than true tragedy. He is said to have written not only his plays but his philosophical works to influence Nero. Certainly his writing reflects that luxurious and treacherous court.

Roman comedy also used two types of subject matter—one which concentrated on Greek materials, and one which used Roman materials. Writers of Roman comedy were no less dependent on their Greek masters than were the writers of tragedy. They used the Greek plays in a somewhat different way, however, cannibalizing scenes and characters from several plays and combining them in an attempt to form something new. Often the borrowed situations were dressed in Roman locales and characters, but the sources are unmistakable. A consistent plot line is often lacking, and where it does exist it is so overlaid with instances, subplots, and counterplots as to be exceedingly hard to follow. Secondary characters, likely to be more important in the staging than the principals, developed as a whole company of stock personages. This is the tradition which descended to the avid copiers of the Renaissance.

It has been noted that some Roman dramatists wrote comedies as well as tragedies. Livius Andronicus' three comedies whose titles are known are *Gladiolus, Ludius,* and *Vergo.* The comedies of Naevius bear the titles *The Charcoal Burners, The Potter, The Soothsayer, The Races, The Night-hawks,* and *The Girl of Tarentum.* Fragments extant from the last of these seem to indicate that it is a play about soldiers on leave and a town girl. The Latin writer of comedy whom scholars of the immediately succeeding generation universally and unequivocally labeled "great" was Caecilius (d. 168 B.C.) who was the author of some forty-two comedies, sixteen of whose titles are identical to those of Menander. Unfortunately, only about two hundred eighty lines of his work have survived. There are thirteen titles and about two hundred lines of Turpilius, and almost a dozen names of other writers of Greek-derived comedy, called by Roman critics *fabula palliatae.* In addition, there were a number of writers who specialized in the *fabula togata*, which were not derived from the Greek but used Roman materials. Casts of the togata tended to be smaller and the plays shorter; the tone was usually lively, amusing, and satirical. From the fragments which remain it is difficult to discern plots, but there is a sharp observation of ordinary Italian lower-class life. The most prolific writer of togata was L. Afrianus for whom there are forty-four titles extant and about four hundred lines. For him and his fellow togata writers, Titinius and Atta, the writing of these plays was a full-time occupation. There remain fifteen titles ascribed to Titinius and eleven to Atta. Typical titles for the togata are *The Match-maker, The Hairdresser, The Rejected Lover, Not What He Seemed to Be, The Divorce, Rescued from Drowning, What You Will.*

The only writers of Roman comedy from whom complete plays exist are Plautus and Terence. Both wrote fabula palliatae. Titus Maccius Plautus (c. 254–184 B.C.), whom we know as Plautus, had had a colorful career as provincial actor, soldier, businessman, and itinerant miller before he took to writing comedies about the year 200 B.C.; in the time that was left him, he turned out one hundred thirty pieces, of which twenty-one are extant—the largest number of plays still in existence of any of the classic playwrights. He based his plays on those of Greek New Comedy, borrowing both plots and characters from the earlier masters. Frequently he Romanized situation, locale, and dialogue. He wrote with far more exuberance than did his Greek prototypes; a quick appraiser of his audience, he wrote into his plays, with robust humor, situations which were native and topical. Thus he continued the tradition, though in paler form, of the great Aristophanic comedy. His plays are exceedingly

ROMAN COMEDY
Left, a bronze statuette of a Roman comic actor. The grotesque mask, the padded body, the short tunic, the vigorous gesture are all typical of his Greek predecessors. Above, a cast for making a comic mask, found at Tarentum in southern Italy. The mask (right) is for the stock character of the comic slave. (Museum of Fine Arts, Boston)

varied in worth, for he wrote with great speed.

He was firmly entrenched in the convention of type characters such as are found in the Greek New Comedy, and these types, often with the same names, appear over and over in his plays. Miles Gloriosus is the braggart soldier who is the prototype of Falstaff; the leading character in *The Crock of Gold* is Molière's model for *The Miser*; his *Amphitryon* had many copiers down to modern times, when Giraudoux produced his *Amphitryon 38; Persa* is the an-

cient version of *The Beggar's Opera; The Twin Menaechmi* is the source of *The Comedy of Errors*. The *Mostellaria* contains what many people have assessed as the most delightful "cunning slave" in all of Latin literature.

Titillating situations, rollicksome dialogue, and vivid characters mark the best of Plautus; at his worst he may be accused of lacking verisimilitude and abounding in bad taste. His plays, however, were received enthusiastically by the Roman audiences; he recouped his arid fortunes and, though a foreigner and an actor, he was granted the privilege of Roman citizenship. Plautus was perhaps the first of all the classic writers to depend for his livelihood solely on the success of his plays with the common people of Rome. He had no patron, but so popular and famous did he become that producers tried to pass off the work of others as being his. (It was the scholar, Varro, late in the first century B.C., who first identified accurately the true Plautine works.) He remained popular for a long time after his death, and even though both Cicero and Horace found fault with his literary abilities, both attested to his vitality and popularity.

Quite different in atmosphere, and in contemporary fame and popularity, were the plays of Publius Terentius Afer (c. 185–159 B.C.), whom we know as Terence. He was born a slave in Carthage, brought to Rome, and educated by his master, Terentius Lucanus, who recognized his talent and set him free. He became the darling of Roman society and frankly wrote for their aristocratic tastes. Taking Menander for his model, he attempted to develop his own style to the polished precision he saw in his master, and indeed there is a refinement apparent from his first play, *Andria*, to his last, *Adelphi*. (In the former of these he added a second lover, and introduced a situation unparalleled in Greek drama: a young man in love with a girl of his own station. Thus, because Roman women enjoyed a freedom not available in the Greek society, which forced an oriental seclusion on its young women, Terence was able to develop a love interest along modern lines.) The other four of his plays which are extant are *The Mother-in-Law*, *The Self-Avenger*, *The Eunuch*, and *Phormio*. This last, adapted from Apollodorus rather than Menander, presents us with a very delightful characterization of a parasite (who has had many progeny in succeeding literary periods). Terence was a talented playwright at war with the tastes of his society. His plays were, indeed, produced, and *The Eunuch* earned him an unprecedented sum of money. But the elegance of his literary style led to accusations by his enemies that the plays had been written by his aristocratic friends, and he was led on more than one occasion to defend himself in prologues written for various productions. The sophisticated humor evident in his plays marked them as high comedy— a quite different genre from the knockabout farce which the Roman populace loved. Legend has it that Terence died of heartbreak on a pilgrimage to Athens when his manuscripts were lost; actually he died at sea when he was less than thirty years old. But his highly polished plays became models for many future writers, including the learned nun Hroswitha, who wrote six plays "after Terence" in the tenth century.

The writing and the performance of tragedies and comedies such as those discussed above were almost entirely limited to the times of the Roman Republic. The only new play officially performed in the Empire was the *Thyestes* of Varrius as part of the games declared for the victory at Actium (31 A.D.). Quintilian (35–95 A.D.) speaks of tragedy as a literary form, not to be staged, and the word *comoedus* was used in the Empire to denote a slave reciting extracts at feasts. One of the favorite pastimes of the Emperor Nero (c. 60 A.D.) was to sing or recite such works as *Oedipus Blinded, Hercules Mad.*

But there was no lack of theatrical fare in the Empire. The mime, the pantomime, and the atellanae, which had shared unofficial attention with the tragedies and comedies throughout the period of the Republic,

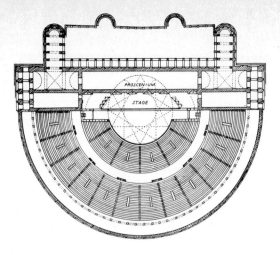

THE MARCELLUS THEATRE AT ROME
The plan of the theatre, showing the precisely symmetrical arrangement of the seats, the integration of stage house and auditorium, and the semicircular orchestra. (Streit, *Das Theater*)

---

became the predominant forms of theatrical entertainment.

Pantomime—an original contribution

The pantomime stands as the only original contribution of the Romans to the art of theatre. Livius Andronicus, mentioned above as actor and playwright, is said to have begun the pantomime as early as 240 B.C. It is said that, finding his voice to be giving out when he attempted to do lines, songs, and dance movements simultaneously in the performance of a tragedy, he assigned the voice parts to a speaker who stood at the side of the stage while he, voiceless, pantomimed and danced the part.

By the first century the pantomimes had become elaborate displays quite distinct from the drama. All the resources of the theatre were used in the service of these performances, the stage pictures and movement being supplemented by orchestral music and choral singing. The pantomimes employed extensive scenery and expensive costuming, and their wonders were extolled by many writers. They were a favorite form of theatrical diversion for the Emperor Nero, who delighted to play in them. The performers were exceedingly popular with members of high society, and it is said that in the later Empire the female dancers often performed on the tables at extravagant banquets of the wealthy. Well-known poets sometimes enriched themselves by writing libretti for the pantomimes, and these libretti were, during performance, sung by the chorus. The choral singing was accompanied by an orchestra of flutes, pipes, cymbals, and trumpets. The subject matter might be anything from mythology or history, primarily in the tragic vein, with the emphasis on love stories. From all accounts, however, neither music nor libretti were of particular artistic merit. The great popularity of the form was due to the skill of the dancer, or *pantomimus*, and the lavish staging. Relying solely upon an intricate system of gesticulation and movement, dressed in rich costume and mask, the performer acted out the story being sung. So all-encompassing did this form become that the old word for actor, *histrio*, came to mean, in the later Empire, "performer of pantomime."

Vulgarity succeeds comedy

The mime, which replaced comedy in the Roman theatre of the Empire, had a long history before its adoption by the Romans. It had originated in the ancient world with public entertainers of all kinds who performed in marketplaces, private houses, or wherever there was an audience. The performers were marked by their skill in mimicry, song, dance, and improvisation. Jesting, buffoonery, and an unfailing aura of indecency were constant elements from first to last. The characters were types, usually drawn from the lower orders of society, the situations titillating, the endings often abrupt. Needless to say, the plays were short. So popular did the form become in Rome that the literary dilettantes of the Empire amused themselves by writing mimes to be read aloud to their friends. But the mime, which drove all other forms of spoken drama from the theatre, was largely subliterary and improvised. Records of its performance may be found up to the beginning of the sixth century A.D.

The only vigorous rival of the mime was the persistent atellana, which eventually, however, also succumbed to the mime. The atellanae were rustic farces, originating in Campania, early imported into Rome. They were played in masks and used traditional figures in ridiculous situations. The emphasis was on horseplay and obscene jest. Originally completely improvisational, they assumed literary form some time in the first century A.D., when Pomponius and Novius began composing them. Fragments amounting to more than two hundred lines and one hundred titles are extant. Something of the character types and subject matter is evident from these titles: *Maccus the Soldier, Maccus the Inn-Keeper, Maccus the Maiden, Pappus the Farmer, Bucco the Gladiator, The Two Dosseni, The She-Ass, The Candidate, The Pimp.* It is an interesting speculation that the character masks of these actors persisted into the Renaissance *commedia dell 'arte.* Maccus, the flat-nosed, stupid country lad, might well be the prototype of Pulcinella; Bucco, the jabbering parasite, the forerunner of that line; Pappus, the silly old man, the ancestor of Pantalone. There seems to be some evidence of the persistence of mime through the Dark Ages, and it may well be that this form, generally played without masks, absorbed the masked atellanae and

emerged in the Renaissance as the commedia.

Bread and circuses

It is no wonder that literary drama was of a comparatively low order and small quantity in Roman times. Not only did the dramatists compete with mimes and pantomimes, but with other "circuses" as well. The bloody encounters of the gladiatorial combats and the animal games in the huge Circus Maximus and the Colosseum drew crowds of eighty thousand and more. Sometimes the Colosseum was flooded for that peculiar institution of the *naumachia*, where slave-manned ships fought each other to the death. The chariot races of the Circus Maximus have become legendary. When the visual capacities of an audience were thus sated, how could it be expected to meet the auditory challenge of real theatre? Splendor was the word for theatre of the Empire; a rather tawdy splendor it became, but nonetheless lavish. Horace bemoaned the materialism of his contemporaries which prevented them from writing dramas as great as the Greek genius had produced. What if he had lived to see the excesses of the later Empire?

Though the Roman theatre never produced great drama, it contributed much of a more material and practical nature to the heritage of the theatre.

Theatre architecture masterful

The Romans were great engineers. Myriad roads, aqueducts, monuments, and buildings attest to the fact. It is natural, then, that their most significant contribution to theatre history is in this field.

The building of theatres occurred late in the history of Rome. Prior to 55 B.C. there were no permanent theatres. When

THE MARCELLUS THEATRE
A Piranesi etching of the Marcellus Theatre in the eighteenth century, when other structures were built inside it. These are the outside walls, and show how the Romans built free-standing theatres where the natural topography could not support the tiers of seats. These thick masonry walls were pierced by passageways leading to the rows of seats in the auditorium.

dramatic performances were to be played, a temporary wooden skene fronted by a raised platform for the actors was built, but this was torn down after the performance. No seats were provided for the spectators, who either had to stand or bring their own chairs for the occasion. As late as 194 B.C., the citizens were outraged to find that special seats were provided and reserved for senators. In 174 B.C., the first skene of stone was built, but the spectators still brought their own seats. In fact, a law had been passed in 185 B.C. forbidding anyone to sit at dramatic performances. As time went on, this law seems to have been observed chiefly in the breach. In 155 B.C., a stone theatre

was planned and construction begun near the Palatine Hill, but public and official outcry was so great that construction was halted and the partially built structure destroyed. The democratic Roman Republic thus showed its scorn of the effete Greeks whom they had conquered, and continued the tradition which looked on theatricals as debilitating to the stronger virtues of the Roman citizen.

Even in 55 B.C., when Pompey succeeded in building the first stone theatre in Rome, he disguised it by incorporating in it, at the top of the rows of seats, a temple to Venus Victrix. He explained that the rows of seats were steps leading to the shrine. The ruse was flimsy and no one was deceived, but at least lip service had been paid to the Republican tradition of austerity. His was the last gesture to the outworn idea, however; and with the coming of the Empire, two more stone theatres were erected in Rome, both finished in 13 B.C. One was built by Cornelius Balbus and seated eleven thousand five hundred; the other, finished by Augustus and named for his nephew Marcellus, seated twenty thousand five hundred. The Theatre of Marcellus is the only classic theatrical structure still extant in Rome, though only a part of the outer walls of the structure remains. The Theatre of Pompey, as reported by the Elder Pliny, seated forty thousand. These three theatres were the only permanent ones built at Rome up to the time of its fall.

Many temporary structures, however, continued to be built. The most magnificent of these by all accounts was that erected by M. Aemilius Scaurus in 58 B.C. The Elder Pliny describes it as having three stories supported by three hundred sixty columns. The lower level was made of marble, the second of glass, and the third was gilded wood. Between each pair of the thirty-eight-foot lower columns were bronze statues. The theatre, according to Pliny, accommodated eighty thousand spectators. After a few days' use the whole thing was torn down.

Another of these temporary structures was a unique swivel theatre erected a few years later by C. Curio. This consisted of two wooden structures whose curving seats were built back to back with each unit on a pivot. After the presentation of plays, the seats were swung around, spectators and all, to form an amphitheatre for athletics and gladiatorial combats. Such was the grandeur of Rome.

About the same time as the Balbus and Marcellus theatres opened, Marcus Vitruvius Pollio completed his ten-volume book, *De*

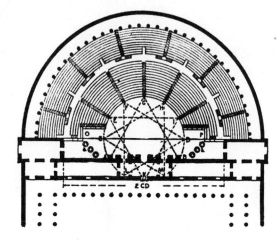

PLAN OF A ROMAN THEATRE FROM VITRUVIUS
This symmetrical arrangement, worked out on geometrical principles, is typical of the plans not only for the theatres which the Romans built but also for those extant Greek structures which they remodeled. (Vitruvius, *The Ten Books on Architecture*, Harvard University Press, 1914)

Architectura, the fifth volume of which takes up theatre architecture. With exposition and illustration, and with the skill of a professional engineer, he describes in detail the plans for an ideal theatre. From this, and from the ruins of actual structures, the Roman theatre building can be realized.

The basic design was a modification of the Greek theatre, with some significant differences. Most importantly, the seats of the spectators (*cavea*) formed an integral structure with the skene; stagehouse and audience space thus formed a single unit, in contradistinction to the two units prevalent in the Greek theatre. While the Romans sometimes built on a natural slope, as the Greeks invariably did, their structures usually were free standing, with the outside walls highly decorated. A system of arched passageways

THE THEATRE OF HERODUS ATTICUS
Present-day view of the theatre in Athens, built in 167 A.D.; seats and stage floor have been repaired for modern audiences. In this case, the seats are built against the steep slope of the Acropolis, at the opposite end from the Theatre of Dionysus. (J. Christopher Roberts)

(*vomitorii*) was included for audience dispersal.

What was the circular orchestra in the Greek theatre was here reduced to an exact semicircle and it was paved. It was not used by any of the performers, but special chairs were placed there to seat the senators watching the performance.

The stage was always elevated, usually to a height of five feet. It was a tremendous area, often more than twenty feet deep and a hundred feet wide. The old skene was now an elaborate stage building, much higher than formerly because of its integration with the cavea. The front of this stage building (*frons scaenae*) formed an architectural background for the stage and was highly elaborate. An ornate center door was flanked on either side by two smaller doors, and the whole area was a symmetrical mass of columns, pediments, niches, and statues. A highly ornamented roof extended over the stage. Around the top of the semicircular seating area was a roofed portico, from the top of which sailors manipulated awnings to protect the spectators from the sun.

This ideal theatre, as described by Vitruvius and built by Augustus and by Balbus, was a development from earlier Roman theatres built at Pompeii, Segasta, and Tyndaris. The latter two were converted from late Hellenistic theatres. At Tyndaris and in the large theatre at Pompeii, both erected about 200 B.C., the auditorium is in the form of a horseshoe built against a natural hill slope. Open passageways lead into the orchestra. Both these theatres were subsequently remodeled—the passageways were vaulted over and special boxes for seating were erected over them. The small theatre at Pompeii, built about 75 B.C. (the same time as the large theatre was remodeled), is the oldest purely Roman theatre preserved. It has the semicircular plan later described by Vitruvius, but the side tiers are cut short to make the building rectangular. A wooden roof was erected over the entire structure. It had a capacity of about fifteen hundred. On theatres of this comparatively small size wooden roofs were usual, as on those at Taormina and Naples. Thus the Roman theatre reached a complete architectural unity such as the Greeks never attained. In the larger Roman theatres, the semicircular plan of seats was complete and uninterrupted, and the awnings mentioned above, invented by Catullus about 80 B.C., were used as roofs upon occasion. In later years, permanent corbels fastened this linen roof into place so that sailors needed no longer man it.

The avid builders of the Roman Empire erected more than one hundred twenty-five of these theatres from England to North Africa and from Portugal to Asia Minor. Where the theatre was a new structure, the form developed at Rome was used. In the eastern provinces, where Greek and Hellenistic structures already stood, they were rebuilt according to the new specifications. Sometimes, as at Aizonoi and Pessimus, the theatre was an architectural unit with the circus of which the Romans were so fond. In the Greek colonies, where the Roman amphitheatre was not popular, extant structures were remodeled by cutting down the orchestra circle, paving it with stone, and building a wall around its perimeter. Thus the theatre could be used for animal fights, gladiatorial combats, and even the simulated sea battles. In this fashion, as indicated above, the Theatre of Dionysus at Athens was reconstructed under Nero. The backless

stone benches for the audience were retained here, however, as they were elsewhere in Roman theatre construction. Along with the marvelous Colosseum at Rome, the ruins of many of these theatres remain as monuments to Roman engineering skill. The best preserved may be found today at Orange in the south of France, at Aspendos in Asia Minor, and at Leptis Magna in Libya.

Innovations in settings

One of the most unusual innovations of the Romans was the use of a front curtain. This curtain, often richly embroidered, was housed in a sort of trough at the edge of the stage area, being dropped at the beginning of a performance and raised at the end of it. Cicero and Juvenal both speak of the use of the *siparium* in the theatre— evidently a portable screen or small curtain which could be used for short scenes. Steps sometimes led from the stage to the orchestra; the front of the stage elevation (*hyposcenium*) was ornamentally decorated, and sometimes had doors, presumably to admit the creatures used in the animal fights.

Vitruvius refers to the use of painted scenery, for which provision was made in the skene. He particularly mentions periaktoi, the painted pieces which revolved to indicate change of scene. He also quite elliptically refers to the three types of scenes: the tragic scene with its "columns, pediments, statues, and other objects suited to kings"; the comic scene with its "private dwellings, with balconies and views representing rows of windows, after the manner of ordinary dwellings"; and the satyric scene with its "trees, mountains, and other rustic objects delineated in landscape style." (*The Ten Books on Architecture*, p. 150.) Just how these effects were achieved is not certain, but we know that there must have been

THE ROMAN THEATRE AT ORANGE
These ruins in the south of France are
among the best preserved of the ruins of
many theatres built by the Romans all over
the Empire. They give a good idea of the
height and massiveness of the Roman stage
house. Typical of the Roman theatre was the
raised stage and the high, intricately decorated front wall of the skene. The stage itself
was covered over with a wooden roof, also
highly decorated. (Theatre Collection, New
York Public Library)

more than rudimentary stage machinery because we have contemporary descriptions of
pantomimes with disappearing mountains
made of wood, fountains, running streams,
and growing trees. It is true that the Romans
were clever in controlling water, and it is
not hard to believe that some of their
theatres were effectively air conditioned by
means of special passages of running water
to cool the air. We also know that in some
instances fine sprays of water mingled with
perfume were blown over the audience to
make them comfortable.

The front of the stage building, in its
fully developed form of actual columns,
niches, and statuary, was a development
from a simpler beginning. The earlier
wooden scaenae evidently had flat walls with
painted decorations, although the traditional
five doors were practical. Under the probable influence of the thyromata panels of the
Hellenistic stages, these painted decorations
became more extensive and rich in the first
century B.C. Pliny tells the story of birds
being lured by the realism of the paintings
on the stage wall erected by Claudius Pul-
cher in 99 B.C. Many other such anecdotes
attest to the realism striven for and apparently attained. The remains of the small
theatre at Pompeii indicate the use of a
painted frons scaenae. But the Roman love
of pomp, luxury, and display made the
splendidly intricate architectural design of
the stage wall the one most typical and most
universal. The earlier flat walls became
broken and elaborated into series of niches,
arches, entablatures, and columns, all
wrought of stone and marble. The first tier

THE ROMAN THEATRE AT SABRATHA
Built c. 200 A.D., this is the largest Roman theatre in North Africa. Clearly visible are the raised stage, the semicircular orchestra, and the three-storied frons scaena.

WALL PAINTING FROM POMPEII
Paintings such as this, from the first century
B.C., are found on the walls of dwellings in
Pompeii. Some have the tragic mask above
them, some the comic mask. They indicate
that the Romans were interested in the dif-
ferentiation of stage setting, and bear out
Vitruvius' prescription of set scenes for the
various types of plays. (The Metropolitan
Museum of Art, Rogers Fund, 1903)

---

alone of Pompey's theatre is said to have
had fifty columns. Though the permanent
decoration of the Roman stage was most
elaborate, special decorations in the form
of bronzes, paintings, and garlands were
evidently added for festival performances.
The stage roof, peculiar to the Roman theatre building, was not only an acoustical
achievement, but served to protect this rich
decoration as well. The linen roof over the
audience was also decoratively painted on
occasion, as Pliny reports of the splendidly
painted roof stretched over the Theatre of
Pompey in 66 A.D. for the visit of the king of

Armenia. In design, form, and decoration,
the theatres were among the most masterful
creations of Roman architecture.

There were no lighting problems in the
ordinary course of the performance, since
productions were given in the daytime. The
roofed-in theatres were no doubt illuminated
equally on stage and in the seating area by
lamps and torches. Occasionally, and as a
curiosity, torchlit night performances were
given.

Music was an important part of Roman
theatricals, especially in the mimes and
pantomimes. Songs were for solo voices or
chorus, and dancing was usually accompanied by singing as well as by instrumental
music. The flute, the lyre, the pipe, cymbals,
trumpets, and the harp were the instruments most frequently used, and dancers
sometimes used taps, called *scabilla*, attached to wooden soles. Musicians were ordinarily seated on the stage, though occasionally they were performers in the show.

Costumes follow the Greeks

Since masks had been a convention of Greek
production, it is likely that they were
adopted by the Romans along with the plays,
costuming, and staging. In the atellanae, of
course, the record is clear: masks were
always a part of their production. That the
use of the mask in tragedy and comedy
might not have been firmly established in
the Roman Republic is plausible when we
read that the actor Roscius (c. 126–62 B.C.) is
credited with making the mask mandatory
for both tragedy and comedy, supposedly because he wished to mask his natural squint.
Whatever the reason, his influence was evidently powerful enough to authenticate and
perpetuate their use. They were much the
same as those that had been in use in the
Greek theatre: old men, young men, old

women, young women, rustics, and slaves. They were usually made of linen stiffened over a mold. As the quantity of melodrama and thrill increased in the stage presentations of the Empire, the masks became more startling and horrible.

The costumes for comedy and tragedy also followed Greek models: long tragic gowns, short comic tunics, elevated tragic boots, and short comic shoes. In the early presentations of tragedy and comedy the two types were separate and consistent. In the Empire, however, several illustrations have shown that the grotesque comic costumes often appeared in the same productions with the traditional costume of tragedy, the juxtaposition being ludicrous in the extreme.

In the mimes the actors were barefoot and wore no masks. They did use makeup, however, and sometimes wore wigs. The typical costume of the mime was a hood which could be drawn over the head or thrown back. One clown-type character whose head was shaven seems to have worn a patchwork jacket, tights, and the phallus. Other characters, both men and women, seem to have worn costumes appropriate to the characters, with increasing emphasis on elaborate display as the mime ascended in popularity with widespread audiences. The mime dancers, particularly the women, became notable for the filminess of their attire and sometimes they wore nothing at all.

However far the pantomime diverged from its inspiration in the tragedy, it did maintain the use of masks. Sometimes as many as five were used by one performer during a single presentation. But since there was no need for his voice to be heard, the mouths of these masks were closed, not open as in the Greek originals. The pantomimist also wore a long tragic gown, now supple and made of silk. As the pantomimes of the

TRAGIC MASKS OF THE ROMAN THEATRE
Above, a tragic mask of terracotta, showing a similar expression and the same dome-shaped protrusion found in many Greek tragic masks. Opposite, masks of the Roman theatre of about 100 B.C., as depicted on a bas-relief. Again, these are the same as were in earlier use in the Greek theatre. (Museum of Fine Arts, Boston; Vatican Museum)

Empire became more elaborate, and women joined the troupes, costumes came to be symbolic and generally scant. Mercury is described as wearing nothing but a short mantle over his left shoulder and a tiny pair of golden wings; a host of Cupids wore nothing but wings and tiny arrows. Beautiful bodies, much admired in pantomime actors, were not concealed or camouflaged.

Acting—a despised profession

The Roman audience expected a high degree of skill from theatrical performers, just as from athletes and gladiators, with whom they classed the performers of theatrical entertainments. But the demands on the individual artist were not so great as in the Greek theatre. Those parts of the plays

which were sung were generally performed by specifically trained singers (*cantores*), while the actor pantomimed the action, and the player in the pantomimes was relieved of all vocalization. Though all actors were expected to have some dancing skill, this was especially stressed in the mimes and pantomimes. There was no limitation in the Roman theatre to three actors as there was in the Greek. Hence there was no doubling of parts except in the early traveling companies of masked players. Actors were cheap and plentiful in the Empire and an acting company could be as large as it needed to be. Often, indeed, it was even larger.

Actors were classified as tragedians, comedians, mimes, or pantomimists. Within these classifications actors specialized in particular roles. Quintilian tells us of the com-edian Demetrius, who specialized in gods, young men, good fathers, slaves, matrons, and respectable old women, while his fellow-comedian Stratocles won his success in the roles of sharp-tempered old men, cunning slaves, parasites, pimps, and other such lively figures. Aesopus, the great tragedian of the first century B.C., evidently played his best roles as Agamemnon in the *Iphigenia* of Ennius, as Atreus in the *Clytemnestra* of Accius, and as the title character in Ennius' *Andromacha*.

The most famous of Roman actors was the comedian Roscius (d. 62 B.C.), who won fame and fortune through his acting. Before Roscius, the accepted style of acting was exaggerated and bombastic. He introduced moderation and a kind of verisimilitude which, in his skillful hands, became quite popular. Both he and Aesopus founded schools of acting, and even today the fame of the former lives in the compliment applied to a good actor: that he is "a veritable Roscius." The early nineteenth century was particularly fond of the designation, and actors were billed as "The Young American Roscius" (Samuel Cowell, 1820–1864), "The Hibernian Roscius" (G. V. Brooke, 1818–1866), "The Scottish Roscius" (H. E. Johnston, 1777–1845), "The Young Roscius" (William Betty, 1791–1874), "The American Roscius" (Ira Aldredge, 1804–1876, the famous black actor), and—rather provincial and somewhat late—"The Ohio Roscius" (Louis Aldrich, 1843–1901).

Among the pantomimists, the most famous were the tragic dancer Pylades and the comic dancer Bathyllus; both gained great personal popularity as well as succeeding in establishing the new art form most firmly. The mime dancer Paris was said to have been the favorite of both Nero and his empress. He suffered for the excellence of his art, for it is said that Nero, himself an actor, had him put to death in a fit of professional jealousy.

The income of Roman actors varied widely from nothing at all to what was evidently the very large annual income of Roscius. So independently wealthy did Roscius become that for some years before his death he could afford to act without compensation—and did. Favorite performers, of course, were also the recipients of lavish gifts from wealthy admirers. It is said that Sulla had a golden ring bestowed upon Roscius, thus raising him to the rank of knight, while Cicero conducted a lawsuit for him against a wealthy citizen whose slave Roscius had instructed.

In spite of the honors and gifts given individual members of the profession, Roman actors as a whole were classed as infami. They had no civil rights, and, as mentioned above, no Roman citizen could earn his livelihood in the theatre without losing all his civil privileges. Actors were, for the most part, slaves trained and supported to add prestige to their wealthy masters or to be hired out to the state or to other individuals as a total acting unit. The marriage of an actor to the child, grandchild, or great-grandchild of a senator was likely to be declared invalid, and any soldier appearing on the stage was instantly punished by death.

Having no basis in religion, acting was admired as an art by the Romans but despised as a profession. Individual performers were patronized by the wealthy and many were intimate with the great and the near-great. Some of the more fascinating female mimes and pantomimists became the mistresses of prominent men. Seneca speaks of the pampered lives led by the slavewomen performers of the pantomimes who were owned by wealthy Romans, and it is said that when Antonius was traveling about Italy campaigning for Caesar, his traveling companion was the mime-dancer Cytheris. In the Empire the attempt to titillate jaded appetites produced shocking scenes in the theatre which were meant to rival the cruel games of the arena. On the day that Caligula was murdered the Theatre of Marcellus offered as part of a mime the actual crucifixion of a captured robber, and Heliogabalus is said to have ordered the realistic performance of adultery on the mime stage.

Thus it was that in the Empire actors as a class acquired a very dissolute reputation, and the early Christian church declared against them. No Christian was permitted to witness a theatrical performance, much less become a part of it. For centuries the ban persisted and until after the

hir meaf frater abierar peregre demipho.
..... achenif amphonefilio.
...... clam habelrut lemni uxorem ......

COMIC MASKS OF THE ROMAN THEATRE
Left, masks for the *Phormio* of Terence,
Ambrosianus manuscript. Above, masks for
the *Andria* of Terence, Basilicanus manuscript. As in the Greek theatre, the masks for
comedy lack the domed top, and their expressions are dictated by the stock characters for whom they were intended. (Vatican
Museum)

time of Molière actors were not even permitted to be buried in holy ground. It is
one of the ironies of history that in spite of
this violent stand against the theatre, it was
in the church that the drama was reborn
long after the fall of Rome.

Summary

The history of theatre in Roman times
divides itself quite naturally into two parts,
just as the political history of Roman times
does: there is the theatre of the Republic,
and there is the quasi-theatre of the Empire.
But in neither case was it whole or indigenous. The theatre of the Republic is chiefly
marked by the writing and production of
literary tragedy and comedy, largely derived
from Greek subject-matter and form, but
nonetheless vital and interesting. At the same
time, there were no theatre buildings, as
such, erected—dramatic materials and dramatic environments did not complement and
influence each other. Nor did they during
the time of the Empire, when there was a
tremendous program of theatre architecture,
but drama had largely ceased to be written
or literary dramas performed. The dich-
otomy between play and its environment
continued from first to last.

Yet, a Roman treatise, Horace's *Ars Poetica* (c. 20 B.C.), was as influential to after-times as Aristotle's *Poetics*. It is a kind of "how-to-do-it" for young playwrights, and sets up the dicta that drama must be written in five acts, and must have as equal aims both pleasure and profit. These criteria, along with examples derived from the tragedies of Seneca and the comedies of Terence, nurtured more than one generation of playwrights after the beginning of the Renaissance.

One quasi-theatrical form the Romans did invent and develop is the pantomime. Yet it was only the technique and form of the pantomime which was indigenous to them; the materials they took largely from Greek legends. The other theatrical forms—mime and atellanae—were so ubiquitous in material and form before and after Roman times that they are the *lingua franca* of mankind rather than the particular province of any one race or nation.

In the practical and tangible arts of theatre the Romans were superb. The great theatre buildings which they planned and constructed are a wonder even today when they are largely in a state of ruin. Roman technicians developed the use of the front curtain, intricate and movable scenery, and a host of stage effects. Roman theatrical producers began the idea of a reserved-seat house. But Rome also put the acting profession into the disrepute which stayed with it for centuries, and instituted claques, whose annoying antics have bothered theatre patrons for centuries.

ROMAN COMEDY SCENE
A wall painting from Pompeii shows a lively scene with a slave, a courtesan, and another male figure. The slave wears the body padding and grotesque mask similar to those found in Greek Old Comedy. (Maiuri, *Roman Painting*, Skira, 1953)

Perhaps the final word on Roman theatre might be something like this: Though there was a great deal of theatrical activity in Roman times, there was never a time when theatre had the respect, love, and admiration of the Roman people. It was always regarded as a species of entertainment, no better or no worse than the multitude of other entertainments provided by the state, and so it never attained its full status as an autonomous and meaningful art form.

Formal theatre in the Middle Ages—performances with recognized and recognizable scripts, performers, and audiences—is a phenomenon of the High Middle Ages: the period from approximately 1000 A.D. onwards. The period of the preceding five hundred years is often called the Dark Ages, and in many ways the appellation is justified. For the second half of the first millennium A.D. was marked by the dissolution of the culture which had been spread throughout Europe and the Mediterranean by the Roman Empire, the decline of trade in Western Europe, the crumbling of the economic system, the devastation of cities, towns, and lines of communication. Yet during the same period a new light was dawning in Europe—that of the Christian church, in whose monasteries and churches were preserved the relics of ancient cultures. It was an embattled church. From its very beginnings it had been in conflict with what it perceived as the sensuality and dissoluteness of the Roman Empire, and had immediately declared its opposition to the "entertainments" of the Romans; theatre in any form was interdicted. After the fall of Rome (475 A.D.), its struggle was with an even more intractable foe—the paganism (i.e., nature worship) of the several native tribes of the continent, as well as with the spread of Mohammedanism after the death of its prophet in 632 A.D. But theatre did not die with Rome, nor was it killed off by the Christian church.

The seeds of drama were long underground and the quickening was slow, but the flowering did come, and even through the long winter of the Dark Ages there were sporadic and weak growths, the evidences of which we can now trace.

It had not been the early Christians alone who had deplored Roman theatre in the time of the Empire, for it is said that the Emperor Marcus Aurelius averted his eyes from the stage when public functions required his presence, and that he complained of the low state to which theatre in his day had sunk. But it was the Christians who were most violently opposed to this pagan activity. The newly converted were most violent of all (see Tertullian's *De Spectaculis*). The Christian church early declared war on the theatre, and waged it vigorously for almost a millennium. Council followed council, edict followed edict, yet the love of many professed Christians for their spectacles was not killed. Even the Christian emperors went no further than to legislate against performances on Sundays and holy days. And in the sixth century, the eastern Emperor, Justinian (483–565), married Theodora, who was said to have been a mime dancer (although it must be recorded that he continued to oppose theatre). The Roman popes and the church hierarchy were implacably hostile; the ecclesiastical writer, Orosius, lays a large share of the blame for the sack of Rome by the Ostrogoths on the decay engendered by theatre. The invading barbarians, however, despised spectacles, though Sidonius, writing in 467, speaks of a theatre still in operation in Rome. In the next century, Cassiodorus suggests that the tastes of the new rulers were more debilitating to theatre than the ethics of Christianity. There is no further mention of theatre by Roman writers after the invasions of the Lombards in 568. In the eastern Empire, Choricius of Gaza (fl. 500) wrote an "Apology for Actors" in which he defended the mime as the "portrayal of life," and a final reference in 692 seems to indicate the existence of theatre there, as does a reference from Barcelona somewhat earlier in the seventh century. In the eighth century, John of Damascus condemned secular performances as rivals of the Mass, and early in the ninth century the church issued a decree forbidding members of the clergy to watch actors at plays given on the stage or at marriages, while Charlemagne forbade actors to don priests' robes. In the tenth century, the erudite nun, Hroswitha of Gandersheim, wrote six moral plays "after Terence," the texts of which are still extant. After this the information becomes more extensive and more definite.

The theatre, then, never really died. Evidently the performers of the Roman theatre continued to ply their craft in some form, their status no doubt the lowest of the low: jugglers, acrobats, dancers, rope walkers, animal trainers, mimes, and musicians continued to amuse and amaze their public wherever opportunity afforded. They performed at fairs, in marketplaces, at crossroads, and—if they were lucky—in the great halls of castles. Often they were beaten, jailed, and driven from town to town. As time went on their repertoires included the stock in trade of the Teutonic gleeman and scop, those wandering tellers of tales, as well as the accomplishments of the earlier theatre. The horizontally stratified medieval society was exceedingly fond of minstrelsy, and the jongleurs were welcomed by peasants, clergy, and nobility, not only because they provided entertainment but also because they brought news of other places. Most socially acceptable of these traveling entertainers were the minstrels who sang the *gestes*.

While these professionals, though neither recorded nor rewarded, were managing to carry on the ragged tradition of theatre, the same evolution of folk festivals evident in primitive man and in the very ancient Greeks was going on throughout what is now Europe. Seasonal festivities and fertility rites —issuing from earliest pagan times—were developing into festival plays and May games, sword dances, and mummers' plays. The church assimilated whatever of the native rituals could be adapted to its purpose, rejecting outright only those which were diametrically in opposition to its doctrine, such as the worship of pagan gods. The celebration of the winter solstice—the victory of the sun over darkness—could be made to fit nicely with the birth of Christ, who brought light to the world's darkness; so Christmas was fixed on December 25. And Easter—the resurrection—was naturally associated with the time of ancient fertility rites, the rebirth of spring. Thus, for its own preservation and growth, the church accommodated itself—where it could—to the archaic practices of its growing body of adherents. It was in the church itself that the most significant drama of medieval times had its birth and development. Thus, ironically, the great opponent of theatre over many centuries became its progenitor; once more a wondrous theatre found its beginnings in religious ceremony, just as it had with the Greeks.

Church influence preeminent

Medieval society was stratified on three levels: nobility, clergy, and peasants. Community of interests existed within these classes, but there was no such thing as nationalism. The nobility were the great landowners, the possessors of wealth. The clergy were the aristocracy of intellect, and, while its individual members supposedly possessed no wealth, the church itself was rich and powerful. The peasants did the work of the world, and owed allegiance to these two masters—first to the church for spiritual welfare, and second to the feudal lords for material welfare. The feudal lords, too, were subject to the church, and medieval history offers a long series of power struggles between nobility and church officials. The church presided over every aspect of existence; it was universally accepted that life in this world was simply a preparation for life in the next and that no one could be admitted to the afterlife except through the church. The individual man counted for little except as he joined the community effort to glorify God and the church. Hence the Middle Ages is a great period of anonymity in art and accomplishment. Who designed the miraculous cathedrals which are the work of this period? Who wrote the plays, composed the music, painted the pictures? The names extant are few indeed, but the wonderful selfless products still endure.

Often the emphasis upon the life to come made existence in this vale of tears incredibly difficult. (Perhaps because life *was* so hard in feudal times the people *had* to look forward to Paradise to make earth bearable.) Few were the pleasures of either peasant or lord; wars were frequent, and the Crusades sapped the wealth and strength of all Europe. In this atmosphere, minstrels were welcomed, and the colorful ritual of the Catholic Church was looked upon with delight as well as reverence. Into this world the new drama was born.

Drama included in the Mass

By the sixth century the Mass, with its celebration of the Eucharist, was the most important service of the church. The service was conducted in Latin and its ritual was fixed and rigid. The pattern of prayer, reading, chant, and song, while invariable in its main outline, took cognizance of special events in the church calendar as well. It was in the Easter Mass that drama began.

One part of the Mass was the singing of "Alleluia" by the choir at various intervals. Some time about the turn of the ninth century, an anonymous monk-musician, thinking to add more beauty to the service (or simply to relieve the monotony), hit upon the idea of holding the last syllable of the "Alleluia," and singing it to more music. These wordless sequences, called *sequentiae*, developed in time into elaborate, beautiful, and melodious tunes for each particular feast day. They were immensely popular, particularly in the court of Charlemagne. They were also very long, very numerous, and had to be memorized by the monks because there were no hymnbooks.

There is a story, probably apocryphal, that a famous musician, Notker Balbulus of St. Gall, in what is now Switzerland, first wrote words to these wordless sequences because he had had a hard time learning them as a choir boy. He himself says that he got the idea from an unknown monk of Jumièges who arrived at St. Gall in flight from the Normans; but he was quite taken with the idea and immediately developed it. He used passages from the Bible suited to the special significance of the particular Mass, and for the first time music and words were paralleled on the basis of one note to a syllable. These worded sequences or *tropes* did indeed make the music easier to remember. Needless to say, the innovation proved immensely popular, was much copied throughout the church, and literally hundreds of tropes were written. Many of these were antiphonal: the choir divided the lines and sang them back and forth. Much of the material was already in dialogue form, e.g., the colloquy of the shepherds and the angels at the birth of Christ, or the questions and answers of the angel at Christ's tomb with the visiting three Marys. Here was one of the elements of drama.

Another element was scenic representation. This was already present in the Mass, for in order to teach its parishioners the important aspects of the faith the church had pictures and statuary as well as pantomime by the priests conducting the services. The Christmas story was made real by showing Mary and the Christ Child in the manger, the visits of the shepherds and the wise men, and the appearance of the star. In the Good Friday service preceding Easter, the cross was taken down from the high altar, wrapped in grave clothes, and deposited in a representational sepulchre. At the Easter service the priests went to the tomb, brought out the cross, and replaced it on the altar. This was a type of dumb show, presented without words, but it certainly and very graphically made the event clear to the illiterate parishioners, who were listening to a service in a language they did not understand and to whom the Bible was a closed book.

The only element lacking was impersonation, and it soon followed. One of the most popular of the tropes was that sung at the Easter Mass, the so-called *Quem Quaeritis* trope, the earliest manuscript of which comes from Limoges and dates back to about 923. This is essentially a drama having three parts: the question by the angels, the answer of the three Marys, and the reply to the Marys' answer. The trope was sung antiphonally by the choir, and because of its hint of dialogue, was very popular. So long as it remained in the Mass, it could be nothing more than a lyrical embellishment. But some time in the tenth century it was transferred to the Matin service (theoretically at sunrise to begin the day with prayer, but actually at seven o'clock), because supposedly this corresponded with the actual time when Christ arose, and also because the plain Matin service needed beautifying. The new order of the Matin service at Easter then included the *Elevation of the Cross* in dumb show; the traditional first, second, and third readings and responses; the *Quem Quaeritis* trope; and the *Te Deum Laudamus*. There were now two dramatic elements in the same service;

because of the comparative informality of the Matin service the trope could be unhampered in its development.

Because of its essentially dramatic character, the trope was soon taken out of the choir stalls and sung before the altar by two boy singers, representing angels, and three men singers as the three Marys. Thus the element of impersonation entered. After the *Elevation of the Cross*, a most dramatic event in itself, the empty sepulchre was left, so it was suggested that the singers sing the trope by the tomb. The boys sat on a rock by the tomb and the men stood near. It was not long until the participants began to dress in costume for the parts, and then true drama was born, even though the parts were still sung.

This dramatic presentation was, of course, under the careful supervision of the clergy. In the tenth century we find in the *Concordia Regularis* of Ethelwold, Bishop of Winchester, most specific and detailed instructions for the staging of the trope. No doubt the dramatic presentation was warmly welcomed by the worshipers, for it was soon expanded. The two episodes found in the Biblical narrative were added: John and Peter at the tomb, and Christ's appearance to Mary Magdalene. The total presentation now required twenty to thirty minutes and constituted a small play.

Imitation of the Easter play for other occasions led to the adoption of a Christmas trope dealing with the visit of the shepherds to the manger. The action of the play was almost identical with the earlier one. It began, in song, *"Quem quaeritis in praesepe, pastores, dicite"* ("Whom seek ye in the manger, shepherds, tell us") and used a manger instead of a sepulchre. The Easter play was known technically as the *Sepulchrum*, the Christmas play as the *Praesepe*. The Christmas play was also expanded by three scenes.

SCENE FROM A MEDIEVAL CYCLE PLAY
One of the typical scenes of the medieval cycle play was that of Christ driving the money-changers from the Temple. Some idea of its interpretation can be derived from this old wood-carving of the scene.

They were the Annunciation, the birth of John the Baptist, and a scene depicting Joseph's doubts about the Virgin Mary—a most popular theme in medieval times.

In the Twelfth Day Matin service there was a dumb show in which a large tin star, hung on a wire extending the length of the church, was pulled along the wire from the entrance to the chancel. Some time in the eleventh century, a Twelfth Day, or Epiphany, play was built around this stage property. Three monks representing the three wise men entered the main door during the singing of the trope and followed the star up the aisle. After presenting their gifts, they sang the *Alleluia* and the *Te Deum Laudamus*. Text and dramatic occasions were expanded by the appearance of angels telling the wise men to go a different way, and by a scene in which Herod boasts of his qualities and asks where the Child is. Herod was the first villain introduced into medieval drama, and what a popular character he turned out to be!

These, and the play of the walk to Emmaus (given the Monday after Easter), as well as the play of the Slaughter of the Innocents (given on December 28), were finally consolidated into two series in chronological order given on Twelfth Day, the greatest feast day of the church calendar, and on Easter. These two plays told the whole story of Christ's life, putting emphasis on the main Biblical events; each occupied the time between the Matin service and the Mass on the day when it was given.

The incorporation of the Christmas material with the Twelfth Day play left the earlier holiday without dramatic representation. But soon St. Augustine's famous *Sermon Against Jews, Pagans, and Arians* began to take on dramatic qualities for the Christmas Matins. In this exceedingly rhetorical sermon, various prophets are called upon to give their testimony of Christ's coming, as are various Gentile sages, all in direct address; the listeners are called upon to mend their ways and do good. Drama entered with the designation of monks to portray the parts of the prophets, each of them in characteristic costumes designed by themselves. Rivalry begot richness, and the people desired to see these costumes more fully. So the *Procession of Prophets* was instituted. Soon more monks than the sermon called for were put into the procession: Adam and Noah were added, then Balaam, who rode an ass (another monk) with beating and braying—a humorous incident which became even more so because an angel followed after the ass and threw Balaam. As others sought prominence in the procession and strove to build their parts into small plays, the *Procession of Prophets* became a series of little plays attached to the Christmas Matins.

Thus there was a series of plays portraying the whole plan of salvation, from the original sin to the birth, death, resurrection, and ascension of Christ. The plays were very effective in teaching the people the history of their religion and the churches were crowded on these great feast days. Gradually another element was added. The dialogue, sung in Latin, was supplemented by an immediate translation into the spoken vernacular. As the incidents multiplied and expanded, singing disappeared, characters not called for in the Biblical narrative were added, the casts grew larger, and the clergy called upon the laity for help. The increased complexity of the staging forced the performances out of the church into the churchyard since there was not room enough inside. This expansion caused further additions to be made; the plays were finally removed from consecrated ground, the clerics withdrew from the performances, and the dramas were secularized. This secularization is significant; from this point on the plays took on a definitely national growth and character.

Thus developed the most typical of the medieval dramas as a direct outgrowth of medieval society and as one of its most representative art forms. There were also other kinds of dramatic presentations in the latter part of the Middle Ages, and these we will consider as we discuss the plays themselves.

Mystery, morality, miracle: sacred drama develops

The dramatic literature of the Middle Ages may be divided into two main types: the cycle plays and the noncycle plays. The first type includes the many series of Biblical plays which developed along the line just discussed; the second includes saint plays, moralities, folk plays, serious plays, and comedies.

At the height of the vogue of the cycle play, each town of any consequence presented its own series. After 1264, when Pope Urban IV decreed the celebration of Corpus Christi Day on the Thursday after Trinity Sunday (two months after Easter), it became customary—particularly in England—to give the whole cycle of plays from creation to the day of Last Judgment on this day. That is why these plays are sometimes called Corpus Christi plays. (The festival was instituted to celebrate the decision that the bread and wine of the communion actually became the body and blood of Christ.) A few of these complete cycles are still in existence, as well as many single plays which seem to have belonged to a cycle.

Among the earliest texts extant today are a few from the eleventh century, such as *The Pastoral Office* (*Officium Pastorum*) and *The Star* (*Stella*) from Rouen, two similar ones from Nevers, and a Herod play from Compiègne. All of these are written entirely in Latin, and are obviously for production in the church sanctuary itself. From the next century we have the *Play of the Anti-Christ* (*Ludos de Anti-christo*) from Tegernsee, *The Promise* (*Sponsus*) from Limoges, and the famous Fleury Play-Book at Orleans containing five plays on Biblical themes. This is the century also of three innovations: the first signed pieces by Hilarius of both French and English background (a *Lazarus* and a *Daniel*), the first play in the vernacular (the Beauvais *Daniel*), and the first play directed to be played outdoors (the Anglo-Norman *Mystery of Adam* (*Mystère d'Adam*) whose stage directions indicate production on the church porch.

The thirteenth and fourteenth centuries are the years of the great cycles, sometimes called mystery plays, covering the whole plan of salvation, and the so-called passion plays confined to the death and resurrection of Christ. Four complete cycles survive: one of

MULTISCENE BIBLICAL REPRESENTATION
While it is not a representation of an actual
cycle play production, this Memling painting
of *The Passion* suggests the atmosphere and
being of the medieval cycle plays.

forty-eight plays from York, one of twenty-
five plays from Chester, one of thirty-two
plays from Wakefield (sometimes called the
Towneley cycle), and one of forty-two plays
from Coventry. There are also separate plays
from Newcastle, Northampton, Norwich,
Tours, and Origny; and there is evidence that
cycles were given also at London, Worcester,
Beverley, Lancaster, Leicester, Canterbury,
Rouen, Padua, Friuli, Ravenna, and many
other places. Of the extant plays, the Brome
Abraham and Isaac (which may be a single
survival of the London cycle) has been highly
praised for its dramatic qualities; the Towneley cycle has been called the most notable for
its literary style, and its *Second Shepherd's
Play* has been performed most successfully
in recent times. Indeed, the whole York cycle
has been enthusiastically and beautifully re-

vived by E. Martin Browne, an English actor-
producer.

The popularity of the cycle plays continued through the fifteenth century; additional ones originated in that time, most notably the *Mysteries and Moralities*, especially
adapted for production by the sisters of S.
Michel at Huy near Liège, and the famous
Mystery of the Passion written by Arnoul
Greban, which is supposed to have taken
forty days in performance.

After 1550, these plays generally ceased
to be produced. The last attempt to produce
the Coventry cycle was in 1591; a revival in
Chester in 1607 was looked upon as an antiquarian curiosity. They had been immensely
popular throughout all of western Europe,
not only in France and England, but also in
Italy and Spain. In both Italy and Spain the

presentation of these Biblical plays endured longer than in England and France. Italian scene designers of the Renaissance used them for spectacular scenic effects, and in Spain they did not finally disappear until midway into the eighteenth century. In modern times, the passion plays at Oberammergau, in Brittany, and at several other places give us a good idea of the survival of this form. Like the Gothic cathedral, added to over many centuries by different artists in differing styles, the medieval cycle play was an accretion of various dramatic elements—serious and comic, tragic and grotesque—all blending into a unique whole which ran the gamut of human emotions. Thus medieval architecture and medieval drama differed basically from their Greek predecessors, in which unity of tone, purpose, and detail were paramount. By using this medieval heritage of multiple scenes transpiring over long reaches of time, Renaissance dramatists would produce a new thing under the sun—romantic tragedy and romantic comedy.

Deriving from the cycle plays were the saint plays, or miracle plays, which had their start in the twelfth century; these, for the most part, used non-Biblical materials. Myriads of saints were celebrated in this fashion, the texts varying in length from what we consider a normal playing time to several days. The two most popular figures in these saint plays are St. Nicholas and the Virgin Mary (who indeed was derived from the Bible, but to whom innumerable apocryphal events are ascribed). More than forty plays of the *Miracles of Our Lady* are preserved in two manuscripts at the Bibliothèque Nationale, and these are evidences of the great cult of the Virgin Mary which was so widespread in the Middle Ages. She seems not to have been so popular, however, in England, where the Reformation no doubt early eliminated traces of Mariolatry. The Fleury Play-

Book, mentioned above, contains four St. Nicholas plays, and Hilarius, whom we have also mentioned, wrote a famous St. Nicholas play. In England, St. George was the subject of many of these plays, notably at Lydd, Bassingbourne, and Windsor. The patron saints of city, town, and village all over Europe were honored with plays, and the hagiology of the church was combed for suitable subjects.

A third type of medieval play, the morality, seems to have begun about the middle of the fourteenth century, flourished through the fifteenth century, and lasted well into the sixteenth. The morality was an allegory which originated in the Lord's Prayer; it was regarded as the ideal prayer, and to make it more effective the clergy divided it into seven parts to combat the seven deadly sins. This exposition became a play of sorts, called *Paternoster*, with a list of characters including the hero, Man, the seven deadly sins, and the seven moral virtues. Like the cycle play, it originally appeared only in the church, then moved outdoors, being given by lay persons rather than priests. In various places, a special group of persons was chosen to perform the play. Only one of these plays, that of Beverly, survives. But there are several texts which use a similar theme and characters, the most important of which is the play called *Everyman*. This is an English play which might be a translation of the Dutch *Elckerlijk*, or the two may be from a common source. It is a very moving exposition of the salvation of Everyman through the offices of Good Deeds, who accompanies him to his judgment. A similar pattern is followed

TERENCE IN THE MIDDLE AGES
An illuminated manuscript page shows Terence being read and mimed in the top picture, while at the bottom the author presents his manuscript to his patron.

in other moralities—the fragmentary *Pride of Life; Purity and the Young Child; Mind, Will, and Understanding; Mankind;* and the *Castle of Perseverance*. As the morality developed it became particularized in its formation and use. It was adapted for production in the schools; education was then made the theme, as in *Wit and Science* and *The Nature of the Four Elements*. Sometimes the play became a propaganda instrument; sometimes it was used as political satire, as in Skelton's *Magnificence* and David Lyndsay's *Satire of the Three Estates*. As in the cycle plays, the character of the devil was a most popular one, and his page or attendant, usually called "the Vice," became the chief funster. His name soon developed into a type name, and became the prototype for many Falstaffian characters. The morality play as a type was transmuted into full-fledged and significant drama in the impressive plays of Ben Jonson.

All of these plays had the moral purpose of edification. Before great drama could flourish this didactic element had to be disposed of. Such a step would not be likely to come from the clergy, but from the common people; the germ of it is found in another type of medieval drama, the folk play. We have already mentioned the development of this type of presentation from rural festivals; it is important because it took the drama out of its religious atmosphere and created pleasure for its own sake. The fusion of the May Day festivities and the legend of Robin Hood—a national hero as far as the peasants were concerned—produced in England such a play as *Robin Hood and the Sheriff of Nottingham*, and in France the pretty pastoral of Adam de la Hale, *The Play of Robin and Marion*. The *St. George Play*, which developed from the Anglo-Saxon sword dance, included impersonations of

heroes, burlesques of these heroes, the killing of a fool who intervenes in the fight, and his resuscitation by a doctor variously named in different localities. The significance of these folk plays is that they stressed drama as pure entertainment, and the pastoral comedy elements were continued into a later age in such plays as Shakespeare's *The Winter's Tale* and *As You Like It*.

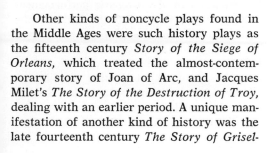

Other kinds of noncycle plays found in the Middle Ages were such history plays as the fifteenth century *Story of the Siege of Orleans,* which treated the almost-contemporary story of Joan of Arc, and Jacques Milet's *The Story of the Destruction of Troy,* dealing with an earlier period. A unique manifestation of another kind of history was the late fourteenth century *The Story of Grisel-*

dis, dramatized from Boccaccio's tale for presentation at a French nuptial festivity.

The comedy accretions in the cycle plays were reflected in the presentation of various farces, *soties,* and humorous monologues as separate entities. Adam de la Hale is responsible for an early farce, *Play of the List,* written about 1267 to amuse a group of his friends. But the most famous, and justly so, of this type is the anonymous *Master Pierre Pathelin*, which is usually dated about 1465. Numerous performances in our own day bear witness to its dramatic vitality. Similarly farcical is *The Wandering Scholar from Paradise* (1550), one of two hundred eight "plays" written by the prolific meistersinger, Hans Sachs. The sotie was essentially a comedy played by fools in their characteristic costume, and was marked by clever repartee and a tendency to satirize, such as in Gringoire's *Play of the Prince of Fools*. In Germany, numerous farces featuring a *Narr*, or fool, were played by lively amateurs. The humorous monologue, while not truly a play, evidently had an important place in dramatic activity, and one of the most interesting of these is Rutebeuf's *Speech of the Herb Peddler* dating from the thirteenth century. An elaboration of the monologue is evident in *The Foure PP*, a dialogue between a palmer, a pardoner, a 'potecary, and a pedlar, written by John Heywood (d. 1580). These short pieces are sometimes called "interludes," and in Italy at least they were sometimes given between the scenes of the more solemn sacred plays. For the most part, however, the occasions upon which they were presented were very numerous and varied—fairs, festivals, banquets, visits, school functions, and so forth. It has been suggested that the mime tradition fostered the production of these secular performances, and that in them the professional actor chiefly appeared.

It seems to be true that in the Middle Ages the lines between types of drama, and between drama and narrative, were very loosely drawn so that no hard and fast distinctions can be made. Indicated here are the most outstanding of the kinds of dramatic performances of the Middle Ages, and it will later appear how these various beginnings

OPEN-AIR THEATRE FOR FARCE
Two woodcuts from a book by Johann Rasser, published in 1574, show scenes from the short, popular farces being performed on a platform stage in Germany.

were consummated in the periods that followed.

Performances abandon church

Occasionally it has been suggested that the magnificent theatre buildings erected by the Romans all over Europe and the Near East must have continued into the Middle Ages the tradition of the dramatic performances of Greece and Rome. But the truth of the matter is that the majority of these structures, long unused after the fall of Rome, fell into decay, were dismantled for their materials, or were put to other uses. It was not until late in the medieval period that we read of an elaborate production of a cycle play in the old Roman theatre at Orange,

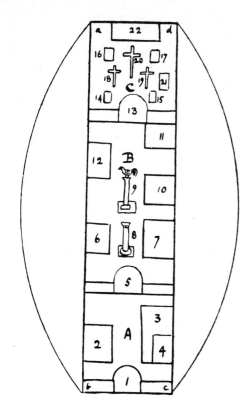

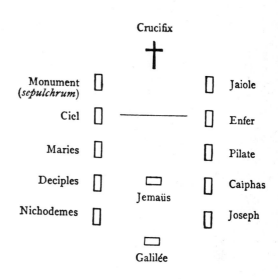

Crucifix

Monument (*sepulchrum*)	▯		▯	Jaiole
Ciel	▯	———	▯	Enfer
Maries	▯		▯	Pilate
Deciples	▯	▭ Jemaüs	▯	Caiphas
Nichodemes	▯		▯	Joseph
		▭ Galilée		

EARLY MEDIEVAL PLANS FOR CYCLE PLAYS
Above, a plan for the mansions in the Play of the Resurrection; left, a plan for the mansions in the Donaueschingen plays. The cycle plays were presented within the churches with just such plans. Each episode had its own platform and all were related to the high altar. (Chambers, *Medieval Stage;* Karlsruhe, *Schauspiele des Mittelalters*)

and of another in the ancient Colosseum at Rome. But in both cases the playhouse was only incidental to the type of production, which had been developed quite independently of Roman theatre.

It seems likely that no permanent playhouses of any kind were built during the Middle Ages, although a dubious reference describes a playhouse at Autun in 1516 as having boxes and a pit with a moat separating the stage from the eighty thousand seats. Actually, the playing place was chosen and arranged for the occasion of the individual performance and varied with the type of play presented. It is possible, of course, to see as a kind of "permanent theatre" the round earthworks such as still survive in the village of St. Just in Penwith, Cornwall,

which the modern British theatre scholar, Richard Southern, identifies as similar to the construction sketched in the *Castle of Perseverence* manuscript of about 1425. If this is so, then James Burbage was not the first Englishman to build a permanent theatre.

Heaven to the right, Hell to the left

The great cycle plays had two main methods of presentation: one on fixed stages and the other on movable platform stages. Both had a similar origin. Detailed above is the fact that the church altar was the place where the first rudimentary dramas were given. As the embryonic drama expanded in incident and dramatis personae, the chancel became too small to be adequate. So the drama expanded into the nave of the church. But here visibility became a problem and platforms were erected so that the action could be seen by the spectators. At first there seem to have been two platforms with the altar comprising a third. Then the number grew as the scripts grew, progressing to the very complicated arrangement of the Donaueschingen Passion Play of the sixteenth century, which used the plan of nave, choir, and sanctuary, and had twenty-two locations or "mansions."

The platform arrangement was maintained when the dramas moved out of the sanctuary. A platform was erected for each locality involved in the action, Heaven being to the left of the spectator, Hell to the right; or, if viewed from the vantage point of the high altar, Heaven was on the right, Hell on the left—an orientation strongly rooted in medieval tradition. Sometimes the church itself figured in the action, as in the *Mystery of Adam*, where it is directed that a character enter or emerge from the church, and as in the Benedictbeuern Christmas Play, where it is directed that the chair of Augustine be set in front of the church, from which position Heaven would be on the occupant's right, Hell on his left. The rectangular arrangement of mansions, which was originally dictated by the shape of the church, was at first maintained in the outdoor productions, with the platforms facing each other and the actors moving from one to another as the action demanded.

When the plays abandoned church property and were presented in the market square, as at Luzerne, the same rectangular plan prevailed. In other places variations were worked out. In Cornwall, as mentioned above, the mansions were arranged in a circle, and in the famous Jean Fouquet miniature of *The Martyrdom of St. Apollonia*, the mansions do not quite encircle the playing area, with much of the action taking

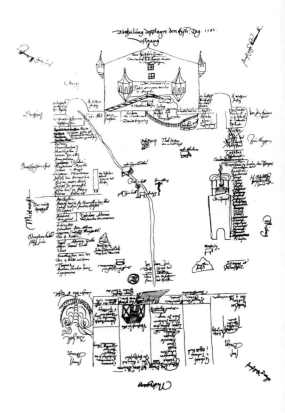

place in the open area. The use of this open area, or *platea*, for unlocalized action was fairly universal, whatever the arrangement of the mansions.

In many places on the Continent the playing area became a long, raised stage on which were erected the various mansions; here also Heaven was to the left and Hell to the right of the spectator, but in reverse if seen from the traditional centerstage point of view. The mansions were erected in a line

THE CYCLE PLAYS AT LUZERNE
Left, a sketch of the setting for the first day
from the prompt book of Renward Cysat,
city clerk of Luzerne and twice director of
the play. This performance is dated 1583.
Above, a model of the setting for the second
day by Professor Albert Koester. The mansions were erected in the marketplace, with
spectators viewing the performance from
windows or from specially constructed
stands. (Luzerne Zentralbibliothek; Theater-
Museum, Munich)

along the stage, often extending for a hundred feet or more. The downstage area was
then the platea, and actors emerged from or
entered into the various structures upstage.
The stage was provided with such trapdoors,
underground passages, and overhead structures as were necessary. Such were the stages
at Valenciennes, at Mons, at Bourges. The
audience sat on scaffolded seats, on the
ground, or on the balconies or at windows of
nearby houses.

Touring pageant wagons

In England, when the cycle plays became
secularized they usually moved to stage-
wagons, or "pageants," rather than to stationary settings. Each separate play of the
cycle had its separate wagon; these generally
consisted of a lower and an upper deck, the
lower curtained off for use primarily as a
dressing and offstage area, the upper as the
playing area. Stations were set up—as many

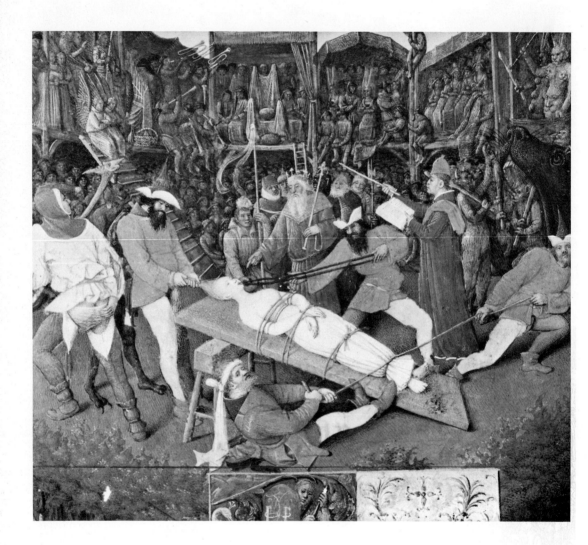

THE MARTYRDOM OF ST. APOLLONIA
This famous Fouquet miniature shows the use of raised mansion stages with the angels to the right of the throne, the devil to the left, and the climactic action of the saint play taking place on the platea, where the priestly régisseur, book and baculus in hand, directs the action. The figures in the foreground are merely the artist's decoration. (Photographie Giraudon)

THE CYCLE PLAY AT VALENCIENNES (ABOVE)
Model of the setting for the play given in France, from a miniature painting by Hubert Calleau, 1547. Though here the platea is evidently raised, the throne is still at the center with Heaven to its right and Hell to its left, other locations distributed between. Actors emerged from the appropriate mansion and used the platea as undifferentiated playing area. (Cleveland State University)

AN ENGLISH PAGEANT WAGON (BELOW)
A conjectural drawing by Richard Leacroft of the Pageant of the Shearmen and Taylors in the Coventry Corpus Christi play. The curtained area below the stage proper was used by the actors as a dressing and retiring room when not on stage. The audience stood about the pageant, or watched from the windows of surrounding houses. (Richard Leacroft Collection)

as were necessary to take care of the people —in the town square, at the town gates, on the green, at the crossroads, and so forth. The procession, headed by the clergy, proceeded in a predetermined order from one station to the next: Mass was celebrated, the first pageant wagon arrived as the church group moved to the next station, the first play was given; then the wagon moved on to the next station while the second pageant arrived and presented its play. Thus, although the plays had to be repeated, all the people could see them adequately. The stations were chosen by the town council and posted a month in advance. There were flags as markers at each station and grandstands for the spectators. Standing room was also sold on housetops. About a thousand people saw the play at each station; the number of stations varied from four to seven, to fourteen, to as many as sixteen. At York the ceremonies began at four-thirty in the morning, in Coventry at six, in Newcastle at noon. At Chester there were three days of plays beginning at noon each day. The pageants were stored in pageant houses from year to year, and were refurbished as necessary or desirable. Extant records at Chester prove these pageants to have been very expensive to prepare. Since one used early in the sequence of plays could be used later (on the succeeding days, say), it was indeed thus used, with the decorations and scene changed for the second use.

There are some records of pageant wagons being drawn up in a circle on the village green for the presentation of the cycle, but for the most part the plays in England were "traveling shows." This phenomenon marks the great difference between Continental and English productions, although it was no hard and fast rule. There is also some indication that wagons were occasionally used in France as well, and certainly in Spain the *fiestos de los carros* (festivals of the cars) was the well-established rule.

Effects lavish and literal

The arrangements for playing dictated the type of settings to be used, although whether the plays were stationary or perambulatory, a verisimilitude in the staging was attempted. The earliest setting utilized the construction of the church, often placing Hell down the crypt stairs, and Heaven up the rood-loft stairs. Frequently a sepulchre was erected near the altar for the Easter play.

When platforms came into use they were beautifully curtained in silk and velvet and as lavishly furnished as possible. Because of their size (six to eight feet wide and eight to ten feet long), there could not be a great number of set pieces, but even here as much richness as possible was the rule. For the *Mystery of Adam*, for instance, we find it is directed that the Paradise shall be hung with curtains of silk, that there shall be many different fruit trees hung with fruit, and there shall be fragrant flowers and leaves. The extant sketches for the two days of the Luzerne play seem to indicate the building of rather elaborate structures with cupolas and a monster-like edifice for Hellmouth. Where the plays were given on wagons the settings perforce remained comparatively simple; even so, however, there are accounts of flaming swords and altars, of leaves opening, and of hell fire.

It was in the horizontal simultaneous settings of France and the elaborate productions of the cycle plays in Italy that very complicated settings and effects were developed. Italian writers speak of monuments opening, of earthquakes, of heavenly beings descending from on high surrounded by the lights of stars, of trapdoors opening to swallow up buildings and persons, and of spotlights, which were evidently highly polished basins reflecting the sunlight. The famous architect, Brunelleschi, designed many of these settings. The elaborate and most mi-

A FAVORITE STAGE SETTING OF MEDIEVAL TIMES
Above, a psalter of Henry of Blois showing an angel locking the damned in Hell; right, an illustration showing Hellmouth, with the damned souls and the attendant devils. Hell was a very literal place to the medieval spectator, and was literally represented not only in the plays but in other illustrations as well. The above representations, although not primarily stage sets, are quite similar to what did appear on medieval stages. (British Museum; Munich National Museum)

nute directions for stage effects at Mons, at Valenciennes, and at Bourges, show that a great deal of time, ingenuity, and money were expended to achieve them.

Contemporary accounts of the 1536 production of *The Acts of the Apostles* describe the rich colors of the canopy spread over the ancient Roman amphitheatre where the performance was given, and speak of the mechanical contrivances used to produce thunder and to simulate dragons spouting flames; of lions, camels, and flying owls; of devices used to raise and lower persons and beasts or to hide them in clouds; of ships sailing;

of fountains spouting; of the burning or decapitation of saints. At Mons, the playbook for the 1501 performance calls for highly complicated technical effects and describes how they are to be achieved. According to its notations, trees and flowers spring from the earth for the creation of the world; Noah's grapevines bear ripe fruit a moment after planting; water for the Deluge is to be piped over the rooftops of the surrounding marketplace, and fall in a downpour; the Hellmouth is to be alive with flame, gunpowder, and thunder; the Crucifixion is to seem meticulously real; clouds are to descend during Christ's transfiguration and then he is to ascend into Paradise. At Valenciennes, a spectator of 1547 speaks of the verisimilitude of the miracle of the loaves and fishes; of the turning of water into wine; of Lucifer coming up from Hell on a dragon; of the souls of Herod and Judas being carried through the air by devils. All of these effects were under the supervision of a *maître des feyntes*, who employed workmen to construct and operate them, and who often went to great lengths to secure some little-seen or spectacular wonder. There is a 1510 record in Vienna of the employment of eight "masters of machines" for a production there. Thus the Middle Ages cared little for symbolic representation, but strove for realism even in supernatural happenings; the spectators were no doubt amazed and delighted, and certainly proud of the unique achievements of their townsmen.

Noncycle plays, as a rule, had a much simpler production, although some of the saint plays were handled in the same way as the cycle plays. Frequently, however, these saint plays were given in schools, as were the moralities and the interludes. Here a simple platform sufficed, as it did for performances in town halls, in the banquet rooms of manor houses, and at court. Sometimes there was not even a platform. The folk plays were usually given on village greens without any particularized setting.

Most typical of the period, however, were the cycle plays; the simultaneous setting and the unparticularized playing area they developed were utilized in later designs for the theatre.

Costuming symbolic and stylized

The passion of the medieval populace for seeming truth and reality made costuming a necessity, although such costuming as there was made no attempt at historical accuracy. We might say that costuming was treated symbolically rather than realistically. Typically, gloves were a sign of high rank. They were worn by God and his angels, by the prophets, by Pilate, and by Herod. The angels wore sheepskins overlaid with gold leaf, had gilded wings and diadems; their faces were often gilded. The fallen angels wore horrible masks, black clothes bristling with hair, cloven feet, and forked tails. Satan typically wore a horrible mask, hose, a hairy coat, and carried a staff and a leather club stuffed with wool with which to beat actors and spectators. Saved souls were dressed in white, damned souls in black. Judas wore a red wig and a yellow robe; Pilate and Herod had splendid clothes and carried clubs. Humble characters wore medieval peasant dress.

Several manuscripts and account books give specific descriptions of specialized costumes. Mezières' *Presentation of the Virgin* directs that Mary shall be clothed all in white and gold, the tunic very white and pleated, the mantle also of white in sendal or silk. Lucifer is to have horns, menacing teeth, a horrible expression, and to carry a bright iron chain with which to bind the archangel Michael. Michael himself is to be garbed "in a most fair fashion," and to brandish aloft a flashing sword. In the *Mystery of Adam*, whose *rubrics*, or production notes, are justly famous, God is to wear a dalmatic, Adam a red tunic, Eve a dress of white silk. For one of the Cornish plays, Adam and Eve wore white leather and had two costume changes —one to garments of fig leaves, the other to costumes made of skins. The devil often appeared in the guise of a serpent, and the animals, when they were not of domesticated variety like sheep and donkeys which could be used live, were simulated by having men wear appropriate skins. Wigs and beards

THE CHRISTMAS PLAY OF ST. GEORGE
The great hall of a medieval castle, with its tall windows, vaulted ceiling, and gallery over the entrance doors, was well suited to the presentation of plays. The far end of the room, with its two great doors and the gallery above them, has curious similarities to the stage backing shown in the DeWitt drawing of the Swan Theatre (page 141). Notice that here the audience surrounds the costumed players. (Richard Leacroft Collection)

were prepared for characters who would need them, as a listing at Twicksbury indicates in calling for "8 heads of hair for the Apostles, and 10 beards, and a face or vizard for the devil."

In the folk plays, the participants were usually costumed and had appropriate props, the clown invariably having a bladder on a stick to beat the spectators. The character of "the Vice" in the moralities carried a similar instrument, a device which was later used by the Elizabethan fool. In the French soties, the dress of all participants was that of the medieval fool, including the cap with long

ears. Interludes were evidently played in the dress of the day.

In the early days of the cycle plays, costumes and properties were supplied by the church. Even when the plays were secularized and moved out of the church proper, the clergy often provided robes, crosses, thuribles, and other items which were in their stores. Otherwise, it seems to have been the general rule, particularly in France, that each actor supplied his own costume. Special items were generally paid for by the general fund, and much of our information concerning costuming comes from inventories and expense accounts.

Though the costuming of the medieval plays would not satisfy a modern audience, and though no attempt was made at historical accuracy, the described results were almost invariably beautiful (or horrifying) and effective. Medieval producers, no less than modern ones, were aware of the aid which costume could give to characterization, and of the satisfaction effective costuming could provide an audience.

Acting largely nonprofessional

The Middle Ages was the heyday of the amateur. By far the greatest number of parts, all through the entire period, fell to those whose means of earning a living was not acting, although various elusive records indicate that professionals were also performing.

In their early stages the cycle plays were entirely in the hands of the clergy; they not only prepared the scripts but acted in them, taking the women's parts as well as the men's (a female character was indicated by the simple expedient of wearing a kerchief over the head and donning a cloak). There was also a clerical master of ceremonies, who held the prompt book and carried a short baton-like staff which was his badge of office.

As the plays expanded in text and the dramatis personae increased in number, laymen were invited to participate. Direction, however, remained in the hands of the clerical *régisseur*, who moved about in full view of the audience, prompt book and staff in hand. In some localities, this responsible position never devolved upon a lay member, but remained the prerogative of the church. However, as the presentation of the plays became increasingly secular, the clergy withdrew from the acting assignments and often from that of director as well, so that the entire production was managed by the laity.

In England, production of the cycle plays was taken over by the guilds, which were powerful functioning units by the twelfth century. The town council usually assigned the episodes to the guilds. The assignments often exhibited a piquant justice: to the plasterers and carpenters went the Creation; to the shipwrights, the Noah episode; to the goldsmiths, the Magi; to the cooks, the Harrowing of Hell; to the bakers, the Feeding of the Five Thousand or the Last Supper; to the scriveners, the Disputation in the Temple. The assignments, of course, varied from town to town, but ordinarily remained traditional in each place. Occasionally the craft guilds did not function, but the corporation of the town or a specially appointed body took care of the entire event.

The guild prepared its pageant with its setting, secured the costumes, hired and trained the actors, and presented its play in the sequence. The actors were paid with funds from special levies, guild treasuries, or town funds; the authorities demanded that the acting be good. Actors might be members of the producing guild or not, depending upon the demands of the parts and the available supply of potential actors. In 1476 in York, for instance, the Mayor appointed a committee of three or four actors at the beginning of Lent to interview aspirants for playing honors on Corpus Christi Day. In the same town, in 1446 and 1447, an expense account shows payments for acting to some minstrels and singers. It would appear that the amateur ranks were swelled by professionals when it seemed feasible and necessary. Some records indicate that actors were paid according to the dignity of the part: God in one instance was paid three shillings sixpence; Noah, one shilling; saved souls in Hell Wagon, twenty pence; damned souls, ten pence. But in other accounts, the length of the acting part determined the payment: for playing God, ten pence; Noah, one shilling; Noah's wife, eight pence. It is easy to imagine that the recruited professionals demanded and got whatever the traffic would bear.

There were frequent rehearsals—three or four times a week for two or three weeks before the play. When the plays were ready, the town council sent out *vexillators*, or standard bearers, to surrounding towns to read the notice of the play. They were usually three in number and were accompanied by two trumpeters.

In England, the production of religious plays was sometimes in the hands of a special religious guild, as at Sleaford, where the Guild of the Holy Trinity performed the play of the Ascension in 1480. Guilds of the same nature seemed to operate in London, and in 1378 a petition from the clerks of St. Paul's to Richard II complained of the rivalry of certain "unexpert people" in the playing of an Old Testament drama. Even here there was rivalry between professional and amateur. In the small towns of the English countryside, Biblical plays sometimes toured from town to town, each vicinity bearing a part of the expense. Generally this type of production was an occasional rather than an annual affair.

TWO SCENES FROM TERENCE
Above, this scene, as presented at Venice, 1467, shows a theatrum, with the audience surrounding the playing area and the actors emerging from opposite mansions to the neutral platea between. Right, only the stage area is represented in this scene, as presented at Ulm, 1486. The costumes are medieval; note particularly the long-toed shoes worn by two of the actors. Cf. page 83: there is no longer a reader. (Venice, *Terence*, 1499)

In France and Italy, on the other hand, the production of plays was, after its relinquishment by the clergy, primarily in the hands of specially constituted organizations rather than the craft guilds. The *Confrèrie de la Passion*, chartered by Charles VI in Paris in 1402, was one of the most famous of these. It was licensed to perform in the Hôpital de la Trinité, and thus became the first permanently established playing company in a permanent playing place in the

Middle Ages. It was the model for many another pious brotherhood in many another French town. Usually these were formed to do honor to a saint; at their annual observance (usually held in the summertime) they presented a dramatic performance, either from Biblical materials or from the lives of the saints. They sometimes recruited actors by means of processions or through the town crier.

Side by side with the brotherhoods were

more secular bodies of performers, the *Sociétés Joyeuses,* or mirthful fellowships. Those of a literary bent no doubt had their origin in the schools and presented soties and farces as well as religious plays. Another type were the fool companies, the most famous of which is that of *L'Infanterie Dijonnaise.* These seem to have been inspired by the semiclerical Feast of Fools, which earlier had allowed the minor clergy to burlesque the offices of the church; the festival was marked by wearing foolscaps instead of cowls. The *Enfants-sans-Souci* of Paris and the *Connards* of Rouen are other famous fool companies. Their chief concern seems to have been with the various forms of contemporary comedy. Allied in spirit was the unique *Basoche,* which, beginning in 1303, united the law clerks of Paris for mutual benefit and entertainment. All these were amateur organizations, although professionals were by no means excluded from their ranks.

In Italy, the dramas were acted by companies of young boys. Modena had its company of *San Pietro Martre,* Rome its *Gonfalone,* Florence its *del Vangelista.* Each company was headed by a person who was at the same time director, head actor, and prompter.

The professional minstrels and mimes evidently had a sort of organization of their own; they even came under regulation by Edward IV of England who, in 1469, placed his own household minstrels in charge of regulating professional activity throughout England. But it was no doubt the amalgamation of these professionals with the various amateur fellowships which produced the traveling companies of the Middle Ages and the beginning of the Renaissance. Companies of this nature, either attached to a noble household and traveling under its protection, or independent of any patronage, played the interludes and moralities in courts, manor houses, town halls, and at fairs. No doubt their repertoires were spiced with the tradition of the Goliards, those satiric wandering scholars of medieval times who so frequently came into conflict with authority.

Whatever the type of producing organization—professional or amateur, religious or secular—a high degree of skill was expected from the performers. In the huge cycle plays endurance was often a necessity, for stage effects such as the crucifixion of Christ and the hanging of Judas were frighteningly real; it was not unusual for the actor portraying one of these actually to faint from the strain. The number of lines assigned the various characters was often stupendous, and it is easy to understand why the régisseur with his prompt book was so universally necessary. Often more than one actor was assigned to a single part, taking the various age levels in sequence; and once at least, at Mons, the voice of God was assigned to three persons who spoke simultaneously. The number of speaking parts grew to tremendous proportions. In the twelfth and thirteenth centuries, casts comprised from twenty to thirty persons, but in the next two or three centuries the dramatis personae rose to two hundred or three hundred, in addition to extras and musicians. In the Bourges performance of the *Acts of the Apostles* there were four hundred ninety-four speaking parts, including five Marys. The deportment of the actors was strictly regulated: they were not to drink before, after, or during a performance; to eat only what was provided; not to leave the theatre during the rehearsal or the performances; to pay fines for any infringement of the rules. Indeed, there is record in England of fines imposed on actors who "spoiled the performance."

The style of delivery was declamatory. Songs were often required, so the actors had to be able to sing. That a high degree of skill in pantomime was necessary can be taken for granted, and what we today call overacting was looked upon with delight in such a character as Herod, who was a ranter always. Not without reason does Hamlet speak of out-Heroding Herod. Although most of the acting chores fell to men, women seem to have been included in the casts at both Metz and Valenciennes, perhaps because the number of men available was not adequate for the number of parts.

In the comedies, the emphasis was upon sparkling dialogue and farcical situations, requiring a great deal of skill from the performers. It was from such a tradition that the acting companies of the succeeding period developed.

Summary

Having no conscious roots in preceding centuries, the great popular theatre of the Middle Ages developed out of church liturgy with accretions from indigenous materials. It was not imitative but original, and this originality was the main source of its vitality. Performances, as in ancient Greece, were linked to religious observance and given only at stated times in the church calendar. From simple beginnings the production techniques developed into marvelously complicated affairs, engrossing the energies of great numbers of people and stimulating communication and trade. The scripts of the cycle plays, deriving from Biblical sequences, also incorporated invented, native characters and often reflected the life of the times in which they were written. They were largely an amateur endeavor, although the participation of "professionals" is frequently enough mentioned to indicate that they were important to the performances.

The various and minor forms of noncycle productions were sporadic in presentation and covered a wide variety of materials and forms of presentation. They introduced wholly secular materials, although many were frankly didactic in intent. The lines of distinction between literary forms were lightly drawn in this period, though the beginnings of subsequent emphases were apparent.

The noncycle plays contributed to the further development of clearcut plot structure, particularly in the moralities. In these and in the interludes, characters were created instead of adapted; the emphasis came to be placed on pure entertainment rather than upon edification—a most important step forward for the drama. The noncycle plays were chiefly played indoors, and this fact had significance for future production techniques.

From the cycle plays came emphases upon realism in stage effects and upon spectacle. More importantly, the cycle play initiated that mixture of comedy and tragedy which became the hallmark of the Elizabethan playwright. And finally, through cycle plays drama achieved widespread popular appeal. Audiences were heterogeneous and enthusiastic, often rising before dawn to see a performance and staying with it for days on end. So important were these performances to the people that businesses were closed during the showing, much as the usual activities had been suspended during the Dionysiac contests of ancient Greece. This involvement of the entire population in dramatic activity, as participant or as spectator, created fertile ground for the development of one of the world's greatest theatres—that of Shakespeare. It is true that many of the ideas and practices of the Middle Ages bore flower and fruit in that later, more expansive era.

Because the pageant of history is so vast and heterogeneous, students are inclined in their zeal to comprehend it, to compartmentalize and divide its wide panorama into neat little packages for easy consumption. They fix upon the date of 1453, the fall of Constantinople, and say it marks the beginning of the Renaissance. And, in a way, there is some truth in this, for that cataclysmic event drove eastern scholars to the West, and they brought with them many Greek manuscripts unknown to Western scholars. But if the Renaissance is defined (and it can be) as the period of the triumph of humanism over medieval scholasticism, when the rebirth of interest in the classics revolutionized man's attitude toward this world and the next, then the date of 1453 is an arbitrary point indeed.

The ideas which became identified as particularly those of the Renaissance had been gestating a long time. Latin manuscripts had been preserved in medieval monasteries, and Horace, Seneca, and Terence were revered by those who were aware of them—the latter primarily for the purity of his Latin style. Even Aristotle was not unknown, largely because of the writings of Boethius, but as his logic was understood to rule out divine intervention in human affairs, he was under interdiction from the church. The primary mode of thought of the High Middle Ages, as influenced chiefly by Thomas Aquinas and Peter Abelard, was that of scholasticism—a method of disputation (setting the question, presenting arguments pro and con, and then striking a balance), which could lead finally to casuistry, aridity, and absurdity: "How many angels," for instance, "could sit on the point of a pin?" But the increasing affluence of the financiers of Italy during the twelfth and thirteenth centuries fostered an interest in the collection of the antiquities which lay everywhere about them. (In 1162 the Roman Senate passed a law

which punished by death anyone injuring a Roman column.) And that interest in ancient artifacts spurred renewed study of ancient writers. Petrarch (1304–1374) is said to have been the first scholar to collect libraries, to advocate the preservation of manuscripts, and to accumulate ancient coins. Dante before him (1265–1321) had devoted his life to scholarship as Petrarch did, trying to reconcile what he could discover of the ancients with his own deep faith in Christianity. It was at about the time that the great cycle plays were turning to the use of the vernacular that Dante wrote his masterpiece in his native Italian, explaining its title by reference to Horace (*Epistola* XI, c. 1318). Shortly thereafter, Petrarch and Boccaccio were also writing their great works in Italian. In 1349, Petrarch even wrote a play, *Philologia* (now lost), as did Pier Paola Vergerio (*Paulus*) a little later. These plays were, evidently, completely different in spirit from the writings of their contemporaries.

Petrarch is sometimes called the Father of Humanism because of his interest in ancient civilizations and his use of the vernacular in his own writings, although he knew little or nothing of Aristotle. It remained for that prototype of the Renaissance man, Leone Battista Alberti (1404–1472), to state most clearly the essence of the new humanism: "Men," he wrote, "are themselves the source of their own fortune and misfortune." It was a revolutionary doctrine in a world hitherto bound in the rigid system of rules, regulations, beliefs, and attitudes of medieval times; it denied the tenet of the scholiasts that theological truth was independent of and superior to philosophical truth—the only order of thought subject to man's reason. It turned men's minds away from the contemplation of eternity to the consideration of the here-and-now: it fostered a spreading belief that all things are possible to man, and it led in turn to the great voyages and great discoveries, to the great music, the great art, and the great literature of this era. The subsiding fear of punishment in the next world led to libertinism, exploitation, political chicanery, and murder. It was the best and the worst of all possible worlds. And the drama, as the true mirror of its age, reflected these often contrary images. The plays of medieval Europe had been largely a looking-glass for morality, not a mirror of man; the new humanists thought them barbarous. They took delight in the tragedies and comedies of individual men and women; they looked for heroes on the one hand and for individual idiosyncrasies on the other. In other words, in their hands drama became completely secular and nondidactic; that is why the Renaissance is the beginning of modern theatre.

It is one of the amazing accidents of history that the influx of eastern scholars into Italy after 1453 coincided with the advent of the printing press developed by Gutenberg and a group of his associates. Now, "pure" texts of the Greek masters could be newly studied, and the new learning could be easily disseminated, so that it no longer was the property solely of a rich and privileged class, but could be widely known. Giorgio Valla published a complete Latin translation of the *Poetics* in Venice in 1498, and the original Greek text was published by Aldus in 1508; by 1549 it appeared in Italian translation by Bernardo Segni. The sixteenth century was marked by a flood of treatises on the art of the drama: commentaries on Aristotle and Horace as well as more or less original formulations, and prefaces to plays. Daniello's *La Poetica* (1536) is the first such original formulation since the ancients, albeit he relies heavily on them. Among the dozens who were caught up in critical theory, the most outstanding

and influential work was done by Minturno, Scaliger, Cinthio, Trissino, and Castelvetro in Italy, and by Thomas Sebillet and Jean de la Taille in France. All of these, to some extent, attempted a synthesis of Horace and Aristotle. Minturno stressed the occupation of tragedy with "serious and weighty happenings" and of comedy with "teaching and pleasing." Scaliger said that it is enough if tragedy concern itself with "horrible events," including "apparitions, or ghosts, or specters," and that comedy should "teach, move, and please." Cinthio stressed the "majesty" of Senecan models because of their maxims, and insisted upon the five-act division. Trissino sternly states that "The action of tragedy should last one day, i.e., one revolution of the sun, or a little more." Castelvetro said that "The time of action ought not to exceed the limit of twelve hours." Sebillet insisted upon "the moral sense of the piece," and de la Taille stated unequivocally that "The story, or play, must always be presented as occurring in the same day, in the same time, and in the same place." These critical tenets became law for generations of playwrights.

Drama secular, not sacred

The early Renaissance theatre was of two distinct types: the select and formal theatre fostered by the humanists, and the popular theatre which, in Italy, came to be called the commedia dell'arte. Both types were secular.

It has been shown that the great drama of the Middle Ages was church drama—universal, religious in subject matter, and under direction of the church. It is also evident how secular elements entered and became a part of this drama, how there was a steady, but perhaps weaker parallel development of nonreligious theatre with different origins and themes. Though the presentation of mysteries and miracles was to continue through many years of the Renaissance period, the animating spirit of the time was secular rather than religious. It gave impetus to secular forms of the drama; the triumph of the Renaissance submerged church drama and favored secular themes. Grotesque and comic elements had been increasingly incorporated into the church drama, and by 1548 the Confrèrie de la Passion in Paris was forbidden by decree to give anything but secular pieces; from that time on French drama developed secularly in both formal and popular types. In Germany, the grotesque and comic elements of the popular Shrovetide Play, as well as the pageantry of the church dramas, were put to the use of the Reformation, which engaged the major vitalities of the German people throughout the sixteenth century.

Two theatres develop

It is in Italy, however, that the force of the Renaissance was earliest and most strongly felt. It is here that the literary and dramatic forms developed which had widespread and continuing influence far beyond their native soil. Here, too, the division between formal and popular theatre was most strongly marked.

It is easy to see in the popular theatre, though a definite connection has not yet been established, the continuation of a mime tradition reaching far back into the earliest days of theatrical history. For the vigor, art, and vulgarity of the commedia are certainly reminiscent of the early Greek comedies and the atellan farces, with overtones of Menander, Plautus, and Terence. Its robustness, sincerity, originality, and theatrical zest infused theater as a whole with irreplaceable benefits. It was a widespread popular comedy originating in Italy and spreading to Spain and to France, where it left the most lasting impression. It was produced by companies of highly specialized professional actor-managers who generally grouped together on family lines, with both men and women participating. The commedia itself, and the playing of specific roles, often became a family tradition. These highly skilled and sometimes very learned performers played before popular as well as select audiences, and so formed the most universal theatre of the day.

The more formal theatre, on the other hand, was the darling of the new intellectual elite who have been called humanists. Its dramatic performances were generally given as special entertainments, or to mark special events. It was patronized and supported by the noble and the wealthy, such as the family of the Medici, the Duke of Urbino, the popes, and their confreres. Its performers were both professional and amateur depending on the occasion, the purpose, and the producer. Its audiences, however, were almost always select. It was, indeed, a minority theatre which nevertheless made significant and lasting contributions to the general stream of theatrical history.

It was from these two types of Renaissance theatre, distinct and yet overlapping, that modern theatre evolved. Though the period itself produced no important dramatic literature, the modern stage was born in the Renaissance theatre.

Few plays of lasting value

With a few minor exceptions, the dramatic literature of this theatre is now the concern of only antiquarians and scholars. Scant indeed are the scripts which have lived beyond their first audiences. Yet to know this theatre one must know the materials with

COMMEDIA CHARACTERS
Left, an unusual print of the character of
The Captain with his oversize wooden sword
and, here, a somewhat Arabic headdress.
This character is often considered the direct
descendant of the Miles Gloriosus. Above, an
old print of the juvenile, of Arlecchino, and
of Columbina, showing the lack of mask on
the first figure, and the masked figures of the
other two. This practice was universal in the
commedia presentations. (Harvard Theatre
Collection; Paris, Coll. Worms)

which it worked and how these materials
were handled.

As a matter of fact, there are no complete playscripts from the commedia. It was
an improvisational theatre using type characters and stock situations. The plays were
simply scenarios freely stolen from novels,
old plays, or any source at all, or ingeniously
invented on the basis of current happenings,
remembered incidents, or spicy gossip. The
scenarios, of which about eight hundred are
extant, were provided by the head of the

company who was, in a sense, the author.
They indicated the cast of characters and
the line of action from situation to situation. Then the performers improvised the
dialogue according to the inspiration of the
moment.

The characters were stock figures, with
specialized characteristics of attitude and appearance and particularized names. Often an
actor assumed one of these characters for a
lifetime. The men's parts were several: there
was Arlecchino, or Harlequin, who was the

clever servant; Pantalone, a ridiculous older man who played duped husbands, old lovers, irate fathers, Venetian merchants; The Doctor (of laws, not of medicine), who served as foil for Pantalone; The Captain, who was the braggart in direct line of descent from Plautus' Miles Gloriosus; then a whole list of servant characters, each with his special characteristics—Pedrolino, Mezzetino, Burrattino, Brighella or Scapino, and Pulcinella, the prototype of Punch. Finally there was the lover, or the juvenile lead as later times would call him, who was never dignified with a type name, but invariably was known by his own—Flavio, Ottavio, and so forth.

His vis-à-vis was the feminine lover, or ingénue, who also bore her own name—Isabella, Flaminia, Lucinda. The other women bore type names: Pasquella, the old woman; Columbina or Corallina, the soubrette—a very clever maid; and the other servant and confidante types, Harlequina and Pierrette.

The scenarios comprised chiefly comedies, but included also were tragedies, tragicomedies, pastorals, and—as the type developed—operas. Flaminio Scala's famous collection of fifty of these scenarios contains forty comedies, one tragedy, and nine operas. Though dialogue was not set down and memorized by the actors, they did have cer-

MORE COMMEDIA CHARACTERS
Above, an oil painting, artist unknown (late
sixteenth century) at the Musée Carnavalet. It
purports to show Isabella Andreini and other
members of the famed I Gelosi. Isabella,
playing the ingénue, wears no mask. Left,
a print of the popular water-gun scene in a
commedia performance, with a masked Arlecchino attacking Pantalone, while The Captain loses his sword in fright. (Musée Carnavalet; Harvard Theatre Collection)

tain speeches and bits of business which
were standard and which were used over
and over. The bits of business were called
lazzi, and these corresponded to the stock
farce situations with which the modern stage
is familiar. There was the recognition lazzo,
the food lazzo, the jealousy lazzo, for instance. The set speeches were of two kinds:
one, the *concetti*, was a type of lyrical out-
burst on subjects such as hope, parting, and
friendship; the other, the *repertorio*, was
more prosaic, and took the form of advice,
tirade, and various greetings—to a lady, to
a gentleman, and so forth. Each actor had
at his command the lazzi and speeches ap-

propriate to his character and used them as
the scenario demanded. Connecting dialogue
and action were always improvised.

The formal theatre, however, used standard scripts of various types: translations of
the Greek and Latin masters, native models
of classic comedy and tragedy, original comedies, tragedies, pastorals, and operas.

In 1429 Cusano discovered in Germany
twelve hitherto unknown plays of Plautus;
after the invention of the printing press, they
received wide dissemination. Terence's comedies were first printed in 1473. Printed
translations of both Roman writers soon
followed and were widely read. Staged read-

ings, as well as private readings, were held and the plays were performed before numerous cultured audiences. In 1502 the Venetian printer, Aldus, published the seven extant plays of Sophocles. A year later he published Euripides, and, in 1518, Aeschylus. Now the theatre was equipped with most of the classic masters, and the humanist writers aped them sedulously.

Even before the vogue of the Greek dramatists, Mussato had produced his *Eccerinis* (1315) on the Senecan model and Petrarch had followed Terence in his *Philologia*. After the printing of the Greeks early in the sixteenth century, Rucellai (1475–1525) produced his own *Orestes;* Dolce (1508–1568), a *Giocasta* using the conflict between the sons of Oedipus; and Speroni (1500–1588) wrote his notorious *Canace.* By and large, these imitators of classic tragedy, though using primarily Greek subject matter, worked in the Senecan technique of stressing the horrible; their plays swam in pools of blood.

Assiduous aping of the ancients was fostered by schools and scholars. The first neoclassic tragedy in France, *Cleopatra Captive* (1522), was written by Etienne Jodelle more to sustain his position as a member of the literary group which called itself the *Pléiade* than as an actable play. It was, however, performed at the court of Henry II, with the young author playing the title role to the great acclaim of his fellow-scholars who awarded him an ivy-crowned goat as a prize. He subsequently wrote an *Antigone* and a *Medea.* The poet Vondel (1587–1679) led the movement of classic revival in the Netherlands at a somewhat later date, choosing Terence as his model; in Germany Hans Sachs (1494–1576) wrote an original *Alcestis*, a strange companion to his two hundred-odd farces and comedies. Beginning in 1551 the schools and colleges founded by

the Jesuits presented plays, chiefly in Latin, drawn from the repertoire of the classics, and written by such extramural scholars as Jodelle, Garnier, and Grévin, or by faculty members or students. Various regulations promulgated by the order from time to time concerning these performances stressed their educational value and limited their subject matter to serious materials in the tragic tradition. These school productions took place in Italy, Germany, Spain, and France with varying degrees of frequency and elaborateness until the suppression of the order in 1773; they thus perpetuated a combination of entertainment and moral purpose, classic in pattern and elaborate in execution, over a very long period of time. So popular were the Latin and Greek plays in Germany that even Martin Luther encouraged Paul Rebhun to write his *Susanna* (1535) in the classic mode.

Both native comedy and native tragedy served theatre, and there were many practitioners. Chief among the Italian writers of comedy were Ariosto and Aretino, though no lesser persons than Machiavelli and Lorenzo de Medici were also writing. Additional names include those of Della Porta, Grazzini, Cecchi, Cini, Caro, and Bruno. From Ariosto's *The Supposes*, first produced at Ferrara in 1502, came Gascoigne's *The Supposes* and the plot of Shakespeare's *The Taming of the Shrew.* Ariosto's *Lena* has interesting situations and is noteworthy for its study of character. Pietro Aretino's comedies—*The Courtier, Marescalio, The Hypocrite, Talanta,* and *The Philosopher*—were produced between 1525 and 1542. They introduced the element of satire, and centered the interest on the principal character who is dominated by some single characteristic—misogyny, hypocrisy, theorizing, and so forth. This type of presentation is a natural development of the stock character, and will be evidenced again in the later and greater plays of Ben Jonson. Of the three plays of Machiavelli— *Clizia*, an untitled comedy in prose, and *Mandragola*—the last is by far the best and most famous. Some writers have called it the best Italian play produced in the sixteenth century. And it has interest quite apart from the personality of the writer. It is one of the few plays of the period in which we witness a real development of character during the course of the play: the heroine changes from a virtuous, chaste wife into a cynical and disillusioned mistress. Its unprincipled clergy, its precipitate and crafty hero, and its cynical morality all effectively reflect the tenor of the age. Like Lorenzo de Medici's *Aridosia*, performed at the marriage of Duke Alessandro in 1536, the *Mandragola* and the comedies of the other writers use stock characters and familiar situations, yet invest these with a native flavor. Marital infidelity is a favorite theme, and the plots abound with young wives married to old and cold husbands; with ardent suitors who go to any lengths to achieve the object of their desires; with cunning priests; with dissolute students; with clever servants, both loyal and disloyal. The picture they give of contemporary life is not a pleasant one by our standards, but it is bustling, vigorous, sensational, sometimes crude, and sometimes over-refined—in short, a rather accurate mirror of the age which produced the plays.

The level of native comedy is low by any dramatic standard, but that of native tragedy is even lower. It is almost completely derivative, tedious, and weltering in blood; early and late examples adhere to the pattern of Seneca. No one now remembers the names of the plays or the playwrights; Tebaldeo, Cammelli, Zinano, Groto are the dust of scholarship.

Trissino lives because his *Sofonisba*, finished in 1515, was widely copied in many places; the type was finally and delightfully travestied in Fielding's *Tom Thumb*. Tasso, now praised in other fields of literature, was lauded by his contemporaries because his *Torrismondo* was so excellent an example of adherence to classic models. Were it not for the sumptuous settings these tragedies commanded, they would not be worth our notice.

Sumptuous also were the settings of that peculiar child of the Renaissance, the pastoral play. This was the escapist drama of the period; its time was always set in The Golden Age, its place was Arcadia, and its characters were shepherds and nymphs. Triggered, no doubt, by the Renaissance affectation for simple and placid country life, the pastorals proved immensely popular in highly sophisticated society and were presented upon many special occasions. Though examples of this kind of spectacle were numerous before 1573, it was not until that year, with the performance of Tasso's *Aminta*, that it was dignified with the name of "art." The triumph of Tasso's graceful gesture was so complete that there followed numerous imitations. Guarino's *The Faithful Shepherd* is the most famous of these. The pastoral had many manifestations all over the Continent, and Shakespeare did not scorn to use the form in such a play as *As You Like It*.

Related to the pastoral drama by reason of its luxuriant production was the one other form of theatrical presentation cultivated in the Renaissance—the opera. Though the chanting of lines and actual singing had been a part of the medieval cycle plays, and though the humanist Poliziano had written in 1422 a dramatic poem set to music and called *The Fable of Orpheus*, it remained for the little circle of musicians and poets gathered at the *palazzo* of Giovanni Bardi in Florence and dedicated to a study of the classics, to produce something new. In their study of the Greek plays they first discovered their musical characteristics, assuming that the dialogue of Greek tragedy had been declaimed or sung. In their zeal to recreate this aspect of the revered art, they created a new form of music-drama. It was *Dafne* (first performed in 1597), with words by Rinuccini and music by Peri, that thus became the first significant opera. *Dafne* was followed by *Euridice*, by the same composers; and then in 1607 and 1608 by the first productions of one of the most highly acclaimed Renaissance musicians, Monteverdi —a *Dafne*, an *Arianna*, and an *Orfeo*. Thus, by accident almost, the humanists produced their only original contribution to theatrical literature, and so popular did it become that from the building of the first public opera house anywhere—that in Venice in 1637— opera captured the imagination of the public. In Italy, and for a long time in Germany, it effectively absorbed practically all of the interest to be exhibited in theatre, and left a tremendous heritage. Opera, of course, went its separate way from theatre, becoming a viable and autonomous art form with a long and intricate history of its own. It was not long until the predominant force in opera was the music rather than the words and actions, hence it belongs not to the annals of theatre but to music. It is the composer who is the focus of attention in opera.

Simple staging in commedia theatre

Being primarily an actor's theatre, the commedia dell'arte placed little reliance upon playhouses or settings, though it did not scorn these physical enhancements when they were offered. The typical background of a commedia performance, however, was a simple platform and a backdrop, sometimes painted, sometimes not. The platform was always of a temporary nature, being erected in marketplaces, squares, open fields, or halls, and remaining only for the duration of the performance. If the platform were high enough, it was curtained off and the understage area used as a dressing room. If not, the area behind the backdrop served the purpose. When the backdrop was painted, the scene was either a street or a forest. Only the most rudimentary of stage props were used—a table, a chair, a basket— and since the performances were mostly outdoors, absolutely no lighting effects were necessary. For music, one of the actors with a guitar played during the performance, or sang the *entr'acte*. The focus was on the actor and there it remained, whether he was attempting by his skill to catch the attention of a noisy crowd at the Parisian *théâtres de la foire*, or whether he had the undivided attention customary at command performances at courts and royal houses.

Court amateurs have elaborate accoutrements

But this simplicity was never practiced in the formal and elite theatre of the day, for which special houses were built and increasingly complicated and magnificent settings invented. It all began simply enough. The early humanists combined what they found of staging suggestions in the texts of Plautus and Terence with what they knew of the medieval custom of mansions. They presented their plays on platforms with backings, indicating three or more individual doorways for the various characters, which grew to be ornamented and elaborated with suggestions of rooms behind them. With the rediscovery of Vitruvius in 1484, attention began to be paid to the accommodations of the audience. The cavea which

EARLY RENAISSANCE PLATFORM STAGES
Left, a model of the simple platform stage erected in the converted Marthakirke in Nuremburg, where many of the moralities of Hans Sachs were presented. A trestle stage in the nave of the church, with a backdrop and side curtains, sufficed for these presentations. Above, stage and players of the fifteenth century, as reproduced in a volume of Terence published by Johannes Trechsel in 1493. Here the backdrop has become a series of curtained archways bearing the names of the various characters. In this way the presentation of the classical plays was related to the medieval ideas of mansions. (Cleveland State University; Henry E. Huntington Library and Art Gallery)

Vitruvius mentions caused much speculation, as well as various designs purporting to recreate a classic theatre. Until 1580, however, theatre buildings remained wholly on paper, or were simply temporary structures (converted halls and such). A more permanent kind of conversion was accomplished by Hans Sachs in 1550, when he transformed a disused Catholic church—the Marthakirke in Nuremberg, Germany—into a theatre with a simple, curtained stage.

In 1580, the Olympic Academy of Vicenza commissioned Andrea Palladio to design and build a theatre according to the best classical ideas of the time, and this Teatro Olimpico, as it came to be called, is the first permanent theatre building of the Italian Renaissance. It escaped the ravages of World

War II and occasionally still houses a production. The theatre designed by Palladio has thirteen tiers of seats arranged in semielliptical fashion around an open floor area called the orchestra, abutting at the ends on a stage which is seventy feet long and eighteen feet deep. The banked tiers of seats are topped by a series of columns. Eighty stucco statues of the Academicians decorated the edifice, and the overall impression, according to the contemporary description by Filippo Pigafetta, was one of an incredible loveliness.

Palladio died before the building was completed, and Vincenzo Scamozzi, to whom the task fell, evidently altered the original plans for the stage proper. Behind the five doors planned for the stage (a "royal" door, designed like a Roman triumphal arch, and four lesser doors, two flanking the royal door on each side) he added perspective vistas. Influenced by the preoccupation of artists with the newly discovered principles of perspective, his vistas—three down the center arch and one each behind the other portals—represented, he said, the seven streets of Thebes. They were constructed of lath and plaster in full relief and in forced perspective. The rest was an elaborate mélange of statues, columns, architraves, and niches after the manner of the Roman theatre. In this building was presented, on March 3, 1585, a production of *Oedipus Rex* which purported to be a faithful rendition of the Sophocles masterpiece, though what with four hundred chairs in the orchestra to accommodate the ladies, with a front curtain which dropped, with the spraying of perfume and the serving of wine and fruit before the performance, the whole thing sounds more like the kind of performance against which Marcus Aurelius railed.

This same Scamozzi, at the behest of Duke Vespasiano Gonzago of Mantua, designed and supervised the construction of a theatre at Sabionetta, which opened in 1588. The commission specified that the theatre be "in miniature" as were the palace, mint, and printing plant with which the Duke had already supplied the town. So Scamozzi designed a single vista for the stage, permanent, like the one at the Olimpico, but beginning almost at the edge of the stage on either side. The tiers of seats were arranged in horseshoe fashion, with a wide space between the front of the stage and the first row of seats; the seating capacity was about three hundred. This building, too, is still standing.

In 1618, in the little town of Parma, about twenty miles from Sabionetta, the Prince commissioned Aleotti, the Ferrarese, to build a theatre. This Teatro Farnese, as it was called, used the same horseshoe arrangement for the tiers of seats, although there were a great many more of them; the theatre seated about thirty-five hundred spectators. It also retained the distance between seats and stage, but included innovations on the stage itself: the first permanent, sculptured proscenium arch, and behind it, a flat-wing system for change of scenes. The proscenium arch and modifications of the flat-wing system persist even in today's theatre. Sometimes the audience occupied the open floor space, but often this was used as a part of the spectacular performances, sometimes even being flooded to make a sea for boats. (Shades of the Roman naumachia!)

By the time the Olimpico celebrated its grandiose opening, Madrid had four permanent theatres, London three, and Paris at least one. This last was a direct line of development from the medieval cycle plays, having been built by the Confrérie de la Passion in 1548 and called the Hôtel de Bourgogne. It seems to have been the first public playhouse built since the fall of Rome; though the Confrérie ceased to produce its own plays there after 1578, they leased the house to other companies and it continued to be an active, producing theatre until 1783. The theatres in Madrid and London will be discussed later.

Another innovation of the Renaissance was a theatre of sorts, built outdoors, with walls and stage wings of clipped cypress and a floor of turf. Such garden theatres were

LATE RENAISSANCE COMMEDIA STAGE
In this eighteenth century painting by Marco Marcola, the commedia stage, which was earlier the simple trestle platform, has been elaborated to contain a front curtain, scenery, and boxes. It is still, however, an outdoor arrangement, and the performers maintain the traditional characters. (The Art Institute of Chicago)

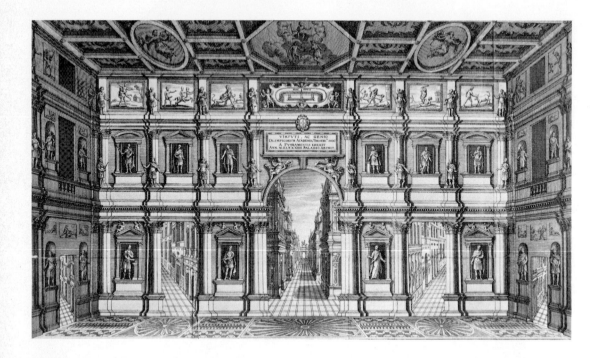

eighty to a hundred feet long, twenty to eighty feet wide, and were built—grown, rather—at such places as the Villa Maria, the Villa Gori, the Villa Serraglio in Italy, and the Schloss Mirabell gardens in Salzburg. Immensely popular for the playing of pastorals, they were an affection of the wealthy copied throughout Europe.

Stagecraft highly skilled

In addition to the building of impressive theatres, the formal theatre of the Renaissance saw stage design carried to increasing complexity and magnificence. The mansion stage of the early classic revival, as seen in the illustrations of the Trechsel edition of Terence (Lyons, 1493), was simple enough, but forces were at work which soon rendered it more elaborate. This stage itself was soon highly decorated with curtains of gold cloth and with tapestries and intricate columns. The early sixteenth-century stage of the *Rederykers* of the Netherlands is an illustration of the elaboration of the simple doorways into an intricately pedimented, two-level edifice (page 135).

Just as the simple mansion settings of the cycle plays became complex enough to require as many as eight "masters of machines," so the stages of the classic revival developed from simplicity to elaboration. To them was added the wonders of perspective representation with which the artists of the Renaissance were so concerned. There is record of a production at Ferrara in 1508 of Ariosto's *Cassaria* with its landscape in perspective of "houses, churches, towers, and gardens." By 1513, the scene was further elaborated. In that year Castiglione, author of *The Courtier*, describes the production of

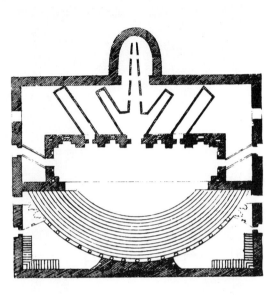

THE TEATRO OLIMPICO, VICENZA
Left, the floor plan of the building with its elliptical seating arrangement, its five doors on the stage, and the vistas in forced perspective behind them. Above, an interior view of the Olimpico, showing the integration of stage and seats, the open orchestra, the raised stage, the colonnade, and the statues of the members of the Academy who commissioned the building. Far left, the stage of the Olimpico as completed by Scamozzi, showing the perspective vistas and the highly decorated walls. (Walker, *Italian Drama*; Victoria & Albert Museum, Crown Copyright)

Cardinal Bibbiena's comedy *La Calandria* (1508) at the court of the Duke of Urbino. He says, "The streets looked as if they were real, and everything was done in relief, and made even more striking through the art of painting and well-conceived perspective" (quoted in Alessandro d'Ancono, *Origini del Teatro Italiano*, Torini, 1891, II. 102). Pillars, statues, altars, and highly decorated stucco temples were a part of this design. The next year the same play was produced for Pope Leo X, with Peruzzi designing a set with "palaces and curious temples, loggias and cornices, all made to make them appear to be what they represented." (Giorgio Vasari, *The Lives of the Painters, Sculptors and Architects*, New York, 1927, II. 297). This continuing emphasis upon realism is a curious echo of the realistic effects constantly striven for in the medieval plays. And, like the earlier plays, these, too, were performed on temporary stages, now erected in great banqueting halls or in courtyards. Often great artists worked in theatre; Raphael, for instance, designed the setting for a production of Ariosto's *The Supposes* in 1519.

When Sebastiano Serlio, who had been a pupil of Peruzzi, published in Paris the second book of his *Architettura* in 1545, he incorporated in it a principle he had used some ten years earlier in designing a setting at Vicenza. This principle was a further application of the idea of perspective; the floor of the rear stage was sloped upward to emphasize the forced perspective which had become so popular. Thus was born the *raked* stage which continued in use even into the twentieth century. In his further descriptions of stage effects, Serlio particularized the reference in Vitruvius to the three types of classic settings—comic, tragic, and satyric—and solidified a convention which was slavishly followed for many years in many places.

For the comic scene he prescribed houses "for Citizens, but specially there must not want a brawthell or bawdy house, and a great Inne, and a Church." He prescribed galleries, windows, levels, some to be in relief and some to be painted. For the tragic scene he planned "none but stately houses . . . Chimneyes, Towers, Piramides, Oblisces, and other such like things or Images . . . cut out round, and well colloured." The satyric scene, he said, "should be made with Trees, Rootes, Herbs, Hils and Flowers, and with some countrey houses." (*The First Book of Architecture*, London, 1611, II, 3, pp. 25 ff.) He accompanied his descriptions with drawings, and it is these visualizations which were so influential with succeeding artisans.

As described above, the principle of the permanent perspective setting in relief was incorporated in the building of the Teatro Olimpico. But the desirability—or necessity—of sets which could be changed during the course of the production led to the development of nested angle wings and flat wings, such as are found in the Farnese Theatre at Parma. When Sabbatini finally published his *The Practice of Making Scenes and Machines* in 1637, he described in detail the various wing systems and methods of changing them.

Serlio, Sabbatini, and Di Somi (whose *Dialogues* on playwriting and stagecraft appeared about 1556) also discuss in their works various stage machines and lighting effects. Since all changes were made in full view of the audience, great care was taken to make the operation smooth and interesting. In addition to the wing system, Sabbatini describes a scene change using an adaptation of the Greek three-sided prism, and cautions that this method requires great care in selecting reliable workers. He tells,

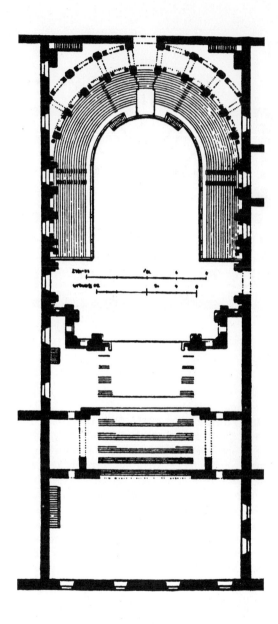

with description and diagram, "How to
Make Dolphins and Other Sea Monsters Appear to Spout Water While Swimming,"
"How to Produce a Constantly Flowing
River," "How to Divide the Sky into Sections," "How Gradually to Cover Part of the
Sky with Clouds," "How to Make a Cloud
Descend Perpendicularly with Persons on It,"
and how to make it descend at an angle (descents and sky effects were exceedingly popular—perhaps an inheritance from the medieval cycles). He discusses how the lights
should be arranged on the stage, and how to
light them. He recommends oil lamps with
strong wicks as most reliable and durable.
Serlio describes how colored lighting effects
may be achieved by using colored water or
wine in glass vessels with lamps and re-
flectors behind them, and tells of the effects
of various ingredients; Di Soma recommends
that the auditorium be darkened so that the
stage lights would appear brighter—a practice which did not become universal until
more than a century later. Angelo Ingegneri,
in 1598, went a step further by urging that

the auditorium be completely darkened during the presentation of a play, and that none
of the stage lights spill over into the auditorium. His system would wait much longer
for acceptance. Methods for moving stars
and suns, for making flashing lightning and
the sound of thunder, for dimming the
lights, and many more are detailed in these
technical discussions.

The most detailed accounts of lighting
practices come from the writings of Joseph
Furttenbach the Elder (1591–1667), who after
spending ten years in Italy returned to his
native Germany to develop there the wonders of the Italian Renaissance. His three
treatises describe in detail many intricate
lighting effects and methods for achieving
them. He also describes and illustrates how
to set up a theatre in which the seating arrangement is on parallel rows of benches
rather than in the elliptical or semicircular
tiers common in Italy. Finally he gives a
great deal of attention to material concerning the construction and use of the rear
stage behind the back shutters which, he

says, may be used as a room or interior, or, with floor boards removed, as a pit for sea scenes. What a far cry from the technically uncomplicated, open-air productions of Aeschylus' theatre!

These intricate stages, whether temporary or permanent, used a front curtain, and there were three ways in which it might operate. A curtain might be arranged to descend into a trough at the front of the stage when the play began (in imitation of the Roman theatre); it might be raised; or it might be drawn in what today is called a festoon drape. Among Furttenbach's works are designs for special front curtains particularly related to the plays presented. In any event, once the curtain was withdrawn it remained so until the performance was over, with all integral scene changes being a part of the performance. Scene changes were cued to the music which always accompanied the performance. This essentially curtainless method of presentation remained till the nineteenth century.

Thus Renaissance stagecraft, profiting from the inventions of medieval artisans and

the development of suggestions found in classic sources, and encouraged by the Renaissance love of opulent display such as was exhibited in the sumptuous *tableaux vivants* of entries and festivities, developed into a highly complicated and skilled art.

Commedia costumes stereotyped

In both the formal and popular theatres, costume and makeup played an important part in creating the scenic illusion. In the popular theatre of the commedia they served to identify the characters, as well as to add to the stage decoration; for this reason, they tended to become stereotyped.

Perhaps a proof of the commedia's ancient heritage may be found in the masks which were made of leather and worn by almost all of the actors. Some scholars see in the black mask of Arlecchino a descendant of the Negro slaves of the Roman mime; in the mask of Pulcinella another hook-nosed descendant of a Roman mime mask; in the dark mask and red beard of Pantalone the Dossenus of the atellanae. The speculation is highly probable, but whatever their ancestry the commedia masks served with the costumes to emphasize the particular characteristics of the various performers.

Pantalone, an avaricious Venetian merchant with a large curved nose, white hair, and a beard, originally appeared in a long red cloak with a red cap and Turkish slippers. Soon the color of the cloak was changed to black, but the red cap and the slippers remained. His foil, The Doctor, also wore black, fashioned in the likeness of a professor's gown, with a black hat. His dark mask had red cheeks and a short beard. The Captain, originally an Italian fighting man, early changed to a Spanish type of braggart. He wore a long-nosed mask with a fierce moustache and carried a wooden sword. Arlecchino, with his black half-mask and chin-piece, began in beggarly fashion with a patched costume which later evolved into the formal checkered design which we know, particularly in his more famous French identity, Harlequin. His companion, Brighella, wore a full mask of grotesque and evil design and he was dressed in wide trousers with a short jacket laced with green braid. Mezzetino's colors were red and white, eventually striped. Pedrolino wore no mask, but had a white powdered face and wore a loose white costume. His French counterpart, Pierrot, became one of the most famous of all these figures. Pulcinella's mask was exceedingly ugly, with a wart, and he generally wore a huge cock's feather in his hat.

Among the women, Pasquella was likely to be masked, with an ugly countenance as befitted the evil old woman that she was; sometimes Columbina wore a half-mask as the feminine counterpart to her partner, Arlecchino. The *inamorate* (juvenile and ingénue) rarely, if ever, were masked, and ordinarily wore contemporary dress as rich as the treasury of the company would allow.

As the popularity of the commedia grew and then waned, the dress of the various characters evolved and changed; but the basic patterns remained the same, always embodying the attitudes and actions of the type characters they dressed.

Classical adaptations and contemporary dress in formal theatre

In the plays of the formal Renaissance theatre the costumes became a part of stage decoration—the richer the production, the richer the costuming. Classical adaptations were used for the Greek and Roman plays. For native comedy and tragedy contemporary dress was the rule. But even here, as Di Somi says, richness was mandatory. Servants were not dressed in torn or mean garments, but in silks and velvets to improve the picture, so long as their masters were clothed more richly with embroidery, laces, and jewels. The aim was to make every actor as unique as possible in style and color, with an emphasis on light and definite colors which would enhance the stage picture. Costuming had another purpose, too. In a production where the players were likely to be drawn from the same social circle as the audience, Di Somi says, "Not only do I try to vary the actors' costumes, but I strive as much as I can to transform each one from his usual appearance, so that he will not readily be recognized by the audience, which sees him daily" (as translated from the MS in the Biblioteca Palatina, Parma, and quoted by Alois Nagler, *Sources of Theatrical History*, p. 105).

In the pastorals, the shepherds wore white silk sleeveless shirts covered over with the skins of animals. Unless they were young and handsome, they also wore a type of fleshings over arms and legs and always some kind of soft shoes. The nymphs were

SERLIO'S TRAGIC AND COMIC SCENES
Prints from Jehan Martin's Paris edition of Serlio's *De Architettura*, 1545. Above, the tragic scene with its classical architecture and triumphal arch; left, the comic scene with its more domestic and contemporary architecture. The effect is achieved by the use of angle wings set in linear perspective, which stage designers adopted from fifteenth-century painters. These are permanent settings, not changed during the performance. (The Metropolitan Museum of Art)

clothed in long-sleeved ladies' shirts, with embroidery and colored ribbons, over which went a long, rich mantle falling from one shoulder and forming the skirt. The animal skins, the mantles, and the ribbons were varied in color and arrangement so that interest would be maintained in the stage picture. Variety in coiffures, some curly, some smooth, some ivy-crowned, was prescribed for the shepherds. The nymphs were uniformly blond (wigs, of course), and golden fillets or colored ribbons and flimsy, floating veils adorned their heads. These visions carried golden darts and bows, while the shepherds bore leafy branches or sticks.

In other specialized types of performances, such as interludes and spectacles, the dramatis personae were garbed as befitted their characters, be they angels, deities, or princes. The only aim was to make the costumes as sumptuous and eye filling as

possible. Expense was never an item for consideration, since these performances in the formal Renaissance theatre were always subsidized by wealthy patrons who vied with each other in lavish display. Furttenbach speaks enviously of the tons of gold the Italian princes were wont to expend on their theatricals while, in the poorer German court theatres which he served, he felt his creative energies shackled by necessary economies.

**Titled dilettantes and scholars
in amateur ranks**

If it were possible to make an arbitrary division one might say that the formal theatre of the Renaissance was a theatre of amateurs, while that of the commedia was a theatre of professionals. One must be careful, however, to confine these labels to acting

only, for certainly in other respects the professionalism of the formal theatre is obvious. In fact, the formal theatre of the period might well be said to have belonged to the stage machinist and the painter. The drawing power for its courtly audience was the magnificence of the spectacle rather than the script or the actor.

The corps of actors in the formal theatre was comprised largely of dilettantes and scholars. The classic revivals were often pre-sented by members of the academies, and these revivals, as well as the other types of formal theatre presentations, were the diversion of the wealthy and the titled. There is record, for instance, of Cesare Borgia being one of the actors in a complicated allegory of Virtue and Fortune in dispute, which preceded the *Menaechmi* given at the marriage of Lucrezia Borgia with Alfonso d'Este in 1502. In the pastorals sported the lords and their ladies, much as the ladies and courtiers

TYPICAL SEVENTEENTH-CENTURY SETTINGS
Left, the design by Lodovico Burnacini for
La Zenobia di Rodamisto produced in Vienna
in 1662. This print includes the very ornate
proscenium arch designed for the production
showing the incorporation of a pit for the
musicians. The stage setting includes angle
wings set in linear perspective. Above, the
design by the same artist for *Il Fuoco Eterno*
produced in Vienna in 1674. Particularly apparent in this print is the use of borders for
ceiling pieces, and the upstage area, or inner
room, of which Furttenbach speaks. (Harvard Theatre Collection; Theater-Museum,
Munich)

of Jacobean England participated in the
masques at a later date. For just such titled
but inexperienced actors Di Somi wrote what
must surely be one of the first handbooks
for actors, when he devoted a section of his
Dialogues to the art of acting. In it he gives
most specific directions about gestures,
movement, and speech, urging that the total
effect should be one of naturalness. No doubt
these amateur groups also profited from
working with the professionals from the

commedia with whom their casts were sometimes augmented. Often the skillful and beautiful commedia actresses became the favorites of the lords of the land. More generally,
however, the commedia companies were invited—or commanded—to present a performance at a marriage, a visit, or at some other
special event. Then the entire company performed, using the technical resources which
the richer private theatre placed at its disposal.

Commedia acting a family tradition

The most famous of the acting companies was I Gelosi (The Jealous-of-Pleasing Ones), but there were many others: I Confidente (The Confident Ones), I Fideli (The Faithful Ones), I Accessi (The Brilliant Ones), I Desiosi (The Desirous-of-Pleasing Ones). Generally, as mentioned previously, the core of the company was a single family, as the Andreini family was in I Gelosi, and the scenarios and reputation of the group descended from one generation to the next. The members were closely knit, with the children being trained to take the place of their elders or to augment the troupe. The training was rigorous. Commedia players were expected to be proficient in song, dance, and acrobatics as well as in the more usual spoken dialogue. They had to have nimble wits as well as nimble heels, for the improvisational nature of the performance demanded it. Sometimes these performers were among the most cultured people of the age. The celebrated Isabella Andreini, star of the latter half of the sixteenth century, was said to speak four languages and to hold intelligent conversations with the most learned men of her day.

Alfoᵛˢ Pariᵍiᵛˢ Jnu Stefaᵛˢ Della
Bella Delⁱⁱ e F   SCENA QVINTA D' INFERNO.

SPECTACULAR STAGE EFFECTS

Left, the design by Bernardo Buontalenti for *Six Interludes* presented at Florence in 1589. This scene shows the continuing popularity of the medieval hellfire, as well as the Renaissance innovation of cloud machines descending from above. The fire, of course, is painted on the flats—angle wings in the foreground, a backdrop upstage. Above, the design by Alfonso Parigi for *Le Nozzi Degli Dei*, presented early in the seventeenth century. Again note the flames, the cloud machines, the angle wings. The centaurs were a particularly popular Renaissance concoction, so constructed as to allow the performer to move in quite realistic fashion. (Stockholm Nationalmuseum; Harvard Theatre Collection)

In addition, she was accomplished in song and dance, exceptionally beautiful—and renowned for her virtue. No less a person than Prince Vincenzo of Mantua acted as godfather at the christening of her child. Her husband, Francisco, was also an accomplished linguist, having five languages at his command. He was a musician and a writer —and an exceptionally popular Captain. Isabella herself played the inamorata, and lent her name to a succession of them. Favorite of the King of Poland was Constantini, who played Mezzetino; and Biancolleli was famous for his Arlecchino. Something of the

TYPICAL COMMEDIA SCENES
Old prints show the physicality of much of the action in commedia performances.

skill of these performers is evident in the fame of Visentini, who could turn a somersault with a wineglass and not spill a drop; of Fiorilli, who as Scaramouche could still, at eighty-three, box his ear with his toe.

The most famous of the troupes played in the courts of the nobles and traveled from city to city. To the commedia performer Marie Fairet goes the honor of being the first woman performer on the professional stage in France, when her company visited Paris about the middle of the sixteenth century. In 1568 a commedia company traveled in Austria, delighting the court at Vienna. In 1571 a troupe was summoned to Paris to play at the marriage of Charles IX. They are reported to have taken Paris by storm, and, indeed, for many decades to come, the Italian comedians were an integral part of the French theatrical scene, where they had a longer and more significant influence than in their native land. A commedia troupe performed before Elizabeth of England in 1577, and Philip II of Spain was greatly pleased

with the troupe which he had invited to play at his court.

The less accomplished troupes traveled to the small towns, and played in the villages. All carried with them costumes, props, and what scenery they needed. The Spanish writer, Augustin de Rojas Villandrando, wrote amusingly in 1603 of the various classifications of traveling Spanish companies, from the *bululu* which is a single player, poor and mendicant, to the grandiose *compañia* with its thirty members, its carriages and carts, and its sixty plays. While Rojas was not writing specifically of commedia players, his descriptions no doubt were applicable to many of these.

But however famous or sought-after performers or companies might become, the implacable church was still opposed to these professional theatre people, and many municipal edicts as well as church pronouncements were issued against them. It is recorded that even so famous a player as Isabella Andreini, who died in 1601 soon after she had been newly honored by Queen Marie, was refused burial in hallowed ground in conformance with the laws of the church.

The commedia flourished during the sixteenth, seventeenth, and early eighteenth centuries; the boundaries of its influence were very wide. What it did was to reintroduce and emphasize the essential nature of theatre: the actor-audience relationship. Moreover, it demonstrated the nature of acting as a skilled profession worthy of respect—although in some places that respect was a long time coming.

Summary

Renaissance theatre, while continuing the production of sacred plays, was predominantly a secular activity. The leading strings of the church were largely severed, and pagan literary influences had widespread effect. The combination of the persisting medieval traditions and the newly found classical materials gave Renaissance theatre a different aim and direction from its immediate predecessor.

It is true that the bustle of the Renaissance renewed interest in theatre, and that the people of the Renaissance probably enjoyed more forms of theatrical activity than those of many another period in history. But it is equally true that no great dramatic literature came out of the Renaissance on the Continent. Perhaps the insistence of the literary men on an adherence to classical models stifled the spirit of originality from which great drama arises. Certainly the informal theatre of the commedia, far less dependent on copying preexisting materials, was more vital and indigenous than the literary theatre of the day. But the Renaissance in Italy, France, and Germany did produce some theatrical manifestations which meant much to later times.

Its early and constant preoccupation with the classical writers set a pattern which was widely followed for many years in many places. The critical dictates of Cinthio and Castelvetro, and the mistaken application of Aristotelian principles put into practice by many playwrights, affected dramatic writing for many generations to come and in many areas of Continental Europe. The period also, of course, developed the opera and the pastoral as distinct theatrical forms.

In theatre architecture it invented the horseshoe type of seating arrangement, which persists even to our own day. It developed the proscenium arch, the painted set, indoor lighting, spectacular effects, and sumptuous costuming—all attributes of what many people today call "modern theatre." Through the commedia it also achieved a high degree of professionalism in the art of acting.

In Italy, especially, the drama of the theatre was played out against a background of almost incessant strife between families and city-states, and under foreign invasions and dominations covering wide areas and long periods of time. In Germany, the involvements of the Reformation tended to turn the populace to interests other than theatre, and the disastrous Wars of Religion in France delayed the consummation of the art of theatre for almost a century in that country. In the face of these adverse conditions, it is a wonder that so much was accomplished. In the next chapters it will be evident what the spirit of the Renaissance could accomplish in more united and comparatively more peaceful countries—the rising nations of England and Spain.

While internal strife and foreign invasion effectively prevented the building of great nation-states in France, Germany, and Italy, Spain and England each succeeded in developing a political and spiritual unity which fostered the development of unique and virile drama. Great dramatic literature and great theatre reached a peak almost simultaneously in these two countries.

The marriage of Ferdinand and Isabella in 1467 and their subsequent defeat of the Moors marked the beginning of Spain's greatness, just as the end of the Wars of the Roses and the accession of Henry VII in 1485 marked the beginning of England's influence and prosperity. These two great powers were briefly united in 1554 by the uneasy marriage of Mary of England and Philip of Spain. But the increasingly nationalistic Englishmen refused to crown Philip, and he left England the next year. By 1558 Mary was dead, Philip was King of Spain, and Elizabeth was on the throne of England. Thenceforth the destinies of these two powers were divided and in conflict. The conflict culminated in the invasion of the Spanish Armada and its defeat at the hands of the English in 1588. England was preserved, Spain looked elsewhere for conquest, and the great age of the drama in both countries was shortly to get under way.

Lope de Vega was born in 1562, Shakespeare in 1564. Both, though exposed to the classical conventions that had made so much headway in Italy and France, blithely ignored them, and produced a peculiarly national, unique drama which operated by its own conventions and was greater than any pale imitation of the ancients could possibly have been.

The Renaissance comes to England

For Englishmen of that day, the period we now call the Renaissance was a bewilder-ingly diverse phenomenon. Early in the century the study of Greek began at Oxford under William Grocyn and Thomas Linacre, and John Colet founded St. Paul's, a school devoted to the new humanist learning. Erasmus visited England and was a familiar of Sir Thomas More, the great English humanist. Though More's *Utopia* (1516) was written in Latin, the language of international scholarship, the precedent of the vernacular established by the great works of Chaucer gained strength, and an increasing number of literary productions appeared in the native tongue.

The individuality of England was emphasized by the quarrel of Henry VIII with the Church of Rome and by the subsequent separation of England from the Papacy in 1533. Though the ties were nominally resumed under Mary (1553–1558), the schism was definite and irrevocable and resulted in the creation of a freer intellectual atmosphere and a sharpening of individual differences such as was not possible, for instance, in Catholic Spain. Indeed, the bold spirit of the Renaissance—with its emphasis upon the things of this world and the infinite capacity of the individual man to determine his own destiny, which contributed to the Lutheran revolt on the Continent—in itself undermined the power of the Roman Church.

The intrinsically political English separation had far-reaching economic, social, and intellectual repercussions. Though Tyndale could be persecuted for his English translation of the Bible in the first quarter of the century, by 1539 Henry VIII could authorize for use in churches an English Bible which incorporated as much of Tyndale's translation as he had been able to finish.

Henry's court was the center of the new learning in England. Here the tentative Renaissance leanings of John Skelton flowered into the literature of two of the most important early English Renaissance writers, the sonneteers Sir Thomas Wyatt and Henry Howard, Earl of Surrey. The court was also the center of very lavish performances of interludes, masques, costume balls, and tournaments, under the supervision of a Master of the Revels, whose office was permanently instituted by Henry in 1544, although it had been sporadically in existence for several years before that time. Elizabeth herself was a product of the New Learning, having been educated first by William Grindall, then (after 1548) by Roger Ascham who wrote *The Scholemaster*, a tract outlining humanist education. Elizabeth developed a mastery of the Greek and Latin classics and was fluent in French, Italian, and Spanish—a true child of the Renaissance and a prototype of the individualism then so admired. A happier consanguinity of ruler and age could scarcely be conceived.

Drama begins to flourish

The schools, encouraged by the example of the court's dramatic productions, began to stage the classic plays which had for some time been used as reading exercises; so Terence, Plautus, and Seneca came to be produced in England. Latin plays for school productions began to be written; then the first school play in English appeared, Nicholas Udall's *Ralph Roister Doister* (c. 1540).

Productions of this kind continued after the accession of Elizabeth in 1558: *Gammer Gurton's Needle* at Cambridge (c. 1562) and the plays at the Inns of Court in London, notably Sackville and Norton's *Gorboduc* (1562). But the accession of Elizabeth caused a significant change in court dramas. She was not so devoted as Henry had been to extravagant spectacle as entertainment. It was useful for political purposes, of course, but Elizabeth was of an inquiring and intellec-

tual turn of mind—and she was also something of a pinch-penny. So she tended to limit spectacle to state occasions and to increase greatly both the quantity and quality of legitimate drama seen at Court.

The acting chores were given to the boys of the Chapel Royal under the direction of Richard Edwards. These boys, chosen from all over the kingdom for their looks and their voices, had been primarily responsible for the musical portions of the court's worship services, receiving both upkeep and education for their work. Edwards, whom Elizabeth appointed to be their master, was a musician, a good lyric poet, and a good dramatist. He wrote plays for the boys and coached them in the parts. Light romantic comedy was his forte; by the time of his death in 1566, he had established a new court drama that was the delight of critics. The production resources of the Office of the Revels were available to him, and the plays were beautifully set and costumed. William Hunnis succeeded Edwards as master at the Chapel Royal. Elizabeth also established boys' troupes at St. Paul's Cathedral under Sebastian Westcott and at her summer palace at Windsor under Richard Farrant.

Farrant conceived the idea of having his boys give their plays before select audiences after the queen had seen them, advancing the argument that such an arrangement would give the boys more practice in public and would also be profitable financially, thus stimulating both master and boys to give more and better plays. Elizabeth approved, and in September 1575, Farrant took a lease on the great hall in Blackfriars, which had formerly been a church holding but was now under jurisdiction of the Crown and was the most aristocratic section of London. When the Windsor boys had a play ready, the Master of the Revels built the set and made costumes, then brought them to Blackfriars. A selected group of nobility was invited to a preview at very high prices. The production was then taken to play before the queen, after which it returned to Blackfriars for a month's run. This scheme was very successful. Hunnis and the Chapel Royal boys joined Farrant in giving their plays at Blackfriars, and one or the other of the troupes gave plays every day. By 1583 John Lyly was writing for the children of St. Paul's to play there; with some intermissions because of litigation over the property, the boys' companies performed at Blackfriars for many years.

Meanwhile, the adult professional companies were also performing at London inns, and the best plays of the best troupes were presented before the court after having been chosen for that honor by the Master of the Revels. Elizabeth told her nobles that she liked these troupes, and many of them thereafter tried to acquire troupes to please the queen. Thus, influenced by court appearances and the competition of the boy companies to improve both their plays and their performances, the professional troupes increased in number and in quality.

The theatre of Shakespeare and his contemporaries—the direct descendant of the popular drama of the medieval period—was significantly influenced by both the court drama and the school plays, both of which existed concurrently with the professional theatre.

The theatrical climate of Shakespeare

The theatre of Shakespeare's day was the culmination of a long development and the amalgamation of many disparate influences. It was also an accurate mirror of the diversity of Elizabethan life. In it was reflected conscious national pride in the achievements of Englishmen. This newly emerging national pride had manifestations in such works as Hakluyt's *The Principal Navigations, Voyages, and Discoveries of the English Nation*, which first appeared in 1559, and Raphael Holinshed's *Chronicle* (1578), that marvelous compendium which was the principal source not only of Shakespeare's historical plays but of other Elizabethan plays dealing with England's past.

The defeat of the Spanish Armada, the voyages of Frobisher, Davis, and Drake, and the consolidation of England's importance in world trade strengthened not only the Englishman's national pride but also his belief in the Renaissance ideal of the heroic proportions of the individual man and his infinite possibilities for a good life here and now.

The characteristics of the Renaissance on the Continent were anglicized in such a figure as Sir Philip Sidney, the courtier-soldier-poet, who was no less renowned for his poetry than for his exploits in battle. The art of living and the art of writing were inextricably combined; conduct and expression marched together in an expanding national consciousness.

The Renaissance Englishman became increasingly acquainted with the literature of other times and places by a swelling tide of translations from Latin, Greek, Italian, and French; if he was wealthy enough, he finished his education with a sojourn on the Continent. Accomplishment was not limited to the noble and the wealthy, however; individual enterprise and ability counted for much. A rising merchant class was changing the face of England. Feudalism was dead; a new world was being born.

As is true everywhere and at all times, the stage in its various forms mirrored the age and the people for which it existed. It reproduced the life of its contemporaries—their beliefs, traditions, emotions, aspirations, aims, and tastes. The Elizabethan theatre was so thoroughly national, so spontaneous and popular, in addition to possessing the more universal and essential qualities of human sympathy, artistic beauty, variety of presentation, and fertility of motive, that no age before or since has produced its equal. The period was one in which, as it were, men stood between two dreams of the past and the future, both colored by imagination, and both shedding glory on the present.

Vigor and pride were combined with a love of learning and elaborate art. Thought and action were no longer fettered; instead of tradition and prescription, instinct and passion ruled. Instead of curbing passions and concealing appetites, the Elizabethans gloried in the outward manifestations of a passionate virility. They were coarse but not vicious, pleasure loving but not licentious, luxurious but not effeminate, violent but not cruel. They were, in the main, law abiding and contemptuous of treachery and baseness; they had an intolerance of political and ecclesiastical despotism, and a fervent love of their country.

For the theatre—which in Elizabeth's day took the place now filled by the novel, the short story, the drama, the newspaper, motion pictures, radio, and television—these conditions were ideal. The demand of the Elizabethans for plays was insatiable, and theatre was a lucrative profession for those who could please the popular taste. Secular fiction and history were ransacked in the search for plots—the legends of Greece and Rome, Italian novels, English history, even contemporary London. It is interesting to note that whatever the locale of the play, the character and development were essentially English: Romeo and Juliet are English youngsters with Italianate names; Hieronimo is a grief-stricken English father who seeks revenge; Hamlet, Prince of Denmark, is a moody Englishman. Someone has said that an Englishman sees little fun in Molière's

Alceste, while a Frenchman sees in Falstaff only a needlessly fat man. It is this quality of intrinsic nationalism that distinguishes the Elizabethan drama from that which had preceded it and that which followed in the Restoration. This quality, dictated by the tenor of the times, contributed to its greatness.

The expanding intellectual horizons of the Elizabethans were evident in the materials of the playwrights. Geography, history, mechanics, recent inventions, popular science, legislation, preventive medicine, astronomy, natural history, civic affairs, and gossip all found their way into the theatre, to be consumed with avid interest by the audiences. In addition to its capacity for welcoming all kinds of information, the Elizabethan audience—like perhaps few others—was marked by its devotion to the spoken word. Listening was easier than reading, and the audience was quick to respond to oratory or repartée. It liked sonorous declamation, and it liked slangy billingsgate. It liked new words and phrases. It even liked classical allusions which it did not understand. It responded to verse, to accent, to the march of the measure. It loved the music and the sentiment of the balcony scene of *Romeo and Juliet* no less than the thunderous rantings of *Tamburlaine*. Because of the tastes, capabilities, and aspirations of this audience, which were accurately gauged by many playwrights, the number and variety of theatrical presentations were astounding, and the affection and loyalty of the audiences unparalleled.

Some idea of the immense popularity of the theatre may be gained from the fact that in a population of about two hundred thousand, no less than twenty-three professional acting companies were performing in London at the height of the period of theatrical activity. In addition eight boy companies, the

Inns of Court, other schools, and the court itself, gave performances. Theatrical fare in the provinces was not as generous, but there were many provincial companies and many of the London companies traveled to the provinces in the off-seasons. English schools and colleges also fostered the production of plays, stressing classic forms and making participation mandatory. Even after the initial strength of classicism had spent itself, school productions of the classics—and especially those of the Inns of Court—remained a significant part of theatrical activity.

The thriving court drama was supervised by an especially appointed official, the Master of the Revels, whose office, as noted above, became permanent under Henry VIII in 1544. It reached the height of its powers under Charles I; the Office of the Revels had then about one hundred employees. During Elizabeth's long reign it concerned itself mainly with legitimate drama. The Office of the Revels selected suitable plays for presentation, drilled the professional troupe selected to act in the plays, provided them with proper costumes, prepared the stage scenery and properties, saw that the players reached their destination, and managed the stage. It also supervised the activities of the various boy companies. With the accession of James I in 1603 the emphasis at court turned to the production of beautiful and elaborate masques, in which form Inigo Jones and Ben Jonson had a long and fruitful association.

For the majority of Londoners—and indeed for all Englishmen—the public theatre with its professional acting companies was not only the most accessible but the most popular form of theatre fare. Because of the tradition behind them, and because of the protection from oppressors thus afforded, these professional companies were nominally a part of noble households. They were the Earl of Leicester's Men, the Lord Admiral's

Men, Lord Hunsdon's Men, the Earl of Pembroke's Men, the Lord Chamberlain's Men, and so on. The members of the nobility named (no one less than a baron was accorded the privilege) were the patrons of the various acting companies. The tradition had originated late in the Middle Ages; when the bands of strolling players were multiplying and ordinances were passed against them, the most competent sought and found the protection of a noble house. They were then at the call of their patron for special occasions but otherwise were quite at liberty to make their own way. The less competent companies were forced out of existence. This principle of patronage lasted through the Shakespearean period and was revived by the royal patents at the Restoration.

The companies of Shakespeare's London were really quite autonomous organizations, looking to the patron simply for the protection of his name and for whatever occasional financial or production aid he might be able to give. For instance, he sometimes gave his cast-off clothing to his company to be used as costumes. Thus the theatre was in actuality a great popular institution operating as a free enterprise. The theatres of Shakespeare's day were controlled by corporations which included housekeepers, actor-sharers, and a business manager; such corporations chose the plays, ran the house, and divided the profits among themselves. They also hired and paid certain classes of actors and other employees.

Performances were usually given in the afternoons. The theatre was considered fashionable and was patronized by all classes of society. In the summertime, performances generally began at three o'clock, in the wintertime at two. Advertising was done through three principal media: the next day's production was announced after the epilogue of a given performance; on the day of the play a flag was set on top of the theatre—white if a comedy were being given, black if a tragedy; and handbills, six by twelve inches, were posted all over London. In addition, parades and criers were often used. Admission prices were so graded that everyone, from apprentice to noble, found a price to his liking. Standing room in the pit cost a penny; seating in the galleries, depending upon location, from two pence to a shilling; and the stools on the stage for the gallants, a half crown plus six pence for the stool itself. There were no reserved seats as we know them, and at very popular plays people had to come early for advantageous locations. The rich sent their servants to reserve seats, the poor sent their wives. The admissions charged made legitimate drama one of the least expensive of entertainments for the average Londoner: admission to the tower of St. Paul's for a view of London cost a penny; the tilt-yard tournaments of the nobles—to which the general populace was admitted—eighteen pence. A book cost, for comparison's sake, sixpence or a shilling; a broadside (a single sheet of paper containing a ballad and a woodcut) cost a penny. No wonder the apprentices of London spent so much time at the theatre.

In fact so many people spent so many hours at the theatre that the city fathers, devoted to the ideal of hard and constant work, and the Puritans, to whom the theatre was anathema, were constantly at war with the players. This dark thread of disapproval runs all through the glory of Shakespeare's day. When the moral opposition joined forces with political expediency the Puritans closed the theatres.

Magnificent drama produced

The plays produced by the Elizabethans comprise the greatest body of dramatic literature in the English language, if not, indeed, in any language. It is easy to identify the plays of Shakespeare as the consummate achievement of the English Renaissance; but those of many of his contemporaries were also of a very high order.

The great stream of professional, popular drama which had developed from the Bible plays, the moralities, and the interludes was augmented by the school plays and the court productions to make a dramatic literature that is the wonder of all who know it. It was the culmination of development in dramatic art, as Shakespeare's plays were the culmination and harmonization of the various disparate elements which preceded him. The nature of the classic Greek play as embodied in Sophocles was a beautiful balance between plot and character. The Romans and their early Renaissance copiers had stressed incident over character, as had the episodic cycle plays and the short interludes, farces, and miracle plays of medieval times. In much of early Renaissance playwriting plot itself was lacking, and the characters were mere stereotypes. Shakespeare's immediate predecessors worked out the problems of plot and character. Thomas Kyd developed a comparatively well-knit plot line, including obligatory scenes and motivations as well as climax and denouement. Marlowe built his plays upon character; what plot there is remained subservient to the title characters. The plays of John Lyly added the element of romance. Shakespeare's nearer contemporary, Robert Greene, worked out a balance between plot and character, and was more skillful than Kyd or Marlowe in reconciling and integrating subplots.

Shakespeare, taking into account all that had preceded him, produced plays as marvelous in their way as those of Sophocles had been: he balanced plot and character; he integrated main and subplots; he used elements of romance; and he reconciled comedy and tragedy by using comedy to heighten the tragic effect. He is our greatest dramatic genius, not only for the characters he created and his magnificent poetry, but also for his consummate skill in dramaturgy, and his most explicit and effective use of the theatre for which he wrote. In his plays the classic tradition and the medieval heritage are wonderfully combined and blended. His followers were not able to maintain this balance of elements, and the decline of the dramatic art was inevitable.

The rise, apogee, and fall of Elizabethan theatre is clearly traceable. Its development covered the period from the accession of Elizabeth to 1594; it reached its climax in the twenty years which followed, and then declined to its eclipse in 1642. It would be impossible even to mention all the names of plays and playwrights of that burgeoning period, so an attempt will be made to present here a more digestible survey by considering the various types of plays which were popular and successful, with some outstanding examples of each.

Four major divisions may conveniently be made: tragedy, comedy, chronicle plays, and masques. Even within these major divisions, however, there are various types, and the school plays must be another consideration. Tragedy, then, was of two types, the classical and the native. Comedy had myriad types: the pastoral, the magical, the bourgeois, the allegorical, the satirical—and combinations of them all. The chronicle plays were historical-legendary, factual-historical, biographical, and popular-legendary. The masques might be anything from the disguisings of the court of Henry VIII to the poetic effulgence of Milton's *Comus*. It was a diverse and prolific age. Often the same materials were treated over and over again by different playwrights, and frequently more than one playwright contributed to a particular script. All the widening horizons of the Renaissance were sources for the dramatists —any incident of human activity from ancient Greece to contemporary London. It was as Thomas Heywood said in his statement of the playwright's function:

To give content to this most curious age,
The gods themselves we've brought down to
    stage,
And figured them in planets, made even Hell
Deliver up the furies, by no spell
Saving the Muse's rapture. Further we
Have trafficked by their help; no history
We've left unrifled: our pens have been
    dipped
As well in each hid manuscript,
As tracts more vulgar, whether read or sung
In our domestic or more foreign tongue.
Of fairy elves, nymphs of the sea and land,
The lawns and groves, no number can be
    scanned
Which we've not given feet to; nay 'tis known
That when our chronicles have barren
    grown
Of story, we have all invention stretched,
Dived low as to the centre, and then reached
Unto the Primum Mobile above,
Nor 'scaped things intermediate, for your
    love.

A noble boast, and nobly was it fulfilled.

The classical tragedy on the Elizabethan and Jacobean stage of the professional companies was an adaptation of Seneca. The most famous of these blood and thunder plays is Thomas Kyd's *The Spanish Tragedy*. Its leading character, Hieronimo, was a favorite bravura part of the renowned actor, Edward Alleyn, as well as of Richard Burbage of Shakespeare's company. The play is an unrelievedly dark revenge tragedy which strewed the stage with bloody corpses, to the great delight of its lusty audiences. It was first played in 1586 and remained popular for many years. The next year saw Marlowe's *Tamburlaine*, and again Alleyn played the title role, a Machiavellian hero who spoke thrillingly in English blank verse. The revenge tragedy with its ghostly visitations and its welter of blood continued through the period. Marston's *Antonio's Revenge* (1599), Chapman's *The Revenge of Bussy D'Ambois* (c. 1600), Massinger's *The Roman Actor* (1626), Webster's *The Duchess of Malfi* (1614), Middleton's *The Changeling* (1622) are but a few examples. Even Shakespeare tried his hand at the type in such a play as *Titus Andronicus* (c. 1594). The type may be said to have been sublimated in *Hamlet*.

The usual classical tragedy, as written and performed at the schools and universities, followed the Continental Renaissance ideal, and was attended by the unities of time, place, and action. In this form, violent events took place off stage and were related by messengers. But the love of Elizabethan popular audiences for action viewed rather than related, led in the public theatres to the wholesale slaughter which takes place in full view of the audience in many of these plays. No wonder that the universities—those keepers and producers of classical plays and their slavish imitations—had no use for professional actors and writers. They were destroying a sacred image by pandering to the public taste.

The classical tragedies written in Shakespeare's day did, however, at least follow the Senecan principle of maintaining an unrelievedly dark tone with a single line of action. Not so the native tragedy, which scorned the classical conventions, mixed in comic scenes, and often had subplots to counterpoint or underline the main plot. Many of Shakespeare's plays well illustrate this principle. The porter's scene in *Macbeth*, the gravediggers in *Hamlet*, which were excised when the eighteenth-century producers "regularized" Shakespeare, show the use of comic scenes in tragedy; the Gloucester story in *King Lear* is a prime example of a subplot.

The native tragedy was a curious amalgamation of Renaissance dramaturgy in main theme, and of medieval holdovers in subplots, clowns, and stage action. Shakespeare and many of his contemporaries, much to Ben Jonson's disgust, gave the people what they wanted. Some other contributors to the native tragic drama were Marlowe, Nashe, Lodge, Beaumont, Fletcher, Ford, Massinger, Heywood, Middleton, Tourneur, and Shirley. If his inheritors were not so overwhelmed by the preeminence of Shakespeare's genius, the plays of many of these would stand higher in esteem than they do today. At its best, Elizabethan native tragedy contributed to a new theatrical form—the romantic tragedy—a panoramic, extended action with a multiplicity of characters related to an integral, central theme, which was derived from that Renaissance philosophy of the freedom and responsibility of man in an ordered universe. Traces of the melodramatic and the sentimental in the writers of the Jacobean and Carolingian period—John Fletcher, Francis Beaumont, Philip Massinger, John Webster, James Shirley, John Ford—mark a decline from the high point reached by Elizabethan writers.

Another union of Continental Renaissance and native English ideals was evident in the pastoral romance, a type of comedy in which is to be found a combination of the Italian pastoral play and the native English love of country life. These qualities combined were greatly in evidence in *The Pinner of Wakefield*, written by Robert Greene (d. 1592), in John Lyly's *Campaspe* (1584), and flowered in such plays as Shakespeare's *As You Like It* (c. 1599). The type was continued in Fletcher's *The Faithful Shepherdess*

(1608) and Jonson's *The Sad Shepherd* (c. 1637).

The magical comedy is illustrated notably by Shakespeare's *A Midsummer's Night's Dream* (c. 1595), Greene's *Friar Bacon and Friar Bungay* (1594), and Marlowe's *Dr. Faustus* (1588), which is indeed not a comedy but illustrates the Elizabethan propensity for magical happenings on stage. In these plays potions, spells, apparitions, and tricks of magic exhibit both medieval superstition and Renaissance love of curious learning.

In the bourgeois drama—to which Shakespeare notably did not contribute—there are Dekker's *The Shoemaker's Holiday* (1600) and *The Roaring Girl* (1611), Peele's *Old Wives' Tale* (1595), Jonson's *Bartholomew Fair* (1614), Greene's *Looking Glass for London* (c. 1594), *Arden of Faversham* (1592), *A Yorkshire Tragedy* (c. 1606, the title page credits Shakespeare), and *A Warning for Fair Women* (c. 1599). *The Shoemaker's Holiday,* one of the most delightful of Elizabethan comedies, is concerned with the wonderful feats of Simon Eyre, an actual master shoemaker who became Lord Mayor of London. The others are also founded upon real characters and contemporary or recent happenings. These plays are a sort of tabloid newspaper of the times.

In contrast to the bourgeois drama and its real characters was the allegorical comedy, whose type-named characters recall the old moralities. But the playwrights of this new age added another dimension to allegory, and produced satires that are apt, biting, and often applicable to the universal shortcomings of mankind. Ben Jonson is the most notable dramatist of this type; Shakespeare played a leading role in Jonson's *Every Man in His Humour* (1598). Jonson's *Volpone* (1607) is one of the most noteworthy of the type. One of the most sensational was Nashe's *Isle of Dogs* (1597), which

satire aroused official ire and caused the closing of the London theatres for a short time in that year.

The chronicle plays, whose plots are based on factual history, are easy to trace in Shakespeare: the Richards, the Henrys, and the Roman plays. The first English play of this sort appeared in 1550, when John Bale wrote his *King Johan*, although he also includes such an allegorical character as Sedition—a practice not followed in subsequent history plays. From that time on there were many anonymous scripts, as well as chronicle plays by Peele, Greene, and Marlowe; Rowley's treatment of the reigns of Henry VIII and Elizabeth in the two curiously named plays, *When You See Me You Know Me* (c. 1604), and *If You Know Not Me You Know Nobody* (c. 1604), were both written after the death of Elizabeth. All of these plays are basically factual, but in practically all of them historical truth is stretched to fit the thesis that Queen Elizabeth was a true, lawful, and strong sovereign of an illustrious house. It was this category of play that the Master of the Revels scrutinized most carefully for possibly seditious material.

The historical-legendary plays may be traced from the first regular English tragedy of *Gorboduc* (1561) by Sackville and Norton, through *Cambyses* (1569), *Locrine* (1591), *The History of King Leir and His Three Daughters* (c. 1590), *Appius and Virginia* (c. 1609), and two plays about King Arthur, *The Misfortunes of Arthur* (c. 1569), and *The Birth of Merlin* (c. 1608). Of the popular-legendary plays we may note Munday's *John à Kent and John à Cumber* (1594), and his two ventures into the Robin Hood legend with Chettle. The biographical plays treated Sir Thomas More, Thomas Lord Cromwell, Sir John Oldcastle, Sir Thomas Wyatt, Perkin Warbeck, and less noble figures like Jack Straw.

INFLUENCES ON SHAKESPEAREAN PLAYHOUSES
Above, an innyard, not only the forerunner
of playhouses, but converted for use as a theatre throughout the period. Spectators paid
their admission fee at the carriage entrance
and stood about in the yard. The stage was
erected in the yard close to one of the four
sides. The galleries also held spectators,
either as guests of the inn or as those who
paid a higher admission to the players.
(Folger Shakespeare Library) Left above, Red-
eryker stage, Antwerp, 1561. On such a stage
the academicians of Antwerp presented their
plays, and some scholars have seen in this
design an influence on the Elizabethan stage
house. It is, of course, a development from
the early Renaissance platform stage shown
on page 109. (Brussels Bibliothèque Royale)
Left below, detail of Hollar's View of London,
showing the circular form of a bear-baiting
pit, establishments which predate The Theatre and which may have influenced the circular shape of the typical public playhouse.

All people, places, and things were the stuff
of the Elizabethan popular drama; and vital
were the characters and events that set the
lusty heartstrings of its spectators vibrating.

Concomitant with the variety of the
popular drama were the continuing productions, chiefly of the classics, at the schools
and universities. The chief products of the
schools were tragedies and comedies on
classic models, written by students and by
faculty. Along with these were continuing
productions of Aeschylus, Euripides, Sophocles, Aristophanes, Plautus, and Terence.
The universities, frowning on professional
actors and professional playwrights, passed
successive ordinances forbidding their performances within a five-mile limit of school
precincts. But the students of the Inns of
Court in London, while producing their own
neoclassical plays, were ardent supporters

of the popular theatre. And when those university men Marlowe, Greene, Peele, Nashe, and Lodge arrived in London, they quickly turned to writing for the popular stage, ignoring the prescriptions of their academic training.

In addition to all this activity, the Elizabethan court was the scene of much theatre. Besides the productions of the professional companies which were often given command performances at court, and the activities of the boy companies for which several of the leading dramatists wrote, the court originated a type of pseudodrama of its own —the masque. Its history goes back to William Cornish in 1512; his *The Golden Arbour of Pleasure* called for thirty courtiers, eight musicians, and eight boys "to sing like birds." Two years later he produced *Love and Duty*, and the elaborately staged, musically accompanied gracefulness of the court masque was under way. As previously described, these spectacular and generally undramatic entertainments were out of favor in Elizabeth's court, fortunately for the legitimate drama. But they returned with the accession of the Stuarts. Ben Jonson wrote thirty-two masques for court production, and many other writers—notably Chapman, Fletcher, Daniel, and Campion—produced them in lesser numbers. William Davenant, later to be of some importance in the Restoration theatre, began by writing and producing court masques, and the contribution of John Milton to this type has also been mentioned above.

The proliferating theatre of the English Renaissance produced all kinds of dramatic literature in various combinations. Polonius' "tragedy, comedy, history, pastoral, pastoral-comical, historical-pastoral, tragical-historical, tragical-comical-historical-pastoral" (*Hamlet*, II, 2, ll. 16–18) is not far from an accurate description of the kinds of things

playwrights were producing for the avid theatre-going public. So few of the scripts have come down to posterity that few people realize the numbers that were written. Thomas Heywood says that he "had a finger in" more than two hundred playscripts; and of Thomas Dekker's seventy, fifty are lost. So the list goes on—myriads of plays are mentioned of which no trace can be found, and doubtless there were many others of which not even the names have lasted. Who can say that the thirty-eight plays now ascribed to Shakespeare represent his total output? The fact that these plays were written for acting companies and, for the most part, jealously guarded from publication, no doubt meant that many would inevitably be lost to succeeding generations. Were it not, indeed, for the loving commemorative labors of two of his fellow-actors, Heminge and Condell, even the Shakespeare canon would be considerably reduced. Of the feverish theatrical activity of Shakespeare's day modern man has little conception. He is simply the inheritor of what can be presumed to be the best of what was written for the theatre then.

London becomes the center

The sixteenth-century Englishman could see dramatic performances throughout the kingdom, but playhouses were built only in London. Traveling companies of players, either the London companies in the summer months or provincial companies, played in towns and villages and manor houses either upon invitation or their own advertisement. The titled patron might present his troupe with a letter of introduction to another noble or to a town corporation. If the traveling company was to play for the household of a noble, a stage was set up in the great hall of the castle. In the towns, the company

THEATRES OF THE BANKSIDE
Detail of Shakespeare's theatre (above), from Visscher's View of London, 1616, and (below) a detail of The Swan playhouse from the same map. (Folger Shakespeare Library)

the Guild Hall at Stratford, when the Earl of Leicester's troupe visited that town.

Sometimes the playing space would be the courtyard of the local inn; in London the innyards were the usual places of playing. The medieval innyard could easily be adapted. It almost invariably had one wide arched entrance for horses and carriages, and was surrounded by a gallery of as many stories as the building was high, behind which were the guest rooms. The company of players stationed one of their number at the entrance to collect admissions from people who stood about in the yard to watch the performance. The performance was given on a platform of boards set upon barrels at some convenient spot in the yard. Guests at the inn sat or stood in the galleries. Depending upon the arrangements of the company with the proprietor of the inn, these privileged spectators were either guests of the house, or they paid to the company a fee which was more than that paid by the standees in the yard. This essential arrangement was retained by the permanent theatres built in London beginning in the fourth quarter of the century.

The passing of laws by Parliament prohibiting tours by masterless men and the requiring of licenses for patronized groups tended to concentrate the playing companies in London, where they played during the greater part of the year, traveling to the provinces only during the summer months. In Shakespeare's day there were six or seven hundred inns in London. The better inns did not allow plays because of the brawls they caused, but others permitted them for a flat rate or on a percentage basis. To advertise the plays, which were usually given in the afternoon, the actors in the morning put on their costumes and paraded the streets with trumpets and drums. As time went on, these temporary playhouses proved unsatis-

would be met by the mayor, who offered them the hospitality of the town and gave a dinner in their honor. Afterwards they performed a play for this select audience. This performance was paid for by town funds, then a subsequent performance was generally given in the town hall and admission was charged. Records of such traveling companies are to be found at Bristol, Bath, Dover, Coventry, Nottingham, and at many other places. Shakespeare himself is presumed to have seen such a performance in

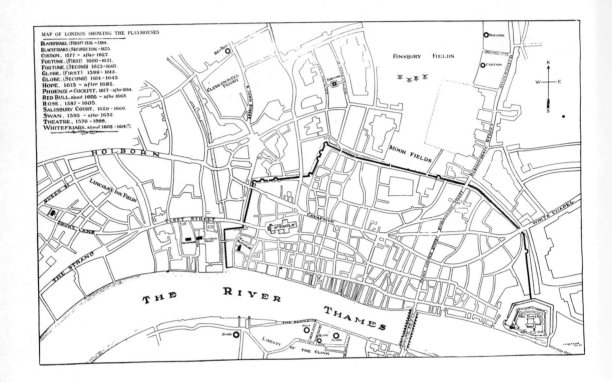

MAP OF LONDON SHOWING THE PLAYHOUSES

BLACKFRIARS, (FIRST) 1576 – 1584.
BLACKFRIARS, (SECOND) 1596 – 1655.
CURTAIN, 1577 – after 1627.
FORTUNE, (FIRST) 1600 – 1621.
FORTUNE, (SECOND) 1623 – 1661.
GLOBE, (FIRST) 1599 – 1613.
GLOBE, (SECOND) 1614 – 1645
HOPE, 1613 – after 1682.
PHOENIX or COCKPIT, 1617 – after 1664.
RED BULL, about 1605 – after 1663.
ROSE, 1587 – 1605.
SALISBURY COURT, 1629 – 1666.
SWAN, 1595 – after 1632.
THEATRE, 1576 – 1598.
WHITEFRIARS, about 1605 – 1614 (?).

factory because the landlords of the inns changed their minds so often, because the actors were not the masters of their fate but at the mercy of the innkeepers, and because these performances naturally were interfered with by the regular commerce of the inn.

Some nameless businessman of vision, aware of the growing popularity of the plays, rented a few of the large inns in London and made them permanent playing places, erecting permanent stages in the innyards. This development permitted very much better staging, the use of more properties, and a measure of security for the acting companies. Benches were put in the galleries for the ladies and gentlemen, and the companies of players who rented the inns thus arranged were masters of the situation. They began to advertise by handbills, and they stationed a man at the gate with an iron box slotted at the top to admit a penny, the price of the general admission. Resident companies were known to have operated at The Bull, The Bell, The Cross-Keys, The Bel Sauvage, The Boar's Head, and the Saracen's Head before any permanent theatres were built.

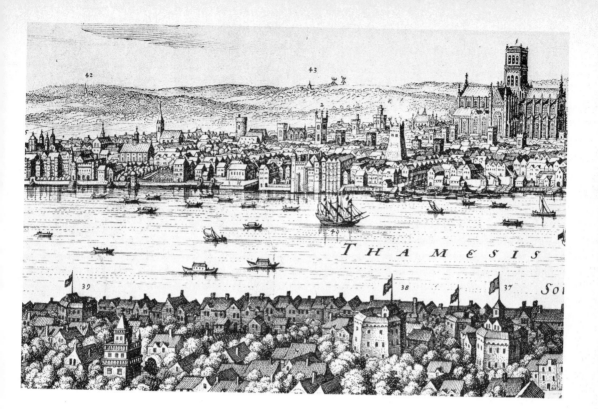

LONDON PLAYHOUSES AND THEIR LOCATIONS
Left, a map of London showing the playhouses erected before 1640. The Theatre and
The Curtain are in the northeast corner; The
Globe, The Rose, The Hope, and The Swan
are south of the Thames River. All except
Blackfriars lay outside the walls of the old
city. Above, Merian's view of London in 1638,
showing The Swan (39), The Hope (38), and
The Globe (37), with St. Paul's Cathedral to the
north. People crossed the river in ferry boats
to reach these. (Folger Shakespeare Library)

The Elizabethan playhouse—
famous and infamous

London now had real playhouses, and the
drama was even more the national amusement. There were two forces working against
the drama, however: the Puritans, who
morally objected, and the city officials, who
opposed the drama because it spread the
plague and caused quarrels, fights, and riots.
Since the players were at least nominally the
servants of nobles and hence wards of the
Privy Council, the city officials could not

molest them. As long as its foes were kept
separate, the theatre was safe. But in 1573,
when the Puritans elected one of themselves
Lord Mayor and dominated the Board of
Aldermen and Town Council, the Town Council put a ban on all plays, saying there was
danger of plague. The ban was not removed
when the danger was over, so the players
complained to their patrons who, in turn,
appealed to the Privy Council, who had the
ban lifted. But the Town Council was not
to be defeated. It met on December 6, 1574,
and passed such stringent restrictions that

it was hard to keep going at all. The Town Council's rules stated that plays could be given on only three days of the week; they had to be censored before being presented; the inns had to be licensed for plays by the Lord Mayor and the Aldermen, and the proprietors had to give a bond that there would be no disorder or immorality in connection with the performances; no plays could be given during the "sickness," during divine service, or when prohibited by the Mayor; and the owners must pay a poor tax.

Again the players asked their patrons to appeal to the Privy Council, which now felt that it could give little help except to define the plague clause to read that plays could not be given on the day after fifty or more had died of the plague. Elizabeth, who loved the plays but who was an excellent politician and careful of her money, went no further than to designate her own Master of the Revels as the censor and the source of licenses. The bond and the tax clauses remained and were serious hindrances.

Finally, James Burbage, ex-carpenter, ex-actor, and utterly devoted theatreman, conceived a good idea—he would build a theatre in one of the "liberties" in London where city officials had no jurisdiction. These liberties were the sites of former Roman Catholic church holdings; by special law they were free of civil authority, being subject only to the Crown. In one of them, Burbage built a theatre for the Earl of Leicester's troupe, of which he was the manager. He was obliged to forgo the liberties of Blackfriars and Whitefriars because, even though they were nearest to St. Paul's and the center of population, they were too expensive. He eliminated the Clink because its moral reputation was very bad. So only Holywell near the Bishopsgate was left. Actually, though somewhat far from the center of population, this was a rather good choice, for it adjoined the

city park and playground, Finnsbury Field. Not being able to get a right of way from the road, he cut a hole in the brick wall separating Holywell from Finnsbury Field and having obtained a twenty-one year lease from Gyles Allen, who owned the plot of ground he wanted, he drew up plans for the first theatre of Renaissance England. The lease was obtained on April 13, 1576, and The Theatre (for so he called it) was opened in the fall of that year. It was the sensation of the season, and influenced all succeeding theatre construction of the period.

The next year Henry Lanman leased a plot of ground close to Burbage's and built a theatre on it which he called The Curtain, probably because the land upon which it was built was called Curten Close. In 1585

INTERIOR DESIGN OF ELIZABETHAN PLAYHOUSES
Far left, the only extant contemporary sketch of the interior of a public playhouse, being that made of The Swan by Arend van Buchell (1565–1641) in his commonplace book, to illustrate the "observations" of his friend Johannes DeWitt, who visited The Swan in 1596. Left, one of the nine panels on the title page of William Alabaster's *Roxana*, 1630, showing spectators in a gallery above the stage and standing in the pit below. Above, a sketch from the title page of *Messalina*, 1640, showing a similar stage, with a curtained inner stage and curtains masking the upper gallery. (Folger Shakespeare Library)

Burbage obtained control of The Curtain, thus becoming the first theatre monopolist.

While this was going on, a very shrewd servant of one Mr. Woodward of the Bankside, Philip Henslowe by name, succeeded to Woodward's extensive property by marrying his master's widow. He was variously in the lumber business, a tavern keeper, a farmer, a pawnbroker, and a real-estate operator, continuing to live on the Bankside. In 1585 he bought a piece of land on the Bankside from the chuch and built a very fine theatre on it, copying the plan from Burbage. He opened it in 1587 as The Rose. It is from the careful records of his operations that we derive information concerning the theatre of Shakespeare's day.

In the next twenty-five years, seven more

such theatres were to be built in London, among them the famous Globe built by Burbage on the Bankside in 1599 from materials salvaged from The Theatre, the rights to which he had wisely kept in his original lease with Gyles Allen. Although there were individual variations the basic plan for all of these theatres was the same.

The outside structure of the Elizabethan public playhouse—that built by Burbage as well as succeeding ones—has been authenticated on practically conclusive evidence. Various extant views of London show the outside structure of several of the theatres. Each is round (or polygonal) except the Fortune (which is square), and each has at one point on the top perimeter a small, gabled, and roofed structure topped by a flag. The inns were not round, nor their yards, nor the town halls, nor great halls of manors. Where did James Burbage, master carpenter, get his idea? Views of London prior to the building of the theatres show a bull-baiting and a bear-baiting "round" in Southwark—accustomed "playing-places" for Londoners. It is conceivable that Burbage appropriated this preexisting design and incorporated into it the stage and stage house which was necessary for his players. In any event, The Theatre provided for about fifteen hundred spectators in three roofed galleries and a standing pit with an open top so that daylight could provide the chief illumination and ventilation could be improved (no small consideration in those bathless days). The building was of timber and stucco with a thatched roof over the galleries. The galleries had wooden benches and standing room. Four special rooms, "the lords' rooms," with locks and keys, were in the galleries nearest the stage. There were no seats for the spectators in the yard or pit.

The interior arrangements of the Elizabethan playhouse, particularly the stage, have been interpreted in various ways because facts are hard to come by. There are only a few pieces of contemporary evidence: the 1599 contract for the construction of the Fortune theatre, the 1613 contract for the construction of the Hope, the DeWitt-van Buchell drawing of the interior of the Swan (c. 1596), and two details of the stage area from title pages of two books late in the period, along with one dated 1672 (page 217). Many scholars have dealt with these materials and have combed the plays and other written matter for clues to the stage arrangements and the actor-audience relationship. It is rather like unraveling a mystery story on the basis of clues which may be variously interpreted. Every person who has dealt at some length with these materials—Cham-

bers, Lawrence, Reynolds, Adams, Thorndike, Hodges, Hotson, Wickham, Nagler, Beckerman—differs from every other in some details to a greater or lesser extent. The audience part of the house—"the fframe" in the Fortune contract—is so well spelled out that there are practically no differences of opinion here. But of the "Stadge and Tyreinge howse . . . erected & settupp within the said fframe, with a shadowe or cover over the saide Stadge" (*ibid.*) there is much latitude for interpretation. The Swan drawing shows, and the Fortune contract confirms, that the stage was raised, was wider than it was

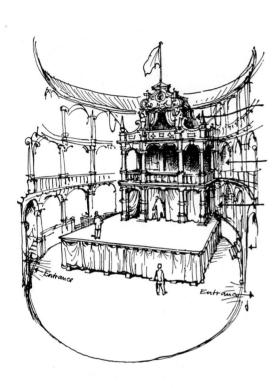

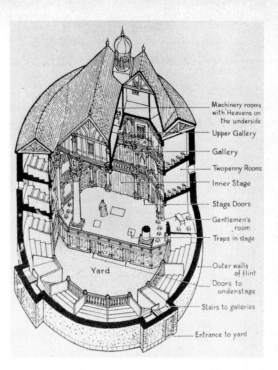

Machinery rooms
with Heavens on
the underside
Upper Gallery
Gallery
Twopenny Rooms
Inner Stage
Stage Doors
Gentlemen's
room
Traps in stage
Outer walls
of flint
Doors to
under-stage
Stairs to galleries
Entrance to yard

Yard

Entrance

Entrance

THE PLAYHOUSE RESTORED: THREE VERSIONS
Differing interpretations of the known facts
provide differing views of playhouse interiors. Far left, a model of the interior of The
Globe by John Cranford Adams. Left, C. Walter Hodges' sketch of the interior of an Elizabethan theatre. Above, Richard Leacroft's
reconstruction of The Globe for Methuen's
outline, *The Theatre.* Compare the differing
interpretations of stage levels, stage house,
pit, galleries, and lords' rooms. (Folger
Shakespeare Library; Richard Leacroft Collection)

deep, and that there was yard-level passage
at the sides of the stage; i.e., the stage projected out into the yard which surrounded
it on three sides. The Swan drawing shows
and the contract confirms that there was a
roof over the stage (sometimes called The
Heavens), and that it was usually supported
by pillars from the audience side of the stage
floor. (The Hope contract specifies that
though the roof should be there, it cannot be
supported by pillars in this building because
the stage was to be a removable trestle-stage
so that the house could also be used for
bear-baiting and other sports.) Three of the

drawings show a gallery over the stage at
the second-floor level; the other shows what
looks like a curtained window in the same
position; there is no mention of either in
the contract. The Swan drawing shows two
very large doors on the face of the tiring
house at the back of the stage level, with
an absolutely blank wall between them. The
three small, detail drawings show a curtain
in this position and no doors at all. That
there were doors, however, is attested by
innumerable stage directions in many stage
scripts. The area behind this facade is the
"Tyreinge howse"—the actors' domain, pre-

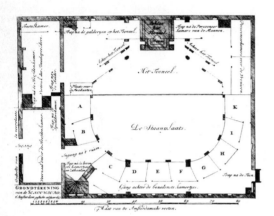

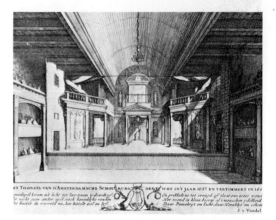

THE SCHOUWBERG, AMSTERDAM, 1637
The floor plan (left); the house, looking toward the stage (above); looking toward the boxes (right). These detailed plans and sketches show an interesting similarity to what Shakespeare's theatre must have been. The standing pit, the two galleries divided into boxes, the architectural stage setting have definite counterparts in England. A unique feature of this house is the interesting roof treatment and the top gallery of steeply raked benches. (Harvard Theatre Collection)

sumably with dressing rooms, prop rooms, and any necessary machinery; it could be entered through a stage door. The open yard of the pit could be—and evidently was on occasion—used for other kinds of "entertainments" than stage plays, whether or not the stage itself (like that of The Hope) was removable. It was an eminently practical house which Burbage built and which subsequent builders copied.

The fiscal arrangement Burbage conceived for The Theatre was also more or less followed by other theatre operators, and was, of course, a refinement of the policies followed by the innyard players. He leased the theatre to Leicester's Men on these terms: the actors were to get all the pennies paid for general admission; Burbage and his brother-in-law John Brayne, who had invested his entire fortune in the project, were to get the extra shillings and sixpence paid for seats in the galleries. It was a profitable arrangement on both sides. The actors, under ordinary conditions, spent about a third of their income for fixed expenses, then divided the rest among themselves. Their income was always assured, since everyone, whatever his location in the house, paid the general admission. And there were sufficient spectators in the galleries to insure the proprietors a good return on their money. Theatre had become a business enterprise as well as an art form.

ZIT EN STAANPLAATSEN VAN D'AMSTERDAMSCHE SCHOU**B**URG.GESTICHT IN'T JAAR 1637 EN VERTIMMERT IN 16..

'tOntbreidelen der Jeugd, noch godloos voedsel van
Vervloekte afgodery, en al wat zy verdichte;
Maar stichtig tydverdryf wast oogmerk van dien Man

YVER

Die, tot een oeffenschool van Deugd, den Schouburg sticht
Der arme Weezen troost, der Ouden stok en staf.
Zo schryft Pompejus niet; maar Kampen op zyn Gra,

J. v. Vondel

In addition to these public playhouses which were most typical of the period, there were sundry roofed-in theatres called, for no clear reason, "private." Such was Blackfriars, where Farrant's boy company had originally performed. James Burbage leased and remodeled the building in 1597 but was restrained from using it as a public theatre. After his death, his sons Richard and Cuthbert leased it to Henry Evans for the Children of the Chapel Royal. Shakespeare's troupe finally installed a "men's company" in the house in 1608. Blackfriars had been converted from the original "great hall" and was rectangular in shape with a stage assumed to be across one end of the narrow dimension, since by this time Italianate scenery was in use in court theatricals. It had benches for the whole audience.

Other private theatres were Whitefriars, Salisbury Court, the Phoenix in Drury Lane, and the Cockpit-in-Court; the latter, designed by Inigo Jones, used a permanent architectural setting in the Italian mode. There were no standees in these private theatres, the capacity of which was very much smaller than that of public houses, and the admission prices were correspondingly higher. Their resources allowed for considerable ingenuity in staging.

Dramatic performances were also given in the great halls of palaces which were converted into theatres for these special occasions, and in specially prepared rooms in the schools and universities. Such a conversion, evidently usual when the students were performing themselves in plays of their own making, prevailed for a recorded performance by Shakespeare's company at Gray's Inn (one of the most dramatically minded of the Inns of Court) on December 28, 1594. In its seventy-foot hall a scaffolded stage was erected. Thus a variety of arrangements was available for the performance of plays in the Elizabethan Renaissance.

Though the exact physical nature of the interior of Elizabethan playhouses is not known, it is known that they were often the colorful scene of boisterous entertainment, and probably the most popular amusement for Englishmen of all social classes. Famous today as the background of the great plays of Shakespeare, they in their own day were both greatly loved and greatly reviled.

"Piece out our imperfections . . ."

The public theatres lacked extensive settings and depended upon the audience, as the Prologue to Shakespeare's *Henry V* requests, to "piece out our imperfections with your thoughts." It is safe to assume that all public Elizabethan playhouses had raised stages, and that these stages had at least one large trap near the center—it is necessary for such scenes as the gravediggers in *Hamlet* and the witches' cauldron in *Macbeth*. There were probably about four smaller traps and what could be more convenient than that they should be approximately in the four corners of the stage? And that the area under the stage should be called "The Hell" since from thence arose spirits and ghosts? From the roof over the stage could be lowered chariots and clouds and airy spirits—so it was called "The Heavens." That gallery

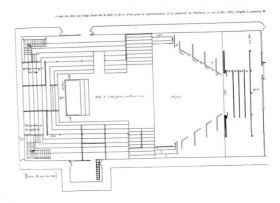

INIGO JONES'S PRODUCTION OF FLORIMENE, 1635
The plan of the set design, and sketch of the border and standing scene, for the isle of Delos. In the court productions, the Italianate system of flat wings behind a proscenium arch was much the vogue. Here Inigo Jones is faithful to the Serlio prescription for the satyric scene with its trees, flowers, and cottages. For such productions, transformations or scene changes were made in full view of the audience. (Reyher, *Les Masques Anglais;* Devonshire Collection, Chatsworth)

over the stage, so apparent in the sketches, could indeed be the "above" which so many plays need, or the "above" could be the tops of trellises, mounts, wooden canopies, stairs, or pavilions mentioned as inventory items in contemporary accounts. If the latter is the case, then the gallery over the stage could be used for members of the audience or for the musicians who always played "above." Or were the musicians ensconced in a third-level gallery above the stage since there were three galleries in the house, even though no third-level gallery above the stage shows in any of the drawings or is mentioned in the contracts? The hardest question deals with the "discoveries" and the "thrusts out" notations of many of the playscripts. The curtains of the detail drawings are pos-

sible answers, for behind them could be the "inner below" where a scene could be set and revealed, or discovered, by drawing the curtains. But what about that blank wall in the Swan drawing? Maybe the variety of set pieces enumerated in the inventories were so constructed as to be used in a variety of ways and were simply brought on when needed, as tables and chairs or stools invariably were, and as were tents for battle scenes. In any event, the stage settings of the public theatre were not realistic (there was no tradition of realistic setting) but symbolic or emblematic.

Various references can be cited to show that in addition to the practice of putting up place names to indicate locations, Shakespeare's contemporaries also utilized set pieces of linen and lath. Evidence can also be mustered for the fact that the stage roof was painted on its inner side to represent the heavens, and that a type of crane was integrated into it for ascents and descents. We also know that effects for thunder were available, that fireworks were employed, that torches augmented daylight, and that the firing of a very real cannon ignited the thatch of the Globe and burned it to the ground during a performance of *Henry VIII* in 1613. Many of the effects called for are reminiscent of the elaborations of the medieval mysteries: angels and prophets descending from Heaven, a serpent devouring a vine, a hand clutching a burning sword emerging from a cloud, Jonah being cast out of the whale's belly, bleeding heads, headless trunks, and many like wonders. Great care was taken to make these effects as realistic as possible, and these tricks were no doubt as highly regarded as had been those of the earlier plays.

The versatility of the setting in the public playhouses, in any event, allowed for multiple scenes moving rapidly, such as many of the plays of the period include. Sir Philip Sidney, writing in the early 1580s, protested this lack of unity:

You shall have Asia on the one side and Affrick on the other, and so many other under-kingdoms that the player, when he cometh on, must ever begin by telling where he is, or else the tale will not be conceived. Now we shall have three ladies walk to gather flowers, and then we must believe the stage to be a garden. By and by we hear news of shipwreck in the same place, and then we are to blame if we accept it not for a rock. Upon the back of that, comes out a hideous monster, with fire and smoke, and then the miserable beholders are bound to take it for a cave.

But Sidney's protest was a minority report. The imagination of the audience was equal to the agility demanded of it. The public theatres most definitely had no front curtain—a fact amply attested to by the endings of plays which provide for the clearing of the stage, even when dead bodies were lying around. In any event, the stage pillars and the entire interior of the house were as elaborately carved and painted as the treasury of the company allowed, and each theatre prided itself on the beauty of its curtains, a fact which indicates that there were indeed hangings of some kind, somewhere—if not enclosing the "inner below," then elsewhere. Contemporary descriptions often mention the sumptuous appearance of the theatres, and this extravagance was one

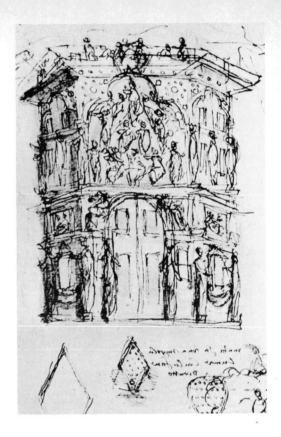

TWO DESIGNS BY INIGO JONES
Above, The House of Fame for Ben Jonson's *Masque of Queens*, 1609. Right, Oberon's palace for Ben Jonson's *Oberon*, 1611; the sketch indicates that this scene is a transformation of a mountain into a palace—only one of the many wonders wrought in these elaborate productions. (Devonshire Collection, Chatsworth)

of the great points of criticism employed by the Puritans. It is fairly certain, then, that within the limits of finances and a daily change of bill, the public theatres attempted to make their scenes as visually interesting as possible.

In the court-subsidized theatres, where the performances were occasional and expenditures far more liberal, the settings were more extravagant. Indications are that these temporary playhouses first employed multiple settings without regard to perspective, after the fashion of the French medieval

mysteries. Perhaps they used the transverse axis of the stage, with stage houses to either side and the audience below and above the stage. Gradually the Italian Renaissance innovation of a single setting in perspective came into vogue, followed by "painty" settings which could be changed at will. These "painty" settings followed the Italian inventions of wing flats and shutters and their use of three-sided prisms as Sabbatini describes them. Various records of the Office of the Revels show expenditures for "apt houses, made of canvas, framed, fashioned and painted," for gilding lions' heads, for making realistic fishes, and for innumerable costume items. Designers for the court theatres became increasingly well acquainted with the Continental stagecraft of the formal theatres and adapted them to English uses. Many of the plans of Inigo Jones, court designer to James I and Charles I, are extant to show us the use he made of elaborate proscenium arches, front curtains, scene dissolves, and cloud effects. He also seems to have utilized Serlio settings upon occasion as well as a raked stage. In fact, so important did scenic investiture become in the increasingly elaborate Stuart masques, for which Jones designed and Ben Jonson wrote, that these two artists quarreled violently about precedence and Jonson lost the argument.

Elaborate settings were often devised for the performances of the boy companies; the workshops of the Office of the Revels were responsible for dressing these shows and for mounting the productions. Frequent entries in the books of the Revels Office show sums paid out for transporting costumes and scenery to various locations, both for the use of the boy companies and for performances of the adult professional companies before the queen and her court. Though the professional companies performed the plays of their repertoire on such an occasion, each play was newly costumed, sometimes given "painty" settings suitable to the court theatre, and rerehearsed. They were almost invariably given in the evening, so lighting was important. The theatrical effectiveness of such performances no doubt influenced both the private playhouses and the public theatres to use as much of their details as possible. By 1639 a special patent was being issued to William Davenant to build a theatre especially for the use of scenes. He never built it, however, for the theatres were closed by the Puritans three years later.

In these indoor playhouses, whether of the temporary type or of the private kind, lighting, of course, assumed great importance, and the effects achieved by the Italians were assiduously copied. The wonders of the Italian theatre were known to the audience of the private theatres and were looked for in these more select playhouses of their native land. These innovations were increasingly adopted.

Music, too, was an important part of theatre, both public and select. There were interludes and postludes as well as integral songs and dances. Performances of the boy companies were frequently preceded by an hour's "musick" in the private theatres where they played. Even the briefest acquaintance with Shakespeare's plays will show the frequent use of songs. So far as the acting companies could afford them, the best musicians were used and every adequate actor was also a competent musician. At court the musicians were very good indeed. Thomas Campion composed for the court masques, as did Ferrabasco. A variety of instruments were available, including recorders, flutes, trumpets, violins, violas da gamba, and harpsichords, as well as drums. Cornets, hautboys (ancestor of the oboe), and the lute were the instruments most

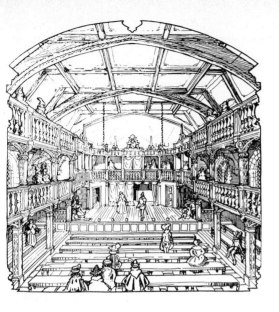

CONJECTURAL INTERIOR OF A PRIVATE PLAYHOUSE
Reconstruction by J. H. Farrar of the second
Blackfriars theatre interior as arranged by
James Burbage in 1597 as a winter home for
Shakespeare's company. It was also leased to
the Children of the Chapel Royal and St.
Paul's.

frequently used by the performers themselves. Much of the music composed for
Elizabethan theatricals is still delightful to
the modern ear.

Though early Shakespearean scholars
tended to stress the simplicity of the Elizabethan theatre, and magnified the dramatists'
greatness in triumphing over the crudity of
their production facilities, it has since become apparent that, as in the Greek theatre,
the playwrights used every device that could
be invented to add to the scenic investiture
of their plays. As the period advanced, one
may be sure, these became ever more complicated and elaborate.

Costumes inaccurate, but elaborate

For many years it was assumed that scant
attention was paid to costuming in the popular theatre of the English Renaissance; the

actors wore contemporary dress and that
was that. But a careful study of the available
sources and the discovery of new ones demonstrates that even the popular playhouses
seem to have paid a great deal of attention
to costuming. The types of costuming in
Shakespeare's day may be divided as follows: classical, allegorical, professional, foreign, and historical.

It is true that many characters in the
tragedies and many more in the comedies
appeared in contemporary dress. But it is
equally true that not a few of the cast of
characters evidently wore "character" costumes. Just as in the theatre of the present
day the presumably authentic costume is in
reality a modern adaptation of a bygone
mode, so in that day noncontemporary costumes were Elizabethan adaptations of other
times and places. Of course, present day
resources for historical accuracy are ever so
much greater and antiquarian zest more fervent; modern theatrical costume, on the
whole, is likely to be a great deal more true
to the character, the time, and the place. But
the Elizabethans, no less than the moderns,
realized the theatrical effectiveness of specialized costuming and used it so far as their
resources allowed.

Inventories revealing such items as
"senatores cloaks" and some extant sketches
show that the Elizabethans sought a flavor
of antiquity in the costuming of classical
plays, though the Roman legionary was likely
to have the full sleeves and plumed hat of
an Elizabethan courtier. The many deities of
classical mythology are listed in Henslowe's
records as having special costumes: "Junoes
cotte," "sewtte for Nepton," "Dido's robe,"
and many others, with appropriate properties. Some idea of how these and others appeared are available in the invaluable
sketches of Inigo Jones.

Inventories and sketches also reveal that

COSTUME DESIGNS BY INIGO JONES
Left, a masker for Thomas Campion's *Lords'
Maske*, 1613, and a naiad for Samuel Daniel's
Tethys Festival, 1610. Above, Queen Henrietta
Maria as Chloris in Ben Jonson's *Chloridia*,
1631, and (right) a Knight masker in *Oberon*,
1611. In all of these, it is apparent that the
basic Elizabethan dress was used, with an
overlay of decoration in a design intended to
convey the atmosphere and special nature of
the character. (Devonshire Collection, Chatsworth; Victoria & Albert Museum, Crown
Copyright)

allegorical figures wore distinctive costumes. Ghosts and witches, fools and fairies, each had distinguishing items of costume in robes and headdresses, in capes and wigs; and the "robe to go invisible in," which Henslowe mentions, must have been a particular convention of the Elizabethan stage. Many are the mentions of bears and lions, of horses, dragons, and dogs, who evidently were costumed entire. Other items mention boar's heads, lion's heads, and, of course, the ass's head that Bottom wore.

Aside from these obviously required costumes, other types were quite evidently in use. Lawyers, doctors, churchmen, and civil authorities wore distinguishing dress. Portia's disguise is a lawyer's gown. Friars, popes, and cardinals wore their typical dress. The figure of "Prologue," who appears in many of the plays, seems to have been particularized with a long black velvet robe, a flowing beard and wig, and a poet's laurel on his head.

Turks, Danes, and Spaniards received particular attention as well. The Turkish costume invariably included a scimitar, a turban, special slippers, and long, loose breeches. Danes and Spaniards are mentioned as having specialized costumes and we know that the Dutchman on the Elizabethan stage always wore wide breeches which were called "slops." He might wear an Elizabethan doublet above them, but the nether coverings displayed his character.

Though the average Elizabethan playgoer could have little knowledge of how his ancestors must have looked, he was certainly aware that Henry V dressed differently from the courtiers of his day, and he must have expected a different costume for such a character. Accordingly, we find Henslowe mentioning "Harrye the V satten dublet," and "harey the fiftes vellet gowne." Various other mentions of robes and crowns, armor and

swords, would indicate a like attention to historical flavor. The Egerton manuscript of *Richard II* even mentions the toe-chained shoes of that day, which must have been a curiosity to an Elizabethan audience.

In the main, the actors appeared in contemporary dress, as rich as they could manage. Critics of the theatre were not slow to point out the gorgeous apparel of the playhouse, where even servants were dressed in satin and lace. It would appear, as mentioned above, that one of the functions of the patron was to present to his acting company his own cast-off apparel and that of his friends. Sometimes new clothes were provided by the Crown for command performances at court, these then becoming the property of the acting companies. It may be supposed as well, that specialized costumes designed and made for the single performances of court masques were sometimes bequeathed to deserving professional companies. These costumes were made of the finest materials available and were a considerable item of expense to the Office of the Revels.

It seems fairly certain that makeup, except where necessary for disguises, was not used. If a character required heightened color on his cheeks, he merely rubbed them before going on stage. But if he needed a red nose like Bardolph, or a beard, then he attached them. Ghosts whitened their faces with white lead, and Negro characters blackened theirs with burnt cork. In the open daylight of the public theatres, no other makeup was deemed necessary.

In the popular theatre, the elaborate and colorful costumes filled the eyes of the beholder, since the settings were comparatively simple and certainly not illusionistic. In the lavish court masques of the Stuart reign, the costumes were as intricate and elaborate as the settings themselves.

Acting demands versatility

Of all the theatre arts, acting is perhaps the most ephemeral. Not until the comparatively recent advent of sound recording and motion pictures has it been possible to make a record of practicing actors. Before the twentieth century there are only the frozen moments of various pictorial representations, the recorded opinions of contemporaries, and the evidence of the dramatic literature itself. What we have to say here of acting itself, then, cannot be entirely accurate but can be reasonable.

The position of the actor in Shakespeare's day was, in many ways, anomalous. Condemned and maligned by some and strictly regulated by various civil ordinances, he was, nevertheless, often a most highly raspected member of society and frequently moved in the best of social circles.

The professional actor had, however, one great advantage: he was a member of a repertory company, which gave a variety of plays over great lengths of time, and he thus had opportunity to grow as an artist. The demands of performance were arduous. The proximity of the audience demanded concentration from the performer, as well as skill in engaging and holding the attention of the sometimes boisterous crowd. The frequent change of bill, a different play every performance, meant that several parts must be kept in mind at once and that the actor be quick in memorizing lines. The intricacy of the lines in many of the extant scripts indicates an exceptional skill in the vocal arts. Contemporary records more often speak of "hearing" than of "seeing" a play, and thus show where the Elizabethan placed his emphasis. The integral songs and dances indicate the actors' proficiency in these skills. Actors are often listed as musicians and instrumentalists in contemporary writings, and

when the actor Augustine Phillips died, he willed his musical instruments to his apprentices as a natural and necessary part of their equipment as actors. Performances often ended with an impromptu entertainment by one or more of the company, called a *giggue*; Tarlton the comedian was so adept at this improvisation, done in verse, that the type of skill has come to be known as "tarltonizing." Since many of the scripts called for some kind of fighting, the actor also had to be an expert fencer, able to make the scene realistic without inflicting harm on his fellow-actors. Fencing was a very popular sport in Shakespeare's London; schools of fencing and public matches were numerous. This same Richard Tarlton, the first great popular star of the days of Elizabeth, was honored by being made "Master of the Fence" the year before he died. A pleasing appearance, grace of movement, a good voice, a ready wit, a lively sympathy, a keen awareness, adaptability, and the capacity for feeling and projecting a variety of emotions were then, as now, essential attributes of the successful actor.

Probably then, as now, an occasional acting genius appeared upon the stage full grown. But for the most part the chief members of any acting company had survived a rigorous training. Sometimes recruits for the professional theatre came from the boy companies (like Saliethal Pavy, whom Jonson memorializes), those carefully selected wards of the Crown who were schooled in rhetoric and song. Sometimes, as was apparently true in Shakespeare's case, aspirants were apprenticed to one of the members of an extant company and received individual tutoring from him. When and if his training was judged to be completed, he was made a journeyman shareholder and could then himself take on an apprentice. The apprentice in the theatre, as in the other vocations, lived in the household of his master, receiving complete training and education from him.

The mature actors tended to specialize either in tragedy or comedy. Richard Burbage, son of James and a member of Shakespeare's company, was famous for his tragic roles, having played Macbeth, Hamlet, Lear, and Othello. His great rival and equal in fame was Edward Alleyn, Henslowe's partner and son-in-law, whose greatest parts were Hieronimo, Tamburlaine, and the Jew of Malta. Among the comedians we may remember Richard Tarlton of the Queen's Company, and her favorite, William Kempe (for whom Shakespeare evidently wrote Falstaff and Bottom), and his successor, Robert Arnim, who played the Fool in *Lear*. Many other names might be listed here, for writers of the Commonwealth and Restoration periods speak nostalgically of the great performances of the bygone day, and laud the skill of them.

It may be supposed that with the comparatively small size of the theatres, and with the close and immediate contact of the audience (some of whom, indeed, sat on the stage), the acting style was what would be called "natural" today. Hamlet's famous advice to the players supports a natural acting style, and comments on the performances of various actors by contemporaries seem to support it. Edmund Gayton, writing somewhat *post factum*, remembers an actor who, in the best Stanislavski tradition, could not be shaken out of his character until the performance was utterly over. Actors were schooled in rhetoric, a popular subject of the day, which included not only voice production, but innumerable and meticulous postures of hands, body, and face. In the class-conscious society of Shakespeare's day, an actor playing a king must move and speak like a king, and so on by degrees to the lowest member of society. A great degree of skill was demanded, and evidently was available.

Although some actors obviously acquired great individual fame, this fame was evidently not as a "personality" actor who transformed every role to his own image, but as a protean creature who could transform himself into many roles.

The actor's life was not an easy one. He rehearsed in the mornings, performed in the public theatres in the afternoons, and spent his evenings either learning new lines or giving performances in the private theatre or at court. In times of plague, or during the summer seasons, the London actor toured the provinces, traveling by horse and cart to the various towns, and carrying set pieces and costumes with him.

New scripts were often prepared under the eye of the dramatist, who might be a member of the company, as was Shakespeare. If the dramatist were not a member of the company but had been paid a flat fee for his script, as was the custom, then the performance was prepared by the stage manager, or bookholder, who also acted as the prompter. When a company was commanded to court, then the Master of the Revels held

SKETCHES OF PERFORMANCES
Left, a woodcut of William Kempe, member of Shakespeare's company, from the title page of a book published in 1600. Above, a scene from *Titus Andronicus;* the sketch is attributed to Henry Peachum and dated 1595.

special rehearsals, censoring and changing script and business where he thought it advisable and often reoutfitting the entire cast.

The professional company included various types of members. In the acting fraternity were the actor-playwrights, who received a flat sum in payment for writing as well as a proportionate share of the profits for acting; the actor-shareholders; and the hirelings who were paid a designated salary. The apprentices, as noted above, were also paid, but the payment went to the master, not the man. The "housekeepers" were the producers and the owners or renters of theatre property. The paid employees, in addition to the hired actors, were the stage manager, the tireman (or wardrobe master), the money takers (or "gatherers"), and the caretakers (who sometimes functioned as extras in the performances), as well as the musicians. Generally, as with the Earl of Leicester's Men, the acting company got the general admissions while the housekeepers collected the additional payments for gallery seats. The actors tolerated the seating of a few well-paying customers on the stage itself since all the

money they paid went to the actors. After the set expenses were paid, the profits were divided among the shareholders. On opening nights the admission was generally doubled; the third performance of a given play was often designated author's night and he collected all the profits. Command performances were paid as flat sums to the company, and these sums were divided proportionately. Varied but typical arrangements were in force for performances in the private theatres and on the road. Sometimes the patrons were called upon for subsidies and loans, though for the most part the major companies were completely self-sustaining.

Though actors worked hard they often made a great deal of money. Edward Alleyn retired at thirty-nine, and lived without remunerative employment for the twenty-two years left him. He endowed Dulwich College, which is one of the richest in England, in addition to supporting almshouses and other philanthropic ventures. Richard Burbage is said to have had a sizable income from his country estates alone. And "that house in Stratford" of Shakespeare's needs no additional comment. In his day the theatre was a burgeoning and profitable business as well as a stupendous art form.

Women never appeared on the professional stage in England; the women's parts were taken by boys. It was an immensely practical arrangement, particularly when the company was on tour. These boys were highly skilled performers and evidently quite satisfactory in their parts. It is to be noted in the playscripts that physical contact is at a minimum between Shakespearean lovers, the most famous of love scenes being played from balcony to garden.

Perhaps it was the Puritan influence no less than medieval tradition which kept women off the stage in England, and the appearance of a French actress on an English stage in 1629 and again in 1632 called down malediction. Only in the court masques did titled women make their dilettante appearance. When the moralist, William Prynne, inveighing against the performance of a French actress in England, said that women players were "notorious whores," he had his ears cut off and was imprisoned for life—at that moment Queen Henrietta Maria was rehearsing for a court performance!

Summary

The theatre of England might be said to have begun its decline with the accession of James I in 1603, although many great and good plays were written after that date. The common people did not like James because he was a foreigner, and because he built up a foreign court which was much more frivolous and unhealthy than the people at large. In the first year of his reign, Parliament passed an ordinance forbidding the nobles to patronize the acting companies, so the King took over half a dozen of the best, Shakespeare's among them. When the first military operations of the Great Rebellion began in 1642, one of the first acts of the Puritan Parliament was to close all the playhouses and forbid all play-acting. Many of the houses were torn down or burned and the actors scattered. Many of them fought with the Cavaliers, earning considerable military distinction. After Charles was beheaded in 1649, some of them fled with the court to France, some companies toured in Europe, and some individuals remained in England to ply their trade surreptitiously and await the turn of the tide.

But their heyday had been a glorious one. Though vestiges of medieval practices had perhaps a more profound influence on the English Renaissance stage than on that of the Continent, purely religious performances disappeared in England long before they did in other parts of Europe. Though the ferment of the Renaissance greatly affected subject matter and many details of production, there was not so close an adherence to classical forms in England as was evident in both France and Italy. The greatness of the English theatre of the period lay in its assimilation of foreign influences to produce a purely native theatre. By the time the period came to a close, it had contributed to the theatre a superb dramatic literature, completed the popularization of the theatre, marked its emergence as "show business," witnessed the development of the proscenium arch and painted settings and the establishment of indoor playhouses.

Theatre in Shakespeare's day was a great popular institution frequented by all classes of society from carter to nobleman. Even the queen was an avid supporter and admirer of theatre. The insatiable curiosity of this large audience made for a wide variety of theatrical presentation and contributed to the greatness of Elizabethan dramatic writing. Artistic satisfaction—and an adequate living

—attracted many good writers to the theatre and held them there. The most important literature of the period is dramatic.

Elizabethan theatre developed an architecture and a stage design eminently suited to the plays and the conditions of production. Multiple and quick-changing scenes could be handled expeditiously on the platform stage, whether by inner recess, galleries, doors and windows, or by temporarily erected, curtained rooms. The construction of the playhouse itself brought the action and the marvelous lines close to every spectator. No fetters were placed on creative imagination by the exigencies of setting; the atmosphere was an utterly free one.

This freedom also challenged the skill of the actor, who rose to great heights of powerful and effective expression. It was the greatest of all ages for playwright, actor, and audience; its fame continues to the present day.

8 Spanish theatre in the renaissance

The medieval history of Spain is marked by violent clashes not only between Moors and Christians, but also between the rulers of the various Christian kingdoms who occupied non-Moorish territories on the Spanish peninsula. Cities and their surrounding countryside changed hands with alarming frequency; wars were constant and bloody. Toward the end of the fifteenth century the alignment of powers centered around the two crowns of Aragon and Castile, with the Moorish possessions lying outside both. The marriage of Castilian Isabella and Aragonese Ferdinand in 1467 united the two leading Catholic powers. When, ten years later, Isabella succeeded to the throne of Castile, and Ferdinand to the throne of Aragon, the stage was set for Spanish national unity. By a series of astute moves these rulers reinstituted the Inquisition as a purely Spanish office, expelled the Moors from the peninsula, exiled the Jews, and emerged with a unified kingdom which rapidly enriched itself through New World conquests. By the time of Philip II (1556–1598), Spanish possessions and powers in Europe and the New World had reached their apogee. The long decline throughout the next century reached its end in 1700, when the War of the Spanish Succession put the Bourbon Philip d'Anjou on the throne of Spain.

The greatest age of Spanish theatre parallels this political stream. Secular drama, tentative and rudimentary at the beginning of the sixteenth century, grew in strength and brilliance in the last half of that period and was most glorious during the first half of the seventeenth century. By 1650 all that is best in Spanish drama had been produced. After the death of Calderon in 1681, no playwright of note appeared in Spain for many generations.

The union of Ferdinand and Isabella had the further effect of making the Spanish tongue as spoken in Castile the predominant language of the Spanish peninsula. From this point on, as elsewhere in the Renaissance, the development of the language became a powerful factor in strengthening national consciousness.

The course of the Renaissance in Spain ran differently than it did in the rest of Europe. There was, for instance, no Reformation and hence no Counter-Reformation. In the same year that Martin Luther tacked his famous 95 theses to the cathedral door at Wittenberg (1517), there died in Spain the redoubtable Cardinal Ximenes, who had by the most drastic discipline raised the Spanish clergy far above the general European level in morals and learning. The Spanish church rejected "Erasmic" leanings. The question of private judgment versus the absolute authority of the church in all matters was hardly even raised in Spain; the church was diligent in suppressing immediately all such heresy. The Inquisition, which had in the late fifteenth century been so effective in helping to consolidate the nation and drive out the Moors, continued with unbated energy. (*Autos-da-fé* were held as late as 1560.) So the phase of the Renaissance which stressed the infinite capabilities of individual man was, in Spain, held in check by the autocratic and authoritarian nature of the society. Indeed, Philip II unquestionably accepted as his prime mission the preservation of the "true church" throughout Europe, and the ill-fated Spanish Armada was commissioned largely to wipe out the heresy of England. The advent of Loyola and the Jesuits (1534) did no more in Spain than to personalize religious commitment and stress the role of the church. Loyola's *Spiritual Exercises* did, however, have something in them of the humanist persuasion in that he urged penitents to use their sensory perceptions to imagine "the length, breadth, and depth of hell," "the infinite sweetness of the divinity," and "Our Lady, Saint Joseph, and the Child Jesus."

The heroes of the Spanish Renaissance were the chivalric knights of history and legend whose stories were the continuing stock-in-trade of the *juglares* (minstrels) and the subject matter of innumerable ballads and epics. After the introduction of printing into Spain in 1475, these *romances* became even more influential as paradigms of subject-matter and style. The devotion to church and state they invariably exhibited formed an unquestioned national consciousness. The sense of mission was fortified by the rapid acquisition of a world empire after 1492: the medieval concept of the devoted *conquistadore* was augmented by authentic real-life counterparts, and the writing of history became a serious pursuit.

Spanish intellectuals and literati were aware of the course of the Italian Renaissance. Naples had been a Spanish dependency from 1443, and several Spanish writers had spent varying amounts of time in the Italian peninsula, some of them even writing plays and poems under the influence of the rediscovery of the classics which marked the Italian Renaissance. But on home ground, the definite and unique national consciousness turned the Renaissance impulse in other directions. There are a few attempts at the picaresque novel as a reaction to the inflated tales of chivalry, but not until Cervantes was able to include the two levels of "poetic truth" in the figures of Don Quixote and Sancho Panza (*Don Quixote* is a masterful amalgam of romance and *picaro*) did such novels succeed. The lyric impulse in Spain took the form of devotional poetry, some of great beauty, such as the mystical poems of St. John of the Cross. And the drama? It burgeoned; an incredible number of plays were written and produced. The literature of Spain —both dramatic and otherwise—reached its greatest achievement in this *El Siglo de Oro.* It even produced the lengthiest and most detailed analysis of the theories and techniques of the new panoramic drama in Lope de Vega's *The New Art of Writing Plays in This Age* (1609). But, in the main, the widespread secularization which everywhere else one of the chief characteristics of the Renaissance was not operative in Spain. Liturgical drama continued to occupy a place of importance in the social scheme; all dramatists, including Lope de Vega and Calderon, wrote liturgical dramas as well as *comedias.* Professional actors came under the jurisdiction of the church and the state, and the church-state (it is difficult to separate them) in various ways exercised both fiscal and artistic control of theatre. Thus theatre never truly became an autonomous enterprise, although it was incredibly popular for upwards of a hundred years.

The Golden Age flowers

The intensity of Spanish theatrical activity coincides with its best dramatic literature. Lope de Rueda, who became so influential that he is said to have founded Spanish national theatre, is first heard of in 1554. He is the first head of a company of players of whom there is any knowledge, and he dominated Spanish theatre until 1565. His activities paved the way for the flowering of the next fifty years.

The Spanish popular theatre, like the Elizabethan, was a direct descendant of the Middle Ages. The medieval pageant wagon had developed in Spain as in England and here, too, performances were often under the auspices of craft guilds. The entire festival was almost invariably under the supervision of the officers of the city; it is from city records that information concerning the Corpus Christi Day celebrations can be studied. The festivities began with the celebration of Mass in the cathedral, followed by a presentation of the sacred drama within the choir of the church itself. The play was ordinarily followed by a dance in the same location; then a procession, including church and city officials moved out of the cathedral to specially designated places in the city where the cars of the players stopped and the performance was given for the people gathered there. Thus Corpus Christi Day came to be known as the Festival of the Cars. The subject matter of the plays themselves included both Biblical material and the lives of the saints, as well as moral, allegorical presentations.

In 1554, the corporation of the city of Seville took over the expense of presentation of the Corpus Christi Day drama from the various guilds, and in the same year there is the first mention, in Benavente, of the presentation of a sacred play by a professional acting company—that of Lope de Rueda. This particular performance was a special one honoring Philip II on his passage through Benavente. The Spanish evidently quite often gave sacred plays on special occasions of this kind, as well as at weddings, and so forth. That Lope de Rueda and his company subsequently performed in the Festival of the Cars is substantiated by the Seville city records. These church-inspired performances continued unabated through the entire Renaissance, as enthusiastically presented in 1679 as they had been two centuries earlier. All of the great names of Spanish drama are of those who wrote both sacred and secular plays, Lope de Vega himself producing nearly four hundred religious plays for the church, along with his phenomenal output for the secular theatre. At the beginning of the seventeenth century the sacred plays seem to have been given in the public playhouses for a limited run after the festival day itself.

The secular drama developed out of the medieval church play, through the *entremeses*, originally of a quasireligious character, which were short pieces accompanying the longer presentations. As time went on, they lost all religious significance. Though this transition from religious to secular themes in the entremeses led to the development of long secular drama, the shorter form maintained its identity as well. At the height of the Spanish theatre the public performance began with a ballad (*jácara*), played and sung by the company musicians. Then followed an introductory piece which was either a monologue or a short dramatic sketch (*loa*), not necessarily connected with what followed but designed to catch the attention of the audience and to put it in good humor. The three acts of the main fare for the day, the long drama (comedia), were interspersed with two entremeses, sometimes supplemented with a ballad or two set to music as requested by the audience; the afternoon's entertainment concluded with a dance.

Theatre atmosphere festive

Performances began at two or three o'clock in the afternoon (depending on the season of the year), and at first were limited to Sundays and feast days. To accommodate the growing demand, Tuesdays and Thursdays were added to the schedule; then, finally, plays were being given in the larger cities on every day of the week except Saturday. Theatres were officially closed, however, during Lent, often during the summer months, and always during epidemics or national disasters like the death of a member of the royal family. Plays were advertised by public crier and by placards. Actors themselves often

ge 180). The same system prevailed in all
wns and cities; traveling companies first
to obtain a license, and then perform
the public.

The same public official also controlled
leasing of theatres to companies for per-
mances, and the remodeling or building
them as well. Theatre buildings were al-
st invariably owned or erected by char-
ble organizations formed to care for the
and the poor. A portion of every admis-
n went to the proprietary organization,
der the supervision of the official, as well
the money from the leases for buildings
ey owned outright. The acting companies
re generally paid a flat sum for each per-
rmance, the distribution of sums within
e company depending upon the company
ganization.

The audiences were boisterous and de-
anding. Hardest to please were the *mos-
eteros*, the standing audience in the pit,
ho were all men. Many of them had made
game of getting into the theatre without
aying—a trick which, if successful, gave the
rpetrator high standing in the eyes of his
llows. Two peace officers were stationed at
e doors of the theatres to prevent riots and
oodshed, but they were often unsuccessful.
omen sat in a separate section of the the-
tre, and the sellers of fruit and drink often
ted as messengers between the women's
allery and the men in the pit. In the boxes
e spectators were mixed, with the women
here generally going masked.

The success of a play often depended on
he reaction of the people in the pit; if they
pplauded and shouted *Vitor!*, the play was
hit; if they whistled and hissed, it was a
ailure. Their approval was often courted by
he playwright in the sketch before the play.
here was much eating and drinking during
he performance, and unpopular actors and
lays were sometimes pelted with orange

skins and fruit pits. So the popular theatre,
as in Shakespeare's England, reflected the
tastes of its audiences, who were sharp in
their judgments and quick to respond. The
popular Spanish stage thus developed types
of plays which varied widely, as did those in
England, from the more formal types of
drama such as were being produced in Italy
and France.

The developing Spanish theatre had one
disadvantage which was the opposite to that
obtaining in England: neither Charles V nor
his son Philip II was interested in drama.
They suffered the usual round of entry processions, special entertainments for important visitors, and the pageantry that was a
necessary concomitant of the kingship. But
neither had a commitment to the emerging
art form. Not until the accession of Philip III
in 1599 did theatre have an advocate in the
highest social circles.

But the Italian commedia companies visited, performing at various places, including
the public theatres. So well received were
they that one critic in 1581 waxed indignant
over the quantities of ducats these foreigners
removed from Spain every year. And the
classic revival was the darling of the schools
in Spain as elsewhere. Performances of plays,
generally in Latin and generally written by
university teachers, are recorded as beginning
in 1530, when the statutes of the University
of Salamanca decreed that Plautus and Terence were to be performed there. Soon after
the foundation of the Jesuit colleges in 1543
they, as they did elsewhere in Europe, took
to producing plays as a part of their regular
activities, calling for the production of "tragedies and comedies" after the manner of and
in the style of the ancients. Often as the
years went by, the school plays used Spanish subject-matter, although they did try to
maintain the style of the classics. Thus, in
spite of royal indifference, various kinds of

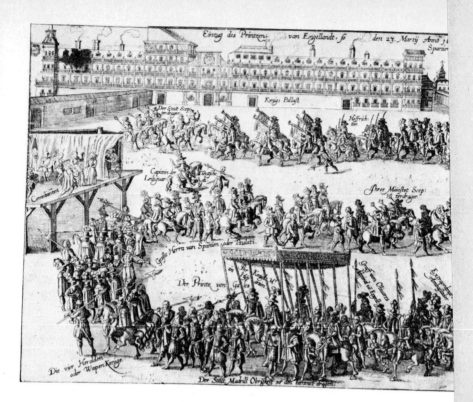

Einzug des Printzen von Engellandt so den 23. Martij Anno 1... Spanier

ENTRY FESTIVAL
Festival given for the entry of the Prince of Wales in Madrid, 1623. At the left is a temporary stage fitted out for the presentation of plays, with a curtained backdrop and musicians and actors performing. Entry processions were popular diversions all over the Continent.

performed the office of crier, and seem to have been acting in this capacity as late as 1638, the year in which a well-known actor, Iñigo de Loaysa, was murdered in the streets of Valencia while announcing the play for the following day. The placards were about twelve by eighteen inches and were usually done by hand. They were posted in prominent places in the city or town some days before the performance.

Every member of the audience paid a single admission price which was quite low compared with the prices of other commodities. The general admission entitled the person to standing room in the theatre. If he

wished a seat he paid extra... ing a sum equal to that ... ready paid; some in the exc... as much as twelve to twen... eral admission price. The ... quently rented for the year... and the rich; and city officia... one for their exclusive use... particular boxes often descer... of a given family.

Theatrical performances... by a city official, a license ... for each performance. Somet... original license was given, ... sisted upon a performance

ANOTHER ENTRY FESTIVAL
Detail from a painting of an entry festival given for Isabella, daughter of Philip II, in Amsterdam. The car pictured emphasizes the medieval character of Spanish preferences, and is reminiscent of the festival cars of the *autos sacramentales*.

---

play production flourished and contributed to the main stream of popular theatre.

Critics were vocal. There were objections to the use of women as performers, to the use of boys in women's parts, to the immorality of players in general, to the rowdiness of the audiences, to the lure of theatre which took craftsmen and merchants from their work, to the subject-matter of the plays themselves. Succeeding decrees, from 1598 to 1682, attempted to correct these abuses. But until theatre itself reached a state of senescence, none of the decrees had a deterrent effect on the robust and burgeoning phenom-

enon that was characteristic of the Spanish Golden Age.

Prolific playwrights produce secular and sacred drama

No English writer has to his credit the phenomenal output of Lope de Vega, who is supposed to have written some eighteen hundred secular plays and about four hundred sacred plays. There are four hundred thirty-one of his plays still on record. It is obvious that in so prodigious a literary output there would be much that is superficial and incon-

sequential. Lope de Vega himself unasham-
edly said that he was interested only in pleasing his public and in giving them what they
wanted. That he was successful in doing this
there is little doubt, for he was almost sen-
sationally renowned, and he most truly represents the national character.

Lope de Vega was preceded by a line of
playwrights who had set the style and the
subject matter which he was to use. Spanish
native drama grew and developed in the first
fifty years of the sixteenth century. Its inheritance from the preceding period was a
tradition of secular pieces performed by
traveling juglares, and a tradition of religious plays as separate entities. The first dramatic text extant in the vernacular is a
twelfth century *Auto de los reyes magos,* a
Twelfth Day play of the Visit of the Magi.
The first name of any consequence in the
annals of drama is that of Juan del Encina
whose *Cancionere* (1496) included a nativity
drama in the vernacular in which the shepherds were easily recognizable local types, as
well as two Easter plays in the vernacular
said to have been done for the Duke and
Duchess of Alba. He also spent some years
in Italy, where it is reported that one of his
more formal, classical plays was performed
in Rome. A Spaniard who settled in Naples,
Bartolomé de Torres Naharro, published
there his *Propalladia* (1517) which contained
six of his eight comedies, all of which had
been performed before noble audiences. One
of these, *Timellaria,* was performed in the
palazzo of the Medicis, another—*Trophea*—
in Rome. All of them are in the classic five-
act form, and at least two (*Comedia Serafina*
and *Himenea*) thematically emphasize the
pundoñor, or point of honor, which would
later be so much the preoccupation of playwrights.

Contemporary with Naharro is Gil Vi-
cente, the Portuguese poet of the court of
Lisbon, who wrote forty-four plays—eleven
entirely in Spanish and seventeen partly so.
Dom Duardos and *Amadisde Gaula* are on
the themes of courtly chivalry; many others
are occasional pieces, eclogues, and semilitur-
gical plays. But all exhibit a facility in natural dialogue and humorous situation, though
the structural necessity of plot is largely in-
effectual. One of the most popular books of
the sixteenth century in Europe was *La Ce-
lestina,* the popular title for an anonymous
Comedie de Calisto y Melibea, written sometime between 1514 and 1519 and now generally ascribed to Fernando de Rojas. It is in
dialogue form in twenty-one acts, and though
obviously not intended for performance, it is
notable for its realistic rendering of characters drawn from all walks of life, its tragic
force, and its impressive conception. Undoubtedly it had influence on sixteenth century Spanish playwrights.

It is Lope de Rueda (1510?–1565) who is
generally called "the founder of Spanish theatre." He was a playwright, a producer, and
an actor. Four of his comedies (*Los Enga-
ñados, Enfemia, Medora,* and *Armelina*), two
of his pastoral plays (*Camilia* and *Tymbria*),
and ten comic *pasos* were published after
his death. (Needless to say, he would not
have published them in his lifetime, since
they were the sustenance of his acting company.) The pasos, which he is said to have
invented as a form, are his best achievement.
Intended for performance between the acts
of the longer plays, they use a common situation, vernacular dialogue, and more than
a little humor. The most famous of them is
The Olives, in which a peasant and his wife
develop a violent argument over the selling
price of the fruit from a tree which has not
yet been planted. The comedies, as we have
them, have no act divisions, and the scenes
vary in number from six to ten. The cast of
characters numbers from twelve to fifteen,

and while the comedies are somewhat clumsy in construction it is easy to see that in performance they would give the delight which is everywhere recorded as the reaction to this company's work. That work was not restricted to plays of Rueda's composition, for the records show that, from 1542 on (when he was commissioned to produce a play for the guild of winemakers in Castile), he toured with his company producing all kinds of performances—sacred as well as secular—in inns, streets, patios, or wherever space afforded. He is even said to have played before the queen in 1561. His activities in the religious theatre, the festival performances, and the popular comedies and farces prefigure the three major divisions into which the theatre of the Golden Age falls: *auto sacramental*, court theatre, and commercial stage.

It was Juan de la Cueva (1550–1610?) who first demonstrated the viability of using the legendary and historical materials of the romance on the stage, and thus provided future writers of comedias with a veritably endless supply of materials. He wrote fourteen comedies and tragedies, mostly in the Senecan manner and following classic form; but three of the plays use the Spanish materials and are free from pseudoclassicism.

Before proceeding to Lope de Vega, it is necessary to mention Cervantes, who was himself proud of his comedias, written for performance between 1582 and 1587. Only two have survived, and only one—*La Numancia*—has any real dramatic force, and that largely through its many fine rhetorical passages. His genius was essentially a narrative one, but he remained interested in the theatre in spite of his lack of success as a playwright. In *Don Quixote*, Part I, Chapter 8, he (much in the manner of Sir Philip Sidney) bemoans plays which were not "more observant of place than of time," as in a comedy where "the first act of which was laid in Europe, the second in Asia, and the third in Africa; and had there been four acts, the fourth would doubtless have been in America."

By the time this statement was published in 1605, the form of the popular Spanish theatre had been established and nothing Cervantes might say could change it. But Lope de Vega felt constrained to defend it in the tract mentioned above: *The New Art of Writing Plays in This Age* (1609). In a series of twenty-eight points he lays down the structure of the new panoramic drama: that there may be comic scenes in serious stories and the other way around; that though there should be but one main action, any time limits other than those prescribed by the story itself are ridiculous; that three acts constitute the proper divisions; that the language be economical and well suited to the characters; that costume be properly devised. The whole tract is replete with the display of his own knowledge of the classics and classical theory, but he says that he is writing "in defiance of art" and in conformance to what he knows will please his audiences "since the crowd pays for the comedies." In spite of its quasi-apologetic tone, the tract is a significant critical paper, and it is certain that the plays he devised were amazingly successful. His long career was marked by widespread adulation and imitation.

Popular Spanish drama, which Lope de Vega brought to its apogee, ignored the divisions of tragedy and comedy. It was universally called simply comedia. The comedia was a three-act play where comedy and tragedy were interfused, drawing subject-matter from heroic legend, recent history, current social problems, and chivalric tradition. The stress was almost universally on incident and plot; characters were stereotyped and but slightly developed during the action of the play. The social milieu in Spain was not conducive to an emphasis on individual will and capacity; the interest of the play is chiefly in its multiplicity of incident and swift movement. Ordinarily written in verse, the best representatives exhibit great ingenuity in verse forms. There have been many attempts to classify these plays, but the form is so diverse as to defy any definite classification. One type of play which Lope de Vega and others wrote with great dash and vigor were the light "cloak and sword" plays founded upon intrigue, mistaken identities, love affairs, and the doings of a flamboyant aristocracy. Though presumably plays of contemporary manners, the picture they give of Spanish society is by no means accurate. But the disguisings, alarums, confusions, and obsession with the *pundoñor* (point of honor) are generally rendered in such sparkling dialogue and dextrous plot that the plays are charming in the presentation. Lope de Vega's most famous of this kind is probably *Madrid Steel*, from which Molière took the idea for *The Physician in Spite of Himself*. It is a complicated love intrigue in which Lisardo masquerades as a physician to court Belisa, while her chaperone is distracted by Lisardo's bosom friend. After many trials, all ends happily. Many of Lope de Vega's contemporaries and followers were expert in the "cloak and sword." Tirso de Molina, in his *Deceiver of Seville*, created the character of Don Juan, who appears with such amazing frequency in other literature. Calderon himself, the last great star of Spain's Golden Age, wrote an ingenious comedy of love in *The Fairy Lady*.

Of the eighteen hundred plays for which Lope claimed authorship (Cervantes called him "a prodigy of nature"), about four hundred thirty comedias are still extant plus fifty autos or liturgical plays. Well-known "cloak and sword" plays are *Punishment Without Revenge, A Certainty for Doubt, A*

Gardener's Dog, and *Wise for Herself.* These lively stories, with invented characters and situations, gave pleasure to audiences by their infinite dexterity. In the legendary and historical materials which were also his heritage, Lope wrote many plays, ranging from conventional histories like *The Crown of Otun* (about a Bohemian king) and *Rome in Ashes* (about Nero), to a type of play drawn from history which could be called "social drama." Powerful is the action of one of the best of these, *The Star of Seville* (disputed authorship), and two others—*The King the Greatest Alcalde* and *Fuente Ovejuna* (*The Sheepwell*). All three of these are built upon the thesis that the king is finally responsible for the administration of justice—and that he does his duty. The second, drawn from the reign of Alfonso VII of Castile, pits the peasant Sancho against the feudal lord Don Tello, with the king finally on the peasants' side. In the third, the adversary for an equally evil commander of a village, c. 1476, is the whole village, who rise to defeat the tyrant, stand together under investigation, and are not only forgiven by the king but taken under his special protection.

Lope de Vega did exactly what he said he was doing: he wrote plays built upon and appealing to the national consciousness of his contemporaries, with little or no regard for any aesthetic principle save that they would work in the theatre and please his audiences. The kind and quality of these audiences determined the content and style of his plays. There is no searching of great moral truths, no questioning of codes of behavior or motivation, no doubt thrown upon the accepted foundations of his society: respect for the crown and the church. Hence his plays are intricately plotted, full of action, unerring in their sense of what would move their audiences, eminent in their stagecraft, delightful in their poetic meters—but ultimately falling short of that universality which would put them in the front rank of world drama forever.

Calderon, the other great figure of Spanish dramatic literature, lived from 1600 to 1681. He was less prolific than Lope de Vega, there being only one hundred twenty of his plays extant, of which eighty are autos. He was no less a child of his time than was Lope de Vega, being concerned with the pundoñor (which too frequently was largely a matter of preserving reputation) and the pattern of beliefs of his society. But Calderon was of a more philosophical and metaphysical turn of mind than Lope de Vega. And he was also caught up in the *culturismo* of his day which attempted to improve the language by re-Latinizing it. The attempt resulted in what is called "Gongorism"—the equivalent of what we know in English as "euphuism." So his plays were long considered the literary superior of Lope de Vega's and his influence on other European drama was great. It is true that *Life Is a Dream* is an effective and chilling statement that it is necessary to realize that life is a dream in order to neutralize one's lust for power. It is true that *The Mayor of Zalamea* is as equally an effective "social drama" as Lope de Vega's *Fuente Ovejuna*. And that *The Fairy Lady* is a delightful comedy of love and *The Wonder-Working Magician* is a thoughtful philosophical work. But *The Physician of His Own Honor* is repellent in its ethics, though accepted in its day, and the others of this type no better. In the final analysis, Calderon lacked the pungent health and theatricality of Lope de Vega, and the extreme punctiliousness of his expression grows tiresome.

Contemporary with these two greatest of Spain's playwrights were literally hundreds of others, few of whom are worth noting. Guillén de Castro in *Las Mocedades del Cid* gave Corneille the character and story for his much more famous play. Tirso de Molina brought Don Juan to the attention of the world in *The Deceiver of Seville*. Juan Ruiz de Alarçon wrote about a prevaricator caught in his own lies in *Truth Itself Suspected*, giving Corneille a model for *Le Menteur*. But the death of Lope de Vega in 1635 marks the beginning of the decline in quantity and quality of playwriting, and by the time Calderon died in 1681, almost all of the practicing playwrights who had been Lope de Vega's contemporaries had disappeared. There would be no further drama of distinction to come out of Spain until near the end of the nineteenth century.

Courtyards converted to playhouses

In Renaissance Spain, as in England, public playhouses developed from space originally intended for other purposes. Strolling companies of players used whatever space they could find for their performances: inns, patios, public squares, the combined yards of houses set around a city block, the streets themselves. Lope de Rueda is said to have planned a special theatre building in Vallodolid in 1558 but there is no record of its having been built. The first space permanently set aside for use by players as a public theatre occurs in Madrid, and is connected with the coming together of the players and the *cofradias*—an association which lasted throughout the period. The year was 1565. It was the *Cofradia de la Pasion y Sangre de Jesucristo* which determined in that year to provide a permanent playing space for performers and to share the income with them. The cofradias were charitable organizations charged with looking after the ill, the poor, and the old. What they did was to acquire the interior yards of a block of houses called a *corral*, and either lease or rent it to the players. They were thus empowered by both church and state. By 1575 there were at least four corrales in Madrid, the most famous being the *Corral de la Pacheca;* three in Vallodolid, one in Valencia, and one in Zamora, where the patio of the hospital was thus converted. By 1600 Madrid had at least eight, Seville six, Vallodolid three, Valencia two, and at least one of record in Barcelona, Granada, Cordoba, Toledo, Marcia, Malaga, Cadiz, and Almagro along with possibly others that have escaped attention. In addition to the Corral de la Pacheca, the most famous and the longest lasting of the theatres of Madrid were the *Corral de la Cruz* and the *Corral del Principe.* In Seville, the *Corral de Doña Elvira, El Coliseo,* and the *Montèria* were the most famous.

The earliest playing spaces in the appropriated corrales were converted by the simple expedient of erecting a broad trestle stage at one end of the corral from one side to the other. Standing room for spectators was in the remaining space of the corral and privileged spaces for other spectators were at the windows of the surrounding houses. Permanent theatres followed the same basic plan. A description of the Corral del Principe in Madrid will illustrate the design of the typical Spanish public theatre of the time.

The space to the sides and the space under the raised stage constituted the dressing rooms of the actors. The open space on the floor of the theatre was paved and provided with raised benches along the sides (called *gradas*) and several rows of benches immediately in front of the stage, both of which areas were reserved for men only. The rest of the space was left open for standees, also for men only. The area opposite the stage was supplied with a balcony, partitioned off and with a separate entrance; this

PRESENTATION OF A SACRED PLAY
The wagon is drawn up before a great house, and the play is being presented while both the gentry and the general populace watch. (Cheney, *The Theatre,* McKay, 1935)

was the *cazuela,* literally "stew pan," and was reserved for women. The side walls of the theatre were supplied with boxes or stalls, called *aposentos,* covered with an iron grating; these were the equivalents of the windows from the rooms of the surrounding houses of the old corrales, and were reserved for both men and women of noble and wealthy houses and for public officials. Just as the owner of a house whose rear wall became a part of a corral might reserve a room for himself and his family, or put in additional windows for others, the boxes of the permanent theatre retained their exclusive character. Stairways led to the women's gallery, the boxes, and the gradas; with the stage, these were roofed over. An awning was stretched over the remaining open space to shield spectators from the weather. Though this basic design was a common one, there were various differences from theatre to theatre. In the Corral de la Pacheca, the roof over the gradas was of canvas instead of being a permanent and tiled structure. At the Corral de la Cruz there seems to have been a gallery immediately behind the gradas extending around the sides of the corral, referred to as the *corredor,* which may have been a part of the original structure of the houses from which the theatre space was converted.

Theatres built after 1600 and called "new"

maintained the same basic design but added some refinements. El Coliseo in Seville, for instance, opened between 1601 and 1607, was extensively refurbished in 1614, and the contract for this reconstruction reveals that at that time the building was provided with a painted wooden roof over the entire open area which had, up until that time, been left open to the sky or covered with a canvas. Twenty marble columns ten feet high and "of the doric order" were set around the open patio on the first level. The twenty on the next level were to be seven feet high and there were to be twenty-nine boxes each with an iron balustrade (the aposentos); above that was another story with five great windows to give the theatre light. The benches in the patio were to have backs (two hundred fifty were made in 1615), and there were to be fifty chairs with leather seats, presumably in the aposentos. The Montèria in Seville was erected in the palace of the Alcazar (although it was a public theatre) in 1626. It is said to have been oval in shape, but otherwise similar to the usual rectangular theatres, with three tiers of balconies, the first containing sixteen aposentos or boxes, the second eighteen, and the third being the cazuela for the women. The building was made of wood with stone pillars and was covered with a wooden roof. Four of the boxes were to be reserved free for the use of the governor and officials of the palace. It was leased to the former producer at El Coliseo, Diego de Almonacid. It has been estimated that the Corral del Principe in Madrid probably provided for seating about seven hundred sixty patrons, and the standing room, of course, could accommodate many more. A sketched plan for the Olivera at Valencia shows three hundred seventy-two numbered seats on benches in the patio, plus boxes and gradas. Thus, capacity audiences in theatres might be anywhere from one thousand to fifteen hundred.

Even more than in England, the Spanish popular theatre seems to have been created almost solely by and for the general public; there is little record of royal activity in theatre-building until the accession of Philip IV in 1621. It is possible that Philip II witnessed the presentation of sacred plays in the Escorial, as well as at their public performances. Under Philip III, who ascended the throne in 1598, there began a more intense interest in theatre on the part of the royal house. Players of comedias were invited to give special performances at royal residences; in 1608 the Duke of Lerma fitted out a courtyard of his Treasure House as a corral theatre so that their majesties could witness plays given as they were in the public corrales. Of course the pageantry, tournaments, entry processions, and other kinds of special theatricals were still being given, and increased in number during this reign. Often professional companies were invited to perform, especially by the queen, who seems to have had a special theatre space fitted out in her private apartments. For the various festival performances, temporary stages were constructed in gardens and patios of noble and royal houses; the open courtyard of the house of the Duke of Lerma was thus arranged to entertain the Earl of Nottingham, ambassador of James I, in June 1605. One of the English embassy described the event thus, saying that after a large banquet

they were carried downe into a faire
court, paued with square stone, in the
middest whereof was a fountaine of cleare
water. The whole court couered with
canuas to defend and keepe off the heat of
the sunne, which at that time shone
extremely. In this Court was of a purpose
a stage erected, with all things fitting for
a play, which his Lordship and the rest were
inuited to behold. The King and Queen
being in priuate likewise Spectators of
that Interlude.

R. TRESWELL
*A Relation of . . . the Journey of . . . Charles
Earle of Nottingham.* London, 1605

But not until the time of Philip IV (1621–1665) did the royal hand become a "first cause" in the building of actual theatres. It was Philip IV who commissioned the Montèria in the Alcazar, and, when planning his new palace at Buen Retiro, included a theatre in the plans. Soon after the opening of the Montèria, the king added to his staff the Italian architect-designer-engineer Cosme Lotti, who helped to plan the new theatre at

RESTORED CORRAL THEATRE AT ALMAGRO, SPAIN
This old theatre, restored in recent years, is in the same form as the more famous corrals of Madrid; the stage is at one end, and galleries are along the sides. Not visible here are the side benches on the ground floor. (Otero Pedrayo, *Geographia de España*)

Buen Retiro. Although parts of the palace were ready for occupancy as early as 1632, the theatre did not open until 1640, when a play of Royas Zorilla (*La Gran Comedia de los Bandos de Verona, The Great Play of the Families of Verona*) specially commissioned for the occasion, was produced. It is, of course, the Romeo-Juliet story. The theatre is described as "sumptuous," and extant floor plans seem to indicate a theatre in the Italian manner, with provisions for a flat-wing system on the stage, a special box or "loge" for the king, and boxes, which the king is said to have allotted to the grandees "by turns." Again, except for special occasions, the public was admitted for a fee, the cofradias profiting as they did at the public playhouses.

Several standards for settings

Renaissance Spain had somewhat the same pattern of stage settings as did early sev-

INTERIOR VIEW OF THE CORRAL DEL PRINCIPE
Conjectural sketch of the sixteenth-century interior by the seventeenth-century artist Juan Comba. Note the barred windows of the houses surrounding the theatre space, and the awning stretched over the yard. (Museo Nacional, Madrid)

enteenth century England. Elaborate, Italianate settings were the rule in the occasional court productions; simplified settings in the public theatres. In Spain, of course, the custom of intricate settings for the sacred plays continued; contracts of the period usually show a certain number of days set aside for the preparation of the public theatres to set up the stage effects for the religious plays which, as we have mentioned, were shown in them after the ceremonial productions of Corpus Christi Day.

One of Aristo's comedies was given in the royal palace at Valladolid as early as 1548, at a wedding celebration, and it was produced with such wonders of scenic display that Caluette de Estrella (*Felicissimo Viage del Principe Phileppe*, 1552), the person through whose writings we know about it, was too overwhelmed by the visual splendor to mention the name of the play. During the reign of Philip II, royal festivities seem to have been limited to special occasions, such as the record of the "entry" festival given in his honor in 1570 in Madrid, when a tank full of water was set up in the Prado, on which sailed eight galleys which attacked and defeated a castle erected at one end. Court masques were revived under Philip III, and the various extant descriptions of these sound like the Jacobean court masque in England, with allegorical figures, sumptuous costumes, reveals, cloud machines, etc. The king even had a special wooden hall constructed in 1605 at the Escorial to house the festivities given in honor of the birth of his son. Another account of 1614 tells of a special open-air theatre built on the bank of the river Arlanza for a production of Lope de Vega's *El Premio de la Hermosura,* in which the curtain at the back of the acting area could be withdrawn to reveal the river, where some of the action took place. Perhaps the most lavish of this type of outdoor production was one planned by Cosme Lotti for the lake of Buen Retiro in 1635. The script was that of Calderon's *El Mayor Encanto Amor,* but the script was incidental to the staging. An artificial island was built in the lake, with a mountain and trees, and a curving staircase from the water's edge. A silver car drawn by fish spouting water brought the goddess Agua to the island; Ulysses arrived in a golden ship; there was thunder, lightning, and an earthquake; Virtue appeared riding on a turtle; Mercury appeared in a cloud machine—the wonders are too many to detail.

Stage machinery, as elaborate as could be devised, was the custom, too, for the sacred plays. Trapdoors were an early device, and seem always to have been necessary to the performances. The cars upon which the actors rode in the procession, beautifully decorated and painted as they were, arrived at the point of presentation and were backed up against a temporary stage for the actual presentation. Here the stage axis was transverse. Each of the two cars bore an edifice of some sort on one end; the actors entered from below and up through these edifices. The honored members of the audience sat on one side of the transverse axis, the majority stood on the

other. Great sums of money were expended on these cars and stages; for a production at Plasencia in 1578, the stage in the square of the city was provided with a tank sixty by twenty feet, filled with water, floating a ship completely rigged, and carrying sailors and passengers. That the artifices, contrivances, appearances, tricks—as stage machinery was variously called—were elaborate and expensive is attested to by many financial records and descriptions of festival presentations in several Spanish towns. Typical is the description of the settings for four sacred plays of Lope de Vega, produced at Madrid in 1609; the settings included a sky with stars, dragon heads spouting flames of fire, a palace with a chapel, a table set with disappearing plates, and many other wonders, including sumptuous costumes.

The school productions also used intricate scenery, such as an interesting performance described as being given by the students of the college of San Hermengildo in Seville. It was a multiple setting, one tower representing a prison, another a great hall, with a large door between them representing the city of Seville. This 1570 description mentions the use of canvas for the painted set.

The public theatres, however, showed no such reliance on painted sets and wondrous effects. Stages of the early theatres were hardly more than the "four trestles, four boards, two actors, and a passion," of which Lope de Vega speaks. This simple platform stage, for most plays, was hung about on three sides with green baize curtains. The curtains on the sides of the stage led directly to the dressing rooms; since there was no front curtain, a person wounded or killed during the course of the action was disposed of by the simple stage direction that he "falls within the dressing room." At the back of the stage the curtain could be drawn to

SPANISH COURT THEATRE
A print of the great lake at El Buen Retiro, scene of grandiose spectacles on floating barges, particularly an extravaganza arranged by Cosme Lotti, the imported Italian designer-architect, in 1635. (Hispanic Society of America)

reveal doors, and the scene was often changed by the simple expedient of having actors exit through one door and come in the other. The second-story level of the rear stage wall was a gallery which sometimes did service for windows and balconies. As in Elizabethan plays, the actors frequently announced the locale of the action and described the surroundings; the audience then imagined the scene. Sometimes simple set pieces of linen or pasteboard appeared on the stage, remaining unchanged throughout the action. Sometimes these set pieces were revealed by drawing a curtain aside. Though no attempt was made at effective illusion, painted canvas set pieces were frequently used to indicate that the stage represented a garden, or was dressed with a fountain, or rocks, or a mountain, or a fort. By the second quarter of the seventeenth century these painted canvases for scenery were more numerous and more frequently used. Lope de Vega complains of this practice, saying that,

Because there are no good actors, or because the poets are bad, or because the auditors lack understanding . . . the managers avail themselves of machinery,

the poets of carpenters, and the auditors of their eyes.
Prologo Dialogistico, 1623, prefixed to Part XVI of his *Comedias*

He evidently never attempted to conceal his contempt for the scene painter and machinist.

Costumes provide the clues

If the stage of the public theatre was lacking in scenic effect, if the audience was asked to imagine what the locale of the play was, costuming was gorgeous and no little help to the audience in imagining locale. Characters dressed in hunting costume could be expected to indicate that the almost bare stage was a forest; sumptuous ball gowns indicated festivities at a palace; and so forth. There was, of course, no pretense at historical accuracy. As in England, playwrights had a tendency to transform past occurrences into current national usages and customs; and audiences, having little sense of the historic past, were not critical of what would seem to us glaring anachronisms. As Ticknor, the great historian of Spanish literature says, "Coriolanus was dressed like Don John of Austria, and Aristotle came on the stage with a curled periwig and buckles on his shoes, like a Spanish Abbé" (*History of Spanish Literature*, II. 539).

Some obvious distinctions, however, were made. These audiences would have been aware that Moors dressed differently from Christians, so stage Moors appeared in turbans and long mantles; but the Roman, who lay outside their immediate consciousness, was dressed in cloak and sword. Lope de Vega complained of the Roman costume in his *New Art*, saying that it was obviously not right. He also was disturbed by such "barbarous things" as a Turk wearing a Christian ruff. In the last decade of the sixteenth century, the learned Alonso Lopez Pinciano urged that actors study history in order to dress themselves properly when playing historical characters, and that due attention be paid to the rank and social class of the characters being represented. This latter admonition was more closely followed than the former. The Spanish were no less class conscious than the English, and did not expect that peasants should dress like princes. Besides, since the scenery was rudimentary, differentiation in contemporary dress was an aid to characterization and to locale.

But everywhere, richness was the rule. A description of the sacred plays of *Job* and *Saint Catalina* presented in Madrid in 1592 is reminiscent of descriptions of medieval English mysteries. Job is to be dressed in a long coat of purple damask and a hat of taffeta, and buskins. God is to be dressed in a tunic of sateen or taffeta in gold and purple with a white taffeta cloak. The three gallants in *Saint Catalina* are to have coats of mail in the Roman fashion, and so forth. The specifications for a 1624 production indicate that the costumes are to be of brocatel and velvet and damask and sateen, trimmed with gold passementerie.

Costumes for the sacred plays were supplied by the municipality, which underwrote all expenses for these presentations. For the performers of secular drama at the public theatres, however, different arrangements prevailed. Principal players supplied their own costumes, while the head of the company provided them for the lesser members. Costuming accounted for a large part of the expenses of actors and managers. In 1589, the manager Sebastian de Montemayor paid eleven hundred reals for a rich skirt and jacket; in 1602, Melchor de Leon paid three hundred thirty reals for a skirt of straw-colored satin; in 1619, the actors Juan Batista Muñiz and his wife paid twenty-four hundred reals for a costume of greenish-gold sateen with gold lace and fringe, red sateen edging, and a red taffeta silk lining. Compare these prices with the top price of five hundred reals paid to Lope de Vega for writing a secular play, and some idea of the extravagance of costuming is possible.

Managers who owned a sizable wardrobe often increased their revenues by hiring out costumes for special performances and for festivals. Actors in financial straits frequently pawned their expensive wardrobes to raise money.

In the poorer traveling companies, of course, the costuming was much more rudimentary and inexpensive. Cervantes, in the Prologue to the volume of his *Comedias* published in 1615, reminisces about Lope de Rueda's little company, and says of its accoutrements that they were all contained in a sack, and consisted of "four white pelices trimmed with gilded leather, and four beards and wigs, with four staffs, more or less." The *Amusing Journey* of Augustin de Rojas (1603), in listing the types and sizes of traveling companies, mentioned the cos-

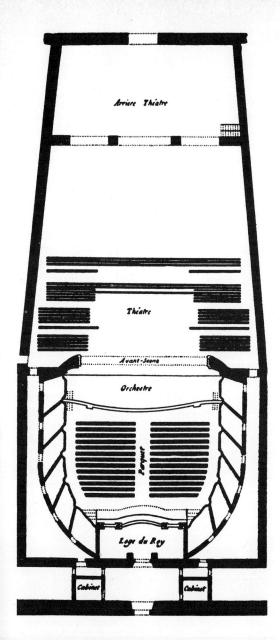

Arriere Theatre

Théatre

Avant-Scene

Orchestre

Parquet

Loge du Rey

Cabinet   Cabinet

SPANISH COURT THEATRE
The plan of the theatre of Philip IV at El Buen Retiro. The space allotted to the stage was greater than that for the audience; the rear of the stage could be opened to a garden; the appointments were lavish. (Dumont, *Parallele de Plan des Plus Belles Salle de Spectacle, Etc.*)

tumes typical of each, from just such a rudimentary supply as Cervantes describes to companies which required two chests to transport their costumes.

But whether actors and managers were a part of an impecunious provincial touring company or of one of the most prosperous organizations in one of the great cities, costumes were an integral and valued part of their possessions, and an indispensable aid to production.

Women on stage

The most significant difference between Elizabethan and Spanish acting companies is that in England no woman appeared on the professional stage, whereas in Spain they were important members of the company, and, for the most part, exceedingly popular. Spanish companies, however, from first to last, must sometimes have used boys in women's parts, as is evident from a series of edicts regulating theatrical entertainment. Allowing women in Spanish companies may have been the result of their popularity in the Italian commedia companies who visited frequently and were highly popular. It may also have been influenced by the undoubted sentiment on the part of many that having a boy act women's parts was somehow immoral. But it probably was the result of the tastes of the audiences who enjoyed seeing women on the stage. Though no licenses were issued for women to act on the public stages of Madrid until 1587, it is very likely that women did act there before that date.

The presence of women made the life of the theatre more complicated than it would otherwise have been, and many are the edicts requiring that any such female member be either married to an actor of the company or be the daughter of an acting couple. Married male actors were required to have their wives with them even though these wives were not actresses. These various rules were no doubt honored as much in the breach as in the observance, for many a Spanish noble took an actress as mistress, and Philip IV himself was the father of Don John of Austria, whose mother was La Calderona, a famous actress. Women seem to have been particularly popular in the various dances, and in "breeches parts," for there are frequent proscriptions against "licentious dances" and the wearing of male attire by females.

There is no record of a female head of a company, but as members of the acting companies they were as well paid as the men; prominent actresses sometimes made considerably more than the male members of the company. Allowances and privileges were extended equally to them as to the men.

Companies of one or many

Acting companies varied widely in composition and quality. The famous *Viage Entretenido* of Augustin de Rojas Villandrando lists the various types: a *bululu*, the lone player traveling on foot; a *ñaque*, two men; a *gangarilla*, three or four men and a boy to play the women's parts; a *cambaleo*, five men and a woman; a *garnacha*, five or six men, a woman to play the first lady's roles, and a boy to play the second; a *boxiganga*, six or seven men, two women, and a boy; a *farándula*, three women besides the men; and the largest, a *compañia*, "sixteen persons who act, thirty who eat, one who takes the money at the door." Costumes, properties, and modes of transportation increase in complexity and cost as the company grows larger.

The more prosperous and well-known companies were organized on two basic principles: those in which the head of the company was the proprietor, paying a fixed salary to the members of the company, and those which operated on shares. In either case definite contracts were drawn to govern the operation of the company. These contracts set hours of rehearsal, with fines for tardiness; payments to each member of the company; traveling and maintenance allowances; and, in the case of sharing companies, a provision for the distribution of parts by mutual agreement. Actors were hired for periods of one or two years, the beginning of the period being marked by Shrovetide. Companies were not resident at a particular theatre, as Shakespeare's company was, but traveled from city to city, generally spending about a month in any given theatre. Various arrangements were made with the owners of theatre properties, generally entailing either a flat sum as rent or a portion of the receipts. For engagements to present the sacred plays on Corpus Christi Day, or for special performances at various other festivities, the companies were paid flat sums agreed upon in advance.

The life of the Spanish actor was strenuous. Rojas describes the daily program:

Actors are up at dawn and write and study from five o'clock till nine, and from nine till twelve they are constantly rehearsing.
They dine and then go to the *comedia;* leave the theatre at seven, and when they want rest they are called by the President of the Council, or the city fathers, whom they must serve whenever it pleases them.
Viage Entretenido, Madrid, 1603, pp. 368–369

In the sacred plays, early morning performances were often required beginning at six even though there had been a festival performance the previous day from two in the afternoon until midnight. The Corpus Christi performances normally lasted two days, with a flat fee as payment for both days. The

STAGE SETTING FOR A SPANISH COURT THEATRE
Design by an unknown artist for a revival in
1690 of a Calderon play. Note the side wings,
backdrop, and cloud borders.

municipalities evidently got their money's
worth!

Actors, of course, were paid only when
they were working. The total number of
days in which a constantly busy actor could
give performances was something less than
two hundred a year, because of all the times
in which performances were prohibited and
the theatres closed. No wonder that the records of litigation and imprisonment for debt
include the names of so many actors and
managers. The average wage for respected
members of the profession seems to have
been in the neighborhood of three thousand

reals a year, plus board and traveling expenses while the company was playing. Adequate but not luxurious living could be had
for about two and a half reals a day in those
times, so the competent performers were not
extravagantly paid. The less competent received considerably less. The apprentices received no wages at all, or only a slight sum
at the end of the season, but did receive all
expenses. Stars were paid, as they have always been, rather extravagantly. There is
record of La Calderona being paid one thousand fifty reals for two days' performance in
the Corpus Christi plays at Pinto in 1632;

SPANISH ACTORS
Left, a member of a traveling company presents his performance before the town officials in order to secure a license for public performance. Above, an old print after an original painting by A. Fabier shows Augustin de Rojas rehearsing. Of special interest here is the elaborate costume so typical of Spanish players.

Maria de Cordoba received eight hundred reals for two performances in secular plays the next year, plus expenses for herself and her maid. Pedro Manuel de Castilla, one of the most celebrated leading men of his time, received twenty reals a day, ten reals for maintenance, and five hundred reals for Corpus performances. But there is no record that any of these Spanish players were ever wealthy enough to buy "that house in Stratford." They were generally considered, and may have been, an improvident lot. But certainly the expenses of costumes, which leading players were expected to bear out of their own pockets, must have taken up much of their income.

History records the names of over two thousand players of the Golden Age in Spain, and by far the majority of these were recruited from the lower and middle classes. There are, however, several outstanding examples of noble gentlemen who were so enamored of the theatre that they became actors or managers. Such a one was Alonso de Olmedo, who was both a distinguished actor and manager, and was, by special authorization of the king, allowed to retain privileges of his rank although he belonged to a generally despised profession. Throughout this entire period all actors were declared without civil rights, and any actor who died in his profession could not be buried in soil consecrated by the church. How paradoxical this sounds when one notes the thousands of church performances that these pariahs gave during the same period! Of course, many of them were highly respected and honored in their lifetimes. In addition, it is interesting to note that both Lope de Vega and Calderon, Spain's two greatest playwrights, died after many years of service as priests of the church. It was not unusual for actresses, particularly, to renounce the stage to enter a convent, as did the famous Maria de Riquèlme. It must have been a comfort for an actress past her prime to know that she had this refuge open to her.

A high degree of skill was demanded of performers in the public theatres. The secular plays were almost invariably written in verse form, and the audiences expected a most felicitous performance. In addition, all actors and actresses had to be proficient in singing, dancing, and playing a musical instrument, for every public performance included these forms of entertainment. A contemporary describes the famous Damian Arias de Peñafiel thus:

Arias possesses a clear, pure voice, a
tenacious memory, and vivacious manner,
and in whatever he said it seemed that the
Graces were revealed in every movement
of his tongue and Apollo in every gesture.
The most famous orators came to hear him
in order to acquire perfection of diction
and gesture.

CARAMUEL
Rythmica, Campaniae, 1669, p. 706

Actors tended to specialize in particular types. Arias played the first leading man;

Carlos Vallego was a well-known second leading man; Cosme Perez was a peerless comic actor. There were also comic actresses; other actresses were designated simply as first, second, or third. Actors also were classified first, second, or third in their particular lines. If the company were large, there might also be a fourth or a fifth. A final classification was that of musician, which might be either a man or a woman. If a playwright were attached to a company, he might function also as an actor or as the manager. Many of the secular dramas of the period were produced by playwright-managers, but the great playwrights were primarily neither actors nor managers, nor, indeed, attached to any acting company at all. By 1631, actors were allowed to band together into guilds or brotherhoods, similar to those of other trades or occupations. (It will be remembered that such an arrangement existed for Shakespeare's colleagues from the first; this may be another reason for the less happy state of Spanish performers.) In 1634 the *Congregaçion de la Novena* (so named in honor of the Virgin Mary) was officially approved by the Archbishop of Toledo. The name is preserved by the organization of Spanish actors today.

Just as there was constant criticism from the Puritans in England, in Spain there was a constant stream of criticism, chiefly from the church. There are frequent complaints of the impropriety of certain actors and actresses in the sacred plays because of their immoral lives. Through the years every form of theatrical entertainment came in for its share of criticism and regulation. Women were successively banned from the stages of public theatres, but the banishment never really took place. Subject matter was censored, costuming supervised, even methods of playing dictated. But all of these successive regulations had no lasting effect until

TRAVELING COMPANY OF ACTORS
This old print shows a traveling acting company c. 1542, such as might have visited the Spanish countryside before theatres were built in Spain.

theatre reached a point where it was itself no longer a vital institution.

Summary

Almost concurrent with the great age of Shakespeare, the theatre of Spain rose to its apogee. It welcomed a veritable flood of playwrights and plays, and saw a host of performers on its stages. The plays differed considerably in kind from those written in England, being chiefly either religious or romantic dramas. But they were indigenous and not copies of Italian neoclassicism; hence they were greater than their Continental contemporaries.

The public playhouses of Spain developed, much as England's did, from space not originally intended for theatre use. In Spain, the audience remained in front of the actors, but did consist in part of standees and in part of persons seated in galleries or boxes.

Here, too, theatre was the greatest of popular amusements. An avid public combined with a fertile theatre produced Spain's greatest period of drama.

Plots and character types produced here were used again in the next period by French playwrights, and it may have been the example of the Spanish stage which made women the rule rather than the exception in French theatre after the middle of the seventeenth century. From there, of course, the custom traveled to England in the Restoration.

This period in Spain saw the complete professionalization of theatre, the establishment of permanent playhouses, and more or less permanent repertory companies. Stage-craft was progressively refined, and costuming expensive and brilliant. The major achievement of the period, however, was that it produced the greatest plays of Spanish literature, notably those of Lope de Vega and Calderon.

After the death of Calderon the fortunes of the public theatres declined, and one by one the old houses disappeared. The famous Corral de la Cruz was demolished in 1743 and an Italian opera house was erected in its stead; the same fate overcame the Corral del Principe in 1745. The theatre at Buen Retiro was completely redesigned in 1738 to house opera, and with the banning of the Corpus Christi autos in 1765 all that remained of the old days had disappeared.

In 1600, when Shakespeare and Lope de Vega were reaching the height of their powers and there were six permanent theatres in London and more than that in Spain, Paris had but one theatre and no dramatist of note. The Renaissance had sparked some little dramatic activity it is true. Jodelet had produced the first native tragedy, *Cleopatra Captive*, in 1552 and an *Antigone* and a *Medea* later; the Italian commedia players were performing in Paris and elsewhere; and there were some bands of native players. But the brilliant staging of the Italian formal theatre, the adroit acting of the popular commedia, and the powerful dramatic literature of the English had no counterparts in France.

The reason for this notable absence of flourishing theatre is twofold. For one, France in the sixteenth century was consumed by the Wars of Religion which ended only in 1594 when Henry IV, the first Bourbon king, entered Paris. The short span of his reign (he was assassinated in 1610), was devoted to consolidating his rule over the whole of France, and to the restoration of order, industry, and trade. It was not until the seventeenth century, then, that France possessed the elements of nationalism and an atmosphere ripe for the development of a national theatre.

A second factor inhibiting the growth of theatre was that since 1402 the Confrèrie de la Passion had held a theatrical monopoly in Paris. It had built its first permanent theatre in 1548; although by that year it was forbidden to present passion plays and mysteries, the Confrèrie turned to the successful performance of farces, soties, and comedies. By 1578 it had ceased to produce its own plays, but its theatrical monopoly was in force and it leased its playhouse to touring companies—a situation which still prevailed in 1600. In spite of growing dramatic activity, the Confrèrie effectively prevented any theatrical performances from being held in Paris and its environs except for those which it permitted and supervised in its own house. There were two loopholes: the Confrèrie had, naturally, no jurisdiction over court performances; and in 1595 Henry IV who was exceedingly fond of visiting the fairs, granted a special license for the performance of plays there. Again, it was not until the seventeenth century that a beachhead was established. From then on, however, dramatic activity spread, and though the Confrèrie did not actually lose its prerogative until 1677, it had ceased to be observed many years earlier.

Theatre awaits its patron

The short reign of Henry IV was marked by increasing dramatic activity in the capital. Two companies were performing there in 1596 since there is extant a record of an official complaint of the Confrèrie against its rivals. In 1598 a company of English actors came to Paris, and in the same year also Valleran le Conte (sometimes written "Le comte" although his signature on legal documents is "le Conte") arrived, the most influential of the early French professional actors. He had had a long and evidently successful career in the provinces, playing comedies as well as Biblical tragedies and the plays of Jodelle. He joined forces with the company of Benoit Petit, then occupying the Hôtel de Bourgogne, and in 1599 that house was leased to him. It was about this time that Alexandre Hardy became the paid furnisher of plays to the company. But the Paris public was not yet to be interested in the new tragedies and pastorals of Hardy and this company, ousted by the farces of Robert Guérin and his troupe, left Paris for several years. By the year 1610, when Louis

XIII succeeded to the throne, le Conte was back again, this time in association with the farce players. After 1613 there is no further mention of him.

Theatrical appetite in Paris was also satisfied by the appearances there of Italian commedia companies who pleased not only court circles but the general public as well with their performances. The mother of Louis XIII, Marie de Medici, was exceedingly fond of this native Italian entertainment, and with her benediction several companies of commedia actors appeared in the French capital. Though they played in Italian, their skill in pantomime and acrobatics made them very popular with the general public. Their influence was to be a potent one for more than a century.

Regular tragedy and comedy made little headway against the farce players and the commedia until the advent of that intrepid statesman and man of letters, Cardinal Richelieu. He reentered the government in 1624, becoming chief minister in 1629. In the latter year the actor Montdory and his company arrived in Paris after enjoying tremendous success in the provinces, chiefly as a result of their production of Pierre Corneille's first play, *Mélite* (1628). Montdory had much earlier been one of the younger members of Valleran le Conte's company, and on several occasions appeared in Paris at the Hôtel de Bourgogne; he had become an actor of great renown. Cardinal Richelieu looked with favor upon his company, and despite the protests of the Confrèrie permitted them to perform in Paris outside the Hôtel de Bourgogne, which was then occupied by the Royal Company headed by the actor Bellerose. Montdory and his actors performed in a variety of locations, chiefly converted tennis courts, finally settling in 1634 in a converted tennis court in La Vielle Rue du Temple in the Marais quarter, then a very

fashionable section of Paris. From its location, the house was named the Théâtre du Marais. Now Paris had two permanent theatres; the long-standing theatrical monopoly of the Confrèrie was effectively broken, and the way paved for the development of a great national theatre.

In the same year that Louis XIV came to the throne, and a year after the death of Richelieu, Molière's Illustre Théâtre was formed and opened in a tennis court near the Tour de Nesle (now the location of the Institut de France, which houses the French Academy). It was New Year's Day, 1644. After slightly more than a year, however, the little company retired to the provinces, where a fruitful sojourn of some twelve years' duration enabled them to return in triumph to the capital to help develop the greatest period of French theatre. This era reached its peak in 1680 with the establishment of the first national theatre in existence —the Comédie Française.

Drama reflects the light of the Roi Soleil

The Golden Age of French theatre is almost completely encompassed by the reign of the *Roi Soleil* (Louis XIV) who declared, "L'état, c'est moi" (I am the state). While to modern ears the statement sounds incredibly arrogant, it is the natural result of the historical and intellectual progression of which Louis XIV was the product. Almost single-handedly, the French invented the Age of Reason, which the English, in the next century, would carry to great heights also. The Renaissance conviction of the infinite possibilities of man was channeled in France toward an emphasis upon that element of humanity which makes man most human— his powers of reasoning. Even in the holocaust of the French sixteenth century, intellectuals were concerning themselves with the exercise of the ordering mind of man. One of the chief aims of The Pleiade (Ronsard, Daurat, Belleau, Bellay, de Baïf, de Tyard) was to bring the French language into an order and regularity founded upon the classical tongues. It would be almost a century later (1636) before Richelieu would succeed in founding the Académie Française to implement, in part, exactly the same aim. John Calvin's *Institutes of the Christian Religion* no less than the essays of Montaigne embody this principle of inquiry and order in quite different spheres. The quantity of critical writing in the French seventeenth century is witness to the absolute devotion of the French to the life of the mind. Philosophers and theologians, historians and literary men poured forth an unprecedented volume of tracts. The progress of intellectual history from 1540 to 1640 was that from a dialectical turn of mind to an analytical one. Descartes (1596–1650) deduced existence itself from thought, and the rationalistic philosophy invaded all areas of human activity. There was nothing that could not be solved, or remedied, by "taking thought." Actual events had seemed to bear out the maxim. After conquest, rebellion, turmoil, and wars, France had arrived at an equilibrium, and through the incredible skill of Cardinal Richelieu had become a unified and powerful state and a model for all Europe. The ordered society, with the king at its head and all elements in proper relation to the throne, was conceived as the ideal state. All elements of that state—economic, social, religious, cultural—were epitomized in the person of the monarch; he was the center around which the whole world swung. Only from this view is the intimate involvement of French theatre with the court understandable—the closeness of Molière and Racine to the king, the frequent intervention of the king in theatrical affairs, the subsidy of playwrights and players by the crown, the commandeering of productions for the delectation of the court, even the royal fiats of consolidation which eventuated in 1680 in the formation of the Comédie Française, the first national theatre of the Western world. For it was no less the king's duty than his inclination which fathered these events, and, on the whole, the issue was admirable.

Social conditions discouraging

Outside of the schools, and excepting the court dilettantes who danced and sang in the court productions, acting was a full-time profession. Often the actors were playwrights as well, as was Molière. Often they were actor-managers, like Bellerose. With minor exceptions, the women's roles were played by women, and, again with minor exceptions, there were no companies of child actors. Sometimes the actors earned personal fame and fortune; sometimes members of the nobility joined the profession. But, barring a repentance which included a renunciation of their profession, actors were considered infamous, and could not be buried in holy ground under the rites of the church. Not infrequently they were despised and abused. Molière himself, though he seems not to have resented them, was often subjected to insults from titled patrons.

The chief spectators at the plays were members of court circles and tradesmen connected with court circles. Courtiers and hangers-on often behaved with an arrogance beyond belief. Many a doorkeeper was wounded or even killed in his effort to extract the admission price from one who thought by reason of his position he should be admitted free. Scuffles in the theatre, even riots, were not unusual. Rostand has immortalized one of these in his play *Cyrano de Bergerac* (1898), which gives a fairly ac-

MOLIERE THE ACTOR
Above, Molière as Arnolphe in *The School for Wives*. In this comedy of his own, in which he was exceedingly popular, Molière wears contemporary dress and wig. Left, in this portrait by his friend Mignard, Molière is dressed for his role as Julius Caesar in *The Death of Pompey* by Corneille. He wears an approximation of Roman dress, but retains the full-bottomed wig (here crowned with laurel) which was customary in tragedy. (Harvard Theatre Collection)

curate idea of the conditions under which players performed in seventeenth-century France. Riotous members of the audience frequently interrupted the plays and sometimes made it impossible for the performance to continue. Members of the nobility demanded—and got—stage seats to which they strolled at their convenience, sometimes long after the play had begun. There they conversed audibly, frequently not about the play, and exhibited their finery and lace. Their sworn enemies were the men standing in the pit, the cheapest of admissions, and frequently word battles between these two groups ended in a free-for-all that had to be put down by civil authorities.

For such an audience Molière, Corneille, and Racine wrote. It is perhaps in no little measure due to the fact that the playwrights had to please two such opposite extremes as the spectators on the stage and those in the pit that they produced the strong and virile drama which they did.

Even the more exclusive court performances were thought of more as purely social events than anything else, and there was a great deal of talk and inattention. In the public theatres, performances were advertised to begin at two o'clock, but since it was extremely unfashionable to arrive on time, they frequently never got underway until nearly five, and this latter hour became the customary one. Not until the establishment of the Comédie Française in 1680 were performances given every day of the week—three or four was the customary number. In

the days when Molière's troupe shared the Petit Bourbon with the Comédie Italienne, they played on Mondays, Wednesdays, Fridays, and Saturdays, with the Italians performing on Tuesdays, Thursdays, and Sundays, the most lucrative days. Even those companies with exclusive occupancy of a theatre did not play every day of the week.

In spite of these conditions, and perhaps partly because of them, the seventeenth century produced the best dramatic literature which France has ever known.

Unity of time, place, and action

France had been stirred by the classically oriented ferment of the Renaissance in somewhat lesser degree than Italy, although as early as 1537 Lazare de Baïf had written his *Electra*, and eleven years later the influence of Aristotle's *Poetics* is to be found in the critical work of Thomas Sebillet, *The Poetic Art*, in which he traces a parallel between the old French moralities and the classic tragedies. By the time that Jean de la Taille wrote his *Saul the Mad* (1572), Aristotle was the authority, and Taille's preface to this play enunciated the principle of the unities of time, place, and action. From that time, many French playwrights, whose names are entirely without significance today, wrote in the new classical pattern of the unities.

Though presumably true to Aristotelian precepts, the French writers of tragedy accepted these conventions as they were enunciated by Horace and practiced by Seneca. They rarely went back even to these sources, but followed the practice of Italian interpreters and copiers of Horace and Seneca. Thus their plays are narrative, oratorical, elegiac; most of them were derivative literary exercises produced, if at all, in the schools and at court.

COURT SPACE USED FOR PERFORMANCES
Right, Jacques Callot's etching of an elaborate entertainment given at the court, *Combat at the Barrier*. The spectators are arranged on temporary bleachers around three sides of the great hall. Above, the king watches a performance in the great hall of the Petit Bourbon palace, converted into a theatre, with the floor free for the royal party, and invited guests in the side galleries. (Museum of Fine Arts, Boston)

In the last few decades of the sixteenth century these literary men falteringly learned to include more action in their plays, to bring their chief characters on stage and face to face; and to work out a plot line. When Alexandre Hardy began writing early in the next century for Valleran le Conte's company at the Hôtel de Bourgogne, the carefully worked out theories came to grips with the practice of a professional playwright producing for a paying audience. Though Hardy was in sympathy with the new classical movement in dramatic art, he had to cope with a medieval theatre where events, not rhetoric, held the stage. So, good theatre man that he was, he made the best of both worlds. He followed the classical conventions of five acts, the Alexandrine line (six iambics with the caesura after the third), messengers, a ghost in the first act, and the sufferings, vengeances, and horrors of the Greek and Roman prototypes. But he banished the chorus and ignored the unities; he placed a series of varied scenes on the stage which told a recognizable story

from beginning to end. Essentially he was more of a romantic than a classicist.

It is said that he wrote more than six hundred plays, of which thirty-four survive. If he had been as skillful in character delineation as he was in plot construction; if he had been able to strike the necessary balance between the two; if, in other words, he had possessed something of the genius of Shakespeare, he might have effectively turned the tide of French playwriting away from the classical unities to a more native, less prescribed drama. Though his plays were full of action and were highly theatrical, they lacked the full measure of genius, and eventually they fell into disrepute because of their romanticism.

It is true, too, of course, that he was writing at a time when the intellectual tides were moving against him, when even the incipient romanticism of Ogier and Chapelain were engulfed by the classic ideal of "right reason." The quarrel was joined—and settled—in the early career of Pierre Corneille, France's first authentic playwriting

genius. Corneille's first play, *Mélite*, written for Montdory's acting company while they were visiting his native Rouen and presented by them in Paris in 1629, turned him from the profession of the law to the theatre. *Mélite* was written after the free-ranging style of the Spaniards and Hardy rather than the style of the classical unities. Corneille was not by instinct, nor by training, observation, and experience (having been away from that center of the "new thought"—Paris), a classicist, and neither his second play, *Clitandre* (1631), nor his highly successful *The Cid* (1636), completely observed the unities.

In *The Cid* (derived from Castro's *Youthful Adventures of the Cid*), Corneille succeeded in proving his genius by producing a play in which the dramatic conflict was that interplay of character on event and event on character from which the plot moves forward. It was deservedly popular, and controversial. Its very popularity called down upon his head the ire of the French Academy. The "Quarrel of the Cid" produced a ver-

itable avalanche of pamphlets. Georges de Scudéry, perhaps piqued by the inordinate public response to the production of the play, fired the opening gun in his *Observations on the Cid*, in which he set out to prove not only that the subject and its handling by the playwright were worthless, but that it violated the chief rules of the drama. Corneille counterattacked. Others took up the quarrel, some championing Corneille, some attacking; notable among others was Jean Mairet, the playwright whose *Sophonisbe*, produced the previous year, had observed all the classical precepts, but had at the same time added a real love interest derived from the pastoral—an innovation which thenceforth added another dimension to tragedy. The Quarrel was finally settled in December of 1637 by the pamphlet *Sentimens* issued from the Academy. It was essentially the work of Jean Chapelain, though ostensibly issuing from a committee and having the editorial approval of Richelieu. Corneille was chastised and defeated. Good Sense and Right Reason—the cornerstones of neoclassicism—had triumphed. Critical dicta from

OPEN-AIR THEATRES
Left, Tabarin's street show in the Place Dauphine. He performed to draw an audience for his brother, the quack doctor Mondor; he was an exceedingly popular entertainer, and the Place Dauphine was his favorite place of playing. The particular kind of hat he wore became his trademark. Above, an elevated outdoor stage in the Fair of St. Germain, evidently built atop the stalls of the market at a particular vantage point. Note the two practical doors on the stage. The actors seem to be wearing masks as in the commedia. (Bibliothèque Nationale; Harvard Theatre Collection)

then to the end of the century exalted adherence to the precepts of Aristotle and Horace, as they were understood in this new society: Unity of Action (no more than one principle action), Unity of Time (no more than a day may transpire in the play's action), Unity of Place (only what could be observed by one person *in situ*), along with a five-act structure, no more than three characters talking in a given scene, a clear ethical demonstration of desirable conduct, and as Boileau (friend of Molière and influential critic) says, "the right decorum . . . that al-

ways pleases by just Reason's rule." Perhaps Saint-Evremond summed it all up when he wrote in 1672:

We ought, in tragedy, before all things whatever, to look after a greatness of soul well expressed, which excites in us a tender admiration. By this sort of admiration our minds are sensibly ravished, our courages elevated, and our souls deeply affected.

On Ancient and Modern Tragedy

Without an understanding of this view of

neoclassic French tragedy, it is impossible for non-Frenchmen to see the great works of Racine and Corneille as other than sententious and barren of action.

In any event, Corneille accepted the decision of the Academy—how could he both succeed in the theatre and fly in the face of so weighty an arbiter of the intellectual mode of the day? So he turned to writing a brilliant series of political tragedies drawn from Roman subject-matter: *Horace* (1640), *Cinna* (1641), *Polyeucte* (1642), *The Death of Pompey* (1643); he was elected to the Academy in 1647, and became the foremost writer of classical tragedy in France. In all of these plays his grandly conceived heroes, speaking in ringing Alexandrine verse, dominate the action of the plot. While this dominance made possible the contribution of an impressive gallery of characters to dramatic literature, the resulting necessity of subordinating plot to character made little contribution to the advance of dramaturgy. Corneille observed the unities of time, place, and action; he barred all violent events from his stage and related them by messenger as the Greek playwrights had done; he wrote in the accepted high moral tone with impassioned affirmations of the heroic spirit. Called "the great Corneille," and much honored throughout his long life (he died in 1684), he wrote many more tragedies which do not today add to his stature. It is thus ironic that he seems never to have been completely at home with the classical conventions; under other circumstances, he might have produced a freer, richer drama.

Racine at home with the unities

Jean Racine, on the other hand, had a genius peculiarly suited to the classical restrictions, and rose to great eminence in the brilliant world of the Roi Soleil. His many successful plays were almost entirely on classical subjects, in wonderfully refined verse, with emphasis upon the inner conflicts of his characters. His plays demonstrate the possibility of perfection within the discipline of the classical precepts. His plots were not complex; but his characters, with their conflict of passion and will power, were very human in their weaknesses and strengths. His expositions were simple and dramatic, his situations real, his materials eminently suited to his technique. The most famous of his plays today is *Phèdre* (1677), though it lacks the serenity of the later *Esther* (1689) and *Athalie* (1691). *Bérénice* (1670), *Iphigénie* (1674), and *Andromaque* (1667), *Britannicus* (1669), *Bajazet* (1672), and *Mithridate* (1673) —his best and most well-known plays—illustrate both his subject-matter and his concern with heroic characters. In a closed room, in a closed situation, elegantly dressed characters explore themselves and their reactions in minute detail, the conflict generally centering upon the opposition between love seen as personal desire and duty seen as social and/or political obligation. The suffering is internal, revealed in long speeches somewhat like arias, the revelation well-reasoned and controlled, so that the whole becomes an abstract moment of experience. It is a theatrical phenomenon exactly suited to the exquisite self-consciousness of Racine's audiences. The continuing popularity of his plays on the French stage, even though styles of playwriting have changed phenomenally since his day, attests to their intrinsic vitality and dramatic effectiveness.

Corneille and Racine were the greatest writers of tragedy in the seventeenth century; only Corneille's younger brother, Thomas, and Georges de Scudéry deserve to be mentioned with them.

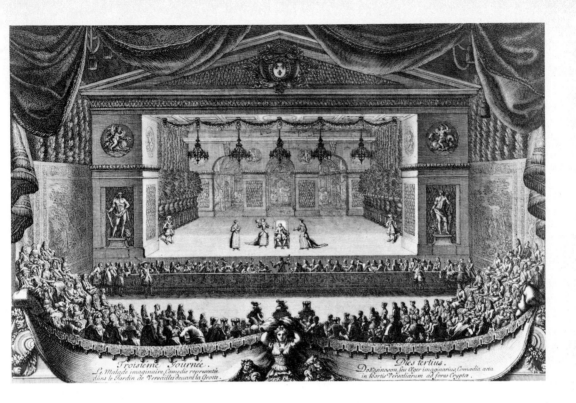

Troisiéme Journée.
Le Malade imaginaire, Comedie representée
dans le Jardin de Versailles devant la Grotte.

Dies tertius.
Ægrotus imaginarius, Comedia acta
in Hortis Versaliarum ad fores Cryptæ.

OPEN-AIR PERFORMANCE AT VERSAILLES
A court performance at Versailles of Molière's *The Imaginary Invalid* in 1674. The king is seated down front center, and the orchestra, which played chiefly for the elaborate interludes accompanying the performance, is placed just below the stage. (Harvard Theatre Collection)

Molière—consummate comedian

Of the writers of comedy only one name is of real importance—that of Molière: writer, actor, producer, manager, director. He himself was a frustrated tragedian. In fact, his Paris debut before the king was almost a fiasco because he presented a poor production of an early tragedy of Corneille—*Nicomède;* the day was saved by appending one of Molière's own little farces, *The Love-Sick Physician.* Molière once tried to write a tragedy, a grand heroic drama called *Don Garcia of Navarre* (1661), which failed miserably after seven performances; Racine's one venture into

comedy, *The Litigants* (1661), was not so bad as this. (Corneille, too, had written several successful comedies for Montdory's company, including *Mélite,* as well as a somewhat later one, *The Liar,* in 1643.)

Molière's consummate skill in comedy was the end product of a development which had refined the medieval farce, added a love interest from the pastorals, incorporated the incidents and tricks of Italian comedy, and used the Spanish technique of developing plot complications within the play itself. Molière's plays perfectly amalgamate all these elements; the ingredient that proves him a genius, however, was his ability to create dramatic action by the effect of events on characters which in turn cause other events to occur. He proved that tricks and intrigue are not necessarily, as Corneille once said, the mainsprings of comedy; but that in comedy, no less than in tragedy, human psychology can be the mainspring. In addition, he had an intense and sympathetic awareness of human character and of society; he drew from life, as it were, and so produced the highest form of comedy.

In fact, Molière is probably the supreme practitioner for all time of the social comedy called "comedy of character," a pinnacle all the more remarkable in that he achieved it practically single-handed, and did so with clarity, grace, and good humor. For its operation, social comedy requires a settled social order with widely accepted mores and collective sanctions; the France of the Roi Soleil was a perfect setting. The province of comedy is to raise critical laughter by the application of reasonableness and common sense; Molière was uniquely fitted to the task by his personal qualities. In the comedy of character which he brought to perfection he presents the ethical points of sanity and reason by selecting certain characters and situations which will demonstrate ridiculous incongruity with sane social standards. It is to the credit of the king that he was always on the side of Molière's endeavor to explode the pretensions of French society, even in the case of *Tartuffe* (1664), which raised a storm of protest and was barred from public presentation for five years after it was written and had its initial performance. When the play was published in 1669, Molière wrote a preface for it which ended:

Nothing admonishes the majority of people better than the portrayal of their faults.
To expose vices to the ridicule of all the world is a severe blow to them. Reprehensions are easily suffered, but not so ridicule.

People do not mind being wicked; but they object to being made ridiculous.

The society which fostered Molière was a fertile field for his probe, and many were the absurdities which he punctured. One of his earliest efforts after his return to Paris pointed up the pretensions of a set of ultra-refined ladies and gentlemen of the court. That was *The Ridiculous Precious Ladies* in 1659. Discretion prompted him to make the silly young ladies of the play provincials and not members of the court, but the point of the satire was not lost on his audience. The immediate objects of his wit were discomfited, but everyone else laughed so heartily that some reform was effected.

Molière had always been a great admirer of the Italian commedia; he had, indeed, taken lessons in acting from Tiberio Fiorillo, the famous Scaramouche. He evidently saw cosmic comic types in the commedia characters, for he adapted them time and again for use in his own dramatis personae. Many of his characters are echoes of the commedia. He learned to know the commedia well during his travels in the provinces and during the years when Italian comedians shared the theatres of the Petit Bourbon and the Palais Royal with him. The Arnolphe of his *The School for Wives* (1662) is redolent of Pantalone, and his many physicians reminiscent of The Doctor of the commedia. With this foundation, or inspiration, Molière's characters emerge as fully rounded, interesting people, lovable or detestable as they reveal themselves. Molière is a master of comic characterization and this is the measure of his genius. The gallery of his memorable characters is a long one, from the Mascarille of his first important work, *The Blunderer* (1655), to the affected ladies, Madélon and Cathos; the various Sganarelles; Ariste in *The School for Husbands* (1666); Alceste of *The Misanthrope* (1666); Harpagon of *The*

Miser (1668); the ladies of *The Learned Ladies*
(1672); and Argan of *The Imaginary Invalid*
(1673), which role Molière was playing at the
time of his death.

Molière's greatest achievement—had he
accomplished nothing else, he might stand
foremost in French letters for this alone—
was that he raised comedy to the stature of
tragedy. Finding a formless and raucous
mass of farce, street entertainment, and acrobatics, he developed a supple and effective
comedy of character which pleased men of

good taste everywhere. Though he laughed at
human nature with its frailties and stupid-
ities, he also knew people thoroughly and
loved them well. Keen observation, coupled
with love and insight, made him perhaps the
greatest writer in the comic vein that the
world has ever seen.

Command performances at court

Molière wrote for the court as well as for
the public theatre. Plays given as parts of

the elaborate court productions also included his keen observation of society; however, they almost invariably incorporated much singing and dancing into the performance. These plays were written upon the demand of the king. Noteworthy in this genre are Molière's *The Bores* (1661), *Monsieur de Pourceaugnac* (1669), and *The Would-Be Gentleman* (1670), in which the inimitable M. Jourdain discovers that he has been speaking prose all his life. *Tartuffe* itself had been a part of the court entertainment *The Pleasures of the Enchanted Island*, given at Versailles in 1664.

Molière was not alone in producing these court performances; both Corneille and Racine, as well as many of lesser note, contributed. Often playwrights collaborated in these productions: Corneille, Rotrou, and three others, upon command of Richelieu, wrote *The Comedy of the Tuilleries* in 1638; Molière, at a somewhat later date, collaborated with Corneille, Quinault, and various musicians. Even the major playwrights of the French seventeenth century were at the beck and call of royalty. The drama, as were all things, was subject to the court.

Playhouses expeditious or elaborate

The court was exceedingly important, also, in providing places for playing; almost all of the playhouses were built and operated by royal permission or upon royal command.

There were three general categories of French theatres in the seventeenth century: the temporary ones, those converted from tennis courts, and the permanent ones built for continuing dramatic performances. Of temporary theatres, there were two types: those erected at fairs, and those built for court performances.

The stages of the fair theatres varied from primitive platforms on trestles to rather elaborate platforms and sets constructed by the wealthier mountebanks for the performances of their hired companies. These mountebanks were the traveling salesmen of the seventeenth century, peddling medicines and cures of one kind and another much in the manner of the medicine-show pitchmen of our own American pioneer days. They traveled from town to town, setting up their platforms in squares, marketplaces, or, in Paris, at the great fairs of St. Laurent and St. Germain. The dramatic performancees were come-ons for their pitch. The lesser entrepreneurs were content to present jugglers, tumblers, and dancers; the wealthier ones often presented complete dramatic performancees. Even so important a commedia company as I Gelosi was brought into France by a mountebank. The acting was often of a high order of excellence; the fair actors frequently graduated to the regular theatres, or alternated between them.

The acting spaces these presentations utilized were all open-air arrangements, with the audience standing around three sides. The ruder sort of platform was backed only by a curtain; the more ornate might use a roofed superstructure with a pictorial backing. In any event, the platform served not only for the dramatic performance, but also for the sales platform of the producing quack.

The other type of temporary playhouse current in the seventeenth century was that used for court performances. These were built from time to time, at great expense, to house the single performances of court spectacles. This sort of temporary playhouse was the French counterpart of the court playing spaces designed by the Englishman Inigo Jones, and of many similar production places in the great houses of Italy. In addition to temporarily converted indoor spaces, the nobility, as in Spain and Italy, often spon-

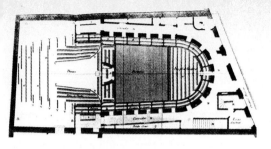

PLAN OF THE THEATRE FRANÇAIS
This is the plan of the first theatre built for
the Comédie Française. The part of the auditorium nearest the stage is provided with
backless benches; part of the auditorium
floor is reserved for standees. The boxes
encircle the pit, and space for seating on
the stage is provided. (Yale Theatrical Prints
Collection)

sored great outdoor festivals which frequently included drama. It was at such a
festival at Chambord that *The Would-Be
Gentleman* had its first performance.

More permanent were the tennis-court
theatres, some of which housed dramatic
performances through most of the century.
By the end of the sixteenth century, it is
estimated that there were several hundred
halls of this sort constructed for the *jeu de
paume*, or "game of the palm" in Paris
alone. This game, unlike today's lawn tennis,
was played with a short-handled racquet on
an indoor court with galleries for the spectators. It had enjoyed a long and feverish
popularity with many segments of the population, particularly the court. The Valois
monarchs had been exceedingly fond of the
game, and the first Bourbon king, Henry IV,
was a devoted player. But he was the last
of the French kings to be really an expert
at the game, and it declined in popularity
after his death. Thus the long, narrow,
roofed-over courts with their side galleries
were left available for other purposes. Acting
companies seeking shelter found the tennis
courts expedient. They would erect a simple
"shelf for acting" at one end, use the galleries for spectators, and put benches around
the sides and down the length of the floor.
Such converted tennis courts in the Rue

Michel-le-Comte and the Quartier Saint-Mar-
tin were the early homes of Montdory's
company. Montdory's final refuge in the
Marais was just such a converted tennis
court; this house continued in use until 1673,
when the company was merged with that of
the Palais Royal. Such also was the house
near the Tour de Nesle in which Molière's
company first opened on New Year's Day of
1644. Functional but not elaborate, these
tennis-court playhouses served a real need in
the growing French theatre.

A few permanent theatres also housed
plays in Molière's day. The earliest of these
was, of course, the Hôtel de Bourgogne, built
by the Confrèrie de la Passion in 1548 and
used throughout the next century. Its construction did not differ from that of the
tennis-court theatres. The auditorium was
long and narrow, with two galleries running
along the walls and the stage across one
end. By putting together clues from various
sources, it is possible to estimate that the
interior dimensions of the space were probably about one hundred two feet long by
thirty-seven feet wide. That the flat floor
was for standees only is attested by numerous prohibitions at various times against the
putting of stools or benches thereon.

Rectangular construction was used also
in the king's private theatre in the Petit
Bourbon Palace attached to the Louvre. This
huge *salle* was approximately two hundred
twenty-one feet by forty-five feet, and prior
to 1635 was used (after the manner of great
halls everywhere) for various festival performances. In just such a manner did the
visiting I Gelosi perform there about the
year 1577. Louis XIII is said to have made a
"theatre" in this room in 1635, probably by
having erected at one end the ubiquitous
"shelf for acting" that was by then widespread in the converted tennis courts. The
floor was left free for the accommodation of

the king and his party, an arrangement which became the custom in subsequent years, although additional seats could be and on occasion were set on the floor. In 1645 (after Richelieu had opened his theatre in the Palais Cardinal), Louis XIV and his new minister, Cardinal Mazarin, had Giacomo Torelli install elaborate machinery, and probably also the proscenium arch to mask the machinery as seen in a popular engraving of the king watching a performance in the Petit Bourbon. This was the theatre which Louis XIII gave to the Italian comedians, and which Molière later shared with them. It was pulled down in 1660, on the sudden order of the Superintendent of Royal Buildings, and Molière, after two years' residence, was ousted without warning. He was able to salvage the boxes and fittings but not the scenes and machines which the famous Torelli had designed. (Torelli's successor, Vigarani, claimed these for the Hall of Machines which he was then building at the Tuileries, and was awarded them, but instead of using them he had them burned. This, apparently, was done out of jealousy, in the hope of destroying all trace of his predecessor.)

Louis XIV gave the homeless Molière and his troupe the theatre in the Palais Royal. This magnificent building was erected by Richelieu as his own residence, and had been called the Palais Cardinal before it reverted to the crown upon Richelieu's death. The original private theatre it contained had been extensively remodeled at great expense, and the cardinal had inaugurated the new house with a spectacular performance of *Miramé* in January, 1641. It seated about six hundred people. At one end of the long rectangle was the stage, with a proscenium arch topped by Richelieu's coat-of-arms. This was the first proscenium arch built into a theatre in France—and for good reason, for behind

it were a front curtain and an elaborate Italianate setting. From the stage there were six broad steps leading down to the floor of the auditorium. At the opposite end of the hall was a kind of lobby formed by three large arcades. The floor of the hall rose from the stage to the opposite end by means of twenty-seven low, broad stone steps on which wooden seats were placed. Along each of the two sides of the hall were two decorated galleries. The rich appointments and the stage machinery were of Italian inspiration. After the property reverted to the king upon the death of Richelieu in 1642, it was used intermittently for court entertainment until Molière and his company moved into it in 1660. It was repaired and redecorated to receive the Molière company. In the plan for what is evidently this redecoration appear the open *parterre* for standing patrons, the seated "amphitheatre" with benches, and the flattened-V shape of the line of boxes—a pattern which was to remain in French theatre architecture for many years, and which differed considerably from the Italian opera house construction elsewhere prevalent in Europe. Then, in 1670, it was extensively rebuilt to house the complicated stage machinery similar to that which Vigarani had destroyed ten years before. *Psyche* was the first spectacular production with the new machines, Molière having moved the play to his theatre after its initial production for the court at the Tuileries. When Molière died in 1673, the composer Lully claimed and received the Palais Royal for his new Academy of Music, and Molière's troupe was ousted. The building burned down in 1763.

When the master designer, Torelli, who lived and worked in Paris from 1645 to 1659, returned to Italy, Cardinal Mazarin had Vigarani appointed court decorator, and it was he who constructed the aptly named Hall of Machines at the Tuileries. It was commis-

sioned to be ready for the festivities surrounding the marriage of Louis XIV in 1660. The house itself was a modified horseshoe, with seating in the parterre and in a gallery to the rear. Its great stage was thirty-two feet wide at the proscenium, and one hundred thirty-two feet deep. It was equipped with the most intricate and expensive of machinery for producing the elaborate court spectacles then in vogue.

When Molière's death in 1673 allowed court musician Lully to claim the Palais Royal for a royal opera house, the Molière company was forced to move to the Théâtre de Guénégaud, newly built as an opera house by the eccentric Marquis de Sourdéac. It had a large and fully equipped stage with a plethora of machinery. The Molière company, under the astute actor LaGrange, and with the financial support of Molière's widow, arranged to purchase from the Marquis his then new but currently unused theatre. It was this well-equipped house which sheltered the first national theatre in the Western world, formed when Louis XIV united the two then remaining Parisian companies (the Italians excepted) into the Comédie Française in October of 1680, giving to them the sole right to perform French plays in the capital.

A new theatre was built for the Comédie and opened in 1689, remaining in use until 1782. It was designed by François D'Orbay, and followed the pattern usual in Franch theatre construction, paying little or no attention to the developments of the Italian opera house plan. It had no royal box, but provision was made for seating on the stage proper, as had been the long-time custom in France. There were two tiers of boxes, with nineteen boxes to a tier, and on the third level an open gallery equipped with benches. The apron of the stage extended twelve feet beyond the proscenium arch, and the floor of the auditorium was divided into three parts: the orchestra pit, with benches for ladies to each side of a protracted center area used by the musicians; the standing pit, reserved for men; and the so-called amphitheatre, or sloping rear section of the floor, which was equipped with benches. Though the boxes tended to be small and dark, the structure was the epitome of French ideas in theatre architecture. Its capacity was about thirteen hundred people.

Thus the playhouse of France in the seventeenth century, begun with the simple stage of the medieval period, developed into a structure which could use the wonders of Italianate scenery in its productions but which maintained a traditionally French arrangement of the actor-audience relationship.

Designers seek complex settings

French settings in the seventeenth century ranged from the simplest to the most complex. Yet it must be remembered that the tendency was toward complexity because of the pervasive influence of the court's love for spectacle and because of the ascendency of the opera. Some of what seem to us today the simplest of Molière's staging problems were often most intricate in their day.

The fair theatres and the provincial companies used, of course, a minimum of settings and properties. Often an undecorated back curtain sufficed for the simple platform stage, though many prints show curious elaborations of this after the manner of the medieval doorways in the production of classical plays. Sometimes the back curtains were painted with landscapes, street scenes, or other pictorial representations. The necessity of portability, however, always limited the possibilities of elaboration on these temporary stages.

Another curious remnant of the Middle Ages was the early seventeenth-century stage of the Hôtel de Bourgogne. Sketches preserved in *Notes for the Decoration of the Plays Presented by the King's Comedians, Reported to His Majesty* show how the chief designer of the house and author of the *Notes*, Laurent Mahelot, produced multiple settings curiously reminiscent of the religious plays of the preceding century. Many of these were for the multiple settings of plays by

Alexandre Hardy, wherein four or five different localities were placed upstage and at the sides, with the central open area being used, as it was in the Middle Ages, as the general acting area. For *Hercules,* a tragedy by Rotrou produced in 1634, the stage showed a practical temple of Jupiter, a practical mountain with a full-grown tree, a funeral chamber, and a tomb. Like the medieval maître des feyntes, the stage manager of this house was charged with all kinds of effects: lightning, wind, thunder, flames, fireworks, simulated deaths, ascents and descents, as well as an occasional hellfire.

It has been calculated that the stage area was about thirty-two feet wide and twenty-eight and a half feet deep, with no front curtain prior to the renovations of 1647, when a ceiling beam was installed to carry one. Recent researches reveal that the earliest stage settings of this house were of the simplest sort—a backdrop and a line of curtained enclosures down each of the two sides through which the actors emerged to the central acting area. This arrangement must have been similar to the curtained doorways of the old Terence engravings. The early stage also had an upper level after the manner of the old mysteries. The balcony stage could be used to increase the number of mansions, or to provide an operating platform for special effects. It was also sup-

TORELLI DESIGN SHOWING SCENE CHANGE
This interesting pair of prints shows a basic principle for transforming scenes. Notice that the downstage décor, consisting of wing flats and borders, remains constant; compare the doorways and urns in the two sketches. The upstage flats forming the perspective and the backdrop, are removed, so that a new backdrop, a sea effect, and a cloud machine can appear. The costumes are also interesting, especially the animated centaur in the first scene. (Harvard Theatre Collection)

plied with a railing and with traps. The stage floor itself had traps. A similar arrangement at the Marais, though with measurements somewhat larger than those of the Hôtel de Bourgogne, made the increasing complexity of production feasible there as well. In its latter days the Marais became famous for its machine plays, while the Hôtel de Bourgogne, swept up in the neoclassic tide, concentrated on building a reputation for the production of tragedy. In this period the multiple setting was replaced by an unlocalized set scene featuring painted representations of temples and palaces.

The early plays of Molière, given on a public stage which was also used to seat some privileged members of the audience, had the most conventional of settings. Folding screens, painted to represent stylized houses, were grouped to show a street or square in perspective. The actors issued from the houses to center stage and performed all scenes, whether domestic quarrels, love-making, or consultations with doctors, in this simulated out-of-doors. The street scene in comedy had a long tradition behind it. It had been a convention from Menander and Plautus to Machiavelli and the commedia. This particular arrangement of folding screens may have been influenced by the frame cubicles used earlier at the Hôtel de Bourgogne, which were, in turn, outgrowths of the medieval mysteries. It also, no doubt, served a very practical purpose in a theatre shared by Molière and the Italian comedians.

When Richelieu opened his newly redecorated theatre in 1641, the stage setting was an elaborated architectural structure in perspective after the Italian style. It was criticized for its elaborateness as detracting from the play, but the criticism affected Richelieu not at all; he added to the performance, on subsequent occasions, extravagant ballet interludes.

ELABORATE DESIGNS FOR COURT PERFORMANCES
Right, one of a number of changing settings designed by Torelli for Corneille's spectacle-play *Andromeda* in 1649. Above, an imposing series of wing flats and borders, with an architecturally designed backcloth, the work of Carlo Vigarani, son of Gaspare, who was Torelli's successor in the French court theatre. The design is for a production of *Alcestis* in 1675. (Stockholm Nationalmuseum)

This interpolation of what would seem to us extraneous material—the more so because of the period's insistence upon the classical unities—became more and more fashionable and sought after. When Molière was ordered, in 1661, to produce a play for Fouquet, the minister of finance, to honor the king, he wrote *The Bores*. The play began with the spouting of twenty natural fountains, during which a large shell opened and an actress, dressed as a naiad, emerged to speak the prologue. *The Would-be Gentleman* was regularly concluded with an elaborate Turkish ballet in which the king himself danced; *The Imaginary Invalid* concluded with an equally elaborate burlesque ballet; *The Misanthrope* was presented with ballet interludes for which the scene was changed. Far from objecting to these interpolations, Molière attempted to preserve the elaborateness of the court presentations when he

moved the productions to his own theatre.

Indeed, not only Molière, but others of his contemporaries, wrote many machine plays designed to exhibit the wonders of the intricately equipped stages designed by Torelli, Vigarani, and their copyists. One of the most elaborate of these was Molière's *Psyche*, designed by Vigarani, and presented first at the Hall of Machines. Among its many wonders was Venus descending from the heavens in a great machine, a magnificent courtyard with a resplendent palace, and a sea of fire. It was to produce this play that Molière spent a great deal of money reequipping the Palais Royal. Though the script seems thin stuff to us today, it was extremely successful in its own day.

Machines and chariots were an integral part, also, of Molière's *Amphitryon*, and the elaborate staging of Corneille's *Andromeda*, as designed by Torelli, was almost incredible.

Mountains appeared and disappeared; gardens sprouted and died; waves engulfed the scene and receded to reveal a palace, which in turn dissolved into a temple. All of these changes, being a part of the show, were wrought in full view of the audience. Extensive substage and overhead machinery was necessary for these effects, and the complexity of their operation does not need to be mentioned. The stage designers were accomplished engineers as well as artists.

The arrival of Giacomo Torelli in Paris in 1645 had brought, for the first time, the wonders of the Italianate scenery to the French capital. Not that changeable scenes had not hitherto been seen on the French stage, but Torelli set up a mechanized system of wheels, levers, ropes, pulleys, and counterweights which allowed elaborations and the spectacular illusion of scenes changing while they were being played. And the substage and overhead machinery which he installed allowed for large-scale scenes of many and varied pieces to move simultaneously without any mechanisms being visible. It was a technical revolution which was very expensive but which every theatre, as they had the means, attempted to install. Torelli was called by his contemporaries "the Great Sorcerer"—and it is easy to see why. Vigarani, who followed him to Paris, used the same systems in the *Salle des Machines*, but increased them in size and complexity.

With the presence of so much spectacle and dancing there was, of course, much music at the performances, and most of it was specially composed for each event. The astute Lully, who enjoyed an almost complete monopoly on music in the court of Louis XIV, composed practically everything for the court performances, including the music for many of Molière's comedy ballets. At one point Molière incurred his enmity by having Charpentier compose the music for *The Imaginary Invalid*, with the consequence that this play was not first performed at Versailles as had been intended, but at the Palais Royal. At one time it seems that the orchestra was installed at the back of the house, but the impracticality of such an arrangement led to its being seated immediately in front of the stage, the present arrangement for musical shows.

Thus, stage decoration in the seventeenth century was of all types and kinds, but the ultimate aim of actors, producers, and audience was always to arrive at the most elaborate and spectacular effects which could be achieved.

Costumes marked by contemporary styles

Costuming on the French stage of the seventeenth century was not dissimilar in type to that of the Elizabethan period. For the most part contemporary costume was worn, save for the kinds of characters to whom this would be completely unsuitable—historical, fantastic, and allegorical figures.

Since actors supplied the costumes they wore from their individual purses, the richness of the dress depended on the affluence of the wearer. Some relief from this expense was afforded through the intrepidity of a M. Bourgeois, a Parisian merchant, who about the middle of the century set up what must certainly have been the first of all costume rental agencies. In addition, there was a lively business in secondhand clothes in the market district of Les Halles near the Hôtel de Bourgogne, and it is likely that many an actor acquired cast-off finery from these merchants.

In 1682, the learned Jesuit Claude-François Menestrier wrote a treatise on ballet, *On the Production of Music Ancient and Modern*, in which he advocated historical accuracy in costuming, keeping always in mind that for dancers, not only the ensemble effect must be carefully observed, but also the individual costume must be functional. His careful descriptions of allegorical costuming are reminiscent of the Inigo Jones designs for the Stuart masques. An examination of costume and stage sketches of the period shows that, in actuality, costuming on the opera and court stages was an adaptation of contemporary dress with a flavor of period and place. Appended comment often reveals that these costumes tended to be made of the richest possible materials with a maximum amount of ornamentation. Particularly lavish are the costumes designed by Jean Bérain for the Paris Opera in the last quarter of the century.

The popular theatres carried over, so far as their finances permitted, the splendid costuming of court spectacle and opera to dazzle the eyes of their public.

A JEAN BERAIN DESIGN
This highly ornate design, with its cupids and cloud machine, was made by the talented Jean Bérain for a production of *Hesione* at the Paris Opera in 1701. It is typical of the lavishness of French taste in scene design. The central figure has descended in a "cloud machine"—a popular contrivance invented in the Renaissance. (Stockholm Nationalmuseum)

The Italian commedia, of course, preserved much of the original commedia costuming, although as time went on these costumes, too, bowed to contemporary taste and took on contemporary touches. It is interesting to note that in the staging of his early comedies (those written for production in the provinces, and now largely lost) Molière retained the masks of the commedia parts from which his characters were derived.

Since long, full wigs were much the fashion for men, they were generally worn on the stage, whatever the character. There is a curiously amusing portrait of Molière himself as Caesar, in a full-bottomed wig crowned by copious laurel leaves—no doubt artificial. The portrait was painted by his friend Mignard and is one of the few truly authentic pictures of the master (page 187).

Since makeup was a prized and devious weapon of at least the feminine half of the society who witnessed the plays, there is little question that it was used on the stage as well. It is probable, however, that actors used it only when required by their parts to alter their appearances materially. They were no doubt schooled in the art of makeup by the Italians, who had perfected its use some years earlier.

Thus, though there were some indications of at least an interest in historical accuracy, the predominant costume of Molière's theatre mirrored the dress of the times, which was in itself widely varied, generally richly decorated, and highly colored—theatrical without being itself of the theatre.

Actors indebted to the Italians

It is of special interest to note that the greatest playwrights in both France and England were first of all actors. Both Molière and Shakespeare began in the theatre as actors; indeed, Molière ended his days as an actor. Most of his contemporary fame rested upon this facet of his ability. Though Shakespeare eventually gave up acting, he spent all of his working life in the theatre. No doubt for both Shakespeare and Molière this close and practical knowledge of what would work on the stage and what would not enabled them to achieve a pinnacle of greatness that might not otherwise have been possible. They were different, it is true, in their views of life—the Englishman's genius was larger, more comprehensive, more sympathetic; he did not have the satiric bent that is evident in all of Molière's work. But then their respective societies were different and the theatre is in large measure a reflection of the society which produces it. To both of them, however, the art of acting was at least as important as that of writing plays—if not more important. When Molière, the year before his death, was proposed for election to the Academy—the condition being that he must renounce his profession of acting—he declined the honor saying, "I will not insult a profession which I love, and to which I am so materially indebted, by purchasing personal advantages at the cost of throwing a slur upon it."

French actors were subject to a constant influence that was not available to those in England: Italian commedia players were almost continuously performing in Paris and other parts of France. With these players, acting was a highly skilled and professional calling, and Molière had a part of his training with Fiorilli, one of the best of the commedia actors. A great deal of the credit for transforming native French actors from mere jugglers and rope dancers to performers skilled in characterization and projection belongs to the Italian companies that toured in France.

Actors of the early French companies in Paris assumed characters taken from the commedia repertoire. In the company at the Hôtel de Bourgogne Gros-Guillaume played Pantalone parts; Gaultier-Garguille, those of The Doctor; and Turlupin, the Harlequin roles. The Players of the Prince of Orange, whose leading player was Montdory, had Jadot as their Doctor, and Jodelet as a Harlequin. Throughout the century, the commedia influence was to be a potent one.

Another great difference between French and English acting companies was that in France, from the first, women played the women's parts and there was no particular prejudice against the practice. There was one exception, however; it was the custom for men, using falsetto voice, to play the roles of character women. Alizon early played these parts with Montdory; Beauval was hired by Molière for the same kind of parts. It is said that the practice was instituted because French actresses, whatever their age or personal appearance, had to be thought of as young and beautiful in order to keep their status. Whatever the reason, we can judge the effectiveness of the practice from

EARLY ACTORS AT THE HOTEL DE BOURGOGNE
Above, Agnan Sarat, here in a farce with a milkmaid and Harlequin, was a very popular farce player. The Italian commedia characters were a continuing influence throughout this period. Right, the most famous of all the French farce players were this trio: Turlupin, Gaultier-Garguille, and Gros-Guillaume. Each essayed roles in serious drama as well, the first being Henri le Grand (or Belleville, as he called himself when playing serious plays), the second Hugues Guéru (Fléchelles), the third Robert Guérin. It was in their farce roles that they were most popular. Turlupin wore the mask and costume of the Italian commedia Brighella; the trademark of Gaultier-Garguille was a pointed beard and a black cap; Gros-Guillaume made the most of his portliness by wearing two belts, one low and one high, and powdered his round face. When he died in 1648 it was said that "farce came down with him." (Bibliothèque Nationale; Harvard Theatre Collection)

the delight with which modern audiences greet Charley's Aunt, though this is frankly a masquerade which the spectators share and so cannot have quite the same effect as serious female impersonation. The women were almost without exception married to actors who were also members of the company. Usually the couple was hired as a

unit. Sometimes it was the woman who was sought and the husband came along as a necessary adjunct; sometimes it was the other way around. Though most of the women on the stage were married, they were invariably called "Mademoiselle," using sometimes their own surnames, sometimes those of their husbands.

The men usually assumed stage names. Molière was legally J. B. Poquelin; Duparc was René Berthelot; Montfleury was Zacharie Jacob; and the long list of actors whose stage names began with "Belle" or "Beau" (beautiful)—Bellerose, Beauchateau, for example—evidences the belief that there was much in a name. Sometimes, but rarely, the men used their own names, as did Joseph Béjart and LaGrange.

Companies of shareholders

The acting companies were closely knit and hard-working units. All persons designated as "actors" were shareholders in the enterprise; other functionaries received fixed salaries. Each company started with a fixed number of shares; the youngest and least efficient members were awarded a fourth of a share; the intermediate class had half a share; mature and leading actors had each a full share. In addition to his share or part thereof, each actor received a small remittance to pay for the expense of lighting and heating his dressing room. The division of the income to the shareholders was made after each performance, every player having the right to be present. Three of these were designated treasurer, secretary, and controller. To them fell the actual work. The first administered the reserve fund which paid fees, expenses, and debts; the second kept the records of payments to actors who held shares; the third, one might say, audited the accounts of the other two.

The paid functionaries, whose salaries were by the day, the week, or the month, and the monies for which were subtracted from income before the shares were divided, included several people—the porter, the ticket seller, the box openers, and the door keepers. Outside employees included a tallow chandler, a printer, and a bill sticker. Nonacting employees for the stage proper included a copyist, who wrote out the parts and acted as prompter and archivist for the company; a stage manager, who might also, on occasion, play small parts; and a designer, who sometimes worked with a mechanic and who not only produced all the scenery for the plays but decorated the auditorium as well. He had to provide his own candle snuffers, and could claim all the candle ends as a supplement to his income.

The playwright was sometimes a shareholding actor, as was Molière. When the playwright was not an actor or a regular member of the company, he was sometimes awarded a share for the run of his play; sometimes he was given a flat payment. He usually helped to cast and direct his play; after it had been accepted by the company, they assembled to hear him read it. The distribution of parts was by mutual agreement, although it might be assumed that in many instances the final decision was far from mutual.

Rehearsals began after the actors felt sure of their lines. The playwright, along with the more skilled members of the company, worked out the stage business and the interpretation of the parts.

A final, and very important office in the company, was that of the "orator," who was essentially the company manager. He called the meetings of the company, composed the poster for the coming attractions, and addressed the audience at each performance, initially quieting the assembled crowd and then attempting by his cleverly worded epilogue speech to entice the spectators back for the next offering of the company.

Players were trained within the company itself, or new players were recruited from the provincial companies or other Parisian troupes. It was the custom, upon the retirement of one of the older actors, that the recruit taking his place pay him a pension. The company at the Hôtel de Bourgogne had a specially established pension plan; Molière's troupe eventually set up one also. Another interesting custom was, that upon the death of one of the troupe, the remaining members made a sizable payment to the nearest living relative as a token of appreciation.

FRENCH TRAVELING ACTORS
In such a troupe as that pictured here in an old print Molière and the Béjarts traveled in the provinces of seventeenth-century France for twelve years.

Though there was no great vogue for companies of child actors, as there had been in England, at least one of these had some small success—The Little Actors of the Dauphin under the enterprising direction of an ex-organist from Troyes, one Raisin by name. From its ranks came one of the great actors of the century, Michel Boyron, called Baron. Early an orphan of two Hôtel de Bourgogne players, he was for some years a member of Molière's troupe and grew to be a widely renowned performer, especially in tragedy. Floridor, who acted first with the Marais and then at the Hôtel de Bourgogne, seems to have had a quiet, authoritative style in tragedy which won the admiration of Molière.

But the approved style of tragic acting—Baron and Floridor excepted—was a kind of chanting declamation, with great bravura exhibitions at the "tirades" or important passages. Such was the acting of Montfleury, of Bellerose, of Montdory, of Mlle. Champmeslé, and of practically all of the tragedians of the Hôtel de Bourgogne where tragedy was most famous and most successful. Molière was naturally and artistically opposed to this style of playing. He sponsored and trained his company in a more natural delivery. He abjured attitudinizing and exaggerated delivery and had his comedies played in an unaffected and lively way. This more natural style worked well in comedy, but the prevailing preferences for the heroic style in tragedy made it impossible to transfer his new techniques to those materials. Not until almost fifty years had passed after the death of Molière was Baron (returning at age sixty-seven from a thirty-year retirement) able to demonstrate that a more thoughtful and "natural" delivery was desirable and effective in tragedy.

By the close of the century the economic position of actors was secure. Many of them had gained wealth and fame; their social position was often enviable, though anomalous. Honors were frequently their lot; they received money grants, special annuities, and such distinctions as the king himself standing godfather to the firstborn son of Molière and Armande Béjart. Often their professional association had a lifetime's duration, as with Molière and the Béjart family: Madeleine, Joseph, Geneviève, Louis, and the young Armande. Many of them lived most circumspectly; yet, as we have said, the church classed them as infamous, and the priest sent for at Molière's death refused him the last rites of the church because he was an actor. His scant and secret burial was in church grounds only because the king himself interposed.

Summary

The greatest period of French theatre coincided, as did those of England and Spain, with a period of great national consciousness. In fact, France in the seventeenth century had an exquisite self-consciousness founded upon its devotion to the tenets of "Right Reason." It reinterpreted the ancients, using classic materials in its tragedies but actually creating a new genre of neoclassic tragedy which might be called "the tragedy of sensibility," or "the tragedy of manners," since its basis was controlled behavior: the intellectual adjustment of the passions of man to the requirements of a social code. Expressed in exalted poetry, these tragedies form the literary heritage of the French. Molière achieved consummate expression in comedy, bringing that form (as he saw his mission) to the same respect and admiration which tragedy enjoyed. The achievement in both forms was possible because of the intellectual and social climate of the times, and the influence of Corneille, Racine, and Molière fathered a host of copyists long after the world that produced them had ceased to exist. But the universals with which they dealt place their works high in the ranks of world achievement in the drama.

Seventeenth century French theatre established women as professional actresses on an equal footing with men. It initiated revolutionary acting styles. It developed a system for the protection of retired actors. It achieved a theatre architecture which was the synthesis of well-established practices in the actor-audience relationship, maintaining to the end of the century and longer the old practice (even in new theatre buildings) of a part of the audience standing to watch the performance.

In the field of production, it brought the proscenium arch with its picture-frame stage into general use, and popularized the conception of the audience viewing a series of scenes which changed as they watched. By the end of the seventeenth century, French theatre exhibited practically all the attributes of modern theatre, in essence at least; surely, it set a production style which would not be replaced for almost two centuries. It developed elaborate staging effects and multitudinous quantities of machinery to operate them. It emphasized extravagant costuming, and an integration of song and dance into the performance. Finally, of course, it saw the beginning of the first national theatre in the Western world, the Comédie Française. The effulgence of the Roi Soleil created a brilliant society. Theatre, which was so much a part of that society, reflected its brilliance.

The Puritan Revolution was fought not only against the king but against theatre. The theatre was never so finally and roundly defeated as the king. The skirmishes and battles were equally protracted and bitter, but the Elizabethan-Jacobean drama was so hardy in its growth and so dear to so many Englishmen that it never completely died. Ordinance after ordinance was passed against stage plays, but there was hardly a year in London from 1642 to 1660 when plays were not being given. The records are full of recurrent raids by the soldiers of Parliament, the seizure of players and their goods, the ransacking of playhouses and their forcible demolition, and the jailing of theatre people. But these records show that the Puritans had not succeeded in destroying theatrical activity.

It is true that dramatic performances were illegal; players were once more branded rogues and vagabonds, as well as suffering the more serious charge of infamy. But incarcerations, floggings, and brandings had no lasting effects. There were always those of the king's party to be played for, always a sizable segment of the population willing to risk inconvenience and prosecution to enjoy theatre. The King's Players had gone with the king to Oxford; other English actors formed the English Company for the Prince of Wales in Paris; others played the English provinces; still others toured the Continent, particularly in Germany and the Netherlands. Some remained in London, to play when and where they could. Parliament was constantly being petitioned in their behalf: Why should these honest artists be deprived of their means of making a living? Why should their families—honest citizens all—suffer deprivation by governmental action? This is the general tenor of all of these petitions; they were of little avail.

Still, at least one of the playhouses seems to have survived intact the depredations of soldiers. The Red Bull escaped all the military wrecking parties and continued in sporadic operation throughout the period of the Commonwealth. In 1661, after the throne had been reestablished, Samuel Pepys writes of attending performances at the Red Bull. The private theatres of Salisbury Court and the Cockpit in Drury Lane, dismantled by the soldiers in 1649, were quickly rehabilitated and continued in use after the Restoration. But the other great playhouses of Jacobean London were effectively destroyed. The Globe and the Blackfriars were both torn down, one in 1644 and the other in 1655, to make way for tenements; the Fortune did not survive the wreckings of 1649. The Hope reverted to bear-baiting, and both bears and house were destroyed in 1655. The great wooden masque house at Whitehall, designed and built by Inigo Jones, was torn down in. 1645; the other Jones-designed theatre at court, the Cockpit, survived but housed no performances until the court was reinstalled.

The theatrical fare presented during the Commonwealth was most likely to be rewritten scenes from the older plays, which were called "drolls," and which were sandwiched between rope dancing, sword tricks, and like secondary fare. Frequently enough, however, whole plays were given, sometimes even new ones, as was the performance of Killigrew's *Claracilla* in 1652 in Gibbon's Tennis Court near Lincoln's Inn Fields. This was, of course, raided, and the performers brought to justice.

During the Commonwealth Gibbon's Tennis Court also housed a performance presented by the devoted adventurer Sir William Davenant. He was responsible for the first legal performance under the Commonwealth, and it is he who figures so largely in Restoration theatre. This thrice-married ex-poet laureate, who in 1639 had been given a patent to build a theatre in London, had fought with the royalist forces. He had been imprisoned in the Tower but was released in 1652. He lost no time in recouping his fortunes by a marriage of convenience, and in making friends with the government in power. By the time he returned from a trip to France late in 1655, he was married to his third wife, and had a sizable theatrical enterprise operating. Taking up residence in Rutland House, he publicly invited, in May 1656, a paying audience to see *The First Day's Entertainment*, a "representation" with music and oratory "after the manner of the Ancients." The careful wording of his publicity was, of course, his evasion of the Puritan ban against "stage plays." The Rutland House performance included a eulogy of the Lord Protector. By September, he was offering, in the hall at Rutland House, the first English opera, *The Siege of Rhodes*, with a minimum of music, no dancing at all, and none of the spectacular mechanical effects that marked Continental operatic presentations. He spent the next year in a series of moves to effect official sanction of public presentations, and by July 1658, his opera was established in the Cockpit in Drury Lane, with new scenes, costumes, and machines—theatre was legally open again in London. He continued with similar presentations, and when it became apparent that the Restoration was inevitable he hurried to Paris to consolidate his position with Charles II, thus becoming one of the two patentees for the London theatres of the Restoration.

Theatre an exclusive entertainment

The theatre of Restoration England was but distantly related to its great predecessor, even though one of its most prominent operators, this same Sir William Davenant, had been a theatre figure prior to the days of the Commonwealth. So agile was he in trimming his bark to the prevailing winds that he became the herald of the new rather than the preserver of the old. Through a series of Machiavellian moves, he effectively killed off all competition and with the courtier Thomas Killigrew established a monopoly of London theatrical activity. This Restoration theatre was by no means the great popular institution which Shakespeare's contemporaries loved; the tide of history had moved beyond the point where such a popular institution was possible. Shakespeare's society had, in spite of a series of dissensions, been largely a homogeneous one, sharing mutual ideals. English society at the time of the Restoration was a deeply divided one—civil war and the Commonwealth had intervened.

Owing their very existence to his majesty, King Charles II, Davenant with his Duke's Company and Killigrew with his King's Company conducted their operations with a view to pleasing the court. If the public were also pleased, well and good. But they were not the main consideration. Restoration audiences were chiefly aristocrats and those pretending to be their associates. Theatre was one of the social activities of a circle brilliantly delineated in Pepys' famous *Diary* —a pleasure-loving, amoral people, contemptuous of what they conceived to be a narrow Puritan view of the world, and determined to enjoy all the sensual aspects of existence. Seemingly unaware that the events of the preceding twenty years had fundamentally changed the structure of the English government—that never again would any monarch be absolute, or irreplaceable— they saw in the return of the Stuarts to the throne a vindication of monarchy. It is also likely that they somehow saw the king as an

English version of the *Roi Soleil*—why not, since they had experienced the effulgence of French society at first hand? But of course, a condition of the return of Charles to England had been that Parliament, not he, would make decisions of policy, a condition amply illustrated three years after Charles' death when the Parliament unseated his Catholic brother James and placed on the throne James' eldest daughter Mary and her husband William of Orange. That singular and bloodless event is known as the Glorious Revolution of 1688.

Meanwhile, the fruits of restored monarchy were to be enjoyed. Charles II was very fond of theatre. He had maintained for a time a company of English players while he was in exile, and he was a frequent spectator at theatrical performances in France, the Netherlands, and Germany. Upon his return to England, he did not confine his attendance to court performances, as his predecessors had done, but went with his favorites to performances at the public theatres where he had a royal box. Such attendance was frequent, and as may be imagined was a significant drawing card for the great and the near-great. Even when the king was not in attendance, the spectators were chiefly of the court party, both ladies and gentlemen in the extravagant dress of the time. People went to be seen quite as much as to see, and a great deal of socializing went on before, after, and during the performance.

Advertising was done by playbills which were posted, thrown into carriages, and delivered at the houses of the gentry. The theatres were opened at one o'clock for performances which began generally at three-thirty, servants being sent to hold seats for their masters since there was no reserved-seat policy. By 1699, performance time had advanced to five o'clock, by 1705 it was five-thirty. The play was always preceded by a series of three "Musicks"; there was music between the acts; and the performance was followed by an afterpiece with music.

The cheapest seats were in the upper gallery (quite the opposite of Shakespeare's house); the most expensive were in the first gallery, or row of boxes. The pit, now provided with backless benches, was the resort of the gallants, the critics, and the poets, and was often the scene of brawls and duels. Theatre police (reminiscent of the Roman custom) were sometimes installed to prevent frays. The royal box was directly opposite the stage, with others on its level being used by court ladies and gentlemen. The more conservative playgoers occupied the middle gallery, which was also in the middle price range. The wearing of "vizard masks" was an affectation of the ladies in the audience, and allowed for ubiquitous circulation of the whores who frequented the playhouses.

Tickets were sold in advance, the usual type being a brass check which indicated the part of the house for which it was issued. Occasionally for special performances printed paper tickets were used. Actors and playwrights were given bone passes for which there was no charge. Gallants attempted, as a matter of sport, to evade the admission price and they often succeeded. It was the custom to make no charge for people who came merely to hear the music and to see the first act of the play; footmen were also admitted to the upper gallery for the fifth act, and were not charged. These privileges were widely abused, and toward the end of the century a "numberer" was installed in one of the boxes, whose duty it was to see that all those who saw the whole play had paid their admission. New plays usually rated double admission prices for their first nights; operas often charged three times as much.

The French custom of seating a selected

portion of the audience on the stage itself did not become a practice in England until the century was almost over, chiefly because Charles II opposed it; once it became entrenched, however, it lasted quite as long as it did in France. The English fops had a special corner of the pit near the stage where they behaved as odiously as their French counterparts and as their Elizabethan forebears had behaved on Shakespeare's stage.

Refreshments (oranges, apples, and sweetmeats) were sold in the theatres by persons holding concessions from the management. Orange Moll at the Theatre Royal was the most famous of these—the actress Nell Gwyn had once been her employee.

Gentlemen of the audience frequented the backstage areas, visited in the dressing rooms of the actors and actresses, and—one must suppose—generally made nuisances of themselves. Actresses were new to the English stage, and were the center of much attention. They were greatly sought after by the young blades, were the recipients of numerous and costly gifts, and moved in the highest social circles; one of them became mistress to the king.

English audiences saw performances of several visiting French acting companies and Italian commedia players (the famous Fiorilli was a member of one of these), both at the Cockpit in Drury Lane and at court. These performances were generally much admired.

Charles II fitted out the Great Hall at Whitehall as a theatre, and there, as well as at the Cockpit-in-Court, he invited a chosen few to see the command performances of native and foreign players. More frequently, however, as noted, he went in person to the public playhouses; the court activities were chiefly balls and maskings.

The Restoration theatre was a place of business, of gossip, of assignation, of style, and, as it often seemed, only incidentally of drama. Like its contemporary French society, this English counterpart was exquisitely self-conscious and self-assured. Events which it chose for a long time to ignore would eventually submerge it in a different pattern.

Neoclassical conventions preside

The Restoration marks the beginning of the neoclassical period in English literature, and as in France the main Greek and Roman influence on the drama was in the writing of tragedy. The works of Shakespeare and his contemporaries were considered to be reprehensible, at the least, for their lack of the classical unities; their plays, when presented in Restoration theatres, were considerably revised and rewritten. The Fool was excised from *Lear*, the gravediggers from *Hamlet*; *Macbeth* was embellished with singing and dancing; *Romeo and Juliet* was given a happy ending. Passages from *Henry IV*, *Henry V*, *Henry VI*, and *Richard II* were cannibalized and transformed into a new *Richard III*. How far this revision extended has been the study of modern scholars, and several curiously "rational" scripts have been published.

As in France, so too in England, the period was marked by an outpouring of critical treatises—in separate pamphlets and as prefaces to plays. The rational mind of neoclassicism was perhaps the world's greatest "explainer," for all matters could be settled by rational discourse. The neophyte English neoclassicists, however, had a hurdle to overcome that did not exist for the French: there was a heritage of great theatre not far behind them. So the argument raged. The formidable erudition of Milton, the wit of Joseph Addison, the earnestness of Thomas

Rymer, Edward Bysshe, and Thomas Blount, for instance, were ranged on the side of the classical precepts. The facility of John Dennis and the skill of George Farquhar protested against Aristotle and the rules. But most importantly and most influentially, John Dryden—in theory and in practice—reconciled the opposing views and popularized that peculiar genre of the English Restoration, the "heroic tragedy." The discourse of his *Essay on Dramatic Poesy* (1668) is divided among four conversants with differing points of view, one of whom (Neander) represents Dryden himself. Though Dryden tells us that his essay is "a dialogue sustained by persons of several opinions, all of them left doubtful, to be determined by readers in general," and though a dispassionate air is maintained throughout, it is Neander who praises the relative freedom of English practice. But it was Thomas Rymer who first articulated the idea of "poetic justice" which would catalyze into a moral argument. Poetic justice demanded, he said, that in the ideal world of the play no man must be punished in excess of his crime nor rewarded in excess of his virtue (*A Short View of Tragedy*, 1693).

So then the English had another critical point to argue: the morality of theatre as a human activity. Argument and counter-argument appeared in quickening tempo from the appearance of Jeremy Collier's *Short View of the Profaneness and Immorality of the English Stage* in 1696 and spilled over into the next century. It is reminiscent of the "Quarrel of the Cid," only here the antagonists are lined up on moral grounds. Social pressures, by the end of the seventeenth century, were on the side of Collier; the stage of the eighteenth century would be very different from that of the Restoration.

Through all these arguments, playwrights (many of them also engaged in the critical ripostes) were writing plays. Sometimes the Restoration writers of tragedy took old stories and retold them in the new style, as Dryden did in *All for Love, or the World Well Lost* (1677), in which he rewrote the story of Antony and Cleopatra to the taste of his times. Although Dryden's play suffers greatly from comparison with that of Shakespeare, it is perhaps the best of the tragedies of the Restoration, illustrating how a playwright of real genius can overcome the most unseemly of obstacles. Probably the most popular of the poet laureate's tragedies was the *Conquest of Granada* (1670) which appeared in two parts of five acts each; his heavily heroic play of five years later, *Aureng-Zebe*, was also quite popular. Dryden wrote operas and comedies as well as tragedies, but the tragedies are his best work. Except for *All for Love*, which is written in blank verse, his tragedies are in the heroic couplet, a somewhat less than supple instrument for dramatic dialogue. Nevertheless, they achieved a kind of nobility and, although not equal to Racine and Corneille, they are nonetheless touched with genius.

Rant, bluster, and hyperbole characterized the typical heroic tragedy, with an emphasis upon the juxtaposition of love and honor between which the hero must painfully choose. Nathaniel Lee (c. 1653–1692) and John Banks (c. 1650–1706) were popular writers in this form in their own day; Banks perhaps deserves some permanent notice for his use of recent history as subject-matter in *Virtue Betrayed* (based on the life of Anne Boleyn) and *The Island Queens* (about Mary of Scotland). The most popular writer of tragedy next to Dryden was Thomas Otway, whose many plays on classical subjects were produced between

1675 and 1682. Two of his plays, *The Orphan* (1680) and *Venice Preserved* (1682), continued to be popular with acting companies and with audiences well into the nineteenth century.

Restoration tragedy, however, was almost no more than an intellectual exercise and a fashionable obeisance to the neoclassical spirit. It is not often read today, and less often produced.

Restoration comedy noteworthy

The best achievement of Restoration dramatists was in the field of comedy. Nowhere else in English literature (if we except, perhaps, Noel Coward) are there plays like these—hard, brilliant, infinitely accomplished, and infinitely remote from the life of the entire population except for that of a very narrow social circle. They are the ultimate refinement of the dramatic genre of comedy. Unlike the universal comedy of character which Molière brought to perfection (dealing, as it does, in the ethical matters of sanity and reason, with the triumph of good sense), this comedy of manners concerns itself with the æsthetic matters of style and sophistication and applauds the triumph of good taste. It is more specialized; it restricts its considerations to the agreed-upon concerns of Fashionable Society, rather than society as a whole. The dramatis personae are drawn from a very limited social circle, the dialogue has a witty brilliance, and the plots are chiefly boudoir intrigues.

There are echoes of Ben Jonson in the names of the characters: Sir Frederick Frolick, Sir Fopling Flutter, Lady Flippant, Lady Wishfort, Mrs. Fainall, Millamant. But the dramatists' treatment of these characters has no undertone of criticism. If we may suppose a single attitude on the part of the Restoration dramatists, it is one of objectivity in the presentation of social types drawn quite unapologetically from their surrounding society. The best of these plays are our best examples of the comedy of manners—the clash of character on character in highly selected situations. Perhaps no other society than that of the Restoration could have produced such playwrights as George Etherege, William Wycherley, and William Congreve. At least no other society has. Others were writing, of course. There was a prodigious amount of dramatic writing going on. But these three are the epitome of what we mean when we speak of the unique quality of Restoration comedy.

George Etherege, fast-living gallant and man-about-town who spent his retirement in Paris, preceded that retirement by a series of plays which took London by storm. The earliest appeared in 1664—*The Comical Revenge, or Love in a Tub*. The best of those that followed were *She Would If She Could* (1668) and *The Man of Mode, or Sir Fopling Flutter* (1676).

The second of the three writers, William Wycherley, had been educated in Paris, and was renowned there as a wit in the circle of the blue-stocking daughter of Madame de Rambouillet, the group which Molière had so neatly pilloried. His first London production was *Love in a Wood* in 1671, which he followed a year later with *The Gentleman Dancing Master*. The most famous of his plays is *The Country Wife* (1675), in which he contrasts the provincialism of Margery Pinchwife with the London society into which she marries; Horner, as catalyst, shows up the deficiences of both milieus. In his last play, *The Plain Dealer* (1676), he exhibits some impatience with the frivolity of his fashionable world, an apt prelude to his own imprisonment for debt and an endless series of lawsuits.

ELIZABETHAN PLAYHOUSE IN THE RESTORATION
Sketch from Kirkman's *Drolls*, published in
1672, showing the leading actor in each
droll, with Robert Coxe playing the simple-
ton. Though this sketch is no longer identified as the interior of the Red Bull, it does
show the persistent platform stage, with
some of the audience standing in the pit
and some seated in a gallery. (Henry E.
Huntington Library and Art Gallery)

The best of the Restoration writers was
William Congreve, whose plays today, in
capable hands, are sheer delight. He belongs
to the last decade of the century, and marks
the culmination of this type of comedy. Not
only does he exhibit supreme genius in the
writing of comic dialogue, but he also
achieves subtle and interesting characterization. Few heroines are so completely delightful as the Millamant of *The Way of the
World* (1700), Congreve's last and best play.
Millamant and Mirabell are the Restoration
descendants of the delightful Shakespearean
couple, Beatrice and Benedick (*Much Ado
About Nothing*). Only a shade less successful
are Prue and Ben, Valentine and Angelica
of *Love for Love* (1695). Congreve's two
other plays of note, *The Old Bachelor* (1693)
and *The Double Dealer* (1693), are hardly
less scintillating. Without any obvious intention to reform the society or the people
whom he observed and used in his plays,
Congreve's work is the epitome of the un-
inhibited, completely infectious gaiety that
pervades Restoration comedy.

Surrounding these luminaries of Restoration comedy were many other writers, such
as the versatile John Dryden whose most
successful comedy was a froth entitled *Marriage à la Mode* (1672); Sir John Vanbrugh,
whose *The Relapse* (1696) was quite successfully revived in the twentieth century;
Charles Sedley; Thomas Shadwell; Mrs.
Aphra Behn (the first successful female playwright); and finally, George Farquhar,
writing at the turn of the century. While
Farquhar belongs to the same tradition as
Wycherley and Congreve, he marks the end
of the type, and points forward to the next
period and the sentimentality of the eighteenth century. His most enduringly interesting plays are *The Recruiting Officer* (1706)
and *The Beaux Stratagem* (1707). Forces had
been at work which doomed the society of
Charles II, and never again would its amoral
glitter light the English theatrical sky.

Beginnings of modern theatre architecture

The Restoration witnessed the passing of the
Elizabethan playhouse and the establishment
of an essentially modern theatre building.
Even the few Elizabethan theatres that had
not been ravaged during the Commonwealth
met their end during the Restoration.

The Red Bull, reaching back (in name
at least) into the Elizabethan period as a

playhouse converted from an inn, was still in operation during the early years of the Restoration. It had been built in 1607 and, although some scholars are inclined to believe that it was roofed over in its later days, the weight of evidence seems to indicate its continuance as an open-roofed, standing-pit theatre such as Shakespeare knew. After Davenant and Killigrew succeeded in enforcing their monopoly, it ceased to be used as a playhouse.

The Phoenix or the Cockpit-in-Drury Lane, one of the private pre-Commonwealth houses (built in 1614), was in litigation during most of the Commonwealth period, and at the Restoration in 1660 was in lease to John Rhodes, whose company of young players were taken over by Davenant to form the Duke's Company. Though the house had been dismantled by the Puritans in 1649, it had been refurbished, and had been used by Davenant for his *Siege of Rhodes* in 1658, with its scenes and machines presumably after the French fashion in stage settings. It was later used by troupes of visiting French and Italian comedians.

Another surviving Elizabethan private theatre was Salisbury Court in Fleet Street (built in 1629). Its interior also had been razed in 1649, but on the eve of the Restoration it had been fitted once more and was sporadically in use by Davenant, George Jolly, and William Beeston until it was utterly destroyed in the Great Fire of London in 1666.

The Red Bull, the Phoenix, Salisbury Court—what echoes of a greater age must have resounded in those old walls as they housed a newer day! But newer walls soon took their places.

The patents obtained by Davenant and Killigrew in July of 1660 empowered each to build a theatre and raise a company of actors. The actors they took from the extant companies. Killigrew chose the company that was then performing at the Red Bull under Major Mohun, who had been an actor of note in Jacobean times and an officer in the royalist army. Davenant, as noted above, took a group of younger actors from John Rhodes' Phoenix. Davenant occupied Salisbury Court, and Killigrew took his company to Gibbon's Tennis Court which had, during the preceding decade, been converted into a theatre.

As French actors had earlier discovered, a tennis court could be made into quite a presentable theatre. Gibbon's Tennis Court in Vere Street, which became the King's Theatre, seems to have been but twenty-four by sixty-four feet in size—an area which would allow of little elaboration. Hence it is assumed that the stage was a platform with a permanent architectural setting similar to the Elizabethan theatre. It opened on November 8, 1660, with *Henry IV, Part 1*. Davenant, on the other hand, established his company at the old Salisbury Court Theatre, opening on November 15, 1660, while he refurbished Lisle's Tennis Court in Lincoln's Inn Fields. The latter opened in June 1661, with *The Siege of Rhodes*. Having used painted perspective-scenery in his productions at Rutland House, he was evidently determined to incorporate this "new" technique in the offerings of his new patent house. Since Lisle's measured no more than thirty by seventy-five feet (larger than Gibbon's but not large enough for his plans), he took over some adjoining property and fitted out his Duke's Theatre with what has been called "a modest imitation of the Italian style." (Mullin, *The Development of the Playhouse*, p. 63). Little is known of its interior design, save that the indefatigable Pepys speaks of sitting "in the side balcony, over against the musick," where he "did hear, but not see, a new play" (*Diary*, May 12, 1669). When

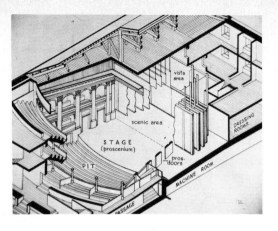

WREN'S DRURY LANE
This reconstruction by Richard Leacroft, of the second Drury Lane opened in 1674, clearly shows the broad and deep apron stage (proscenium here) which was the most typical characteristic of Restoration and later English theatres. Actors entered from one of the four proscenium doors. The wing-flat system behind the proscenium arch functioned largely as a scenic background for the action. The pit has backless benches; there is a double row of boxes and a gallery on the third level opposite the stage. The decoration is simple and classical in line. (Richard Leacroft Collection)

---

it was ready, Davenant's company moved into the newly fitted house, where it remained until some years after his death in 1668, not moving into its sumptuous building in Dorset Garden until November of 1671.

It was primarily because Davenant's newly converted theatre in Lisle's Tennis Court was a formidable rival to his old-style playhouse at Gibbon's that Killigrew rushed completion of the first Theatre Royal, into which his company moved in May of 1663. The year before he had taken a lease on an unused riding yard between Bridges Street and Drury Lane; on it he constructed the first new theatre building of the Restoration. This house, popularly called the first Drury Lane, was fifty-eight by one hundred twelve feet, and was built at an approximate cost of twenty-four hundred pounds. Very little is known of the design of the house, except that Pepys speaks of attending it on May 8,

1663, the second day of its being opened:

The house is made with extraordinary good contrivance, and yet hath some faults, as the narrowness of the passages in and out of the pitt, and the distance from the stage to the boxes, which I am confident cannot hear; but for all other things it is well, only, above all, the musique being below, and most of it sounding under the very stage, there is no hearing of the basses at all, nor very well of the trebles, which sure must be mended.
PEPYS
Diary, May 8, 1663

Equally little is known of the design of the exterior, except that panoramic maps of the period show a long, narrow hall capped at the center by a large, shallow dome. It is possible that by 1665, when Killigrew planned a refurbishing and enlarging of the house while it was closed during the plague, Sir Christopher Wren had a hand in that reconstruction. At any rate, it was he who designed the second Drury Lane, constructed on the same spot after a disastrous fire destroyed the original structure. (Drury Lane had escaped destruction in the Great Fire of 1666, only to be completely destroyed by fire in 1672.) While the new theatre was being built, Killigrew took his company to Lisle's, which had been vacated the year before by the Duke's Company.

The second Drury Lane, built at an approximate cost of four thousand pounds, was fifty-eight by one hundred forty feet. The stage area covered about half the length of the building, with an apron as deep as the stage behind the proscenium. Both apron and stage are slightly raked, and a wing system is indicated for the stage furnishings. There are two proscenium doors on either side of the apron, with a box above each. The sloping pit is supplied with backless benches and is surrounded by two tiers of boxes, with an additional upper gallery at the end opposite the stage. The decoration indicated is not ornate, and, indeed, contemporary writers are one in declaring that the second Drury Lane was much plainer than the theatre at Dorset Garden. The interior walls of the building narrow slightly toward the stage, focusing on the apron, and fostering a good actor-audience relationship by de-emphasizing the division between house and stage. Three floors of dressing rooms are provided behind the stage. When the then-manager Christopher Rich remodeled the inside of the building in 1696, he shortened the apron by four feet, converted the downstage proscenium doors into boxes, and installed additional benches in the pit.

The Duke's Theatre in Dorset Garden, opened in 1671, was evidently much more elaborate. It was one hundred forty feet by fifty-seven feet, and cost nearly nine thousand pounds. Though no floor plan has been discovered, contemporary references indicate a house arrangement similar to that at the second Drury Lane. A series of engravings published in 1673, with the text of Settle's *Empress of Morocco*, shows much of the stage design. From the elaborately decorated proscenium, a half-roof extends out over the apron; above this is a pair of windows flanked by full relief figures of Thalia and Melpomene. The windows open into a room behind, which was evidently the music room —Pepys' "music above" is further evidence. The stage seems to be raked and supplied with grooved wings and shutters as was the Drury Lane. Again, there are proscenium doors with boxes above them, evidently two on each side. The house is decorated with statues and busts in relief and much gorgeous ornamentation. It would appear that the additional length of the auditorium,

coupled with the heavy ornamentation of the walls containing the proscenium doors and the overhanging "music above," gave the interior a tunnel-like feeling that became oppressive. When, after a series of unfortunate circumstances, the acting companies of the two patent houses were amalgamated in 1682, the United Company chose to continue its repertory at Drury Lane—a house more suitable for the performance of plays. Dorset Garden was evidently used for the occasional performance of opera after this time. There is no more mention of it beyond 1706.

These were the theatres of the Restoration, influenced in their decoration and use by those of France, but incorporating traditionally and peculiarly English characteristics —the deep apron and the proscenium doors and boxes. The characteristics of this stage shaped the kind of acting seen upon it as well as the plays written for it.

Staging flexible and effective

Some continuity of Restoration stage design with that of pre-Commonwealth times is evidenced in the person of John Webb, who had been assistant to Inigo Jones; Webb designed the settings for *The Seige of Rhodes* when Davenant presented it. He also redesigned the two court theatres, the Cockpit and the Great Hall, laying out both the stage plans and the house. Plans and sketches for *The Siege of Rhodes* and for a court performance of Orrery's *Mustapha* reveal that he was following the ideas of Inigo Jones in court presentations. The designs show a highly decorated proscenium arch, backed by a series of wing flats and shutters. The *Mustapha* plan indicates a sky cloth from the top of the proscenium to a lower point in the back wall; the musicians were placed in an

THE DUKE'S THEATRE, DORSET GARDEN
Left, exterior view; above, interior, looking toward the stage. These two prints, from Settle's *Empress of Morocco*, show the elaborate Dorset Garden theatre. The music room is above the stage, flanked by full relief statues of Thalia and Melpomene, and there is a suggestion of proscenium doors to either side. The stage is raked, and the decoration is rich and intricate. It is highly likely that the proportions of the set are elongated to fit the page of a book. (Henry E. Huntington Library and Art Gallery)

elevated gallery behind the back wall. In both designs the stage is raked to enhance the perspective.

This plan, in essence, is the one followed throughout the period in practically all theatrical productions. The stages of the public theatres built during the Restoration were provided with grooves to receive the wing flats and shutters which formed the staple set. Both the patent houses had stock sets, one for tragedy and one for comedy. That for tragedy included a grove, a temple, a palace hall; for comedy there was a bedroom, a

boudoir, a park. These were painted on flats, and in the comedies the pictured representations of places in London aspired to be as accurate as possible.

The operation of this set was easy and quick. After the "Third Musick" the actor speaking the prologue emerged from one of the proscenium doors onto the apron, spoke his lines, exited, and the front curtain rose. It was generally the festoon kind of curtain. Entrances and exits of the actors were usually to the apron from the proscenium doors, the upstage area serving as a kind of background. Sometimes the actors went within the scene by moving upstage and having the side flats click together to cover them. Sometimes scenes and players were revealed by an opposite arrangement. When the play was over, the epilogue was spoken while the curtain was still up. If the play was a tragedy, it would be followed by a jig or comic afterpiece. Then the curtain would fall. Many stage directions in scripts of the time indicate that the scene "draws off," or "draws over," thus showing the method of operation. There were no waits between scenes; the action was continuous as on Shakespeare's stage.

Sometimes this flat and backcloth system included *relieves*, or set pieces in three dimensions. Sometimes the flats themselves were cut out to form trees, temples, and so forth, revealing the backing behind them. Sometimes they were transparencies, through which a back scene was dimly shown. Moonlight effects were generally achieved in this manner. For special performances, new scenes were sometimes prepared, and, by 1690, an act-drop curtain made its appearance in cases where the element of surprise was important in revealing a scene, or when there was a particularly difficult change to be made. These act-drop curtains were not popular in the public theatres, and their use was generally confined to the opera. An interesting and peculiar convention of the Restoration theatre was the green baize carpet of tragedy. For the presentation of tragic plays the floor of the stage was covered with green baize—a very useful convention in preserving the costumes of the actors who expired in the course of the performance.

Though most plays were given with a minimum of emphasis upon elaborate settings, stage effects were as popular as they have always been with theatre audiences.

Stages were equipped with traps for graves and for the emergence and disappearance of ghosts and the like. Flying arrangements were made for such characters as the witches in *Macbeth*. Lifelike dummies of bodies and heads were made for tortures and dismemberments. Blood effects were eagerly worked over to achieve a sense of realism. The fires painted on the scenes were augmented by fireworks and smoke. Lightning and thunder were manufactured. Ascents and descents were arranged on movable platforms. Cloud effects were popular. Restoration staging was a curious mixture of the real and the conventional. Chairs, tables, and books were often painted on the flats; but when a character was stabbed, he had to bleed what looked like real blood.

Since Restoration theatres were entirely roofed in, lighting presented a problem. The general practice was to have both stage and house well lit throughout the performance by many chandeliers. Pepys complains of the glare of these lights when he was sitting in the gallery. The stage sometimes had a short strip of footlights down center, most frequently candles but sometimes oil lamps. One ingenious arrangement for lowering the lights was the substitution of "floats" for the footlights. These were wicks in cork floating in oil, the whole tank of which could be lowered into a trap. Candles and oil lamps lit the area behind the proscenium. Few changes in lighting were attempted in the course of a performance.

The preferred position for the musicians was backstage or above stage, although at Whitehall there seems to have been some rather clever arrangement to seat them in a pit to one side of the stage, at its front, or in the end of the gallery nearest the stage, as seemed to suit a particular performance. The prelude, entr'acte, and postlude were played from the designated spot; music called for in

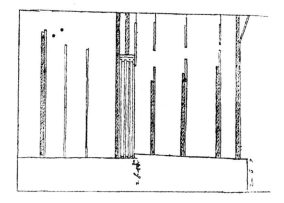

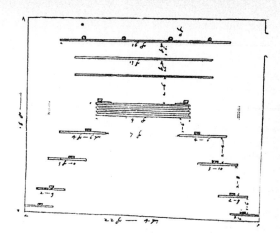

the play itself was generally furnished by musicians who came on to the stage in the course of the action.

Restoration staging was a curious compendium of practices both native and foreign. The raked stage, the wing and shutter system in perspective, the flyings, and the front curtain were all imported from Continental practice. Trapdoors had been a part of Elizabethan staging, and the ubiquitous and unique proscenium doors and deep apron were, no doubt, remnants of the forward-thrusting platform of Shakespeare's day and the doors of his stage house. Or perhaps the doors were derived from the mansions on a transverse stage axis which Shakespeare's stage may have inherited from medieval practice. In any event, the realistic stage effects went beyond Shakespeare to medieval practices. Thus the Restoration stage was the descendant of differing traditions, all of which were combined to produce a flexible and effective instrument for the plays which were written for it.

Costumes blend many traditions

Restoration practice in costuming descended from the Elizabethans, with a curious admixture of what had been customary in both the public and private theatres and in the court masques.

The Restoration theatre had a costume "à la Turque," which always included a turban and wide trousers, and a costume "à la Romaine," which nodded in the direction of breastplate and short tunic but always included a Restoration wig. In historical plays, the leading characters were apt to be dressed in a reproduction of a known painting of the figure, as Henry VIII was dressed after Holbein's famous portrait, but other characters in the piece would wear the dress of Restoration courtiers.

These slight attempts at accurate costuming were confined to the men; women wore contemporary dress whatever the period of the play. Head feathers were always the sign of heroism and dignity, worn by men and women alike. Tragic actresses were almost universally garbed in black velvet. They had a special appurtenance in their gowns' long trains—cared for by a page boy, presumably invisible, who followed the actress about the stage, arranging the folds of the skirt and seeing that the train was well disposed when, as often happened, the action of the play required that the wearer die.

In the comedies, contemporary dress, enriched as much as possible, was usual. The leading characters wore the richest costumes; those less important might be rather indifferently dressed. Often the feminine stars blazed with jewels either borrowed for the occasion, or received as gifts from admirers. Because these costumes were exceedingly expensive they were, in the ordinary course of events, for only the most important performers. Where expense was no object, or where costumes were subsidized by a wealthy patron of the court, even the blacksmiths might be clothed in satin. The men, whatever the part, almost invariably wore the usual Restoration wig, with the villain wearing a black one. A curious convention of disguise, similar to the Eilzabethan "cloak to go invisible in," was the use of an eye patch, which presumably completely disguised the wearer, although he otherwise looked exactly as he had before donning the patch.

Like Elizabethan actors, those of the Restoration were sometimes recipients of gifts of clothing. Downes records in his *Roscius Anglicanus* (1708) that for the opening of Davenant's play *Love and Honor* in October of 1661:

This play was richly cloath'd; the King gave Mr. Betterton his Coronation suit . . . the Duke of York giving Mr. Harris his . . . and my Lord Oxford gave Mr. Joseph Price his.

On the other hand, the usual costume was not quite so splendid, for Pepys remarks, after an investigative visit backstage at the Duke's Theatre in 1667, that "how poor the men are in clothes, and yet what a show they make on stage by candlelight."

A great deal of makeup was employed. False noses, beards, and mustaches were used by the men. Powder, rouge, pencil, lip rouge, and the ever-present beauty patch were standard with the women. Colley Cibber once complained that the actresses would use no facial expression because they were afraid they would crack their heavy and stiff makeup. The outstanding exception to this seems to have been the beautiful Elizabeth Barry, who evidently customarily wore little or no makeup and thus could use a full measure of facial expression.

Though the disparity in costuming and its lack of fitness to the historical periods of the plays no doubt strike the modern person as inartistic, it must be remembered that the majority of Restoration playgoers had no historical sense and looked only for brilliance and charm in the performers and their clothes. Needless to say, the novelty of actresses on the public stage engendered great interest in the contemporary fashions in which they appeared.

Innovations in acting styles

The greatest difference, of course, between acting companies of the Restoration and those before the Commonwealth is that the newer groups included women. The impetus for this came from the Continent, but Restoration managers justified it by the specious argument that it was immoral to have men in women's parts. Certainly the inclusion of women in the acting companies allowed dramatists to expand the female roles and to write some of the most brilliant characterizations ever to adorn the English-speaking

EPILOGUE to SIR PATIENT FANCY.

"That we have nobler Souls than you we prove,
By how much more we're sensible of Love."

TWO RESTORATION ACTRESSES
Left, Nell Gwyn as Epilogue to *Sir Patient Fancy;* above, Anne Bracegirdle as the Indian Queen. In both these costumes, the basic Restoration silhouette is maintained, an Elizabethan ruff being added to the first, a feather headdress and fan transforming the second into an Indian costume. There is also a page, in a curious version of an Indian headdress, to bear the train of the Queen. (Harvard Theatre Collection)

stage. For here again, as always, playwrights wrote with particular performers in mind— Araminta, Angelica, and Millamant were created by Congreve for Anne Bracegirdle.

Early in the period, some women's parts were still being played by boys, and throughout the period, children were popular for the prologues and epilogues. One of the most noted of these was a seven-year-old girl who was evidently very effective, even though she could have had little conception of the meaning of the sentences she spoke. The most outstanding of the boy players were Edward Kynaston, whom Pepys praises, and Charles Hart, said to be a grandson of Shakespeare's sister Joan. As these boys outgrew their parts, they were replaced by women. Some performers specialized in tragedy, as did Elizabeth Barry; some played only comedy roles, as did Cave Underhill and the new female stars, Anne Bracegirdle and Nell Gwyn. More frequently, however, performers played both tragedy and comedy.

At first the actors who had survived the Commonwealth continued in prominence in the Restoration. Major Michael Mohun was one of these; he had his own company at the reopening of the theatres, and later was chosen by Killigrew to head the King's Company. It was to this company that Nell Gwyn belonged, along with Mistress Knepp (Pepys' friend) and Rebecca Marshall, another of Pepys' favorites.

Davenant's rival Duke's Company began with a group of much younger actors, the best of whom was Thomas Betterton. His is the greatest name of the period. His Hamlet, played in wig and frock coat, was famous; he supposedly played it as Shakespeare had instructed, having been coached by Davenant, who had the role from Taylor, himself instructed by Shakespeare. In any event, contemporary comments agree that it was a great Hamlet. Practically all the Shakespearean heroes came within Betterton's compass, and he played the leading roles in the new comedy as well. His style is reputed to have been free of rant and exaggeration and to have been in character throughout. At one point he was sent by Charles II to study French theatre; he returned with some interesting ideas of picturesque and plastic grouping for ensemble playing, no doubt observed at the French opera, and formulated some rules for acting. These are reminiscent of the Elizabethan "rhetorics" in the careful attention given to the disposition of every part of the body for the achieving of certain emotional effects: eyes uplifted for one effect, downcast for another; head turned left with right hand extended to signify rejection, and so forth. Whatever his technique, and it seems to have been most carefully thought out, the total effect was evidently one of naturalness and rightness. He won great fame in spite of an unprepossessing appearance and a total inability to dance or sing.

It must be remembered, of course, that not only Restoration playwrights but audiences as well considered the first qualification of an actor to be his voice—that all other attributes were thereunto added. "Natural-

ness" in those neoclassic times would be "art"—"nature methodized," as Pope would later put it. What Restoration audiences probably saw on the stage was delivery and gesture larger than life, rhythmic and impressive. In any event, Betterton was held in such esteem by his contemporaries that he was buried in Westminster Abbey, as was his acting partner, Anne Bracegirdle. She is reported to have been a pleasant singer and a charming dancer, exceedingly comely, and very popular in "breeches parts." She seems to have had that indefinable charm without which no performer rises to greatness.

Actors were trained not only by being taken as apprentices in an established company, but by being enrolled in that peculiar institution of the Restoration, the Nursery, which maintained classes and gave student performances. The history of its establishment leads one to suppose that it was simply Davenant's invention to get rid of a formidable rival in the person of George Jolly, an itinerant English actor who had received permission from Charles II, in the first days of the Restoration, to form an acting company and to present plays in London. How Davenant scotched the plan is a story too long for telling here, but George Jolly ended up as mentor to the fledgling actors of the Nursery. These students graduated into the established companies in London, or into touring companies of the provinces, some, perhaps, as far afield as the Irish Theatre at Dublin (which, for once, Davenant was unable to control, the managership being awarded to one John Ogilby).

The companies were run by royal patentees who, under the issued patents, had great powers. As in the French companies, a specific number of shares were divided among the actors, but in England the manager retained as many shares as he could justify. English actresses, unlike the French,

BETTERTON'S HAMLET
Illustration from Nicholas Rowe's 1709 edition of the play. Betterton plays Hamlet, and his stance and forceful gesture lend credence to his reputation as one of the best actors of the time. The costumes of Hamlet and his mother are of Restoration times; note particularly the wig that Betterton is wearing. Not much can be surmised about stage setting from this background, since books in those days were frequently illustrated as if from life. (Harvard Theatre Collection)

were not awarded shares. Davenant maintained the actresses in his company from seven shares allotted to him for the purpose; Killigrew paid his actresses as hirelings. Managers were permitted to sell their shares to nontheatrical people—thus beginning the domination of the theatre by businessmen and the subsequent abuse of the managerial

system. These nontheatrical participants were called "the adventurers," and often they were all that the name implies. Such an adventurer was the Christopher Rich who took over the management of the United Company in 1693. His sharp practices drove a company of actors headed by Betterton to revolt; they seceded and formed their own theatre under special royal permission, performing once more at the old Lisle's Tennis Court. Abuse of his position as manager had indeed caused the demise of Killigrew's King's Company, and the amalgamation of the two patent houses in 1682.

Since the basis for payment of actors was the division of shares, their incomes were exceedingly variable. These were often augmented by tutoring and by the receipt of gifts. The best of the actors fared well, the others rather poorly. Fixed and occasional expenses, as well as the salaries of nonacting employees, were either paid from the manager's shares or were deducted before the income was divided among the shareholders. It is interesting to note in some of the documents of the time that the patentee-manager was sometimes called the "Orator," as was the manager of French companies.

Mention has been made of the conviviality between performers and spectators, fostered by the freedom of the playhouses and the narrowness of the social circle from which spectators came. Companies made frequent appearances at court, and the court appeared frequently at the theatres. No such assiduous participation by court amateurs in court performances was evident in the Restoration as had been the case in pre-Commonwealth court circles. Some there was, but little in comparison with the older times. Actors approved by a benign court were beginning their climb to the social acceptability that was to lead, almost two hundred years later, to the knighting of Henry Irving.

Summary

Though the Restoration theatre began its decline in 1688, when the Glorious Revolution exiled James II and established William and Mary on the throne, it still had many brilliant moments. A more telling blow was delivered ten years later when Jeremy Collier launched his indignant *Short View*, which began a series of persecutions that eventually changed the whole character of English theatre. The end of the period may be marked by the accession of Queen Anne in 1702. She was completely disinterested in the arts, literature, and theatre. That special darling of the court and court society would henceforth have to find a new audience. From this point a new era begins, with the middle classes and sentimentality replacing aristocratic flippancy.

But the Restoration, in its short and brilliant career, added to the store of English drama the best examples of the comedy of manners that the literature possesses. It also began, through the writings of John Dryden, a tradition of insightful dramatic criticism. Though the tragedies produced by its dramatists have largely not been remembered, they were a peculiarly English amalgam of classic and Elizabethan characteristics.

Other areas of theatrical activity initiated features that became characteristic of later theatres. Restoration theatre achieved the modernization of audience accommodation with a seated pit, galleries, and boxes. It introduced a new kind of managerial system involving people primarily nontheatrical. It initiated and popularized on the English-speaking stage feminine stars. It advanced the complexity of stage design, with emphasis upon a wing-flat system of painted scenes. It standardized the roofed-in theatre building. It established, in the amalgamation of painted settings with the old Elizabethan platform stage, the peculiarly English construction of forestage and proscenium doors which was to remain for many decades the English and American tradition.

In many respects, Restoration theatre was unique. It was not (as Elizabethan theatre before it and eighteenth-century theatre after it) the popular pursuit of wide segments of the population. It grew from and spoke to an exclusive, aristocratically oriented society—that Fashionable Society of the court and its immediate followers. Yet within that narrowly circumscribed orbit it spoke brilliantly and uniquely. Times were changing, and more rapidly than the contemporary *afficionados* of Restoration theatre realized. The eighteenth century would be a whole new scene.

11 Developments in england and america

The eighteenth century is a watershed in the history of theatre in England. Before it, theatre had been sanctioned and supported by the ruling authorities: church and/or state. After it, theatre in England (and from the first in America) stood in the marketplace and sold its wares like any other merchandiser. It took most of the century to work out the arrangement. A series of historical accidents had brought about a situation which existed only in England and from there journeyed to America.

The predominant theatre of the Middle Ages (the cycle plays) had been supported and supervised by the church. The theatre of the Renaissance developed because it had the support and encouragement of the state and the intellectual community. But even at the height of its accomplishment, the Puritans frowned upon theatre as inimical to the fundamental precept that "Thou shalt not make unto thee any graven image, or any likeness of any thing . . ." Besides, in the first half of the seventeenth century, theatre became identified with the Cavaliers, or court party, so that at the opening of the civil war it was outlawed. For more than twenty years it was a fugitive, and when it returned with the Restoration, it was still more closely identified with court and aristocracy. Indeed, its very life depended upon court patronage, which continued until the accession of Queen Anne in 1702. (When Betterton broke with the United Company in 1695 he had appealed to the Crown and been given a special patent by King William to have his own company in Lincoln's Inn Fields.) Interest ceased with Queen Anne; the function of government with respect to theatre in the eighteenth century became adverse rather than supportive. The period is marked by a series of "regulating acts" which, on the whole, inhibited rather than encouraged theatre. Intellectuals and aristocrats gradually withdrew their support from what was now, in essence, a bastard whose very life-blood depended upon finding a new audience which would support it. By the end of the century that new audience was assured, and theatre was the property of the citizens—both in spirit and in fact—a commodity of the marketplace competing for attention with a variety of possible items for purchase.

There was much intellectual ferment in the English eighteenth century. The neoclassic mode of thought begun at the Restoration flowered in the first half of the century and did noble battle throughout the second half with the slowly gathering forces of romanticism. Yet so self-assured was this development that during the course of the eighteenth century, literary England became a creditor nation rather than the debtor nation it had been before. The Age of Reason, the neoclassic period, the Augustan Age (terms applied to the greater portion of the century), though ostensibly drawing its inspiration from the French, but really going back to the ancients, was sanguine enough to believe that it was doing for England what the writers of the Augustan period had done for Rome. Not only were the rules and order of the ancients to be applied to English literature, but they were to be improved upon, for obviously their practice had violated their precepts—and there would be none of that in England! The literary arbiters of the day—Pope, then Johnson—were confirmed neoclassicists, and their influence spanned the century. Respect for science and logic, rationality, an ordered society, a pleasing style that never descended to dullness—these were the characteristics of the time. Antiemotionalism was the creed. Paradoxically enough, the very period saw a rise in sentimentality, and a slow but certain undercurrent of real feeling which gathered strength throughout the century and burst into the glory of the romantic revolution just at its end. The contradictions of the age—its serenity, its tempestuousness; its logic, its inspiration; its doctrine of deism, its Wesleyan doctrine of personal salvation—made it a seedbed of ideas and practices which spread throughout Europe, often with startling manifestations.

It is a fascinating century in many areas of human thought and action. Science, government, economics, and philosophy were seething with discovery and change. John Locke (1632-1704), originally a student of chemistry and medicine and a practicing physician, became the outstanding political philosopher of the Age of Reason. In his political doctrines the American colonists found justification for their War of Independence. As an empiricist he was confident that adequate observation and discussion could sift truth from error. His *Essay Concerning Human Understanding* (1690), one of his most significant writings, examined the origin of ideas and predicated the new concept that the mind at birth is a *tabula rasa* upon which experience writes. Hence came the various manifestations in the century to follow of the theory that environment, the conditions of society, contained the roots of good and evil —that man was the product of his environment. George Berkeley (1685-1753), David Hume (1711-1776), and William Godwin (1756-1836), all speculated concerning Lockean principles, engendering considerable philosophical activity which had political and social repercussions in both Europe and America.

Political events, also, engendered closer contact with other European nations. Queen Anne's War, concluded in 1714, caused England to be more politically involved with the Continent; the Seven Years' War (1756-1763) won an empire in America; and the campaigns of Clive in India (1756-1760) won that jewel for the English crown. Then came the American War of Independence and the es-

tablishment of a new nation. Meanwhile, the involvement of the Crown in the day-to-day affairs of government dwindled. The accession of the House of Hanover, whose first representative, George I, could not even speak English, led eventually to the establishment of the office called "Prime Minister"; he became the real manager of the state and, with his associates, dominated Parliament. Robert Walpole and the elder Pitt perfected the system whereby such a "government," defeated by Parliament on an important bill, would resign and new elections of Parliament would be held. Thus the government became more responsive to the people. George III was the last king who made an effort to recapture royal power and prerogative; one result of his failure was the establishing of the United States of America.

In literary circles authors were declaring their independence of patrons, and, for the first time in many generations, not only making a living but sometimes even earning a fortune solely by their pens. Alexander Pope, for instance, received his generous support solely from the general public, and Samuel Johnson wrote his famous letter to Lord Chesterfield, stating his success independent of patronage. The new patrons of literature were the political factions, and through them, the general public. The battle for freedom of the press was fought through most of the century; by 1776 there were fifty-three newspapers in London alone. Essay, poem, novel, and pamphlet proliferated. There were more avenues for literary expression than ever before. Philosophical, economic, social, scientific, and literary ideas were not only rushed into print, they were also discussed at great length in the coffee houses, popular meeting places of the age and, as Addison said, the means of "bringing philosophy out of closets and libraries, schools, and colleges, to dwell in

clubs and assemblies, at tea-tables and in
coffee-houses." Discussants in various fields
congregated at particular coffee-houses, as
the literati did at Will's—and any member of
the general public could drop by to listen
or to participate or to hear read the latest
information from the periodicals. In the rush
of experiment in new literary forms playwriting was often neglected; in the press of
concern for philosophical, economic, and social ideas theatre was often an unimportant
consideration. It was, nevertheless, an effect-
tual mirror of the times, and had an interesting life of its own.

Theatre a middle-class amusement

During the eighteenth century English theatre was forced to broaden its base. Royal
sanction had been withdrawn, and there were
decreasing numbers of devotees from court
circles. The new audiences were of a new
social class: London was the seething center
of an expanding empire, the economic and
social hub of far-flung mercantile ventures,
the Athens toward which the outlanders
yearned. Very early in the century John
Dennis, critic and playwright, was complain-
ing of three categories of people who patronized the eighteenth-century theatre, who, he
says, had no education at all: younger brothers suffering under the laws of primogeni-
ture; merchants; and foreigners. All, he says,
contributed to the debility of theatre. In any
event, wealthy tradesmen had evidently replaced the gallants and the men of letters
in the pit, though the front and side boxes
were still occupied by the *beau monde*.

The new playgoers, the tired businessmen of the age, demanded and got plays
which were not mentally taxing but were
interesting and entertaining. At least this
was the aim. And when the two patent
houses, largely dedicated to pure drama, did
not pander to their tastes (Garrick over and
over again tried to elevate English taste in
theatre), audiences resorted to the five or six
other theatres of London for opera, pantomime, and puppet shows.

The rise of other forms of entertainment
was not solely due to public demand, but
was in some measure a way to circumvent
authority. During most of the century only
two theatres were licensed for dramatic performances—Drury Lane and Covent Garden.
But many another theatre presented plays,
both long and short, under the guise of con-
certs, much as in our Boston plays for many
years were advertised as "moral discourses."
Also the enterprising John Rich (c. 1682–1761),
son of Christopher Rich of Drury Lane
fame, made a very good thing of the pantomime originated by one John Weaver, dancing master at Drury Lane. These pantomimes
were spectacular presentations in dumb
show with music, and used as plot the stan-

dard texts; one of the most famous of these was Marlowe's *Dr. Faustus*. The pantomime had a lasting popularity, enduring down to modern times in the celebrated English Christmas pantomimes.

John Rich, under the name of Lun, was his own performer in the pantomimes, just as quite universally the chief managers of the day were also actors. Drury Lane was long under such management: first the trio of Cibber, Wilks, and Doggett beginning in 1710; then, after a slight interval, for thirty years under The Great Garrick; and again toward the end of the century under John Kemble. Kemble also managed at Covent Garden; Rich had been its first actor-manager. And both William and Lewis Hallam, proprietor and manager, respectively, of the company which gave the first professional performances in America, were actors. Most famous of these, of course, is David Garrick who in many ways symbolizes this Age of Great Acting, as it has been called. In addition to his innovations in the art of acting, he introduced many improvements in staging, design, and theatre management. For a time, at least, these men succeeded in warding off the complete domination of theatre management by nontheatre people. How completely the theatre was later taken over by businessmen is easily seen in the paucity of actor-managers today.

Though the theatre of the period was essentially that of the upper middle class, in many ways the audience was heterogeneous. Its composition dictated a later opening hour, with performances beginning at six so that those who worked might attend. Those of the working classes, whose day invariably extended from six in the morning to six at night and often to nine, were admitted late, with reduced prices if they came only to see the afterpiece. (The main performance of the evening was always followed by a musical

OLD DRURY LANE
Above, a 1775 print of the old Drury Lane during Garrick's term as manager; the rear boxes have been converted to galleries on the first and second levels. See page 219. Right, Richard Leacroft's redrawing, amended in accordance with scale drawings of ceiling and proscenium opening in the Soane Museum. This corrected drawing gives more reason to believe the designation of old Drury Lane as an intimate house where the features of the actors were clearly visible from the farthest gallery. (Richard Leacroft Collection)

farce or a condensed comedy which was advertised with the main piece and which closed the evening about ten o'clock.)

For the first time in the history of theatre, advertising could now be done through the newspapers, which got their start in 1706, as well as through the use of playbills. Programs and printed tickets were in use, although individually reserved seats did not become customary until the nineteenth century. Admission was generally by brass checks to a particular part of the house, with the beau monde in the front and side boxes, the wealthy tradesmen in the pit and first gallery, and the mob in the upper gallery.

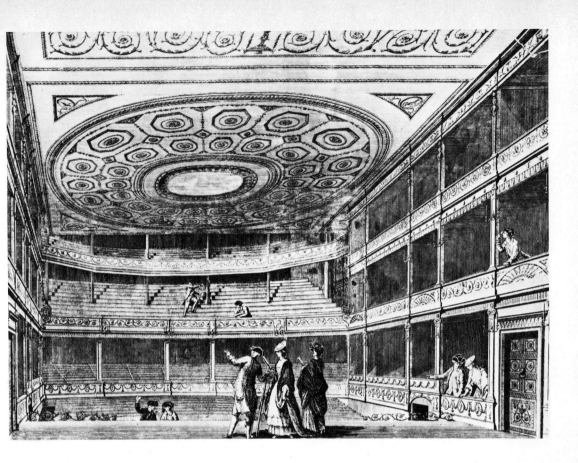

Prices were higher than today, and considerably higher than under Elizabeth I. Places in the pit cost about two shillings sixpence, in the boxes four shillings, in the middle gallery one shilling sixpence, and in the upper gallery one shilling. Prices in Shakespeare's theatre were from one penny to one shilling (except for stage seating), with the bulk of the seating costing two pence. The custom was to allow half-price admission after the third act, and all actors, managers, and playwrights were on the "free list."

As can be imagined, the upper gallery was a rowdy place, although serious disturbances were surprisingly few. Prostitutes were pre-sumably confined to the upper boxes, but pickpockets were rife. To combat the deplorable practice of some dandies and poetasters who often took it into their heads to damn a play by hisses and catcalls, managements employed claques who were instructed to applaud and cheer at the right moments. It would appear that though this eighteenth-century audience was by no means so boisterous as Shakespeare's, nor so quick with the sword as the somewhat later "dandies," it was certainly not the quiet and well-behaved crowd usual to the theatre today. By its likes and dislikes, made vocal and visual, it determined the types of plays, to a large extent their physical production, and the style of acting. Great talent on the other side of the footlights sometimes dictated public taste, then as now, but as always the audience was the supreme arbiter.

English theatre in America

Opposition to theatre continued to be felt throughout the century, with more than fifty diatribes against it being published during that time. In America, dramatic performances were almost completely prohibited by the religious scruples of the New England colonies and the middle colonies; Virginia, that Cavalier settlement, was the one to which Hallam's company journeyed. Virginia had been the scene of the first recorded English production in the New World, that of a now-lost play entitled *Ye Beare and Ye Cubbe,* for which presentation the author and actors were brought into court in 1665. This inauspicious beginning of theatre in America was typical of conditions in the colonies. In 1709 the Province of New York forbade play acting along with cock fighting and other "disreputable" forms of entertainment, and both the New England colonies and Pennsylvania—the one basically Puritan, the other Quaker—were deeply opposed to any kind of theatrical entertainment.

By 1716, however, there was a small native company performing in Williamsburg, Virginia. In 1723, there is record of performances by strolling players outside of Philadelphia, and by 1749 the company of Walter Murray and Thomas Kean was performing in a warehouse within the city limits. The next year they performed in New York and in Williamsburg, and in 1752 the Hallam Company came to Virginia. They made significant progress during the next twenty years up and down the coast, but dispersed in 1774 when the First Continental Congress passed

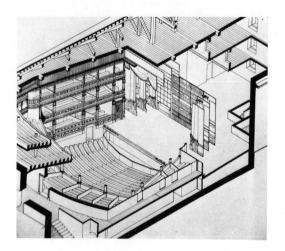

OLD DRURY LANE, CONTINUED
Above, Richard Leacroft's reconstruction of the Drury Lane of Garrick's time, with a single set of proscenium doors, an orchestra pit, and three galleries opposite the stage. Note that the stage is set for *School for Scandal* (cf. page 239). Right, the interior of Drury Lane in 1792, after more seats had been added in the boxes and new candelabra installed. (Richard Leacroft Collection; Henry E. Huntington Library and Art Gallery)

a resolution, which among other things, discouraged all "expensive diversions and entertainments." During the Revolutionary War, British soldiers presented plays in Boston, New York, and Philadelphia, and even the American soldiers, though having both less leisure and less inclination for theatre, presented Addison's *Cato* at Valley Forge. When the war was over, the self-exiled Hallam Company, now calling itself The American Company instead of The English Company, returned and professional dramatic activity resumed.

The nascent theatre in Scotland suffered similar difficulties. Glasgow's first theatre was burned by a mob in 1752, at the insti-

gation of the militant Methodist, George Whitfield (1714–1770). The Presbytery of Edinburgh suppressed plays and outlawed playwrights for several decades; when the Reverend John Home had his patriotic *Douglas* (1756) produced, he was asked to resign from the ministry. But there was a flourishing theatre in Dublin which sent many performers to the stages of London, and smaller theatres were establishing firm hold in the English provinces.

Age undistinguished by its plays

The eighteenth century is universally known as the Age of Great Acting; the plays of the age were largely undistinguished. Altered versions of the classics were given and were immensely popular. Shakespeare, too, suffered at the hands of producers. *Romeo and Juliet*, in Garrick's version, had one hundred forty-two performances in twenty-five seasons. Of the Shakespeare canon, Garrick produced twenty-four at Drury Lane, most of them changed. *The Tempest, The Winter's Tale, A Midsummer's Night's Dream,* and *The Taming of the Shrew* were made into opera-like plays with music and dancing. The Gravediggers were cut out of Hamlet. Macbeth made a dying speech. When the American Company presented *Othello* in Newport in 1761, Desdemona was smothered "in an adjoining room." The tragedies of Racine were offered in translations by Ambrose Philips and Charles Johnson, and those of Voltaire by Aaron Hill. When comedies of the Restoration period were revived (as they frequently were), they were often bowdlerized. Public taste favored comedy; tragedy was usually propped up with the presentation of a comic afterpiece that was as liberally advertised as the main play.

The original dramatic writing of the period may be conveniently divided into seven types: classical tragedy (or, more exactly, pseudoclassic tragedy), domestic tragedy, comedy of manners, sentimental comedy, farce, ballad-opera, and pantomime. The last two are decidedly less literary than the first five, and worthy of notice only because they occupied so large a portion of the theatrical scene.

Samuel Johnson, that eminently "reasonable" man, speaks for classical tragedy when he says in *The Rambler* (No. 125, 1751):

As the design of tragedy is to instruct
by moving the passions, it must always
have a hero, a personage apparently
and incontestably superior to the rest,
upon whom the attention may be fixed
and the anxiety suspended.

Firmly adhering to the accepted pattern of classical tragedy as interpreted by the French, English tragic dramatists of the eighteenth century dipped once more into the traditional materials, producing verse plays of almost startling stiffness. The general worthlessness of this genre is illustrated by the fact that the best of them was the *Cato* of Joseph Addison (1713), which owed its immediate popularity to its seeming application to the then-rife speculation over Queen Anne's successor and was thus widely translated, produced, and imitated on the Continent. There was a *Siege of Damascus*

by one John Hughes, a *Miriamne* by Elijah Fenton, and a *Sophonisba* by James Thomson, who belongs, not to the tradition of classical tragedy, but to the beginnings of romantic poetry. Delicious fun is poked at the sonorous inanities of this play, as well as at many other things, by Henry Fielding in *The Tragedy of Tragedies, or The Life and Death of Tom Thumb the Great* (1730).

Using the form, though not the materials of classical tragedy, James Young, another preromantic poet, wrote three plays, *Busiris* (1719), *The Revenge* (1721) using the Othello theme, and *The Brothers* (1735). The first American play to be produced by professional actors, Thomas Godfrey's *The Prince of Parthia* (1767), was another of this kind, as were Arthur Murphy's two English plays, *The Grecian Daughter* (1772) and *Alzuma* (1773). The one play of Samuel Johnson (*Irene*, 1736), with which he came armed to London, is little more than a series of dialogues on moral themes between Mahomet, Emperor of the Turks, and various Greek captives. It was not produced until 1749 when Garrick performed this act of kindness for his old friend and mentor.

Heroic drama was almost alien to the taste of eighteenth-century theatregoers; dramatists met those tastes by the development of a comparatively new genre, the domestic tragedy, or pathetic tragedy, which used materials closer to the understanding and sympathy of its audiences while retaining the rudiments of classical form. Some starts had been made in this direction during the Elizabethan period, when Thomas Heywood wrote *A Woman Killed with Kindness;* but the writers of the eighteenth century, in once more taking up domestic materials for tragedy, handled them with a sentimentality foreign to the Elizabethans. Such were the plays of Nicholas Rowe, poet laureate at his death in 1718—notably *Jane*

Theatre Royal in *Drury-Lane*,
This present *Saturday*, being the 9th of OCTOBER,
Will be presented a PLAY, call'd
ROMEO and *JULIET*.
Written by SHAKESPEAR.
Romeo by Mr. GARRICK,
Escalus by Mr. BRANSBY,
Capulet by Mr. BERRY,
Paris by Mr. JEFFERSON,
Benvolio by Mr. USHER,
Mountague by Mr. BURTON,
Tibalt by Mr. BLAKES,
Fryar *Lawrence* by Mr. HAVARD,
Mercutio by Mr. WOODWARD,
Lady *Capulet* by Mrs PRITCHARD,
Nurse by Mrs. MACKLIN,
Juliet by Miss PRITCHARD,
(Being the *First Time* of her appearing upon ANY STAGE.)
With the ADDITIONAL SCENE Representing
The Funeral PROCESSION
To the MONUMENT of the *CAPULETS*.
The VOCAL PARTS by
Mr. *Beard*, Mr. *Champness* and *Others*.
In Act I. a *Masquerade Dance* proper to the Play.
To which will be added a FARCE, call'd
The ANATOMIST.
Monf. *Le Medecin* by Mr. BLAKES,
Crispin by Mr. YATES,
Beatrice by Mrs. BENNET.
Boxes 5s. Pit 3s. First Gallery 2s. Upper Gallery 1s.
Places for the BOXES to be had of Mr. VARNEY, at the Stage-door of the *Theatre*.
† *No Persons to be admitted behind the Scenes, nor any Money to be returned after the* Curtain *is drawn up*. *Vivat* REX.

AT THE
THEATRE ROYAL
In COVENT-GARDEN,
This present *Monday*, being the 29th of *November*,
Will be presented a TRAGEDY, call'd
ALL FOR LOVE:
OR,
The WORLD well LOST.
Marc Antony by Mr. BARRY,
Dolabella by Mr. SMITH,
Alexas by Mr. DYER,
Serapion by Mr. MARTEN, *Myris* by Mr. REDMAN,
Ventidius by Mr. SPARKS,
Octavia by Mrs. ELMY,
Charmion by Mrs. BAKER, *Iras* by Miss MULLART,
Cleopatra by Mrs. WOFFINGTON.
With DANCING
By Mr. GRANIER, Mr. LEPPIE, Mrs. GRANIER, and OTHERS.
To which will be added a *Ballad* FARCE, call'd
The LOTTERY.
With the SCENE of
The DRAWING in *GUILD-HALL*.
Lovemore by Mr. LOWE,
Stocks by Mr. DUNSTALL,
Jack Stocks (*alias* Lord *Lace*) by Mr. DYER,
Chloe (*alias* Lady *Lace*) by Mrs. BAKER.
Boxes 5*s*. Pit 3*s*. First Gallery 2*s*. Upper Gallery 1*s*.
PLACES for the BOXES to be taken of Mr. *CRUDGE*, at the Stage-Door of the *Theatre*.

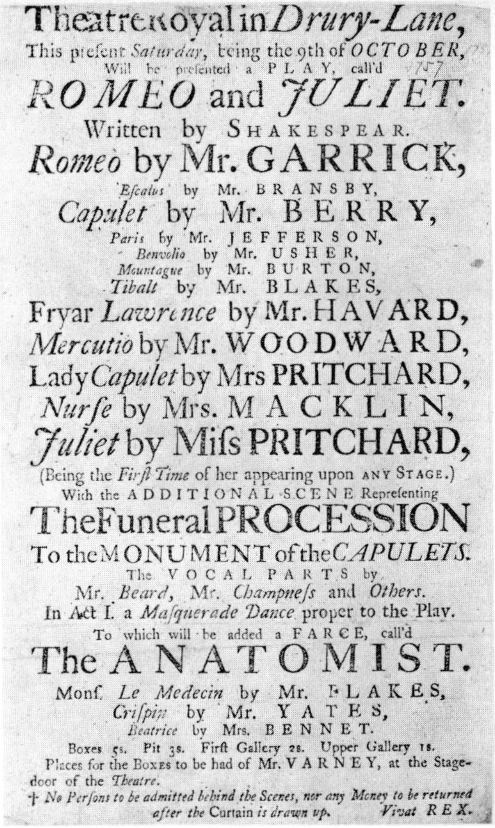

TWO EIGHTEENTH-CENTURY PLAYBILLS
These two playbills, from the middle of the century, show a typical evening's entertainment: a tragedy followed by a farce. Notice that dancing is added to *All for Love* at Covent Garden, and a Funeral Procession to *Romeo and Juliet* at Drury Lane, while the masquerade dance of Act I, "proper to the Play," is also advertised. (Henry E. Huntington Library and Art Gallery)

Shore and *The Fair Penitent,* in which Mrs. Siddons starred for many years. The *Douglas,* already mentioned, of the Reverend John Home, was a combination of classical and domestic models, using materials from a Scottish ballad, and providing in Young Norval, the hero, one of the most popular acting parts of the century. The most famous of the genre, however, and the most influential was George Lillo's *The London Merchant, or The History of George Barnwell,* first produced in 1731. It was epic-making in that it was written in prose rather than verse (except for the prologue). In the preface to the printed edition, Lillo states the credo for the new form:

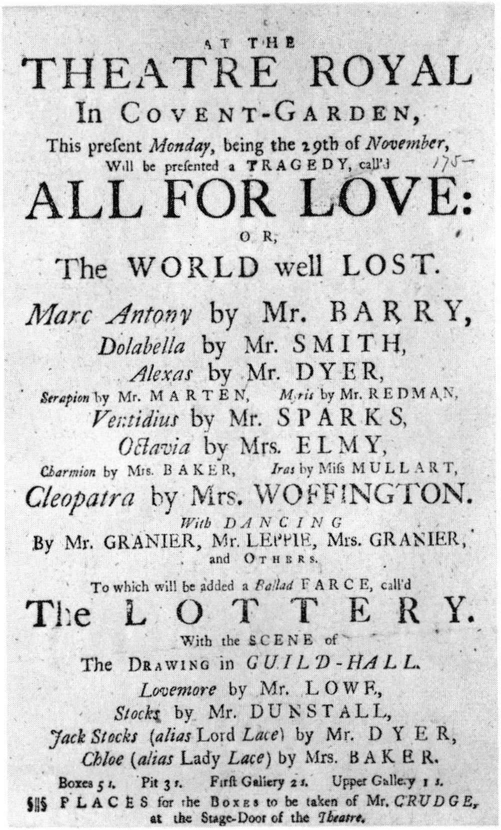

> tragedy is so far from losing its dignity
> by being accommodated to the
> circumstances of the generality of mankind
> that it is more truly august in proportion
> to the extent of its influence and the

numbers that are properly affected by it . . . Plays founded on moral tales in private life may be of admirable use, by carrying conviction to the mind with such irresistible force as to engage all the faculties and powers of the soul in the cause of virtue, by stifling vice in its first principle.

So by example he would teach his new audiences the code of behavior of his mer-

chant prince, Mr. Thoroughgood, and the dire consequences in Barnwell of a breach of that code. Lillo's play supplied Diderot, the great French critic, with his theme that plays should be serious, bourgeois drama of real life. The same theme was then successfully expounded by Lessing and long had a great effect on German stage literature.

The shallowness that marked much of the domestic tragedy of the period was evident also in the comedy of sentiment, begun in

TWO FAMOUS PLAYS
Left. engraving of the famous screen scene in Sheridan's *School for Scandal*, 1777. The bookcase and window are painted on the backdrop; the actors are playing on the apron. Note the effective use of side-lighting. Above, Addison's *Cato* as presented in the Niewe Hofzaal, Amsterdam, 1766. The stage decoration consists of wing flats, borders, and backcloth; the doors are in the proscenium. The actresses are in contemporary dress. (Harvard Theatre Collection)

reaction to the amorality of Restoration comedy. An early example is Colley Cibber's *Love's Last Shift* (1696) in which the roving husband completely reforms. Sir Richard Steele, of *Tatler* and *Spectator* fame, produced his first comedy of this kind in 1701. It was called *The Funeral, or Grief à la Mode*, in which he said he intended to present virtue and vice in their true form. This was followed by *The Lying Lover* (1703) and *The Tender Husband* (1705); he did not

return to playwriting until 1722 with his final play, *The Conscious Lovers*. Here the conscious morality and sentimentality of the chief characters are delightfully relieved by the realistic comedy of the servants. In the preface to the printed version of the play (1723) Steele states the purpose of sentimental comedy:

For the greatest effect of a play in reading is to excite the reader to go and see it;

and when he does so, it is then a play has the effect of example and precept.

What the upwardly-mobile audiences wanted and got—in characters, in dialogue, and in plot—was not life as they knew it but as ideally they would have liked it to be, with cogent examples (both good and bad) of how to make it so.

Among the many sentimental comedies of Richard Cumberland, the best and most often played were *The Brothers* (1769) and *The West Indian* (1771); ruses, mistaken identities, and trials of character were Cumberland's favorite themes. Mrs. Elizabeth Inchbald, actress-playwright, had a successful comedy in 1785 with *I'll Tell You What*. She also wrote *Every One Has His Faults* and *Wives as They Were and Maids as They Are*, which have some moments as sprightly as their titles. Thomas Holcroft, friend of Tom Paine and William Godwin, wrote many sentimental plays, the best known of which is *The Road to Ruin* (1792). Thomas Morton introduced the name of "Mrs. Grundy" in his *Speed the Plough* (1798); this play had been preceded by *The Way to Get Married* (1796) and *A Cure for Heartache* (1797). Additional representatives of the type are Arthur Murphy's *Three Weeks After Marriage* (1764), and *The Way to Keep Him* (1760), whose subject matter is obvious.

The most prolific of these dramatists was John O'Keefe, among whose fifty-odd productions were *Tony Lumpkin in Town* (1778), obviously derived from Goldsmith's famous *She Stoops to Conquer, Wild Oats* (1791), and *The Castle of Andalusia* (1782). Almost equally prolific were the George Colmans, Senior and Junior. The elder Colman, erstwhile manager of Covent Garden and the Haymarket Theatres, wrote and adapted some thirty plays, notably *The Jealous Wife*

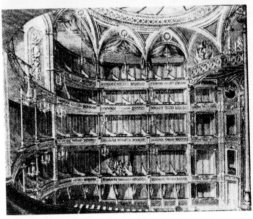

(1761), and, with his good friend David Garrick, *The Clandestine Marriage* (1766). The younger Colman, among many less important pieces, immortalized the famous British character in his *John Bull* (1803).

Some reaction to the sentimental comedy is evident in the truly comic scenes of Oliver Goldsmith's *The Good Natured Man* as early as 1768, and again in Samuel Foote's *The Handsome Housemaid* (1773), which is a burlesque of the sentimental comedy. Indeed, in his *Essay on Theatre* (1772), Goldsmith stated his opposition to sentimental comedy which, he said, "flatter(s) every man in his favorite foible." But representatives of the true comedy of manners are very few and somewhat late in the century's development. The rash and protean Richard Brinsley

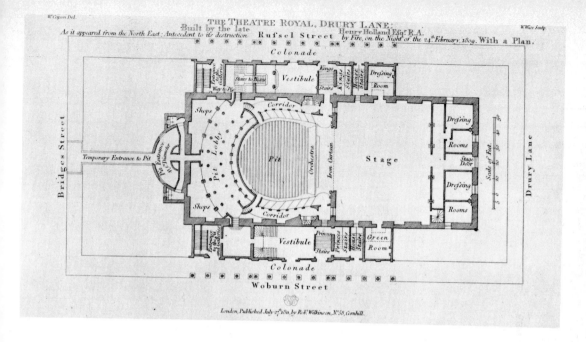

THE THEATRE ROYAL, DRURY LANE;
Built by the late Henry Holland Esq. R.A.
As it appeared from the North East; Antecedent to its destruction by Fire, on the Night of the 24. February, 1809. With a Plan.

London, Published July 27, 1811 by Rob.t Wilkinson, N.o 58, Cornhill.

NEW DRURY LANE
Facade, interior, and plan of the New Drury Lane, opened in 1794, as the "largest theatre in all Europe." Note the abbreviated stage apron and the increased stage area for scenes and machines. The actors are now performing largely "within the scene," i.e., behind the proscenium arch. (Yale Theatrical Prints Collection; Henry E. Huntington Library and Art Gallery)

Sheridan recovered something of the brilliance of Restoration comedy without its obscenity in two of his most celebrated plays, *The Rivals* (1775) and *The School for Scandal* (1777), whose characters and situations continue to delight audiences today. The former is not without its passages of high-flown sentiment, and the way in which Charles Surface, in the latter, wins his uncle's heart by cherishing the old man's portrait is also purely sentimental. But the total tenor of both plays is sharp, incisive, and refreshing. Still very popular, too, is Goldsmith's *She Stoops to Conquer* (1773), which, while not so incisive as the plays of Sheridan, is still in the comedy of manners tradition. And the first native American comedy, Royall Tyler's *The Contrast* (1787),

was of this genre, pointing up the superiority of the homegrown American to the Anglophile society in which he is deposited.

Criticism is implicit also in the many satirical portraits in the plays of Samuel Foote, and in the dramatic pieces written during the American Revolution by Mercy Otis Warren and John Leacock. As literary satires, Sheridan's *The Critic* (1779) and Fielding's *Tom Thumb* (1731) are unparalleled.

Farce, with its total emphasis upon amusing situations, was domesticated to a thoroughly English species during the eighteenth century with such lively pieces as *The Lying Valet* (1741), *Miss In Her Teens* (1747), *The Irish Widow* (1772), and *High Life Below Stairs* (1759). Garrick was its chief protagonist.

The ballad-opera, in which the text of a burlesque farce was interspersed with songs written to popular tunes, was an eighteenth-century English growth. The most notable of the type, and certainly good theatre in any age, is John Gay's *The Beggar's Opera* (1728), with its immortal characters, whom nobody any longer thinks of as being satiric. Sheridan also wrote in this genre; his delightful *The Duenna* (1777) is also good theatre today.

Of the pantomimes brief mention has already been made. In addition to garnering the fare for these "harlequinades" from previous and present theatre, the producers of the increasingly popular pantomimes often made up their presentations entirely. But since the pantomimes were primarily spectacle, and only very secondarily literary drama of any sort, there is no need to linger over them.

Playwrights of the eighteenth century, following popular taste, tended to stress the rewards of virtue, the demands of gentility, and the trials of character, with much emphasis on disguises, surprises, and unexpected wealth. Though many of the plays are quite lively, and certainly pleased contemporary audiences, their artificiality and superficial treatment of character have rendered the majority of them quite without interest to today's audiences. The very existence of theatre depended upon the number of tickets sold; the number of tickets sold depended upon how accurately the plays reflected the tastes of the audiences

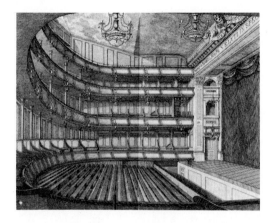

COVENT GARDEN INTERIORS
Left, old print of a riot at Covent Garden in 1763 during a performance of *Artaxerxes*. Note the lighting arrangements, the stage boxes, the orchestra pit, and the actors performing on the apron stage with the scenic background behind the proscenium. Above, the interior of Covent Garden in 1794, its final remodeling before it burned down in 1808. Note the benches in the pit. (Henry E. Huntington Library and Art Gallery)

who bought them. Eighteenth-century play-writing is a mirror of that taste.

Culminating developments in playhouses

That theatre was successful in meeting the tastes of its new audiences is attested by the fact that those audiences grew larger and larger: the eighteenth century shows a record of ever-increasing size and number of playhouses. Drury Lane in London will illustrate this tendency. As earlier detailed, the first small house, built by Killigrew in 1663, was burned to the ground in 1672. The somewhat larger second building on the same plot was designed by Christopher Wren and opened in 1674. During most of the succeeding century, it underwent extensive remodeling and enlargement until it was condemned and completely torn down in 1792.

Also mentioned was the fact that the first remodeling was done by the then-manager Christopher Rich in 1696, when he provided for more seats by cropping the apron four feet and converting the downstage proscenium doors into boxes. But so firmly entrenched was the use of the double proscenium doors that the loss of the lower pair was compensated for by adding a pair to the area above the proscenium arch, to either side of the stage.

Lacy and Garrick enlarged the seating capacity somewhat when they took over the patent in 1747. Then in 1762 a major change occurred. Garrick had long been wanting to banish from the stage those spectators who, relying on the tradition of stage seating (which had begun in England about 1690), had spoiled performances. But stage seating was a good source of revenue, particularly on actors' benefit nights when patrons crowded the area, their total admission price going to the actor whose benefit it was. Often they formed a complete amphitheatre on the stage, effectively screening out the scenery and making entrances and stage movement difficult. Garrick knew that he could not deprive his company of the money represented by stage seating without compensating for it elsewhere. So he remodeled the interior of the theatre to provide more seating space (*cf.*, pages 219, 234) and the next year prohibited the public from behind the scenes, with little protest from his company.

Sheridan enlarged the house once more in 1781, increasing the capacity to two thousand. These successive enlargements were demanded by attendance; average daily attendance swelled from about six hundred fifty in 1742 to almost twelve hundred by 1775, with the theatre capacity enlarging from about one thousand to about fourteen hundred.

This Drury Lane Theatre, which was in constant use for a hundred years, was an intimate playhouse with three galleries opposite the stage, the lower two of which had been converted from boxes, and three rows of boxes along the sides. In this old house, as one of the critics of the New Drury Lane remarked,

The moving brow and penetrating eye of
that matchless actor [Garrick] came
home to the spectator. As the passions
shifted, and were by turns reflected from
the mirror of his expressive countenance,
nothing was lost.
RICHARD CUMBERLAND
Memoirs, London, 1807, Supplement, p. 58.

But the old house was replaced in 1794 with the largest theatre in all of Europe. It had a capacity of over thirty-six hundred seated in an almost semicircular auditorium, with five rows of boxes along the sides and two opposite the stage, topped by two galleries, in addition to the pit. The portion of the proscenium arch over the stage apron was also fitted with boxes, there was only one pair of proscenium doors, and a spacious lobby was provided for the pit patrons. Richard Cumberland complains that

Upon the scale of the modern Drury
many of the finest touches of his
[Garrick's] art would of necessity fall
short. The distant auditor might chance to
catch the text, but would not see the
comment, that was wont so exquisitely to
elucidate the poet's meaning, and impress
it on the hearer's heart.
Memoirs, p. 58

Many similar complaints were lodged against this cavernous house.

The stage was, likewise, of impressive proportions—forty-three feet wide by thirty-eight feet high at the proscenium opening, extending to ninety-two feet in depth. The backstage area was eighty-five feet wide and more than a hundred feet high, so that none of the scenery from the old house could be used, and all had to be built anew. The house was equipped with water piped to every part in case of fire, and an iron curtain was hung at the proscenium to shut off the stage in such emergency. Nevertheless, the theatre was completely destroyed by fire in 1809, the interior, as an economy measure, having been built entirely of wood, and the fire precautions having been neglected.

The other patent house of eighteenth-cen-

OTHER LONDON THEATRES
Left, one of the small, speculative houses
was the Regency, 1815, so named when it was
refurbished. It had been built originally in
the 1790s as the Scala. Above, Astley's Amphitheatre, 1780, a much larger house with a
variety of uses. (Henry E. Huntington Library and Art Gallery)

tury London was the Covent Garden Theatre,
built and opened by John Rich in 1732. At
that time it was eighty-six feet long from
the proscenium opening to the opposite wall
(almost twice the depth of Drury Lane) and
fifty-six feet wide. This rectangular area had
a row of boxes opposite the stage, with two
very deep galleries above, and three rows
of boxes along the sides. Its capacity was
about two thousand. It was highly decorated
with draperies, pilasters, and friezes. The
stage apron was reduced in depth, and the
single pair of stage doors was set back from
the edge of the apron far enough to allow,
on the stage level, a pair of double boxes.

But the long and comparatively narrow
house had the same difficulties as Dorset

Garden. In 1784 it underwent alterations to
try to improve the difficulties of hearing and
seeing from the farthest seats. Then again
in 1791 and 1794 the interior was reconstructed, including the provision of more
boxes for the growing affluence and affecta-
tions of the audience, and a resonating
chamber was installed beneath the floor. The
stage area was also enlarged. But the edifice
burned to the ground on September 20, 1808.

Before moving to Covent Garden, Rich's
company had been playing at Lincoln's Inn
Fields, in the old, converted Lisle's Tennis
Court of Restoration days. This theatre
continued in sporadic use through most of
the century. Dorset Garden, the grandiose
structure of the Restoration, was soon aban-

doned in the new century because of bad acoustics, and the Queen's Theatre in the Haymarket, built for Betterton by Vanbrugh in 1704, was turned over to opera for the same reason. Contrary to the Continental practice of building elaborate structures primarily for opera, English practice tended to consign to the musical form whatever houses were unsuitable for plays. Vanbrugh had incorporated into his house a large lobby for the box patrons, and added a large entrance foyer and salon with fireplaces.

The Little Theatre in the Haymarket opened in 1720 and was in operation through most of the century. At one time it was under the management of Henry Fielding, whose sharp satires are said to have instigated the Licensing Act of 1737 which restricted the production of legitimate drama to the two patent houses. It had been erected by a builder named Potter and was a very modest building, with but one gallery and no special accommodations for the audience. It became a protype of the small, speculative playhouse which would meet the needs of the growing theatre audiences of London in areas away from the main theatrical center. It was taken over by Samuel Foote in 1776 when he obtained a patent for performances in the summer months. He took over some additional property to provide a portico and entrance lobby. Corridors and entrance doors were enlarged and a second gallery added. In 1777 George Colman purchased it and was successful there for many years. (In 1820 the old building was demolished and the theatre called the Haymarket today was erected on the spot.)

In 1765 the old wooden "music house" at Sadler's Wells (the site of a medicinal spring) was pulled down and a modest theatre building of stone was erected, and enlarged in 1778. Another of the small, unlicensed theatres was one called The New

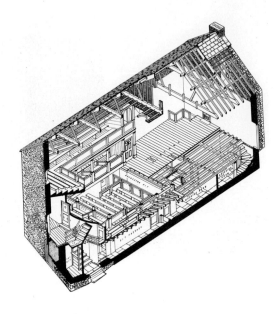

Wells, which had been built by Thomas Odell in 1729 in Leman Street in Goodman's Fields. It was under the managership of William Hallam from 1740 to 1751, when it was closed and the Hallam company set out for America in an attempt to recoup their fortunes. Astley's Amphitheatre opened in 1770—a building originally no more than a sawdust ring with covered benches at the side for patrons to watch the performing horses. But in 1780 the structure took on the formality of a complete building, with an ordinary galleried playhouse where a major section of the pit was made into a circular riding ring. Portions of the program offered were dramatic in nature and, for these, benches were set up in the riding ring and removed for the "hippodrama" which ordinarily came later in the program.

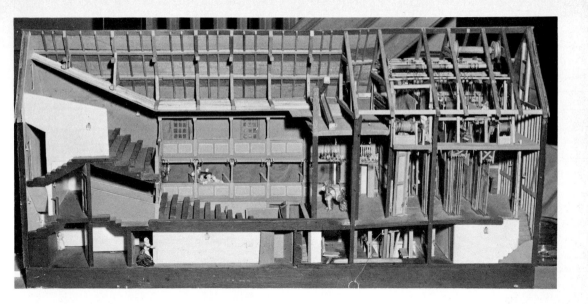

PROVINCIAL THEATRES
Left, the Georgian Theatre, Richmond, Yorkshire, 1788, measured and drawn by Richard
Leacroft. Above, a scale model of the theatre
built at Williamsburg, Virginia in 1751. The
similarities of construction are plainly evident: the single pair of proscenium doors,
the orchestra pit, the side boxes, and the
galleries. This plan was to remain standard
in theatre construction for a very long period of time. (Richard Leacroft Collection;
Colonial Williamsburg)

Thus Astley circumvented the licensing laws
and at the same time pleased his patrons.
His idea was widely copied both in England
and in America.

Other theatres built during the century
include the Pantheon (1770), but it had disappeared by the end of the century; the
Royal Circus (1782), which was converted
to the Surrey Theatre in 1805; the Royalty
Theatre (1785); the East London Theatre
(1787); and the pretentiously named Theatre
Royal English Opera House, which replaced
in 1789 an old music hall called the Lyceum,
devoting its programs to variety acts, music,
and dancing.

Few of these unlicensed theatres were as
large as the patent houses, and those in the
provinces were also small. For instance, the
New Theatre Royal, built in Edinburgh in
1768 and in operation for ninety years, was
a building only fifty by a hundred feet, built
at a total cost of fifteen hundred pounds
including scenes, wardrobe, and decorations.
It is supposed to have seated six hundred
thirty and was, at the beginning of the next
century, taken over by no less a person
than Sir Walter Scott.

Typical of these provincial stages is that
of Richmond, in England, built in 1788 and
still standing. It is a rectangle, measuring
twenty-four by fifty-four feet inside, and seating about four hundred people. The sloped
floor of the pit has eight rows of benches,
terminating in a row of boxes with a gallery
above and a single row of boxes along the
sides. The stage is twenty-seven feet deep,
including a five-foot apron, and is raked. The
proscenium arch is seventeen feet high,

about fifteen feet wide, and has a single set of proscenium doors.

Dublin had had a theatre since 1635, and the Smock Alley Theatre, opened in 1662, was a fertile source of talent for the London stage, as well as a rewarding stop for visiting actors. From 1758 to 1819 a second theatre, the Crow Street, also flourished there.

Theatres built in America

In America, the Hallam Company, arriving in 1752, played in a series of temporary structures. In Williamsburg, their first stop, they performed in a converted warehouse which had been in use sporadically for various amateur performances. It had pit, boxes, balconies, and a gallery. No doubt it was very small. They played in other make-shift buildings in New York, Newport, Annapolis, Charleston, and in Philadelphia, where the first permanent theatre in America was built by David Douglass, who had taken over the company by reason of marrying Lewis Hallam's widow. The Southwark Theatre opened in November 1766 (in its first season it produced *The Prince of Parthia*, as mentioned above); it was a substantial structure of brick below and wood above, painted red, with interior pillars to support the roof. It was used continuously as a theatre for more than thirty years, and was used for other purposes for more than a century.

The other theatre of importance built in America in this period was also constructed by Douglass, and was called the John Street Theatre. It was opened in New York in 1767. William Dunlap (*History of the American Theatre*, 1833), the first historian of American theatre, says it had two rows of boxes, a pit, and a gallery, and was "an $800 house." It probably seated about a thousand people.

During the Revolution, the British requisitioned the house for amateur theatricals, but it fell again to the American Company after the Revolution, when Lewis Hallam, Jr. returned with them from Jamaica. One other playhouse of brick was erected at Annapolis in 1771. But the majority of "theatres"—and they were many—erected before the Revolution were converted spaces or ephemeral wooden structures. The spate of permanent theatre buildings in America came in the last two decades of the century; they were solidly built houses. Such theatres were erected in Charleston and in Richmond in 1786, in New Orleans in 1792, a second theatre in Charleston in 1793 as well as a "circus Pantheon" (like Astley's Amphitheatre) in Philadelphia. In 1794, the Chestnut Street Theatre in Phila-

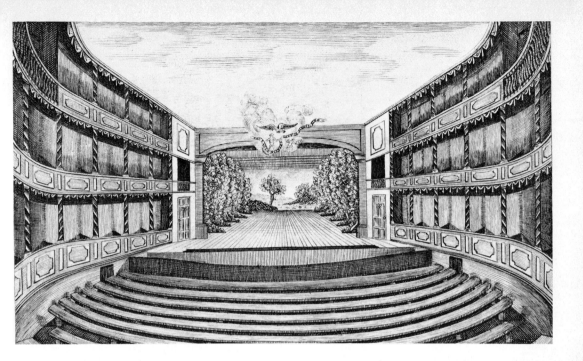

delphia and the Federal Street Theatre in
Boston were built; in 1795, the Theatre in
Providence; in 1796, theatres in Norfolk and
Petersburg in Virginia and the Haymarket
in Boston; and finally the splendid Park (or
New) Theatre in New York in 1798 with its
"Shakespeare box"—properly a gallery on the
second tier where ordinarily the front boxes
would be, an early evidence of the comparatively quick elimination of boxes from
American theatres. With the minor exception
noted here for the Park, all were of the
accepted design, with sloped pit floor, two to
three rows of boxes, one or two galleries,
a raked stage, an apron, and usually a set
of proscenium doors. It would be a long time
before theatres broke this mold and branched
out to new forms.

New departures in settings

As the playhouse increased in size, scenic
investiture increased in complexity. The pantomimes and operas, which relied on visual
interest, eventually affected design for the
legitimate theatre. For almost two-thirds of
the century, however, the patent houses relied on the use of the stock sets developed
in the preceding period, and they were put
upon the stage time after time in many
different plays. Tate Wilkinson, writing in
the 1780s, speaks of a particular set at Covent
Garden which had been in use since 1747, and
which he looked upon as "a very old acquaintance." The palace, garden, temple, and
prison were in constant use, as a 1743 inventory of Covent Garden illustrates. These

were, of course, painted on flats, backcloths or shutters, and borders. The flats were operated in grooves, as Inigo Jones had long ago prescribed. Interiors as well as exteriors were handled in this way, the walls of a room being formed by a triangular arrangement of wing flats ending in a back flat, and exteriors using the same arrangement except that the flats were now trees or buildings of one sort and another.

Theatres had permanent rigging to take care of the movement of this universal system of stage decoration. All that needed to be done was to change the flats, borders, and backcloth from play to play. Traveling companies could even remove painted canvases from their frames, roll them up, then retack them to frames in a new location. Thus the Hallams brought with them to Williamsburg "the Scenes . . . painted by the best Hands in LONDON, excell'd by none in Beauty and Elegance." Even the reportedly spectacular scenic effects achieved by the Alsatian Philippe Jacques de Loutherbourg for Garrick at Drury Lane after 1771 were basically operated by the same system. The painting on the flats, however, brought, for the first time to England, realistic illusionistic scenery.

True, de Loutherbourg rarely designed for legitimate drama, concentrating on the dramatic entertainments which were a part of the Drury Lane repertory, but his ideas and production methods were important for the future of scenic art. For the flat backcloth he sometimes used three-dimensional forms, giving the illusion of great distance. He achieved spectacular effects in outdoor settings, journeying to Derbyshire for on-the-spot sketches to be translated to the stage for *The Wonders of Derbyshire;* he started with authentic sketches in his recreation of a scene in the South Seas. He employed cloud effects and transparent scenery, and experi-

mented successfully with new ways of using elemental effects. He tried stained glass and colored silks for lighting effects, and dispensed with the hot and smelly footlights in favor of side and top lighting on the stage itself. The influence of his work is apparent when we read of no less than a member of the Royal Academy designing stage scenery in 1780, by which time it had become the custom for the scene designer to be called in for consultation at the beginning of production on a play. And it is obvious from the record that "Loutherbourg pieces" were frequently given for the express purpose of displaying his unique faculties.

With William Capon, who came to Drury Lane when it moved into its new and greatly enlarged house in 1794, the old wing and border systems for the standard plays were almost completely discarded, and new sets, obviously intended to become standard, were designed. Capon was a romanticist imbued with the artistic possibilities of the Gothic style, and this style he transposed to the stage with careful research and draftsmanship. His work marked the end of the temples and palaces which had dressed the theatre for so long, and ushered in a new era.

By this time, also, the use of forced perspective had practically disappeared, and all the grooves, when used, were of one height. The front curtain was still raised at the beginning of the show and lowered at the end, but there was an increasing use of act drops, often specially prepared for particular performances.

The wonders of the new scenery were employed in the provinces as quickly as possible, though often the reincarnation was, of economic necessity, on a much less ambitious scale. When the Hallam company came to America, it brought with it a complete set of cast-off scenery from London, including the green front curtain which was standard

for a long time in both English and American theatres. But even here, as the century progressed, spectacular scenic effects were tried. There is an interesting and minute description of the stage effects for John Burk's *The Battle of Bunker's Hill*, produced in Boston in 1796, which tells of practical hills, houses on fire, and a quite realistic battle. Some of the effect was achieved by means of painted cannons and painted smoke borders and flats, but these were coupled with actual gunfire, real smoke, and flame. In Charleston, a production of *The Tempest* opened with an attempt at a real storm and shipwreck.

All during the century, theatres struggled with the problem of lighting, using oil lamps which gave better illumination but smelled and smoked, or candles, or a combination of the two. They would wait long for gas, and then electricity, to make spectacular developments in lighting possible.

Music was almost always a part of theatrical representation, even in straight dramas, with a special section of the pit, that nearest the stage, usually assigned to the musicians. The arrangement was much like the present-day "orchestra pit."

Within the limits of economy and possibility, the visual aspect of theatre received increasing attention.

Innovations, too, in costumes

Eighteenth-century costuming followed the practice of the Restoration theatre, which in turn derived much of its method from Elizabethan playhouses. But there were some interesting innovations of significance to be observed.

Study of various theatrical prints of the time, as well as of printed records, indicates that the men and the women performers followed separate systems. The actors' costumes for tragedy were of four types: contemporary, Roman, Eastern, and special. Garrick played Macbeth in knee breeches, a scarlet and gold coat, and a tie wig. Hamlet was played in the same contemporary dress, but all in black. Woodward played Mercutio in colorful eighteenth-century costume and a tricorne hat; Romeo was similarly attired. In plays with Roman backgrounds, the actors retained the knee breeches, but often wore tunic-like tops and mantles and sometimes breastplates and plumed helmets. Quin played Coriolanus in the stiff *tonnelet* (an umbrella-like skirt reaching to the knees) of the Paris Opera and the plumed headdress that was usual for heroes. Many prints show lacings up the calf as if sandals were being simulated. In parts like Othello and Bajazet, the costume consisted of roomy, full trousers, a loose coat often trimmed with fur, and a turban, sometimes with plumes. Boots and a scimitar completed the outfit. The special costumes were traditional, and generally wigless. Such a one was Falstaff, who appeared in an Elizabethan collar, large buskins, and a cloak. The print of Garrick as Richard III shows the slashed sleeves of the Elizabethan period; the slashing on Mrs. Barry's dress and the pointed collar and cuffs of Mr. Barry have something of the flavor of the supposed period of the play—1616. Shylock wore long, wide trousers, a long black gown, and a red tricorne. For comedy, contemporary dress was universally worn, whatever the period of the play. The richness of the actor's wardrobe was often enhanced by gifts of cast-off garments from the nobility. In the pastorals and pantomimes, individual and fantastic garments were worn.

It was the general rule, however, that no matter what the costume of the actor, the actress playing with him appeared in the most fashionable dress of the eighteenth century. The plumes were added for tragic heroines, but Cleopatra, Andromache, Merope, or Queen Elizabeth were clothed in the highly decorated, hoop-skirt fashion of the times, with hair dressed high and usually powdered. An occasional print indicates a bow in the direction of historical costuming, but such hints are more of the eighteenth century than otherwise. Due to the influence of Mrs. Bellamy, the traditional black velvet gown of the previous period's tragedy queen was given up and the richest possible dress substituted. She tells

of preparing a costume for Cleopatra by adding many diamonds to the silver tissue gown once worn by the Princess of Wales. With the allowance made her by the manager for costuming herself, she sometimes had her gowns made in Paris, and, by her own account, sometimes changed costumes from night to night for the same character and play. The only governing principle apparent in the costuming of women (in this day when players largely costumed themselves) was that the actress should look as bewitchingly fashionable and beautiful as possible. Chambermaids, country wenches, and servants all appeared in hoops and powdered hair and satin shoes, with no thought of authenticity, and this practice continued throughout the century in spite of many criticisms of it. Reform would require a stronger managerial hand as well as a concern by the ensemble for the total stage picture.

Almost the only exception to the uniform fashionable dress for women was taken by Sarah Kemble Siddons (1755–1831) who, even when she early appeared in the stays and hoop petticoats usual with the other actresses, did not powder and curl her hair but wore it smooth and braided. This delighted the great artist Sir Joshua Reynolds because it truly showed the size and shape of her head. She later became enamored of the Greek style, and gave up the stays and hoops for tragedy, adopting the drapery of Greek statuary for these roles.

The men were more adaptable to change, perhaps because their longer tenure on the public stage lessened the compulsion to present an invariably fashionable appearance. As early as 1721, Aaron Hill was urging costumes more nearly like the period the character was portraying, and in 1734 he provided sketches "in the old Saxon dress" for a play of his own. Macklin caused a sensa-

Mr. Quin

in the Character of Coriolanus.

QUIN IN TWO SHAKESPEAREAN ROLES
Left, Quin as Coriolanus. He wears the stiff skirt (tonnelet) which was popular on the French stage, and the head feathers which were usual for heroic characters. Above, as Falstaff, he again has a feathered hat, but wears a ruff and boots with his eighteenth-century dress. These touches were sufficient for his audiences, to make him a noncontemporary or "historical" character. (Harvard Theatre Collection)

tion in 1773, when he played Macbeth in "the old Scottish garb" even though his Lady appeared in the costume of contemporary fashion. Garrick followed with a *King Lear* in old English costume. Kemble dressed the witches in Macbeth as weird creatures, and attempted a reform in the Hamlet costume. Toward the end of the century actors began to realize that when the script called for disheveled dress, it was right to wear it so, and not accede, as Garrick earlier did in his Macbeth, to wrongheaded demands for perfect grooming no matter what the circumstances in the play. By this time the stars

at least made an attempt at correct costumes, although the rest of the cast might be in all sorts of contemporary dress. To the eighteenth-century mind, "historical" meant simply "not conventional or contemporary," and it remained for succeeding periods to develop a semblance of historical accuracy in costuming.

On the whole, eighteenth-century costuming would appear to be a hodgepodge, and no decent order was to come from this chaos for some time.

Makeup was more universally used by women than by men, and was basically a

powder makeup. White, black, red, and pink were the prevalent colors, applied from papers or pads of carded wool. Men ordinarily did not use makeup except when playing parts of a much greater age than their own, or for disguises. In the former instance, lines were drawn on the face with ink; in the latter, the use of false noses, beards, and wigs predominated. Lampblack was sometimes used for traditionally Negro characters. Makeup was removed either with cocoa butter or with plain soap and water. Although Garrick has been pointed out as being proficient in makeup, the general practice must have been rather crude, the effects garish.

Makeup was to improve in refinement and effectiveness as stage lighting improved.

The age of great acting

It is sometimes said that the eighteenth century was the Age of Great Acting because there were no great playwrights; that if the critics and writers who began to proliferate in that period had had challenging dramatists to deal with not so much would have been written about the actors. There may be some truth to this contention, for acting is surely one of the most ephemeral of all the

TWO FAMOUS PLAYERS IN TWO FAMOUS PLAYS
Left, Mr. and Mrs. Barry as Jaffier and
Belvidera in *Venice Preserved;* above, as
Bajazet and Selima in *Tamerlane*. Both these
plays and players were exceedingly popular
on the eighteenth-century stage. (Henry E.
Huntington Library and Art Gallery)

arts, and the art of this period is known only
by what can be read. Yet the actors of the
century did have Shakespeare, Congreve,
and Jonson to deal with, and from all
accounts met the challenge successfully.

If the critiques are read judiciously, and
the various sketches, prints, and portraits of
actors in various roles are studied with care,
one can only come to the conclusion that
eighteenth-century acting was a powerfully
developed art, and that it no doubt produced
at least two of the greatest talents the English stage has even seen—David Garrick and
Sarah Kemble Siddons.

In the first quarter of the century the

accepted style of acting—particularly in tragedy—was the sonorous line, the strutting
effect. It is best exemplified by James Quin
(1639-1766), a great hulk of an Irishman
ideally suited to comedy parts. Although he
made a superb Falstaff, he yet insisted on
being a tragedian. He performed in a bellow-
ing recitative with labored movement and
incongruous gesture. He was the product of
the elocutionary style which had been championed by Colley Cibber and was enshrined
in his *Apology* (1740). It was no doubt grand-
iloquent and formalized.

A transitional figure was Charles Macklin
(c. 1700-1797), also an Irishman come to Lon-

don, who took issue with the grand style and opposed too much elocution in the theatre. He felt that the actor should not "mould and suit the character" to his own gestures and manner, but rather that he should "suit his looks, tones, gestures, and manners to the character." He caused a sensation when in February 1741, he did a Shylock unknown to any living person. The interpretation assigned to Shylock by the usual "lines of business" of repertory playing was that of a comedian; at Drury Lane that year the part fell to Macklin, because he was a comedian. Over the protests of Fleetwood, then manager of Drury Lane, he completely changed the interpretation. The applause with which he was greeted caused Fleetwood to say, "Macklin, you *was* right, at last," and Alexander Pope to remark, "This was the Jew that Shakespeare drew." In preparation for his part, he is said to have spent hours on the Exchange, studying the Jewish money-lenders there.

Later that same year (October 19, 1741), David Garrick startled the theatre world in his appearance as Richard III at the Goodman's Fields Theatre, his first professional appearance in London. Quin's comment on first seeing Garrick is famous: "If this young fellow is right, then we are all wrong." During the season of 1745-1746 Quin and Garrick appeared on the same stage when Rich hired them both at Covent Garden. Public acclaim veered from one to the other and the season seems to have ended in a draw. But the next year Garrick took over the management of Drury Lane with James Lacy as his partner. He assumed responsibility for the artistic side of the productions, leaving the business details to his partner. From that point on he became the arbiter of acting in England; Quin and his old-fashioned style faded from view and Macklin lived in the shadow of Garrick's greatness. For thirty

ALL FOR LOVE.

MRS YATES as CLEOPATRA.
I'll die, I will not bear it, you may hold me.
Act V. Scene 1.

years at Drury Lane he was star performer, director, manager, playwright, and adapter. He set a standard of production and performance that was truly memorable. He acquired the best performers available for his company, whether or not he agreed with their artistic principles, and whether or not they were his rivals in popularity. He exacted "order, decency, and decorum" from them,

Mr. HARTLEY *in the Character of* CLEOPATRA.
I'll die I will not bear it.

TWO CLEOPATRAS AND A SHYLOCK
The actresses are playing in Dryden's *All for Love*. At the far left, Mrs. Yates in a 1777 production; above, Mrs. Hartley in a production of 1776. Eighteenth-century actresses generally wore the most elaborate possible dress in contemporary style, whatever the part they were playing; these two Cleopatras nicely illustrate the principle. Left, Macklin as Shylock, with curious long trousers over which he wears an eighteenth-century waistcoat, and the long Jewish gabardine. (Henry E. Huntington Library and Art Gallery)

set up a rehearsal schedule to which he demanded absolute adherence, expected his company to be letter perfect in their parts, and eventually provided them with the best that could be secured in the way of plays, costuming, and scenery. He even gave them a heretofore unheard of security by setting up his Actors Fund to take care of their old age and incapacitation. He was, withal, an astute businessman, who made a fortune for himself and a sizable income for his fellow-players. He was truly a protean genius. His activities called such attention to acting that many critics wrote articles, pamphlets, and books trying to analyze this "science"; among them were Aaron Hill, Frances Gentleman, John Hill, Roger Pickering, and Thomas Sheridan. Addison, Boswell, and Johnson also commented on acting as an art, Boswell particularly showing great insight when he wrote in 1770 that an actor "must have a kind of double feeling. He must assume in a strong degree the character which he represents, while he at the same time retains the consciousness of his own character." Garrick is usually credited with reforming acting in his day although, of course, what he did was to build upon the work of his predecessors, bring it to perfection, and demonstrate in his own performance that "perfectly right, perfectly natural" style for which he is commended.

From the plethora of materials written about him, one can today gather that his attraction on stage was that he could seem to *be* the character he was impersonating rather than to *recite* it, and that he could assume a wide variety of characters all different from what he was. In modern parlance, what he evidently achieved was an ideal characterization *in the circumstances* and *in the style* conceived by the playwright. Edwin Duerr (*The Length and Depth of Acting*, pp. 225 and 226) sums up Garrick's achievement as being due to his Versatility, his Vitality, and his Veracity (or truth). So long as Garrick held the stage, he could do no wrong, and all other contemporary performances are compared with his.

During his last year of tenure at Drury Lane, a young actress from the provinces joined his company—Sarah Kemble Siddons. But so inauspicious was her accomplishment that when Sheridan took over the management of the theatre the next year, he did not hire her. Back to the provinces she went and did not return until 1782 when Sheridan did make her a member of the company. Her first appearance was as Isabella in *The Fatal Marriage* and she was sensational. From that time until her retirement in 1812, she was the darling of the London public quite as much

GARRICK IN PERFORMANCE
Above, the closet scene from *Hamlet*. See page 227. The Ghost is still dressed in armor; the background is now mid-eighteenth century; the costumes belong also to the period of the production. Betterton's full-bottomed wig has given way to the periwig. Right, the tomb scene from *Romeo and Juliet* with Mrs. Bellamy. In this version Juliet happily awakens before Romeo kills himself. Again the costumes are contemporary with the actors rather than with the period and place of the play. (Harvard Theatre Collection)

as Garrick had been before her. But by that time either the theatres had become so big, or the tastes of the public so changed that her acting style was less natural, more declamatory than that of Garrick. Everything she did was deliberately designed, thought through with penetrating intelligence and insight, performed with meticulous attention to detail—in other words, done with complete artistry so that it *seemed* right. She was perhaps the most famous Lady Macbeth ever to appear on the English stage.

Another of the twelve children of the provincial actor Roger Kemble was Mrs. Siddons' brother John Philip Kemble, whose ability and fame were only a shade less than hers. He, too, managed Drury Lane and later Covent Garden, but his genius was not so many-sided as that of Garrick. He was a far better actor than manager, although he did spend much time in the preparation of production books for his performances, particularly the Shakespearean revivals. He is said to have been a superb Hamlet, and played a distinguished Macbeth to his sister's Lady. He, too, lived on into the next century.

Other notable names of the older generation are those of John Wilks (1665–1732), who was good in both tragedy and comedy, and was one of the managers of Drury Lane before the advent of Garrick; Barton Booth (1681–1733), who was reputedly unsurpassed in his attitudes, or poses assumed while listening to other performers; Colley Cibber (1661–1757), who was a versatile utility actor and became a significant theatre historian;

and Anne Oldfield (1638–1730), whose career of unbroken triumph ended with a burial in Westminster Abbey which greatly impressed at least one of the onlookers, Voltaire. Contemporary with Garrick was Spranger Barry (1719–1777), whose very good looks and superior ability made him a rival to Garrick in the esteem of the public, their playing of the same parts often being minutely compared; his wife Ann (1734–1801), who is said to have been unsurpassed in comedy, especially as Millamant; Kitty Clive (1711–1785), who frequently battled with Garrick over her desire to play tragic roles although, as Garrick insisted, she was far more suited to the comic roles in which she was eminently successful; and Peg Woffington (c. 1714–1760), sometime mistress of Garrick who was greatly admired for the spirit and elegance of her performances, no less than for her natural ready wit and intelligence. Of less skill but of some importance were the actor-soldier-of-fortune Anthony Aston, who first came to America in 1703, and who wrote a play for his own performance; and the whole Hallam Company, who later performed with such success in America. Though as in other aspects of theatre the acting of the eighteenth century was a mixture of the old and the new, it presaged a development which eventually revolutionized the art.

Though Garrick attempted to discipline rehearsals and performances, with no small degree of success, the usual practice was somewhat chaotic. These were repertory companies, with each actor having at his command the roles of his "line," and being engaged for a particular company because of his proficiency in these roles. Parts in new plays were assigned by the company managers in conformance with these established lines. Stage business in the traditional roles was based on the performance of the actor who first created the part, and the attempt

was made to maintain this conception— hence the furor over Macklin's reinterpretation of Shylock. Since so little in the way of originality was expected or demanded of actors, rehearsals were rather peremptory and lackadaisical affairs. A revival ordinarily entailed one quick runthrough at ten in the morning on the day of performance, and from many accounts actors were prone to miss even this. New plays were prepared in a week to ten days, the rehearsals being held in the same four-hour period in which the revivals were rehearsed. If, by reason of the particularity of the author or manager, a new play took as long as two weeks to prepare, the situation was considered quite unusual. No wonder there are many derogatory contemporary comments about the laxity of performers who were not in command of their lines, whose stage business faltered, or who had grown too old for effectiveness in particular parts. There was evidently a great need for a disciplinarian such as Garrick.

Benefit nights, first instituted by Betterton about 1690, continued in full swing in this period, the end of each season being devoted to them, and seats on the stage being allowed for them, even after stage spectators had been generally abolished. Actors usually worked on fixed salaries which varied from about seventy pounds to about three hundred pounds for the season, depending upon their position in the company. Sometimes stars were engaged for great sums per season, as was Peg Woffington, at a thousand pounds—a really immense sum considering that when Garrick first became the chief actor of Drury Lane his acting salary was exactly half that amount. Mrs. Oldfield is said to have earned six hundred pounds for sixty nights, and Quin eight hundred for a season. These salaries were augmented by the benefit nights (at which seventy-five to two hundred pounds were raised for the individual), by special gifts and subscriptions on the part of the public, and by teaching fees. Prominent actors took apprentices and also tutored members of the nobility.

Neophytes in the acting companies worked for a six-month probationary period with no salary at all, and then were paid from ten to thirty shillings a week, depending on their ability and the parts they played.

The eighteenth century marked the height of the provincial circuit system. Acting companies, in an earlier age known by the names of their patrons, now called themselves by the names of the towns which constituted their headquarters. From such a town the individual acting company journeyed to surrounding towns for varying periods of time, ranging from two to three or four months. There were many such provincial circuits throughout England; the most famous were at Bath, Norwich, York, Liverpool, Manchester, Bristol, and Newcastle, all of which operated under royal patent. Special licenses were issued by the Lord Chamberlain (who had replaced the Master of the Revels as an officer for this function) for Brighton, Windsor, Richmond, and Surrey, since these were places of royal residences. These and many other companies not only supplied the provinces with continuing dramatic fare, but served as training grounds for the London theatres. As in the London companies, benefit nights supplied a good share of the actors' incomes, which were otherwise fairly small.

The tradition of the author's third night (when he received all the profits) persisted, but his payment for the play was now no longer a flat fee; it was tied in with production expenses. He could also realize something for publication rights, an advantage which became increasingly important in an age of increasing printed materials. For the most part, writing for the theatre was not a full-time profession; the outlets for new plays were too limited. Actors and managers found it expedient (and cheaper) to prepare their own scripts, as Garrick and Colman did. And besides, there were so many other outlets for the written word—newspaper, periodical, pamphlet, essay, novel—that writers of real talent could find immediate gratification in these forms without waiting for the tedious production process in the theatre and its comparatively tenuous rewards.

Theatre workers in England in the eighteenth century enjoyed a better reputation than their predecessors generally, and better than their counterparts on the Continent. Garrick moved in the very best social, literary, and artistic circles of his time, and many other performers were held in high esteem. Perhaps their own preparation and performance had something to do with this, but the increasing democracy of their social milieu had more to do with it. Learned and worthy men and women had been in the theatre before, but not for a very long time had actors been accorded the honors given those of eighteenth-century England—and those honors were to increase in succeeding generations.

Summary

In the eighteenth century, England began that domination of world affairs which continued into the present century. Not only in politics, but also in literature, English ideas penetrated to other cultures and had lasting influences. America, too, though declaring its political independence from England, was in all other ways, and particularly in theatre, a reflection of the older society.

In the profusion of human concerns which characterized the eighteenth century, theatre was seldom of prime importance. With the notable exceptions of Goldsmith and Sheridan, writing for the theatre engaged the attentions of only second- or third-rate writers. Even Goldsmith owes a part of his fame to fields of writing other than drama, and Sheridan was vigorously concerned in other activities for a good part of his life. Some worthwhile plays were written by such theatre people as Garrick and the Colmans, but they are not of the first order of literary merit.

The old dependence of theatre on the aristocracy was being replaced by the patronage of less cultured members of society, with a consequent proliferation of nonliterary entertainment. Even in those theatrical presentations most closely approximating literature, there was a marked tendency to meet the tastes of the new audiences by an emphasis upon sentimentality and bourgeois drama. Not until the tastes of the public could be educated to demand the best would superior dramatic fare once more appear.

In the art of acting, however, the period reached great heights and contributed great acting talents which have become legendary. David Garrick, the greatest of these, is in many ways the most typical mirror of his age, developing a perfection of art by rule and precept, much as Pope did in the writing of poetry and as Sarah Kemble Siddons did in the next generation, although both were extolled for the "truth" and "naturalness" of their skill. Partly because acting dominated the arts of eighteenth-century theatre, it may be charged with the rather dubious distinction of being the seedbed for the star system. But the prevailing practice of the day was that of permanent repertory companies performing continuously, mainly in revivals and adaptations.

On the production side this period developed very large theatre buildings and established the picture-frame stage as a preferred, if not exclusive, method of production. Both of these items were to dominate theatre practice for many years. In addition, the period introduced the use of act drops, and made some slight progress in authentic costuming, though only for actors, not for actresses. Staging grew increasingly complex, with a definite tendency to stress the spectacular and the extravagant.

In the final analysis, what was probably most unique about theatre in eighteenth-century England and America was that, for the first time ever, it had to be independent—without sanction or subsidy—and find its own audience. That it succeeded in doing so is its chief credit.

Theatrical conditions on the Continent in the eighteenth century were significantly different from those in England. Theatre was never thrust out on its own but continued to be subsidized and extended by the state. As one of the sanctioned activities of the social whole it received the attention of both the intellectuals and politicians throughout the century. The results of such attention were both good and bad.

On the one hand, the state-supported and sanctioned Comédie Française, entrenched as the most powerful producing agency of the period, preserved an adherence to the works of Racine, Corneille, and Molière, tended to denigrate new plays unless they were "regular" like those of the great seventeenth-century writers, and even then produced new works only after long delays. New playwrights and new ideas were forced to seek a home in the playhouses of the boulevard, which were largely commercial ventures. The many playwrights who wrote for these houses were, as the century progressed, influenced by their less cultivated audiences to an overemphasis upon incident, single-facet characters illustrating pure virtue and pure vice, tricks of staging, and spectacular presentations. These circumstances caused the development of escapist melodrama and extravagant and sentimental romance rather than works of more honest dramatic content. The prestige of French neoclassicism as enshrined in the Comédie also dictated the course of development of German theatre for the first half of the century.

On the other hand, the influence and example of France and its national theatre maintained the interest of persons in power in the establishment of similar organizations elsewhere on the Continent. National theatres opened in Copenhagen in 1722, in Sweden in 1737 (with a second one in Stockholm in 1757), in Russia in 1756, in Vienna in 1776, and in various duchies, principalities, and imperial cities in German territories from 1767 on. The establishment and operation of theatres became the concern of the politically powerful on the Continent in the eighteenth century; in the German, Russian, and Scandinavian countries, theatre begins to be significant in this century. The building of theatres was a concern of civic authority and of temporal power, not of private enterprise as in England. Continental theatre architecture was mostly monumental in concept and execution—the visible embodiment of civic pride, or aristocratic largesse, or the display of new wealth. Because the predominant theatre installations of the Continent were not tied to private enterprise, they developed lavishness of scenic investiture to a fine art, contributing the names of many men who became famous in this field. All areas of theatre activity on the Continent were influenced by the continuation of official sanction and support.

Almost a hundred years after the establishment of the Académie Française and the "Quarrel of the Cid," neoclassic precept was still the predominant intellectual mode. Voltaire, writing his *Discourse on Tragedy* in 1731, protested the necessity for maintaining "the fundamental laws of the theatre, which are the three unities," and he greatly admired the *decorum* of Addison's coldly classical *Cato*. His neoclassical allegiance had been shaken, however, by a three-year stay in England (1726–1729), where he had been impressed by the productions of Shakespeare, albeit at that time even these had been "purified" by Tate, Dryden, and other adapters. His *Discourse* constitutes a kind of apologia in which he says that the difference between English and French audiences ultimately accounts for the differences between English and French plays—the English being "more fond of action" and the French

giving "more attention to elegance, harmony, and the charms of verse." In succeeding years, he moved farther away from the neoclassic tenets, partly because of his disenchantment with the traditionalists of the Comédie and partly under the influence of his fellow-encyclopedist, Denis Diderot, whose essay *On Dramatic Poetry* (1758) defended a new antiaristocratic, antiheroic theatre as one of the greatest and most effective means for teaching and influencing opinion and action, for training the emotions and sympathies. Diderot had been greatly impressed by the bourgeois drama of George Lillo, believing that this genre of domestic tragedy would have an immediate and powerful effect on its spectators. He said that there should be a "serious comedy" which would deal with "the duties of man" as well as his "follies and vices." Lillo also influenced an early dramatic work of Gotthold Ephraim Lessing, the young German critic and play-

FAMOUS THEATRE PERSONALITIES
Far left, Carolina Neuber as Elizabeth. Left, Adrienne Lecouvrier as the tragic muse. Above, Talma as Nero. Right, Clairon as Electra. (Theater-Museum, Munich; Yale Theatrical Prints Collection)

wright who would, in his *Hamburg Dramaturgy* (1767–1769), produce the first considerable body of dramatic criticism in Germany and would turn the attention of German playwrights and audiences to the superiority of English models (including Shakespeare) over the French ones which had been upheld by his earlier fellow-countryman, Johann Christoph Gottsched.

All of this intellectual activity, this passion for analysis, classification, and observa-
tion, was the normal result of the neoclassic reliance upon reason—upon the ordering mind of man. Treatises in abundance were also issued on the art of acting, notably by the Riccobonis (father and son) in 1728 and 1750, and by Diderot in 1778 (*The Paradox of Acting*). The nature of the various theatre arts (among, needless to say, all sorts of other human activities) was endlessly argued, and the various arguments would produce at the end of the century and the

beginning of the next a wholly different intellectual and cultural atmosphere—what we have come to call the Romantic Revolution. Ironically, it was one of the contributors to the French *Encyclopedia* (that ultimate product of rationalism), Diderot's good friend Jean-Jacques Rousseau, who would be hailed some years after his death as the patron saint of romanticism and the French Revolution. And a contemporary of Lessing, Immanuel Kant, would in the year that Lessing died (1781) publish his *Critique of Pure Reason* which demonstrated that there is something in the mind of man which is not put there by his senses, thus turning John Locke upside down and initiating the transcendental philosophy which was so influential with the romantics.

England and Spain influence the Continent

It seems to be true that the development of great theatre is concomitant with the rise of nationalism: Sophocles in Greece, Shakespeare in England, Lope de Vega in Spain, and Molière in France all flourished in periods of intense patriotism and national consciousness. Yet the nature of theatrical art is such that its influences, ideas, and practices transcend national boundaries and, largely disregarding politics, form a world community of their own.

Continental theatre in the eighteenth century graphically illustrates this statement. France, which had provided inspiration for the English Restoration theatre, now for the first time began to see the glories of "that inspired barbarian," as Voltaire called Shakespeare; in addition, the French developed a sentimental drama of their own from the example of English writers. Spain, too, had its influence on French theatre through the predilections of Beaumarchais; Spanish

theatre in the eighteenth century, on the other hand, was almost completely "Frenchified." In Paris, with a most vigorous theatrical tradition behind it, there were five public theatres in operation in addition to numerous and varying court theatres. Foremost was the Comédie Française, charged with the production of legitimate drama, and leaning toward tragedy. A vigorous rival was the Comédie Italienne, no longer solely devoted to the commedia dell'arte, but producing most notably the plays of Marivaux, as well as several other French writers. In addition, there was the Opéra and two houses devoted to spectacle, farce, and pantomime—Nicolet's and l'Ambigu-Comique. By 1784, there were ten theatres in Paris; in 1791 there were fifty-one.

For a considerable period the nascent drama of Germany aped that of France, performances themselves being given in French. Frederick the Great, for some time a patron and admirer of Voltaire, preferred French to German all his life, and Gottsched, the critic, forced the French mold upon German dramatic practice with singular persistence. The so-called *Aufklärung*, the Age of Enlightenment, in Germany, was the result of French-worship and the neoclassic spirit. Reaction against this arbitrary standard produced a style of theatre called *Sturm und Drang* (Storm and Stress), and a shift to English models more compatible with the German national character. Ultimately a truly German style emerged.

Russian theatre was first German and then French before it became Russian. In Italy there was war between Goldoni, whose leanings were French and who spent his last years in Paris, and Gozzi, whose popularity was great in Germany. And in tiny Denmark the genius Ludvig Holberg ridiculed Frenchified Danes as well as Germanic excesses to foster a vigorous and typical national drama.

"SEMIRAMIS" IN PERFORMANCE
A drawing by St. Aubin of a performance of
Voltaire's play at the Comédie Française in
1748. Note the privileged members of the
audience sitting left and right on stage.

Theatre employment respectable and admired—but not settled

This century marked the decline of the
dilettante and the part-time worker in the
theatre and the rise of theatre as a distinct
art and employment. This development is
particularly notable in acting, which took on
stature as a respectable, even an admired
employment in many areas.

In Germany, however, where the imported opera had achieved respectability and
aristocratic sanction long before theatre did,
there were no permanent theatres until the
last third of the century. Dramatic performances were given by companies of wandering players, much as had been the custom in
pre-Shakespearean England and provincial

France. Indeed, the first companies in Germany seem to have been English ones. The
Elector of Saxony received a company of
English players in 1586, and in 1592 a troupe
under one Robert Brown was performing at
Frankfort-on-Main. The companies of Reynolds, Roe, and Spencer continued the tradition through the Commonwealth period,
first performing in English, then in a mixture
of German and English with much and exaggerated pantomime, then finally in German
entirely. The programs were mixtures of improvisation, low comedy, exaggerated tragedy, and farce. But in 1727, when the gifted
actress Carolina Neuber met and was
charmed by Johann Christoph Gottsched,
they formed an association to reconstitute
German theatre according to the classical

rules as received from the French. The theatrical public, however, was still so sparse that until the end of her life (1760), Neuber was essentially a traveling player. The German companies differed from their earlier English predecessors chiefly in that many of the players were students who left their books either temporarily or permanently to join the strolling players.

In Italy, Goldoni began writing for the Teatro Sant'Angelo in Venice in 1734, where a capable company of commedia artists were in residence. He there attempted to substitute regular comedy, written rather than improvised, for the horseplay and buffoonery of the commedia. At the time there were seven playhouses in Venice, with resident companies who toured the peninsula in off-seasons. Here the tradition of aristocratic participation in theatrical activities, as a parallel to the professionalism of the commedia players, endured perhaps the longest. A member of the Arcadian Academy at Rome (Joseph Cooper Walker) wrote in 1799 that Italian towns abounded in private theatres, and that theatrical activities were the favorite amusement of the Italian nobility. Many of the nobles maintained private companies of actors and musicians, and in addition all the large cities had public theatres for both opera and drama.

In Russia as the century progressed the companies were either groups of free citizens —the "independent" companies—or troupes of serfs, trained and maintained by the landed nobility for their amusement, often bought and sold. When a noble acquired a freeman to augment his serf company, the newcomer was allowed the distinction of prefixing the equivalent of "mister" before his name on the programs.

Leading players, and even whole companies, sometimes traveled outside their national boundaries to perform in foreign cities: French companies played in London, German ones in St. Petersburg, and Italian ones in Paris. In the settled centers of theatrical activity, the ranks of metropolitan players were being constantly enlarged or changed by accessions from the provinces. Not only plays traveled from country to country, but also players and production techniques.

Audiences set the pace

Whatever the origins of the stage presentations, the audiences everywhere were supreme and dictatorial. The German public defeated Gottsched's attempt at purification of their theatre fare, insisting on the *Nachspiel*, or farce, no matter how serious the occasion, and clinging to their love of native comic characters even to the extent of enjoying a Hanswurst or Pickleherring in *The Merchant of Venice*. The Italian public's love of the riotous and irregular commedia temporarily defeated Goldoni's attempts at reform and led to his removal to Paris, where the sophisticated public often unmercifully derided an actor whose enunciation slipped or whose gesture was not in the accepted mode. In Spain, the theatres were general meeting places, with admission to the house separate from that required for a seat; also, the bullfight was beginning to displace the theatre as the national amusement.

In the theatres of Paris, still the most brilliant on the Continent, there was seating on the stage for more than half the century. Voltaire, convinced that this practice spoiled the reality of the performances, as Diderot had previously maintained, succeeded in abolishing spectators from the Comédie stage in 1759 by soliciting a gift of sixty thousand francs from the Count de Lauraguais to compensate the actors for the decreased revenue they would thus suffer. The pit was still the resort of the quarrelsome element of the masculine public, and guards (Diderot complained that they "stifled his enjoyment") were assigned to keep order. Boxes were rented for the season by the noble and the wealthy, a practice which assured a basic income for the actors. But that very basic income, complained Mercier, tended to make them lazy.

In almost all areas, eighteenth-century Continental theatre was more sensitive to the demands of a changing audience than had been its immediate predecessors excepting only the theatre of Shakespeare, whose audience so largely determined the direction of its accomplishments.

Translations and adaptations

During the whole of the eighteenth century, there was a lively business in translated and adapted plays. Corneille, Molière, and the lesser French dramatists were translated or liberally adapted in Italy, Russia, Germany, and the Scandinavian countries, as well as in Spain. The previous chapter told how George Lillo's *London Merchant* invaded the Continent, as did Cumberland's *The West Indian* and Addison's *Cato* which appeared in 1732 under J. C. Gottsched's aegis. For all its lack of appeal to modern tastes, this was one of the few English plays which Voltaire praised. Richardson's novel *Pamela* (1740) influenced a number of plays in a new type called the *drame*, and was at least once directly rendered into another language. Goldoni produced his *Pamela Unmarried*, taking the liberty to make Pamela's father an exiled Scottish count because an Italian audience would not tolerate the marriage of a gentleman to a plebeian.

Shakespeare was increasingly influential in original playwriting, and was often translated into French and German. J. F. Ducis had a very great success with *Hamlet* in 1769 by rewriting it in alexandrine verse. He then did the same with *Macbeth*. The great German actor Schroeder made several of Shakespeare's plays popular with the German public, taking some interesting liberties with them: Hamlet did not die in Schroeder's version, and there was no duel with Laertes; Cordelia came to life again in *Lear*, and the old king did not die (this was, of course, the standard happy ending that was also played in England throughout the century); *Othello* had a happy ending. Aside from the pervading influence of eighteenth-century neoclassicism to prune Shakespeare in conformity to those tenets, the growing sentiment in audiences of the second half of the century was that things should turn out well for the hero or heroine of a play (especially if the audience liked the character) whether or not there was any dramatic justification—hence the "happy endings."

A curious holdover from earlier times was still evident in the writing and elaborate production of church drama and religious plays in Spain, Italy, and Russia. Some of these were adaptations of Biblical stories, like the ten sacred dramas of Annibale Marchese; some were of the morality type, like *About the Penance of a Sinful Man*, written by the churchman Dimitry, Metropolitan of Moscow, given in St. Petersburg in 1752. But most of the theatres of Europe had long outlived this type of play, and turned to other things.

Original writings stale and slavish

As one would expect, it was in the writing of tragedy that tradition remained strongest. For tragedy has always been the most highly regarded of dramatic forms, the least subject to tampering. Of the numbers of

tragedies that Voltaire wrote, the earliest are almost unadulterated Racine, the very first being *Oedipe* in 1718. But after his English sojourn and his deeper contact with the intellectual currents of his day, he came to include themes and emphases which altered the substance of pure neoclassicism, although he continued to maintain that what he was doing was revitalizing tragedy. Believing with Diderot that theatre was an admirable rostrum for the inculcation of moral truths, he not only implied a moral in the tone of his plays but often made it explicit in the plot and dialogue. In *Alzire* (1736) for instance, he insists that humanitarianism is the hallmark of religious values; in *Mahomet* (1741) he argues a religious thesis. He was quick to catch the winds of interest current in his day, and in *Zaïre* (1736)—perhaps (with *Merope*, 1741) the best that he wrote—love supplies the motive of the action. In *Semiramis* (1748) he introduces a ghost, and in *Tancred* (1760) he foreshadows romanticism in his interest in the Middle

TWO PLAYS BY SCHILLER
Left, a scene from *The Robber*, 1781. The costumes are presumably sixteenth century but succeed only in not being eighteenth century. Above, a scene from *The Bride of Messina*, 1803. Here the presumably classical costumes include long tights for the men and some wreaths of laurel leaves. (Goethe-Nationalmuseum, Weimar)

Ages. Voltaire in his long life wrote more than fifty plays, about half of them tragedies. He was the ultimate spokesman for his age and incredibly famous during his lifetime. Modern judgments of his work are not so kind.

Voltaire's influence was potent in Germany, where he had spent some time in the court of Frederick the Great. In the second quarter of the century (aided and abetted by the neoclassical convictions of Gottsched) numbers of neoclassical tragedies were writ-

ten; for instance, Behrman's *Horace*, Koch's *Titus Manlius*, and a lengthy list from J. E. Schlegel which became ornaments of the German *Aufklärung* (Age of Enlightenment). Voltaire's influence extended to Russia, where Alexei Sumarokov (1718–1777), the first Russian dramatist of note, wrote a long list of plays adhering to the unities and using the heroic style, though he often took his materials from Russian history. Nikolev was his contemporary in tragedy, but used materials chiefly from the classics.

The influence of neoclassicism even routed Lope de Vega and Calderon from the stages of Spain, and the tragedies of Garcia de la Huerta and Lopez de Ayala were admired. But not even the prizes offered by aristocrats for the writing of tragedies here and in Italy could inspire great works. Italy even had an Arcadian Academy to perpetuate classic ideals. In the opinion of their contemporaries, the outstanding dramatists of the first half of the century were Apostolo Zeno, Metastasio, and Scipione di Maffei. About the middle of the century, Gasparo Gozzi, elder brother of the more famous Carlo, wrote a number of strictly classical tragedies. Then in the latter half of the century came the fiery patriot, Count Vittorio Alfieri of Asti, who saw in the materials of classic times a good vehicle for the expression of his own convictions about popular liberty fighting against tyranny. His sizable list of plays almost all bear the classic titles (*Oreste, Agamemnone, Antigone*, etc.), the plots are the classic plots, but the characters are made to speak always in support of Alfieri's own ideas.

Others were writing neoclassic tragedies in the eighteenth century; it was a persistent form. But only one deserves mention here: the Frenchman Crébillon, and that for only one of his plays, *Rhadamisthe and Zenobie* (1771), because it held the stage until well into the next century.

Comedy, having arrived at its zenith so recently with Molière, was less fixed, more subject to change, more amenable to the inclusion of the concerns of new audiences. The closest to Molière in time and in character is J. F. Regnard (1656–1710), who drew on the humors of the provinces as did Molière. Another writer much like him is Dufresny (1648–1724). Marivaux (1688–1763), who wrote chiefly for the Comédie Italienne, was the best of the comedy writers of the

early century, injecting psychological analysis of character into comedy as Molière had done. His best two plays are still popular: *The Surprises of Love* (1722) and *The Game of Love and Chance* (1730). The first significant writer of comedy in Russia, Fonvizin (1745–1792), wrote realistic satires in the tradition of Molière, such as *The Minor* and *The Brigadier*.

The eighteenth-century insistence on opinions and social conditions increasingly deployed attention from the character conflict which had been the main concern of earlier comedy writers. Even Marivaux, albeit unwittingly, participated in the genesis of the sentimental comedy with such plays as *The Confident Mother* (1735), *The Faithful Wife* (1755), and *The False Confidences* (1737), the first play in French theatre ending in a marriage that cut across the boundaries of social class. Dancourt (1661–1725) and LeSage (1667–1747) both concerned themselves with middle-class manners; they used traditional names for their characters, but were realistic in that they worked out the plot to what seemed a logical conclusion rather than a manufactured denouement. The latter's *Crispin, Rival of His Master* (1707) is one of his most delightful and successful plays. Toward the end of the century, Beaumarchais (1732–1799) produced a series of comedies in which he said he tried to combine the fun and intrigue of comedy with the emotional appeal of the drama. How successful he was is attested by the continuing appeal of *The Barber of Seville* (1774) and *The Marriage of Figaro* (1784), the best of his many plays. Because in these he showed the servant, Figaro, to be the superior in intelligence and cunning to the aristocratic personages, and because he included sentiments expressing sympathy with the common people (a position at that time politically hazardous), he had some difficulty getting

TWO FAMOUS PLAYS, ONE FAMOUS PLAYER
Left, Goethe as Orestes in his own *Iphigenia*, with the title character in a voluminously draped pseudo-Greek robe. Above, a scene from Schiller's *Wallenstein*, showing the Gothic influences on stage décor typical of the late eighteenth century. (Goethe-National-museum, Weimar)

these plays produced. But later he became a hero of the Revolution. Today Figaro seems but the culmination of the long line of clever servant characters, and the plays not at all revolutionary in intent, but merely very delightful comedies.

The volatile nature of comedy and its changing materials and methods were evident in countries other than France, which remained, however (as it did in tragedy), exceedingly influential. There was no high comedy in Spain and Portugal and none in Germany. The few comic plays in Russia, by Sumarokov and Knyazhnin, were true to type in using contemporary events and criticizing the foibles of society. *The Mother-Rival, The Querulous Woman, The Braggart, A Petty Quarrel* are the names of some of them. The chief inheritor of Molière's mantle

was the Italian Carlo Goldoni. He began his career in Venice, writing plays in the Venetian dialect; he hoped to transform the now-debased improvisations of the commedia dell'arte. He moved to Paris in 1761 at the invitation of the Comédie Italienne, where he wrote more plays in both Italian and French. He was tremendously successful in both Venice and Paris, retiring with a pension from the king; he was deprived of the pension by the Revolution and ended his days in poverty. He is supposed to have written about two hundred fifty plays. The most popular with English audiences has been *The Mistress of the Inn* (1752), which afforded a favorite part for Eleanora Duse in the next century. *The Boors* (1759) is said to be his masterpiece and has been used as the libretto for an opera. *The Fan* (1765) is typical in its new and rather charming insistence by the young women therein on their right to marry where and whom they pleased.

But even Goldoni said that he chose to picture virtue rather than to ridicule vice; thus he departed from the spirit of Molière and entered into the spirit of the new age. His rival Carlo Gozzi (1720–1806), beginning with the established commedia, injected fantastic elements, producing what he called "fairy dramas," and presaging the coming period of romanticism. His best known play has been translated into English as *The Three Oranges* (1761). Holberg, in Copenhagen, the only other writer of the type in the eighteenth century, did not eschew ridicule, but reflected his age in his evident social consciousness. *Jeppe of the Hill* (1722) is his best play; in it he evidences his belief that changes in society should not take place too swiftly, and thus he allied himself with Diderot who preached the didactic mission of drama.

The drame—a popular catchall

The outstanding genre of the eighteenth century was the drame, which may be said to include domestic tragedy, sentimental comedy, romanticized history, and possibly fantasy. All audiences everywhere were demanding it. Voltaire's *Nanine* (1749) was an attempt to satisfy this taste; in its preface he, like Lessing a few years later, justified the type by saying that true comedy may contain both humorous and emotional scenes. Nivelle de la Chaussée, in *The False Antipathy* (1733), produced a play primarily designed to arouse tender emotions rather than to excite laughter. In this and in his succeeding plays, the comic elements are merely episodic, becoming less and less frequent, until in *Mélinde* (1741) there is no humorous

SIMPLE AND ELABORATE SETTINGS
Above, a drawing of a late seventeenth-century German stage. Four sets of wing flats, a backcloth, cloud borders, and candelabra are all clearly visible. Right, Giuseppe Galli-Bibiena designed this elaborate proscenium and stationary set for an opera in Vienna in 1716. (Theater-Museum, Munich)

line or role at all. One of his later plays, *The Governess* (1747), was a precursor of *East Lynne*.

This drama of sensibility, which broke down the distinctions between comedy and tragedy, was often called by that paradoxical name, *comédie larmoyante*, or tearful comedy. Diderot, primarily a critic, found the type useful for didactic purposes and produced three plays of the kind, notably *The Father of the Family* (1758). Mercier was another practitioner. In Russia tearful comedy also flourished, with Lukin writing *Rewarded Constancy* and *The Spendthrift Reformed by Love*. In the same period, toward the end of the century, Plavilshchikov produced *The Store Clerk* and *Wretched and*

Solitary One, whose very titles are typical of the genre.

It was in Germany that the new type had its chief impact. J. E. Schlegel (1719–1749) anticipated it with his two comedies, *The Triumph of the Good Woman* and *The Silent Beauty*, though these were written in verse and hence were not true to the genre, in form at least. (Diderot, in laying down rules for the drame, had said that realistic drama must be in prose.) C. F. Gellert, with a play each in 1745, 1746, and 1747, truly established the type in Germany as La Chaussée had in France.

Lessing was perhaps its outstanding exponent. Under the influence of the English novelists and writers of domestic tragedy, he produced in 1755 *Miss Sara Sampson*, a play which was immensely influential with other writers. In Lessing's play the situation is real, the development logical. It does not depend, as do so many of La Chaussée's plays, upon mistaken identity and the long arm of chance. In it, of course, audiences of today find too much didacticism, too much sentimentality, and too many scenes designed to elicit tears. Nevertheless, the fame of this play influenced a whole generation of German writers. Lessing had preceded it with *The Young Lady-Scholar* (1748), written for Carolina Neuber, whom he greatly admired.

Though Lessing was primarily a critic, and did immense service to German literature by successfully combatting the French

pseudoclassicism of Gottsched, two others of his plays, *Minna von Barnhelm* (1772) and *Emilia Galotti* (1772), were of great significance. In the first, he created two memorable characters: Tellheim, a manly but sensitive soldier with a most punctilious sense of honor; and Minna, one of the most charming heroines in German drama. In the latter, he took the classic story of Virginia, killed by her father to save her from the lascivious decumvir Appius, and translated it to a tragedy of common life. His final dramatic work *Nathan the Wise* (1779), is a plea for religious tolerance, and presents the first noble Jew in German literature. His chief disciples in the theatre were J. F. von Conegk, J. W. von Brawe, and C. F. Weisse, who was perhaps the most successful German playwright of his day.

Lessing was the finest flower of the German Age of Enlightenment. His unwavering faith in classicism took him back to Aristotle without the filtering screen of French neoclassicism; he even insisted that Shakespeare, for all his irregularities, was a more cogent example of Aristotle's spirit than

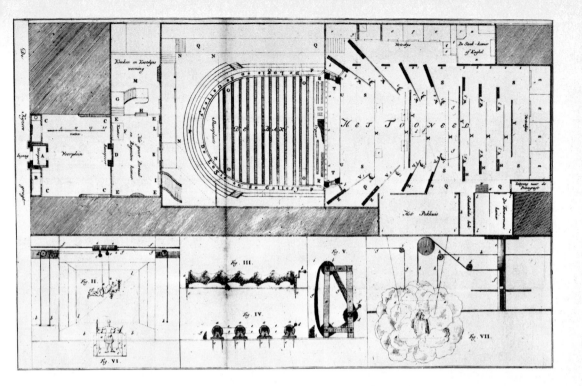

THE SCHOUWBERG, AMSTERDAM, 1772
Left, an interior view toward the stage, showing the symmetrical perspective scenery
which was prevalent throughout the period
and the lighting of the stage apron by
chandeliers in the proscenium arch. Above,
the floor plan of the house and stage, with
sketches showing how various machines are
contrived and operated. The plan indicates
the use of several sets of wing flats, some set
on an angle, and three backdrops. (Harvard
Theatre Collection)

were the French dramatists. His skill and
generosity in expressing his ideas and calling
attention to English models led to the short-
lived period called Sturm und Drang in German literature which, if it had not been for
the youthful participation of that consummate genius Johann Wolfgang von Goethe
(1749–1832) and his brilliant friend Johann
Friedrich Schiller (1759–1805), would be of
no more significance today than are the contemporary writings of Gray, Young, and Mac-
pherson in England. Writers of the German
romantic movement at the beginning of the

next century would look back to Sturm und
Drang as partial inspiration and example;
therefore it will be treated in more detail in
a later chapter. It was largely exhausted
after 1780, and the century ended in the
classicism of the mature works of Goethe
and Schiller which dominated German literature. Schiller's trilogy of the Thirty Years
War, *Wallenstein*, his *Maria Stuart* with its
obligatory scene of confrontation between
Elizabeth and Mary (which did not historically take place), his *Maid of Orleans, Bride
of Messina*, and *Wilhelm Tell*—all written in

a final burst of creativity between 1798 and 1804—are a series of splendid classical dramas. And Goethe's late works—*Iphigenia in Taurus* (1787) and *Torquato Tasso* (1790) —are his testament to the classic mind. Even *Faust*, Part I, which appeared in 1808, is more a testament to the rational than to the romantic, for in conjunction with Part 2 (which finally was published in 1832), it is the summation of Goethe's vision of fulfill-ment of life by striving and selfless activity. Thus, from complete dependency at the be-ginning of the century, German dramatic lit-erature had achieved by the end a complete independence and had produced the greatest works of its entire history.

Many playhouses, all alike

The development of the playhouse in the eighteenth century illustrates in some sense the search for the perfect theatre interior. For more than half the century French theatres went their separate ways while Italian practice dominated structures else-where on the Continent; i.e., from the first,

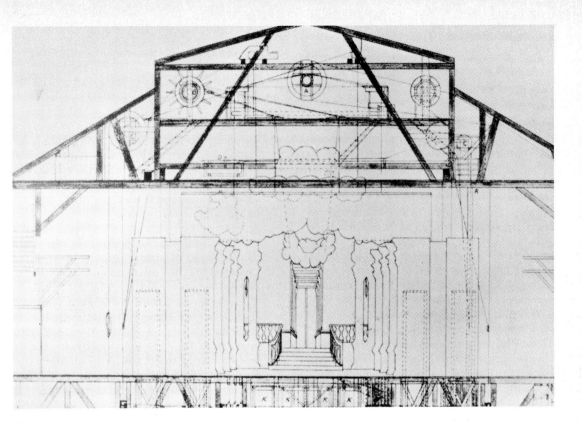

THE DROTTNINGHOLM THEATRE
The prison scene, left, is one of several still extant at this marvelously preserved theatre, which opened in 1766. It, like the others, was fastened to the permanently installed machinery, shown in detail in the drawing (above). All flats moved simultaneously to change from one scene to the next—a system of scene-change prevalent on eighteenth-century stages.

Italian practice provided seats for the entire audience, whereas French practice until well into the last quarter of the century maintained a portion of the pit for standees. Everywhere private theatres were different from public ones, and those built in restricted sites different from those where there were no such restrictions. But houses built for opera were almost invariably in the Italian style. And everywhere, playhouses proliferated.

Paris, which began the century with three theatres in operation, had five in 1754,

and fifty-one in 1791. In Italy, every city of any size had one or more theatres, and Venice had seven. The most celebrated public theatres were in Parma, Verona, Turin, Rome, Bologna, and Naples. Vienna had two famous playhouses, the Burgtheater and the Kärtnerthor. Though there was no subsidized national theatre in Spain, there were many playhouses scattered throughout the provinces. Lisbon's theatre was burned by the Inquisition in 1745, however, and the drama languished. Peter the Great established a theatre in St. Petersburg and built a playhouse in 1702. After his death theatre stagnated except for private amateur performances at the holidays. Anna Ioannovna opened a special theatre room in the Winter Palace in 1734 to revive interest, but there were no regular theatrical performances in Moscow until 1756. In 1787 a ballroom was transformed into a theatre in Kharkov, in honor of the empress' visit, and about the same time, Count Sheremetev, on his estate in Kuskovo, built a theatre designed by Valli, a famous architect. The first issue of Reichard's *Theater-kalender* in 1776 lists fourteen German theatres, to which six more were added the next year. By the last decade of the century, there were well over thirty. Notable among these were the rejuvenated Hamburg Theatre under Schroeder's management, that of Koch in Berlin, Seyler in Gotha, Döbbelin in Dresden, Marchand in Frankfort, and Goethe in Weimar.

The wooden structure built by Peter the Great near the Kremlin in 1702 was one hundred forty feet by one hundred five feet, and forty-nine feet high. It is described as having a gallery, benches, doors, windows, and a lined ceiling. The one converted from a ballroom at Kharkov is described as being lined throughout with red woolen cloth, as having armchairs and benches in the orchestra, and large boxes seating twenty each, with a total seating capacity of four hundred.

These were, of course, court theatres, with interior arrangements guided by the necessities of court protocol. In the Kleine Komoedienhaus in Dresden, built in 1697, there was armchair seating for royalty in the open space of the pit fronting the stage, with the rest of the sloped pit fitted with benches, and three tiers of boxes. The small stage was fitted with four sets of wings and a curved backcloth. In the same year the tiny house at Weimar, later to be made famous by Goethe, was built. Here there were no boxes

at all, except on either side of the proscenium, but a U-shaped gallery surrounding the sloped pit floor, and the same stage arrangements as in Dresden. (By Goethe's time, the benches had been replaced by the individual seats with numbers, and the stage had oil lamps that could be dimmed.) The special, down-front and upholstered seating for the royal patron was maintained in the little theatre built at Drottningholm in 1776 for Gustavus III, and at the more elaborate theatre at Versailles designed by Jacques-Ange Gabriel and opened in 1770. Here the shallow U-shape of the sloped pit is surrounded by an amphitheatre of benches divided into boxes, and the stage is provided with twelve sets of wings and three back-shutters. An unusual feature of the house is a cylindrical reverberation chamber under the orchestra pit between the stage and the audience. A different arrangement for the royal patron (one that was to become standard) was incorporated into the charming little Residenztheatre in Munich designed by François de Cuvillies and opened in 1752. Here the royal seat was a grandiose box immediately opposite the stage, occupying the second and third levels of the U-shaped boxes, with the entrance door to the pit below it on the first level.

Provision for a royal box in this manner became usual, in opera houses especially, although when Burnacini designed the new Vienna Opera House, which opened in 1667, the royal seat was still on a dais in the pit immediately in front of the stage, and de la Guépierre's plan for the massive Opera House at Stuttgart provides for the royal seat on a dais mid-point in the auditorium, probably because in a house of that size acoustics would be a problem and the favored seat must be in a spot good for hearing. A different solution to the problem was incorporated into the Paris Opera House, designed

Coupe du nouvel Opéra de Stuttgardt esquissé pour en voir l'effet sans aucunes règles de Perspective

Plan ou Projet de la restauration de l'Opéra de Stuttgardt.

OPERA HOUSE AT STUTTGART, 1759

De la Guépierre's plan for the opera house at Stuttgart, with a cutaway sketch of the interior, as published in Diderot's *Encyclopedia*. The floor plan shows more space allotted to the stage than to the auditorium —a usual custom for a theatre which stressed spectacular productions. Note the interesting seating arrangement in the plan, which includes a special box in the center of the auditorium.

by Moreau and opened in the Rue St. Honoré in 1764. Here there was a "loge" within the proscenium arch on each side for royalty, large boxes with benches on either side of the apron for special guests, and fourteen shallow boxes on the first tier. Although the basic plan of the interior was that of the ellipse developed by the Italian architect S. M. Sarda, the disposition of the elements of stage, forestage, and standing pit was strictly in accordance with customary French practice.

Not until 1782 would France have a theatre in which the entire audience would be seated; fittingly enough it was the building which was at that time used by the Comédie Française, the Théâtre de l'Odéon. The stage area was about half the total length of the house, there was no extended stage apron, no standing pit, no amphitheatre, and three rows of boxes with a gallery above them. The horseshoe-shaped auditorium floor was completely equipped with benches for spectators, much to the disgust of the dramatist Mercier, who loved the standing pit. The shallow curve of the front of the stage heralded a new relationship between audience and players in that actors would now be forced behind the proscenium arch and would play in the midst of the scenery rather than in front of it—a situation long since arrived at by performers in Italian-style houses elsewhere in Europe. The house designed by Victor Louis in 1787, into which the Troupe de Molière moved in 1791, was similar, but larger. With various refurbishments and reconstructions, this building still houses the Théâtre Français. It is typical of another tendency in theatre architecture of the time: there are various salons, foyers, and special rooms appended for the comfort of the audience. Earlier, such accommodations would have been restricted to court theatres. It is also illustrative of the final settlement of the space and hearing problems in its rows of boxes ranged one above the other, so that the maximum number of people could be as close as possible to the stage. By the end of the century most of the building problems had been solved, and the changes of the next century would be chiefly those of comfort and convenience for patrons. The end product of eighteenth-century experiments in theatre architecture is still with us today in many cities and towns of the Western world.

Settings keyed to variety

The predominant mode of dressing the stage during the eighteenth century, whether that stage was in a court or public theatre, an opera house or playhouse, was that of flat wings set parallel to the edge of the stage, in pairs progressively closer together, closed off at the back of the stage by a backcloth—essentially the same system developed in the Italian Renaissance and brought to perfection in the seventeenth century by Torelli. It had been Torelli who had substituted mechanical changing apparatus for the earlier system of numbers of stagehands at each position pulling flats at the sound of the stage-manager's whistle. Now each flat was attached to a long pole which protruded from a slot in the stage floor, being attached under the stage to a system of ropes, pulleys, and winches whereby a single operator could move all the flats at once. These changes were made in full view of the audience, and the effect must have been something like the dissolve in moving pictures—one scene fading while another comes into view. Overhead were similar provisions for changing the borders that finished off

ELABORATE STAGING
Left, Louis Jean Desprez design for *Gustaf Vasa* in Stockholm, 1786. Above, Giorgio Fuentes design for Mozart's *Titus* in Frankfort-on-Main, 1799. Elaborate sets and huge crowd scenes were popular on the Continent, as these two designs indicate. (Stockholm Nationalmuseum; Theater-Museum, Munich)

the tops of the flats, plus machinery for descents and ascents of clouds, chariots, etc. Whether there were five sets of side wings, or fifteen, the system was the same. It can be examined even today at the Drottningholm Theatre in Sweden, where the complete system, with all its painted scenery, is preserved intact. The theatre was closed at the death of Gustavus III in 1792, not to be reopened until 1922; it has been preserved as a museum since.

In the poorer theatres, the hand-moved system of flats and back-shutters was, of course, maintained. The investiture of the smaller German and Russian theatres operated as a system of "long and short" scenes; i.e., flats could be clicked together for a "short scene" while a set piece or two was brought on, and then the flats opened for a "long scene." It was a primitive but effective means for change of scene. And changing scenes was the order of the day, not only because they were interesting in themselves, but because the "new" drama needed them.

Banishing the spectators from the stage of the Théâtre Française had made it possible to expand the use of scenery there, and the stage of the new Comédie Française had seven sets of side wings and a backcloth; that of La Scala at Milan had ten sets of grooves, with the possibility of using backcloths at seven of these. Moreau's Paris Opera House had twelve, plus an extra space at the back of the stage to extend the vista, and a system of counterweights in the stage walls to assist in the shift of scenes. The stage plan of the Hanover Opera (1746) called for three vistas behind a conventional wing and backcloth system on a stage twice the size of the auditorium, and Ledoux's interesting Théâtre de Marseilles provided for two vistas on an immense stage. In the less highly developed theatres, the settings were simple; the small ballroom theatre of Kharkov had but two stage settings, an interior and a forest, and a single front curtain. But often the stage appointments in Russia, as elsewhere, were sumptuous. Count Sheremetev's Valli-designed theatre is said to have had eight curtains, almost two hundred settings, fifty-two sets, sixty-eight minor decorative accessories, seventeen large chests of wardrobe, and seventy-six chests of hand props.

In Germany particularly, the love for metamorphoses, machines, and disguises was evident from handbills, and here as throughout most of Europe, elaborate stage effects wrought with pulleys and platforms and the various machines of the Renaissance came to enjoy high favor. Transformations, wherever they could be achieved, were tried. The fame of the Hall of Machines persisted as a model, and the relaxing of the classical rules of unity in time and place made changes of scene mandatory. When the Berlin Opera House was built in the middle of the century, a canal supplied water for two great "water machines" to give the effect of cascades on the stage.

During the eighteenth century, the popularity of machines was challenged, if not displaced, by the magnificently conceived settings of the members of the Bibiena family and their followers. This family, devoted to stage design, covered four generations, from the middle of the seventeenth century to the end of the eighteenth. The designs of the older members stressed the forced diminishing perspective in absolute symmetry which marked the theatre artists of the Renaissance. These were almost invariably highly ornamented in profuse baroque style, giving a feeling of immense space and magnificence. In the second and third generations, the designers tended to substitute for symmetrical perspective the much more interesting angular perspective, keeping, however, the same grandeur and ornamentation. Often stairways and platforms, which may have been practical, were included as a part of their designs. The Bibienas worked in Italy and also in Russia and Germany.

One of their followers, Servandoni (1695–1766), brought the principle of angular asymmetrical perspective to Paris, producing a grandeur and spaciousness which Parisians had not seen before. The Roman, Juvarra (1676–1736), working from the same artistic principle, produced designs which seem to provide for a permanent architectural setting downstage, with changes of scene by means of painted drops or flats behind. The Venetian, Piranesi (1720–1778), primarily a graphic artist whose techniques in etching created a

TWO BIBIENA DESIGNS
The most influential scene designers of the eighteenth century were the Bibienas, whose ideas found wide acceptance throughout the Continent. These two designs illustrate a principle which they are said to have discovered—the use of diagonal or asymmetrical linear perspective. The intricacy and massiveness of the stage picture are typical of the many designs from Bibiena hands. See page 244. (Harvard Theatre Collection)

peerless series of prison scenes and another of the antiquities of Rome, did theatrical designs notable for their grandeur and for the masterful use of light and shadow.

All of these effects would seem to have been achieved by the use of careful scene painting on flats and an appropriate arrangement of these on the stage, although a few of the forms might well have been partially sculptured.

Algarotti (1712–1764), for nine years advisor to Frederick the Great on operatic problems, urged the addition of chiaroscuro lighting to the effects these designers achieved by use of line and of dark and light areas in order to underline the mood of the production. Thus, said he, the lights and darks of the scenic designer could be embellished by light rather than destroyed by it. Not only should lighting enhance the theatrical effect, he thought, but all illusion in scenery, costume, and acting, as well, should be aimed to this end. Algarotti has a very modern sound.

During the course of the century, variety in scenic investiture became the rule, with the type and kind dependent upon the species of play to be presented.

Attempts at costume reform

As in eighteenth-century England, so on the Continent there were various attempts at costume reform, not all of them successful. If anything, the traditional Continental costumes at the beginning of the century were more formalized, and in many ways more ridiculous, than those of the English. German actors of the early century used a standard costume that was as curious, in its way, as that of the French; all wore black velvet knickerbockers, which each actor himself supplied. Atop this he wore a brown cloth coat and a silk waistcoat given him by the manager. If he were to play the part of a king, the waistcoat would be gold embroidered; he would wear a full-bottomed wig, a hat with feathers, and would carry a scepter. Classic heroes were distinguished by a scarf tied across the brown cloth coat, a helmet, and a sword. Sometimes a breastplate of sham gold replaced the scarf for Greek heroes. For these characters, the hair was worn pigtail fashion, topped with a headgear of feathers. In the poorer companies, lace was often cut from paper, gold embroideries from gold paper. Whatever the period

JUVARRA
These two designs are in the nature of working drawings, showing how the effects are to be achieved. Left, the elevation is accompanied by a rough floor plan showing how the painted flats are to be set; above, numbers on the wings at the left and the cloud borders show how these are to be arranged. (Victoria & Albert Museum, Crown Copyright; Museum of Modern Art)

or the character, the black velvet breeches were mandatory. Gottsched, to his credit, realized the ridiculousness of this outfit and urged that his *Cato* be played in Greek robes. But when Carolina Neuber, quarreling with him in 1741, presented the play with authentic costumes, he was made as ridiculous in the eyes of the audience as she desired he should be. The departure was too radical. Five years later, the actor Ekhof was playing J. E. Schlegel's *Canut* in a red velvet coat instead of the brown cloth, a full-bottomed wig, and a cane hooked over his left arm.

By 1773, German audiences were ready to accept Goethe's *Goetz von Berlichingen* at Hamburg in historically correct costumes, but such costume seems to have been the exception rather than the rule.

In France, too, there were reforms. Those which were not violent were well received; those which were too drastic were as ill-received as Gottsched's *Cato*. As in Germany, the early eighteenth-century French company had a standard method of costuming. The women were garbed in contemporary court dress, with large paniers, much fringe, lace, and bright ribbons on the dress, and diamonds and feathers in their elaborately dressed hair. The men had a hero's costume consisting of a large full-bottomed wig, three-cornered hat with many feathers, elaborately worked gilt armor, wide silk sleeves with lace cuffs, tonnelet, a sword belt, a small ornamental dagger, gilt-fringed gloves, silk stockings, and embroidered half boots trimmed with gold, with high red heels. In the hand was either a fan, a wand, a scepter, or a cane, depending on the character. These were magnificent, expensive costumes, often costing from three to ten thousand francs. They were used even in the "antique" plays, with the sole exception that here the lover (an eighteenth-century innovation in the classics) wore the contemporary court dress without the tonnelet.

In 1751, the accomplished actress, Mlle. Clairon, discarded the panier to play Electra, to Diderot's great delight; but the costume, even without the panier, was far from Greek. Indeed, Mlle Clairon felt that the true Greek costume belonged on statues, and that her representation of the style on stage need only follow the general outline.

The same sort of mild reform was effected by Voltaire four years later, when he asked the designer Joseph Vernet to create costumes "neither too Chinese nor too French" for his production of *The Chinese Orphan* at the Comédie Française. The result would seem hardly effective to us today—trousers showing below full skirts and elaborate headdresses marked by the usual feathers—but the innovation was greeted with enthusiasm. When, the next year, Mme. Favart at the Comédie Italienne appeared in her own *The Chinese* with costumes actually made in China, she was received less enthusiastically. She had been severely criticized three years earlier, as well, in *The Loves of Bastien and Bastienne*, for appearing in the title role

in a plain linen dress, simply dressed hair, and wooden shoes such as village women wear. But she persisted in her search for authenticity, and in 1761 appeared in *The Three Sultanas* in costumes made in Constantinople.

The ballet master Noverre had long inveighed against the panier and the tonnelet, but so advanced were his recommendations concerning costume and movement that he had little practical effect. More telling was the appearance of the actor Lekain as Genghis Khan in *The Chinese Orphan*, minus tonnelet and dressed in long Turkish trousers, fur-trimmed cloak, and turban with ostrich plumes. He used an adaptation of the same costume when he appeared as Orosmon in *Zaïre*.

But as in England both actors and actresses were very fond of their sumptuous dress, the actresses particularly always wishing to appear at their most beautiful and magnificent regardless of the part they were playing, and verisimilitude in costuming made headway very slowly, despite the urgings of Voltaire and Diderot.

The universal use of white makeup (powdered pearls or a starch-bismuth mixture applied with a wash) was slowly displaced. Mlle. Clairon said that it precluded all facial expression—so much a part of characterization—and urged that others use, as she did, nothing but an artistic heightening of the natural features, and a coiffure suited to the character.

Thus did a few practical visionaries point the way for things to come.

Reforms effected in acting

More reforms were effected in acting than in theatre design and costumes, for this was the Age of Great Acting on the Continent, as well as in England.

Paris was the theatrical center of Europe

WATTEAU'S "THE FRENCH PLAYERS"
This famous painting from the first quarter of the century shows the typically elaborate contemporary costume of the women, and for the men, the fringed tonnelet, the high-heeled fringed boots, the feathered hat, the intricate decoration. (The Metropolitan Museum of Art; The Jules S. Bache Collection, 1949)

and the Comédie Française, in all its aspects, had counterparts throughout the Continent. The accepted style of acting in tragedy was bombastic and declamatory, and hedged about with conventions. For more than half the century, the acting area at the Théâtre Français was restricted to an open square about twelve feet on a side because of the audience seated on the stage. The players formed a semicircle on the stage, moving front and center as they spoke, declaiming their lines with sonorous delivery in tragedy and a chanting singsong in comedy. Movement was graceful and studied, gesture restrained. Michel Baron caused a sensation in his younger days by letting his hands go above his head—a gesture scandalously against the rules. These practices were affected even by the most lowly of the German traveling companies.

The attempts at a more natural style which were tried during the century were the work of individual gifted actors and actresses, reinforced by precepts set down from time to time by critics, playwrights,

and managers. Luigi Riccoboni, star performer with the Comédie Italienne, wrote a treatise on acting in 1738 in which he urged that one of the chief attributes of the actor was *enthousiasme*, which he defines as "feeling the thing he pronounces." In 1750, his son Francesco stated that the actor's chief requisite is "insight." Sainte-Albine and Diderot both speak of *sentiment*, or the "disposition to be affected by the passions." In France, the final banishment of the audience from the stage of the Théâtre Français allowed more freedom of gesture, more attention to motivated action and to stage pictures, which contributed toward underlining and enhancing the emotional impact of given scenes. Voltaire and Diderot were exponents of a more natural style of acting; in Italy, Goldoni prefaced his sixteen famous comedies with a set of rules for actors which included audible, clear enunciation; natural gestures; ensemble playing; and a decorous offstage life. In Hamburg, in 1753, Konrad Ekhof declared that "Dramatic art is copying nature by art and coming so near it that semblance is taken from reality," and "The actor must not enter into the real emotion that he is to represent but must do everything by means of art." About ten years later, when the great Friedrich Schroeder was performing at the Burgtheatre in Vienna and astonishing audiences with his excellence, he said that the skilled actor conceives each character so that it "not merely suggests a type, but distinguishes it from kindred characters by individual features which the performer finds in his own experience." Yet when the great Goethe formulated his *Rules for Acting* just after the turn of the century, most of his ninety-one axioms concern themselves with the details of deportment and movement on stage. Perhaps these kinds of rules were necessary for the unskilled amateurs with whom Goethe largely had to make do, but the important concern of those who were involved in analyzing acting was that the "art" in acting should be at least partly *feeling* and not merely skill in semblance.

These rules had been preceded by a number of experiments in the training of actors. The playwright Capacelli had founded a theatre at Bologna to institute a new style. Ekhof started his Academy for Actors in 1753, and Russian theatre might be said to have begun with an official decree in 1756 providing for the training of an acting company as a part of the royal Corps of Cadets. By 1782, a theatrical training and acting company had been established at the Imperial Russian Theatre in St. Petersburg, with the actor Dimitrevsky at its head.

As might be expected, the major changes came through successful individual endeavors. Michel Baron (1653–1729), who began so auspiciously in Molière's theatre, retired from the stage at the peak of his career, leaving the boards to the howlers, like Pierre Beaubour (1662–1725) who took over his place at the Comédie. His feminine counterparts were Mlle. Champmeslé (1642–1698) and Mme. Duclos (1668–1748). Encouraged by the success of Adrienne Lecouvreur (1692–1730), Baron returned to the stage in 1720, at the age of sixty-seven, after almost thirty years of retirement. Though Baron and Lecouvreur, who played together, acted with more seeming truth than their contemporaries, their performances were far from what we would call natural. Neither ever fell below a certain level of heroic grandeur, though gesture and movement were freer. Voltaire, admiring Lecouvreur after her death, called her "this incomparable actress," who spoke to the heart and showed feeling and truth where formerly had been artificiality and declamation.

For all his lip service to naturalness in the art of acting, though, Voltaire really championed a speaking style which, while

differing from formal declamation, stressed the sound of the words over their content. When Mlle. Clairon (1723–1803), contrary to his coaching, acted his *Electre* speaking naturally, he was led to exclaim, "It is not I who wrote that, 'tis she; she has created the part!"

Clairon was one of the most talented actresses of the French theatre, pronounced by Garrick "a perfect actress." Endowed with much physical beauty and a vivid imagination, she studied her parts in minute detail,

COSTUMES AND COSTUME REFORM
Left, Lekain and Vestris in Voltaire's *Semiramis* in 1748. The tonnelet of the men and the elaborate court dress of the women were the admired and accepted costumes for eighteenth-century French actors. Above, costume design "neither too Chinese nor too French" for Voltaire's *The Chinese Orphan*, 1755. Far left, Mme. Favart in *The Three Sultanas*, 1761, authentic in detail. Voltaire's reforms were moderate and fairly well accepted; those of Mme. Favart more extreme and less well accepted.

planning every aspect of vocal inflection, gesture, and movement, so that the result was an artistic unity with a feeling of truth. Her rival, Mlle. Dumesnil (1713–1803), was a purely inspirational actress who scored in the passages of great emotional stress, but might otherwise be most commonplace. She depended upon inspiration rather than studied art, but through her long career had many ardent partisans. She, like Clairon, was more effective in tragedy than comedy, but a popular contemporary, Mlle. Gaussin (1711–1767),

was unique in being equally effective in both types.

Among the men, the two great names of French eighteenth-century theatre are Lekain (1729–1778) and Talma (1763–1826), the one unprepossessing in appearance, the other darkly handsome; the one to die a decade before the Revolution, the other to become its darling and live beyond it. Both studied to produce a unified characterization which carried the sense of the scene and the intention of the playwright in voice, costume, gesture, and carriage. They are nearest in effect to natural acting in this century—a movement which was greatly aided by the appearance of the drame, a type of play mainly realistic, requiring natural movement and conversation.

Perhaps because tradition was not so strong in Germany as elsewhere in Europe, and forms other than classical tragedy were more popular, there was more scope for the development of new skills in acting. In any event, one of the world's greatest actors developed in Germany in this period—Friedrich Ludwig Schroeder (1744–1816). Tall, handsome, graceful (he had been an acrobat and a dancer), he was an inspired actor and a talented director and manager. Born into a theatrical family, he lived all his life in the theatre, playing more than seven hundred parts. In his long management at Hamburg, beginning in 1771 and lasting with two intermissions until his retirement in 1798, he insisted upon company discipline and ensemble playing, requiring strict order and punctuality in rehearsals and performances. At the same time, he managed his own theatrical education. Having been inspired by the acting of the older Konrad Ekhof, he put himself under strict discipline, carefully progressing from light comedy to more complicated parts, then to the greatest. In his first presentation of *Hamlet* at Hamburg, he did not play the lead but took the part of the Ghost, though he later triumphed in the title role. He also played Macbeth, Shylock, Falstaff, Richard II, Iago, the Miser, Arnolphe, Orgon, Angelo in *Emilia Galotti*, Werner in *Minna von Barnhelm*, and hundreds of other roles. Dissatisfied with his tenor voice, he finally achieved a full, rich baritone, and, by force of will power, curbed his passionate temperament to serve his clear intelligence. He was immensely successful, made a fortune, and retired to a large estate.

Popular also during most of Schroeder's career was the older Ekhof (1720–1778), first theorist of the German stage, who insisted that acting must come from within. Two more erratic talents were those of Iffland (1759–1814) and Fleck (1757–1801). The first, like Mlle. Dumesnil, had brilliant moments but found difficulty in sustaining a long part; the second was so temperamental that it is said audiences never knew if they were to see "the great or the little Fleck."

There are no names among the women to compare with these, although one must admire Carolina Neuber (1697–1760), not so much as an actress, but as a devotee of theatre who did much to establish the future greatness of the German stage. Schroeder's mother, Sophia (1714–1792), and his sister, Dorothea (1752–1821), were both much admired in their day, as was Charlotte Ackermann (1757–1774). But the bright star of German theatre was unquestionably Friedrich Schroeder.

Company organization changed little

The development of the art of acting tended to make actors more versatile, but companies were generally organized to employ actors for special lines, as had been the case in the previous period. In Paris at the Comédie, male parts in tragedy included kings, tyrants, lovers, and the secondary roles; female parts were princesses, mothers, lovers, and the seconds. In comedy, the male parts were financiers (a type new to this age), *manteaux* (or old comic parts), lovers, valets, and peasants; for the women, *duègnes* (or old comic parts), coquettes, lovers, and maidservants. Foremost in each part was the master of the line, and each had his double or understudy. The actors were engaged by the First Gentlemen of the Chamber (the group of nobles charged by the king with

overseeing theatrical affairs), who also issued regulations concerning the finances and discipline of the theatre. The company met weekly on Monday mornings to discuss affairs of the theatre, to hear new plays, and to distribute parts. The male members took weekly turns being business managers, and one of them was stage director, except when a playwright like Voltaire took over the directing of his own works. The freedom of the players to control their own company still existed to an extent, but was not so great as in the days of Molière.

In Germany, such a democratic organization would sometimes exist, as at Mannheim where committees chose the plays and cast them and everybody aired his opinions about everything. But more generally companies were under the supervision, more or less autocratic, of an appointed superior, like Iffland at Berlin, Schroeder at Hamburg, and Goethe at Weimar.

Russia had a system all its own. The players were classified and hired to these parts: leading tragic and comic lover, second tragic and comic lover, third tragic and comic lover, noble father, comic father, first domestic, second domestic, moralizer, clerk, and two confidants; women's parts were the same three lovers, two chambermaids, an old woman, and two confidantes. Companies were generally supervised by an aristocrat; members were not permitted to marry except with the supervisor's consent. Salaries were fixed by imperial budget; in the serf companies, owned and operated by wealthy landowners, there were, of course, no salaries. The serfs were whipped for bad performances, and often traded or sold. Sometimes they earned their freedom by good performances, and once, at least, a serf actress married into the nobility, after her master had duly elevated her, of course.

While the lot of Continental actors and actresses was not, on the whole, as salutary as that of the English players, it was constantly improving. Church opposition was still strong, particularly in Germany and Russia, and even in France the "infamous" stigma had not entirely evaporated. Evidenced chiefly by edicts against Christian burial for actors, the opposition, for instance, caused Carolina Neuber's coffin to be lifted over the churchyard wall rather than be carried through the gate, and her monument to be erected in a public crossroads. It constantly criticized actors' morals; members of the profession countered by urging decorum in private life and often insisted on it. But one of the early acts of the Revolutionary National Assembly in Paris during 1790–1791, which prided itself (and was regarded as) a wholly *rational* body, was to restore to actors the right to holy burial (which had so long been denied them by the church), to place Parisian theatres under the control of the municipality instead of the Gentlemen of the Chamber, and to declare that "any citizen may erect a public theatre, and give performances therein of plays of every description." The Reign of Terror was still to come.

Summary

Just as the literary influence of England spread to the Continent in the eighteenth century, there were recurring mutual influences among the theatres of the various countries with, toward the end of the century, the German theatre emerging as a significant national entity.

On the Continent, more men of literary persuasions were involved in theatre than in England and America, primarily because theatres on the Continent continued to have the sanction and support of governments and ruling classes. Both Voltaire and Diderot in France, with sizable reputations in other fields of writing, devoted a large part of their attention to theatre, both in playwriting and dramatic criticism. In Germany, Lessing and Goethe, with prodigious accomplishments in other fields, were among the most significant of theatre workers. On the Continent, more time and attention were given to criticism and theory, all those mentioned above making important contributions to this field. As for the plays themselves, the Continental versions of the domestic tragedy turned out rather better than the English varieties, though outside of Goldoni and Beaumarchais no comedy touches that of Sheridan.

Acting, of all the arts of theatre, showed the greatest advances on the Continent, as it did in England, with the great names of Schroeder, Talma, Lekain, Lecouvreur, Clairon to match those of Garrick and Siddons. All of these performers were members of permanent theatre companies, and developed within the framework of a constantly producing unit. Some of them were managers as well as actors, and all succeeded, to some extent, in developing new techniques in the art of acting.

The number of theatres increased greatly everywhere in the eighteenth century, with many national theatres being established on the Continent. The trend in theatre architecture was almost universally toward large and highly decorated houses, with audience accommodations in the opera-type, horseshoe auditoriums, and stages effectively pushed behind proscenium arches. Magnificent effects were popular in stage design, with the architectural emphasis of the Bibiena tradition the paramount style. A few designers and producers concerned themselves with the total stage picture, and this aspect of production was to receive increasingly effective emphasis in the next century.

For many centuries, the Eastern Hemisphere was itself divided into two distinct parts—the world of Asia and the world of Europe. This history has been dealing with the theatre of Europe, and may seem to have implied that no other existed. Quite to the contrary, however, Asian lands developed, independently, unique and highly civilized cultures, including remarkably advanced theatre. A form of drama, roughly paralleling that of ancient Egypt, was evidently extant in China about 2000 B.C. It seems to have been a dance-drama commemorating religious festivals, military successes, and ancestors, and was confined to the nobles and the priests. The epic period of Hindu literature began about the same time as the institution by Pisistratus of the Great Festival of Dionysus at Athens. The greatest Hindu playwright, Kalidasa, flourished about 350 A.D. Chikamatsu, the Shakespeare of Japan, was born about thirty-five years after Shakespeare's death.

Over many centuries, there were contacts between these two worlds. India saw its first Aryan invasion from the north about the tenth century B.C., and Alexander the Great (356–323 B.C.) had conquered a large portion of that country before his death. From the eighth to the eleventh century A.D. the Arabs and Mohammedanism came to India. In the thirteenth century, it was threatened by the greatest conqueror of them all, Genghis Khan, who took his Mongol hordes even into Europe after consolidating his conquests throughout most of Asia. In 1500 the Portuguese came then a century later the Dutch and the English, to be followed by the French about 1670. The early Christian church had arrived in India by the third century, and in China by the fifth, but was slowly strangled by the Moslems and the barbarians. Christian and Moslem contended over Indo-Asia for the next thousand years (indeed, the struggle still progresses, with various other, less violent faiths also entering the field from time to time). In any event, from 1500 on, the church was a significant factor in bringing elements of Western culture to all parts of the Far East. These evangelistic endeavors, coupled with various commercial and military operations culminating in the opening of Japan by Commodore Perry in 1854, brought East and West into ever-increasing contact. Despite westernizing influences the culture of these lands remained essentially indigenous, and markedly different from that of the Western world.

Eastern culture penetrated the Western world slowly. Everyone knows of the long sojourn of Marco Polo in the court of Kublai Khan toward the end of the thirteenth century, which had been preceded by an earlier voyage on the part of his father and two uncles. Both before and after that, the wonders of gunpowder, spices, silks, and the printed book were brought from Cathay to Europe. Columbus discovered America on a fruitless search for a western passage to those fabulous lands. In the sixteenth and seventeenth centuries, the Portuguese, Dutch, English, and French traders brought back from India, China, Japan, and the Malay archipelago, spices, textiles, and precious gems, along with other, less commercial evidences of Eastern civilization. Willow-ware plates and other china pieces, Canton wallpapers, and furniture incorporating oriental motifs appeared in many well-to-do and noble houses during the late seventeenth and early eighteenth centuries. The French court held Chinese masquerades; a Chinese pavilion was built in Kew Gardens; Catherine the Great built a little Chinese village as a playground.

In the middle of the eighteenth century, oriental influence reached into theatre. The

MANUSCRIPT OF KALIDASA
The illustrations on this ancient manuscript convey something of the grace and emphasis of gesture which actors in the old classical drama of India possessed. Differentiation of costume, particularly in color, is also apparent. (Museum of Fine Arts, Boston)

fourteenth-century Chinese play, *The Romance of the Western Chamber*, had been translated, and Voltaire, sails trimmed to the currents of his age, had taken his theme for *The Chinese Orphan* from *The Little Orphan of the House of Chao*. Oriental influence on eighteenth-century costuming was indicated above and the same period saw the introduction of the eastern shadow show to western audiences. Dominique Séraphin established a Shadow Theatre in Versailles in 1774, and the "Chinese Shadows" were taken to England by Ambroise the next year. In 1789, Sir William Jones translated Kalidasa's *Sakuntala* into English, and it earned high praise from many, including Goethe. Early nineteenth-century romanticism quickened interest in the remote culture of the Orient, with several literary works deriving from the East and more plays being translated. There is record of a company of Chinese actors playing for Napoleon III in Paris in 1860, having previously performed for thousands of Chinese in California soon after their immigration for the famous Gold Rush. In the 1880s, the Jackson Street Theatre in San Francisco was converted to oriental drama, and in 1930, the Chinese actor Mei Lan-fang was received with great acclaim in Europe and America, Stanislavski naming him one of the world's great actors. The twentieth century also saw western productions of Hindu and Chinese plays, as well as several instances of English-language dramas in the oriental manner. It is chiefly in the traditional forms of Oriental theatre that western interest has been manifest. Visits of *Kabuki*, *Noh*, and *Bunraku* companies as well as appearances of individual artists in increasing numbers in the twentieth century have sparked investigations of oriental forms. The 1920s saw several scholarly books published and after World War II the volume of such investigations increased enormously. Various groupings of scholars have systematically pursued the history, theory, and production styles of the traditional oriental theatre.

Though theatre in Asian lands is changing drastically in form and content today, those kinds which had by the mid-eighteenth century entered the theatrical consciousness of the West remain of prime interest. The following account will, therefore, deal primarily with traditional forms and will end with a brief consideration of the changes and additions of recent years.

Brahma begets theatre

As in the West, so in the East, theatre grew out of religious observance. The origin of theatre in India is traditionally ascribed to the supreme god Brahma, who ordered the

SCENE FROM A CHINESE PLAY
In this scene from *Killing the Tiger General*, the male character wears a long beard and stylized face makeup. The female characters wear the "rippling water" sleeves. (Zung, *Secrets of the Chinese Drama*)

sage Bharata (now one of the words for "actor" in India) to set up a playhouse, instructing him in the four Vedas—dance, song, mime, and sentiment (or *rasa*).

Whatever the legendary character of this creation, these elements have remained constant in Hindu theatre. Developing from the dialogue form of the Vedic hymns which date to 1500 B.C., real theatre actually emerges from the great source books of Hindu drama, the *Mahabharata* and the *Ramayana*, epics which appeared about the fifth century B.C. The most important period of Hindu drama follows these and takes inspiration almost wholly from them. In the lands east of India—Burma, Thailand, Java, and the Malay Peninsula—theatre sprang from the same sources and developed similar forms. Tibet, also, was influenced early by Buddhism and

the drama to be found there was and still is religious in origin and under the direction of the Buddhist church. In China, where the beginnings were rooted in religious observance, additional influences such as the celebration of military victories, honoring ancestors, and observing harvests also crept in. The Chinese tradition spread to Korea and thence to Japan.

Theatre for aristocrats

In all of these lands the drama was long and chiefly confined to the nobility and the upper classes since they were the only persons thought capable of understanding and appreciating (and, incidentally, of paying for) theatrical productions. In both China and India, seedbeds of all oriental drama, the

TWO NOH CHARACTERS
Above, a seventeenth-century painting of a character in the Noh drama. The fan is a ubiquitous hand prop used to simulate many objects. Left, a different type of fan is used by this fierce character who is masked and wigged. (Museum of Fine Arts, Boston)

earliest serious theatre was under the direction of the priests and was performed for the nobility. The first treatise on theatre in India, dating from the third century B.C., relates that theatrical performances would take place in connection with some festival or public celebration, upon which occasion the king or some other rich patron would call upon a group of actors to perform in either temple or palace.

Actors formed a distinct caste and were held in low repute, though some few of them might gain the friendship of influential patrons. A Chinese emperor of the third century B.C. is said to have employed many troupes of actors, whose chief duty was to perform at court banquets. At the same time, in the Buddhist monasteries the priests embellished for their humbler listeners the stories of which they were masters. These priestly performances were forbidden after the tenth century. The performers in the court plays were taken from the lower ranks of society, and for a very long time in China as in India actors were little regarded as persons. Theatre was a diversion for the leisure class, and the lower orders had largely to be content with puppets and shadow shows when, indeed, they had any time at all for diversions.

All during its great period, Hindu drama paid at least lip service to its religious origins, performances beginning invariably with a musical program, then an invocation or prayer, then proceeding to a dialogue between the director and the chief actress to let the audience know that, after all, this was merely entertainment. The ensuing plays were likely to be very long—eight or ten acts of exceedingly varied content and an inevitable happy ending. The increasing pressure of the Moslem invasions had, by the eleventh century, virtually destroyed this theatre, though some degenerate types of farce lived on, and various subliterary species of dance performances persisted in the many isolated regions of that teeming subcontinent with its more than sixty languages. Various incursions of European cultures did no more than impose western forms, and there was no true revival of Hindu theatre until the advent late in the nineteenth century of the neoromantic Rabindranath Tagore.

Chinese theatre more literary, more literal

In China, on the other hand, the Mongol invasion under Kublai Khan in the thirteenth century paved the way for greater participation in theatre, because Chinese literary men, heretofore engaged in public office through the elaborate system of literary examinations, were debarred by the new conquerors from office; they turned to theatre as a means of livelihood.

Their themes began to embrace all classes and ideas and the plays became, in time, an exceedingly popular entertainment, reaching a peak in the nineteenth century. Plays were usually of four acts with a prologue and prefatory poem and many diversions between the acts. Often a theatrical performance consisted not just of a single play, but of scenes from many plays arranged after some predetermined plan and lasting from early morning to late afternoon or from early afternoon to late evening. As can be imagined in such a theatre, there was much eating and drinking, and coming and going, and the playhouses were designed to encompass these activities.

Japan—entertainment and theatre

The derivative theatre of Japan developed along class lines, with the classical and traditional Noh drama reserved at first for the emperor (or the shogun who usurped his power), then much later becoming the diversion of aristocrats and wealthy commoners as well—but always playing to a highly restricted audience.

The popular traditional theatre of Japan is the Kabuki, which incorporates some aspects of the Noh as well as of the Bunraku, or marionette theatre. Its presentations are far more variegated and spectacular than the more classic Noh, combining for popular appeal most of the elements which are called entertainment as opposed to theatre. As in the Chinese theatre, a typical program might consist of scenes from well-known plays, interspersed with dance or pantomine, with perhaps a melodrama in addition, and a final dance number.

In the 1890s, there was a movement to bring occidental methods to the Japanese

stage, and in 1909 a Free Theatre was established after the pattern of the Moscow Art Theatre. Twentieth-century Japanese theatre has been marked by various repressions, as well as a second influx of occidental influences, so that Noh, Kabuki, and Bunraku have experienced some difficulty in maintaining themselves. But a quite recent resurgence of interest in the old forms has strengthened the hope that increasing westernization will not utterly destroy this "theatre theatrical."

Situation, sentiment, and a happy ending

The oriental theatre was for long periods and in many places almost completely unliterary.

Many of the so-called playscripts are no more than a framework for the actors who are by all odds the most important elements in the total theatrical picture. In Java, for instance, spoken parts were added to the traditional dance and pantomine only under western influence. In the shadow plays, the leader recites all the lines, often improvising on the well-known plot lines, and directs the orchestra which always accompanies the performance. In the plays using live actors, a similar convention is observed; the actors, in pantomime and dance, simply act out the lines spoken by someone else. In the few Tibetan scripts which have been translated it is obvious that they are but fragmentary

BUNRAKU THEATRE
Left, a detail from a seventeenth-century screen painting shows the puppets, the operators, and some members of the audience during a performance. Above, two puppets and an operator in a modern Bunraku theatre. Some idea of the size of these dolls may be gained by comparing them with the figure of the operator. Chikamatsu wrote many of his plays for the Bunraku. (Museum of Fine Arts, Boston; Japan Tourist Association)

guides, large portions being improvised during performance. In Burma and Cambodia the few extant texts are based on the *Mahabharata* and the *Ramayana;* theatre performance is, and always has been, a combination of dance and pantomime with an integral musical accompaniment. Only in China did dance cease to be an integral part of dramatic production (probably the result of Confucian influence), although stylized movement and gesture persisted.

In considering the plays of India, where there is a considerable body of literary drama, one must forget the accustomed designations of tragedy and comedy, for the Hindu plays cannot be made to conform to this pattern. Hindu criticism set up ten forms of the drama, the divisions being determined by material, type of hero, and sentiment to be evoked. In no case was the tragic denouement to be allowed; no matter what the vicissitudes of the characters, the ending must be a happy one.

The highest form of drama was the one in which the subject was legendary, the hero royal or divine, and the sentiment heroic or erotic. The best of the Hindu dramas, Kalidasa's *Sakuntala*, is of this genre; the hero is the legendary king Dushyanta, the heroine is the divinely guarded Sakuntala, and the story is of the star-crossed love of these two who are finally reunited. It was evidently written about 400 A.D., and besides seeing some performances on western stages, it was made into a beautifully evocative motion picture in 1943. It is typical of all Hindu drama in its long lyrical passages, its emphasis upon situation and sentiment over character conflict, and its inclusion of humorously playful characters as servants and officials. In conformance with Hindu tradition, the noble characters speak Sanskrit, the literary tongue, while the lower orders speak in Prakrit, the popular tongue.

Kalidasa mentions as his predecessors other playwrights of some renown. The most notable of these is probably Bhasa, whose play *The Poor Charudatta* provided the basis for a later play, *The Little Clay Cart*, traditionally ascribed to King Shudraka, also a predecessor of Kalidasa. Though a play of great interest and charm, *The Little Clay Cart* differs in species from *Sakuntala*, for it takes its characters from ordinary life. It is again a love story, this time of a Brahmin and a courtesan (not, indeed, a mistress in the occidental sense, but a socially approved, skilled, and intelligent companion, like the Japanese geisha). It was produced in the 1920s by the Neighborhood Playhouse in New York.

The first dramas of known authorship in India are fragments dating to the first century. They are of two plays by the Buddhist Asvaghosa and deal with religious conversion. Bhasa is somewhat tentatively credited with thirteen plays discovered as late as 1912. But the name of Kalidasa is supreme in India's golden age; his three plays (among other works of poetry) are generally conceded to be the finest flower of Hindu literature. *The Hero and the Nymph* is of the epic stamp; *Agnimitra and Malavika* of *The Little Clay Cart* type.

After Kalidasa, there are few names of importance. Harsa, a seventh-century king of northern India, is notable for his three plays about love triangles. Bhavabhuti in the eighth century has three outstanding plays, again on the theme of star-crossed lovers. Bhatta Narayana and Rajasekhara in the next century deserve mention, the latter for *The Camphor Cluster*, written entirely in Prakrit. Before the eleventh-century submersion by the Moslems, two other playwrights of note appeared: Vishakhadatta whose *Raksasa and the Seal* deals with political intrigue, and Krishnamisra whose *The Rise of the Moon of Knowledge* personalizes abstract qualities like Error and Reason and their conflict in man's mind. There was no further native Hindu drama of any literary merit until Rabindranath Tagore in the nineteenth century. Intellectual, poet, and mystic, Tagore concerned himself with the revivification of the essential and timeless spirit of India divorced from the influence of colonialism. Among his prolific writings are a series of plays which successfully establish a connection to the golden age of Kalidasa. Best known to western audiences are *Chitra, The King of the Dark Chamber*, and *Red Oleanders*.

China's dramatic output cannot be classified by western divisions, for in the main the plays include both tragic and comic events and justice is always done even though it means employing a quite obvious deus ex machina, such as bringing back the spirits of the dead to settle matters.

The evolution of the plays had much to do with their form. In addition to origins in religious observance, there were three other early influences. About the time of Confucius (c. 551–478 B.C.), there were in the emperor's court actors who gave heroic scenes in praise of ancestors as well as a special company of dwarfs or fools who presented short sketches which pointed out in story form the faults of the administration. That this was sometimes perilous is attested by the fact that the great Confucius himself once felt impelled to order the death of an actor who had carried his criticism too far. During the T'ang Dynasty (720–907 A.D.) the populace was amused by professional story tellers who embellished their historical, heroic, melodramatic, or tragic tales with song and dance. In much the same fashion, the Buddhist priests told stories from the scriptures, which brought large audiences to the temples to hear them. Often the songs incorporated in these stories were set to popular tunes and dance was included whenever possible. By the Sung Dynasty (960–1127 A.D.) these forms had been amalgamated into long performances of dancing, singing, and narrative; an early Chinese theatre historian reports some two hundred eighty of these plays from the Sung Dynasty, and six hundred ninety from the next, the Chin Dynasty.

When the Mongols came and literary men turned to writing for theatre, the performances became more truly plays. Dialogue and dramatic action were substituted for the long poetic and narrative passages. Hundreds of these plays were written during the rule of the Mongols (1280–1368) and one hundred sixteen still survive. Chinese

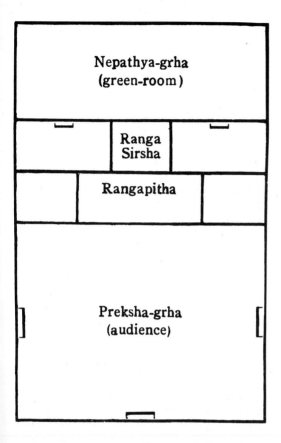

Nepathya-grha
(green-room)

Ranga
Sirsha

Rangapitha

Preksha-grha
(audience)

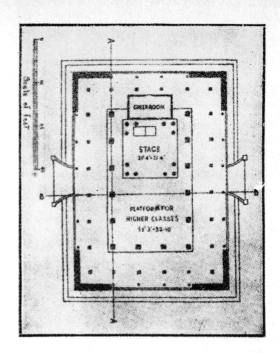

FLOOR PLANS OF ANCIENT THEATRES OF INDIA
Left, the final form of the classic Hindu theatre, rectangular in shape, with equal space allotted to actors and to audience and the stage divided into its traditional areas. Above, the plan of an old temple theatre at Trichur, in the Cochin state, Kerala. The rectangular form is maintained, as is the relationship of greenroom to stage area, but the stage itself differs from the plan at the left. (*The Theatre of the Hindus*)

scholars say the best of these is *The Sufferings of Tou-E*, but the first to be translated into English was *The Romance of the Western Chamber*, which, in a later version by S. I. Hsiung, was successfully performed in England in 1938. It was from this period that Voltaire was inspired to his *The Chinese Orphan*; and *The Chalk Circle*, in a translation by Klabund, received a beautiful German presentation in the 1920s.

The Ming Dynasty (1368–1644) produced more than six hundred plays, the most famous of which is *Romance of a Lute;* as *Lute Song*, this play had a fairly successful run on Broadway in the 1940s. In all of these plays, there is no thought for the unities of time, place, or action, and the subject matter is extremely varied, taken from all walks of life. The Chinese classify their plays by subject matter: historical, military, civil, romantic, criminal, ethical, fantastic, problem. Toward the end of the nineteenth century there developed a new form of play, without music, but it has never been as popular as the traditional form. The Sino–Japanese War in the 1890s brought a rash of patriotic plays, as did the Japanese invasion of 1937. The advent of Communism in 1950 brought the same kind of doctrinaire plays that have marked Soviet theatre production.

Korean drama, which began in the Buddhist temples, was secularized by historical epics and by ancestor worship; these morality performances are still popular. Literary influences came from the Chinese. In the tenth century, the persecution of Buddhist monks caused a wave of propaganda plays both for and against them. The most important Korean drama was written in the fifteenth and sixteenth centuries, but the Western world knows little of it because of the difficulty of translating the many puns and plays on words of which it is chiefly composed.

Kabuki and Noh

The drama of Japan, on the other hand, is fairly well known to us, consisting of two main divisions, the Noh and the Kabuki. The Noh dates from the fourteenth century, presumably having its origin in the Shinto-worship dance called the *Kagura*. This ancient worship was modified by the coming of Buddhism in the sixth century, and the Shinto dances were supplemented with dance-dramas written by Buddhist priests and called *Saragaku*. The consolidation of the form is credited to one of these priests, Kwanami Kiyotsugu (1333–1384), fifteen of whose plays are still extant. More famous was his son, Seami Motokiyu; more than one hundred of his plays are still extant. They are the length of a one-act play and deal with historical or religious events commemorating heroes or declaiming the virtues of the Buddhist philosophy.

Typically, the Noh play consists of a slow-moving and stylized dance by the *Shite* (or Doer) preceded by a dialogue which explains the circumstances leading to the dance. The explainer is called the *Waki* (or Assistant); both he and the Shite may have Adjuncts, called *Tsure*, and all are assisted by a chorus of ten or twelve men who sit motionless to the side of the stage and chant parts of the dialogue to the accompaniment

of a flute, two hand drums, and a stick drum. Four to six of the plays are given at a single performance, a fixed order of types having evolved by the sixteenth century. The presentation of the serious Noh plays is interspersed with *Kyogen*, short, farcical incidents involving two or more characters, performed without chorus and musicians, and sometimes parodying the more serious Noh. A typical "wig play" is Kwanami's *Sotoba Komachi;* a typical "battle play" is Seami's *Atsumori;* a typical Kyogen is *The Bird-Catcher in Hell.*

The Kabuki had its origin about 1600 with the renegade temple dancer O'Kuni, who began dancing in a dry riverbed (thus lending the name "beggars of the riverbed" to actors). She soon gathered about herself a company of women, children, and then men, and her success generated numerous imitations. Charges of immorality eventually suppressed these performances, and in the final form of the Kabuki only men performed. The word Kabuki is written with three characters that mean song, dance, and performance. In contradistinction to the esoteric and aristocratic Noh plays, Kabuki took for its themes the concerns of daily life and presented them to popular audiences.

Much of the early Kabuki was purely improvisational, but with the advent of Chikamatsu in the latter half of the seventeenth century it acquired literary distinction. His first known play appeared in Tokyo in 1677 and was called *The Evil Spirit of Lady Wisteria.* He is supposed to have written more than a hundred plays, as long or longer than those of Shakespeare. They include history, comedy, tragedy, melodrama, realism, and romance. Violent action marks many of them. Chikamatsu is credited with initiating a highly influential genre in his *Shinju* plays, which revolve about the idea of double suicide for love. Current happenings,

A CHINESE COURT THEATRE
Model of the traditional classical court theatre of China as it looked in 1830. It has an
apron stage, surrounded by pit and galleries,
with a formal background and no scene
changes. (Cleveland State University)

such as the scandal of the Ronins in 1701,
were sources for Kabuki plays, as were the
legendary and historical events of both
China and Japan. Murder, torture, suicide,
battles, frequent changes of scene, long
periods of elapsed time, characters from all
walks of life—these are to be found in the
Kabuki drama, with, of course, the integral
song and dance which pervades oriental
theatre.

Chikamatsu also wrote for the Bunraku,
or puppet theatre, which enjoyed popularity
from its inception in the fifteenth century to
its height in the eighteenth. It had been preceded by *Joruri* (doll theatre) practitioners
from the seventh century onwards; Chikamatsu is said to have favored the puppet-
theatre and to have written for it because
the actors in the Kabuki (accustomed as
they were to improvisational techniques)
took liberties with his texts. Subject-matters

of the plays are about equally divided between historical dramas concerning the
heroes of the past and domestic tragedies
with characters from everyday life. Over the
years, there has been frequent borrowing of
materials back and forth between Bunraku
and Kabuki, and when Kabuki actors perform a Bunraku play they use the jerky
movements associated with the puppets. Performance chores in Bunraku are shared
among the puppeteers, the chanters, and the
samisen players, although the chanters (who
provide description, narration, and dialogue)
are the most revered members of the company.

Since the nineteenth century when the
Shakespearean scholar Tsubouchi began to
bring decided western influences into Japanese drama, Japan has seen productions of
Ibsen, Wilde, Shaw, Strindberg, Maeterlinck,
and O'Neill, but its typical and indigenous

drama remains the Noh, the Bunraku, and the Kabuki.

Playhouse is the setting

In oriental theatre it is impossible to consider settings apart from the playhouses, since "setting" as western theatre knows it does not exist, except in the Kabuki. Theatre types range from a mere space for acting to the elaborateness of the Japanese houses.

In Tibet, plays were, and still are, given in the open space before temples, sometimes using the temple steps, while the audience sits or stands about as it chooses. Performances in the lands east of India were also generally outdoors, with a roof of matting supported by pillars protecting audience and actors. Such even was the Dancing Shed, which was the Royal Theatre of Cambodia as late as 1883—a thatched-roof structure open on three sides, with space behind the stage wall for dressingrooms. The Burmese theatre building is similarly rudimentary, with bamboo platforms on three sides to hold the distinguished guests, the balance of the audience sitting or standing on the ground around the stage, which is simply a floor of matting. A tree is the only stage decoration, either stuck in the ground at stage center, or attached to one of the poles supporting the roof. Lighting, when necessary, is supplied by earthen pots of petroleum-soaked flares. The orchestra sits on the ground to either side of the stage. The playhouse of the Chinese traveling companies was a similar temporary and portable structure, with roofed bamboo platforms around three sides and standing room in the center on the ground. Here, however, the stage was a fourth platform, larger than the others, and roofed.

The courtly drama of India, China, and Japan might be given in specially built structures in gardens or in the converted halls of palaces and temples. In the whole period of classic drama in India, there may not have been separate and permanent theatre buildings. Researches seem to indicate that the earliest arrangement of playing space was triangular in form, then square, and finally rectangular, although the three may have existed simultaneously. Each of these basic shapes could be of three sizes, the smallest for monologues (one of the divisions of playwriting), the largest for spectacles, and the middle size preferred for all other presentations. The space was about equally divided between players and audience.

In the rectangular theatre the stage had two equal major divisions, front and back, and two doors connected these; the back area was a greenroom for the actors. The playing area was again divided equally from side to side, with the central portion at the back elevated. In the square theatre and the triangle the same division of stage areas prevailed, but there was no elevated platform and but one door to the greenroom. The auditorium was richly decorated with woodwork carved to represent creepers, birds, and animals. The walls were covered with beautiful paintings on a variety of subjects prescribed in one way only—they must be "pictures of pleasure." One ancient reference mentions a theatre at Ikkeri, built by King Venkatappa, which was worked in ivory and sandalwood and inlaid with precious stones, surrounded by a garden. Another refers to a circular theatre, but details are lacking.

In the Cochin state, Kerala in southern India, some old temple theatres are still extant, such as the one at Trichur. This is a rectangle, with a floor about four feet above ground level, the intervening space being of intricately carved granite. There are two entrances, north and south. A raised plat-

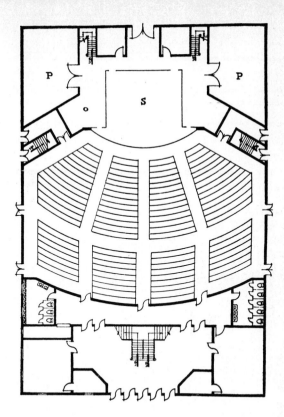

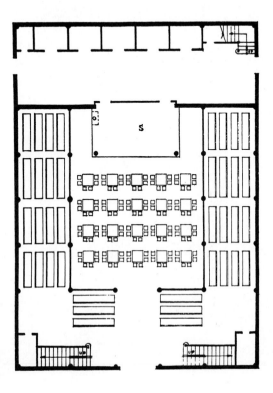

FLOOR PLANS OF CHINESE THEATRES
Left, the traditional Chinese teahouse theatre, with tables and chairs for the gentry on the main floor and galleries for the women and less affluent members of society. Above, a modern Chinese theatre, with rows of seats substituted for the tables and chairs, but with stage appointments still approximating those of older times. (Zung, *Secrets of the Chinese Drama*)

form in the center of the wooden superstructure runs east and west and is divided into three sections. The westernmost is the greenroom and is marked off by screens. Two doors lead to the central portion, which is slightly raised to form the stage. This is a square area with an ornately carved ceiling supported by ornamented pillars. The rest of the interior is for seating the audience. A row of carved pillars around the entire structure supports the roof. The modern scholar of South Indian theatre, K. R. Pisharoti, says that the old Sanskrit dramas

are still occasionally performed in this theatre temple.

In the ancient theatres the audience was seated on stone or wooden benches placed on a rising series of stepped platforms, with the downfront-center space reserved for the patron or the guest of honor, and the remaining seating space divided by pillars into sections for the four castes.

Though stage walls and curtains were richly decorative, there was no attempt to change or localize this decoration for individual plays. Properties were sometimes used,

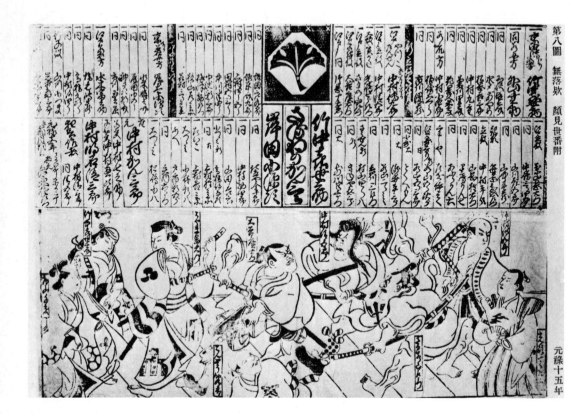

such as the toy cart in *The Little Clay Cart* or the artificial elephant employed in the story of the Udayana. Such properties, as well as arms and accessories, were said to have been made of stiffened cloth, wood, metal, mud, and wax. But for the most part, properties were indicated by the gestures of the actors, gestures which became highly conventional and significant. British domination brought in an infusion of western the-atrical customs, and theatres on the Euro-pean model were built in the chief centers of population, incorporating, to some degree at least, English theatrical traditions and practices.

In China the early plays were performed in the halls of great houses or in pavilions in the gardens or orchards. The most famous of the orchards was that of the Emperor Hsuan Hsung, or Ming Huang (713–756),

第五十一圖　無落景　大判漆繪

起言几年

KABUKI THEATRE
Left, an early eighteenth-century playbill. In addition to the names of plays and characters, this interesting advertisement shows sketches of the performers, each with a title. Above, an eighteenth-century print of a Kabuki theatre, clearly showing the elevated stage, the galleries, the standing pit with its penlike subdivisions, the runway through the audience over which an actor is making his entrance. The setting is less austere than in the Noh theatre, with set pieces and backgrounds in use. (Museum of Fine Arts, Boston)

whose troupe performed in his pear garden where he founded a school for actors. It was called, literally, Young Folks of the Pear Garden. He thus became the patron saint of Chinese theatre, and even today before going on the stage Chinese actors burn incense to his image which stands in all greenrooms.

When the first public theatres in the large cities were built they were called tea houses, and the drinking of tea and the eating of sweetmeats by the audience are still accompaniments of Chinese performances. The typical structure was a squarish rectangle, with about one-fourth of the total area devoted to backstage space. The stage itself projected out into the auditorium and was raised. Tables and stools for the wealthier patrons filled the ground floor, with a railed gallery supplied with benches around three sides for the less wealthy. A second-floor gallery provided boxes and benches for the women spectators. The stage, whether indoors or out, was roofed, being supported by two columns at the downstage corners. The wall at the back of the stage, beautifully painted or hung with an embroidered curtain, terminated at either side in a curtained doorway to the backstage area. The door at stage left was for entrances, at the right for exits. The orchestra had a small balustraded section upstage right, where it remained throughout the performance. In the modern Chinese theatre the tables have disappeared, although tea drinking still remains a pastime of the audience. The seats are now arranged in curved rows with aisles, each row provided with a shelf for the ubiquitous teapots, and the stage has retreated to an almost proscenium-like form, with a wide, curving apron to which a door opens on either side. The upstage right and left entrances have been retained, and the orchestra now sits backstage.

There are no stage settings as such. Whatever things are necessary for the drama in hand are supplied from the property rooms by the two property men, clothed in black, who are supposed to be invisible to the audience. An ordinary table may be a wall, a mountain, an altar, a bridge, a battlement. Chairs placed on the left indicate the high rank of their occupants. Several chairs covered with a cloth may be a bed. An actor carrying an oar is in a boat. City gates are a cloth banner supported by two sticks in the hands of the property men. Banners represent armies; four black flags flourished by the property men indicate a violent wind; four white ones painted with waves represent water; two yellow ones painted with wheels make a chariot. A red flag held before the face of an actor means that his head is cut off, and a red sack tossed on the stage represents the severed head. Small bits

of paper tossed on the stage make a snowstorm. A tassled horsewhip enables the actor to ride an invisible horse; if he falls then or at other times, the property man supplies him with a cushion upon which to land. Physical topography and architectural details are supplied by the actor's pantomime: if he is climbing a hill or a flight of steps, he raises his knees high to indicate it; an exaggerated step over an imaginary doorsill indicates a door. Thus, the visual elements of Chinese theatre are highly conventionalized, placing primary emphasis upon the skill of the actor to supply all the necessary details.

In Japan, the acting area of the classic Noh play is adapted from the ancient Shinto dancing platform, being of highly polished cypress and hollow below so that the feet of the dancing actors will resound. It is about three feet high, about eighteen feet square, and is covered over by a pointed temple roof supported by four pillars which have significance in the actors' movements. Downstage left, a short extension of the stage accommodates the singers; upstage left a short, railed enclosure houses the musicians and stagehands. The flute player sits at a pillar also upstage left. A door in the stage wall behind this pillar is for the musicians and chorus. Actors enter from stage right over a long, roofed bridgeway running diagonally back to a curtained doorway. The back wall of the stage is painted with a formalized pine tree; three potted pine trees are spaced along the actors' bridgeway to symbolize heaven, earth, and humanity. A few short steps lead from downstage center to the pebbled path surrounding the stage, but they are never used in performance. The audience sits or stands in the open area surrounding the stage. The properties are as rudimentary and symbolic as those of the Chinese theatre, and perhaps are even more austerely used. Four poles with a flimsy roof make a palace; if the roof

SHADOW PUPPETS FROM JAVA
These fantastic figures, made of pierced
leather and mounted on sticks, are operated
from below against an illuminated backdrop,
while the lines are spoken and sung by offstage voices. The intricate lines of the figures
are indicative of the highly decorative costume in oriental theatre. (The American
Museum of Natural History)

is thatch, it is a cottage. A fan, in the use of
which the Japanese are particularly adept,
may be a dagger, a tray, a knife, or almost
anything else. Again, the skill of the actor
rounds out the visual scene.

In the Kabuki, however, both properties
and setting are apt to be more literal. The
Kabuki theatre naturally derived from that
of the Noh, but the bridgeway for the actors
early became a runway, generally extending
from the down right corner of the stage out
through the audience. The temple roof of
the early stage was later reduced to a
painted representation. The audience stood
in walled-off pens on the auditorium floor,
the walls being convenient runways for the
purveyors of tea and sweetmeats. The more
affluent spectators sat on cushions in the
boxes surrounding the three sides of the
roofed-in playhouse. The stage was higher
than that of the Noh, stage and runway be-

ing elevated to the heads of the standing
spectators. As this theatre gained in popularity, the stage became wider and shallower,
and was, after 1760, equipped with a revolving stage. Both this and the runway were
adopted by western theatre, the latter being
a feature of Max Reinhardt's production of
Sumurun early in the twentieth century, and
then being taken over by the burlesque
houses. The revolving stage, also, was built
into the Munich Theatre by Lautenschläger
in 1896.

The oriental Kabuki stage and runway
were frequently supplied with traps, and
the revolving stage often moved with actors
on it, while they walked presumably from
one location to another. A part of the stage
was recessed and was revealed by a curtain
that rolled back to one side. The scenery and
properties of the Kabuki are factual and
elaborate (within the limits of Japanese

artistic asceticism), and the traditional invisible stagehands are present to keep things moving. But even in this most literal of oriental theatres, the effect is far from the reality expected and demanded on occidental stages; it remains a stylized art, incorporating not only the spoken word but dance and music as well.

The Bunraku stage is typically much wider than it is deep or high, and it has an extension downstage left in the form of a platform on which sit the chanters and the samisen player. Scenery may be as intricate as that on the Kabuki stage, but the stage floor is marked by a trough fronted by a platform and backed by scenic elements. In this trough the puppeteers move, manipulating the dolls on the knee-high platform in front of them.

In the traditional oriental theatre, house lights are not extinguished during the performance, but merely dimmed. In consequence, stage lighting tends to greater brilliance than it does on occidental stages. This greater brilliance, coupled with the gorgeous appearance of the actors, makes for a dazzling effect.

Costume and makeup heighten stylized effects

If settings are largely nonexistent in much of oriental theatre, costumes and makeup are varied and elaborate, achieving an intricacy seldom found on the western stage.

Costuming in the classic theatre of India was more realistic than the later uniform gorgeousness of China and Japan. The dramas of Kalidasa and his near-contemporaries were carefully costumed to indicate the characters' differences in class, profession, and nationality. Gods and demigods appeared brightly arrayed like kings; nobles wore elaborate and many-colored garments. But cowgirls wore plain garments of dark blue; ascetics, garments of rags or bark; people engaged in religious services, plain, uncolored robes. Physical and mental states were reflected in the costuming, dirty and ragged clothes connoting misery or poverty. Faces were painted to reflect the area from which the character derived, as well as his station in life. Brahmins and kings, as well as people from the north and west, wore reddish yellow; persons from the Ganges valley and members of the two lower castes wore dark brown; those from the south of India, as well as members of primitive tribes, were painted black.

Masks were and still are used in the religious dramas of Tibet and the dance-dramas of Java, and were also used in the early Chinese theatre. In China, however, they were quickly replaced by face paint, which over the centuries has achieved a high degree of elaboration and significance. The patterns and combinations of colors are standard for specific character types: predominant white indicates treachery; black, bluntness and integrity; blue, stubborness and ferocity; red, loyalty and courage; yellow, strength and cunning; pink and grey, advanced age. Outlaws and demons wear green; gods and immortals wear gold. The patterns are stylized, such as that of the Monkey God, who paints his face in a triangle of crimson, with golden circles around the eyes and nostrils; for Tou Erh-tun, the brigand chief, a blue face is lined with curves of black and white, a second pair of eyes is painted below the actor's own, and the forehead painted to represent many-colored gems. Types of beards also help to indicate age and character. They may be red or blue, black or brown, long or short, divided or straight—each quality signifying a definite attribute. Cunning characters generally wear long moustaches, good characters never. "Painted face" roles (of which there are at least two hundred

fifty) are specifically male roles. One classification of male role which is not a painted face is that of the "scholar," a gentlemanly, handsome young man who uses white makeup accentuated with a touch of red around the eyes and a red line on the forehead. The *tan*, or women's roles (also played by men), use stylized and heightened natural makeup on a white base.

Both men and women are gorgeously appareled. The styles are adaptations of the noble dress of the eighth to the sixteenth centuries, but there is little attempt to make them historically accurate. Again the symbolism of color is used, with emperors in yellow, officials in red, civilians in blue, old people in brown, and rough characters in black. They are splendidly decorated; the stage warrior, for instance, appears with embroidered tiger heads on his heavily padded shoulders and long, scalloped panels dropping from his waist. He also wears thick-soled shoes, reminiscent of the Greeks, to give him height. If he is a general he also wears four small, triangular flags across his back at the shoulders, and a magnificent headdress trailing two long pheasant feathers. Elaborate headdresses surmount the female characters, and on ceremonial occasions many of the characters wear long, full sleeves ending in a filmy, wide white silk cuff which covers the hands and waves gracefully through the vari-

ous gestures of the pantomime. Both costuming and makeup are not realistic, but rather conventional and stylized, telegraphing to the audience the disposition, station, and function of the character as soon as he appears.

Masks are retained in the Japanese Noh theatre. There are fifteen standard masks, beautifully carved of wood and painted, which are reserved for the use of the First Actor who may change masks many times in the course of a performance. Other actors in the Noh, as well as all of those in the Kabuki, wear face paint in brilliant designs and colors. The female characters, like those on the Chinese stage, wear natural makeup, slightly heightened and stylized. The costumes are magnificent in color and highly decorative. No less rich than the nobles are the garments of the commoners, being differentiated only by cut and color. High and elaborate headdresses are often featured, and

JAPANESE NOH THEATRE
Left, in this performance in a Noh theatre
the masked leading actor is portraying a
woman. Visible at the left is the bridgeway
for entrances of the actors, with one of the
three pine trees in view; at the right is the
formal pine tree painted on the back wall
of the stage. The steps leading to the pebbled
path around the stage can be seen in the
lower left corner. Above, Noh masks ready
for painting. The creation of masks for this
drama is a revered art form in Japan; this
photograph shows two types of masks. (The
American Museum of Natural History)

there is much jewelry and ornamentation.
Like the costuming of the Chinese theatre,
that of Japan makes little pretense to reality, relies largely on symbolism and formalism, and gives an effect of oriental splendor.

Stage belongs to actors

Theatre in the Orient is supremely the actor's
theatre. It is his skill which commands the
attention of the tea-sipping, morsel-eating
audience, and which stirs their imaginations
to set the stage with whatever intricate
scenery and properties are called for. The
oriental actor is a highly skilled practitioner.

In the classic theatre of India, and in the
lands to the east which took their dramatic
inspiration from India, the custom was generally to have the women's parts played by
women. Indeed, in Cambodia, the entire responsibility for the training, rehearsing, and
costuming of the royal company of actors
falls to one of the principal ladies of the
court, who has a corps of women to assist
her. Here, women players predominate, men
being used chiefly when the plays are from
the *Ramayana*. In Tibet, on the other hand,
women never participate. Male characters
are acted by the priests, female characters
by laymen.

Actors in classic India formed a special
caste, and the various acting companies were
each under the direction of a leader who was
married to one of the actresses. The leader
was called a *Sutradhara*, or "Stringholder,"
from the ancient puppet plays. He was an
actor-manager-director, and on occasion supervised the construction of the temporary
theatre buildings as well. He also, as noted
above, addressed the audience directly at the
beginning of the production, remarking on
the play, its author, and the occasion, and
complimenting the audience on their refinement and taste. His wife ordinarily assisted
him in this presentation. In the operation of
the company, he had two men to help him,
and the other eight or ten players worked
under these men. The companies were mostly
itinerant, seeking patronage for their repertory from city to city. Except in unusual
cases, the actors were generally despised as
a caste, even though their art was admired.

The characters they portrayed followed
definite classifications. There was the noble,
handsome, and brave hero; the resourceful
but wicked enemy of the hero; his companion or confidant; the rake; the manservant;
the comic; the beautiful and accomplished
heroine; her confidante; and so forth. It is
to be assumed that each actor specialized in
a "line," for the demands on each were arduous. Series of conventionalized gestures indicated going on a journey, mounting a
chariot, climbing a mountain, groping in the

dark, and so on. The system seems to have had many parallels with the later commedia companies of Italy.

In China and Japan, acting is traditionally a male vocation. It is true that when Ming Huang established his College of the Pear Garden in the eighth century, both men and women were among the trainees. In fact, the original Japanese Kabuki was established by a woman. But women were banned from the Chinese stage in the eighteenth century, when, it is said, an emperor married an actress; in Japan they were forbidden by imperial edict less than a hundred years after they began. It is true that in the twentieth century women again appear on Chinese and Japanese stages, more in Japan than in China; there have even been all-girl companies in Japan. But men have long been preferred, even in female roles; the greatest actor to come out of China in recent times has been Mei Lan-fang, an *onnagata*, or performer of female roles.

The training is long and arduous, beginning in early youth. Each actor is expected to master a hundred to two hundred roles, each with its special characteristics, gestures, and movements. In China, there are four large classifications of types: males in general, robust males, females in general, and broad comedians. An actor generally makes his reputation in one of these types. Within each type there are numerous subsidiary types, each interpreted in a specific way. Vocal characteristics are important. Robust males and broad comedians speak in a forced bass, other types in falsetto. They sing to the accompaniment of string, brass, and percussion instruments, and must master the art of making themselves heard above these piercing sounds. Each character has his own walk and set of gestures. There is a "language of the fan" and a "language of the sleeve," and every movement follows a strict convention. Actors enter and exit to a tempo set by the orchestra, and every movement is a studied rhythm. The female impersonators work to emphasize the difference between the sexes, with even the slightest crook of the little finger designed to emphasize the fragility and delicacy of the fair sex. It is a triumph of art over reality.

Since there is little or no opportunity for change of facial expression because of the painted faces and, in the Japanese Noh, the masks, performers must rely on other means to communicate emotional effects. In the Noh, this communication is aided by the construction of the stage on which the dancing feet of the actors beat a rhythm that reveals emotional states. It is obvious that the oriental actor must be skilled in prose and verse, in song and dance, and pantomime; that he must have his voice and every muscle of his body under absolute control at all times. Continuing application and constant discipline are his lot. Yet with few exceptions, such as the general esteem for Noh performers, he has long been held in low repute. Occidental standards have changed this opinion in modern times, and the great success which Mei Lan-fang had in Europe and America did much to raise the status of his fellow-actors in Asia. And, of course, the motion pictures have created stars in the western tradition.

Changing values and changing theatre

The traditional forms of theatre in Japan are alive and comparatively well today because of various forms of government subsidy, tax abatement, designation as "valued national cultural properties," and special efforts at audience development. But many Japanese theatre people regard them as ossified and not in step with the changing face

CHINESE ACTORS IN COSTUME
Left, Mei Lan-Fang, the great female impersonator, with the props and gesture to indicate starting on horseback in *The Rainbow Pass*. Above, a female and a male character (with beard) are posed in the traditional gesture which indicates they are on board ship in the play *The Valiant Fisherman and His Daughter*. (Zung, *Secrets of the Chinese Drama*)

of modern Japan. At about the same time that Tsubouchi began to introduce western drama to Japan, the theatrical form of *Shimpa* (a kind of hybrid, half-naturalistic Kabuki theatre) was introduced, and some years later the all-girl, musical-comedy form of *Takarasuka* became popular. But the most significant departure from the traditional forms was in *Shingeki* (new theatre), based on European ideas in which actor, dancer, and singer were separate entities, and theatrical forms stressed the actor's skill. Beginning with the Tsukiji Little Theatre in 1924, many subsequent troupes produced not only the plays of western cultures, but also many native plays written to nontraditional patterns. Shingeki is still a viable and popular theatre form in Japan, but since World War II several Japanese playwrights and performers have been working through new performance groups to reincorporate the music and dance of the older forms in socially relevant materials. They have criticized Shingeki as too closely tied to the playwright's words, and declare themselves antiestablishment in stressing the capabilities of actors. They travel in "mobile theatres," perform in tents or in makeshift quarters, and see themselves

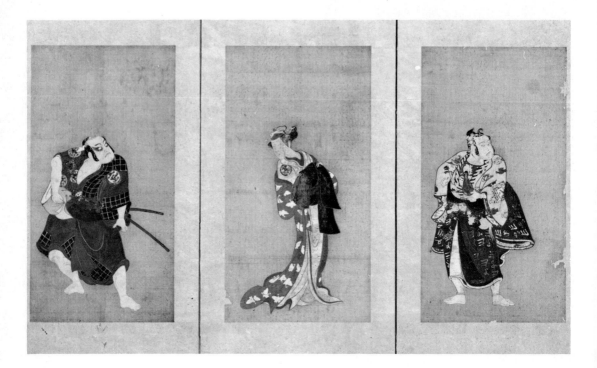

JAPANESE ACTORS
Costumed figures on a six-panel screen of
the Ukiyoe period. A comparison of these
will show the variety of masks and costumes,
the vitality of the gestures, the grace of the
postures common to these oriental performers. (Museum of Fine Arts, Boston)

(like their counterparts in other countries)
as the wave of the future.

Similar troupes have been at work in
India, combatting western dominance of
Indian cultural centers such as Madras, Calcutta, and Bombay with indigenous language
performances which utilize adaptations of
traditional techniques such as *Jatra* to bring
social and political materials to the attention
of the wider population.

In China, art has been declared "political," and during the Cultural Revolution of
the 1960s, all traditional theatre pieces were
barred from performance. The form, however, of the beloved "Peking Opera" (the traditional Chinese play) was applied to socio-
political materials, and, with the abolition of
such "outmoded" practices as the appearance
of the property men on stage, the government has thus far given approval to five
"Peking dramas with contemporary themes"
(such as *Red Detachment of Women*) which
have been played throughout China. This
new and approved form has replaced not

only the traditional Chinese theatre, but also the Russian-inspired spoken drama which had made some headway in China during the period of Sino-Russian friendship immediately following the Russian Revolution.

Summary

The oriental theatre has proved through many centuries that realism is not a necessary concomitant of theatre.

The traditional dramatic literature of the Orient has little in common with that of the Western world. It makes no attempt to hold the mirror up to nature; it is in no wise realistic. Virtue is always rewarded, evil always punished; happy endings are universal. We might call it escapist drama, but it has an undeniable charm, a touch of fantasy that is genuinely appealing. It represents an abstraction of reality, a symbolization of character and experience rather than verisimilitude, and therein lies its universality.

JAPANESE THEATRE IN JAPANESE ART
Above left and right, in this seventeenth-century, screen, stage, actors, audience, and box office are arranged in decorative fashion. Below left, costumed actors in *The 47 Ronins* carry the props and assume the characters of the parts they play. (Museum of Fine Arts, Boston)

Its manner of staging is well suited to its subject matter. In the Orient theatrical presentation has been almost without exception a highly refined and symbolic art form. The essence of human experience, not a representation of life, is the goal of drama, evident in themes, staging, costumes, and acting. Oriental abstractions are sometimes meaningless to western eyes, their prolixity often tedious. Yet the kernel of oriental theatre art has been an emphasis upon the skill of the artists, and in the timeless atmosphere of Asia this art has reached a great refinement. The splendor of the costumes and the skill of the actors have had some effect on western theatre, both in design and performance, and certainly two very practical contributions to western theatre technique have been the revolving stage and the runway through the audience.

Not only the pronouncements of the *philosophes* of the Enlightenment but historical events themselves had challenged the divine right of kings, and during the century the challenge was extended to the right of any human being to sovereignty over any other human being. Slavery and serfdom were eliminated in all parts of Europe (including Russia) by 1863, and in many other parts of the world which were influenced by European thought and practice. In 1848 Karl Marx published the *Communist Manifesto* in which he summarized the conditions of the working classes and prophesied an historical process based on the changing economic structure in which the industrial working class—bearers of the new social order—would emerge triumphant. Then in 1859 Charles Darwin shook other preconceived beliefs with his *Origin of Species*. And when Freud would begin to publish at the end of the century, the works of these three men would indeed create a new world order.

Revolution and romanticism were both the result of and the reaction to the Age of Reason. On the one hand, the confidence of the neoclassic period in the reasoning powers of the mind led to the questioning of all institutions and received cultures, and to the individuation which is the mark of romanticism. On the other hand, the essence of neoclassicism was the searching for *ideal* forms, for the suppression of individuality to the service of the ideal. Romanticism became a *reaction* to the neoclassic, asserting individual rights, privileges, abilities, transcendencies, and inspirations, and insisting on the primacy of feeling over thought, hence a wide diversity in the expression of those ideas. The romantic spirit infused most areas of human activity in the nineteenth century; the concern here is primarily with its effect on theatre. It is interesting, however, to note that it was in the Romantic Age that the novel—the most highly personal form of literary art—came to full power.

Theatre under strict control in surging political turmoil

Diversity—and a lamentable divorce from literature—marks theatre through most of the nineteenth century. With few exceptions, plays of real literary merit did not emerge until the revolutionary inspiration, which had already wrought great changes in political, economic, and social fields, reached the theatre itself. But throughout the century the number and kinds of theatrical productions increased enormously, and the numbers and kinds of people who went to the theatre likewise increased. Often the unsettled and unsettling times made theatre seem escapist and crowd-pleasing, devoid of ideas as well as reality. Often the subject-matter of the drama seemed inconsequential, and seldom profound. But in Europe in the nineteenth century theatre was learning to do what English theatre had already done: earn its way by pleasing its new audience. State-supported and subsidized theatres continued to exist (and here and there to predominate) but by and large the initiative in production tended to move to nongovernment hands, though supervision and surveillance of theatrical activities by public officials continued.

In the political turmoil of a large part of the nineteenth century in Europe, the theatre was sometimes neglected, sometimes banned, sometimes put to uses far from artistic. Caught up in the conflicting loyalties of the French Revolution, the century-old Comédie Française was split into opposing factions; Talma became the darling of the Republicans, and moved with his company in 1791 to the new theatre of Les Variétés Amusantes. (In this house, remodeled since, the Comédie

GERMAN ROMANTIC DRAMA
An 1813 painting of a scene from Schiller's *Wallenstein*, a typical romantic tragedy in both content and setting. (Goethe-National-museum, Weimar)

plays today.) The Loyalists, after a short interdiction when there were no dramatic performances in Paris, continued at the old house. Talma called his company the Théatre de la République, while the older company was known as the Théâtre de la Nation.

These companies were reunited in 1799, the year in which Napoleon became First Consul, though during the period of the Republic more than fifty theâtres had sprung up all over Paris—then as now, the center of French theatrical activity. Napoleon thought of himself as (among other things) a patron of the arts; in 1812 he signed the famous Decree of Moscow, which limited the number of Parisian theatres to eight, each with its sphere of activity defined, and reserved the production of classic plays, as heretofore, to the Comédie Française. The management as set up by this decree, with some modifications by decrees of 1850, 1859, and 1945, is still in force today. Thus has the continuity of French theatre descended in unbroken line from Molière to the present time, with an emphasis upon repertory and the production of classics both new and old, and a strict insistence upon training for membership in the company. The manager was and is appointed by the government, though the shareholders, as in Molière's day, have a voice in the affairs of the theatre, exercising it vigorously or weakly as the abilities of the incumbent manager permit. But the monopoly of the state theatres was effectively broken and the theatres of the boulevards would wield increasing influence.

The head of state in Russia also dictated and regulated theatrical activity there. Tsar Nicholas I (reigned 1825–1855), in his drastic reorganization of Russian life, brought the theatre under the regulation of the Third Department, or secret police, arrogating to himself as head of the department all theatrical matters, including the selection of the repertory and the distribution of the parts. There were two theatres in St. Petersburg at this time, one devoted to ballet and opera and one to drama. Although under Nicholas' successor and through the rest of the century many theatres were built in many provinces, and theatre managers and owners frequently came from the merchant class, all theatres continued under the jurisdiction of the secret police. They exercised a strict censorship on the performance of plays, as well as on the number and kind of playhouses allowed. Thus, though there was a gradual transition from a theatre dominated by the aristocracy to one owned and managed by the middle class, government participation in theatrical activity was strong throughout.

Censorship was also strong in the theatres of Vienna, where other companies rivaled the government-patronized Burgtheater. Censorship was implicit, at least, in the court theatres of the German principalities and the Italian city-states. Though theatrical production in most places tended to pass from the hands of the aristocracy to those of middle-class entrepreneurs, the ruling classes were keenly aware of the potential use of theatre as a progaganda instrument. Just as the French theatres of the Revolution became the mouthpieces of the new sentiments, so Italian theatres saw a wave of patriotic and nationalistic plays, and the Russian theatre was organized in defense of the status quo through the secret police of the Third Department.

This widespread regulation had its reaction toward the close of the century in various "free" theatres set up as private producing agencies in various parts of the Continent. That is another story and belongs to a later chapter. Another kind of freedom from government restriction—or rather, circumvention of it—was found by those producers who instituted in their playhouses various forms of bastard theatrical art like melodramas, vaudeville, pantomimes, *opéras comiques*, and so forth. Convention and reaction, the struggle of the new against the old, were as evident in theatrical activity as they were in other fields, though until the last quarter of the century no great or lasting changes were effected in theatre.

Further inroads on the tradition of actor-managers were made during this period, with more and more nonacting managers coming to the fore. The fortunes of actors were as unstable as ever, except in such permanent companies as the Comédie Française, though even there merit often suffered at the hands of influence, as in the case of an inferior actress being elected shareholder over the very able M. Worms because she had an influential friend in the imperial government. Criticism of the free lives of players was still current, being directed notably against such an eminent performer as Sarah Bernhardt. But the rising respectability of the acting profession went steadily forward in the public regard. When Régnier (François Toussez) retired from the Comédie Française in 1872 after forty years of "uninterrupted ser-

ANOTHER SCHILLER PLAY
Sketch by the Duke of Saxe-Meiningen, later in the century, for the scene in Schiller's *Maid of Orleans* in which Joan is captured. The sketch is typical of the Duke's practice in carefully working out the disposition of each individual in the great crowd scenes for which his productions were famous. (Collection of Duke George II, Meiningen Museum)

vice on the first stage of Europe," he was admitted to the Legion of Honor, and ten years later the same accolade was bestowed upon Edmond Gôt.

The relationship between actors and audience was still a close one, Parisian playgoers expressing their disapproval of play or player in quite definite terms, with frequent police intervention. Often the hisses of a dissatisfied audience were fought by the hired claques who sat, under the direction of a leader, in the seats just beyond the orchestra pit. They were an accepted institution in French theatres until 1878 when the Comédie

dispensed with them. These claques often made or broke a performance.

Playgoers in Paris purchased their tickets from any one of half a dozen ticket offices throughout the city, or at the theatre just before the performance, paying then as now in New York an extra sum for the convenience of the ticket office. Playbills cost extra, as did the footstools which the old female ushers could supply. Advertising was under government regulation, with each theatre being assigned a particular color for its posters, with all printing in black and the size a uniform fifteen by thirty inches. These were displayed throughout the city on posts and walls. It is said that when an enterprising American wished to display his large, colored circus posters in Paris in 1867, he had to obtain special permission to do so. By the last decades of the century, performances in the theatres began at seven o'clock and lasted until midnight or after. The chief offering was preceded by one or more short pieces which often operated as proving grounds for new writing and acting talent.

Throughout these years, amid all manner of change, the French audience maintained its love of and interest in theatre, and it constantly grew in size and range of interest. In Russia, theatrical interest and activity spread so rapidly that before the end of the century, Russian dramatists had contributed some of the most significant plays to be written in that era. Germany made rapid strides in theatrical development, and there was a resurgence of theatrical interest in Spain and Italy. In the smaller countries of Scandinavia and middle and southern Europe, national theatres were founded and native playwrights, like Ibsen, sometimes rose to international stature.

Extravagance and escapism

New plays of this period displayed some marked divergences from earlier types, and a wide diversity of subject matter and treatment. Romanticism brought many changes in matter and manner; but toward the end of the century tastes turned to "the light of common day" which marked the so-called realistic school.

Translations and adaptations, unprotected by international copyright, were produced on stages everywhere. The Shakespeare cult in Germany, begun by Schroeder, was carried on by an excellent series of translations under the editorship of Ludwig Tieck. Shakespeare was produced in France, in Czechoslovakia, in Russia, and in Italy, with increasing reverence for the original texts. The other classic dramatists continued to hold the boards, with more or less success depending on their interpreters, as did the playwrights who wrote "copies of copies," as Schiller called them, from the more recent past.

But the chief concern here is with the playwrights contemporary with the theatre which produced their work. Napoleon, eager to have his own great tragic poet, as Louis XIV had his Racine, tried to elicit great tragic plays by edict and subsidy. But the effort was fruitless; the genre was dead. Napoleon had to content himself with criticisms of Talma's interpretations of the great classic parts, and with ordering the Comédie company to play, often at a moment's notice, in all the great capitals of Europe so that their admiring peoples might see the glory of France. He was slightly more successful in his patronage of comedy, for under his prompting Louis Picard produced *The Small Town* (1801), which traveled to Germany and thence to England as *The Merry Widow*.

Of the few names which could be mentioned in tragedy and comedy as previous ages knew them, none would be significant today, except perhaps that of the Austrian Franz Grillparzer, who wrote on classic themes at one point in his career, and the Dane Adam Oehlenschlaeger, among whose thirty-odd plays are numerous tragedies influenced by his study of the Greek drama.

Romanticism was the prevailing spirit of the first half of the nineteenth century. The long-regarded rules of the neoclassicists were abandoned in favor of freedom of form and content. Romanticism as a literary movement first developed in Germany where the insistence of the Reformation on the immediate

THE "HERNANI" RIOTS
Sketch of the disturbances at the Comédie Française occasioned by the production there, in 1830, of Victor Hugo's romantic drama.

relationship between man and God was reinforced in the latter half of the eighteenth century by the idealistic philosophy of Kant, and the new direction given literary criticism by the forceful writings of Lessing. Concurrent with Lessing's strictures against French neoclassicism and his own study of English criticism and playwriting, there arose tremendous interest in England's greatest playwright. Shakespeare was now explained not as being great in spite of his flouting of the Aristotelian rules but precisely because of it. His plays were considered vast pictures of life itself having no unity of time or place; the only unity the plays needed, or knew, was the unity of the hero. All one needed to do to produce great drama was to create many outstanding personalities and have them go through many events.

The young Goethe was caught up in this mistaken interpretation of Shakespeare's greatness, without giving due consideration to the fact that the Englishman wrote primarily for the theatre he used, his plays being fashioned for the Elizabethan playhouse and its spectators. Thus Goethe published, in 1773, his *Goetz von Berlichingen*, with fifty-four changes of scene and forty-one speaking characters, outdoing his master, whose *Antony and Cleopatra* (most lavish of the Shakespearean canon in change of scene) had but thirty-eight. Goethe's play was fashioned for the contemporary reader rather than for contemporary theatre in which each of these fifty-four scenes would require a shift in the stage decoration. Nevertheless the play was produced, and its success in book form as well as its production gave impetus to an increasing looseness of dramatic form—"the technique of the curiosity box," as Goethe called Shakespeare's plays—which completely disregarded the English master's logical plot development.

On this pattern F. M. von Klinger produced his *Storm and Stress* in 1776, from which the Sturm und Drang movement takes its name and J. M. R. Lenz his *The Soldiers* (1776), which is a series of sensational events loosely related to a single character. To the literature of the movement, Goethe added *Clavigo* in 1774 and *Stella* the next year, while Schiller closed the cycle with *The Robber* (1781) and *Intrigue and Love* (1783). Lack of a coherent aesthetic, and the turning of Goethe and Schiller (the only men of real genius in the movement) to classical forms, caused a temporary hiatus in the developing romantic movement.

It was Schiller's study of Greek drama that led to the inclusion of the idea of Nemesis in his own plays, and thence to a whole series of fate-tragedies based upon the operation of a curse. Such were the widely popular plays of Werner and Müllner. Both the *Ritterdramen* (plays of chivalry) and the *Rührstücke* (sentimental melodramas) were outgrowths of the early Sturm und

Drang movement in Germany. They proved more popular on the stage in their own day than did the plays of Schiller. Kotzebue's plays were Rührstücke in their most extravagant form, and were widely copied and translated in other parts of Europe, in England, and in America.

The romantic movement per se was founded in 1798 by Ludwig Tieck at the University of Jena as the result of his lifelong interest in Elizabethan and Spanish drama. Its theoretical basis was laid by August Wilhelm and Friedrich Schlegel in their joint volume of essays published in 1801. In it they maintained that the first duty of criticism was to understand and to appreciate, that the right of genius to follow its natural bent was sacred. As the romantic movement developed in Heidelberg, Würtemberg, and Berlin, it incorporated the beliefs and interest of the earlier Sturm und Drang, as well as stimulating interest in the German past, which in turn led to a passionate nationalism. Heinrich von Kleist (d. 1811) wrote a series of plays (unproduced before his death) which stressed the belief that the only security in life is to be found in the unconscious voice of instinct and feeling, and E. T. A. Hoffmann (d. 1822) added the final ingredients of supernaturalism and melancholy in his widely popular novels.

It was this brand of German romanticism that Mme. de Staël (who had spent most of the years of the Age of Napoleon in Germany) wrote about in her widely popular book, *On Germany* (1810). But it was Stendahl in his *Racine and Shakespeare* (1823) who called for a new literature to replace the outworn style of the Age of Gold.

Meanwhile, the private enterprise theatres of the Parisian boulevards had developed a highly popular dramatic form called melodrama (from the old French term *mélodrame*, meaning a musical passage in-

A CONTRAST IN PARIS THEATRES
Right, the grandoise Paris opera house, opened in 1874; the elaborate design and spacious appointments of this theatre influenced many subsequent theatre buildings. Above, an Honoré Daumier lithograph of the interior of the Théâtre Ventadour, showing the cramped interior and the dark little boxes that were typical of Paris theatres. (Photo Cinemati, Paris; Museum of Fine Arts, Boston)

tended to convey the actor's emotions in theatrical forms where he was unlicensed to speak). René Guilbert de Pixerécourt had first used the term in 1800 to designate the new theatrical form which accompanied a highly moral plot with music, ballet, combats, processions, and intricate theatrical effects—the ingredients of his dramatization of Ducray-Duminil's novel, *Coelina, or The Mysterious Child.* This most popular form of theatre in the nineteenth century had its sentiments, extremes of character, thrilling music, spectacle, blood, violence, and emotional agony. Virtuous though outraged heroines, manly but misunderstood heroes, diabolical villains, plots consisting of spectacular obstacles to be overcome—and a

happy ending—these constitute the dramatic form which swallowed up the drama of the previous century in all its forms and filled most of the theatres of the world for most of the 1800s. Needless to say, it was highly satisfying to its audiences—and sold like hotcakes!

But melodrama was far from respectable in the minds of the intellectual leaders of the day. There would have to be other grounds for unseating the outmoded classical tragedies and comedies from that bastion of respectability, the Théâtre Français. Mme. de Staël's book, Stendahl's book, the visits of Charles Kemble, Edmund Kean, and William Charles Macready in various plays of Shakespeare—these all led the young bo-hemian playwrights of Paris to storm the doors of the Comédie with "romantic" dramas. One of the most vocal of the playwrights, Victor Hugo, wrote the manifesto for the new form in his preface to *Cromwell* (1827), beginning in an evangelistic tone: "Behold, then, a new religion, a new society; upon this twofold foundation there must inevitably spring up a new poetry," and going on to detail passionately the task of the new playwright who will,

with the same breath mold the grotesque and the sublime, the terrible and the absurd, tragedy and comedy . . . take the hammer to theories and poetic systems. . . . there are no other rules than the

general laws of nature . . . Genius resembles the die which stamps the king's effigy on copper and golden coins alike.

Cromwell was not produced, but the next year the Comédie accepted a prose tragedy by Alexandre Dumas *père, Henry III,* the first romantic play granted production there. In February 1830, Hugo's *Hernani* was announced, and the battle lines were drawn: conservatives versus radicals. It is to the credit of Baron Taylor, manager of the Comédie, that the play preparation went forward, but when it opened there were hoots, catcalls, skirmishes, and open battles. For forty-five nights hardly a word of the play could be heard. It was a battle to the death of the

general laws of nature . . . Genius resembles cleared, Hugo was clearly the hero and romantic drama became acceptable. Ironically, the actors of the Comédie, having a long tradition and training in a style antithetical to the new materials, were not particularly successful in presenting them, and the Odéon and the theatres of the boulevard proved more congenial homes.

Hugo went on to great popularity with *Marion de Lorme* (1831), *The King Amuses Himself* (1832), and—most famous of all—*Ruy Blas* (1838). They are theatre pieces above all; in reading them today one needs to stage them in one's mind to savor the excitement of many scenes and characters, intricate lines of action, and extravagant dia-

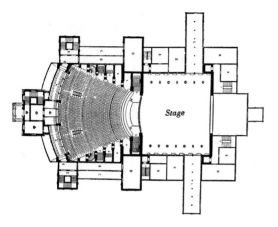

logue. Alexandre Dumas *père*, writing for the Théâtre de la Porte Saint Martin, produced many plays of the same type, notably *Antony* (1831) and *La Tour de Nesle* (1832). Then he turned to dramatizations of his own novels of which he had written more than one hundred; the formlessness of the typical romantic play was well suited to the discursiveness of the novel form.

Alfred de Musset, writer of exquisitely witty dialogue, had little influence on contemporary theatre, because after an initial failure on the boards he wrote solely for publication. But his skillful plays have more interest and genuine literary merit than those which were produced when written; they have since been widely played. Perhaps his

most famous is *Lorenzaccio* (1831), a Renaissance tale of Florence.

In Germany, after the death of Goethe (1831), romantic drama flourished in the work of Heinrich Laube, C. D. Grabbe, Georg Büchner, and Friedrich Hebbel. Though Hebbel was by far the most popular in his day, modern critics see more value in Büchner's presentation of the inevitable suffering attached to greatness (*Danton's Death*, 1835) and his proletarian tragedy, *Woyzeck* (1836).

In Italy, romanticism was channeled into the service of the nationalist cause, as in Niccolini's *Nabucco* (1819), which, paying lip service to the unities, is sometimes claimed by the classicists. But his later plays, with their impassioned outcries against foreign powers and the absolutism of the church, mark him definitely as a romantic. Manzoni's lyrical historical tragedy, *Il Conte di Carmagnola* (1820), and the early plays of Paolo Ferrari are other examples of this type.

In Spain, the earlier romantic tradition of Lope de Vega and Calderon received new impetus in the work of Francisco Martinez, Juan Eugenio Hartzenbusch, and Antonio Gutierrez whose *El Trovador* (1836) served, some twenty years later, as the basis for Verdi's opera, *Il Trovatore*.

By far the most popular and most prolific playwright of the mid-nineteenth century in France was Eugène Scribe (1791–1861) who wrote or adapted (sometimes with collaborators) about four hundred plays—all carefully calculated to leave undisturbed the moral and social prejudices of the bourgeois audience for which he wrote. Though he is now held in a contempt as great as his fame in his own day because of the ultimate insignificance of his subject-matter and the obvious mechanics of his technique, his influence was salutary. Scribe developed the "well-made play," neatness itself, though no less romantic than the type of play he set out to reform. To its clear-cut structure and easily identified character types could be tacked all kinds of improbabilities and theatrical effects. None of his plays is remembered today except perhaps his least typical: *Adrienne Lecouvreur* (1849), which gave a spectacular acting part to Rachel, Bernhardt, Ristori, Modjeska, and others. His successor in the well-made play was Victorien Sardou, who like Scribe was immensely successful, widely copied and translated, and remembered today mainly because of George Bernard Shaw once epitomized his type of writing as "Sardoodle-dom."

Occasionally a well-made play rose to greatness. One of the earlier ones contains keen insight into human motivations and a superior literary style; this is Gogol's *The Inspector General*, produced in 1836 at the Moscow Maly Theatre, and still very interesting and playable. Perhaps it was both the incipient realism and the folk quality of Gogol's play that interested the eminent Pushkin (1799–1837), who had spent his life in pursuit of these qualities and whose powerful play, *Boris Godunov* (1825), was banned from the stage in Russia for many years. Pushkin was the first writer of eminence to insist that the vernacular, as opposed to French, German, or church Slavonic, was the best medium for literary and dramatic expression in Russia; it is interesting to note how quickly after him Russian playwriting rose to greatness.

A wave of patriotic plays had been made to order for Tsar Nicholas I, who also encouraged melodrama and vaudeville as escapist theatre for the masses. In spite of political interdiction (or perhaps because of it), the mid-nineteenth century saw the emergence of the great national drama—and playwrights such as Gogol (1809–1852), Turgenev (1818–1883), the two Tolstoys (Alexei, 1817–1875, and Lev, 1828–1910), Chekhov (1860–1904), and Gorki (1868–1936). Alexei Tolstoy's historical trilogy, *The Death of Ivan the Terrible, Tsar Feodor Ivanovich, Tsar Boris*, was written between 1866 and 1870, but was banned by the Third Department and not produced until the opening of the Moscow Art Theatre in 1898. The reception accorded Gogol's *The Inspector General* caused his self-exile. Turgenev's most famous play, *A Month in the Country* (1850), was not staged until 1872 because of censorship. And Chekhov, perhaps the greatest playwright of them all, would wait for the new theatre movement to give him adequate production.

The development, after the middle of the century, of realism and naturalism had some roots in the romantic's concern for common things and common people, for nature in its primitive state, and thus parallels the continued production of the still popular romantic drama. One of its chief exponents in France was Alexandre Dumas *fils* who, in his preface to *The Prodigal Father* (1868), pays tribute to Scribe for his technical facility, but deplores the fact that he did not incorporate moral or social theses into his plays, as he, Dumas *fils*, was devoted to doing. Ironically the play for which Dumas *fils* is best known today is the sentimental *Camille* (1852). Even Ibsen, who is the cornerstone of this "new theatre," progressed from romanticism through historical drama incorporating psychological insights, to the powerful social and psychological studies which are the basis for his widespread fame and influence. Again, as in the preceding century, new forms grew slowly beneath the pattern of the established, breaking through in the last decades of the period to triumph.

French playhouses typical of Continental theatre architecture

Though the First Empire attempted to limit the number of theatres in Paris, the proscrip-

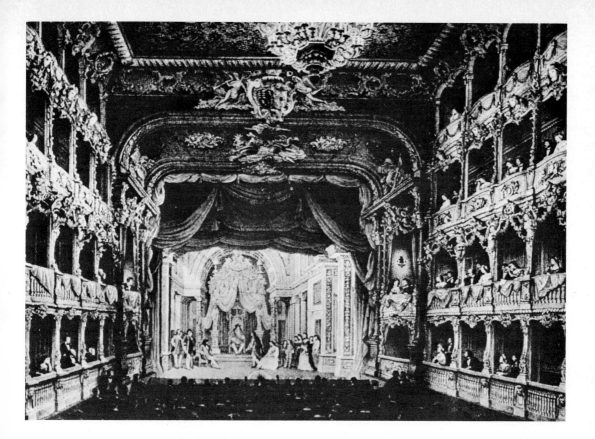

RESIDENZTHEATER, MUNICH, 1867
The highly ornamented interior has a deep
proscenium arch—containing four boxes—two
on a side. The stage is set with side wings
and backcloth; the main curtain falls at the
edge of the stage.

tion was of comparatively short duration;
it was totally abolished in 1867, and by the
third quarter of the century there were again
upwards of fifty houses in the metropolitan
area, including one in almost every outlying
ward of the city proper. Of these, about
twenty might be called leading houses, patronized chiefly by the upper classes; the
rest were secondary houses, devoted to the
entertainment of the middle and lower
classes.

Among the leading theatres, the first was,
of course, the Théâtre Français, housing the
venerable Comédie. The house to which
Talma and his insurgents moved in 1791, in
the Rue de Richelieu, is the one still occupied today, although it has gone through
various renovations and rebuildings, notably
after a disastrous fire in 1900. A renovation
in 1864 provided for a fine foyer, or public
reception room, in which the audience gathered between scenes and before and after
the performance. The building in the nineteenth century was a free-standing structure,
seating fourteen hundred spectators, with a
colonnade marking the front of the ground
floor. In addition to the auditorium, it housed
(as it still does) a valuable museum of portraits and statues, including Houdon's
famous bust of Molière; dramatists as well

as players are included in the galleries, and the list of artists who are represented is an impressive one. The library on the fourth floor houses, in addition to the complete records of the long history of the Comédie, many precious manuscripts of plays first presented there. Here is the record of a theatrical organization older than any other in the Western world, housed in a building which is still an active theatre center.

Other theatres of the nineteenth century which offered Parisians the same fare at the Comédie were the Odéon or Second Théâtre Français, the Gymnase Dramatique, and the Vaudeville. The original Odéon had been built during the reign of Louis XIV and was occupied for a while by the Comédie Française. It was destroyed by fire in 1799, rebuilt, and for a time called the Théâtre de l'Impératrice. It burned again in 1818, but Louis XVIII ordered it rebuilt at once and gave it permission to act all the plays of the classical repertory, which had hitherto been the exclusive right of the Comédie. It was at this time that the Odéon was called the Second Théâtre Français, but it never rose to the eminence of the first house, functioning somewhat as a "bush league" for aspiring players and playwrights. In 1959, it was officially designated Le Théâtre de France, under the directorship of the renowned Jean-Louis Barrault. The Gymnase Dramatique began in 1820 as a sort of public practice room for students of the Conservatory, the government-supervised school of theatre. Its function became much like that of the Odéon in relation to the first theatre of France. The Vaudeville was founded in 1792 by two secessionists from the Opéra Comique, and devoted about fifty years of its existence to the production of the light, topical amusements set to music that were called vaudevilles at that time. Then, in 1852, it produced Dumas *fils' The Lady of the Camellias*, a straight play which met the requirements of the theatre's operation by including one song. So successful was this innovation that the Vaudeville continued in the new genre from then on.

Another group of somewhat larger theatres devoted themselves to drama and spectacle. The most famous of these was the Théâtre de la Porte Saint Martin, which housed most of the plays of the insurgent romantics. It had been built in 1781 to house the opera but closed in 1796 when the opera moved out. It reopened in 1802 with melodrama and was closed again from 1807 to 1810. From then on it concentrated on spectacle and melodrama and the plays of the new romantics. At the Gaîté were offered "fairy pieces" and musical extravaganzas, enlightened now and then by the music of Offenbach and Gounod. The Châtelet was devoted to spectaculars of military or geographical persuasions, often having whole menageries parade across the stage. The Ambigu Comique, early in the century the scene of many of Pixerécourt's fabulously successful melodramas, eventually became the refuge of the naturalists.

The *opéra bouffe* (comic opera), which rose to great popularity in the later nineteenth century, was housed chiefly in the Bouffes Parisiennes, the Renaissance, the Folies Dramatiques, and the Variétés—the last of which was the chief home of Offenbach. But all through the century, the Opéra Comique remained, as it had been previously, the chief house for light opera.

The most imposing of theatrical buildings in Paris was the Opéra, or National Academy of Music, built at great expense, through good times and bad over a period of twelve years, and finally opened in 1875. It is a grandiose structure, in an extravagantly decorated style, designed by Charles Garnier, and often copied throughout the

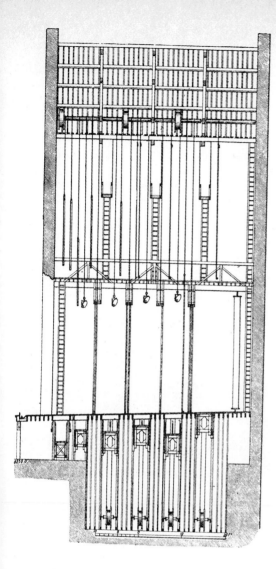

CONTINENTAL STAGE MACHINERY
This sketch shows the complications of stage machinery necessary in the large theatres. Much understage and overstage construction was demanded by the complicated scene changes. (Sachs, *Modern Opera Houses and Theatres*)

Paris built or remodeled was fairly standard. The arch contained three tiers from which stretched th horseshoe galleries, one built almost directly over the other. The first of these had two or three rows of chairs, backed by a row of boxes; the second was generally all small boxes; the third was furnished completely with benches. Where a fourth gallery was included, it too was given over to benches, inhabited by the "gallery gods." The floor of the orchestra was still divided into three parts: orchestra chairs nearest the stage, a pit with seating on benches, and under the first gallery a tier of dark little boxes. Brander Mathews complained in 1880 that even the best of Parisian theatres were very uncomfortable, with narrow aisles often crowded with extra chairs and very hard and narrow seats. Consideration for the comfort of the audience would wait for a future time.

This style of interior incorporating boxes and galleries stacked one above the other (in spite of interesting alternatives developed in the previous century) was largely dictated by the necessity to get the most people into the smallest space and assure that each of them was as close as possible to the stage. The expanding theatre audiences, the growth of theatre production as private enterprise business, and the restriction of available space in the urban settings where theatres were generally erected dictated a capitulation to this "hencoop" construction.

Only in exceptional cases could theatre design depart from this norm. Financed by King Ludwig of Bavaria, Richard Wagner, for instance, could conceive and build a notable exception, which became the herald of a new era in theatre building. It was the Festspielhaus at Bayreuth, sketched by Wagner and built by Otto Brückwald in 1876. Asking that every spectator have a full view

Western world. Seating twenty-one hundred persons, it replaced the old opera house in the Rue Le Peletier with an opulence almost unbelievable, and a tremendous stage most intricately fitted out with machinery.

The general design of the theatres of

of the stage, Wagner demanded and got a house without galleries, the floor of the auditorium inclined, the rows of seats slightly curved. It was the first radical change in a style which had endured for two hundred years and it had significant influence on both the design of new theatres and the renovation of old ones. It is apparent that though revolutionary for its day, it was no more than a return to the basic plan of the old Teatro Olimpico, and beyond that to the theatres of ancient Rome.

It might also be worth noting that the success of Astley's Amphitheatre in London was not lost upon the new Parisian entrepreneurs. In 1807 there appeared the *Cirque du Mont Thabor*, in 1814 the *Cirque du Temple*. Both had the large riding ring and a proscenium stage as well. Interestingly enough, neither had the arc of boxes which at Astley's, like a regular playhouse, surrounded the riding ring, but banks of seats arranged *en amphithéâtre*.

It will not profit us significantly to enumerate all the theatre buildings on the Continent. By and large there were two sizes: the larger theatres housing opera and spectacle, and the somewhat smaller ones

ELABORATE STAGE SETTINGS
Left, Joseph Quaglio's design for Schiller's
Wilhelm Tell, given in Munich in 1806. This
romantic setting is typical in its elaborate
picturesqueness. Above, Friedrich Beuther's
Temple of Isis for Mozart's *The Magic Flute*,
given in Weimar in 1817 under Goethe's direction. The massive structural forms and
the diagonal linear perspective show the
Bibiena influence. (Theater-Museum, Munich)

housing the drama. Indeed, in Moscow and
St. Petersburg the two officially sanctioned
theatres were named just that: Bolshoy, or
Great; Maly, or Small, with the Moscow
Maly, opened in 1824, developing into perhaps the most famous of Russian theatres.
The tiny Maly in St. Petersburg was replaced
by the Alexandrinsky, a larger house, in 1832,
about the same time that a third house, the
Youth Theatre, was opened for light comedy
presented by the graduates of the Government Theatrical School. The removal of the
ban on theatre construction in 1882 encouraged the opening of many private theatres, chiefly modeled on the French style,
both in the capitals and in the provinces.
The numerous theatres of middle Europe
and Italy, many of them first built in the
eighteenth century, persisted in the opera-
type house. Not without reason was the
theatre called an auditorium, a place for
hearing, rather than a spectatorium, or place
for seeing. Even the popularity of spectacles
did little to alter the design of theatres for a
long time, and the revolution was accomplished only when theatre people realized
that all those who came to the plays should
both *see* and *hear* them advantageously.

The romantic imagination and set design

Playhouses at the opening of the century were, of course, equipped with the old Torelli permanent-rig system, with flats attached to the poles which went through slots in the floor to the carriage system below stage and the backcloth lowered through a long thin slot while another was raised by pulleys to take its place. But the rise of melodrama with its snow storms, floods, the uprooting of trees, earthquakes, and other phenomena ("so terribly lifelike," as one contemporary remarked, as to excite "cries of admiration mingled with fright") dictated changes, as did the ensuing popularity of romantic drama. Machines now had to be built especially for each production, since each had specific and integral requirements. The stage floor developed into a total system of traps so that it could be opened at any spot for ships sinking, earthquakes, or even the installation of aquatic tanks. The old under-stage machinery then had to be banished and the space over the stage elaborated to take care of changes. So the fly loft developed, with the possibility of raising and hanging scenery aloft in the system of ropes, pulleys, counterweights, and fly-galleries. The substitution of three-dimensional set-pieces for the old flat wings also presented problems in scene shifting. Complicated systems of rising and falling platforms with ropes and counterweights or hydraulic installations were devised.

Thus stages increased in size and complexity, often being one and a half to twice the size of the auditoriums. The expense of the new stage equipment and the necessity for new arrangements or different "riggings" for various productions led to a gradual increase of the number of consecutive performances of a play, since one could not move so easily from play to play as was possible

under the old flat-wing system. Thus, over the century repertory was phased out and the long run instituted. So, too, developed the intermission, with the curtain lowered to mask changes of scenes. Engineers struggled with the problem of making these changes as rapidly as possible, and in addition to hydraulic lifts, invented wagons upon which whole scenes could be set in the wings and rolled onto the stage at the appropriate time; these, of course, were very large and heavy and often took some time to be put into place. Toward the end of the century audiences were sometimes advised to leave the theatre for dinner at the end of one act and come back again for the next act. Interestingly enough, for all its innovation with respect to the auditorium of the Festspielhaus at Bayreuth, the immense stage areas were devoted to a tremendous complication of machinery for the spectacular stage effects of which Wagner was so fond. Smaller and less affluent houses had to "make do" with the old system or with a minimum of new machinery.

MORE ELABORATE STAGE SETTINGS
Left, Sanquirico's temple setting for a melo-drama given in Milan in 1826. The dark forms downstage and lighter ones upstage are reminiscent of Piranesi. Above, Simon Quaglio's Roman Hall for a production in Munich about 1850. The same characteristics, but not in so marked a degree, are evident here as in the setting at the left. (The Metropolitan Museum of Art; Theater-Museum, Munich)

Theatre's Industrial Revolution

As time went on, the wing flats were sometimes hinged to provide a "return" on an oblique angle from the flat itself which paralleled the footlights, and this finally developed into the box set. The new scheme did not entirely replace the wing set but simply became another means for dressing the stage. At first the overhead borders were retained with the box set; then, as better means of lighting were developed, the borders were replaced by a ceiling, and the box set reached its apogee.

Another development of the period was the use of multiple sets, not like those of the medieval mysteries with mansions stretched in a horizontal line across the stage, but with rooms above rooms, as for the plays of Nestroy in Vienna in the 1830s. Though each part of this compound set comprised an acting area, stage properties and furniture were likely to be painted on the scene rather than to be practical.

During the nineteenth century the candle, which had lighted theatres for many generations, and the oil lamp were replaced first by gas and then by electricity. Gas was patented for manufacture in 1781 and was installed as a lighting system in 1816 in the Chestnut Street Theatre, Philadelphia. In 1817, the Lyceum in London converted to gas, and finally, by 1830, it reached the Continent via Berlin. Light sources for stage and auditorium were now controlled by literally miles of flexible tubing attached to a gas table behind scenes, where all or some of the lights could be dimmed or brightened as the production demanded. Concomitantly, theatre fires increased in number.

The brilliance of stage lighting was enhanced by the development of limelight (produced by heating a cylinder of lime to incandescence by the use of a gas mixture) as early as 1816, and in 1846 the Paris Opéra was using an arc light formed by passing an electric current between two rods of carbon. The same designer, M. J. Duboseq, who perfected the arc light from the original experiments of Sir Humphry Davy earlier in the century, also developed a lightning machine, a rainbow projector, and a luminous fountain—all based on the arc-light principle. But adequate theatre lighting awaited the invention of the incandescent lamp by Thomas Edison in 1879; its first installation was made in 1880 and 1881 at the Paris Opéra. Four theatres in Germany became completely electrified in 1883: the Landestheater in Stuttgart, the Residenztheater in Munich, the Staatsoper in Vienna, and the Stadttheater in Brünn. Theatres in London and New York quickly followed. Now a light source was available capable of infinite variation, and for the first time in theatre's long history, lighting became an integral and sometimes all-important feature of the total production.

Along with the changes in the mechanics of staging went an increasing attention to accuracy and authenticity. The reforms regarding costumes urged by Diderot and Mlle. Clairon in the preceding century began to have some effect in settings as early as 1810, when Joseph Schreyvogel at the Burgtheater in Vienna strove for historical accuracy, and had his designer, Antonio de Pian, make suitable settings for Schiller's *Wallenstein* in 1814, and for Grillparzer's *The Ancestress* in 1824. His successor, Heinrich Laube, carried this idea forward. A similar interest was evidenced by Count von Bruehl in Berlin, who, in addition to stressing historical accuracy, seems to have been the first to utilize projections from a type of magic lantern as a part of the stage setting. Franz Dingelstadt, appointed director of the Munich Theatre in 1851, gave the minutest attention to his stage settings, and the climax was reached by Duke George II of Saxe-Meiningen, called "the theatre Duke." He expended much time and effort on research so that every detail of his productions would be most minutely accurate, even engaging an armorer to recreate outmoded ways of dress. From 1874 to 1890 he made theatre history, influencing theatre in all parts of the Western world and inspiring Stanislavski in Russia.

But the theatre Duke never solved the problem of quick set changes. The use of platforms to achieve different acting levels in different scenes, a worthy innovation in itself, often caused interminable waits at intermissions, particularly in multiple-scene plays like those of Shakespeare. Three other Germans—Gottfried Semper, Ludwig Tieck, and Karl Immerman—tried to simplify the Shakespearean performance by simulating what they thought to be Shakespeare's own stage. The first two collaborated on a design to create what they thought the Fortune must have been, and six years later, in 1840, Immerman designed for Düsseldorf a fluid stage with an architectural setting which was

MORE QUAGLIO SETTINGS
These are by Angelo Quaglio, whose family worked as designers for most of the century in Germany. Above, his setting for *Die Meistersinger* at Munich in 1868, showing a vista in linear perspective. Right, the original model of a set for Schiller's *Maid of Orleans* at Munich in 1875. (Theater-Museum, Munich)

imposed on the standard proscenium-arch stage of the theatre. Thus the Germans led the Continent in the progress of theatre art.

Historically accurate costumes

During the nineteenth century, costuming developed authenticity as it is known today—that is, an historical accuracy in line and detail adapted to the configuration of the contemporary actor or actress, and not necessarily presenting an exact duplicate of the original appearance. Ellen Terry's Portia, for instance, really looks quite different from that of Katherine Hepburn although each is authentic or true to the time and place of Shakespeare's original character.

As detailed previously, the mild costume reforms effected by Voltaire and Mlle. Clairon in the 1750s were accepted by their audi-

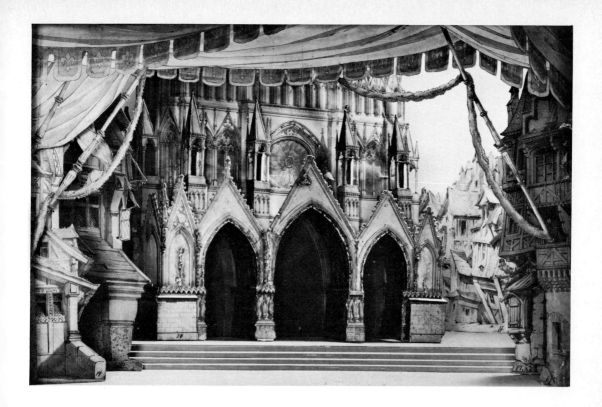

ences, but the more truthful authenticity of Mme. Favart at the same time evoked only opposition. In the last years of the eighteenth century, Talma, influenced by the painter David, made himself an authentic Roman costume for his part (a minor one) in Voltaire's *Brutus*. In those days, there were no dress rehearsals and actors supplied their own costumes. Imagine the shock of both players and audience when Talma appeared in Roman tunic with bare arms and legs. Contrast his appearance with the hoop-skirted actresses and the beplumed and beribboned actors. He scandalized his older colleagues, but evidently pleased the younger portion of his audience. As he gained prestige as an actor he was able to win others to his costuming principles, but not without protest from such a one as his father-in-law, the actor Vanhove, who when

presented with his first correct Roman costume protested that it had no pocket for his handkerchief, and how was he to play tragedy without that indispensable prop?

In the very year of Talma's death, 1826, Ludwig Tieck was writing (in his collected *Dramatical Papers*, from his experience as director of the Dresden Court Theatre) that historically correct costumes were not even desirable in the theatre, but that actors should use a "poetic and pictorial" costume, such as "had perhaps never been worn by anyone in real life." And he further maintained that Othello should not be dressed in oriental costume, for instance, because it "of necessity must always produce a disturbing and repellent effect."

But in Vienna, Schreyvogel and then later Laube, directors of the Burgtheater, carried on their battle for historically cor-

SIMPLIFIED SETTINGS
Above, Immerman's Shakespearean stage, Düsseldorf, 1840. This structural stage setting was superimposed upon a regular proscenium stage, and remained unchanged throughout the performance. Left, the stage for the Passion Play at Oberammergau. This, too, is a permanent structural setting and is very similar to the one above. It is, however, built for an outdoor production. (Theater-Museum, Munich)

rect costuming, and Count von Bruehl at the Royal Theatre in Berlin is said to have done an historically correct *Henry IV* in 1817. When Koch did Goethe's *Goetz von Berlichingen* in medieval costume in 1774, it was more for reasons of avoiding censure for the political topicality of the play than for the sake of accuracy, but Goethe himself appeared as Orestes in something closely resembling classical garb only six years later (page 273).

In France, Paul Lorimer, designer for the Paris Opéra, strove unceasingly for accuracy in costuming, but, in general, until near the end of the nineteenth century, historical costuming consisted merely of the addition of period details to dresses which followed the current mode in their main outlines.

A genuine and lasting reform was effected by the theatre Duke of Saxe-Mein-

ingen, whose exhaustive researches and careful attention to detail made memorable stage pictures. He gave the minutest attention to details of every costume, and since his productions were usually plays demanding great crowd scenes, the number of costumes required was staggering. The pictorial effect of the crowds, arranged and moved to underline the emotional intent of the particular scene, was rendered outstanding not only by the costumes and sets, but by virtue of the fact that in this company the members of the crowd were not the usual supernumeraries, but polished actors who might in other plays of the repertoire play leading roles, and who were studiously coached in every movement and utterance. The carefully staged crowd scenes and the meticulous costuming made a deep impression wherever the Meiningen company appeared in

THE THEATRE DUKE
George II, Duke of Saxe-Meiningen, prepared these sketches for a production of *Fiesko* by the Meiningen company.

their various tours. It was not until the fame of these players had spread throughout Europe that the propriety of truly accurate costuming was generally accepted.

One must, however, be aware that the very development of plays of everyday life fostered a recognition of the aptness of costume in helping to project character. Then it follows that the historical dramas of which the romantic writers were so fond would also benefit in the same way by having the correct dress for the personages represented. The disappearance of the stage apron, which tended to emphasize the actor in his own person rather than as a dramatis persona also sped the time when he would be integrated into the total stage picture. In other words, the "theatre Duke" did not single-handedly change the course of stage costuming, but the loving and effective work he did was the culmination of a number of trends in the nineteenth century.

Grease paint, at last

Modern theatrical makeup was a nineteenth-century development, too. For more than half the century, stage performers were dependent upon powders of various colors and composition for stage effects. The whites, generally made from lead, often proved poisonous to the users. Reds and yellows, derived from cochineal and umber, respectively, were more or less harmless. Blacks were generally burnt cork. Lines were achieved by the use of india ink under the powders, changes in shape of nose or cheeks by gumming on appropriate wads of wool or forming a piece of paste from powder and gumming it on.

In about 1865, the German Wagnerian singer Ludwig Leichner, through study and experiment at the University of Würzburg, developed the formula which resulted in the first appearance of grease paint. He developed and numbered a series of colors and liners in stick form and as a part of his sales technique recommended their use. By 1873, his manufacture of the new makeup had become a thriving business enterprise. By 1895, a wide range of colors could be obtained and their use had almost completely supplanted the older powder-based makeup techniques. For removing the grease paint, Leichner recommended liberal applications of cocoa butter. A lanolin-based cream has now supplanted the cocoa butter, but in most other details, the Leichner makeup is still being used.

Romantic spirit encourages individual eccentricities

By 1800, the great Schroeder had retired from the stage, Iffland was near death, and the only actor of magnitude on the Continental stage was the Frenchman, Talma. His star shone brightly for a few years beyond the First Empire, but in spite of his many reforms in acting and in costuming, he was essentially a classical actor in the tragic-hero line. It is true, of course, that he was restricted in his interpretations by the materials with which he worked (the classical tragedies) and that his methods might have been better suited to the newer romantic plays which came into recognition after his death. In any event, the rise of the romantic drama brought in a whole new school of actors and acting styles.

Most typical of the newer type was Frédérick Lemaître (1800–1876), whose career lay chiefly outside the Comédie Française. An increasing number of his contemporaries made careers outside that venerable house— another mark of the emphasis on individual freedom which the romantics stressed. Lemaître was the first French actor to be equally at home, and equally successful, in comic as well as tragic parts, and he rose to great eminence. His training had been in the Conservatory, but much of his early experience was in playing melodrama, farce, and extravaganza, and he became equally adept in all styles. His most signal victory was the creation of the character of Robert Macaire in an otherwise insignificant melodrama called *The Inn of the Adrets*, which he played not straight as it was written but as a comedy part. He played many of Victor Hugo's parts, and that great Frenchman on Lemaître's death in 1876 put the actor in the proud line of Thespis, Roscius, and Talma as one of the great actors of all time.

If one were to choose a prototype for the nineteenth-century romantic actor, however, the choice would without question be the German, Ludwig Devrient (1784–1832). He presented a grandly wild appearance, with

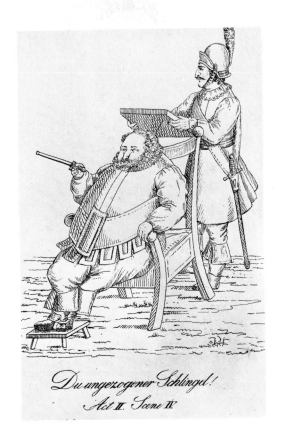

Du ungezogener Schlingel!
Act II. Scene IV.

long dark hair, pale face with melancholy eyes and a sorrowful smile, and a general remoteness from the world in which he moved. He was greatly admired in romantic parts in Germany, and especially at the Burgtheater in Vienna where he made an amazing success. In his later career he played a wide variety of character parts, particularly Falstaff, in which he was said to be outstanding. He has often been likened to the great English romantic actor, Edmund Kean (1787–1833).

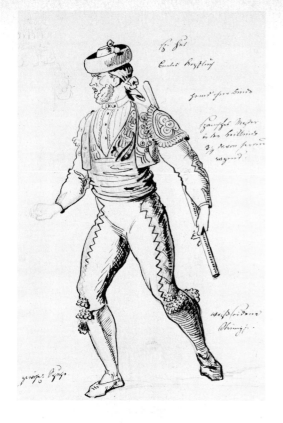

COSTUMES AND CHARACTERS
Left, the great romantic actor Devrient as Falstaff. Note the closer approximation to Elizabethan dress evident in this sketch. Above, a sketch by the Duke of Saxe-Meiningen for a character in *Don Giovanni*. Here the authenticity is undoubted and the details carefully worked out. (Theater-Museum, Munich; Theaterwissenschaftliches Institut der Universität Köln, Sammlung Niessen)

The famous Russian tragedian, Pavel Mochalov (1800–1848), was of the same type —wildly romantic and relying entirely on intuition and the inspiration of the moment. Laceration of personal feelings to create stage characters, rather than studied technique and discipline in their realization, was the stock-in-trade of the romantic actor. Mochalov lived and performed in Moscow, as did his contemporary Michael Shchepkin. There the atmosphere seemed more favorable to developing new techniques than in

St. Petersburg which was wedded to French neoclassicism. It was at the Moscow Maly that Stanislavski, in the second half of the century, complimented Maria Yarmolova as the greatest actress he had ever known, not excluding Duse, and called Alexander Lensky "the most talented and attractive actor" he had ever seen.

The greatest names in the nineteenth-century theatrical firmament are women: Rachel, Ristori, Bernhardt, Réjane, Modjeska, and Duse—two Italian, three French, and one Polish.

Rachel (1820–1858), often called one of the greatest actresses the world had ever seen, was a typical romantic in her short, brilliant, and recklessly intense career. But her great fame was made in classical tragedy, her greatest part generally conceded to be Phèdre. She was accepted by the Comédie Française in 1838, and died twenty years later at the age of thirty-eight after a stormy association which saw her playing as often outside the Comédie as in it. She created the first Adrienne Lecouvreur in Scribe's play, and triumphed as Marie Stuart in Lebrun's drama. She was fabulously successful in the French provinces, in London, all over Europe including Russia, and in America. Her style was an intensely emotional one, suffusing the old classical tragedy with new life.

Rachel, in her last years, saw the rise of a serious rival in Adelaide Ristori (1822–1906) who came to Paris from her native Italy in 1855. She, too, made her great reputation in tragic parts, her most noteworthy being Maria Stuart in Schiller's tragedy. She traveled to London, Spain, and America, and in her later years was often compared most favorably to Sarah Bernhardt, the flaming star of the last three decades of the century.

Bernhardt (1845–1923) became a byword quite as much for her flamboyant personal

RACHEL IN TWO COSTUMES
Left, the renowned French actress appears in her most famous role as Phèdre, wearing classic drapery and a fillet; above, as Rosalind in *Bajazet* she wears a richly decorated oriental costume fitted to her well-corseted figure. (Henry E. Huntington Library and Art Gallery)

life as for her undoubted skill on the stage. Painter, sculptor, poet, and playwright, she was also adept at self-advertisement, managing through her long career to keep her name ever before the public. Her star propensities caused her to break with the Comédie Française, into which she had been accepted in 1862. It was, and is, the policy of the Comédie to acknowledge no stars but to list the members of the acting company in the order of their seniority. To this practice Rachel and Bernhardt both objected. After

1880, Bernhardt never acted there again, traveling through Europe, America, and even Egypt and Australia. At times she herself managed three various Paris theatres, to one of which she gave her own name. She did all the parts in which Rachel had become famous, and added the great romantic heroines as well, particularly Marguerite Gautier in *The Lady of the Camellias*. She loved breeches parts, made a great success in Rostand's *L'Aiglon*, and, curiously enough, triumphed as Hamlet.

Preferred by many in comedy parts was another Frenchwoman, Réjane (1857–1920), who, realizing her potentialities and limitations, confined herself to light comedy. She became as famous in her line as Bernhardt in tragedy. She traveled to New York, London, and South Africa with immense success. Helena Modjeska (1844–1909), on the other hand, made her worldwide reputation in the great tragic roles of Mazeppa, Mary Stuart, and Lady Macbeth.

The final star among the actresses of the century was the Italian, Eleanora Duse (1859–1924), whom Shaw preferred to Bernhardt. She, too, did best in the tragic line. Duse became a public personality by a technique the obverse of Bernhardt's. She professed to hate publicity and built up a legend of an enigmatic personality, which was as effective a technique with the theatre-going public as was Bernhardt's flashier approach. The legend was heightened by her unhappy passion for the poet Gabriel D'Annunzio, and her far-flung, highly successful tours.

Only slightly less famous was Tommaso Salvini (1829–1916), perhaps the greatest Othello ever to appear. He played this famous part in his native Italian with companies all over Europe and America, who spoke in their own tongues, and evidently played it with an intensity and ferocity that was sometimes frightening.

Debates persisted through the century about the nature of the art of acting, and occasional treatises (chiefly by nonactors) dealt with the subject. One of the most "scientific" of these analyses was done by the Frenchman François Delsarte (1811–1871) in a series of lectures, classes, and demonstrations founded upon various "trinities," like life, mind, and soul; language, thought, and gesture; nature, humanity, and divinity. His ideas influenced both Adolphe Appia in Switzerland and Percy MacKaye in America. But the definitive statement on the art of the actor came from an actor (and a great one), Constant Coquelin (1841–1909), who issued in 1880 his *The Actor as Artist.* An incomparable comedian of the French national theatre, he brilliantly played all of Molière's heroes and was legendary in Rostand's *Cyrano de Bergerac* (1898). He was one of the few actors who set down something of the technique by which they achieve their ends, saying that the good actor must be two people—the one who performs and the one who regulates and criticizes the performances. Thus he argued for a disciplined art which would not be solely a matter of inspiration, but also of technique.

Repertory framework still prevails

Acting is usually remembered by the brilliance of its individual artists, but the advancement of theatrical art does not depend solely upon these individuals. At least equally important is the work of repertory companies, which develop the difficult technique of ensemble playing, doing justice to the playwright and, in the long run, being a more fully satisfying kind of theatre. All of the great talents mentioned here were developed in repertory companies, though each, in some measure, flourished outside that system.

The great strength of Continental theatre through most of the nineteenth century was still within the repertory framework. Schreyvogel and Laube in Vienna, Tieck at Dresden, von Bruehl in Berlin, the theatre Duke of Saxe-Meiningen, though they produced no stars of the magnitude of these mentioned, kept alive and vital the concept that "there are no small parts, only small actors"; that the performance of plays requires the best of an *ensemble* and not a quasi-solo performance by a theatrical personality. The star system never became as firmly entrenched on the Continent as it did in England and, more particularly, in America. The next chapter therefore, will give fuller consideration of both its glories and its evils.

Summary

The nineteenth century in Europe was a period of great upheaval with many significant changes in governments and in social structures. Theatre, as a mirror, reflected those changes and upheavals. During the century, neoclassic drama largely disappeared from the theatres, and in its place the new forms of melodrama and romantic drama developed. Melodrama quickly filled the increasing number of theatres with spectacular shows of breathtaking complexity in scene and situation, but of uncomplicated morality—good and evil stock characters with the good always triumphing over many perils. It was a form very popular with the great proletariat which was now coming into

SALVINI IN TWO COSTUMES
Left, the great Italian actor as Othello, his
most famous role, with authentic oriental
touches to the costume; above, as Macbeth,
looking somewhat like a Viking. (Harvard
Theatre Collection)

the theatre. Romantic dramas—chiefly distinguishable from melodrama by a higher order of literary merit, acceptance by the higher orders of society, and justifications in critical theory—used primarily historical materials, with many scenes and characters and a wide range in time. After the middle of the century, many plays were written with some attention to contemporary social problems. In form they were "well-made," but they contain no profound philosophical concerns and very little true analysis of charac-

ter. Few plays of lasting literary merit appeared then.

Playhouses, even when new, tended to continue the previous plan of pit, box, and gallery for audience seating, as being the most economical of space and most efficient for hearing and seeing. The one great innovative design—the Bayreuth Festspielhaus—would influence future construction. Stages grew larger and stage decoration intricate and often flamboyant, with an increasing complexity of machinery to handle the multiple scenes and the spectacular effects. Gas and then electricity initiated experimentation and advance in the separate area of lighting.

Historical accuracy in costuming developed to the point of complete acceptance and, indeed, there was often an overemphasis upon antiquarianism. Grease paint was developed for use as makeup. Though repertory companies continued to be the chief home of actors, there was a growing tendency for individual performers to disasso-

ciate themselves from such companies and function as single agents, or stars. During the century, nonacting managers and producers became the rule rather than the exception.

Finally—and perhaps most importantly for the future of theatre—the audience was almost completely democratized, with hitherto unreached segments of the population being brought into the theatre for the first time.

The American Revolution was genteel in comparison with many revolutions in the Western world that followed it. Its architects and engineers were neoclassic rationalists, and its result—the creation of a new nation —was in many ways a political accident. There were many on both sides of the Atlantic who deplored the expedient which divorced the colonies from Mother England, and the population of the new country lost a great number of able men when the Loyalists moved out. Political independence had been gained, but a true national identity and a cultural independence would be a long time coming.

The Articles of Confederation bound together thirteen sovereign colonies in a loose union; but the colonies had little in common and not much interest in common goals. The struggle to establish an effective national government was long and hard, engaging the best minds of the day. When Washington was inaugurated President on April 30, 1789, under the new Constitution, there were still many who were actively opposed to the federal form of government which he administered. Though the framework of a democracy was present, the true democratic spirit was largely lacking. The successful War of 1812 gave the new nation more of a sense of national identity, and with the election of Andrew Jackson, a man of the people indeed, democracy became more of a reality. Then the Civil War, a revolution almost as far-reaching as the preceding one, finally established the sovereign power of the federal government. The struggle had taken almost a century.

Having arrived at an answer to the basic political question, the United States after the Civil War saw an expansion and consolidation that made her at the beginning of the next century a world power. America and England were linked by the transatlantic cable in 1866 and on May 10, 1869, a gold spike was driven at Promontory, Utah to mark the completion of the transcontinental railroad. The gold was symbolic, for the post-Civil War period was the era in which great fortunes were made and the prowess of the American Businessman (the undoubted national hero) spread throughout the world. The frontier—so potent a factor in the growth of the United States—disappeared and urbanization spread rapidly. Education, sanitation, road building, and the like became public responsibilities, and increasing attention was given to the welfare of larger and larger segments of the population.

Though the violence of civil war did not touch England in the nineteenth century despite the European conflagrations of 1848, revolutionary events were nonetheless taking place there. George III was so ardently disliked by his subjects that the wave of republican sentiment lasted through the reigns of George IV and William IV, and was not dissipated until well along in the reign of the circumspect Victoria who came to the throne in 1837. The long series of reforms which preceded her coronation and followed throughout her reign constituted, in essence, a far-reaching revolution broadening the base of suffrage, clearing up various political and economic inequities, and assuring the emergence of middle-class domination of the constitutional monarchy. Disraeli presented Victoria with the title of Empress of India in 1875; it was during her sixty-three-year reign that England became, substantially, the British Empire, upon which the sun never set. The long rivalry for world domination which had existed between France and England was settled in England's favor. Though Victoria's visit to Paris in 1843 was greeted with something less than enthusiasm by the anglophobic French, by 1856 the rivals were partners in the Crimean War, and from that point on were increasingly cooperative and respectful of each other, developing a partnership that was not to be disrupted until the rise to power of De Gaulle in 1958.

In both England and America, huge strides were made in scientific invention. Coal, iron, steam, and electricity brought changes that have since been called the high point of the Industrial Revolution. Railroads, typewriters, telephones, phonographs, streetcars, agricultural and industrial machinery, automobiles—even the airplane and the motion picture were among pre-World War I innovations which rapidly became an indispensable part of life. So numerous and prolific were developments and inventions that the scientist bid fair to replace the businessman as the national hero. The Great Exhibition in England in 1851 was intended as an illustration that England was "the workshop of the world" and in 1893 the World Columbian Exposition was held in Chicago.

The old *laissez-faire* policy was still the predominant philosophy of politics and economics. Utilitarianism, invented as a term by Jeremy Bentham early in the century, was defended as an ethical position by the formidable John Stuart Mill later in the century, and was the underlying philosophy of the period: that position or action is right which brings the greatest good to the greatest number. In the increasing prosperity and sense of well-being which characterized the period, the plight of the exploited working classes, the slum conditions in the great cities, the frequent corruption of local governments were generally lost sight of, although from the middle of the period on, a vociferous minority had been voicing socialist principles. Marx's *Communist Manifesto* (1848) was not translated into English until 1886, and the first International Workingmen's Association, formed in England in 1864, was dissolved by 1874; not until 1905 did the

I.W.W. appear, although the first successful organization of labor unions (the American Federation of Labor) was organized in 1886. Not many voices were raised in protest against obvious abuses: the Fabian Society in England, Frank Norris and Lincoln Steffens in America, a few forward-looking writers on the Continent were voices crying in the wilderness. The twilight of Victorianism and the Edwardian era were suffused with the false glitter of material well-being, a prevailing optimism, and the panacea of a false internationalism which was to be swallowed up in the bitter rivalries of the First World War.

Both England and America were shaped by the revolution in thought instigated by Darwin, and by the developments of the Industrial Revolution, just as Europe was. England and America each had its own Romantic Revolution, America's coming somewhat after that of England. Both countries were open to continuing influences from the Continent. The world of art is one world. Though it may be temporarily influenced by political nationalism (there are examples of that from the earliest times to the present), it has more similarities from one people to another than dissimilarities; it deals not primarily with temporary political divergences, but with the feelings, dreams, and aspirations of mankind, which are more alike than different. Art has always overstepped national boundaries, theatre no less than other forms.

Theatre develops as a commercial enterprise

Before the middle of the century theatre in both England and America had become a thoroughly and completely commercial venture and was to develop by the end of the century into a really "big business." The Theatre Regulation Act of 1843 in England removed the last features of the old series of

FAMOUS VISITING PERFORMER
Rachel receives the plaudits of the audience
after her performance in Corneille's *Horace*
at Covent Garden in 1841.

licensing acts (often in the past respected
more in the breach than in the observance), and thence all kinds of plays could
be produced by any theatre with the approval of the Lord Chamberlain. (That approval was not finally eliminated until 1968.)
Any governmental regulation of the theatre
in the United States did not occur until
"show business" was challenged under the
1890 Sherman Anti-Trust Act.

For the greater part of the nineteenth
century, English and American theatres were
not only similar but interchangeable. Players,
plays, designers, and producers freely crossed
the Atlantic in both directions in a more or
less amicable commerce. Theatre entertainment grew to be completely universal in both
countries, reaching upward and downward
into every segment of society. The growth of

railroad traffic led, in England, to the attrition of the hitherto prosperous provincial
circuit system and the final substitution by
1880 of an almost universal plan of touring
London plays with either first or second
companies.

In America, with its larger territory, the
death of provincial repertory took a little
longer. The thirst of the westward-moving
pioneers for theatre was met, in part, by that
uniquely American phenomenon of the showboat, which through most of the century
plied the great interior rivers. Companies
also traveled by stage and railroad throughout the interior of the continent. By 1806
there was a professional company of actors
in Pittsburgh. By 1815 "Old Sam" Drake was
playing in Lexington and Louisville, and
Noah Miller Ludlow opened his St. Philippe

Street Theatre in New Orleans just three years later. He removed to St. Louis in 1820, leaving New Orleans to James H. Caldwell. St. Louis remained the theatrical center of the west until 1837, when performances were first given in Chicago, whose phenomenal growth soon insured its supremacy. Sacramento had a theatre in 1849—a year memorable for other reasons, and San Francisco in 1850, the same year in which the Mormons opened a theatre at Salt Lake City. Seven years later there was a theatre at Omaha, and in 1859 one at Denver. This wave of theatre openings followed the movement of the western frontier, leaping from the Mississippi to the coast and then doubling back. It is estimated that whereas in 1800 there was but a handful of theatres and a mere one hundred fifty professional actors in the United States, by 1885 there were five thousand theatres in more than thirty-five hundred towns. The frontier theatres were rough affairs, and hazardous for ladies in the audience (of whom, fortunately, there were few) by reason of the eating, shouting, and roughhousing that characterized them. The showfolk were a hardy race, much put upon their mettle not only for mere survival but also to engage the attention of the rough audiences. Before the end of the century the western theatres were sending back to the more refined East Coast such capable people as David Belasco from San Francisco and Lotta Crabtree from the mining camps.

Philadelphia was the early theatrical capital of America, but the Erie Canal was opened in 1825 and New York rapidly outstripped Philadelphia as a commercial and transportation center. The population of New York City exploded from a mere eighty thousand in 1800 to five hundred thousand by 1850. From the thirties onward New York preempted Philadelphia's importance and became the center of theatrical activity in the United States, as London was in England. More than forty theatres were built in New York during the century, their construction following the movement of the population from the City Hall area to Fourteenth Street, to Herald Square, and thence to the present theatrical center between Forty-second Street and Fifty-ninth. Unhampered by prohibiting legislation, theatre proliferated in all the centers of population.

London, the center of the world to English-speaking people, increased in population from one million to five million between 1800 and 1880, and theatres proliferated accordingly. The 1843 Theatre Regulation Act, which removed the limitation of "regular drama" to Drury Lane and Covent Garden, had the effect of increasing both theatre activity and theatre competition. Melodrama had never been considered "regular drama" and the number of London houses offering that fare, along with other variant forms of entertainment, simply continued in the same vein. But the formerly privileged "patent houses" were obliged to add to their offerings the popular fare so much in demand.

The outstanding theatres of England and the United States were, for the most part, under the supervision of actor-managers. John Philip Kemble managed at both Drury Lane and Covent Garden at the beginning of the century, as did William Charles Macready about the midpoint in the century. Charles Matthews at the Lyceum, Mme. Vestris at the Olympic, Charles Kean at the Princess's, Samuel Phelps at Sadler's Wells, the Bancrofts at the Prince of Wales' and the Haymarket, at various times made their theatres famous, as did Laura Keene at her own theatre in New York, Mrs. John Drew at the Arch Street Theatre in Philadelphia, and James Wallack and William Burton in theatres named for themselves in New York. But the tendency toward nonacting managers

TYPICAL NINETEENTH-CENTURY THEATRE
An old drawing shows a scene from an 1859 production of Dion Boucicault's *The Octoroon*, one of the most popular of nineteenth-century plays, particularly in England, where the American playwright-producer spent much of his time.

known
with t
Garder
not a
Siddon
above
mandir
had pr
and lar
in. A
famous
1849. It
tween
Macrea
Forrest
sides in
York. S
angloph
York, M
series c
in the
injury o
market
the Ban
the old

But
or by p
box offic
It is the
bulk of
to nonli
merit we
new the
develope
years in
largely a
the last
turn, eve
have visi
occasions
there (18
Shakespe
tations o
longer fo

culminated in the latter part of the century with Augustin Daly and David Belasco.

It was in England and America—both without the established and subsidized national theatres possessed by most of the European countries—that the star system entrenched itself, and that theatre took on many of the aspects of a business rather than an art. Through most of the century, name actors visited or went on tour, generally appearing with local companies for stated performances without benefit of rehearsal, the local actors accommodating themselves to the visitor as best they could.

Toward the end of the century, when the idea of ensemble playing was gaining ground, stars began carrying with them at first a few supporting players and later whole companies. But to the very end of the period there were those theatre personalities who appeared in "foreign" theatres, relying on themselves alone to impress the local company and the audience.

A new audience with old habits

These audiences now embraced all segments of society and they made their sentiments

mained unproduced until first acted by the Shelley Society in 1886. Wordsworth and Coleridge wrote, respectively, *The Borderers* and *Remorse*, both of which reflected the Gothic aspects of romanticism, and *Remorse* was actually produced at Drury Lane (1813). None of these men, however, had any real affinity for theatre.

Byron, on the other hand, had at least served on the Drury Lane Committee of Management from 1812 to 1816, and had written a prologue spoken at the opening of the new house in 1812. He wrote six dramas, two of which—*Manfred* and *Cain*—are not really stage plays. The other four are more stage-worthy: *Marino Faliero, The Two Foscari,*

Sardanapalus, and *Werner.* Macready successfully produced the latter two in 1830 after Byron's death, and Charles Kean subsequently revived *Sardanapalus* in 1834. Only one had been produced during Byron's lifetime, *Marino Faliero* at Drury Lane in 1821. *Manfred* and *The Two Foscari* were produced at Covent Garden in 1834 and 1837, respectively.

Charles Lamb's second play, *Mr. H.* (1806), was an instant failure, tradition having it that Lamb, in the gallery, hissed louder than anyone else. His first, *John Woodvil* (1802), was never produced.

Only two of Browning's plays were produced: *Strafford* (1837), written at the re-

THE ROYAL HAYMARKET THEATRE, 1821
Left, the exterior as designed by John Nash, and above, the interior and floor plan. Notice the rectangular arrangement, and the persisting side boxes. (Henry E. Huntington Library and Art Gallery)

quest of Macready and produced by him, and *A Blot on the 'Scutcheon* (1843). *King Victor and King Charles* remained unproduced. Three decades later, Irving produced three plays by Tennyson: *Queen Mary* (1876), *The Cup* (1881), and *Becket* (1893). Also produced in other theatres were three more: *The Falcon* (1879), *The Promise of May* (1882), and *The Foresters* (1892). None of these plays would deserve mention here except for the fame of their authors.

Lesser men were writing for the theatre and reaping its rewards, such as they were. In English and American playwriting— more so perhaps than that of Continental writers—it is possible to see the continua-

tion of recognized and recognizable dramatic forms. The tradition of classical tragedy died hard. Joanna Baillie in her *Plays of the Passions* (3 vols., 1798-1812), James Sheridan Knowles in *Virginius* (1820), and Sir Thomas Talfourd in *Ion* (1836), *The Athenian Captive* (1838), and *Glencoe* (1840) tried to keep it alive. So, too, did the American James Daly Burk in *Female Patriotism, or The Death of Joan of Arc* (1798), as did the transplanted American, John Howard Payne in *Brutus* (1818). All of these were produced but none was successful except *Ion* and *Brutus*, the first because of Macready's playing, the second because of Kean's; it is true, though, that Payne's play, by its frequent revivals through the century, proved itself the more durable.

There is also traceable mild social comedy which had some popularity. Anna Cora Mowatt Ritchie's *Fashion* (1845) is often called the first American social comedy, and has some merit in the playing even today. Less well known, but equally good, are James K. Paulding's *The Bucktails* (1847) and William Henry Hurlbert's *Americans in Paris* (1858), the former playing his Americans against an English scene, the latter using France. Dion Boucicault's earlier *London Assurance* (1841) and Bulwer-Lytton's *Money* (1840) represent this genre in England. Social comment became more basic and implicit with the plays of T. W. Robertson: *Society* (1865), *Ours* (1866), *Caste* (1867), *Play* (1868), and *School* (1869) paved the way for the end-of-century realism. The sentimental comedy popularized toward the end of the previous century lived on in this one. In England, Tom Taylor and Charles Reade were its chief purveyors. Among the best of Taylor's seventy-odd plays are *Masks and Faces* (1852), *Still Waters Run Deep* (1855), *Our American Cousin* (1858), and *The Ticket-of Leave Man* (1863). Reade's *Gold* (1853) and

The Courier of Lyons (1854) were his most successful. And in America, the phenomenal success of *Rip Van Winkle* in various renderings throughout most of the century marked the triumph of sentimental comedy.

Romantic dramas like those of Victor Hugo and Alexandre Dumas *père*, new to English and American audiences, also had a great vogue. Typical are such plays as Bulwer-Lytton's *Richelieu* (1839) and *The Lady of Lyons* (1838), both eminently successful in their day, and in the romantic plays of Robert Montgomery Bird in America, chiefly *The Gladiator* (1831), written for Edwin For-

rest, and *The Broker of Bogota* (1834). These, with *Bianca Visconti* (1837) and *Tortesa the Usurer* (1839) by Nathaniel Parker Willis, *Leonor de Guzman* (1942) and *Francesca da Rimini* (1855) by George Henry Boker, represent the best of the type, mostly in verse, which enjoyed lavish success in both England and America. A resurgence of interest in romantic verse drama in the 1880s led to revivals of some of these, and to a few new representations of the type by William Gorman Wills in England and Henry Guy Carleton in America. But by that time the main interest of playgoers was in another field.

THEATRES LARGE AND SMALL
Left, Interior view of the Olympic, 1816. This
is one of the smaller, speculative houses, but
still conforms to the general pattern; note
the dark little boxes on the first level. Above,
the somewhat larger theatre at Sadler's
Wells, showing the tank installed in the stage
in 1804 to accommodate "aquatic drama."
(Henry E. Huntington Library and Art Gallery)

The "drama of common life," growing out
of another facet of romanticism, increased in
popularity through the century. One of its
manifestations was in national types, like the
Irish of Dion Boucicault's *The Colleen Bawn*
(1860) and the title character of *The Octoroon*
(1859); in frontier types like James Kirke
Paulding's *Lion of the West* (1830) and
Joseph Stevens Jones' *The People's Lawyer*
(1830), which fathered a whole line of Yankee
characters; in German, Negro, and Italian
types in the farces of Edward Harrigan; and
in the somewhat different dramatization by
George L. Aiken of Harriet Beecher Stowe's

Uncle Tom's Cabin (1852), although this is
more melodrama than anything else.

In America, especially, the romantic idea
of "the noble savage," first popularized by
Rousseau, was largely responsible for a wide-
spread interest in Indian plays. And Edwin
Forrest's announced competition for plays
whose leading character should be "an orig-
inal of this country" added to the stimulus.
Examples include James Nelson Barker's *In-
dian Princess* (1808), and also *The Indian
Prophecy* (1827) of George Washington Parke
Custis, the *Metamora* (1829) with which John
Augustus Stone won Edwin Forrest's prize,

THEATRE INTERIORS AND PERFORMANCES
Left, Macready's production of *As You Like It* on the stage of the new Drury Lane in 1842. The theatre had opened in 1812, with seating capacity for twenty-eight hundred people—somewhat smaller than the house it replaced. Above, a performance of *Our American Cousin* on the stage of the Sans Pareil theatre, which opened in 1808 with John Scott's innovation—no bottom row of boxes, the pit extending to the walls all around. (Henry E. Huntington Library and Art Gallery)

Penn Smith's *Pocahontas* (1830), the *Forest Princess* (1844) of Charlotte Barnes Conner, and a myriad of others copied on both sides of the Atlantic. The vogue reached its end in 1855, when John Brougham laughed it off the stage with his burlesque *Pocahontas, or The Gentle Savage*.

Melodrama pure and simple, in direct descent from Pixerécourt, was the genre that filled most of the theatres most of the time, and many of the plays named above have melodramatic characteristics. It was a pirated translation from Pixerécourt, made by Thomas Holcroft, that first appeared in England at Covent Garden on November 13, 1802, billed as a melodrama and called *A Tale of Mystery*. It was the beginning of a deluge that swamped the century and lives on today in many movies and television series. To name even a small percentage of the writers and their plays would be impossible. Materials varied as popular interest was caught by different subject matters. There were "Eastern" melodramas like *Cataract of the Ganges, or, The Rajah's Daughter* (W. T.

Moncrieff, 1823) and *Mazeppa, or The Wild Horse of Tartary* (H. M. Milner, 1831); nautical melodramas like *Black Eyed Susan, or All in the Downs* (Douglas Jerrold, 1829); crime melodramas like *Jonathan Bradford, or Murder at the Wayside Inn* (Edward Fitzball, 1833) and *The Bells* (Leopold Lewis, 1871) in which Irving starred for many years; melodramas of common life like *Luke the Laborer* (J. B. Buckstone, 1826) and *The Poor of New York* (Dion Boucicault, 1857) which the author successfully adapted for both London and Liverpool, changing the name accordingly; animal melodramas like *The Dog of Montargis* with its canine star and *Hyder Ali, or The Lions of Mysore* with a whole menagerie, including elephants; "fantastical" melodrama like *The Black Crook* (1866), which played for sixteen weeks at Niblo's Garden in New York City; and even Henry Arthur Jones made his first success in the melodrama, *The Silver King* in 1882. The melodrama theatres often had a "house playwright" who produced scripts in record time to take advantage of fast-breaking

THE "OLD VIC"
Interior of the Royal Coburg Theatre, 1848. This theatre, built in 1818, is still an active theatre today. The interior is not substantially changed, except that individual seats have replaced the benches in the pit.

items of popular interest or to write appropriate surrounding adventures for a newly developed spectacular effect, like a railway wreck or a ship sinking or a bridge being blown up. The writing and production of melodrama was a highly competitive business.

A few other kinds of theatrical entertainments ought, at least, to be mentioned. J. R. Planché in England and John Brougham in America produced a whole series of burlesques on varied literary, political, and social topics which are not only interesting and often delightful in themselves, but are accurate mirrors of the ideas and issues which were engaging the attentions of their contemporaries. Certainly, too, the tuneful operettas of Gilbert and Sullivan, that marvelous culmination of musical theatre in the nineteenth century, should be noted here. Sir William Schwenk Gilbert, librettist of that famous series, had a considerable reputation as a playwright in his own day, quite aside from his association with Sir Arthur Sullivan. It is one of the ironies of theatrical

history that neither the plays of Gilbert nor the other music of Sullivan lived beyond the lifetimes of their creators, while the products of their collaboration are as alive and wonderful today as they have ever been. In England, the music halls (still a lively tradition) offered serious competition to the theatres from 1850 on, adding to their staple fare variety acts, sketches, and short plays, and developing skilled individual performers. Finally, perhaps a passing word should be given to the birth and heyday of that indigenous American entertainment, the minstrel show. Initiated by the solo performances of Thomas D. Rice (1808–1860) as "Jim Crow," it developed, with the addition of other performers, as the "Ethiopian Opera" and reached its typical form with E. P. Christy, who first called it "The Minstrel Show" in 1846. It was at its peak of popularity from that time until at least 1870 and declined thereafter until it had entirely disappeared by the 1920s. The first half of the show was a series of jokes in dialogue between "Mr. Interlocutor" and the "end men," Tambo and Bones, interspersed with musical numbers. The "olio," or second half, was a series of specialty numbers. All performers were in blackface.

By the 1890s in England, literary men of ability were again writing for the theatre; it took a little longer in America. But, as in Europe, by the end of the century dramatic writing had reassumed literary respectability.

New theatres for old

The significant development in theatre architecture through the nineteenth century was the increasing attention paid to amenities for the audiences. In the large state theatres of the Continent such amenities were earlier and more lavishly accomplished. But even in the private-enterprise houses of England and

America, the succeeding decades brought more in the way of comfort for those who paid the bills by their admissions. Gradually the dark little passages to pit and gallery were replaced by lobbies and salons. Systems were devised for heating auditoriums and for bringing in fresh air. Cloakrooms were added, and washrooms. Benches were replaced by upholstered individual seats. "Every man a king" meant that more and more of the perquisites of royalty should be allotted to the theatre patron, especially since he was paying for them.

Drury Lane and Covent Garden, the traditional strongholds of the drama in London, saw, during the nineteenth century, invasions of other forms of entertainment. The official removal of their monopoly in 1843 soon caused Covent Garden to turn entirely to opera, while at Drury Lane pantomime and melodrama, as well as visits of the Comédie Française in 1879 and the Meiningen company in 1881, helped to keep it going through the century. Other theatres were challenging the venerable two.

The Covent Garden building, erected at great cost and opened in 1808, burned down in 1856. It had been planned by Robert Smirke with statuary by Flaxman. The 1808 building was slightly smaller than the one it replaced but was still of cavernous proportions; there were a pit, two galleries, and three tiers of boxes, one of which was private with its own entrance. The Grand Salon was eighty-six feet long, and had coffee rooms at either end. The stage was sixty-eight feet deep and forty-two feet wide at the proscenium, which was constructed like a columned triumphal arch, with a door on either side leading to the forestage. It was replaced in 1858 by the present structure.

Drury Lane, opened in 1812, was designed by Benjamin Wyatt after the universally admired theatre of Bordeaux. It, too,

CHANGING INTERIORS IN AMERICAN THEATRES
Above, the interior of the Park Theatre, New York, as painted by John Searle in 1822. The house was erected in 1820. Note the three tiers of boxes with a gallery above, and the proscenium doors. Right, Augustin Daly's Fifth Avenue Theatre, New York, in 1867, with no boxes at all except those in the proscenium arch, two stepped-back galleries, and seats with backs in every part of the house. (New York Historical Society; Henry E. Huntington Library and Art Gallery)

was slightly smaller in dimensions than its predecessor but still seated about twenty-eight hundred. The pit was approximately three-quarters of a circle, with seven private boxes to each side and a front lobby. This use of a front lobby as an entrance to the pit marked a distinct departure from preceding designs in which the pit was entered by side doors or long, narrow passages. Above the lobby and the lower boxes was a circle of twenty-six "dress boxes" with a private entrance for select members of the audience. Then came the first tier, giving into the rotunda and grand salon at the front

of the house, and having two private boxes at each end nearest the stage. Then came the second tier, above which were placed, at the sides of the house, fourteen boxes (seven on a side) with the lower gallery on the same level opposite the stage. Above the lower gallery rose the upper gallery, now on the sixth level. In the proscenium arch were four boxes, two to each side. The proscenium opening was thirty-three feet wide and nineteen-and-a-half feet high. The whole house was richly decorated, with crimson carpeting in the salon and coffee rooms. This is the house which, with many subsequent interior renovations, is still in use. Both Drury Lane and Covent Garden persisted in the opera-house tradition, with the pit enclosed by tiers of boxes.

A new kind of seating arrangement got its start in 1806, when John Scott, a color maker, built the little Sans Pareil, later the Adelphi, for his daughter and her one-woman entertainments. Here there was no bottom row of boxes, but the pit itself extended under the first tier to the walls all around. The same plan was followed in the Coburg (later the Old Vic), built in 1818. By the 1830s and 1840s the front part of the pit had been con-

verted into orchestra stalls, and in mid-century they were furnished with comfortable individual seats called *fauteuils*. Thus was the Olympic built in 1850; with the opening of the new Adelphi in 1858, the backless benches disappeared entirely and comfortable armchairs were installed throughout.

By 1860, when Phipps built the Queen's, the first tier of boxes projected so that there were two or three rows of seats free of supporting columns, backed by the usual boxes, above which rose the other tiers, still sup-

ported by columns. Progress in cantilever construction caused the removal of the supporting columns in the Gaiety (1868), the Vaudeville (1870), the Savoy (1881), the Prince's (1884), Terry's (1887), and the Garrick (1889). Pillars to support the boxes had been omitted in the building of New York's first fine theatre, the Park, as early as 1798, and contemporary comment remarked on the unobstructed vision thus possible from every part of the two-thousand-seat house. There were but three rows of boxes, with the

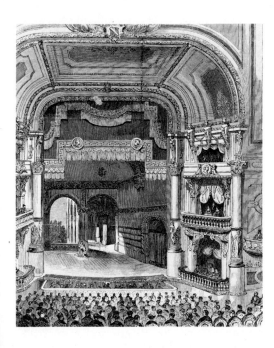

POPULAR THEATRES, ENGLISH AND AMERICAN
Left, the interior of the Princess's Theatre, London, in 1876, and above, the interior of Booth's Theatre, New York, in 1869. Note that in each case the proscenium is ornate, there are stage boxes, and that each member of the audience now has an individual seat with a back. (Harvard Theatre Collection)

gallery rising from the top of the first row. In 1807 the English architect J. J. Holland brought the Park more into conformity with English houses by installing four rows of boxes with the columns usual in England. This building was destroyed by fire in 1820 and rebuilt the next year. The new house, designed by Hugh Reinagle, held twenty-five hundred; a sloped pit extended under the first row of boxes and three tiers of boxes of fourteen each were supported by iron posts covered in gold leaf, with a gallery above.

The stage was forty-five feet wide and seventy feet deep, and there was a single proscenium door to each side.

It is manifestly impossible to give here detailed descriptions of all the theatres built in the United States in this century, but a few items are worth noting. The first Bowery Theatre (1826) was designed in Greek revival style by Ithiel Town and was greatly admired by contemporary English architects. It burned, and was replaced in 1828 with an equally Doric facade. When the National Opera House (which gave up opera and became simply the National Theatre in 1836) was built in 1833, a sloped parterre fitted with upholstered chairs and sofas displaced the first tier of boxes as well as taking up the "pit" space, and the whole was fully carpeted. In the Astor Place Opera House (1847) there were no plaster walls, but the interior was entirely of wood paneling, including the sounding-board ceiling covered with painted canvas. Acoustically the building was a great success, financially it was a failure. Brougham's Lyceum (1850) included not only a theatre, but a ballroom, a lecture room, and salons. The apotheosis of nineteenth-century American theatres was the one opened by Edwin Booth in 1869. It was a splendid, solid stone structure on Twenty-third Street, expensively decorated in second Empire style. The only boxes remaining were three on each side in the deep proscenium arch, which no longer had the old proscenium doors. The pit was now the orchestra as we know it, sloping from a sunken orchestra pit to the entrances. Three galleries, stepped back, sloped around front and sides of the house and over a portion of the orchestra. There were no supporting columns, and the rows of seats on every level were equipped with arms. It had ducts to bring in warm air in the winter and cool air in the summer (the former from furnaces in the basement, the latter from fans above the ceiling). There was an admirable expanse of work space in the structure, and an apartment for Booth. It was the acme of developing theatre styles in architecture, and was much copied in succeeding years. It has long since disappeared as a building, but something of its style and atmosphere is still observable in the old Lyceum on Forty-fifth Street east of Broadway, built by Daniel Frohman and opened in 1903.

There would be little profit in naming all the theatres built in New York and London, and in other cities of America and England, for they almost invariably followed the plans of these described. It is interesting to note that boxes, often with private entrances, persisted longer in England than in America where the weight of aristocracy is not so heavy. But even theatres having these boxes with private access devoted most of their space to less specialized seating—an indication, perhaps, of the increasing democratization of the audiences.

Individual innovations in set design

It is highly likely that the wing-and-shutter system initiated by Inigo Jones in the court masques of James I had a life of almost three hundred years because it was a very practical and economical arrangement for theatres offering a constantly changing bill. The stock set, consisting of palace, garden, cottage, woods, cave—more or less, as the affluence of the particular theatre indicated—was standard throughout the eighteenth century and persisted through much of the nineteenth. It was a system capable of infinite refinement, particularly adaptable to theatres where set changes were done in full view of the audience. (Act drops to conceal changes of scenery were not usual in the theatre until the 1870s and 1880s.)

In England the usual method of handling the wing-and-shutter system was different from that in Continental theatres. Here the wings and back shutters were arranged in grooves which consisted of shallow wooden troughs in groups of three to eight, fastened to the floor of the stage and to the underside of the fly-gallery above, into which the wings and shutters were slid from offstage. Sometimes there were ingenious arrangements of pulleys and ropes which allowed one set of pieces to be drawn off, revealing the set immediately behind, or, where the number of sets exceeded the number of grooves, for a new set to be drawn on. Sometimes these changes were individually operated by hand upon signal from the stage manager's whistle but this method could not be as smooth and coordinated as the rope-and-pulley system. Many elaborations of the system were developed, whereby the centerstage portions of the upper and lower grooves were loose rather than fixed so that if a particular scene demanded a vista, the empty loose grooves, being hinged, could be drawn out of sight so as not to spoil the vista. Loose grooves were sometimes arranged on a pivot so that their scenes could be pushed to a diagonal position instead of remaining parallel to the footlights. The difficult movement of the larger and heavier back shutters was sometimes overcome by having the back scene painted on cloth backed by thin strips of wood which could be rolled much in the manner of the old rolltop desk.

The Continental system of changing scenes by understage machinery through slots in the floor was never universal in England or America, though Covent Garden in 1857 and the Lyceum in 1863 did install it, and there is some mention of its earlier use at Drury Lane and in Dublin. But by 1880, the grooves were back in use at the Lyceum, for in that year Irving again re-

EARLY NINETEENTH-CENTURY SETTING
Capon's design for a stage setting for the new Covent Garden Theatre, 1810. In its use of the Gothic motif it announces the romantic movement.

moved them to install a system of scene support by braces, much in the modern manner. At the same time he initiated the practice of dropping the curtain for scene changes, which custom was no doubt necessitated by the now obvious inability to change all the flats simultaneously.

Increasing attention was paid to the preparation of the stage flats, scene painting becoming an important aspect of theatrical production. The nineteenth century gives us the name of the Grieve family, who became as important to scene design in nineteenth-century English theatre as the Bi-

bienas had been earlier on the Continent. The work of another scene painter, Charles Stanfield, became so popular that his name frequently appeared on the playbills in larger type than those of the principal actors. Ingenious effects were achieved by painting scenes on thin cloth in transparent colors, so that they could seem to disappear and reappear as the lights were changed before and behind them. Cut cloths became so intricate, particularly in the spectacles and the pantomimes, that the stage must often have appeared like a lace-paper valentine.

Mme. Vestris and J. R. Planché, at the

Lyceum, early introduced as much verisimilitude and historical accuracy as could be achieved with the groove system, and Mme. Vestris is said to have established the success of the box set with the English public through a production of Boucicault's *London Assurance* at Covent Garden in 1841. Planché, a self-styled antiquarian, had designed an authentic *King John* for Charles Kemble at Covent Garden as early as 1824, and in 1838, the actor William Charles Macready played *Coriolanus* in a setting of the Republic, a distinct contrast to a contemporary production of Kemble's against the background of Imperial Rome. Samuel Phelps, at Sadler's Wells from 1844 to 1862, initiated a series of Shakespeare revivals which became noteworthy for their authenticity and Charles Kean carried this practice to an almost pedantic extreme in his productions at the Princess's from 1850 to 1859. Elaborate, pictorialized settings were continued by Henry Irving at the Lyceum in the last two decades of the century. These were generally magnificent, although founded on research into the supposed periods of the plays themselves, and firmly established the tendency to produce Shakespeare in highly elaborate settings. In some of these, live crowds were augmented with painted crowds to produce spectacular effects, and scenic vistas enlarged the stage pictures.

The elaboration of the wing system during the nineteenth century was accompanied by increasing complexity in stage effects, particularly in the use of various traps in the stage floor. The Corsican trap, invented for a production of *The Corsican Brothers* (1848), allowed figures to appear from below as if they were rising and gliding across the stage, by means of an ingenious slot which opened before the platform, drawing the actor up an incline, and closed behind him. The Vamp Trap, developed for Planché's *The Vampire*

CHARLES KEAN AT THE PRINCESS'S
In the 1850s Charles Kean produced a series of Shakespearean plays at the Princess's in London notable for their settings and costuming. Here the usual wings and borders are carefully designed to simulate columns and arches. Above is a model for his production of *Hamlet;* right a scene from his *Macbeth*. (Cleveland State University; Victoria & Albert Museum; Crown Copyright)

in 1820, consisted of two spring leaves, in the stage floor or the scenery, which enabled the actor seemingly to pass through a solid. The Star Trap, the Cauldron Trap, the Bristle Trap, and many others were developed to such an extent that the so-called trickwork of English nineteenth-century theatre became famous throughout the world. Various ascents, descents, and flyings were also continued and developed in this period, with overhead machinery to operate them, even to the extent of performers seeming to fly out over the heads of the audience and back again. The counterweight system for handling scenery was perfected, being used both below and above stage. These elaborate, and expensive, developments were made practicable by the growing institution of the long run as opposed to the hitherto prevailing

repertory system. The long run was initiated in the spectacles and extravaganzas, but gradually through the century, aided by the star system in acting, became entrenched in the legitimate theatres as theatre became a business rather than an art form.

It must not be supposed that any of these innovations received universal approval and widespread adoption at any one time; traditional, outmoded, and antiquated methods of stage presentation often existed side by side with the new. Indeed, the American producer W. B. Wood was bemoaning the practice, in 1852, of the use of stock sets, often glaringly incorrect, which was still general in American theatres. The opening of the Booth Theatre in 1869 was a signal event, for in addition to being a beautifully and comfortably appointed house, the stage was marvelously equipped. The stage floor was flat rather than raked, and portions of it were supplied with traps operated by hydraulic rams. There was seventy-six feet of space from stage floor to gridiron, so that drops could be raised entirely out of sight. The ultimate complexity of stage equipment in America was achieved by Steele MacKaye when he opened his Madison Square Theatre in 1879, with a double-level elevator stage to allow whole scenes to be set in the basement or overhead and raised or lowered to stage level.

The change in theatre lighting from candles and oil lamps to gas and then to electricity during this century has been discussed above. It is interesting to note that the Chestnut Street Theatre in Philadelphia was the first house to use gas for illumination. That was in 1816, and the next year, Drury Lane in London advertised itself as being entirely lighted by gas. The introduction of gas was the cause of controversy, the light being considered by some as too brilliant, by others as a great advance. Theatres installed, and then sometimes removed, the innovation. By the middle of the century, however, gas lighting was universally accepted, and was controlled by the prompter from behind the scenes. Gas lights were installed vertically inside the proscenium, and across the top of the stage on battens, with colored cloths to produce red, green, or white light from these or from other strategically located outlets in the stage area. Controls for the stage and the house were separate, and the first practice was simply to dim the house lights while the performance was in progress. Irving is credited with initiating the practice of blacking out the house while the play was being performed, thus first using a technique urged three centuries before by the Italian, Ingegneri. Colored glass began to replace silk and paper as the medium for color effects, and in the use of colored lights Irving again made great contributions.

Electricity went through the same period of installations and removals, disapprobation and approval, that had been the lot of gas. Limelight and arc light preceded the use of electric bulbs, invented by Edison in 1879. Two years later, Covent Garden installed stage lighting by the new bulbs, which was evidently coupled with a dimmer system allowing variation in illumination from a bright glare to total darkness. By 1887 electricity had been installed in most of the important theatres of Europe and America. The first experiments in lighting the stage from the front of the house were performed by David Belasco at the Grand Opera in San Francisco in 1879, when he used an old bulls-

eye lantern from a locomotive as a light source. The advent of electricity meant a decrease in the number of theatre fires, which had assumed alarming proportions during the sixty-year reign of gas. During that time there had been a total of three hundred eighty-five disastrous fires in England, France, and America.

Historical costuming gradually evolves

As pointed out earlier, the nineteenth century is generally conceded to be the period in which costuming historically correct for the period in which the play supposedly takes place became universal. And, in the broad

Mrs Alsop as Rosalind

"But you are no such man."

As you Like It, Act II Scene 3.

TWO POPULAR PERFORMERS
Left, Mr. Wrench in the part of Benedick.
Above, Mrs. Alsop as Rosalind. In the early
part of the century there was little concern
for authentic costume, as the portrait of Mr.
Wrench attests. Even somewhat later, the
female silhouette, in presumed rustic dress,
was that of the fashionable lady of the day.
(Henry E. Huntington Library and Art Gallery)

outlines of the statement, it is true. But the
initiation was by no means sudden or exact.
Though the French theatre in the eighteenth
century made indubitable progress in accurate costuming, the reforms effected on the
English stage in the same period were comparatively meager.

During the first quarter of the nineteenth
century, the same conditions prevailed. The
popularity of the novels of Scott caused
some interest in historical costuming, but the
net results were simply the adding of Elizabethan details, for instance, to contemporary
dress. The first attempt at historical accuracy for every character in the production
was evidently that of J. R. Planché for

Charles Kemble's production of *King John*
late in 1824. Planché, after indefatigable research, dressed the cast in authentic thir-
teenth-century costumes, receiving for his
effort the scorn of the actors who had to
wear his "stew-pans" for hats, but receiving
also, as he tells it, the unmitigated praise of
the public.

In 1838 Macready did *Coriolanus* "with a
true sense of antiquity," albeit the dress was
no more than "an approximation to the toga,"
according to a contemporary report. That the
majority of the so-called historical costumes
of the period were just such approximations
is evident from the fact that Macready as
Macbeth is described by a German visitor as
wearing a "fashionable flowered chintz dress-
ing-gown" in the murder night scene. Another evidence is the fact that in the Shakespeare productions with which Charles Kean
made the Princess's Theatre famous from
1851 to 1859, Mrs. Kean as Hermione in *The
Winter's Tale* wore a perfectly correct Greek
dress but wore it over a crinoline. And she
was not alone in her adherence to this un-
dergarment. For so long as it remained in
style, all kinds of costumes were superimposed upon it. And whatever the style of
dress they were wearing, actresses persisted
in having their coiffures the latest in attractive nineteenth-century styles.

The vogue for domestic dramas—which
were played, of course, in contemporary
dress and (notably at the Prince of Wales
Theatre under the Bancrofts in the third
quarter of the century) with real furniture
and box sets with practical doors and windows—furthered the demand for real properties and realism in dress in other types of
drama. Thus the antiquarian fervor of Kean
and Irving as applied to historical plays received additional impetus. The visits of the
Meiningen players to London in 1881 brought
an example of how effective truth to time

JOHN PHILIP KEMBLE
Left, Kemble as Hamlet in the painting by Sir Joshua Reynolds; above, as Macbeth in a contemporary lithograph. The tradition of feathers for the tragic hero persists in both of these costumes. The difficulty of appropriate dress for Macbeth is here fully illustrated—though he wears a kilt, he also dons mailed gauntlets, armor, and classical sandals. See page 35. (Henry E. Huntington Library and Art Gallery)

and place could be, and spurred the efforts of English producers to this end. By the close of the century, accurate historical costume was the rule rather than the exception—quite the reverse of the century's beginning.

As on the Continent, the art of makeup was modernized in nineteenth-century England and America. The first description of the use of grease paint in English theatre occurs in 1877, some years after its introduction on the Continent. That these paints had

been imported from Germany is evident from the listing of colors given with the instructions for their use—the same numbers given by Leichner himself. Many actors still clung to the old powder makeup; as late as 1883 a writer on the art of makeup talks only in terms of powder and does not even mention grease paint. By 1890, however, powder was largely superseded by the more versatile and more durable grease paints. This somewhat slow adoption was no doubt aided by the advent of gas and then electricity, for the addi-

EDWIN BOOTH
Left, Booth as Benedick in *Much Ado About Nothing;* above, as Hamlet. This most renowned of American nineteenth-century actors wears, for both of these characters, costumes whose elements are the same: tights and a long-sleeved tunic. The decoration varies, but neither costume observes strict historical authenticity. (Harvard Theatre Collection)

tional illumination required more care and more verisimilitude in the application of makeup. Care in the dressing of the actors paralleled care in the dressing of the stage, with realistic effects the ultimate goal.

Stars are born

Though the eighteenth century is generally called the Age of Great Acting, the term is no less applicable to the nineteenth. In England, the century opened with John Philip Kemble and Sarah Siddons as the outstanding pair, and closed with Henry Irving and Ellen Terry. America moved from dependence on imported English actors to the development of great native talents, notably Edwin Forrest and Edwin Booth, both of whom had a European as well as an American reputation.

The nineteenth century was the age of great stars whose appearance generally assured the success of the pieces in which they were playing. In view of the commercialism

EDWIN FORREST
Left, Forrest in one of his favorite roles, as Spartacus; above, as Coriolanus. See Quin in the same role (page 253). Something of the force and fury that characterized Forrest as an actor is evident in the portrait of Spartacus. (Harvard Theatre Collection)

of the nineteenth-century English and American theatre, it is easy to see why the star system became greater and more entrenched than it did on the Continent. Stars were generally assurance of good houses; they were excellent drawing cards for those ever-so-necessary audiences. And those audiences who made the stars shine ever more brightly —were they perhaps responding to some deeply felt need for heroes, for almost mythical and unearthly perfection? At any rate, Americans have made royalty of various ilk, no doubt because they have never had any royalty of their own. Stars toured widely, in the early years traveling at first individually, then with a few supporting players, and finally with complete supporting casts. Acting was a family tradition, and there were many outstanding acting families: the Kembles, Keans, Tearles, and Trees in England; the Jeffersons, Booths, and Drews in America. Lacking the tradition of a great national theatre such as that of France, both England and America witnessed the death of repertory companies during the nineteenth century and the rise of long runs. Particularly

in America, the uneconomical and in many ways inartistic method of assembling a cast for a particular show, playing it, and then disbanding the company, gained firm foothold.

As on the Continent, acting styles moved from the classical to the romantic. Just as Talma began the century in classical style in France, so in England John Philip Kemble (1757–1823) and his sister, Sarah Siddons (1755–1831), represented the acme of classical acting there. Dignity was the keyword of their performances. Though, like Talma, they were both interested in more truth in costuming and stage presentation, their style of acting was measured and conventional, commanding and powerful. Each was best in the great tragic parts, working on a preconceived plan for a calculated effect.

Deliberately opposed to the "cold" classical style, with what often descended to monotony of delivery, was William Charles Macready (1793–1873), who varied his delivery with calculated pauses to the extent that "the Macready pause" became famous in discussions of Victorian theatre. Of an un-

WILLIAM CHARLES MACREADY
Left, Kean's great rival playing Iago in a costume which is neither Elizabethan nor sixteenth-century Venetian but a curious mixture of both; above, playing Orestes in a costume more accurately Greek. (Harvard Theatre Collection)

governable temper, he made many enemies but also did much to advance the art which he professed to hate, insisting on stern rehearsal discipline, doing praiseworthy revivals of Shakespeare, and bringing Byron to the English stage. He traveled to France and to America, appearing here first in 1823 and last in May 1849, when his rivalry with the American actor Edwin Forrest led to the infamous Astor Place Riot. The critic William Hazlitt said of Macready that this actor was the best tragedian he had known next to Edmund Kean.

Kean (1787–1833) was the true romantic, and rival of Macready in tragic roles, doing best in those that required some madness or frenzy. Coleridge's comment is still the best epitome of his style: to watch Kean was "like reading Shakespeare by flashes of lightning," a quotation which is sometimes interpreted to mean that his bursts of emotion coincided and blended with those of Shakespeare. He relied on gesture and facial expression more than on voice, and excelled as Shylock, Richard III, and Iago. He was of the inspirational school of acting, as was George Frederick Cooke (1756–1812), the first English star brought to America by William Dunlap. Cooke's performances varied from brilliance to bathos, and much of his inspiration is said to have come from the bottle.

The extravagant romantic drama demanded extravagant acting, but there were always voices raised against it, such as those of Charles Matthews (1776–1835), his son Charles James (1803–1878), and Mme. Vestris,

Mr KEAN in the Character of RICHᴰ. III.

THE KEANS
Left, Edmund Kean as Richard III in 1824; above, his son Charles as Hamlet in 1858. The elder Kean had a flashing brilliance which his son never achieved, although the latter was far steadier and more meticulous in his performances. The costuming in both portraits, while not nineteenth century, is not historically accurate either, but more nearly Elizabethan. (Henry E. Huntington Library and Art Gallery)

whom the younger Matthews married. They practiced and preached a more temperate style. It is true that the newer, realistic play which the latter two chiefly produced was more conducive to realistic acting—indeed demanded it. Thus, the total effect was quite salutary.

The first home-grown American actor to appear on the English stage was John Howard Payne (1791–1852), known chiefly today because of the song "Home, Sweet Home," which was originally a part of his light opera *Clari* (1821). He was one of a vanishing breed of actor-playwrights. After some small success in New York, he went to England in 1813, where he appeared with greater success in London and the provinces, writing many plays and acquiring the friendship of Talma.

Another American emigré was Ira Aldridge, billed in London as "The African Roscius" when he made his debut at the Royalty Theatre in London in 1826. He, too, never returned to the United States, touring widely and popularly in Germany, and becoming an English citizen in 1863.

More flamboyant was Edwin Forrest (1806–1872), whom William Winter once characterized as "a vast animal, bewildered by a grain of genius." He was a belligerent American, proud of his nationality, and the bitter rival of Macready. Large and imposing of figure, with a big voice, he excelled in bold and forceful roles such as Spartacus, Jaffier, Metamora, and Richelieu. He made many enemies, and was often accused of ranting. He had been one of the first native

MISS ELLEN BATEMAN
AS RICHARD 3RD

MISS KATE BATEMAN
AS RICHMOND.
RICHARD 3RD

talents to score a success at the Bowery Theatre in New York, whose astute manager Thomas Hamblin devoted himself in the 1830s to enlarging the audience of his theatre. He capitalized on what he called native American talent in order to attract the new audiences who were not steeped in the tradition of English plays and players.

Quite the opposite of Forrest in personality and style was the greatest of nineteenth-century American actors, Edwin Booth (1833–1893). Booth appeared not only in England, but in Australia and Germany as well, bringing honor to himself and to his country. His career was temporarily halted when his brother, John Wilkes Booth, assassinated Lincoln, but he was well received on his return to the stage. Impressive in appearance, he was a careful theatre workman, studying his parts with great depth of understanding

CHILD PERFORMERS
Far left and left, Ellen and Kate Bateman, popular child stars in both England and America. After various successes in America, they appeared in London in 1851, when Kate was eight and Ellen seven. Kate appeared as Richmond, Portia, and Lady Macbeth to Ellen's Richard III, Shylock, and Macbeth. Ellen retired from the stage, but Kate went on to success as an adult actress. Above, William Henry West Betty, known as "The Young Roscius," took London by storm when he was thirteen, in 1804, ousting even Sarah Siddons and John Philip Kemble in public favor. His triumph was short-lived, and he died in obscurity. (Henry E. Huntington Library and Art Gallery; Harvard Theatre Collection)

---

and projecting the characters sympathetically and fully rounded. He was a magnificent Hamlet, playing the part for one hundred consecutive performances in 1864.

As in the earlier days of American theatre, in the nineteenth century some English actors came to America and made it their home. Such were William Burton, John Brougham (another actor-playwright whose burlesques at the midcentury form an inter-

esting chapter in theatre history), and the Wallacks, whose second-generation Lester became one of the outstanding actors and managers of the latter part of the century. Laura Keene also came from England to establish an excellent repertory company in New York, and Louisa Drew to operate similarly in Philadelphia. One of Mrs. Drew's daughters married the English-turned-American actor, Maurice Barrymore, to found America's royal family of the theatre. The three Joseph Jeffersons were also of English origin, the first arriving in 1795, the last dying in 1905. There were also three generations of Davenports on the American stage in the nineteenth century. In the latter part of the century the great names were James H. Hackett, E. H. Sothern, Julia Marlowe, Mary Anderson, and Lotta Crabtree who began as a child actress in the western mining camps and rose to great fame. The American theatre also cheered a woman who, like Bernhardt, was fond of playing men's parts, Charlotte Cushman. She appeared as Romeo in London in 1845 to her sister's Juliet. Ada Rehan and Mrs. Leslie Carter also fluttered pulses toward the end of the century, and Minnie Maddern Fiske, once a child actress, became famous for her realistic, natural acting in the plays of Ibsen.

Dominating the English stage in the latter half of the century were Charles Kean, not so erratic or brilliant as his father; the Bancrofts and John Hare, who, under Tom Robertson's direction at the Prince of Wales Theatre, brought natural acting to a degree of perfection; and Henry Irving and Ellen Terry, whose names have come down as the epitome of excellence. Irving, at least, was not considered perfect in his own day, Henry James, for one, finding considerable fault with his art. But Ellen Terry seems to have been the ideal artist—sensitive, warm, and in complete command of her craft. Irving was knighted in 1895 for his services to theatre, and was the first English actor to be so honored.

Two years later, Squire Bancroft was knighted, like Irving, for his services to theatre. His had been a lifelong endeavor to make theatre respectable, to achieve greater realism in stage production, and to raise the status of actors. He and his wife, in conjunction with Robertson, made material increases in actors' salaries, and early paid for the ladies' dresses—hitherto an almost unheard-of practice. They were also the first to institute a single play as the whole bill for their theatre, in the 1860s. They demanded long and careful rehearsals, much as did the nonacting Augustin Daly in the American theatre.

Actors' salaries varied greatly, as might be expected. A star commanded a truly fabulous sum while lesser players got a mere subsistence. The star system worked great havoc in the old repertory system with its assured income. It was also instrumental in destroying potential talent by long runs and one-part players, as Eugene O'Neill's father, James—potentially perhaps a great star—wasted his life playing a perpetual Count of Monte Cristo. For a good part of the century, actors' incomes were supplemented by benefit nights (that venerable institution which came in for much criticism); it was finally abolished by theatres like Wallack's in New York in 1868 when Wallack raised actors' salaries to do so.

Training was chiefly by family tradition, and the great vogue for child actors produced some competent persons as they matured. Otherwise, actors acquired skill by taking parts in whatever vehicle offered itself—mainly in the hinterlands—and through actual stage experience moved on to better parts with better companies in the more well-known theatre centers.

Extremes of affluence and poverty were perhaps more marked among the nineteenth-century actors than ever before, but their social status definitely improved. By the end of the century, only the die-hard puritanical element was still opposed to them.

Changes in the tastes of audiences, in types of plays, in methods of production, and in producing agents, all played a role in altering both actors and acting styles from the classical actor who played a line of parts throughout his lifetime, to the romantic, then the realistic actor who either played himself no matter what the part or created a variety of parts of varying kinds. With the production scheme in operation in the commercial theatres toward the close of the century, the actor was likely, in his lifetime, to play far fewer parts with far less variety than in previous ages of theatre. His training was usually haphazard, and his security—at least in England and America—practically nonexistent.

The position of playwrights with respect to their work improved during the century. The first dramatic copyright act in England was passed in 1833 and is commonly known as Bulwer-Lytton's Act. It, as did the subsequent act of 1842, protected the right of presentation only within the judicatory of England. The United States passed a similar law in 1856, but none of these "protections" prevented theatre managers from using outright or adapting the plays of extranationals. It was not until the last decade of the century that a series of meetings produced the International Copyright Union, originally with nine members, but now (1973) embracing all countries which have a significant literary output excepting the Soviet Union.

Summary

In England and America, no less than on the Continent, theatres of the nineteenth century were largely filled by spectacular and extravagant melodrama with little literary value. Perhaps more so than on the Continent, plays of the accepted genres were written and produced in England and America. But with few exceptions, even these have little literary worth or lasting significance.

So far as the resources of theatres and producers allowed, the presentation of entertainments and plays was lavish and intricate. A special aura of glamor attached itself to theatre and theatre personnel, creating great stars and popularizing touring and one-part actors. The creation of a special "aristocracy" in the acting profession, particularly in democratic America, got its start in the nineteenth century. Great new audiences looked to the theatre as a passionately loved entertainment. And since these new audiences were largely uneducated, the philosophical and literary content of the entertainment was necessarily at a minimum. They got what they paid for.

Repertory almost completely disappeared, and the long run became firmly established, making possible ever-increasing complexity of stage setting and elaborate production. The theatre grew to be as commercial as amusement parks, as much a big business as oil or railroads.

Both in England and America, more attention was paid to the comfort of the audience in the construction and appointments of theatre buildings, and the practice of a single play as an evening's entertainment was initiated. Though stages remained elaborate, the proscenium doors finally disappeared. Costuming developed true authenticity, and acting achieved such power as to engender extreme adulation in the treatment of theatre personalities. Finally, this period began the decided differentiation and specialization in production personnel which has reached a high point in the modern theatre. That is, the functions of producer, director, actor, and designer more frequently were performed by four different people rather than, as in many periods of theatre, by one or two.

At the outbreak of World War I, Europe had enjoyed an unprecedented forty-three years of freedom from general conflict. Alignments and realignments of powers had flourished, but the constant shifts in diplomacy had succeeded in maintaining the so-called balance of power which insured a general, though fully armed peace. The predominant mood was one of optimism. Goods and people moved freely, without major tariff barriers or passports to check them. It was a time of colonialism and empire, and a time of general prosperity throughout Europe and America which brought a higher standard of living to more people than had hitherto been possible. Goods and services were increasingly available to larger and larger sections of the population, and the urban centers grew apace.

Theatre was included in the general prosperity and growth. Not only was the long run indicated by the complication of scenic investiture, but it was also economically feasible because of the tremendous increase in the population of cities and the increasing affluence of more people. The development of railroads made it possible to pack up shows which originated in the great centers of population and transport them to outlying places, and hence continue their financial success. Of course, such "road shows" caused the death of provincial stock companies eventually, but then the "locals" also had the advantage of seeing the best that was offered in cosmopolitan centers and of enjoying the great stars who traveled with the shows. Tremendous business organizations evolved to administer the attendant complications, as well as to "corner the market" insofar as possible in the cosmopolitan centers themselves. Such theatrical trusts came into existence in England (Cochran, Butts, Grossmith), in the United States (Klaw, Erlanger, Frohman, the Shuberts), and even in France

(Franck, Trébord, Volterra). All were dedicated to "giving the public what it wants," and the subsidized theatres of the Continent offered approximately the same fare.

In France there were plays like the farces of Georges Feydeau (*The Girl from Maxim's*, *A Flea in Her Ear*), the grand romantic dramas of Edmond Rostand (*Cyrano de Bergerac, L'Aiglon*), and the Folies Bergère, which had begun its long life in 1869. In Italy there was the poetic effulgence of Gabriel D'Annunzio (*The City of the Dead, La Gioconda*), and in Russia the middle class characters of her first professional playwright, Alexander Ostrovsky (*The Diary of a Scoundrel, Enough Stupidity in Every Wise Man*). In Germany, Wagner was producing his spectacular operas; in England Gilbert and Sullivan were triumphing at the Savoy, and Irving was giving extravagant productions of both Shakespeare and melodrama at the Lyceum. In the United States James O'Neill was perpetually on tour with *The Count of Monte Cristo*, Harrigan and Hart were "rolling 'em in the aisles" with *The Mulligan Guards*, and Lew Wallace's panoramic *Ben Hur* was spectacularly filling the Broadway Theatre. And all of this was being applauded by one of the most influential critics of the time, Francisque Sarcey, who had declared in 1876 that "There is no other rule of the theatre than that of pleasing the public" (*A Theory of the Theatre*).

But three years before that pronouncement—which might be the total raison d'être of theatre in the last quarter of the nineteenth century and (at least in the United States) the first decade and a half of the twentieth—two events had happened which would change the face of theatre all over the Western world. In that year (1873) Emile Zola in Paris finished the dramatization of his 1867 novel, *Thérèse Raquin*, writing a trenchant preface for its publication, and

Henrik Ibsen in Norway completed *Emperor and Galilean*, which marked the end of his earlier romantic style and the beginning of his new style.

In the same year that August Strindberg, another "giant from the North," wrote *The Father* (1887), André Antoine in Paris opened his Théâtre Libre to give a hearing to the plays which avante-garde dramatists, following the lead of Zola and Ibsen, had been writing over the past ten years, and which the commercial houses were not, for a variety of reasons, interested in.

An avant-garde of amateurs

So it happened that the rebirth of theatre fell once more largely to the hands of amateurs, to individuals and groups outside the established playhouses. Once the innovators had proved their worth by gathering a sizable audience to support them, the commercial houses were quick enough to adopt the changes.

André Antoine (1858–1943) was an amateur only by virtue of the fact that his theatrical training was more or less unacademic and that at the time he started his unique Théâtre Libre he was employed as a clerk in the Paris gas company. He had spent much time in study of the new literary movements of the 1870s and 1880s. From the time that he took his first job as an errand boy at the age of twelve, his reading had been avid and he continued it through a period as a bookseller's assistant. At this time he also enlarged his study program by attending lectures at the Ecole des Beaux-Arts and by frequenting museums and libraries. His evenings were spent in the theatres, as a claque at the Comédie Française, and as a supernumerary there, where he took part for years in the whole repertory and learned the actor's art by observation and imitation. He also joined an evening class in recitation and diction, and became the producer of classical plays for the group. After his rejection by the Conservatoire in 1876, chiefly because he lacked private recommendation, he spent five years in military service after which he returned to the job at the gas company. Late in 1886, he joined the Cercle Gaulois, one of the many amateur dramatic clubs of Montmarte which gave conventional plays once a month. Encouraged by Arthur Byl, a budding playwright, he urged upon the group the production of unpublished plays, and collected a program of four short plays, including a dramatization of a short story of Zola, *Jacques Damour*. Against the alarmed opposition of Krauss, the retired army officer who shepherded the Cercle, Antoine produced his program and the Théâtre Libre, or Free Theatre, was launched.

The program appeared March 30, 1887, to general critical approval, including that of Zola, who came and was impressed with both Antoine's acting and directing. Antoine was thirty at the time. One more program appeared that spring, to be followed by a season which included seven programs, at the beginning of which Antoine left the gas company to devote himself thenceforth to theatre. He much later divided his warfare against established theatre into three campaigns—the first from 1887 to 1895 at the Théâtre Libre against "the upholders of the theatre of the past"; the second from 1896 to 1906 at the Théâtre Antoine "for the conquest of the general public"; the third from 1906 to 1914 at the Odéon, his "last fight against official traditions and administrative routine." Antoine's raison d'être was to give a hearing to new playwrights of whatever dramatic genre; the course of events, however, made him the chief spokesman for naturalism even though he always fought against such a narrowing emphasis.

The immediate and almost fantastic artistic success of Antoine (he faced financial disaster throughout his career) inspired the opening, in September 1889, of the Freie Bühne (Free Stage) in Berlin. This institution, fostered and administered by nine young men of whom Otto Brahm, a critic, was chairman, aimed to found a stage free of the existing theatres, censorship, and financial preoccupations. As did the Théâtre Libre, the Freie Bühne operated with a small subscription audience drawn from the intelligentsia, played each production only once or twice, and rose to great critical acclaim. These two theatres inspired similar organizations in many parts of France and Germany, the most notable of which was the Freie Volksbühne (Free People's Stage), initiated by Bruno Wille, which produced plays for the working classes, also on a subscription basis, at a very nominal cost. The Volksbühne movement was to enjoy great popularity in Germany.

By 1891, London had its Independent Theatre, run on the same plan established by Jacob T. Grein, an immigrant Hollander. It was for the Independent Theatre that George Bernard Shaw produced his first play. The organization lasted for seven years, and in large measure inspired the founding of the Stage Society in 1899 and the Abbey Theatre at Dublin in 1901. All of these organizations were devoted to the developing of new dramatic writers and of a style of acting more suitable to the new materials.

Each of these "free" theatres became almost completely concerned with naturalistic writers. But there also were established a number of independent theatres which called themselves "art" theatres, devoted to new works of other than the naturalistic school. Such was Paul Fort's Théâtre d'Art in Paris, which lasted from 1890–1892 and devoted itself to symbolist plays. On its

demise, the mission was carried forward by Lugné-Poë at the Théâtre de l'Oeuvre from 1893–1897. In 1898, Adria Gaul opened his Teatro Intim in Barcelona to experiment in production styles for a wide range of drama, and in 1907 the Intimate Theatre was opened in Stockholm, primarily as a showcase for Strindberg's plays. Between 1904 and 1907, the Court Theatre in London produced chiefly Shaw's plays, and in 1907 Georg Fuchs and Fritz Erler opened the Munich Art Theatre to "retheatricalize the theatre."

Perhaps the most famous, and certainly one of the most enduring, of these new theatres was that established by Constantin Stanislavski and Nemirovich-Danchenko in 1898 as the Moscow Art Theatre. By reason of his comparatively prolific writing, Stanislavski's is perhaps the best-known in modern theatre. He had early been involved in amateur theatricals on his father's estate, continued these activities in Moscow with the Society of Literature and Art, which he helped to found even while he kept working in his father's business establishment, and finally attained fulfillment in the Moscow Art Theatre. He had long been disgusted with the formalism of conventional theatre fare, was inspired by the performance of the visiting Meiningen troupe, and eventually developed the so-called Stanislavski method of acting which is devoted, as he says, to "the inner truth, the truth of feeling and experience." His theatre weathered the October Revolution of 1905 and the Bolshevik Revolution of 1917, and is still today one of the major theatrical establishments of Russia and the world.

In America, stronghold of the theatre as big business, the establishment of the new theatres lagged almost a generation behind Europe. There was no significant contribution by an established acting company presenting the new drama until 1915, when the Washington Square Players—later to develop into the powerful Theatre Guild—began producing for a subscription audience in the tiny Bandbox Theatre in New York. In the same year the Provincetown Players began activities in Massachusetts and the next year moved to Greenwich Village. This was the group which produced the first plays of Eugene O'Neill. Meanwhile, the little theatre movement spread across the country, from Baltimore to Chicago and the West Coast, taking its inspiration from the European free theatres and placing itself in opposition to the theatre trust of the commercial houses. In England, also, little theatres, generally offering plays in repertory with a more-or-less permanent company, were established in Glasgow, Manchester, Liverpool, and Birmingham. Thus the attrition of professional theatre, caused by the death of repertory and the rise of the long run, was somewhat compensated for by a resurgence of amateur participation which some enthusiastic writers of the time compared to the great amateur participation of the Middle Ages. Universities also began to contribute to the new spirit in theatre with the establishment at Harvard of the famous 47 Workshop (1907) of George Pierce Baker, and the founding of the theatre school at the Carnegie Institute of Technology in Pittsburgh, under Thomas Wood Stevens (1914).

Commercial acceptance alters emphasis

Almost universally, the first aim of the free theatres was to present new and untried plays such as the commercial houses would not accept. As the appeal of these productions was proved, and the playwrights accepted for the professional houses, the experimental impetus was directed to the reform of acting and stagecraft. Acting indeed, had metamorphosed concomitantly with the

new plays, since they demanded a new and different histrionic embodiment, and the emphasis of both Antoine and Stanislavski, for instance, had been quite as much on acting as on playwriting. Stagecraft followed, and the period immediately preceding World War I in Europe was marked by the influences of Gordon Craig and Adolphe Appia, and the application of their principles by such an energetic dreamer as Max Reinhardt. Though innovations in stagecraft and production were numerous in Europe prior to World War I, they were almost nonexistent in America until after the war, in spite of the visits of various European troupes, and the urgings of such visionaries as Sheldon Cheney, Kenneth Macgowan, and Robert Edmond Jones. First America would have its new playwrights, as Europe had first had hers. America was not to succeed to theatrical preeminence until the postwar period.

The new movement in the theatre also gave importance to two specialized theatre workers—the director and the designer. Both Antoine and Stanislavski had been greatly influenced by their observations of the work of the Duke of Saxe-Meiningen, the nineteenth-century régisseur who brought the idea of a single, overriding, and unifying force to theatrical production. The idea, in itself was not new; Pixerécourt early in the century had voiced and practiced the identical principles. But the theatre Duke applied them to far more significant materials, and hence had an influence which the earlier Frenchman lacked. David Belasco and Augustin Daly in America and Granville-Barker in England became exemplars of the type. Then the infusion of Gordon Craig's ideas of symbolic design and simplified staging, with the actor no more than a supermarionette performing at the behest of the director-designer, added a new concept to the role of the director. But supermen are rare in any age, and the postwar generation witnessed the division of labor in theatre into the differentiated roles of director and designer, with both specializations gaining increasing importance.

The forty years preceding World War I saw the introduction of practically all of the elements of today's theatre. The revolution in playwriting, acting, and production which was effected in that period almost completely changed the end-product of theatres everywhere. It was a revolution as vast in import and effect as any that had hitherto taken place—its result was what we know as the modern theatre.

Naturalism and realism provide the materials of the revolution

It is significant that a play from one of Zola's short stories was on the opening bill of the Théâtre Libre and that Ibsen's *Ghosts* was the first offering of both the Freie Bühne and the Independent Theatre. For the genius of these two men—Zola (1840–1902) and Ibsen (1828–1906)—brought to the drama the new elements of realism which had triumphed in the novel and which would seriously challenge the romantic outpourings of the hitherto accepted dramatists. As late as 1880 there were two literatures in France— the novel and the drama. Zola was the recognized leader of the naturalistic novel but had made no impression on the theatre. All three of the plays which he had written prior to this date had been failures, although *Thérèse Raquin* (1873), dramatized from one of his novels, had shown elements of great tragedy. Zola, with his characteristic extravagance, declared that the French theatre was a void, that the Augier–Dumas–Scribe– Sardou school of playwrights were mere hacks, presenting completely unlifelike characters and events in meticulously realized settings. The literary naturalist, he declared, must be as much of a scientist as a biologist or a chemist, restricting himself to stating facts exactly as he found them, exhibiting no sympathies, passing no judgments: the naturalistic play would become a scientific study of man, with a minutely realized setting which would perform the same function as description in the novel. It would be true to life—a slice of life or *tranche de vie* (as the genre came to be called), with no more organization or artifice than life itself possesses. It was chiefly through his dramatic criticism, published between 1876 and 1880, that Zola influenced the new movement in the theatre and became master to a line of disciples that included Antoine, Becque, Hauptmann, and, to some extent, Ibsen himself.

Like Zola, Ibsen was greatly interested in the new scientific discoveries of his time. Darwin's *Origin of Species* (1859) was translated into Norwegian in the early 1870s; lectures and discussions of heredity and environment, of the survival of the fittest, ensued. In all this Ibsen was tremendously interested, as he also was in the series of Zola's novels which had begun in 1867. His earlier plays had begun in the romantic tradition, the best of them being *Peer Gynt* (1867), that marvelously bewildering study of universal man, written in a style full of grandeur and deep understanding. With *Emperor and Galilean* (1873) he renounced the poetic form as being antithetical to realism; although the play is inordinately long and set in Roman times, it does incorporate a psychological analysis of character which would become more pronounced in his later plays. With *Pillars of Society* (1877) he began the series of realistic social plays upon which his international fame chiefly rests. He became the darling of the Germans, among

whom he was then living. There followed, at two-year intervals, *A Doll's House, Ghosts, An Enemy of the People, The Wild Duck, Rosmersholm, The Lady from the Sea, Hedda Gabler,* and *The Master Builder.* It was in his subject matter, and his demonstrated concern with the effects of heredity and environment, that Ibsen partook of the new thought, for he by no means illustrates the formless slice-of-life technique advocated by Zola. His plays, like those of Sudermann in Germany, are well plotted and meticulously structured. It is not difficult to see why some critics have classed his dramas as the acme of the well-made play. Yet he is more the herald of the new than the flower of the old; he is, in a very understandable sense, what he has often been called—the father of modern drama.

It was his subject matter that caused him to be censored and banned in the state and commercial theatres, and which caused the free theatres to champion him. He did not regard his mission in the same objective, amoral light as Zola did his; when compared with Zola, he answered that he was similar, "Only with this difference, that Zola descends into the cess-pool to take a bath, I to cleanse it." Ibsen had an almost incalculable effect on dramatists everywhere, even to the far reaches of Italy where the realistic dramas of Rovetta, Praga, Traversi, Giacosa, Bertolazzi, and others took as their subject matter the daily lives, problems, and idiosyncrasies of the people they knew.

One of the most perfect examples of the slice-of-life play ever written is Henri Becque's *La Parisienne* (1885), whose central character is a frivolous, extravagant, and coldly calculating society woman who escapes being a monster by virtue of the playwright's skill. Becque (1837–1899) had previously written *The Vultures* (1882) and several other plays in the naturalist genre, and found so much difficulty in getting them produced that in 1882 he rather cynically and bitterly called for a new theatre which would give plays like his a hearing. Antoine answered five years later, and the *pièces rosses* (literally, "nasty bits") became, in spite of Antoine's efforts, indelibly linked with the Théâtre Libre. Antoine himself insisted that his theatre was open to all types and kinds of plays so long as they were new and original, but the force of circumstances made pièces rosses predominate. François de Curel, Eugène Brieux, Georges Ancey, Porto-Riche, Hennique, and Méténier are but a few of the native dramatists whom Antoine brought to public attention, and the first three of these, at least, achieved lasting reputations.

Antoine also first produced the great Tolstoy's *Power of Darkness* on February 10, 1888, thus introducing a new foreign playwright, and paving the way for subsequent productions of Ibsen, Hauptmann, and Björnson.

Hauptmann's *Before Sunrise* (1889) had been the first native German play presented by the Freie Bühne; it deals with the jilting of his sweetheart by Alfred Loth, idealist and reformer, when he finds that she is the daughter of an inveterate drunkard and sister of a dipsomaniac, and the subsequent suicide of the jilted Helen. Hauptmann (1862-1946) continued in the naturalistic vein with *Lonely Lives* (1891), *The Weavers* (1892), *The Beaver Coat* (1893), *Drayman Henschel* (1898), and *Gabriel Schilling's Flight* (1912). His romantic tendencies, however, became apparent as early as 1893 in *The Assumption of Hannele*, and flowered in the symbolic fantasy of *The Sunken Bell* (1896) and *And Pippa Dances* (1906). The total body of his work makes him the foremost of modern German dramatists. His development reversed that of Björnson (1832–1910) who, like his compatriot Ibsen, had turned from the romantic drama to naturalism, producing *Leonarda* as early as 1879, and *The Gauntlet* and *Beyond Our Powers* in 1883. He, too, was much admired by the Germans, but turned to novel writing in disappointment over the reception accorded his plays.

The third great Scandinavian, the Swedish August Strindberg (1849–1912), was also a novelist, although he never forsook one form for the other. His commitment to naturalism began with *Sir Bengt's Wife* (1882), was most notable in his two most famous plays, *The Father* (1887) and *Miss Julie* (1888), and appeared as well in *Easter* (1901) and *The Dance of Death* (1901). The preface which he wrote for the production of *Miss Julie* remains the most comprehensive description of naturalism—its materials, means, and effects. When Antoine produced the play in 1893, he translated this preface and distributed it to his audience, probably because Strindberg's clarion call for the rethinking of actor-audience relationships, costuming, makeup, setting, and lighting were so precisely what Antoine was doing in his Théâtre Libre. Like Hauptmann, Strindberg also wrote nonrealistic plays (which will be dealt with below) as well as novels. The number and variety of his works have made him Sweden's greatest writer.

In addition to Tolstoy, the realistic movement in Russia produced Maxim Gorki (1868–1936), whose *The Lower Depths* (1902) might stand as the perfect example of naturalism, and Anton Chekhov (1860–1904), one of the world's great dramatists. Although he had written a number of highly successful vaudeville sketches and short, popular farces before

STANISLAVSKI REALISM
Working along the same lines as Antoine,
Stanislavski produced at the Moscow Art
Theatre in 1902 the play shown above—Gorki's *The Lower Depths*. Stanislavski himself can be seen as one of the characters in
the upper left of the picture.

---

he turned to longer plays in the new form,
Chekhov's first two long plays were poorly
received. *Ivanov* (1887), the grimmest of
his plays, was hissed at its first performance; *The Seagull* (1896) was greeted
with unseemly laughter on its first presentation. Neither play was fully appreciated
until given later by the Moscow Art Theatre.
In 1899 the same group produced *Uncle
Vanya*, in 1901 *The Three Sisters*, and in 1904
The Cherry Orchard. In this last play, a
"tragedy of life's trivialities," as Gorki called
it, Chekhov reached the pinnacle of his
career; Madame Ranevskaya, Trofimov, Lo-
pakhin are memorable characters in the
finest tradition of theatre, each drawn from
the life around him as Chekhov had observed
it. Though his contemporaries were in-
capable of recognizing the fact (Chekhov
was unhappy over Stanislavski's insistence
on the seriousness of the plays which he himself considered "comedies"), what Chekhov
had actually produced in his four great plays
(upon which his international reputation is
founded) were excellent tragi-comedies—a
genre which would become predominant in
the twentieth century.

Such observation and fidelity to reality
sustained the Abbey Theatre in Dublin at its
first inception in 1899, although the nature of
its founders rendered the Irish movement
far more poetic than those of other lands.
William Butler Yeats (1865–1939) was first
a poet, then a playwright, and even in one
of the most famous of his plays, *Deirdre*
(1906), dramatized from Irish heroic legend,

he is more the lyric poet than anything else. One of his co-founders, Edward Martyn (1859–1924), was fired by both Ibsen and Irish nationalism, but never succeeded in mastering natural dialogue, while the third founder, Lady Augusta Gregory (1852–1932), was successful only in the short plays which displayed her strong feeling for the everyday problems of the Irish people. The greatest of Ireland's dramatists was John Millington Synge (1871–1909), who at Yeats's behest spent several years in close observation of the common people of Ireland and then produced a series of unparalleled plays, including *The Shadow of the Glen* (1903), *Riders to the Sea* (1904), *The Well of the Saints* (1905), *The Playboy of the Western World* (1907), *The Tinker's Wedding* (1909), and the unfinished *Deirdre of the Sorrows*, produced in 1910 after his death. To these outstanding names should probably be added those of Lord Dunsany, St. John Ervine (whose *John Ferguson*, 1915, gave the Theatre Guild its first great success in 1920), and Lennox Robinson, whose most famous play is one of the best of Irish comedies—*The Whiteheaded Boy* (1916).

In England, the realist movement had for precedent the genre pictures of Tom Robertson as presented by the Bancrofts. Influenced by Ibsen, Sir Arthur Wing Pinero (1855–1934) produced a series of social dramas which, though superficially of the new genre, basically were well-made plays in the tradition of Scribe, revealing little comprehension of complexity of character or of original observation. *The Second Mrs. Tanqueray* (1893), *The Notorious Mrs. Ebbsmith* (1896), and *Midchannel* (1909) are his most famous plays. Fresher observation and a keener appreciation of character are evident in the plays of Henry Arthur Jones (1851–1929): *Saints and Sinners* (1884), *Wealth* (1889), *Michael and His Lost Angel* (1896),

which Shaw considered to be his best play, and *Mrs. Dane's Defense* (1900). Jones was an ardent champion of the "new" drama, although his plays today seem pale imitations of the "real thing"—Ibsen. A real concern with social problems, and the penetration of character which marked his series of great novels, made John Galsworthy (1867–1933) a significant contributor to the stream of English naturalism. His best plays are *The Silver Box* (1906), *Strife* (1909), *Justice* (1910), and the later *Loyalties* (1922).

But the true dramatic renascence of English theatre sprang from George Bernard Shaw (1856–1950), whose *Widowers' Houses* (1892) was the first native play produced by Grein's Independent Theatre. The following year he wrote *The Philanderer* and *Mrs. Warren's Profession;* then on the heels of the furor kicked up by these "unpleasant" plays, he turned to the far pleasanter *Arms and the Man* (1894), in which he satirizes the taste of critics for romantic drama. A mere listing of the plays he wrote between the opening of the Independent Theatre and the beginning of World War I will demonstrate his undisputed preeminence in British dramatic writing, if not, indeed, in world literature during that period: *The Man of Destiny, The Devil's Disciple, You Never Can Tell, Caesar and Cleopatra, Captain Brassbound's Conversion, Man and Superman, John Bull's Other Island, Major Barbara, The Doctor's Dilemma, Getting Married, Androcles and the Lion,* and *Pygmalion.* The vitality and variety of this impressive list show how Shaw was able to turn the new impulses in theatre to his own purposes, producing inimitable and great plays. Though he began as an Ibsenite, blaming Mrs. Warren's predicament on the capitalist society that forced her into an unsavory profession, he soon transcended both realism and naturalism and became purely Shavian, that blend of iconoclasm,

BELASCO REALISM
Scene from Belasco's famous production of
Rose of the Rancho, a highly romantic script,
which Belasco dressed in the trappings of
realism with very literal setting and lighting.
(Theatre Collection, New York Public Library)

intellectualism, restraint, revolution, and
delight which made him a world figure.

In America only the most tentative of
beginnings were made in the new drama
prior to World War I. Bronson Howard
(1842–1908) in 1882 treated the problem of
divorce in *Young Mrs. Winthrop.* Then, influenced by William Dean Howells' championing of the European writers, James A. Herne
(1839-1901) produced his *Margaret Fleming*
in 1892. It is a serious domestic drama,
devoid of big scenes, and relatively unconventional. It failed in New York, but he was
able to recoup his fortunes with *Shore
Acres* (1892), a genre study of New England
characters. In 1906 and 1908 there appeared
The Great Divide and *The Faith Healer,* both
by William Vaughn Moody (1869–1910),
which, though somewhat banal to present-

day audiences, were fresh and new in subject
and treatment when they appeared. Eugene
Walter (1857-1941) in *Paid in Full* (1908) and
The Easiest Way (1909) showed a desire to
deal frankly with social and economic problems. But none of these plays had the intrinsic dramatic worth of their European
counterparts, and they were few indeed when
compared with the bulk of American pre-
war playwriting. Owen Davis with his melodramas, George Ade with his gay satires,
Charles Hale Hoyt with his rollicking farces,
Clyde Fitch with his social comedies, Augustus Thomas with his local color plays, and
David Belasco with his flagrant romanticism
clothed in a deceptively realistic setting,
were the most prolific and the most highly
successful dramatists of the new world.

But there was a second path—a path

apart from naturalism which avante-garde writers contemporary with the naturalists were exploring. As early as 1884, Ibsen himself had taken a step along this path in *The Wild Duck*, where the bird and its capture, its life in the garret, and its death epitomized the illusions of several of the characters and how they are destroyed when these illusions are shattered. Such an invitation to an audience to find private meanings in the imaginative substrata below the logical action is approaching the quality called symbolism. Ibsen explored it further in *The Lady from the Sea* (1888) and *The Master Builder* (1892). They move toward a deintellectualization of the drama, toward making it subject to private interpretation, toward an intuitive grasping of hidden meanings rather than a clear understanding of precise

statement. When the playwright deliberately intends to build effects by symbols, to make the symbols stand out *as symbols*, then the antirealistic mode is called symbolism.

The year before the appearance of *The Master Builder*, a young Belgian poet, Maurice Maeterlinck, influenced by his acquaintanceship with Philippe Villiers de l'Isle Adam during a visit to Paris (at the exact time when Antoine was including in his first program of the Théâtre Libre Arthur Byl's short nonrealistic fantasy), began to pursue the divergent, nonrealistic path. In 1891 appeared *The Intruder* and *The Blind*, tiny gems of poetic expression, in which the characters seem like somnambulists "who are a little deaf and are being continually awakened from a painful dream," as he puts it. In this quest to invoke the invisible, the

THE PRINCE REGENT THEATRE, MUNICH
Left, an exterior view; above, interior view.
The Prince Regent Theatre in Munich is
typical of new theatre construction in Europe at the turn of the century. It follows
the Festspielhaus plan of a fan-shaped bank
of widely spaced seats in continuous rows
and many exits in the side walls. (Theater-
Museum, Munich)

intangible, the subconscious, he wrote *Pel-
léas and Mélisande* in 1893, *The Interior* in
1894, and *The Bluebird* in 1908. It is the *inner*
action, the action *behind* the visible action he
is trying to show; the movement culminates
in expressionism just after World War I.

Strindberg, who admired Maeterlinck,
turned away from the naturalism of *Miss
Julie*, and in 1898 produced the first play of
the trilogy *To Damascus* (the entire work was
completed in 1904). In 1902, upon the appearance of *A Dream Play*, he wrote an "Author's
Note" to accompany the play which is as
important for subjectivist drama as his
earlier preface to *Miss Julie* is to naturalism.
It opens:

In this dream play, as in his former dream
play *To Damascus*, the Author has sought

to reproduce the disconnected but
apparently logical form of a dream.
Anything can happen, everything is
possible and probable. Time and space
do not exist . . . The characters are
split, double and multiply; they evaporate,
crystallize, scatter and converge. But a
single consciousness holds sway over
them all—that of the dreamer.

He went on to write, in 1907, *The Ghost
Sonata*, which has proved to be the most
durable of his subjectivist plays.

In Germany, Hauptmann moved from
naturalism to symbolism, as noted above.
But Frank Wedekind (1864–1918) was totally
a symbolist in *Spring's Awakening* (1891),
Earthspirit (1895), *The Marquis of Keith*
(1900), and *Pandora's Box* (1903). His pre-

vailing preoccupation with erotic themes aroused such opposition that at one point he was imprisoned in Munich, but his works were influential in Germany's new theatre movement after his death. In Vienna, Hugo von Hofmannsthal (1874–1929) began a series of plays in 1891 with *Yesterday*, one of the best of which is *Oedipus and the Sphinx* (1906). He is best remembered today, however, for the libretti he wrote for his friend, Richard Strauss.

The most respected of the symbolist drama in France was written by Paul Claudel (1868–1955); during the early part of his career it was published anonymously. Only a few of his plays were produced before World War I. (He was not a professional playwright, but a diplomat.) *The Exchange*, written in 1893, was not produced until 1913 by Copeau; *The Tidings Brought to Mary* (1912) was, however, produced by Lugné-Poë in the year it was written. *The Hostage* (1911) was produced in 1919, but *The Satin Slipper* (1919) was not done until the 1940s. *Crusts* (1918) and *The Humiliation of the Father* (1919) are now also available in English. His plays, along with his other writings, make Claudel a major figure in French literature.

In England, there was no strong antirealist movement, perhaps because of Shaw's and William Archer's indefatigable championing of Ibsen. But perhaps the fantasies of James M. Barrie (1860–1937), which delighted London audiences, show some of the "otherworldliness" of the symbolists: *Peter Pan* (1904), *The Admirable Crichton* (1903), *A Kiss for Cinderella* (1915), *Dear Brutus* (1917), and *Mary Rose* (1920)—in all of which there are "otherworldly" elements, though also frequently more than a hint of sentimentality. And it is possible to conceive that Oscar Wilde (1865–1900), particularly in *Salome* (1892), has an affinity with the symbolists. And maybe even that masterpiece *The Importance of Being Earnest* (1895) could be called antirealistic, since he declares with it, "The real is dead, long live artifice!"

For the future, the most significant of the nonrealistic writers of the period was perhaps Strindberg, for his dissection of personality in his dream plays was soon to be fortified in the public mind by the expanding fame of Sigmund Freud (1856–1939). Freud's influence would also permeate the realistic theatre in its materials as well as its means, and become an overriding concern of twentieth-century theatre.

Organized monotony in popular theatre

At the beginning of the present century, theatre everywhere was marked by an appalling standardization—playhouses, playwrights, producers, plays, players, decorators, and playgoers. The theatrical trusts which dominated show business operated on a mass-production basis. The Theatrical Syndicate (Klaw, Erlanger, Hayman, Nirdlinger, and Zimmerman) and the Shuberts between them controlled practically all of the five thousand legitimate playhouses in the United States, including thirty-eight in New York City, twenty-one in Chicago, fifteen in Philadelphia, and seven in Washington, D.C. Over two hundred fifty traveling companies employed the services of twice as many railroad agents in arranging their tours. Charles Frohman organized a central booking system for the Syndicate, and those stars who wished to remain independent, like Richard Mansfield, William Faversham, Joseph Jefferson, and Sarah Bernhardt, were forced to play in tents and skating rinks. The expansion of railroad facilities and the clutch of the monopoly effectively strangled hundreds of local repertory companies throughout the land.

TWO SETTINGS FOR "THE VALKYRIES"
Above, Max Bruckner's setting for Act I at
Bayreuth in 1896. The emphasis here is upon
a grand pictorial setting. Right, Adolphe Appia's design for Act III. As Appia planned it,
these massive shapes do not come to life
until properly lighted and until actors move
upon them. (Theater-Museum, Munich; Fondation Adolphe Appia, Berne)

The same conditions prevailed in England,
where the London companies, or special road
companies assembled in London, toured productions to the provinces while making
money for the theatrical trusts in the capital.

Against such entrenched standardization
the European free theatres took their stand;
the little theatres spread across America; and
such a hardy pioneer as Miss A. E. F. Horni-
man subsidized the Abbey Theatre in Dublin
and established the Manchester Repertory
Company in England. Protest and reform
also began in the colleges and universities
with the establishment of the 47 Workshop
by George Pierce Baker at Harvard (to develop workers for the "new theatre," a task
in which he was phenomenally successful),
the opening of the School of Drama at Carnegie Institute of Technology in Pittsburgh
in 1914, under Thomas Wood Stevens, and the
establishment of the Wisconsin Players by
Thomas H. Dickinson in 1911, each with a
developing curriculum in theatre arts. The
full development of this type of theatre
would come in the postwar period.

The many theatres built in Europe and
America tended to follow one of two patterns
—either the metamorphosed "hen coop" of
the earlier nineteenth century, or the Bayreuth Festspielhaus plan. The former type appeared chiefly in England and France, the
latter in Germany and America, although the
continuous rows of seats characteristic of
the Bayreuth plan tended in America to be
cut by wide aisles, as dictated by the more
stringent fire laws.

As early as 1875, two French architects
designed a house with a "dished" floor, the
slant increasing sharply toward the back,
thus overcoming the disadvantages of the
straight slant used in the Bayreuth plan.
But this new idea did not become current in
theatre architecture until well into the twentieth century.

The orchestra pit was almost universally
just below the stage, between it and the first
row of seats, although when Steele MacKaye
built his Madison Square Theatre in New
York in 1880, he housed the orchestra in an
opening above the proscenium arch, in order
not to impose them between actor and audience. Outstanding practitioners of the new

TWO MORE APPIA SETTINGS
Left, design for *King Lear*, Act II; above, design for *Parsifal*, Act III. These austere settings with many levels are typical of the revolutionary designs of Adolphe Appia. With this type of setting, lighting and costuming gained new importance. The emphasis was on the actor, and the setting simply attempted to give him adequate space through which to move. (Fondation Adolphe Appia, Berne; Gabriel Jacques-Dalcroze, Geneva)

theatre architecture in Germany were Max Littman and Oskar Kaufmann, with the Prince Regent Theatre in Munich the outstanding example of the former's work and the Volksbühne in Berlin, with its immense stage space, of the latter's. Littman was also responsible for designing the Munich Kunstlertheater in 1907, which maintained the same auditorium design as his 1901 house, but at the request of the proprietors, George Fuchs and Fritz Erler, the stage house was entirely different. There was no scene loft,

TWO DESIGNS BY GORDON CRAIG
Left, a setting for *Macbeth;* above, a setting for the ideal theatre. The generally perpendicular treatment of Craig is evident in these two designs, and the massive proportions of many of his settings are illustrated particularly in the *Macbeth* sketch. (Theatre Collection, New York Public Library; Museum of Modern Art)

no great stage area, no extensive mechanical equipment. The acting space was relatively shallow and unadorned, with a door on each side of the proscenium opening. It was intended as an "art" theatre, according to the new mode, and eschewed illusionistic scenery.

In theatres of the basic Bayreuth design, the side walls were liberally supplied with exits, and the wider space between the continuous rows of seats allowed for quick movement of the audience in or out. H. C. Ingalls, in designing the two hundred ninety-nine-seat Little Theatre for Winthrop Ames

in New York in 1912, used the continuous bank of seats, but cut it with two aisles, in conformance with American law, and had exits only at the front of the house. Other larger American theatres, built somewhat later, used a dished orchestra floor and a sharply sloped balcony. In America, too, stages tended to be more restricted in area than those of European houses, being neither so wide nor so deep. The average seating capacity of these houses tended to remain between fourteen hundred and seventeen hundred, although there were extremes in both directions. Theatre economics dictated a capacity large enough to cover mounting expenses and the heavy costs of elaborate productions.

The amateurs improvise

The amateur producing groups used whatever space was available. The Théâtre Libre opened in a little wooden building in the Passage de l'Elysée des Beaux Arts (now known as the Rue André Antoine), with a seating capacity of three hundred forty-three, then moved to an old eight-hundred-seat house in the Rue de la Gaîté. Brahm gave the first productions of the Freie Bühne in the Lessingtheater. The English Independent Theatre, and its successors, the Stage Society and the Incorporated Stage Society, used whatever theatres were available for their sporadic performances. In America, the Provincetown Players began producing in a wharf building in Massachusetts, then moved to a converted stable (still standing and still in use as a playhouse) in Macdougal Street, New York. The Washington Square Players, which became the Theatre Guild, produced first in the Bandbox, then in the Comedy Theatre, and finally, after ten years, built their own Guild Theatre. Warehouses, storerooms, school halls were pressed into service by the various little theatre groups, transformations great or small being made in them as resources permitted. The English repertory companies in Manchester, Liverpool, and Birmingham used extant theatres, and both the Little and the Haymarket theatres in London struggled to establish repertory. The Vedrenne-Barker company, which performed with such distinction at the Court Theatre in London beginning in 1904, moved to other houses as exigencies demanded. A permanent home, however, had been built at

TWO REINHARDT PRODUCTIONS
Above, Oskar Strnad's design for *Danton's Death*, and right, the setting for *Sumurun*. The vast settings for these two massive productions were typical of one phase of Reinhardt's work. That indefatigable producer worked in many widely differing styles and types of plays, playhouses, and productions. (Max Reinhardt Archive; Theatre Collection, New York Public Library)

Stratford-on-Avon for the Shakespeare Festival Company; it opened in 1879, incorporating, in a style peculiarly unfit for its material, the traditional accoutrements of nineteenth-century theatre architecture. When this antique building burned down in 1926, G. B. Shaw sent a letter of congratulations to the manager.

The new movement which instigated major changes in playwriting and acting, and to some extent in stagecraft, had very little influence in theatre architecture until the postwar period. With the variety of production styles being tried, it is understandable that anything so permanent and expensive as a theatre building would await develop-

ments and a more settled aesthetic view before there would be a new spate of building.

Realist settings—true to life and false to art

It is true that the Duke of Saxe-Meiningen deserves immeasurable credit for the care with which he prepared his *mise-en-scène*. Yet it must not be forgotten that he worked within the limitations of the stage settings current in his day. Though he used platforms to vary the acting levels, he assumed that stages would continue to be set with scenery painted in perspective; he merely cautioned the stage director to so plan the actors' movements that probability would not be violated when the player was seen against the set. He assumed that roses, for instance, would continue to be painted on the set, then warned that great care must be taken so that the practical rose needed in the production would blend artistically with the painted ones. He did insist that objects on the set to be used by the actors—doorways, windows, benches, steps—should be plastic or three-dimensional and that the prevalent *ozones*, or strips of blue cloth in the flies to represent sky, should be replaced by arching foliage, rooftops, or, if necessary, by painted clouds.

The influx of the new realism did nothing for stagecraft but intensify what Sheldon

Cheney called "the perfect realization of a false ideal." The box set had developed during the nineteenth century and actual furnishings had been gradually substituted for painted properties. But the literalness of many a stage set was at variance with the romantic and melodramatic properties of many of the plays themselves. It is interesting, and perhaps commendable, that David Belasco experimented for three months to find exactly the right color lights for a California sunset in *Girl of the Golden West*, and that for *The Easiest Way* he transferred to his stage, intact, wallpaper and all, the in-terior of a down-at-the-heel boardinghouse room. Indeed, Belasco was nothing if not a meticulous workman. Every scenic detail, to the smallest of properties, was arduously sought out or carefully created so that, unpeopled by the players and devoid of the play, his sets were the marvels of his audiences for their literal truth. His attention to detail went so far as to extend stage carpeting offstage and into the dressingrooms, so that actors would thus be helped to prepare for their entrances.

When truth began to be conceived as necessary not only in setting but in acting

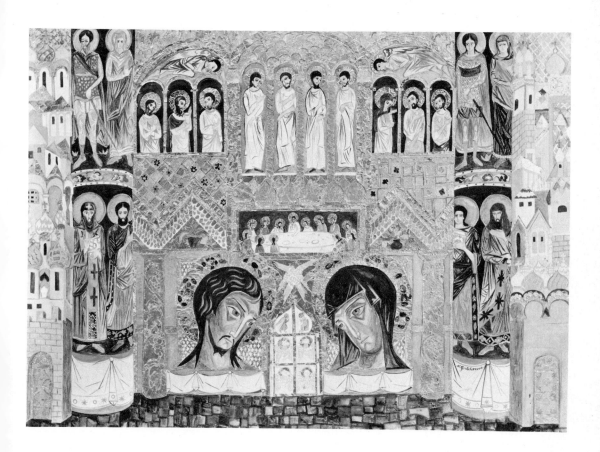

TYPICAL DESIGNS FOR THE RUSSIAN BALLET
Left, Léon Bakst's design for *Scheherezade.*
Above, design for *Liturgy* by Natalie Gontcharovna. These richly decorative pictorial settings are at the opposite pole from the
Appia–Craig objective. They are well suited
to the visual appeal of the ballet, but over-
whelming when used in the production of
plays because they divert attention from the
spoken word which is the essence of drama.
(Museum of Modern Art)

and writing as well, the realistic stage
setting was even more admired. Antoine exalted the idea of the "fourth wall," saying
that the ideal way to prepare a play was to
set it completely, as if there were to be no
audience, and then when the décor and action
were determined, decide which wall would
be removed so that the audience could see
what went on. He even did a lot of actual
building on the stage, and sometimes installed plumbing in the interest of "reality."
For a production of *The Butchers* (1888) he
hung real carcasses of beef on the stage.
Here is the application of Zola's principle of

scientific observation, of the stage milieu replacing the passages of description in the novel. Nothing is to be left to the imagination of the audience—every detail is to be explicit.

The basic fallacy of this point of view is that it seems to exclude the audience from the production, that it makes them, as it were, eavesdroppers rather than participants. More than a hundred years before, when Diderot was urging realism in stage settings he had been careful to point out that the audience was included within the fourth wall— they were silent spectators to what went on within the room represented by the stage. The realist movement ignored the audience almost entirely.

The new aesthetic—illusion via atmosphere

Yet at the very moment when this photographic realism was reaching its height in practice, insistent voices were heard saying that this surface truth was not a central truth, could not be true to the spirit of drama, was indeed a denial of aesthetic truth. For the theatre is not life itself, but an art form, based on selectivity and aiming for unity of effect. Even the most realistic of stage settings cannot transfer the actual lath and plaster of a room, the literal stones of a wall into the theatre. The most that can be accomplished is to strive for the *illusion* of reality through the use of artificial substitutes in paint and canvas. Then arises the paradox of real people and plastic properties seen against a manifestly unreal background —a painted backdrop, canvas trees.

Why not, said Adolphe Appia (1862–1928), as early as 1895, put the emphasis where it belongs—not on the set, but on the actor. Instead of presenting a forest, for instance, with an actor moving about in it, show a scene which will give the *impression* of an

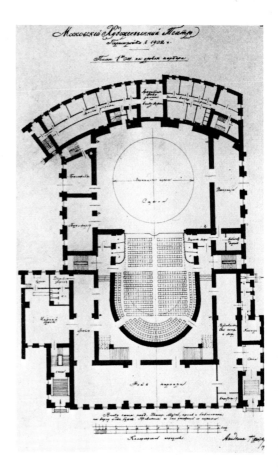

actor who is moving about in a forest. Why not concentrate on the essential *feeling*, the essential communication between actor and audience? Now you can throw away all paint and canvas. By the proper combination of color and intensity of lights you can create whatever *mood* you need to enhance the performance of the actor. You can give him a neutral background of levels and space that does not come alive until it is lit and he

THE MOSCOW ART THEATRE, 1902
Stanislavski's famous theatre, showing (at left) a floor plan, with the stage area larger than that alloted to seating, and above, two views of the stage. The upper one is a photograph, the lower a design. Note the inclusion of the seagull which became a trademark with this theatre.

THE VIEUX COLOMBIER
Two stage settings in the theatre of Jacques Copeau. Eschewing both realism and pictorialism, Copeau developed a basic architectural platform stage which could be changed by minor props and set pieces for various scenes and plays. It was often called Elizabethan, and, in truth, it does seem to have its inspiration from the earlier period, placing the emphasis upon the play and the players rather than upon the setting. (Macgowan and Jones, *Continental Stagecraft*, Harcourt Brace Jovanovich, 1922)

is moving upon it. Thus the central truth of theatre is reached—the creation of atmosphere.

This is the essence of the new aesthetic movement in the theatre, conceived by Adolphe Appia, preached by Gordon Craig (1872–1966), put actively to work by Max Reinhardt (1873–1943). The effect of space, of noble architectural settings, could be brought to the theatre only by leading the spectator

to imagine them. A single column, a soaring arch lost above the proscenium, a lone candelabrum could *give the effect* of a cathedral. A garden wall, a few pots of flowers, a conventionalized tree would make a garden setting. Interiors would use neutral hangings or screens with only the most essential of furnishings. Nothing would distract from the movement of the actor in the space provided for him. The set would be backed by a curving neutral dome (the Fortuny sky dome, at first made of silk, later of plaster) upon which the lights could play and which would put the emphasis on the forestage and the actor. There would, of course, be no footlights.

The extreme of this aesthetic ideal was the suggestion of Gordon Craig that the live actor be replaced by a supermarionette who could be counted on not to disturb with his personality the visual harmony created by the stage director, and various marionette theatres were actually established, chiefly in Germany. In Germany, also, Max Reinhardt took the live actor as far toward this ideal as possible in his wordless productions of *The Miracle* (1910) and *Sumurun* (1911), which toured Europe and America. Even the Moscow Art Theatre, a stronghold of realism, was touched by the new aesthetics. Gordon Craig designed a *Hamlet* (1912) for them, using a series of movable screens for the various scenes. On paper and in prospect the idea looked ideal; in practice it was a fiasco, because Stanislavski was never able to conquer the problem of anchoring the screens and moving them as the design required. They all fell down at dress rehearsals, then had to be firmly anchored and immovable during the run of the show. Hence the effect Craig intended was largely lost. Craig was a theorizer; he conceived designs often too grand to be realized on any theatre stage. Few of his plans were ever put to practical use. But through his basic ideas he influenced a line of disciples who destroyed the false ideal of the imitation of reality, and who set the theatre back on the path where it belonged—theatricality.

The insistence of Appia and Craig on visual felicity in stage setting had another manifestation in the movement developed by the Russian Ballet under Diaghilev (1872–1929). To enhance the visual appeal of this

THE APPIA-CRAIG INFLUENCE
Costume designs by Norman Wilkinson for *Love's Labours Lost.* Austere settings with colorful and lavish costumes were typical of Wilkinson's work. (Museum of Modern Art)

form, painters were called in to the service of the theatre, and such ones as Léon Bakst and Alexandre Benois produced infinitely varied and rich décor in which the dancers became part of an intricate and lush stage picture. Their *Scheherazade* (1910) was an unbelievably rich and sensuous oriental spectacle, for instance. Some misguided theatrical managers, envious of these ballet performances, thought that they could titillate their audiences by splendid pictorial settings, not realizing that the drama, after all, has a reliance on the spoken word which ballet has not. So they fell into the same error that

MORE OF THE APPIA–CRAIG INFLUENCE
Claude Bragdon's design of a setting for *The Glittering Gate*, illustrating the use of line, with no decoration except for the focal gate. (Museum of Modern Art)

had engulfed the realists—they produced settings which overwhelmed both actor and play.

In the larger houses, huge turntables were installed, such as that which Lautenschlager first built at Munich in 1896, and Stanislavski built into the new Moscow Art Theatre in 1902. Elevator stages, like that of Steele MacKaye at his Madison Square Theatre, were tried, as well as wagon stages with whole sets moving off into the wings. At the other extreme stage settings were reduced to the barest minimum. When Jacques Copeau (1878–1949) opened his Vieux Colom-

bier in 1913, he dispensed with the proscenium arch and footlights, as Antoine had dreamed of doing, but, contrary to Antoine's minutely conceived realistic scene, he used a permanent architectural setting upon which he placed only the most essential properties for the play in hand. Granville-Barker (1877–1946) ignored the proscenium arch when he took over Wallack's Theatre in New York for an American season in 1915, building out the stage to cover the orchestra pit and the first two rows of seats, and playing Shaw, Ibsen, Galsworthy, and Shakespeare in a style which completely ignored the picture-frame setting and the footlight tradition. William Poël (1852–1934) in the 1890s gave Shakespeare on a simplified architectural stage. Aided by the exigencies of war scarcities the so-called simplified staging received great impetus during the war years. Lush décor was reserved largely for escapist musicals and ballets; legitimate drama profited by a simpler production. The two divergent streams of the aesthetic movement, rich pictorialism and tasteful sparseness, were to undergo further interesting development after the war.

Authenticity replaces beauty as costume standard

By the time that the new movement of realistic drama was in full sway in theatre the principle of careful and accurate costuming had been universally accepted. The Duke of Saxe-Meiningen had insisted not only upon historical accuracy in costuming, but on proper carrying of the costume by the actor. Helmets were to be worn straight over the brow; stances for persons wearing classical garb were to differ from those of eighteenth-century dandies. Costumes were to be worn as early as possible in the rehearsal period, so that the performers could grow into them.

David Belasco displayed the same zeal for correct costuming as he did for detailed settings. He tells of buying from a person met on the street the exact worn coat or pair of shoes that he needed for a character in a play, or of sending to France or Japan for costumes and materials for other productions. Antoine objected to the white hands and knees of the mountaineers in the Meiningen *Wilhelm Tell* which he saw in 1888, saying that it violated reality, and the Moscow Art production of Gorki's *The Lower Depths* spent much time and effort in achieving the requisite amount of filth and raggedness. Stanislavski made it a practice to visit the actual scene of plays he undertook, if at all possible, and to bring back to Moscow not only many sketches but also materials, properties, furniture, and costumes, so that his stage pictures would be as *actual* as he could make them.

When Strindberg wrote his preface to *Miss Julie* (1888), he urged that actresses cease insisting upon being beautiful, but be lifelike; that they use little or no paint on their faces so that their emotions may be clearly visible; and that actors do the same. Appia and Craig both maintained that the director must have absolute control of all the elements of production, including costuming and makeup, so that a unified effect could be achieved.

In the pictorial settings of the Russian Ballet, the costumes were designed and executed so that they became a part of the décor as the dancers appeared on the stage. In the more austere Appia-Craig settings, the costumes formed the chief decoration of the stage, standing out in brilliant contrast to the neutral backgrounds. When Granville-Barker produced *Twelfth Night* early in this century, Norman Wilkinson and A. Rothenstein designed a plastic neutral background and colorful costumes in a style Sheldon Cheney called "representative of the best staging being done in England."

Costuming now was conceived of not chiefly as a means of dressing the individual characters of a play to their individual advantage, but as a contributing element to the whole mood and style of the play. The long, flowing robe of crepe de chine in which Reinhardt dressed the Lady Diana Manners for *The Miracle* was prophetic of the many innovations in costuming which that wizard would introduce in the postwar years.

Costuming for women, of course, adapted

itself to the full bosom, tiny waist, and generous hips which was the ideal of feminine beauty in the days before World War I, and coiffures took into account the universally popular center part with the long hair drawn backwards in a slant over the forehead. Henrietta Crossman as Rosalind, Edith Wynne Mathison as Viola, Julia Marlowe as Juliet may have been correctly garbed from an historical and artistic point of view, but the style of their own day comes through in their photographs. This contemporaneity (perhaps anachronism) is more noticeable in women's costumes than in men's because, of course, the stylish female figure has changed so radically in the decades of this century. And stage costuming, however accurate and artistic, must always be affected by the people who wear it. Perhaps Gordon Craig was right in wanting to substitute supermarionettes for live actors!

New acting methods necessary in the new theatre

For the advent of the new realism at the end of the nineteenth century actors found themselves largely unprepared. In spite of the work of the two Matthews, of Mme. Vestris, and of the Bancrofts, the predominant style—as exemplified by Sir Henry Irving and Ellen Terry—was dignified and more declamatory than intimate. Actors were still complimented on their points, much as singers were, just as if almost a century had not passed since the tirade was the true test of an actor's ability. Romanticism, also, had introduced a flamboyant manner to the stage, and the vestiges of it persisted.

But neither declamation nor flamboyance was convincing in the new theatre. Perhaps this is one reason why the earliest of the new theatres used amateur actors, training them in the new skills required. Antoine

cautioned his players to disregard the admonition of Goethe and the theatre Duke about facing the audience when they spoke, and tried to orient them to the scene on the stage rather than to the house. Having been himself well trained in the prevalent style of the Comédie (it is said that he could give a perfect reproduction of the great favorite, Gôt), Antoine quickly realized its inadequacy for the plays he was presenting. It had no simplicity, no life, no naturalness. It was bound by conventions that insisted no actor speak while walking or sitting down, that lines be recited elegantly, that bodies appear statuesque and dignified. So he started with entirely new personnel, and taught them not to recite, but to live their parts. He taught them that movement is the actor's most intense means of expression, that the whole physical makeup must "speak" for the actor, that vocal expression must be natural, conversational. He taught them that each scene in a play has its own movement, which is a part of the total movement of the play; that no actor is more important than the play itself. He taught also by example, playing in such a way as to receive many critical plaudits for his truth to character. Wonderingly, one critic remarked that Antoine and his company played as if there were no stage, as if they were unconscious of being watched. Observing that the famed crowd scenes of the Meiningen were right pictorially but not vocally, in that the actors spoke in unison, he taught his crowds to speak as a real crowd would—now one, now another, over and under each other. So he produced a new kind of actor, and lost his players constantly to the commercial and state houses. He became, in effect, a training school for a new generation of actors in France. At the end of the first season, Mevisto went to the Porte Saint Martin, and Mme. France to the Ambigu. By the end of the third season, ten of his amateurs had passed on to the professional stage, five of them to the Odéon alone. Lugné-Poë, who founded the Théâtre de l'Oeuvre in 1893, had been one of Antoine's actors, as had Firmin Gémier, assistant to Antoine at the Théâtre Antoine, and later director of the Odéon. The Théâtre Libre ceased to exist after about eight years, but its work had been sound; its principles were everywhere applauded, and Antoine went on to many more years of work at the Antoine and the Odéon.

The Moscow Art Theatre, too, began with amateurs, and Stanislavski constantly found it difficult to reteach professional actors in the new style. Early under the influence of the pictorial qualities of the Meiningen troupe, he soon found it difficult to accept their somewhat declamatory style of acting. As a result of the famous eighteen-hour conversation between himself and Nemirovich-Danchenko, the Moscow Art Theatre was founded in 1898, and he began the system which made his theatre the home of theatrical naturalism.

Stanislavski possessed that rare ability to analyze and systematize, and he set down his own development, plans, experiments, and conclusions in a series of books which have become gospel to many twentieth-century actors. The essence of his so-called system is the careful training of the actor's perceptions and imagination, and the use of these abilities in the preparation of a role. This preparation must proceed over a long period of time, and concern itself not only with the outward manifestations or projection of character, but also with the inward feeling, or soul. Indeed, he stated, a complete realization of the "inner man" would lead to the projection of it, which must then become systematic through long and patient practice. Some of his productions were in preparation for over a year before they were

seen in his theatre. The actor, according to him, needed to perfect his art through a lifetime of study and playing. He insisted that action or speech, merely for the sake of action or speech, was bad; that every player must have a definite motivation for speaking and acting, in every scene an objective toward which he played. This, in itself, was nothing new, for the American director Augustin Daly had insisted on the same

TWO POPULAR AMERICAN STARS
John Drew and Ada Rehan as Petruchio and Kate in *The Taming of the Shrew*. While these very popular performers are dressed with a great deal of attention to authenticity, Drew still wears the mustache which was his invariable adornment, and Ada Rehan exhibits the hourglass figure which was so much admired before World War I. (Henry E. Huntington Library and Art Gallery)

discipline for his acting company a generation before; Belasco prided himself on the discussions and character analysis that preceded every rehearsal period; Antoine had worked along the same lines ten or fifteen years previously. Nor was Stanislavski's "inner emotion" new to the stage—many fine actors preceding him had used just such a method, even including the meditative preparation which he recommended before each performance. But Stanislavski happened along at the right moment in theatre history and he had the talent, rare among performers, of codifying his ideas and explaining his method. Through many years of trial and error, in a constantly producing theatre and with a stable company of actors, Stanislavski at last discovered what was for him "the primal source of theatre art"—the actor and his "truth." The truth is double: an *inner* and an *outer* truth, with which the actor projects the *lived experience* of the play in the theatre. His system was to achieve worldwide prominence, and the Moscow Art Theatre was to become the hallowed shrine of the postwar generation.

Another group which was to rise to prominence and influence got its start in 1913 when Jacques Copeau, erstwhile critic and writer, trained a group of amateurs and with Roger Martin du Gard and Georges Duhamel opened the Vieux Colombier. His primal source of theatre art was the *poet*, or *playwright*, and the actors (as well as the director) were to perfect themselves to give "scenic life" to the original vision of the playwright. The French government sent this group to America in 1917–1918, and the interior of the old Garrick Theatre was transformed to Copeau's neo-Elizabethan style. The players were received with great interest, and influenced both acting and production methods here. The whole succeeding generation of French actors and directors were influenced by Copeau's ideas and his work.

The Freie Bühne and the Independent Theatre did not have so great an influence upon acting. Their personnel was recruited chiefly from the ranks of the professional actors who were interested in the new materials and who lent their spare time to the new theatres. Otto Brahm sometimes despaired of the resultant intrusion of "Weimar classicism" into the performances, and with the hope of developing a true acting ensemble, accepted the directorship of the Deutsches Theater in 1894. In England Grein's venture influenced the establishment of several repertory companies where ensemble playing was the ideal.

At the time that Stanislavski was perfecting his actor-centered, true-to-life techniques, Vsevolod Meyerhold (1873–1935), one of the Moscow Art Theatre's original company, was insisting that art is not life and that actors should not imitate life. His experiments in St. Petersburg before the Revolution were extended and refined after it. The strength of naturalism and those directors who believed in it submerged any antirealistic attempts through the years preceding World War I, but after it there would be many questions raised concerning naturalistic acting.

The rise of the modern director

Before Antoine (if we except Pixerécourt), there had been no director in the modern sense of the term—a unifying intelligence that directs all aspects of a given production. After him hardly a play has been given without such direction. Both he and Brahm let the play develop through rehearsals, setting only the environment beforehand. Stanislavski, on the other hand, prepared elaborate production books covering every aspect of the play before it went into rehearsal. This was the method of Max Reinhardt, too. The realist movement in the theatre, focused primarily on plays and actors, gave a new theatre worker to the world—the director (in the modern sense). The aesthetic movement which received its impetus from Appia and Craig also stressed the importance of the director, but would also, in the years after the war, bring a final contribution in the development of the specialized work of the designer.

Summary

Theatre of the twentieth century began before the close of the nineteenth. Theatre's own revolution started outside the commercial houses, but successfully transformed that protean creature by dispelling its false theatricality and bringing it closer to truth of materials and methods.

A whole new generation of playwrights, devoted to meticulous observation and objective presentation of situation and character, wrote many plays of significance. Literary men were once more involved in dramatic writing, developing new forms and new expression with skill—and often with genius. The new theatre produced the greatest English playwright since Shakespeare—George Bernard Shaw. Concomitantly, a growing number of theatre people were concerned with theatre as an art rather than theatre as life; nonrealistic works were done with a frequency which would lead to a predominance shortly after World War I.

The new theatre also developed the intimate playhouse, exalted and then almost discarded the "fourth wall" of the stage. It brought photographic realism to an acme of perfection, then made beginnings in replacing it with a more disciplined theatricality. It made direction an art in itself, and not an adjunct as it had largely been for many years. And it gave a new significance to stage design.

Finally, and perhaps most significantly, the art of acting was transformed: it found new methods to produce a new end product, and it codified techniques which were to have inestimable influence in the years to come.

17 The great world wars and the time between

In less than a generation, all the major powers of the Western world were twice engaged in general and brutal conflict, and in the second outbreak the Orient as well was involved. The mere twenty-one years intervening between the cessation of hostilities in World War I and the Nazi invasion of Poland with which World War II began may well disappear in future chronicles of the early twentieth century, and the whole era from 1914 to 1946 be regarded simply as The Great World War. But this close at hand, and in the United States, those twenty-one years are distinct; even within them are marked two separate periods—one of great and unprecedented prosperity, and one of deep and humiliating economic depression. The combination of Great Depression and World War II gave the longest Presidential tenure in the history of the United States to Franklin Delano Roosevelt: 1932 to his death in 1945, shortly after he had been elected to a fourth term. For the survivors of the first conflict in Europe, there was no happy time. The war had been fought largely on French soil, with great devastation to property and life; *La belle époque* of the Third Republic was gone forever, and in twenty years there were forty-three different ministries in the French government. England was in dire economic condition and troubled by strikes and the Irish question. So harsh were conditions in Italy that by 1925 Mussolini was in power, and in Spain there was civil war. The stringent provisions of the Treaty of Versailles engendered a German climate which led to the elevation to power of Hitler in 1933. The Russian Revolution precipitated a power struggle there which was not decided until 1929, when Stalin succeeded in expelling Trotsky and became undisputed master; in the decade of the thirties Stalin in a wave of purges effectively eliminated all possible opposition to his dictatorship.

In contrast to the general international good-feeling of the last quarter of the nineteenth century and the first decade of the twentieth, the war era was marked by intense national concern; each nation and people looked with suspicion and hostility on peoples outside its national boundaries, built high tariff walls, restricted immigration, and often imposed harsh censorships. Isolationist elements in the United States defeated its entrance into the League of Nations, and as late as 1937 Congress passed another "neutrality act." Hardly more than a year passed, however, from the outbreak of hostilities in September 1939, until the United States was at full-scale war, triggered by the Japanese attack on Pearl Harbor on December 7, 1941. It had taken three years (from 1914 to 1917) for America to join her Allies in World War I. The world had shrunk in the interim, and the United States was, perforce, obliged to assume a more international view. The harsh realities of four years of war, and the effectiveness with which it was brought home to the general population, changed public opinion to the extent that the United States became the leader in setting up the new international organization of the United Nations, even giving it a home on American soil.

Science and invention continued to multiply goods and services. In addition to the perfecting and continued spread of the telephone, radio was added as a means of communication, and government-enfranchised corporations were set up to administer the airwaves which were considered "public domain." Governments also made special provisions for extending road systems, which were made necessary by the increase of the automobile as a means of transportation. So, too, the airplane, speculatively used in the last months of World War I, developed into a major means of transportation and figured largely in World War II. The idea of "public domain" grew apace, with governments postulating the idea of "public enterprise" not only in transportation and communication, but in trade and power as well. Public enterprise in the United States even embraced theatre in the 1930s, which witnessed the four-year life of the first, last, and only federally subsidized theatre in this bulwark of individual enterprise—the Federal Theatre Project of the Works Progress Administration lasted from October 1935 to July 1939. At its peak, it employed ten thousand people, operated theatres in forty states, published a magazine, and sponsored a play and research bureau which served not only itself, but school, church, and community theatres throughout the nation. It fostered Negro theatre, and developed the unique production technique of the Living Newspaper, which engendered so much criticism that a hostile Congress finally liquidated the whole program.

Everywhere, in the private as well as the public sector, it was the collective voice which was heard. Literally thousands of organizations, both national and international, spoke for political parties, social institutions, economic segments, and minority groups. Labor unions reached a peak of power in their confrontations with management; this confrontation was evident in theatre as well as in other areas. The American Actors' Equity, founded in 1912, enforced a major and costly strike in 1919, which effectively demonstrated its power. In the same year, the International Labor Organization was founded, and in 1935 the Congress of Industrial Organizations split from the American Federation of Labor in the United States. In France and England, too, organized labor made great gains. By 1926, the Dramatists Guild in America (founded in 1912) had negotiated a Minimum Basic Agreement with producers, to complete the unionization of theatre workers.

The period also saw the establishment, in many countries of the Western world, of news agencies, chains of newspapers, and a tremendous number of daily papers. As of 1930, there were more than two thousand daily newspapers in the United States, and more than three thousand in Germany alone, while France had two hundred and Italy one hundred twenty. For theatre, the widespread circulation of newspapers meant an increase in the number of reviews and notices, although (except in major metropolitan centers) no noticeable improvement in the quality of criticism. This mass circulation of printed materials in the form of newspapers was augmented by hundreds of magazines, one of which was *Theatre Arts Magazine*, initiated by Sam Hume and Sheldon Cheney at the Detroit Arts and Crafts Center in 1916. It moved to New York City in 1918 and became perhaps the most influential theatre publication in the United States for about thirty years. Mass circulation also became operative in book publishing, with the founding of the Book-of-the-Month Club in 1926 and the growth of paperback book publishing during the 1930s.

Moving pictures challenge theatre

But the most sensational factor contributing to the mass culture—and the one with the most implications for theatre—was the moving picture. The first public showing of this "scientific" development was in the form of animated drawings done by Reynaud in Paris in 1892. When in 1896 the first public showings in the United States took place in Koster and Biall's Music Hall in New York as a part of its vaudeville bill, one of the one-minute sequences was a scene from Charles Hale Hoyt's play, *A Milk White Flag* (1894).

In 1905 John P. Harris opened his Nickelodeon in McKeesport, near Pittsburgh, Pennsylvania, showing fifteen-minute programs of these short films. Within two years there were three thousand of these nickelodeons throughout the United States, and by 1910 there were ten thousand. In 1915 D. W. Griffith (an ex–stage actor and director) issued his still famous *Birth of a Nation*—a three-and-a-half-hour epic in twelve reels. The incredible growth of the movie industry was launched, and the prosperous economy of the United States in the 1920s fostered its growth. But not until 1927 (the same year in which the sixty-two hundred fifty-seat Roxy Theatre, devoted to film, was opened in New York City) did the new medium become a threat to theatre. For it was in October of that year that the first successful "talkie"—Al Jolson in *The Jazz Singer*—was released. That season also marked the high point of production in the eighty first-class legitimate theatres of New York of three hundred two productions. By 1931, the number of professional Broadway houses had shrunk to sixty-six, and the number of houses available to stage plays outside of New York City had declined from fifteen hundred in 1920 to about five hundred in 1930. Of course, the stock market crash had occurred in October of 1929, and this signal economic disaster had the effect of curtailing both the commercial production of plays in New York City and the sending out of road companies, since theatre is, by its nature, an expensive art form. But the movie industry, which had consolidated its gains and equipped houses for sound between 1927 and 1929, could supply entertainment on a widespread basis and at minimum cost. Hollywood never felt the Depression at all, except that many stage performers moved to the West Coast during the 1930s. (By the 1939–1940 season, the number of productions on Broadway had shrunk

to eighty.) In fact, Radio City Music Hall was opened in 1932, in the midst of the Depression. Eventually, however, the popularity of film led theatre people to a rethinking of their own uniqueness, and a considerable change not only in *what* was being presented on stages, but also on *how* it was presented and through what administrative structures. In the long run, these considerations gave the theatre new life.

The commercial, private-enterprise theatres of England and the United States were supplemented outside the metropolitan centers by producing units, largely amateur to begin with, which operated on the principle of creating their own theatre with the talent at hand. The Drama League of America, founded in Evanston, Illinois in 1910, continued, as the pioneer organization of the little theatre movement, to organize play contests, sponsor special performances, and act as a center for the dissemination of information for nonprofessional theatre. In England, the British Drama League was founded in 1919 for the same purposes, with the Scottish Community Drama Association functioning similarly in Scotland. Following the precedent set by Maurice Brown in establishing the Chicago Little Theatre in 1906 to produce plays (in his ninety-one seat house) which were not available in the commercial theatre, Thomas H. Dickinson established the Wisconsin Players in 1911, and Sam Hume (out of George Pierce Baker's 47 Workshop) set up the Detroit Arts and Crafts Theatre in 1916. The year before, Livingston Platt had opened the Boston Toy Theatre, and in the next two decades there would be established the Pasadena Community Playhouse, the Dock Street Theatre in Charleston, the Hedgerow Theatre in Moylan, Pennsylvania (by another 47 Workshop participant, Jasper Deeter), the Théâtre de Vieux Carré in New Orleans, the Goodman Theatre in Chicago, the Cleveland Playhouse, and Little Theatres in Dallas and Omaha. A "civic center" theatre was completed in Kalamazoo, Michigan in 1931, and a similar house in Colorado Springs in 1936. In England, the number of provincial repertory companies was augmented in 1923 by the Oxford Repertory Company, and in 1926 by the Cambridge Festival Theatre. In 1929, Barry Jackson at Birmingham inaugurated the Malvern Theatre Festival which was to become a prototype, and in 1935 his Birmingham Repertory Theatre (first established in 1913) became the first English theatre to be supported by civic funds as a civic activity. Reinhardt had established, in 1929, the Salzburg Festival, giving, in addition to what was to become a world famous outdoor production of *Everyman*, other performances of other plays in the Salzburg Theatre. In France, Firmin Gémier toured the provinces with a tent theatre and a professional company—known as the Théâtre Ambulant—between 1911 and 1914, and persuaded the government to establish the Théâtre Nationale Populaire in 1920, with a token government subsidy. Even in Spain there was a brief period in the early 1930s when Alejandro Casona toured a government sponsored People's Theatre, and Federico Garcia-Lorca did the same.

Colleges and universities—particularly in the United States—contributed to developing theatre studies and performance. The Wisconsin Players (1911) affiliated themselves with the State University; Frederick Koch started the Carolina Playmakers at the University of North Carolina in 1918; Yale University became the second school to offer a complete curriculum in theatre with the opening of the School of Drama in 1925; by 1937 there was sufficient theatre work being done in educational settings to warrant the establishment of the American Educational Theatre Association. By World War II there were some three hundred schools where students could major in theatre studies, and many hundreds more with fewer course offerings. In 1935, the American National Theatre and Academy was authorized by Congress, and, though no funds were appropriated to sustain it, the organization began to function on several levels to stimulate theatrical activity on a nation-wide basis. In 1936, the Academy of Dramatic Art was chartered in Rome for similar purposes but the war shortly stopped its activities. From 1927 to World War II there was also an International Theatre Congress—an outgrowth of the international meetings held occasionally since the first important International Music and Theatre Exposition held in Vienna in 1892.

Many new theatres established

Theatre professionals themselves also began to work widely outside the established state or commercial theatres. Largely they were motivated by interest in new plays and new production methods, although occasionally economic factors persuaded them to operate thus. In Spain, the internationally known playwright Gregorio Martinez Sierra (1881–1947) opened his Teatro Eslava in 1917 to produce the new plays of his European colleagues by the new production methods; he introduced the first plays of Federico Garcia-Lorca to the Spanish public. In Italy, Enrico Prampolini (1894–1936) opened his Teatro Magnetico in Rome in the early 1920s to produce the plays of the futurist dramatists who glorified the machine and espoused the elimination of all stage effects except those which were truly functional, as a machine is functional. In 1925, Luigi Pirandello (1867–1936), Italy's greatest playwright, opened his Teatro Odescalchi to produce his own plays.

In Moscow, experimentation in production methods and the presentation of new materials were effected by the establishment of the "Studios" of the Moscow Art Theatre. The First Studio was opened in 1912 by the innovator, Eugene Vakhtangov (1883–1922). The Second Studio was formed in 1919 under the actor Mchedelov, the Third Studio in 1920 evolving from the First, with Vakhtangov moving to the new organization and Michael Chekhov (1891–1955), nephew of the playwright, remaining as head of the First Studio; the Fourth Studio began in 1921. In 1924, upon Stanislavski's return from an extended foreign tour, all the studios were liquidated. The actors of the Second Studio were absorbed into the main company, whose ranks had been decimated by defections on the tour; the First Studio was officially designated the Second Moscow Art Theatre; the Third officially became the Vakhtangov Theatre; and the Fourth Studio was officially designated (in 1927) the Realistic Theatre. It was at this last that Nikolai Okhlopkov became director in 1932 and served for a few brilliant years as one of the most creative of nonrealistic directors. Besides these offshoots of the Moscow Art Theatre, consistent experimentation was carried on for twenty years, beginning in 1914, by Alexander Taïrov (1885–1950) at the Kamerny Theatre in Moscow, set up for that purpose. In St. Petersburg, renamed Leningrad after the Revolution, experimental productions were sometimes done by Komisarjevsky and Meyerhold, but there was no house devoted to that sole purpose.

In Germany, Max Reinhardt (1873–1943) was, until 1933 (when he left the country), a kind of one-man total experiment. In addition to his chief job as director of the Deutsches and Kammerspiele Theatres in Berlin, he also set up there the Grosses Schauspielhaus, the Redoutensaal in Vienna, and began the Salzburg Festival. Since there was already a system of Volkesbühne and state theatres in Germany, other directors like Jürgen Fehling (1890–1968) and Leopold Jessner (1878–1948) tried out the new techniques in these. Erwin Piscator (1893–1966) founded his Proletarian Theatre in 1920, and developed the theatrical form known as "epic theatre."

In France, the new and largely antiestablishment theatres were inaugurated by a number of men who had, at one time or another, come under the influence of Jacques Copeau, who reopened his own Vieux Colombier when he returned from New York in 1919, continuing its operation until 1924. Louis Jouvet (1887–1951), who had been a member of Copeau's company during its American visit and thereafter, formed his own company in 1924 after the dissolution of Copeau's group and became famous at the Théâtre de l'Athenée in his collaboration with Giraudoux in producing the latter's plays. Another was Charles Dullin (1885–1949), who had his own Théâtre l'Atelier in 1922, then became director at the Théâtre Sarah Bernhardt in 1941. The third director of note in this period was Georges Pitoëff (1884–1939), originally from Russia, who at his Théâtre Mathurins produced principally foreign drama in the new style. All three of these had been actors before becoming directors, and, with Gaston Baty (1882–1951), formed an alliance in 1927 called the Cartel des Quatre for mutual aid and assistance. Baty worked primarily at the Théâtre Montparnasse. Other directors of note who formed companies of their own in the 1930s were Michel Saint-Denis (1897–1972), Copeau's nephew; his son-in-law, Jean Dasté; André Barsacq; and Maurice Jacquemont. Thus Copeau influenced two succeeding generations of French actor-directors; he himself came back to the Comédie in 1936, where he remained until dismissed by the Vichy government in 1941.

England, too, had a spate of producing organizations, inaugurated by actors and directors, which reinvigorated its theatre. Aside from the spread of repertory in the provinces, there were a few production units of note in the capital. The first was that initiated and supervised by Lilian Baylis (1874–1937) at the Old Vic, which from 1914 on gave an enviable series of Shakespearian productions under the direction of Ben Greet. It was at the Old Vic that Tyrone Guthrie (1900–1971) began his notable directing and producing career in 1937, and many other English actors had their start. Nigel Playfair (1874–1934) did a notable series of Restoration and eighteenth-century plays at the Lyric in Hammersmith. The Gate Theatre and the Mercury Theatre were run as private clubs by Peter Godfrey and Ashley Dukes, respectively, doing new works which could not obtain a license from the Lord Chamberlain.

Like Copeau in France and Lilian Baylis in England, it was George Pierce Baker at his Harvard 47 Workshop who inspired a formidable list of playwrights, directors, critics, actors, and designers who rejuvenated the American theatre. Robert Edmond Jones (1887–1954) and Theresa Helburn (d. 1965), at one time members of the Workshop, were instrumental in starting the Washington Square Players in 1914, which became the Theatre Guild in 1919, producing notably the plays of George Bernard Shaw and Eugene O'Neill (another member, for a brief time, of the Workshop). George Abbott, also a Workshop participant, was briefly associated with the Neighborhood Playhouse (begun in 1915 by Alice and Irene Lewisohn), then went on to develop a spectacularly successful career as a director. Though the originators of the Provincetown Playhouse during its first season on the fish wharf (1915) were not Work-

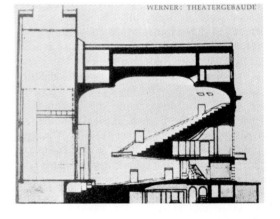

WERNER: THEATERGEBAUDE

shop people, one of their second season's productions was an O'Neill play, and when they opened a fall season in 1916 in a remodeled brownstone at 139 Macdougal Street in New York, some of the Board members were former Workshop people. In the fall of 1918 they moved to a converted stable at 133 Macdougal Street—the building still known as the Provincetown Playhouse, the site of the first performances of *The Emperor Jones*. They were devoted entirely to the production of American playwrights, and be-

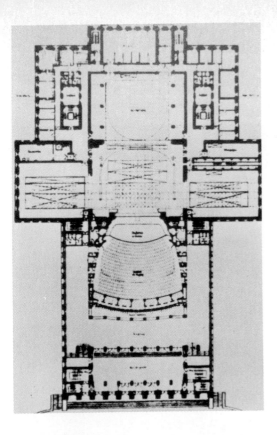

TWO TYPICAL THEATRE PLANS
Left, side view of the Ziegfeld Theatre, New York, built in 1927, showing the small stage space, the great overhanging balcony, and the lack of working space typical of construction in American commercial theatre buildings. Above, plan of the Dessau Landestheater, 1938, showing the typical arrangements of Continental, state-supported theatres, with great stage space and much ancillary space.

---

sides O'Neill, fostered the not inconsiderable talent of Susan Glaspell along with a host of lesser talents. The subsequent success of O'Neill on Broadway and the death of George Cram Cook (an essential "motivator" for the group) in 1924, diminished the effectiveness of the Provincetown Players, but their contribution to the American theatre scene was enormous. From 1926 to 1929, John Howard Lawson (another 47 Workshop member) and John Dos Passos devoted themselves to "radical" plays, chiefly in the expressionistic style, in their New Playwright's Company, first located on West Fifty-second Street, then in Greenwich Village. From 1926 to 1933 Eva Le Gallienne ran the Civic Repertory Theatre, devoted chiefly to the classics, with a policy of low ticket prices and subscriptions, in a house on Fourteenth Street. During the Depression years of the 1930s, several "workers" groups formed theatre producing units. The Theatre of Action first produced Irwin Shaw's *Bury the Dead;* the Theatre Collective first produced Paul Green's *Hymn to the Rising Sun;* the New Theatre League first did Clifford Odets' *Waiting for Lefty;* and the International Ladies' Garment Workers Union, through its Labor Stage, Inc., produced Marc Blitzstein's *Pins and Needles.* The Theatre Union during its four-year life (1932–1937) devoted itself chiefly to new, full-length labor plays, producing the works of George Sklar, Albert Maltz, John Howard Lawson, and others. The Mercury Theatre (1937–1938) grew out of the Federal Theatre Project, chiefly to do works not possible under that aegis. In its short but brilliant career, it produced Marc Blitzstein's *The Cradle Will Rock* (a labor musical), the antifascist, modern dress *Julius Caesar,* Dekker's *Shoemaker's Holiday,* Shaw's *Heartbreak House,* and *Danton's Death.*

But the most important and the longest lasting of these was the Group Theatre, founded in 1931, whose story is told in Harold Clurman's stimulating book, *The Fervent Years.* Inspired chiefly by Stanislavski principles (or their understanding of them), the founders aimed to build a permanent acting company which would revitalize the relationships between actor and author, actor and actor, and actor and society. Over a period of nine years (until 1940), they produced a remarkable series of plays and contributed to the American theatre a whole generation of playwrights, directors, and

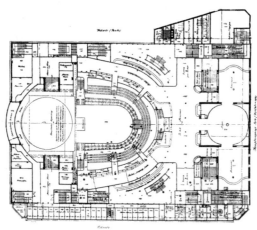

Grundriß des Großen Schauspielhauses
Parkettgeschoß

TWO VERY LARGE THEATRES
Interior (above) and plan of the Grosses
Schauspielhaus, Berlin. This "theatre of the
five thousand," conceived by Max Reinhardt,
combines the features of both the proscenium stage and the platform stage; it has
seats for thirty-five hundred people. The
ceiling treatment is interesting and unique.
Opposite, exterior and plan of the Red Army
Theatre, Moscow. This large theatre seats
over two thousand people, and has a unique
architectural plan, incorporating a vast stage
area in addition to the large number of
seats. (Herold, *Das Grosse Schauspielhaus*;
Architecture de l'USSR, Moscow)

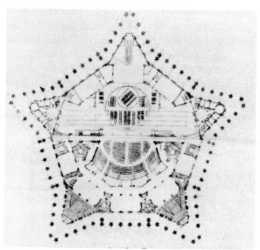

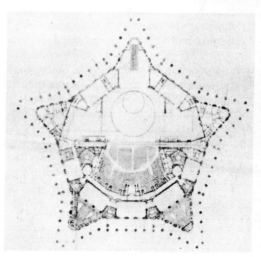

actors, whose names comprise a significant portion of the population of modern American theatre. Finally, in 1938, the playwrights Sidney Howard, S. N. Behrman, Maxwell Anderson, Robert E. Sherwood, and Elmer Rice formed the Playwrights' Company, chiefly a producing venture, to do their own plays. It lasted for many years, later adding John F. Wharton, Roger L. Stevens, and Robert Anderson as partners.

In 1919 the first Negro theatre was organized in Harlem: the Lafayette Players. Then in 1928 the Harlem Experimental Theatre came into being, and the next year the Negro Art Theatre. In 1935 Rose McClendon opened the Negro People's Theatre, and in 1938 Langston Hughes formed the Harlem Suitcase Theatre. This significant activity was consummated in 1940 with the famous Negro Playwrights Company which functioned for three years on Broadway, offering notably Paul Robeson in *Othello*.

In 1941, Antoinette Perry began the Experimental Theatre of the Dramatists Guild; in 1944 Sam Jaffe and George Freedley persuaded Actors' Equity to initiate the Equity Library Theatre, which is still a functioning unit; and in 1945–1946, Eva Le Gallienne (along with Margaret Webster and Cheryl Crawford) had another try as the American Repertory Theatre. And all this while, of course, commercial producing in the regular Broadway houses was going on, just as it was in the West End theatres of London, the Comédie Française and boulevard theatres in Paris, and in the state theatres of Germany and Russia. What all this activity meant, of course, was that theatre in the Western world was broadening its base, was successfully meeting the challenge of the movies, and was showing a renewed inerest in being the mirror of the times which produced it.

Playwriting gains literary respectability

Some conception of the prodigious amount of playwriting going on in this period may be formed by noting the fact that of the three hundred two productions mounted on Broadway during the 1927–1928 season, two hundred were new plays. That not many of these would live is perfectly true; but then that statement might be made of any theatrical season anywhere at any time. One need only remember the wide stretches of the nineteenth century, when hundreds of theatres were offering thousands of performances to hundreds of thousands of people, and then ask how many of those productions were based on scripts which had such lasting value that they became a part of the significant dramatic literature of the culture. What was apparent, however, in the decades under consideration, is that several people of real genius were writing plays, and many people of considerable talent, so that the literary respectability of playwriting (so largely in doubt during most of the nineteenth century) was now unquestioned. What this fact means, of course, is that by the early years of the twentieth century there were audiences of sufficient size and number, well enough educated, to receive and applaud plays with significant philosophical and literary content. The advent of the movies—fortunately for theatre—siphoned off to the new medium with its mass audience those tailored farce-comedies, melodramas, romances, and period pieces which had bulked so large on theatre stages in pre-movie days.

Though stage melodramas, farces, and domestic comedies continued to be produced in large numbers, and though the period saw the development of the musical show as a particular variety of romance, comedy in general became more topical and outspoken,

THEATRE INTERIOR FOR "THE MIRACLE"
Two sketches by Norman Bel Geddes for
Reinhardt's production of *The Miracle* (1924)
for which the interior of the Century Theatre
in New York was transformed to the likeness of a cathedral, except that the theatre
seats remained in place for the audience,
visible at the bottom of the sketches.

more realistic, rising even to the comedy of
manners in the works of Noel Coward,
Terence Rattigan, S. N. Behrman, and Philip
Barry. The themes of the realists were drawn
from the social, ethical, political, and moral
revolution which followed World War I and
from the interest in psychology generated by
the writings of Freud. All of these themes
were also exploited by the theatrical forms
of symbolism, expressionism, surrealism, and
epic theatre, and there was even a spate of
poetic plays. The three outstanding makers
of modern thought—Darwin, Marx, and Freud
—found expression in a variety of theatrical
forms. The Darwinian emphasis upon the
physical and social environment and the survival of the fittest, the Marxian emphasis
upon the historical imperative and the struggle between the haves and have-nots, the
Freudian emphasis upon the subjugation of
the individual to his inner drives of the
libido and the ego so fragmented man's
view of his world that the theatre, being the
reflection of that world, contained a wider
variety than ever before of materials, means,
and effects. The best plays of the best playwrights struggled with these modes of
thought in the effort to give man a meaning-

ful image of himself. The first (Darwinism)
continued in the long list of Shaw's Ibsen-
influenced "idea plays"; the second (Marxism) in the proletarian dramas of the 1930s
and the epic theatre of Brecht; the third
(Freudianism) chiefly in expressionism and
its variant forms, like the plays of Pirandello,
and the realistic "psychological dramas" of
O'Neill. To the present view it would appear
that not since the eighteenth century have so
many plays of lasting value been written, but
modern criticism may yet be too close in time
to make such a judgment.

Significant experimentation in Germany

During the time of World War I and the
period of the 1920s, no national theatre was
so innovative as that of Germany. Not only
were the eclectic presentations of Reinhardt
startling and pleasing wide audiences, but also
the experimental techniques in production of
Jessner, Fehling, and Piscator were calling attention to the viability of nonrealistic theatre.
It was also in Germany that literary expressionism reached its most widespread practice
and perhaps its most memorable plays. Stimu-

TWO RUSSIAN THEATRE INTERIORS
Above, the Realistic Theatre, Moscow, which Okhlopkov transformed when he took it over in 1932, arranging the space so that the performance surrounded the audience and encompassed them. Right, the interior of the Meyerhold Theatre, Moscow, c. 1934, designed from his conviction that curtains, lights, and realistic scenery were outmoded in modern theatre.

lated by the controversial and grotesque plays of Wedekind, and inspired by the pacifist and anticapitalist mood engendered by the war, young playwrights spoke their views in a series of antirealistic plays which came to be called "expressionist," a mode defined by one of its practitioners, Herworth Walden, as "an attempt to give by means of concentration and intensity in word, sound, color, and movement a material abstraction of reality, and in a manner that violently excites the playgoer" (as paraphrased by Huntly Carter, *The New Spirit in the European Theatre*, 1914–1924, p. 222). In other words, it is a movement which is at the opposite pole from realism, extracting from a given situation and set of characters only the essential emotional content, and projecting this in deliberately theatrical and nonrealistic terms. George Kaiser (1878–1945) and Ernst Toller (1893–1939) are the chief exponents of the style and the material. The former, an exceedingly prolific writer, with more than forty plays to his credit, most of them in the expressionistic style, is best known for *From Morn to Midnight* (1916) which satirizes through the person of a bank clerk, whose bid for freedom ends in his suicide, the robot-like men who are caught in the meshes of modern industrial society; and the powerful *Gas I* and *Gas II* (1918–1920) in which the whole industrial society crashes to destruction. Toller's first play, *Change* (1918), written while he was imprisoned for pacifist activities, is a plea for the abolition of war; *The Machine Wreckers* (1922) is based on the Luddite riots of 1815; but his most famous play is *Man and the Masses* (1921), in which Sonia Irene (as described by Toller himself) projects through a dream medium "her horror of capitalistic control, of proletarian warfare, and her pity for its victims." Several other German dramatists produced expressionist plays: those of

Reinhard, Sorge, Walter Hasenclever, and Karl Sternheim preceded the major works of Kaiser and Toller; those of Fritz von Unruh, Paul Kornfeld, and Reinhard Goering appeared at about the same time, and those of Hans Chlumberg followed.

Germany's major playwright of the twentieth century, Bertolt Brecht (1898–1956), had also been a part of the expressionist movement. Two of his early plays, *Baal* (1918) and *Drums in the Night* (1919), are in this style. The essence of the expressionist credo—the theatrical presentation of inner states—used a technique of many scenes which were often dissociated and dreamlike in quality (the heritage from Strindberg). The epic theatre form, which is associated most closely with Brecht, eliminated the subjectivity of expressionism, but used its form of many, often dissociated, scenes. Disillusioned with Freudian exploration of the psyche and coming more and more to believe that the Marxian dialectic was the inevitable hope of man, Brecht turned to a "social" theatre which forbade the exploration of the inside of the head, and set out to make his audiences *think* instead of *feel*. His first venture of the kind was *A Man's a Man* (1924), a vaudeville-like antiwar play where sympathy and empathy for the antihero, Gayley Gay, are effectively strangled by the episodic structure, the interpolation of songs, the constant disruption by attention to mechanics of staging, the puppet-like conception of the characters. The effect Brecht was striving for was to send his audience out to act on the ideas presented. The technique sharpened after his first great theatrical success—his adaptation of *The Beggar's Opera* as *The Three-Penny Opera* (1928) with music by Kurt Weill, which ran for four hundred performances, but which is not typically epic theatre. In 1931 he used the cinematic techniques of Piscator's experimental productions in *The Ex-*

pedient to propound a justification for a revolutionary course of action. During his exile from Germany (1933–1947), he wrote those thesis plays for which he became famous: *The Private Life of the Master Race* (1935), *Mother Courage* (1937), *Galileo* (1939), *The Good Woman of Setzuan* (1940), *The Resistible Rise of Arturo Ui*, a satire on Hitler (1941), and *The Caucasian Chalk Circle* (1945). In explaining what he meant by *verfremdungseffekt* (inadequately translated as "alienation effect") Brecht said that his epic theatre was the opposite of the "dramatic" theatre; in epic theatre the stage *narrates* the sequence rather than representing it, thus making the spectator an observer rather than a participant, so that his energies are awakened, decisions are demanded of him, and insights developed. Brecht, being a poet as well as a playwright, does not always maintain the detachment he aimed for, but the body of his work has made him the most significant German writer for the theatre since Hauptmann.

German expressionism also produced Franz Werfel's *Goat Song* (1921) and two important plays from Czechoslovakia: Karel Čapek's *R.U.R.* (*Rossum's Universal Robots*) with its devastating attack on mechanization, and *The Insect Comedy* (1921) which he wrote in collaboration with his brother Josef. Other middle European writers of note were the Polish surrealist S. Witkiewicz, and the Germans Carl Zuckmayer, Friedrich Wolf, and Ferdinand Bruckner. The triumph of the Third Reich in 1933 led to a widespread emigration of many writers and theatre workers; those who remained turned largely to the writing and production of ultimately insignificant patriotic dramas and pageants. The most widely innovative and creative theatre of the early part of the twentieth century was stilled by a political opportunist who went mad with power.

New forms in Italy, Spain, and Russia

Surprisingly, after centuries of some good but hardly ever great playwriting, Italy produced in Luigi Pirandello (1867–1936) a truly seminal genius whose influence has expanded continuously since his death. The way had been prepared for him by the disillusionment and pessimism of the "Theatre of the Grotesque" school of writers which included Luigi Chiarelli, Luigi Antonelli, and Rossi di San Secondo—which, because of the war and succeeding fascism, had replaced the optimism of the Futurists and the romanticism of D'Annunzio. Turning from novel writing to the theatre during the days of World War I, Pirandello brought to the theatre a consideration of the same problem which he had been exploring in his novels—the nature of reality and of human personality conceived as an aggregate of conflicting and shifting selves. He is expressionist in theme (the exploration of subjective states) and in form (episodic, often unstructured, and lacking a final resolution), but realistic in mode (real people in real settings speaking understandable language); the genre is best called "tragicomedy." Calling himself "a philosophical writer" he explains in his preface to *Six Characters in Search of an Author* (1921) that his "maidservant," Fantasy,

amuses herself by bringing to my house—
since I derive stories and novels and
plays from them—the most disgruntled
tribe in the world, men, women, children,
involved in strange adventures which they
can find no way out of; thwarted in
their plans; cheated by their hopes; with
whom, in short, it is often torture to deal.

In addition to *Six Characters*, which is perhaps the most famous of his plays, the most frequently performed are: *Right You Are— If You Think You Are* (1915), *Henry IV*

REALISM
Norman Bel Geddes' design for *Dead End* (1935) by Sidney Kingsley, in which tenements crowding a run-down river pier are made as factual as possible.

(1922), *Each in His Own Way* (1924), *Tonight We Improvise* (1930), and *As You Desire Me* (1930). "I see life as a tragedy," he said, and "I have tried to tell something to other men, without any ambition, except perhaps that of avenging myself for having been born." It is a statement like that, as embodied in his work, which made him the precursor of the "absurdist" school of modern playwrights. He was awarded the Nobel Prize in 1934.

The Spanish Nobel Prize winner (1922), Jacinto Benavente (1886–1954), was past his prime as a dramatist by the time he won the prize, but his "theatre of ideas," along with the more romantic plays of Gregorio Martinez Sierra and Joaquin and Alvarez Quin-

tero, continued to dominate the Spanish stage. With the exception of a few plays of novelist Ramon del Valle-Inclan, the most potent contribution to Spanish theatre was by Federico Garcia-Lorca (1899–1936). Rebelling against foreign influence in the theatre, and inspired by his involvement with a traveling troupe of university students, he wrote a small body of plays which have achieved world renown. They are all poetic, deeply imbued with the feeling and texture of Spanish mores and society, and impassioned in expression. The most notable are *The Shoemaker's Prodigious Wife* (1930), *Blood Wedding* (1933), *Yerma* (1934), and *The House of Bernarda Alba* (1935). His death in the Spanish Civil War robbed the world of a more-than-promising playwright, and Spain of a career which bid fair to rival those of its Golden Age.

Revolution in Russia had the initial effect of stimulating playwriting as well as innovative production techniques. Since the Soviet hierarchy regarded the theatre as a collectivist art, they fostered its growth. The preservation of the traditional drama was accompanied by the creation of the new. Taking their name from the earlier Italian school of writers, the Futurists, believing firmly in the Revolution, called for a revolution in the art of theatre as well. Outstanding among these was Mayakovski, who wrote the first important new play of the Soviet regime, called *Mystery Bouffe* (1918), a mock-heroic travesty subtitled "An Heroic, Epic, and Satiric Representation of Our Epoch." He went on to write *The Bedbug* (1929) and *The Bath* (1930), both praising the new regime. Anatol Lunacharsky, as People's Commissar of Education, not only encouraged a rereading of the past in the light of the present, but wrote several plays in this reinterpretive style: *Faust and the City, Oliver Cromwell, The Emancipated Don Quixote,* and *Napoleon Intervenes.* Glorification of the new regime appeared in the work of many other dramatists: Ivanov's *Armored Train 14–89* (1927), Kirshon's *Bread* (1931), Pogodin's *The Poem of the Ax* (1931), and many others. The early days were unique in tolerating such a play as Bulkagov's *In the Days of the Turbins* (1925), which showed some sympathy for the White Guard, and Katayev's comedy, *Squaring the Circle* (1928), which amusingly presented the individual's problems when confronted with Soviet rules and regulations. As Stalinism tightened its hold, however, the creed of the Soviet theatres was handed down to be new socialist realism. Mayakovski committed suicide; Meyerhold, the great

innovator in staging, disappeared; and playwrights wrote to the prescription of the state, which outlawed romantic love and the inner conflicts of human beings and glorified collectivism, the machine, and its own supremacy.

New playwrights in France and England

Though there was no political revolution in France following World War I, the unsettled and unsettling times are reflected in the wide variety of dramatic writing which marks the period. There was a continuation of the "light entertainments" preoccupied with the "eternal triangle," notably in the plays of Sacha Guitry and Georges Feydeau, of Louis Verneuil and Jacques Deval. Equally popular were the plays of Marcel Achard, Armand Salacrou, and Marcel Pagnol. There was a resurgence of religious drama in the plays of Léon Chancerel and Henri Ghéon, along with productions of the earlier-written plays of Paul Claudel and Paul Demassey. Expressionism in France produced particularly the plays of Henri-René Lenormand (1882–1951) wherein he explores the subconscious, notably in *Time Is a Dream* (1919), *The Dream Doctor*

TWO FAMOUS PLAYS
Left, the final scene of O'Neill's *Mourning Becomes Electra* (1931) as designed by Robert Edmond Jones, and above, the final scene of Thornton Wilder's *Our Town* (1938), which dispensed with settings entirely. (Theatre Collection, New York Public Library)

(1922), *Man and His Phantoms* (1924), and *The Coward* (1925). At one point in his career critics dubbed him "the Eugene O'Neill of the French stage," but his vision was not so wide as that of the great American. Fernand Crommelynck (*The Magnificent Cuckold*, 1921) and Jules Romains (*Donogoo*, 1926, employing film effects, and *Dr. Knock*, 1925, a harsh satire) were others who worked in the expressionist style. By 1924, the French had adopted the word "surrealism," applying it to painters as well as writers who had the positive intent of governing the entire content and creative principle of a work of art by the workings of the subconscious mind. The term had first been used by Guillaume Apollinaire (1880–1918) to explain what he was doing in his 1903 play, *The Breasts of Tiresias*, which was revised and produced in 1917. He said surrealism was a new kind of "imitation of nature," such as "When man wanted to imitate the action of walking, he created the wheel, which does not resemble a leg. He has thus used surrealism without knowing it." Roger Vitrac and Raymond Roussel, working in the 1920s, have also been called surrealists. But the most famous is Jean Cocteau (1892–1963), whose movie, *Beauty and the Beast*, is the best

permanent record of the surrealist style. His earliest theatrical work was a cubist fantasy for the Ballet Russe called *Parade* (1917). which was followed by a pantomime for circus clowns, *The Ox on the Roof* (1920). The next year came *The Married Couple of the Eiffel Tower*, a surrealist fantasy in which all the dialogue was spoken by phonographs. In 1922 he produced his *Antigone*, with scenery by Picasso, music by Honegger, and masks by himself. In 1926 came *Orpheus* which he intended should "work on people like music." In *The Infernal Machine* (1934) and *The Terrible Parents* (1938), he again mined the classic materials with startling results. Though Cocteau has sometimes been accused of striving for effect simply for the sake of effect, his work at its best has all the power and strength of a waking dream.

Cocteau's preoccupation with classic materials (in spite of his declared surrealism) is a typically French preoccupation. No national group has so consistently reworked the classics as have the French. In fact, the most prestigious of modern French playwrights, Jean Giraudoux (1882–1944), built the largest part of his considerable reputation on his novel reinterpretations of ancient stories: *Amphitryon 38* (1929) in which the Lunts

starred, *The Trojan War Will Not Take Place*
(1935) which was a starring vehicle for
Michael Redgrave, and *Electre* (1935)—all
"language" plays largely written under the
influence of Copeau, to whom the language
and the playwright were the most important
elements in the theatre. In addition, Giraudoux used legend of another kind in *Judith*
(1931), the haunting *Ondine* (1939), and the
fantasy-drama *The Madwoman of Chaillot*
(1945). In all of these the language is paramount, the action moves by the language—
and beautiful language it is. Similarly inspired was the lesser talent of André Obey in
Noah (1931) and *The Rape of Lucrèce* (1931).

Finally, the Belgian, Michel de Ghelde-
rode (1898–1962), in a series of tragicomedies
episodic in form and bitter in mood, echoed
Pirandello in his mourning for lost faith and
his conviction that "particularly in our time,
the Innocents must be slaughtered: that has
been the law since the time of Jesus";
Escurial (1927), *Chronicles of Hell* (1929),
Pantagleize (1929), and *Hop, Signor* (1938)
are his most significant and well-known plays.

No such experimentation and variety
were evident in the English theatre. The
English public and playwrights remained almost exclusively wedded to realistic theatre
and "idea plays." Part of the reason for this
devotion, of course, was the tremendous
reputation and the equally amazing output of
George Bernard Shaw, who continued to his
death in 1950 to write incisive and interesting plays for the British and American stage.
Heartbreak House (1919) was premiered in
America by the Theatre Guild. Twenty more
plays were written before his death, notably
Back to Methuselah (1920), *Saint Joan* (1923),
The Apple Cart (1929), *Too True to Be Good*
(1931), *The Millionairess* (1935), and *In Good
King Charles's Golden Days* (1939). Shaw has,
perhaps, been the only British playwright to
rival Shakespeare in the last three hundred

years—an opinion of which he would
approve!

Following in the footsteps of Galsworthy
in being both novelist and playwright were
Somerset Maugham (1874–1965) and J. B.
Priestley, the first of whom wrote a series
of delightful social comedies like *The Constant Wife* (1927) in which Katharine Cornell
starred in America, while Priestley is mostly
noted for more serious plays like *Dangerous
Corner* (1932). The poet W. H. Auden collaborated with Christopher Isherwood on *The
Dog Beneath the Skin* (1935) and *The Ascent
of F6* (1936) in an attempt to bring poetry
back into the theatre; and T. S. Eliot wrote
Murder in the Cathedral (1935) for perfor-

AMERICAN DESIGNERS FOR AMERICAN PLAYS
Left, Jones's design for *Desire Under the Elms*. The siding of the house can be removed in sections to reveal interior scenes. Above, Jo Mielziner's design for *Winterset*. Both of these designs are excellent examples of the principle that the play is interpreted by the décor no less than by the actors. (Theatre Collection, New York Public Library)

mance at Canterbury, and *The Family Reunion* (1939). Poet laureate John Masefield and A. A. Milne also tried the poetic form in theatre, as did John Drinkwater (most famous for his prose drama, *Abraham Lincoln*, 1919) but the effort would have little success until after World War II—and little even then.

Comedy thrived—as usual—on the English stage, most notably in the witty and sophisticated plays of Frederick Lonsdale (like *The Last of Mrs. Cheyney*, 1925), Noel Coward (*Hay Fever*, 1925 and *Private Lives*, 1930), and Terence Rattigan (*French Without Tears*, 1935). Emlyn Williams titillated audiences first with melodramas like *Night Must*

Fall (1935), and then with the sentimental *The Corn Is Green* (1938). Even the war did not become a subject for the drama until 1928, when R. C. Sherriff's *Journey's End* and *Wings over Europe* by Robert Nichols and Maurice Brown were produced. Regional characters and themes were used in realistic plays by Dodie Smith, James Bridie, and notably Sean O'Casey (1884–1964) whose first play, *Shadow of a Gunman* (1922), heralded a new ironic viewpoint on cherished Irish beliefs. He followed this with *Juno and the Paycock* (1924) and *The Plough and the Stars* (1926), both viewing in realistic tragicomedy the lives of the Dublin lower class. Then, at last, in 1928, O'Casey injected the long-exiled expressionism into English letters in *The Silver Tassie*, with its phantasmagoria of the horrors of modern warfare, and followed up the strain in 1934 with *Within the Gates*, with its chorus of Down-and-Outs and its figure of the Dreamer. J. B. Priestley, then, surprisingly, wrote the expressionistic *Music at Night* (1938) and *Johnson over Jordan* (1939), but with a few other exceptions, the new wave of theatrical statement had little effect in England.

American playwriting comes of age

In the United States, on the other hand, expressionism influenced the major dramatist who marked the "coming of age" of American theatre—Eugene O'Neill (1883–1953) was so influenced early in his career, though not to the exclusion of other modes. In fact, the dramatic *oeuvre* of O'Neill stands as a paradigm of the eclectic influences characteristic of American theatre. His trenchant initial series of one-act plays were naturalistic in content and form, as was his first Broadway production, *Beyond the Horizon* (1920). Immediately he was hailed as the great naturalist genius of America. But concurrently he was working on the expressionistic *Emperor Jones* which was produced at the Provincetown Playhouse late in 1920 and subsequently moved uptown. *Anna Christie* (naturalistic) was produced in 1921 with Pauline Lord in the title role, and the next year came another expressionistic play, *The Hairy Ape*, with Louis Wolheim. So he alternated, never settling into a single style: *Desire Under the Elms* (1924, and all naturalistic), *The Great God Brown* (1926, symbolism and with masks), *Marco Millions* (1927, epic but realistic satire), *Strange Interlude* (1928, with unrealistic asides), *Dynamo* (1929, realistic), *Mourning Becomes Electra* (1931, a New England apotheosis of Greek legend),

Ah! Wilderness (1931, straight realistic comedy), and *Days Without End* (1934, expressionistic). In 1936 he received the Nobel Prize. No wonder, for his restless genius had explored, with searching penetration, not only the "relation of man to God"—which he once said was his primary concern—but also the relation of man to man and man to his world, of man's effort to find a meaning in his existence and a belief to which to commit himself. It was a large vision that O'Neill brought to the American theatre; although his skills in language were sometimes not commensurate with his concepts, his dramatic imagination was larger than any which had heretofore grown on American soil.

In a more minor way, this ability to use more than one dramatic style is evident in Elmer Rice (1892–1967) who, among other works, produced the apotheosis and paradigm of expressionism (*The Adding Machine*, 1923) on the one hand, and an equally effective and landmark naturalistic work, *Street Scene* (1929), on the other. George S. Kaufman (1889–1961) could write a paradigm of realistic comedy with Moss Hart (*You Can't Take It with You*, 1936) and a biting expressionistic criticism of capitalism with Marc Connelly, *Beggar on Horseback* (1924). Paul Green could write a realistic *The No 'Count Boy* (1924) and the expressionistic antiwar *Johnny Johnson* (1936). Expressionism was the mode also of Irwin Shaw (*Bury the Dead*, 1936), John Dos Passos (*The Moon Is a Gong*, 1925), John Howard Lawson (*Processional*, 1925 and *Marching Song*, 1937), and Sophie Treadwell (*Machinal*, 1928), among many others who were influenced by this antirealistic mode.

The chief rival in fecundity and reputation to O'Neill was Maxwell Anderson (1888–1959), whose first success was the war story told in naturalistic tones, *What Price Glory?* (1924), written in collaboration with

Laurence Stallings. Six plays later, in 1930,
the Theatre Guild produced his verse drama
Elizabeth the Queen with the Lunts, which
started him on a series of verse plays including *Mary of Scotland* (1933, starring Helen
Hayes), *Winterset* (1935, on the Sacco-Vanzetti
case), and *The Wingless Victory,* which won
the Drama Critics' Award in 1936, and starred
Katharine Cornell. Before the end of World
War II twelve more of his plays had been
produced, including the abrasive *Key Largo*
(1939) and the delightful play with music by
Kurt Weill, *Knickerbocker Holiday* (1938). In
1942, he would say (in *The Basis of Artistic
Creation*), "the theatre at its best is a
religious affirmation, restating and reassuring
man's belief in his own destiny and his
ultimate hope." Though the future may
charge Anderson with a certain facile ease
and lack of depth, he was a very influential
and admired writer during his lifetime.

American comedy of manners spoke in
largely realistic and often admonitory tones
in the more than a dozen plays which each

of the following wrote: George Kelly, whose
Craig's Wife, 1925, won a Pulitzer Prize; S. N.
Behrman, in whose plays the Lunts more than
once starred; and Philip Barry, in whose
Philadelphia Story (1939) Katharine Hepburn
made her mark on Broadway. Other less
prolific writers of the comedy of manners
included John Van Druten, Susan Glaspell,
Samson Raphaelson, Rose Franken, and Howard Lindsay and Russel Crouse. It was a
genre which pleased the increasingly sophisticated theatregoers, although it made few
demands on either intelligence or commitment.

Farce and melodrama were also popular,
and in both forms refinements in wit and in
style brought many of the productions to a
comparatively high order of excellence.
Among the best of the former were John
Cecil Holm's *Three Men on a Horse* (1935)
with its inimitable greeting card salesman,
and Sam and Bella Spewack's enduring
spoof of Hollywood, *Boy Meets Girl* (1935).
Among the many melodramas those thought

best are Ben Hecht and Charles MacArthur's *The Front Page* (1928), Edward Chodorov's *Kind Lady* (1935), and Joseph Kesselring's *Arsenic and Old Lace* (1941).

Another type of "light entertainment" brought to a high point of effectiveness during this period was the unique American musical comedy. In the 1920s, Florenz Ziegfeld had done a series of *Follies*, with music, dance, and spectacle; George White had done a *Scandals* with the same ingredients; and the Marx Brothers had appeared in *The Coconuts* (1925). Then, in 1927, Jerome Kern and Oscar Hammerstein offered *Showboat*, with a coherent story, recognizable characters, and well-integrated musical numbers. From then on, the American musical comedy (perhaps the only native form) had many adherents and practitioners. Hardly a season

has passed from that day to this without at least one new musical being presented, and often more than that. Surely the best of all musical satires ever written on American politics is *Of Thee I Sing* (1931), a collaboration among George S. Kaufman, Morrie Ryskind, and George and Ira Gershwin. And everyone still seems to agree that *Oklahoma!* (1943), prepared for the musical stage by Richard Rodgers and Oscar Hammerstein from Lynn Riggs' earlier play, *Green Grow the Lilacs* (1931), marked a high point.

Plays using regional characteristics—always present from the beginning in American theatre—also flourished; from Hatcher Hughes' Pulitzer Prize *Hell Bent fer Heaven* (1924), through Marc Connelly's *The Green Pastures* (1930), to Richardson and Berney's *Dark of the Moon* (1945), this type of play

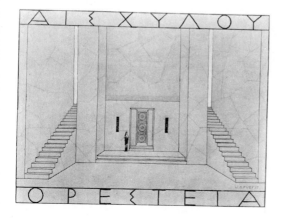

UNIT SETTINGS WITH CHANGING ELEMENTS
Left, Lee Simonson's design for *Marco Millions*. The large architectural forms remain constant throughout the play; the inserts change for the various scenes. Above, René Fuerst's design for *The Oresteia*. This set operates on the same principle as the other; but here changes are made within the central arch only. (Theatre Collection, New York Public Library; Mme. Fuerst)

used realism as well as fantasy to bring to the stage American types of characters.

More serious, and perhaps ultimately more significant, was the work of Sidney Howard (1891–1939), whose best plays are considered to be his ironic comedies: *They Knew What They Wanted* (1924) and *Yellow Jack* (1934), the latter about the fight to control yellow fever. Robert Sherwood (1896–1955) also commanded respect for his insights concerning society in *The Petrified Forest* (1935), *Abe Lincoln in Illinois* (1938), *Idiot's Delight* (1936), and *There Shall Be No Night* (1940). Sidney Kingsley with *Men in White* (1933, concerning problems in the medical profession) and *Dead End* (1935, concerning the effect of slum life on children) commanded respect, as did Lillian Hellman's plea for tolerance in *The Children's Hour*

(1934) and her exposure of a nest of vipers in *The Little Foxes* (1938). The "proletarian plays" of Clifford Odets chronicled the stories of frustrated little people in naturalistic terms: *Waiting for Lefty* (1935), *Awake and Sing* (1935), *Paradise Lost* (1935), *Golden Boy* (1937), *Rocket to the Moon* (1938), and *Clash by Night* (1941), and marked him as one of the most able of the new writers. Perhaps the most innovative—and certainly one of the most serene—of the new playwrights was Thornton Wilder who, in *Our Town* (1938) and *The Skin of Our Teeth* (1942), easily contained the past, the present, and the hereafter, and voiced in frankly theatrical terms his confidence in the durability and ultimate victory of the human race. These, with the sizable list of his shorter plays and a few other long ones, make him one of the most interesting of modern American playwrights. It remains to mention William Saroyan, poet of desperation, who sings of the joys of life in opposition to the threat of death in such plays as *The Time of Your Life* (1939), *My Heart's in the Highlands* (1939), and *The Beautiful People* (1941), to demonstrate that American playwriting from World War I through World War II had indeed, in quantity, in quality, and in kind, arrived at a level which assured its prominence on the world scene.

Theatres, theatres everywhere

As might be expected, the renewed theater interest and activity occasioned a tremendous spurt of playhouse building. In the United States, the prosperous years of the 1920s further spurred such activities. From 1917 to 1928, two dozen new theatre buildings were erected in New York City alone; by 1928 there were eighty "legitimate" houses in that theatrical center. But the ensuing Depression and the increasing popu-

larity of film effectively halted all theatre construction. Several extant houses were turned over to film showings; by 1945 there were only thirty-six theatres in the theatre capital offering "legitimate drama." The same year there were but two hundred houses outside of New York as compared with the five thousand that had been in operation at the turn of the century. But the decade of the 1930s also witnessed the construction of a number of notable community or civic theatres and college and university theatres, as well as the continuation of numerous other "little theatres" which had begun earlier (many of which took over dark commercial houses). What was happening was the beginning of the decentralization of American theatre from New York, and a change in its nature which would become very clear in the years after World War II.

Even in England, where the years of the 1920s were not so prosperous as in America, more than a dozen new theatres were built in London and a few in the provinces, where also the newly forming provincial repertory companies sometimes established themselves in disused commercial houses. Several of the London theatres were turned over to cinema, but not in as great numbers as was true in New York City. On the Continent, where theatre production has never been so totally a commercial venture as it has been in England and America, the fluctuations in the building and abandonment of theatres were

EXPRESSIONISM
Left, Otto Reigbert's design for Brecht's expressionist play, *Drums in the Night* (1919). The effort to "make the décor act" is apparent here. Above, Mordecai Gorelik's design for John Howard Lawson's *Processional* (1925), an American version of expressionism.

not so marked, although during the days of the Third Reich in Germany the existing theatres were augmented by a unique production style for frankly propagandistic purposes. These were the so-called *Thingstatten*, which were spacious natural sites of hilly slopes or ancient ruins used as staging areas for massed choral presentations or pageant-like productions. In Russia by the beginning of World War II, there were about a thousand theatres for "legitimate drama" plus additional ones for children's theatre and amateur groups. The Soviet hierarchy after the Revolution had embarked on a deliberate policy of developing indigenous theatres in all of the republics, sending out theatre workers from Moscow and Leningrad

to aid in the process, and often bringing provincial troupes to the capital to play. It even organized and sent out a Traveling Arctic Theatre in 1935 to perform in the frozen north. Several of the theatres had, of course, been in existence in the big cities before the Revolution and, with some attention to repertory and management, were allowed to continue. The Moscow Art Theatre, the Maly, and the three main houses in Leningrad are examples. But most of the post-Revolutionary theatres were founded and organized by the People's Commissar of Finance and bore such names as Theatre of the Revolution, Realistic Theatre, Red Army Theatre, Trades Union Theatre—all very proletarian titles. The Red Army Theatre, Mos-

cow, opened in 1940, is an extravagant example of the lavish building program.

The hiatus in theatre construction caused by the Depression and the ensuing world war was, in the long run, probably healthy, for it gave an opportunity for aesthetic ideas to crystallize and for structures more nearly approximating new theatre necessities to be developed. The dozens of new theatres which had been erected in London and New York were frankly commercial ventures, dictated in form more by economics than aesthetics—namely, how to get the optimum number of paying audience-members into the smallest amount of space without too many complaints that many of them could not see or hear the performance. So the urban playhouses in these metropolitan centers were generally of the pattern of the Ziegfeld Theatre in New York built in 1927, where steel and cantilever construction allowed a tremendous balcony overhang. The concept is that of two amphitheatres, one above the other, the top one having seats at a steeper slope or rake than the bottom one, so that the patrons at the rear of the balcony could see the stage. In this arrangement, there are no side-boxes, and the shelf-like balcony does not extend as the old boxes did to the proscenium frame. Thus there are wide expanses of bare wall space, which architects treated by various decorative devices. Joseph Urban decorated the interior of the Ziegfeld; Komisarjevsky did the interior of the Phoenix in London. The elimination of boxes made for more democratic seating arrangements, as had Wagner's plan in the Festspielhaus, but the large overhang of the balconies destroyed whatever feeling of community might have been engendered by the Festspielhaus plan because orchestra floor patrons and balcony patrons were effectively cut off even from sight of each other. The stage areas were no larger than necessary to mount a produc-

CONSTRUCTIVIST STAGE SETTINGS
Above, Exter setting for *The Merchant of Venice.* Though there are few painted flats in this set, the arrangement of the structural forms gives a feeling of time and place and offers many interesting possibilities for the movement of the actors. Right, Kurt Söhnlein's setting for *Orpheus in the Underworld.* The repetition of the curved line with strong perpendiculars makes for a completely unrealistic, but interesting, setting. (Kurt Söhnlein)

tion (the set was built elsewhere in such a fashion that it could be easily moved from one theatre to another). The form of the playhouse and its stage tended to favor single-set productions since there was little space for handling scenery. The new stagecraft, therefore, tended to concentrate on unit or multiple settings, and a minimum number of set pieces augmented by increasingly sophisticated lighting schemes.

Continental theatres, though, which were largely devoted to repertory and permanent theatre companies, were much more elaborate and intricate houses. Not so limited by economics and the necessity of portability in scenery, the stagehouses were often larger than the audience spaces and equipped with revolving stages, wagon stages, and much ancillary space in the form of scene shops, electrical shops, machine rooms, etc. German and Russian theatres especially, tended to develop into such "factories." The seating plan of the Festspielhaus was the general pattern, with no great overhanging balconies as in the commercial houses of England and

America. Audience spaces in lobbies and salons were usually provided for, in contra-distinction to the "commercial" houses where these were inclined to be very small or non-existent, like the typical Broadway house of today where audiences at intermission are forced to spill out onto the sidewalks.

Experimentation in theatre architecture

More experimentation in architecture was done in Germany and in Russia than in England and the United States. Max Reinhardt, in an attempt to erase the inviolable line of the proscenium arch from theatre production, created the Grosses Schauspielhaus with a tremendous acting area surrounded on three sides by audience, and a fully equipped proscenium stage intended for use primarily as background to the action. Called the "Theatre of the Five Thousand" and opened in 1919, it proved impractical for any but the largest kind of production. (Actually, it seated about thirty-five hundred.) The attempt was made to give smaller productions on the stage itself, putting seats on the great thrust stage, but then the sight lines from the surrounding arc of seats were bad and the attempt was not a success. Reinhardt's conviction was that audience and actors should be housed *in the same room* (and not in two separate rooms, as the typical proscenium house put them); he tried again in the Redoutensaal in Vienna, using only a minimum number of screens to mark off the acting area, and this experiment was successful. Also, his touring company of *The Miracle* transformed interiors of theatres into a cathedral for purposes of the performance, as the Olympia Hall in London was transformed, and the Century Theatre in New York, in a design by Norman Bel Geddes.

The great wave of experimentation in the Russian theatre took place largely in theatres which were inheritances from older times, although when Okhlopov took over the Realistic Theatre in Moscow in 1932, its interior was completely redesigned to his plans to allow for variable space staging (with audiences in varying relations to the players). The theatre was, however, closed in 1938 and, with the growing strength of Soviet socialist realism, returned to its previous proscenium form. An interesting experiment in housing actors and audiences in one room was Terence Gray's at the Cambridge Festival Theatre in 1926, when the old stage was completely torn out and a platform installed with steps leading down into the audience. This type of "end-stage" would receive further development after World War II.

All the new theatres everywhere tended to be called "large" and to be used often for musicals or opera, or "intimate" and to be confined to drama. The former generally seated from fifteen hundred to two thousand, the latter nine hundred to twelve hundred. Recognition that a different size of theatre interior was desirable for spoken drama and for musical drama or spectacle, led to plans for variable-spaced interiors or for more than one theatre under the same roof. One of the few such plans to be actually built was the Malmö City Theatre in Sweden, which opened in 1944. Two theatres are incorporated into it. The smaller house seats two hundred four, but the larger one, by a cleverly arranged series of laminated maplewood screens hung from rails, can vary its capacity from four hundred, to eight hundred, to twelve hundred, to a maximum of seventeen hundred. As planned by Sigurd Lewerentz and a group of associated architects, it incorporates a semicircular apron stage projecting thirty feet into the auditorium. This forestage can be lowered to form an orchestra pit, and the proscenium itself varied in size by raising up or sliding off the four sections into which it is divided. The building also houses extensive foyers and lounges, workshops, and a restaurant.

Houses containing large and small theatres were also seen as the answer to the

problem of civic and university theatres in the United States, where the necessity to perform in houses big enough to be economically viable was matched by the equal necessity of a smaller, more experimental space both to keep the volunteers upon whom production depended interested in the theatre activities, and to try out new works. Thus, when the Cleveland Playhouse opened its new plant in 1927, it incorporated both a large and a small theatre along with ancillary spaces for both theatre workers and patrons. Theatre plants were also planned at the State University of Iowa and partially realized by 1935. It was a concept that would be widely adopted in both "art centers" and universities after the war.

One of the projects of the famed Bauhaus in Weimar (1919–1933) was an investigation of the "autonomous laws of the stage, removed from all naturalistic imitation." And in 1926, Walter Gropius drew up plans for a "total theatre" which, by mechanical means, could change the actor-audience relationship by moving banks of seats and stage space

TWO EUROPEAN DESIGNS
Left, design of Nicolai Akimoff for the production of *Armored Train 14–69*, in Russia, 1927. Above, design of Vlastislav Hofman for *R.U.R.* in Prague. Both these settings are nonrealistic and exhibit some characteristics of constructivism. (Museum of the State Dramatic Theatre, Leningrad; Museum of Modern Art)

into different configurations. The theatre was never built, but the plan is an interesting solution to the aesthetic problem which was troubling theatre people throughout the period. It was a healthy troubling—how to bring the audience into the performance and not shut them out, as the "peep-show" proscenium arch of realism had done, and to conquer that "fourth wall" which was basically untheatrical. Extreme measures would be taken in the decade after the war, but no completely satisfactory solutions were forthcoming before.

Settings create only the illusion of reality as design becomes an art

Even within the predominant proscenium style, many attempts were made in particular productions to dispense with the fourth wall, the natural concomitant of realism and naturalism. If reality were to be duplicated on the stage, then the setting must be solid and exact, the properties must be "real." Let there be tons of real dirt for *Tobacco Road*

(1933) and real food for *Life with Father* (1939). Let the actors ignore the audience and play their scenes as if only they were concerned. But what to do about that blank space between actors and audience? Pretend that it does not exist. Dress it with the logs of a fireplace, or call it the end of a dock, with the audience sitting in an ocean, as it were (*Dead End*, 1935). In other words, ignore the fact that theatre is theatre, and let the spectators eavesdrop on a slice of life.

Needless to say, the excess of this practice could lead only to the excess of the ridiculous. The theatre is an art form, frankly depending on audience and the relationship of the play thereto. So even though the very real kitchen, with oilcloth-covered table and solid doors could be welcomed in John Van Druten's *I Remember Mama* in 1944, the idea became current in this century that the most effective, perhaps even the most desirable form of production was not, of necessity, the minutely realistic. Indeed, the method suited only particular types of plays, and even then the production profited from a selection of details rather than a faithful reproduction of reality. If a fireplace, a sofa, and a couple of chairs in one scene and a section of steps with a railing in another could suggest an interior and a train pulling out of a station in Jo Mielziner's design for Sherwood's *Abe Lincoln in Illinois* in 1938, of what use was further documentation? Lights could create mood and focus attention and the effect was theatrical.

Inspired by the ideas of Appia and Craig, a whole generation of scene designers in both Europe and America achieved an importance hitherto unprecedented—or perhaps unprecedented since the days of the Bibienas and Piranesi.

Typical of these new designers was Robert Edmond Jones, who perhaps more clearly than the others set forth in precept and practice the guiding principle that the scene must enhance the play, not from a pictorial basis primarily, but from the fundamental premise that the play is interpreted and made meaningful by actor and décor. He once said that the obligation of the scenic artist was to "see the high original intention of the dramatist" and to work to "affirm and ennoble the art of the actor." Then, in 1941, he summed up his thinking and practice in a challenging book, *The Dramatic Imagination*. He concerned himself with every detail of the visual aspect of the production—settings, lights, costumes, properties—working with a dedication and an intensity that inspired others and that produced many memorable designs.

For him, as for those who espoused the new principles everywhere, scene design was a creative act, imbued with high and artistic purposes. This creative act he performed for all types of plays from Shakespeare to *The Philadelphia Story* (1939), one of his most famous and effective designs being that for O'Neill's *Desire Under the Elms* (1924). With its brooding tree and clapboard house that opened to show various interiors at the times when action took place in each, it made this type of multiple setting (though not a new idea in itself) one of the popular styles. The creative management of Arthur Hopkins (1878–1950) brought Jones to the attention of the Broadway commercial theatre, and his successes—along with attention paid to the new stagecraft by the Theatre Guild—helped to establish new ways of thinking about design in American theatre.

Another type of setting adapted to multiple use was the so-called unit set with changing elements brought to significant development by designers like Donald Oenslager, Lee Simonson, Adolph Linnebach, Gamrekelli, and Roger Furse, to mention a

ARTISTS AS THEATRE DESIGNERS
Above, setting by Salvador Dali for the ballet, *Labyrinth*, 1941. Right, Marc Chagall's design for *Congratulations, That's a Lie and the Police*, 1919. These highly individual and theatrical designs are typical of the work of the many artists, particularly in France, who have designed for the modern stage. (Museum of Modern Art; Marc Chagall)

few. This type stresses a basic arrangement of platforms, steps, columns, or other vertical masses which can be changed for various scenes by curtains, screens, or other set pieces. It has, of course, a direct relationship to the permanent architectural stage setting of such theatres as Copeau's Vieux Colombier and Reinhardt's Redoutensaal but is more directly concerned with the basic needs and shape of an individual play. Lee Simonson's design for O'Neill's *Marco Millions* (1927), and those of René Fuerst for *The Oresteia*, are examples of this type. Sometimes these unit settings are enhanced by projections or painted backdrops, and sometimes the planes of the architectural forms are also painted. Another type of unit setting which gained currency was that of a single sculptural form, usually set on a revolve,

which met the needs of varying scenes in a given production. Here again, lighting was of utmost importance to the mood and the flow of the performance.

These developments had their source in the theories of Appia and Craig. Great practical impetus was given to these ideas in the work of Leopold Jessner (1878–1948) in Berlin, who became famous for his *Jessnertreppen*, which Macgowan and Jones have translated as "those crazy steps of Leopold Jessner." By breaking up the stage floor with a series of levels in steps of varying form and size, Jessner gave his actors another dimension through which to move. He further made wide use of colored planes and surfaces and great variation in lighting. He developed the symbolism of color to a very high degree in settings, costumes, and lights,

and in the 1920s staged many memorable productions.

This effort to "make the décor act" came to be called expressionism in design, just as the attempt to give a material abstraction of reality in playwriting was called by the same name. Erwin Piscator, Theo Otto, P. Schillingowsky, and many others experimented along these lines. Often projections of signs or numbers, or moving pictures, became a part of the staged play with the avowed purpose of having greater impact on the audience. Modern spectators may derive a feeling of the expressionistic technique of "making the décor act" through Carl Mayer's famous landmark film, *The Cabinet of Doctor Caligari* (1919). Sketches of designs for the theatre, as well, convey something of the impression.

In Russia, these nonrealistic techniques reached an apotheosis in the constructivist settings which had their greatest vogue there. The movement was partly a revolt against painted settings, and in essence stripped away the paint and canvas, leaving only the basic forms of the constructed scenes for the actors to use. Partly, it was a further development of the idea that setting should be conceived as an arrangement of forms to display the agility of the actor and to enable him to project various moods and emotions by large movements through space, and highly variable relationships in space with other actors. In many of the productions of Taïrov and Meyerhold, chief exponents of the form, the curtainless stage was filled with strange and unreal constructions of wood, glass, or metal, over, around, and on which the acrobatic actors could move. Often the action took place in the auditorium as well as on the stage, audience and play becoming one. Okhlopkov applied this technique by sometimes having several stages scattered through the audience, with the actors moving from one to another. But the fertile inventions of these Russians in the 1920s and early 1930s came under official interdiction before 1940, and the stress on new socialist realism after that time stifled experiment and tended to turn back the clock in Russia to an outmoded theatrical form, the literal realism of the turn of the century.

Expressionistic setting was seen in America as early as 1923, when Elmer Rice's *The Adding Machine* was produced, but the extremes of this and the constructivist forms never won wide popularity. They did, however, in a most fundamental way bring about a realization of the validity of Meyerhold's "theatre theatrical"—not, to be sure, in the identical way he conceived it, but in a freeing of scenic conceptions, so that the designer asked first what production method would best convey the essence of the dramatist's thought, and then created his details to carry out this image. Curiously, in the midst of all of these innovative techniques in stage design, there was a continuation of the use of painted settings by such eminent artists as had startled earlier audiences of the Ballet Russe. Thus, by World War II there was a greater variation in types and kinds of scenic investiture than ever before in the history of the theatre, varying all the way from minute fidelity to reality to the most unrealistic of abstractions. Scenic design came of age in the present century. As never before, lighting came to play a fundamental role in theatrical interpretation, with lighting designers assuming importance as separate and significant entities. The development and perfection of lighting equipment made this possible. Footlights, except in deliberately antiquarian performances, were banished, and light sources were often not confined to the stage itself but emanated from all parts of the house.

Staging utilized all devices from the simplest to the most complex. Revolves, wagons, flies, platforms, flats, plastic set pieces, curtains, painted drops—all the resources of past and present found their place, depending on the play at hand. There was one resounding success which dispensed almost totally with scenic investiture—the remarkable production of Thornton Wilder's *Our Town*, which opened in 1938 and gave proof that there is room for all kinds of

AMERICAN DISCIPLES OF APPIA AND CRAIG
Above, design for *Macbeth* by Robert Edmond Jones; below, design for *King Lear* by Norman Bel Geddes. These drawings, by two of the most outstanding American designers, not only illustrate the importance of design in the modern theatre but also emphasize the importance of lighting to design. Sources and areas of light are shown in both. (Museum of Modern Art; Barbara Bel Geddes)

visual techniques in theatre, but that after all the whole structure of scene design need not be a prerequisite for effective theatre.

Artistry gains in importance with authenticity in costuming

The various experiments and trends in scene designing had their counterparts in costuming. The pictorial effects achieved by the painters working in theatre were aided by costumes designed in color and line to enhance the stage picture. Historical accuracy was taken for granted in noncontemporary plays, though even here the costume designer worked not so much in authentic materials and styles as in authentic effects, using whatever materials would lend themselves to this result. Canvas was painted to look like brocade under the stage lights, silk jersey to drape like Egyptian cotton or Greek linen, bulky knit yarn silvered like coats of mail— these were the working materials of costumers. Sometimes noncontemporary plays were costumed in accordance with an overall production style, as was Max Reinhardt's famous production of *King Lear* in which he conceived the characters as statues cut from stone. The costumes here were made from rubber sheeting, carefully draped, folded, and painted in highlights. Sometimes, with a special interpretation in mind, noncontemporary plays were costumed out of period or in modern dress. Barry Jackson, of the Birmingham Repertory Company, startled London theatregoers in 1925 when he brought there his production of *Hamlet* in modern dress—the first time the play had been done in this fashion—and followed it in 1928 with a *Macbeth* similarly clothed. Though the innovation was both praised and damned, other directors, upon occasion, did the same, notably Orson Welles and John

Houseman in their 1937 Mercury Theatre production of *Julius Caesar* in modern military uniforms.

Even where contemporary dress was demanded by the play, players ceased to wear whatever they thought appropriate from their own wardrobes, but each detail was as carefully planned as if the setting were in remote times. Costume design became an art, its basic theory being that each individual costume must bear a relationship not only to the time and place of the play, but to the character's function in the play structure and to his psychological orientation as well.

Costumes of the period, then, were planned to harmonize with the stage setting, to render the actor visible at all times when he should be visible, and to make less conspicuous the less important characters. Line and color became of paramount importance, with details used only where they could enhance the total picture, and included only if they were large enough to register with an audience. Lynn Fontanne wore a floating evening gown in *O Mistress Mine* (1946) which probably would not appear at an actual party but which was right for the character in the play; Alexander Woollcott wore a battered raincoat in *Wine of Choice* (1938) exactly suited to his character.

In addition to their mission of projecting character and its relation to the play, it was realized that modern costumes must be wearable and durable, not hampering the actor and lasting through many performances. So costumes came to be, whether contemporary in period or not, designed with all these things in mind, as well as the necessity for taking into account the individual actor who would wear them.

Costuming is, of course, in many ways even more important than scene design, for plays can be produced on a bare stage, with

TWO DESIGNS FOR "THE EMPEROR JONES"
The convict scene in the O'Neill play as designed by Cleon Throckmorton, left, and Donald Oenslager, above. Both show the influence of the Appia-Craig theories in the use of light and shapes rather than details. (Museum of Modern Art; Donald Oenslager)

curtains, or with elaborate scenery, but there must always be actors and they must always be dressed in some way. In plays with little or no scenic investiture, the costumes must be relied upon to convey time, place, and mood, so that the choice of dress for a play like *Our Town* is of great importance.

In the period following World War I, the excessive zeal of theatre people for the visual aspects of production almost drove drama out of the theatre. This was the period of great experimentation in line and color, the period when a "blue *Lear,*" a "red *Hamlet,*" a "grey *Resurrection*" were popular. It was the time when Jessner produced a *Richard III* with Gloucester in the coronation scene dressed all in flowing red, with his courtiers, likewise dressed, below him on a flight of red steps with a red sky overhead. It was the time when in *Masse-Mensch,* a woman dressed in blue in a cage of scarlet bars was surrounded by dark, formless figures. Expressionism in stage décor made the individual less important than the mass effect. A similar aim was evident in the use by Meyerhold of uniform blue denim coveralls

for both actors and actresses in his constructivist productions. Subsequent developments tempered these extremes in the West, and of course in Russia the official new socialist realism completely stifled them.

Nonrealistic theatre generally gave costume designers opportunity to let their imaginations flower, and romantic and fantastic costuming often achieved startlingly artistic effects. In Europe, particularly, many easel painters designed for the theatre: Derain, Picasso, Matisse, Laurencin, Gris, Braque; from Russia came the richly oriental designs of Léon Bakst and Natalie Gontcharovna. The musical stage was particularly fruitful of imaginative costuming, for here unusual design, sharp contrasts, and interesting line could have freer play than in more conventional drama. A large number of costume designers, some of great talent, appeared as a result of the dissemination of new stagecraft ideas and ideals: Jean Victor-Hugo in France; Ernst Stern and Oscar Schlemmer in Germany; Nivinsky and Varpekh in Russia; Nadia Benois, Oliver Messel and Roger Furse in England; and Robert Edmond Jones, Norman Bel Geddes and Stewart

Chaney in America. Often the same artist would design both sets and costumes, but increasingly the costume designer was recognized as a separate and important artist contributing to the unity of production.

The emphasis upon lighting inherent in the new stagecraft and the intensity and variability of electric power caused additional attention to be paid to the art of makeup. The influence of the movies, also, where the eye of the camera so easily picked up discrepancies and inadequacies, brought makeup techniques to a high order of refinement. Various types of grease, pancake, and panchromatic makeup were developed to enable actors to enhance their good characteristics, subordinate the undesirable, or assume ages or stations in life not comparable to their own. Makeup was brought into line with the desire for unity of effect, fantastic face painting being in order with fantastic costuming and decor, and actresses, for the most part, no longer insisting upon being beautiful at the expense of the part they played. The theatre profited from the necessary attention paid to makeup by the moving picture industry, using the new products and techniques for its own purposes. Wigs and beards could now be so carefully constructed that the wearing of them would hardly be suspected, so natural they looked. Or they could be completely stylized, for special effect, as was the case with Alfred Lunt in *Amphitryon 38* (1937). Harking back to other periods of theatre history, masks again began being used, as they were in O'Neill's *The Great God Brown* (1936), or for Yeats' *The Only Jealousy of Emer* (1924). By the advent of World War II, it might be said that the "new stagecraft" which had heralded a new period in theatre history was so universally accepted in theory and in practice (except in Russia) that one could no longer speak of it as "new."

Stanislavski method takes root in America

In the period following World War I, Russia was theatre's Mecca, and, for actors, Stanislavski was its saint. Americans, in particular, took up the Stanislavski cult with a fervor that was amazing. The Group Theatre, whose existence spanned the 1930s, was inspired by and dedicated to Stanislavski's principles. Organized and directed by Harold Clurman, Lee Strasberg, and Cheryl Crawford, it included the already experienced Stella and Luther Adler and Morris Carnovsky, and developed the talents of Franchot Tone, John Garfield, Lee J. Cobb, Elia Kazan, Sanford Meisner, Robert Lewis, Clifford Odets, Irwin Shaw, Frances Farmer, Jane Wyatt, and John Howard Lawson. A glance at this list will show actors, directors, and playwrights still active, who have contributed many stellar moments to theatre in the last thirty-five years.

The Stanislavski influence in America is

RUSSIAN DESIGNS FOR TAIROV PRODUCTIONS
Left, Ryndin design for a production at the Kamerny Theatre of John Dos Passos' *Fortune Heights*. Above, the same designer's setting at the same theatre for *The Optimistic Tragedy* by Vishnevski, both c. 1934.

easily enough traced. The Moscow Art Theatre played for three months in New York beginning in January 1923, then went on to Chicago, Philadelphia, and Boston. They played for another three months in New York beginning in November of that year, then appeared for shorter periods in Chicago, Philadelphia, Boston, Washington, D.C., Pittsburgh, New Haven, Hartford, Newark, Cleveland, and Detroit. By the end of this tour they had performed in the United States for a total of forty weeks, everywhere to critical acclaim. Stanislavski's *My Life in Art* was first published in Boston in 1924 at the conclusion of this lengthy tour. Richard Boleslavsky and Maria Ouspenskaya of the MAT company remained in New York to teach at the American Laboratory Theatre, offering occasional performances by their students. By 1928, Lee Strasberg and Harold Clurman, who had studied there, collected a group of young performers to work on materials in the new "method," and by 1930 had even

persuaded the Theatre Guild to give a "studio" performance of Kirshon's *Red Rust* (1927). The Guild did not repeat the experiment, but from it grew the Group Theatre.

Established actors, of course, were in no way caught up in the Stanislavski fever. Lionel, Ethel, and John Barrymore, Alfred Lunt and Lynn Fontanne, Helen Hayes, Jane Cowl, Otis Skinner, Katharine Cornell, Walter Connolly, Pauline Lord, Roland Young, Laurette Taylor, Clifton Webb, Ina Claire, Basil Rathbone, and many more than can be mentioned here, pursued their successful way in spite of the criticisms of the "young Turks" of the Group Theatre. But the dedication and artistic success of that unit contributed a large number of talented people to the decade of the 1940s and later.

The French method in England

Though Michael Chekhov, originally a member of Stanislavski's group, worked for a time in England, the chief influence there came from France and the principles of Jacques Copeau. Copeau voiced no allegiance to Stanislavski, though he worked essentially by the same methods toward the same results, placing perhaps a somewhat more definite emphasis on developing vocal qualities and speaking lines beautifully. Emphasis upon voice training and effective delivery has been characteristic of French theatre from the first. The immediate channel of Copeau's influence in England was Michel Saint-Denis, who first founded his own London Theatre Studio in 1926 and then went on to the direction of the school at the Old Vic, returning to France again in 1947 to become director of the Eastern Center of the nationwide *Direction des Arts et Lettres*. From the Old Vic came such actors as John Gielgud,

Laurence Olivier, Michael Redgrave, Anthony Quayle, Peggy Ashcroft. In the late 1920s and early 1930s, the leading actors of England, like Sir Gerald du Maurier, were called "leading" by virtue of their skill in light comedy and romance. The style was easy and polished, natural and realistic, and set a tone to which a whole generation of actors aspired. Du Maurier had been for some years an actor in the company of Sir Herbert Beerbohm-Tree, who had founded in 1904 the Royal Academy of Dramatic Arts, which is still a major training center in England. The Continental influences, however, developed a new ideal for leading players in England; they began to be judged by their ability to match the great classic—and, above all, the Shakespearean—roles.

The principles expounded by Granville-Barker in 1922 state the English point of view about acting. He says that actors should first "break their shins, so to speak . . . over voice production, elocution, dialectics, eurythmics" and then "upon the lines of a seminar" they should participate in "the cooperative study of widely different plays." Something of this nature was what actually transpired in England. Maurice Evans, Sybil Thorndike, Cedric Hardwicke, Donald Wolfit, Edith Evans, Ralph Richardson, Flora Robson, along with those named above, constituted a whole new generation of English actors whose skill not only in the classic roles, but in a wide variety of characterizations won them worldwide attention. There were a few, like Noel Coward and Gertrude Lawrence, who still shone best in light comedy roles, but the thrust of English acting in the period was to a skilled versatility, which encompassed not only acting, but directing as well. Almost all of the actors named here have also directed, notably Olivier, Evans, and Redgrave, and the

Englishman who would have tremendous theatrical power in the postwar period—Tyrone Guthrie—also began as an actor and then turned to directing.

Versatility, flexibility on the Continent

Great versatility also became the mark of French actors of repute, with Jouvet, Pitoëff, Dullin, Dasté being both actors and directors, and Baty an outstanding director. It was in this period too, that the great talents of Jean-Louis Barrault and Madeleine Renaud had their first successes; they would become more important in the postwar years.

The ideal, at least in both Germany and Russia, was that the individual performer

DIRECTORS' HANDLING OF CROWD SCENES
Left, Sudakov's production of Ivanov's *Armored Train* at the Gorki Theatre, Moscow. Above, Meyerhold's production of *The Inspector General* at his own theatre. In both pictures the careful attention given to each of the many performers is evident in the variety of postures, attitudes, and expressions.

should be flexible in all dramatic types. The Brechtian epic theatre injected an interesting new idea into the art of acting in its insistence that the actor must not be so involved in his part that he cannot stand aside and comment on it as well—a distinct departure from the prevalent practice of an actor living his part, of "being" and not "commenting." This departure from the Stanislavski "living the part" was not so startling in Germany itself, since the Russian's theories never took firm root there, but it would have wide repercussions after the war. In Russia, of course, the imposition of restraints in the 1930s effectively strangled the interesting antirealistic experiments of Meyerhold and Taïrov, and would delay for

a very long time any other departure from realism, for which the Stanislavski teachings were particularly apt.

In Germany and Russia, theatres with permanent acting companies have long been in existence; state and municipal funds have been allotted as a matter of course to support staffs of one hundred or more in many towns and cities. Schools and academies have often been attached to these, and acting training has gone forward along carefully laid out lines. The Conservatoire and the many theatres of Paris have also offered training to French actors, and plans were laid before World War II to extend these possibilities through the dramatic centers; the plan would be implemented after the war. In England, not only the Royal Academy but also the special theatre groups and the provincial repertory companies gave many opportunities for actors to develop their skills.

Training and security more accessible to European actors than to Americans

In America, however, with its emphasis upon Broadway success and long runs, and its complete lack of permanent theatre companies, there had been little opportunity for "on-the-job" training, and no sort of security in the commercial theatre. With the demise of the old stock companies, there were attempts at establishing repertory. Eva Le Gallienne attempted such an organization in 1926 with the Civic Repertory Theatre. The Group Theatre was such an organization, and the various "little theatres" gave opportunities to actors, although mostly not on a professional level. In the United States, the chief impetus for training came through the colleges and universities, beginning with the 47 Workshop, then the establishment of full or partial programs in many educational settings.

It was during this period that the supremacy of the director emerged to an unchallenged position in the theatre, and directing became a separate and distinct art. The individual practitioner, called in America "the director," in England "the producer," and on the Continent "le régisseur," represented the "guiding intelligence" of which Craig spoke, the counterpart of the Duke of Saxe-Meiningen and before him René Pixérécourt. Mostly they were actors who became directors: Reinhardt, Meyerhold, Copeau, Granville-Barker, and the whole "second generation" spoken of above. But here and there a nonactor rose to eminence as a direc-

A FAMOUS ACTING PAIR
Alfred Lunt and Lynn Fontanne in Giraudoux's *Amphitryon 38*, as they appeared in the 1937 production in New York. Their reputation reached its height about midcentury, and they have now become legendary.

tor, like Gaston Baty in France and Guthrie McClintic in the United States.

The old proscriptions against the theatre completely disappeared; many actors and directors were knighted in England during this period, and Russia created the special designation of "People's Artist." By the beginning of World War II, theatre everywhere was the concern of cultured and intelligent people, and even in England and America (where commercialism had so long dominated), significant changes were being brought about. After a long period of neglect, theatre was once more a respectable and respected art form.

Summary

Though theatre, especially in England and America, remained to a large extent a business in this period, it did present some heartening innovations. Primarily, more people of genuine creative ability concerned themselves with theatre. Production became an art, with special fields for scene, costume, and lighting design, and practicing artists in each received due credit for their work. Acting profited by new impulses, and new methods of working were developed. Directing, too, rose to the level of an art, with separate, and sometimes overriding, credit. Playwriting became highly diversified, with many outstanding names. For the first time in theatre history American dramatic writing dominated the world scene. New and interesting production styles were tried: expressionism, surrealism, constructivism, epic theatre, and a host of less well-defined techniques appeared. There were many reforms in theatre architecture, which bid fair to eliminate the old opera-type house in new construction, and stressed the development of flexibility in theatre interiors, coupled with adequate working space.

Most significant of all, however, was the increasingly widespread interest and participation in theatrical activity, even though motion pictures claimed a large share of public attention. The withdrawal of the theatre experience from wide segments of the population occasioned by the demise of stock companies and the attrition in road shows was beginning to be compensated for by the growth of theatrical activity outside metropolitan centers by both professionals and amateurs. And in America, many colleges and universities were increasingly concerning themselves with both training and production. By mid-twentieth century it looked as if a "cultural explosion" in theatre was near at hand. Though World War II would curtail progress, particularly on the Continent, it actually gave impetus to production in England through the establishment of C.E.M.A. (Council for the Encouragement of Music and the Arts), which with both private and public funds sponsored performances throughout Great Britain. The success of this venture and the favorable public response led to the establishment of the Arts Council of Great Britain, and the allocation of public funds to the arts, including theatre —a situation hitherto unprecedented in England. That left the United States, at the end of World War II, the only major power in the Western world not allocating portions of public funds to theatre. It would take several more years before that would happen, even in a token way.

Now that the last quarter of the century is about to begin, it is easier to see that the conclusion of World War II was not just the ending of another of a long series of conflicts, but the beginning of a new age, no less far-reaching in eventual importance than those which began after the Wars of the Roses and the Hundred Years' War. Though the world is yet on the brink of its new age, it is still possible to chart some of the signposts. Chiefly, the new age owes its birth to revolutions in energy sources and in communications, and may come to be known either as the Atomic Age or the Electronics Age. The use of the atomic bomb to end the war called attention to the destructive possibilities of that new energy source, and raised worldwide debate concerning whether or not man's technical competence had not outrun his ethical judgment. The subsequent effort of scientists to put atomic energy to peaceful uses has run into questions of ecology and the pollution of the environment. The atomic revolution has brought home to most of the peoples of the world the realization that earth is a much smaller place than any previous cultures had imagined, and that, for better or for worse, nations had best hang together or they would hang separately. This conviction has been reinforced by the revolution in communications, wherein television (tentative and experimental before the war) has spread to the four corners of the globe with phenomenal speed; by 1969 it was estimated that four *billion* people all over the world watched the spectacle of man's first step on the moon—an event that in its being and its reporting would have been inconceivable a mere twenty-five years earlier.

Television has given immediacy to a host of limited conflicts that have been continuously erupting, and several of its critics would say that it has even fomented some of

these. In any event, the third quarter of the century has been marked not only by an enforced world-consciousness, but, ironically and paradoxically, by an unprecedented upsurge of unique identities of all kinds: the fragmentation of which Francis Fergusson wrote in 1949 has become a splintering. Commercial and political interests of the great powers in geographically removed parts of the world have been labeled "colonialism" with pejorative connotations and almost without exception former empires have dwindled. Hosts of newly independent countries have entered upon the international scene and the United Nations, accepting as equals all duly constituted governments, has swelled from an original membership of forty-eight to a number two-and-a-half times greater than that.

Though political alignments in the postwar period tended to follow a division between totalitarian and democratic powers, even these divisions are becoming increasingly ambiguous and nonoperative. In the cause of self-determination, there have been unsuccessful revolts against Soviet domination in Hungary, Czechoslovakia, and Poland, and more successful ones against English, American, and French domination in other parts of the world. Conflicts have not been limited to national groups, but special-interest groups within specific political boundaries have also been at war. Minority groups, political parties, economic and social institutions have been belligerently self-assertive. The 1960s were marked not only by ethnic riots, but by student revolts, one of which caused the dismissal of Jean-Louis Barrault from his post as director of the Théâtre des Nations in Paris in 1968. (He was reinstated in 1971.) These events, coupled with a series of horrifying assassinations of public figures —all made instantaneously vivid by the communications networks—have generated a chaos and frustration that are typical of the present day. This atmosphere is reflected in literature in all its forms. Nihilism, despair, and frustration have tended to picture modern man (in exactly the opposite stance from his Victorian forebears) as living in the worst of all possible worlds.

The course of human events has given wide currency to the philosophy of existentialism, with Sisyphus as the exemplar of the disillusioned, hopeless—and therefore eminently courageous—striving individual. (In contradistinction, the Marxist ideal is Prometheus—example of hopeful and inventive courage.) The modern existentialist, as exemplified by Jean-Paul Sartre, is an antirationalist with no belief in natural social harmony and no hope in man's perfectibility. Though enunciated in France in the years immediately preceding World War II, existentialism had no wide influence until after the war. By now many thoughtful people are declaring, with Lionel Trilling, that "the Age of Reason is dead," although some equally thoughtful people, like Buckminster Fuller, are also declaring that man is capable of dealing with whatever problems confront him, of willing his own salvation. What the outcome of it all will be is still very much an open question (to paraphrase Thornton Wilder).

Though the extreme of fragmentation reduced man to a lone figure in a godless world struggling to make an assertion through which he could define himself (hence the modern emphasis upon "doing your own thing" and on self-expression), there has been at the same time a geometric multiplication of organizations of all kinds; there is hardly a segment of society which does not speak with some collective voice. These groupings are ideological, economic, social, artistic—and on local, national and international levels. Never in the history of the world have there been so many associations of so many kinds. It is a rare person who does not belong to one or more of these multifarious groupings. The urge to "do something" seems unquenchable in the human psyche, and the number of things being done in the current world is astronomical.

Theatrical production highly diversified

Theatre, being always and everywhere the reflection of the society which produces it, has mirrored all these various images until it would seem that, like Humpty-Dumpty, it can never be put together again. The kindest and most hopeful statement concerning the position of theatre today is probably that it is in a period of transition, and that new forms and ways of being will emerge. On the other hand, it would seem equally likely that theatre as a viable human activity may very well cease to exist. Cases could be made for both points of view. At any rate, the task here is to chart (insofar as it is possible) the life of the "fabulous invalid" in the present day.

From the number and kinds of theatrical events taking place in the present world, one would have to conclude that more people are involved in theatre today than ever before—and this in spite of the advent of cinema and television. But it would also seem to be true that modern theatre illustrates more vividly than ever before the fact that it has ceased to be a unifying activity of humankind; that audiences are irrevocably and increasingly specialized; and that "great diversity" is about the only generalization it is possible to make concerning theatrical activity in the present world. Great diversity exists—and evidently the feeling that somehow theatre is an important human activity. For the United States finally (although minimally) joined its companions in the rest of the Western world in allotting some pub-

lic funds to theatre. In 1965, the Congress passed legislation setting up the National Council on the Arts, of which Roger L. Stevens (long a Broadway producer) was named chairman. A National Endowment for the Arts was allotted $17.5 million for a three-year period to "encourage" theatre, music, radio, television, films, dance, and the visual arts. Subsequent legislation continued allocations of funds, but never in the proportion of Germany, for instance, where public funds support about 80 percent of all theatre production. State councils on the arts, however, have supplemented this minimal assistance in many parts of the United States, and in 1967 a Business Com-

mittee for the Arts was formed to expand private participation by leadership and advice. In the same year, the AFL-CIO set up pilot projects to sponsor arts activities, and several foundations (chiefly the Ford and the Rockefeller Foundations), before and after that date made allocations of funds to specific arts organizations. Thus a combination of public and private interests spurred theatrical activity throughout the United States. In 1961, the Ford Foundation allocated monies to set up its Theatre Communications Group for exchange of information and assistance among resident professional companies countrywide. Within a few years, thirty professional companies were associated with TCG, and by the

1970s there were more than seventy professional regional theatres scattered throughout the United States (some affiliated with
TCG, some members of the University Resident Theatre Association, a division of the
American Theatre Association, and some independent of both).

Decentralization and internationalism spread

The number of productions each season on
Broadway—hitherto the theatrical capital
of the United States—continued to shrink to
below fifty new productions per season, but
semiprofessional and amateur community
theatres continued to be established by the
hundreds, with the American Community
Theatre Association banding them together,
and the number of college and university theatres exceeded two thousand. The special
interests of hundreds of groups performing
for children were looked after by the Children's Theatre Association, and a growing
emphasis upon theatre in the secondary
schools caused the formation of the Secondary School Theatre Association. Each of
these special interest groups performed excellent services in building audiences, as the
growth of professional theatres will attest
and the construction of art centers (discussed hereafter) verify.

Decentralization of theatres from metro-

politan centers went on apace in England and France as well. By 1958, the establishment of dramatic centers in Strasbourg, St. Etienne, Toulouse, Rennes, and Aix-en-Provence had caused a 25 percent decline in receipts in Paris theatres, and by 1964, Minister of Culture André Malraux was announcing twenty such centers either built, building, or planned. Since that time, new theatres have indeed opened in Lyons, Tourcoing, Bourges, and Brest. To each is attached a company which not only plays at its center, but also tours the surrounding territory (except at Lyon, where director Roger Planchon brings audiences from afar by special buses). In England, the movement toward the establishment of repertory theatres in the provinces, which had begun before the

war, quickened its speed, with practically every population center now boasting its own theatre and company, and often more than one. Added to Birmingham, Cambridge, and Oxford were Bristol, Coventry, Nottingham, Salisbury, Manchester, Leeds, Liverpool, Newcastle, York, Sheffield, Edinburgh, Glasgow, Dublin, and Cork to a total of fifty resident companies. And in 1946 Bristol University opened the first Department of Drama in a British university, adding a specially designed theatre in 1951.

The state-supported theatres of Germany (East and West), of Czechoslovakia, Poland, Hungary, Yugoslavia, Rumania, and Russia continued to grow in number, and many of them (as the years passed) added small, experimental studio theatres to the larger

NEW THEATRE PRODUCTIONS
Left, the original production of *Hair*, directed by Gerald Freedman and produced by Joseph Papp at the Astor Place Theatre, New York. Above, the English National Theatre production of Tom Stoppard's *Rosencrantz and Guildenstern Are Dead*. Both of these new plays had great success both in initial production and subsequently. (George E. Joseph, Martha Swope)

institutions. By 1970, in Prague alone, there were thirty theatres, all resident-repertory, and all state-supported, and state theatres were also to be found in Greece and Israel. Even in Italy, ten resident theatres were established, the most famous being in Milan, Genoa, Turin, and Rome.

The quantity and quality of theatrical production (along with improved communication and means of travel) led to the establishment of innumerable theatre festivals throughout Europe and America. Some were specialized, like the Shakespeare festivals at Ashland (Oregon), Antioch (Ohio), Stratford (Ontario, Canada, and Connecticut, as well as "on Avon" in England), and Central Park in New York City; or like the Shaw Festival in Niagara-on-the-Lake, Ontario; or the classic revivals at Athens, Epidaurus, and Delphi. Some were eclectic in content, like those at Berlin, Dubrovnik, Malvern, Glyndebourne, Canterbury, and Aldeburgh. And some were truly international, with performing groups from many parts of the world, like those at Edinburgh, Spoleto, Paris, London, Nancy, and Avignon. In the last years of the 1960s, such festivals numbered well over fifty; all were for a short time of concentrated production, usually during the summer months, and made for an exciting interchange of ideas and perspectives. International theatre organizations were soon added to national ones, with the most wide-reaching one being the International Theatre Institute, founded in 1947 under the auspices of the United Nations Educational, Scientific and Cultural

Organization (UNESCO). But there are also international organizations in children's theatre, community and amateur theatre, theatre research, and theatre criticism.

Aside from the international festivals, there has been a not inconsiderable traffic in national troupes playing set engagements in countries other than their own. The Moscow Art Theatre played return engagements in New York in 1958 and 1965, and the Comédie Française came in 1955, 1961, and 1965. The Teatro Piccolo of Milan visited in 1960 and the Deutsches Schauspielhaus of Hamburg in 1967. In 1971, the Teatro Libero of Rome appeared in New York, and continuing exchanges of productions have gone on from one European theatre capital to another, while such United States productions as *Hair, Fiddler on the Roof,* and *The Boys in the Band* played stands in European cities, and British productions formed an ever larger part of Broadway seasons. In spite of language and cultural differences, theatre workers everywhere are more and more involved with each other on a worldwide basis, and this tendency can be expected to grow, rather than to diminish.

Theatre professionals also decentralize

One of the most significant trends of the period was the movement of theatre profes-

BLACK THEATRE
Left, the original production at Arena Stage, Washington, D.C., of Howard Sackler's *The Great White Hope* (1967), with James Earl Jones in the title role. Above, a scene from Ed Bullins' *The Electronic Nigger and Other Plays* (1968), first performed at the American Place Theatre and then later at the New Lafayette Theatre. (Arena Stage; Martha Holmes)

sionals away from metropolitan centers to aid in the burgeoning decentralized theatre. Typical is Tyrone Guthrie (1900–1971), who went to Stratford, Ontario in 1953 to help local afficionado Tom Patterson establish the Shakespeare Festival Theatre there, and in 1963 presided over the opening of the Minnesota Theatre Company in Minneapolis in the theatre which he had aided in establishing and which bears his name. Michel Saint-Denis' taking over the direction of the dramatic center at Strasbourg in France in 1953 is another example, as is the formation of the Association of Producing Artists (APA) in New York City in 1958 under the direction of Stuart Vaughan, and its subsequent migra-

tion and return under the actor-director Ellis Raab to play two seasons at the Lyceum (1967–1969) in association with the Phoenix Theatre, and the establishment of the American Conservatory Theatre (ACT) under William Ball in San Francisco. Conversely, regional theatres developed talents which later enriched the metropolitan centers, as John Neville, after five years at Nottingham, went to London (1967) to act and direct; as Jules Irving and Herbert Blau, after a dozen years at the San Francisco Actors Workshop, took over the direction of the Vivian Beaumont Theatre in Lincoln Center in 1965. But often directors were content to stay with the regional theatres which they had helped to develop: Frederic McConnell (d. 1958) at the Cleveland Playhouse (from 1921), Zelda and Tom Fichandler at Arena Stage in Washington, D.C. (from 1951), Robert Porterfield (d. 1970) at the Barter Theatre in Abingdon, Virginia (from 1932), Nina Vance at the Alley Theatre in Houston (from 1947), George Touliatis at the Front Street Theatre in Memphis (from 1951), Adrian Hall at the Trinity Square Repertory Company in Providence, Rhode Island (from 1963), Harlan Kleiman and Jon Jory at the Long Wharf Theatre in New Haven (from 1964), and Gordon Davidson with the Center Theatre Group in Los Angeles (from 1964). They were following the pattern laid down by Barry Jackson at the Birmingham Repertory Company many years before. By 1966, more professional actors were employed outside of New York than on Broadway; the next year the Minnesota Theatre Company did a New York season; the 1967–1968 Broadway season produced three plays which had originated in regional theatres; the next season there were seven. By the 1971–1972 season the number had risen to fifteen, and here was a reversal indeed. For noncommercial theaters were now infusing a healthy dose of lifeblood into the increasingly moribund stream of commercial Broadway, and the United States could feel that at last it was following a pattern that had obtained in England for almost fifty years.

Noncommercial theatres in metropolitan centers

Within the great theatrical centers themselves, but outside of the establishment theatres, many creative people also worked. In London there were, typically, Joan Littlewood at the Theatre Workshop, George Devine and William Gaskill at the Royal Court (still devoted to new plays and playwrights, and adding an experimental "Upstairs" in 1969), Frank Marcus at the Hempstead Theatre Club, Bernard Miles at the Mermaid, Peter Brook at the Roundhouse, and after 1968, when the Theater Act discontinued licensing, many others in numerous "studio theatres," which now functioned much in the way that off-Broadway had for a number of years in New York.

Though actually any production not presented in the few blocks of commercial theatres in New York is an "off-Broadway" production, the term acquired special meaning in the 1940s when Actors' Equity recognized productions in small houses (one hundred ninety-nine-seat limit), done with economy and not as a potential profit-maker, to be an acceptable showcase for performers who could work there for less money than in a "regular" production. The most famous of the establishments that began operation as an off-Broadway house was the Circle in the Square, under the direction of Theodore Mann and José Quintero in 1950, which has continued its policy of tasteful revivals and has introduced new talents to the New York scene. The Theatre de Lys on Christopher Street was converted to a platform-stage house from an old movie theatre in 1952, and presented in the 1950s a renowned revival of *The Three Penny Opera* and another of Calder Willingham's *End as a Man*. It also continues, but not with a constant director-producer. The Cherry Lane, the Provincetown, the Sheridan Square Playhouse, the Greenwich Mews Theatre, and many other small theatres—usually converted or rehabilitated space, like church basements, lofts, warehouses, etc.—have been and still are being used as off-Broadway houses. Some have special orientations like the Shakespeare-wrights at the Jan Hus Theatre during the 1950s; the Fourth Street Theatre in the same period which produced a notable series of Chekhov plays; the Equity Library Theatre which has been "showcasing" talents since 1946; the American Place Theatre under Wynn Handman, devoted to new plays; the whole complex of theatres built into a landmark building in Astor Place by the intrepid producer Joseph Papp, in one of which *Hair* got its start and where the production of new plays is paramount; the theatre of the Negro Ensemble Company, under the direction of Douglas Turner Ward and Robert Hooks, which since 1966 has been giving productions of plays by black playwrights; the Chelsea Theatre Center under Robert Kalfin; and the Judson Poets Theatre, directed by Al Carmines, which devotes itself to new and experimental works, as also does the Cubiculo. There are also a number of off-Broadway houses which are available for rental to groups who use them on a one-show basis, like the Village Gate, the Eastside Playhouse, the Sullivan Street Playhouse, and many others, with a great deal of fluidity and no constant policy. At the present time, off-Broadway tends to be considered an alternative to Broadway production for plays with limited appeal.

The experimental thrust which was, fifteen or twenty years ago, typical of off-Broadway has now moved to an area called off-off-Broadway, where the newest plays of the newest playwrights are presented. It was Joe Cino, in 1958, who cleared a space in his Café Cino (a coffeehouse in the Village) and invited young playwrights, actors, and directors to present their works—their pay being simply what they could collect as a contribution from the audience, who, it was hoped, would also purchase coffee and sweets. It was the Café Cino which introduced the first productions of Lanford Wilson. Though the Cino disappeared with Cino's death in 1967, the same tradition is still maintained at the Old Reliable, an otherwise obscure tavern in the Village. It was in this pattern, too, that Ellen Stewart, an intense and creative black woman, began the Café La Mama in 1962. But her organization grew and became the LaMama Experimental Theatre Club, now housed in its own building with three theatres, and companies which tour in Europe.

Noncommercial (a term now preferred to regional, community, off- or off-off-Broadway) theatres which have become more or less permanent, and which have gained reputations, are chiefly those which are "the lengthened shadow" of one or two persons, like the Cleveland Playhouse, the Mermaid in London, Arena Stage, American Place Theatre, Theatre Upstairs at the Court, Theatre Workshop in London, etc. Though no one makes a great deal of money in any of these theatres, they are constantly-producing units where participants of all kinds can keep their tools sharp and develop their abilities. They often make for the most exciting theatre available.

One other type of theatrical production should be mentioned: summer outdoor drama, now grown to such proportions in the United States that there is an Institute of Outdoor Drama to look after its interests.

These historical pageants, along with the institution of various festivals, have largely displaced summer stock as a major theatrical activity during the summer months. What summer stock remains these days consists of star vehicles and/or "package shows" which move from one summer theatre to another. The first of the historical pageants was *The Lost Colony*, continuously presented in Virginia since 1939, except for the years of World War II. Between then and now, many similar productions have been mounted across the United States, and they form a likely place for students and young professionals to work through the summer months.

Finally, recent years have seen the formation of "theatre collectives" like the Living Theatre of Julian Beck and Judith Malina, the Open Theatre of Joseph Chaikin and Roberta Sklar, the Performance Group of Richard Schechner, the Manhattan Project of André Gregory, the Polish Laboratory Theatre of Jerzy Grotowski, and the Institute of Contemporary Arts of Peter Brook, which are dedicated to exploring the nature of the theatrical act from many points of view. Since their impact is chiefly on acting techniques, as has been the long-term influence of the Berliner Ensemble under Brecht, they will be discussed in greater detail later.

French playwriting opens new paths

By midcentury the great playwrights of the previous period were gone: O'Neill, Shaw, Pirandello, Giraudoux, Brecht, and Garcia-Lorca. But many playwrights who had come into prominence in the 1930s and 1940s were still writing. Newer impulses would come first from France and Switerland, with England, then America and Germany following. By the 1970s, new dramatic forms and new materials were everywhere in evidence.

The disillusion engendered by the Nazi occupation of France during the war years supplemented and strengthened the existentialist point of view and produced a genre of playwriting synthesized and heralded by Jean-Paul Sartre in his 1946 essay "Forgers of Myths," in which he declared that the "theatre of characters" (typical of England and America) is an outmoded and no longer relevant indulgence. Down with Freud and the analysis of character, the clash of character on character! Man is not "a reasoning animal" but entirely indeterminate and dependent for identification on his series of free choices in "certain situations." The successor to the theatre of characters, therefore, is the "theatre of situations," and those situations "show the public the great myths of death, exile, love." The aim is "to forge myths" in

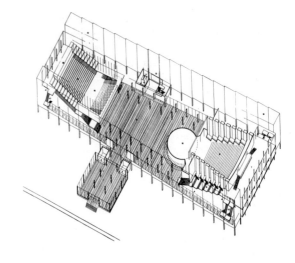

dramas which are short and violent . . . usually a conflict of rights, bearing on some very general situation . . . this is the theatre, austere, moral, mythic, and ceremonial in aspect which has given birth to new plays in Paris during the occupation and especially since the end of the war.

Sartre's own first play, *The Flies* (1943), uses the Orestes myth to explore the definition by action of the character of Orestes and his achievement of dignity for himself and for "the freedom of Argos." He followed this with *No Exit* (1944) and *The Respectful Prostitute* (1946), both of which enjoyed great popularity in New York's off-Broadway theatres, *Red Gloves* (1948), *The Devil and the Good Lord* (1951), *Kean* (1954), *Nekrassov* (1956), and *The Condemned of Altona* (1960), which was played by the Lincoln Center Repertory Company in the 1960s.

The most outstanding French dramatist in the same genre is Jean Anouilh, who before the war had gained some reputation

with *Thieves' Carnival* (1938) and other plays, but sprang into real prominence with the production of his *Antigone* in 1943. For Sartre, Anouilh's plays became the epitome of the "theatre of situation." Anouilh has been an incredibly prolific playwright; hardly a theatrical season has passed in Paris without a play from his pen. A selection of some of the more outstanding of these would include *Invitation to the Chateau* (1947), *Waltz of the Toreadors* (1952), *The Lark* (1953), and *Becket* (1960). Another playwright whom Sartre recommends is Albert Camus (1913–1960), both for his 1944 play, *Cross Purposes*, whose misunderstandings "can serve as the embodiment of all misunderstandings," and his *Caligula* (1946) which Sartre also praises. Though Camus wrote other plays, his chief influence on the course of French drama was his essay "The

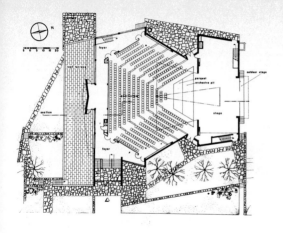

FLEXIBLE THEATRE PLANS
Left, plan for the theatre at Mannheim, Germany, completed in 1957. A large house, with a revolving stage, is on the right, a smaller house on the left, in which the performance space and audience seating can be changed. The two theatres share lobby space. Above, plan for the theatre in the Student Art Center at Sarah Lawrence College, designed by Marcel Breuer. Alternate rows of seats are removable; an elevator stage can be lowered for an orchestra pit or for parquet seating; the rear stage wall can be converted to a proscenium for playing to an audience seated out-of-doors. (Nationaltheater, Mannheim; Sarah Lawrence College)

Myth of Sisyphus" (1942), which contributed to the development of absurdist drama. Another existentialist of the Sartre stamp was Simone de Beauvoir (*The Useless Mouths*, 1945).

Camus' essay gave name to the new form of French theatre typified by Ionesco, Beckett, Tardieu, Genet, Adamov, Audiberti, and Arrabal. The pertinent passage is this:

A world that can be explained by reasoning, however faulty, is a familiar world. But in a universe that is suddenly deprived of illusions and of light, man feels a stranger. His is an irremediable exile, because he is deprived of memories of a lost homeland as much as he lacks the hope of a promised land to come. This divorce between man and his life, the actor and his setting, truly constitutes the feeling of Absurdity.

Existentialists, in spite of their austerity, were optimists in that man could define himself by action, and their plays used recognizable characters in a carefully structured form. The absurdists, on the other hand, are intensely pessimistic, viewing all action as pointless, using improbable characters which often carry type-names, substituting tensions and/or states for plot, and relying heavily on sight and sound images. They are the direct descendants of Alfred Jarry's *Ubu Roi* (1896), of which Sacha Guitry said at the time, "It is not related to any other form of literature." Aside from the definition contained in Camus' essay, the best presentation of the theory of absurdism is contained in Antonin Artaud's *The Theatre and Its Double* (1938), which is a series of essays, manifestos, letters, and notes. In it he calls for the abolition of the "tyranny of the word," and the substitution of a "marvelous complex of pure stage images," so that the spectators will be "put in a state of deepened and keener perception." These are the effective prescriptions from the work for the absurdists; other declarations therein would later lead to the performance concepts of the theatre collectives.

The most consistent and productive of the absurdists has been Eugene Ionesco, whose generally short "antiplays" (as he calls them) comprise a lively catalog of absurdist characteristics. The earliest is *The Bald Soprano* (1948) which annihilates the ritual of social intercourse. *The Lesson* (1950) does the same for all teaching and learning; *Jacques, or The Submission* (1950) for courtship; and *The Chairs* (1952) for communication of any kind. By the time *Amédée*, with its hideously growing corpse, appeared in 1952, Ionesco's reputation was spreading and with *The New Tenant* (1957) it was firmly established. Since that time he has written many more well-known plays, notably *Rhi-*

noceros (1960), *The Aerial Pedestrian* (1963), *Exit the King* (1963), and *Hunger and Thirst* (1966).

If one were to choose the absurdist play which above all is most definitive of the absurdist tenets, it would have to be *Waiting for Godot* (1952) by Samuel Beckett. It was his first play. In it, Beckett presents in dramatic terms the precarious balance between hope and despair, between humanism and nihilism with which modern man lives. No positive act is possible; the only posture is that of waiting. Beckett's later plays are less successful in total configuration, although still intriguing: examples of these later works are *Endgame* and *Krapp's Last Tape* (1957), *Happy Days* (1961), *Play* (1964), and *Back and Forth* (1966).

The other major writer in the absurdist genre in France is Jean Genet who carries nihilism to even greater lengths, insisting that deviation is essential and as valuable as accepted virtues. His first play, *The Maids*, appeared in 1947. Of the others which followed, *Deathwatch* (1948), *The Balcony* (1956), and *The Blacks* (1959) had great successes in New York, while *The Screens* (1961) waited for five years before it was produced in France, and in 1972 had a great success at the Chelsea Theatre Center in New York. Other absurdist writers in France, with typical plays, are: Arthur Adamov (*The Parody*, 1952), Jacques Audiberti (*The Landlady*, 1960), Jean Tardieu (*The Keyhole*, 1955), and Fernando Arrabal (*And They Put Handcuffs on the Flowers*, 1967). More conventional plays continued to be written by Henry de Montherlant, André Roussin, Marcel Achard, Félicien Marceau, Marcel Aymé, and George Schéhadé, plus the more recent addition of Eduardo Manet, Jacques Mauclair, and Rémo Forlane. It has been a provocative and productive period in French playwriting.

German language playwrights also experiment

The most significant new playwrights in the German language are two Swiss writers, Max Frisch and Friedrich Duerrenmatt. Each is more akin to the point of view of Sartre and Anouilh than to that of the absurdists, for each admires the courage of man and sees it as a possible hope in an otherwise frustrating and incomprehensible world. Frisch's first play, *Santa Cruz*, appeared in 1944, and of the several which he has written since that date the most favorably received have been *The Chinese Wall* (1946, revised 1955), *Biedermann and the Firebugs* (1956), and *Andorra* (1961). Each of these has been translated and played in either England or America. Duerrenmatt also has been popular in translation. Although his first play appeared in 1947, his first great success was *The Marriage of Mr. Mississippi* (1952). Then came *The Visit* (1957), in which the Lunts starred, and *The Physicists* (1962), *The*

A MODERN FLEXIBLE THEATRE
Left, the exterior of the Kalita Humphreys Theater designed by Frank Lloyd Wright for the Dallas Theater Center. Above, the interior, with a forty-foot revolving stage and concrete drum overhead to assist in quick scene changes. Charles Laughton has called this "the most beautiful theatre in the world." (Dallas Theater Center)

Meteor (1966), *Play Strindberg* (1970), and *Portrait of a Planet* (1971).

The creative force of Brecht, both in plays he wrote after his return to Germany and in his productions at the Theater am Schiffbauerdamm with his Berliner Ensemble, dominated German playwriting. Even when significant new plays were written after Brecht's death, they tended to be polemical. One of the earliest and most startling of these was *The Persecution and Assassination of Jean-Paul Marat as Performed by the Inmates of the Asylum of Charenton Under the Direction of the Marquis de Sade* (1959, and usually called *Marat/Sade*), which caused a sensation in New York when the English director Peter Brook brought his London company for a visit in the 1960s. Its author, Peter Weiss, then turned to more purely "documentary" playwriting in *The Investigation* (1965), which purportedly was an arrangement of actual documents pertaining to Auschwitz. It is a dramatic technique with some relationship to the newsreel, which

German playwrights (presumably in the expiation of guilt, or the concern with social problems—or both) have particularly practiced. *The Investigation* had sixteen simultaneous stagings all over West Germany and was widely hailed. But when he applied the same techniques to Portuguese colonialism in *Song of the Lusitanian Bogey* (1967), a formal protest was entered by the government of Portugal. He has since followed the same vein in *Trotski in Exile* (1970) and *Hölderlin* (1971).

Rolf Hochhuth followed the same pattern in his attack on Pope Pius XII in *The Deputy* (1963), presented with designs by the great Czech designer, Joseph Svoboda. It caused a sensation worldwide. When *The Soldier* was produced in 1967, England objected to its interpretation of Churchill's wartime actions. In 1970, Hochhuth had *The Guerrillas* produced. The documentary play has quite thoroughly consumed the energies of German playwrights on both sides of the division between East and West. Heinar Kipphardt, after two plays of nondocumentary style, wrote in 1964 *In the Matter of J. Robert Oppenheimer,* in 1965 *Joel Brand* (one of Eichmann's assistants in the annihilation of Jews in Nazi Germany), and in 1967 *The Night They Slaughtered the Boss.* Günter Grass, a novelist who started his playwriting career in 1957 with an absurdist *The Wicked Cooks,* turned in 1966 to polemic in *The Plebians Rehearse the Revolt,* and to the student revolts in 1969 with *Beforehand.* Hans Helmut Kirst made a play out of the 1944 plot against Hitler, *The Officers Revolt* (1966), and Harmut Lange wrote an anti-Prussian polemic in *The Countess of Rathenow* (1969). East German writers Helmut Baierl, Armin Stopler, and Hans Magnus Enzenberger all wrote polemical plays, the last offering *Inquiry in Havana* (American intervention in Cuba) in 1971. The 1967 play of Armand Gatti, *The Passion of General Franco,* elicited protests from Spain. Other writers in a similar vein are the more recent Fritz Hochwalder, Matthew Braun, Hans Gunter Michaelson, and (in Vienna) Peter Handke, who has written and had produced five plays since 1966, and bids fair to make a real name for himself. Absurdism has hardly touched Germany; its focus and attention seem to be elsewhere.

Italy, Scandinavia, Middle Europe, and Spain

The same passion for the expiation of guilt, the crisis of conscience, is evident in the later plays of the Italian, Ugo Betti (1892–1953): *Corruption in the Palace of Justice* (1948), *The Queen and the Rebels* (1951), and *The Burnt Flower Bed* (1953), which, along with many other plays, make him an important Italian writer. The documentary play was evident in Primo Levi's *If This Be a Man* (1965) about Nazi death camps; the

continuing religious influence in Diego Fabbri's *Christ on Trial* (1955); a nod toward absurdism in Dario Fo's *Death and Resurrection of a Puppet* (1971). But Italian playwrights have written mostly realistic comedies, like those of Eduardo de Filippo about Neopolitan characters: *Naples Millionaires* (1946), *Filumena* (1955), *Saturday, Sunday, and Monday* (1959), *The Boss* (1960). Chiefly the theatres of Italy have been filled with plays from other countries.

Thus filled also were the chief theatres of Scandinavia, Belgium, and the Netherlands. In 1969, a native Belgian dramatist had an antiwar play produced—*To Die a Little* by George Renoy. In the same year the Finnish dramatist, Paavo Haavekko wrote an anti-Stalinist documentary, *Agricola and the Fox,* to follow it the next year with *The Bratteras Family.* Social consciousness marked the premiere of Swedish dramatist

THRUST STAGE CONCEPT
Left, the interior of the Guthrie Theatre in
Minneapolis, designed by Tanya Moiseiwitsch,
showing the interestingly varied seating possibilities, and the use of light sources from
the house. Above, a scene from Anthony
Burgess' new adaptation of *Oedipus*. The
thrust stage is fixed, but the surrounding
space can also be used in performance. (The
Guthrie Theatre)

Vainno Linna's *Up the Slaves* (1966), but it
was the old classics of Ibsen and Strindberg
that Ingmar Bergman directed for his yearly
stint at the National Theatre. The theatrical
experimentation that had begun in Poland
with Slawomir Mrozek's *Tango* (1968) was
muted with the 1968 Russian occupation;
Mrozek fled and from Zurich wrote of his
exile in *Wroclaw* (1970). In Rumania Jose
Lacour, in Hungary Gijörgy Szabo, in Yugoslavia Primos Kozak and Dusan Joosnovic
tried out the antirealistic forms and Meodred
Bulatovic wrote *Godot Has Arrived* (1966).
Czechoslovakia, in addition to Josef Topol
and R. J. Clot, had a playwright of international potential in Vaclav Havel whose *The
Memorandum* (1965) was translated and
played in England and America.

In Spain, two playwrights, both born in
1926, represent the two sides of dramatic
writing—Alfonso Sastre in what he calls "the
theatre of anguish," and Alfonso Paso, prolific
writer of comedies. In the nearly twenty
plays that Sastre has written, his concern is
always with the persons and places where
"there is hunger, misery, and the knives are
being sharpened." Typical titles are: *The
Condemned Squad* (1953), *Everyman's Bread*
(1955), *Death in the Neighborhood* (1959),
and *Red Earth* (1960). Lauro Olmo shares
Sastre's social concerns, and has had some
of his plays banned by the Spanish censors.
Also in the realistic tradition is Joaquin
Calvo Sotelo. Paso, on the other hand, has
written over a hundred plays since 1955—all
comedies, short and long. His *Song of the
Grasshopper* (1960) was produced in New
York in 1967; other typical titles are: *The
Poor Little Thing* (1957), *The Girl's Wedding*
(1960), and *Dear Professor* (1965). Miguel
Mihura also writes the popular Spanish
comedies, and Antonio Buero Vallejo tends

toward the symbolic in such a play as *The Story of a Stairway* (1949).

Playwriting in Russia was at a virtual standstill during the years of World War II, and the tightening of censorship in 1949 (with party administrators in each theatre) virtually assured that none but explicitly patriotic plays would be produced. In this vein Nikolai Pogodin wrote *The Missouri Waltz* (anti-American, naturally), *The Aristocrats,* and *Kremlin Chimes* (glorifying the Revolution). After Stalin's death in 1953, and the general relaxation after the 1956 denunciation of Stalin by Khrushchev, he wrote a family problem play called *Sonnet of Petrarch* (1957). Anatoly Safronov and A. Stein wrote similar plays, but the satires of Evgeny Shvarts (*The Naked King,* 1934, *The Dragon,* 1943, *The Shadow,* 1940, *The Story of the Young Marrieds,* 1955) remained unproduced until after his death in 1958. Censorship is still in force in Russia, for even in 1970, Mikail Bulkagov's early anti-Stalinist *Master and Marguerita* was refused permission to be staged. Nevertheless, a new group of playwrights seems to be working: Victor Rogov, Edward Razusky, Vasili Aksenov, Leonid Zorin (with a 1966 play, *Dion,* which pokes fun at Khrushchev), Alexander Volodin, and Yulian Semynov. There have been two evidently popular plays by the famous poet Andrei Voznesensky—*Antiworlds* (1964) and *Watch Your Faces* (1969) which was closed by the censors after two performances. Aleksei Arbuzov in 1969 and 1970 wrote *Happy Days of an Unhappy Man, Faith Hope and Charity,* and *Fairy Tales of Old Arbato*—titles that are reminiscent of an earlier day. It may be that, even though there are no absurdist plays as yet in Russia (and may never be so long as the Soviet system endures, since the absurdist philosophy is the exact opposite of Marxism), there is again enough creative energy stirring to augur well for the future.

England and the United States

For almost ten years after the war, English playwriting pursued the same paths as it had before the war. Two more O'Casey plays were added to the canon during the war years—*Red Roses for Me* (1943) and *Purple Dust* (1945). It looked as if Eliot's earlier venture into poetic drama might become a trend, and the great poet added three more poetic dramas dealing with modern subject-matter in *The Cocktail Party* (1949), *The Confidential Clerk* (1953), and *The Elder Statesman* (1958). Christopher Fry added to the splendor of language on the English stage with the production of *A Phoenix Too Frequent* (1946), *The Lady's Not for Burning* (1949), and *Venus Observed* (1949), in addition to a number of translations from Giraudoux. He later added *The Dark Is Light Enough* (1954), *Curtmantle* (1961), and *A Yard of Sun* (1970). But no other poets took up the challenge; poetic drama was just not resuscitated. The novelist Graham Greene contributed three plays in the 1950s: *The Living Room* (1953), *The Potting Shed* (1957), and *The Complaisant Lover* (1959); Terence Rattigan turned from his previous preoccupation with light comedy to write three very serious plays: *The Winslow Boy* (1946), *The Browning Version* (1948), and *Separate Tables* (1955); and the very literate Enid Bagnold wrote *The Chinese Prime Minister* (1963), *The Chalk Garden* (1965), and *Call Me Jacky* (1968). But the new wave of playwriting would make all these, in time, seem curiously old-fashioned.

It was George Devine's idea at the Royal Court in London that seemed to trigger a new vitality in English playwriting. He de-

voted his managership to the discovery and
production of new plays, and beginning in
1956 with John Osborne's first play, *Look
Back in Anger*, the Royal Court in ten years
introduced a formidable array of new talent
and sparked a revival of playwriting that has
continued to the present day. So invigorating
was this new talent that the venerable Shakespeare Company (now designated the Royal
Shakespeare) not only extended its activities
to the production of new plays, but also set
up an affiliated experimental "collective" in
1963; and the Old Vic (becoming, in essence,
the National Theatre Company headed by
Laurence Olivier, in 1963) also sought out
new plays and playwrights. The theatre collective of Joan Littlewood at the Theatre
Workshop (which had preceded by ten years
the formation of the English Stage Company
at the Royal Court, but was not so much in
the public eye) developed the special talents
of Brendan Behan (1923–1964): *The Quare*

Fellow (1945), *The Hostage* (1958), and *Bor-
stal Boy* (1961); as well as of Shelagh De-
laney, whose first work, *A Taste of Honey*
(1958), was done there, with the second, *The
Lion in Love* (1959), appearing at the Royal
Court.

It is obviously impossible (to say nothing
of undesirable) to list here the names of all
the plays written by the "new wave" of English playwrights. John Osborne has been producing almost a play a year since he began in
1956, with one of the most famous being
The Entertainer (1957), in which Laurence
Olivier starred as Archie Rice, and another
the Paul Scofield vehicle, *The Hotel in Amsterdam* (1968). Three others who have
demonstrated staying power and continuous
creativity are John Arden, Harold Pinter, and
Arnold Wesker. Characteristically, they deal
with lower-middle-class life in a kind of
neorealism which is not psychological but
"situational," in the way that Sartre had

described in his 1946 essay "Forgers of Myths," except that the English playwrights are using situations and characters from the English contemporary milieu. The results are no less disorienting and disturbing than if the method had been attached to legendary materials, as the French were wont to do. As a matter of fact, with Pinter especially, it is likely to be *more* disorienting, especially in such plays as *The Dumbwaiter* (1957), *The Birthday Party* (1958), *The Caretaker* (1960), *The Homecoming* (1965), and *Old Times* (1971). Pinter bids fair to be the most important of the new English writers. Running him a close second is John Arden, whose first real success was with *Live like Pigs* (1958), followed notably (but not exclusively) by *Serjeant Musgrave's Dance* (1959), *The Work-house Donkey* (1960), and *Armstrong's Last Good Night* (1964). Wesker's first success was with *The Kitchen* (1958); *Roots* appeared in

1959, and, along with other plays, *Their Very Own* and *Golden City* in 1966. Other playwrights "discovered" at the Royal Court (listed with a representative play) include: N. F. Simpson (*One Way Pendulum*, 1959), Ann Jellicoe (*The Knack*, 1961), and Edward Bond (*Saved*, 1964). Each of these has gone on to write more plays, but in not nearly the number of those named earlier.

John Whiting (1918–1963) began his writing career with the British Broadcasting Corporation (BBC), and before his untimely death had produced a sizable body of work including *Marching Song* (1954) and *The Devils* (1960). Before 1965, Peter Shaffer had produced both *Five Finger Exercise* (1958), a Pinteresque domestic drama, and *The Royal Hunt of the Sun* (1964), a Brechtian exploration of the conquest of Peru, along with other plays; and works of David Mercer, Fred Watson, Henry Livings, Alun Owen, and

EARLY ARENAS
One of the earliest of arena stages is that of the Penthouse Theatre at the University of Washington (left), opened in 1940 by Glenn Hughes, with an elliptical acting area and auditorium. Above, the Margo Jones Theatre in Dallas, named for one of the pioneers in arena staging techniques.

Bernard Kops had been produced. Since 1965 the not inconsiderable talents of David Storey, Joe Orton, and John Mortimer have come to the fore. David Storey is a young novelist turned playwright who gave an austerely moving play to the talents of John Gielgud and Ralph Richardson in *Home* (1970), the fourth of his plays which now seem to be appearing at yearly intervals. In a brief career, Joe Orton wrote several plays, including *Entertaining Mr. Sloane* (1965) and *The Good and Faithful Servant* (1971). John Mortimer, who is a novelist and screenwriter as well as a playwright, has fewer plays, the latest of which (*Come as You Are,* 1971) starred Glynis Johns and Denholm Elliott in a wry four-part comment on British social classes. Other, newer playwrights have included Alan Ayckbourn, Giles Cooper, George Hulme, Frank Marcus (*The Killing of Sister George,* 1965), John Bowen,

Peter Barnes, Barry England (*Conduct Unbecoming,* 1969), E. A. Whitehead, Charles Wood, Christopher Hampton (*The Philanthropist,* 1970), Tom Stoppard (*Rosencrantz and Guildenstern Are Dead,* 1967), and Anthony Shaffer (*Sleuth,* 1970). All of the plays named here were exported to New York. Also traveling west was Robert Shaw's *Man in the Glass Booth* (1967), the first of a spate of English documentary plays which included others by Charles Wood, Peter Nichols, Frank Norman, Ewan Hooper, and John Hopkins.

Meanwhile, actor-director Peter Ustinov was writing an occasional play (*Romanoff and Juliet,* 1956, *Photo Finish,* 1961, *Halfway Up the Tree,* 1967). Along with several screenplays (notably for *Tom Jones*), Robert Bolt pursued his individual way with such plays as *A Man for All Seasons* (1960) with Thomas More as the hero, and *Vivat! Vivat Regina!* (1970), starring the first Elizabeth and her rival, Mary. Also meanwhile, and not incidentally, the renascence of playwriting was operating in Ireland, producing Bill Naughton (*Alfie,* 1962), Hugh Leonard (*Stephan D.,* 1962), James Saunders (*Next Time I'll Sing to You,* 1962), Conor Cruise O'Brien (*King Herod Explains,* 1969), and Brian Freil (*Philadelphia, Here I Come,* 1965, *The Lovers,* 1967, *The Munday Scheme,* 1970). It might well be said that playwriting in the British Isles has now reached an almost unprecendented quantity; a great deal of it seems to be of very good quality, but the future will be the best judge of that.

When one reads that there were almost a thousand new plays premiered in the United States in the year 1970 alone (a year when Broadway offered as few as thirty-four new shows), some idea may be derived of the upsurge of playwriting in America as well as of the decentralization of theatrical production. Both these tendencies are the predominant movements in American theatre since World War II.

There were a few more plays from the great names of the preceding period. William Saroyan's *The Cave Dwellers* was produced in 1957; Lillian Hellman's *The Autumn Garden* in 1951 and *Toys in the Attic* in 1960; Odets had a lively revival with *The Country Girl* (1950) and *The Flowering Peach* (1954); Behrman produced *The Cold Wind and the Warm* (1959) and *But for Whom Charlie* (1962), the latter for the new Lincoln Center Repertory Company; Thornton Wilder's *The Matchmaker* appeared in 1954; and of the several plays that Maxwell Anderson wrote after the war, the best are *Joan of Lorraine* (1946), which starred Ingrid Bergman, and *Anne of the Thousand Days* (1948), which had Rex Harrison as Henry VIII. The most amazing holdover was Eugene O'Neill. His corrosive play, *The Iceman Cometh*, appeared in 1946, and the haunting *Moon for the Misbegotten* in 1947. O'Neill died in 1953, after presumably having destroyed much unfinished work, particularly of the nine-play cycle upon which he had been working for several years. Two of these, lovingly rescued by his widow, appeared in 1957 and 1967—*A Touch of the Poet* and *More Stately Mansions*. The play which O'Neill had insisted not be shown until twenty-five years after his death appeared in 1956—*Long Day's Journey into Night*, certainly one of his most powerful plays and a grim but understanding picture of his own family and their problems. In addition, a one-act play, *Hughie*, has been performed. Presumably the canon is now complete, and the posthumous additions have, if anything, increased his reputation.

In the United States, there was no turning to poetic drama, perhaps because Maxwell Anderson had tried it earlier. The only major effort in this regard was that of Robinson Jeffers in the 1950 script he pre-

DESIGNING FOR ARENA
Above, a scene from *Playboy of the Western World* in the converted movie house which was the first home of Arena Stage in Washington, D.C. The acting area was rectangular, with four tiers of seats. This scene demonstrates the importance of the floor in arena stage design. Right, a scene from Robert Lowell's *The Old Glory* at the Trinity Square Repertory Company in Providence, Rhode Island. Here the overhead is also used as a means of dressing the volume of stage space.

pared for Judith Anderson on the Medea story, *Tower Beyond Tragedy*, which she played to great acclaim. Gertrude Stein's early work, *Four Saints in Three Acts*, was performed in 1952; Truman Capote essayed a few works in the dramatic form, notably *The Grass Harp* (1952); and in 1970 Kurt Vonnegut's *Happy Birthday, Wanda June* appeared in New York. But almost without exception, writing for the theatre in America was in the hands of those who were solely or primarily playwrights.

A new triumvirate is now challenging the "greats" of the earlier period: Tennessee Williams, William Inge, and Arthur Miller. The most prolific of the group is Tennessee Williams, with a long list of one-act plays in addition to many full-length ones. More than

any recent playwright, his plays are very theatrical, using multiple scenes, dissolves, music, and poetic prose. Though his range of characters is not wide, and his earlier work is better than his later, he is truly in the front rank of modern American playwrights. One of his earliest works, *The Glass Menagerie* (1945), continues to be his most popular, although equally strong are *Streetcar Named Desire* (1947), *The Rose Tattoo* (1951), *Cat on a Hot Tin Roof* (1954), *Sweet Bird of Youth* (1957), and *Night of the Iguana* (1961). A new play by Williams, whenever he has one ready, continues to be an event in the New York season.

Arthur Miller evidently works more slowly and thoughtfully, with a shorter list of plays to his credit, but with every one meticulously wrought, and showing his concern for the simple and downtrodden, his scorn for the exploiters. His most widely known and revered play is *Death of a Salesman* (1949); *The Crucible* (1953) is very possibly his best; *After the Fall* (1964) his most autobiographical. *The Price* appeared in 1968, and *The Creation of the World and Other Business* was produced in the 1972 fall season.

William Inge made his first real impression in 1950 with a touching play that brought Shirley Booth to fame, *Come Back, Little Sheba*. *Picnic* (1953), *Bus Stop* (1955), and *The Dark at the Top of the Stairs* (1957) —all in the vein of psychological realism— made his reputation seem assured. But the plays which followed through 1966 were dis-

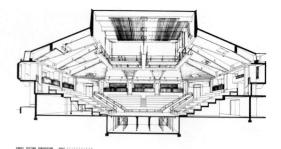

ARENA THEATRE
Left, an exterior view of the theatre plant opened October 9, 1961, showing the entrance to the building which houses offices, dressingrooms, and workrooms, and the theatre building adjoining. Above, a cross-section perspective of the theatre building, showing the arrangement of the seats with the tier at the left being movable, the boxes, the light bridge, and the grid. Right, a photograph of the interior, with set pieces at two of the entrances for actors. This plant, designed by Harry Weese, is unique in arena theatre construction. (Arena Stage)

appointing, and his death in 1973 closed the canon. Of the other writers who were prominent in the 1950s—Arthur Laurents (*The Time of the Cuckoo*, 1952), Carson McCullers (*The Member of the Wedding*, 1949), John Patrick (*Teahouse of the August Moon*, 1953), and Robert Anderson (*Tea and Sympathy*, 1953)—only Anderson is still writing, his last Broadway work—*Solitaire, Double Solitaire*—appearing in 1971.

Of the group of playwrights coming into prominence in the 1960s, the most prolific—and perhaps the most outstanding as well—are Edward Albee and Neil Simon. They stand on opposite sides of the theatrical fence, as it were. Albee began with short plays in the absurdist manner—*The Sandbox* (1959), *The Zoo Story* (1960), and *The American Dream* (1961). But in the year 1961 he also wrote the brutally realistic *The Death of Bessie Smith*, and the next year what is

probably his best and most famous play, *Who's Afraid of Virginia Woolf?* None of his subsequent productions have earned the regard of that one, although *Tiny Alice* (1964), full of metaphysical mysteries, aroused much comment. It would appear that he is now moving toward the "theatre of situation," since in his *All Over* (1971), he simply presents characters who are reacting to the death of a great man.

Nothing could be farther from the stylistic progression of Albee than the plays of Neil Simon. From first to last (with the possible exception of *The Gingerbread Lady*, 1971), he has written a kind of inventive and infectious comedy such as has not been seen since Kaufman and Hart. *Barefoot in the Park* (1963), *The Odd Couple* (1965), *Last of the Red Hot Lovers* (1969) are only three of the plays that seem to come at yearly intervals, each one more widely heralded

than the last, and each destined for a comfortable run on Broadway. Other writers of some reputation through most of the 1960s were: Paddy Chayevsky (*The Tenth Man*, 1959; *Gideon*, 1961), Jack Gelber (*The Connection*, 1959; *Square in the Eye*, 1962), Frank Gilroy (*Who'll Save the Plowboy?*, 1962; *The Subject Was Roses*, 1965), William Gibson (*Two for the Seesaw*, 1958; *The Miracle Worker*, 1959), William Hanley (*Slow Dance on the Killing Ground*, 1964; *Mrs. Dally Has a Lover*, 1965), Murray Schisgal (*The Typist* and *The Tiger*, 1962), John Lewis Carlino (*Cages*, 1962), Gore Vidal (*The Best Man*, 1960), and Hugh Wheeler (*Big Fish, Little Fish*, 1961).

With the exception of Robert Marasco, whose *Child's Play* appeared new and unheralded on Broadway in 1970, other playwrights whose names promise to become memorable have largely worked off-Broadway, off-off-Broadway, and in the regional theatres. Ronald Ribman writes beautifully literate plays like *Journey of the Fifth Horse* (1966) and *Ceremony of Innocence* (1968), as does Jack Richardson in *The Prodigal* (1959). Absurdist and melodramatic in technique, but with a social conscience, is the sizable list of Sam Shepard's plays, a recent one being a major production by the Lincoln Center Repertory Company in 1970—*Operation Sidewinder*. Absurdist in technique and meaning are the plays of Arthur Kopit, among the best of which is *Oh Dad, Poor Dad, Momma's Hung You in the Closet and I'm Feeling So Sad* (1961). But true absurdism still sits a bit uneasily in the American psyche, and most of the newer playwrights are actually in the "theater of situation" scheme with Pinter and his like. Worthy of notice are John Guare, Terence McNally, Paul Zindel, Lanford Wil-

son, Israel Horovitz, Frank Gagliano, Jason Miller, Paul Fisher, Marie Irene Fornes, Leonard Melfi, Rochelle Owens, Dale Wasserman, and David Rabe. Neither has there been much of a thrust toward documentary plays in the United States, with perhaps the most outstanding of the less than a dozen that have appeared being the 1971 *Trial of the Catonsville Nine.*

The 1960s have also seen a flowering of plays by black playwrights. Early, and successful on Broadway, was Lorraine Hansberry's *A Raisin in the Sun* (1959), Ossie Davis' *Purlie Victorious* (1961), and James Baldwin's *Blues for Mr. Charlie* (1963). But the bulk of the increasingly significant black plays have been written for black theatres, like the Negro Ensemble Company, the New Lafayette Theatre, and their counterparts. Significant in the group of black playwrights are Ed Bullins with a sizable list of plays, including *The Electronic Nigger* (1968) and *The Fabulous Miss Marie* (1971), Douglas Turner Ward with *Day of Absence, Happy*

Ending (1966), and *The Reckoning* (1969), LeRoi Jones (*The Slave, The Toilet,* 1964; *The Dutchman,* 1963), Lonnie Elder III (*Ceremonies in Dark Old Men,* 1969), Charles Gordone (*No Place to Be Somebody,* 1969), Errol Hill (*Man Better Man,* 1969), John C. Scott (*Ride a Black Horse,* 1971), and Derek Walcott (*Dream on Monkey Mountain,* 1970). Martin Duberman's *In White America* (1964) and Howard Sackler's *The Great White Hope* (1967) also speak of the black experience, but being written by white men are not in the same category.

Not a year has passed since World War II without one or more musicals being created, the most outstanding in a long list probably being *My Fair Lady* (1956), based upon Shaw's *Pygmalion; West Side Story* (1957) made by Leonard Bernstein and Arthur Laurents from a modern Romeo-Juliet tale; *The King and I* (1951), based on the novel *Anna and the King of Siam; Camelot* (1960) by Richard Rodgers and Oscar Hammerstein, using the King Arthur legends; *Hello, Dolly!*

THE ARTS CENTER IDEA
The John F. Kennedy Center for the Performing Arts in Washington, D.C., was designed by Edward Durrell Stone. It is typical of one kind of arts structure, in that all facilities are contained under one roof. This center houses a concert hall, an opera house (above), a proscenium theatre, and an open theatre, along with ancillary spaces. (The John F. Kennedy Center for the Performing Arts)

(1964) by Jerry Herman, based on Wilder's *The Matchmaker; Fiddler on the Roof* (1964) by Joe Stern, Jerry Bock, and Sheldon Harnick, based on Sholom Aleichem's stories; *Man of La Mancha* (1966) by Mitch Leigh and Joe Darion based on *Don Quixote;* and *1776* by Peter Stone and Sherman Edwards (1970), telling of the Founding Fathers. For their freshness, appeal, and long runs, we might also mention the off-Broadway musicals *The Fantasticks* (1964), by Tom Jones and Harvey Schmidt, and *Your Own Thing* (1968) by Hal Hester and Danny Apolinar.

Finally, mention must be made of a new kind of play, created by theatre collectives, like Jean-Claude van Itallie's *America Hurrah!* (1967), which was worked through with the Open Theatre, and Megan Terry's *Vietrock* (1966), which was similarly produced, or *Paradise Now* (1968), created by The Living Theatre. These are like the productions which emerged from Joan Littlewood's Theatre Workshop—*Oh, What a Lovely War!* (1963) and *Mrs. Wilson's Diary*

(1967). The expansion of the number of theatre collectives indicates that there will probably be more plays in this fashion.

Playhouses and art centers proliferate

The theatre-building boom that followed World War I has been matched and exceeded by that following World War II. Untold numbers of theatre buildings have been erected all over the Western world. In Germany and Russia many of the theatres erected were replacements for structures destroyed during the war. Russia lost more than two hundred; by now all have been replaced and additional ones built. The total number of theatres in Russia stands now at a figure well over one thousand. In Germany, one hundred fifty-five theatres were destroyed. Again, all have been replaced, at a cost of more than four hundred million dollars. The number of theatres in West Germany alone is now one hundred seventy (all but twenty of which are state-supported). And there are an additional one hundred thirty-five in East Germany, all of which are state-supported. Add to that the thirty professional theatres in Finland, the thirty-six of Austria, the sixty-six of Yugoslavia, not to mention Poland, Hungary, and Czechoslovakia, and some idea of the widespread concentration of theatre in middle and eastern Europe alone may be gained. The ardor was only a little less intense in Western Europe and America. Everyone, it seems, has been building theatres—and at the very time when avant-garde playwrights are saying that theatres are not necessary!

German theatre building took two paths. Sometimes a building was carefully restored to former splendors, as was the National Theatre at Munich, which reopened with great fanfare in 1963, after careful research and planning and the expenditure of tremendous sums of money. Sometimes an entirely new structure, like the theatre at Mannheim, was planned and built, incorporating the best of modern ideas about theatre complexes. Opened in 1957, it incorporates two houses under one roof with mutual large lobby space. The larger house has fixed seating after the Bayreuth plan and a revolving stage; the smaller house dispenses entirely with the proscenium and seats the audience on two sides of an open space which is itself capable of alteration. The reconstruction of the National Theatre at Munich, of course, restores an ornate and marvelously equipped nineteenth-century theatre, with its five decorated tiers, its stage boxes and royal box, and its spacious lobbies and salons. The best of modern lighting equipment and control was added. The house is best suited for opera, but Munich also has the Residenztheatre for drama, plus several other theatres.

France took a similar path of restoration and/or new building. By 1960, the sixty theatres of Paris were offering two hundred productions each season, and the decentralization of theatre was going on apace, with professional companies in six dramatic centers, and three more added during the 1960s. Political and economic crises have delayed somewhat the twenty such centers projected by then Minister of Culture André Malraux in 1963, but the idea still lives. The interior of the old Théâtre Sarah Bernhardt was replaced with a single-tier auditorium and a new stage and the house was renamed Théâtre de la Ville in 1968. A new and modern two-thousand-seat house was built in Lyons for Planchon's Théatre de la Cité, and the interior of the Théâtre Nationale Populaire in the Palais de Chaillot (which had been built in 1937) was remodeled in 1954 with a thrust stage.

The expansion of theatre activities in Great Britain also caused similar restorations and new building. Bristol's more than two-hundred-year-old Theatre Royal has been restored for the use of the fine Bristol Repertory Company, as has been the Georgian Theatre at Richmond, in Yorkshire (see page 247). In Coventry, target of saturation bombing during World War II, the new Belgrade Theatre (named because of a gift of Yugoslav timber) was opened in 1958, and new, modern theatres (usually incorporating small, experimental stages as well as the major house) have been built in Nottingham, Guildford, and several other provincial centers. The new Abbey Theatre in Dublin, opened in 1966, includes the small Peacock Theatre for experimental work, while the main house—a gem of wood-paneled walls and upholstered seats in ascending fan shape —has a low stage where the proscenium has been suppressed and the feeling is that actors and audience are occupying the same room. The outside of the building, however, with its four-square, concrete-and-brick, functional construction looks a bit like a parking garage. The Chichester Festival Theatre, opened in 1961, is of the new thrust-stage design, and the complex on the South Bank of the Thames in London which will be completed in the 1970s as the National Theatre, will contain a twelve-hundred-seat house and a nine-hundred-seat house in variant theatrical forms.

In the United States and Canada some old theatres have also been restored, like Sullivan's unique Auditorium in Chicago, the Ritz in New York City, the Avon in Stratford, Canada, and the Royal Alexander in Toronto. A great many old theatres, however (especially in New York), have been pulled down to make way for new construction, which sometimes includes theatres. To date, four of these have been opened: one is the Amer-

DEATH OF A SALESMAN
One of the most famous plays of modern times—the 1949 production of Arthur Miller's play was designed by Jo Mielziner. His setting became as famous as the play itself. (Theatre Collection, New York Public Library)

ican Place Theatre in the lower reaches of an office building on West Forty-sixth Street, two others are the Circle in the Square and Uris Theatres in a building on West Fiftieth Street, and the Minskoff on Forty-fifth Street. Recent changes in the New York City building code have allowed such construction, and additional ones are in the planning stages. The most unprecedented and widespread architectural movement, however, has been the construction of "centers," like the O'Keefe Center in Toronto, Lincoln Center in New York City, the Music Center in Los Angeles, the Art Center in Atlanta, the John F. Kennedy Center in Washington, D.C., and complexes of greater or less size in Birmingham, Milwaukee, Fort Worth, and many other places. In the United States alone the number of facilities either being built or being planned is well over three hundred, and one prediction has it that by about 1980 no self-respecting community of more than one hundred thousand population will be without such a center, either actual or planned. Impetus for such a building spree has come not only from growing civic pride, but also from the implementation of states' arts councils which now function in every state, and from the encouragement (and sometimes the financial assistance) of the National Council on the Arts. Colleges and universities have added to this proliferation of architecturally elaborate arts centers, notably Dartmouth College, the University of Michigan, Southern Methodist University in Dallas, the Krannert Center at the University of Illinois, Brandeis University, the State University of New York at Albany, and innumerable others, all built since World War II but motivated by the same reasons that led the University of Iowa to plan such a facility as early as 1935.

The uncertainty regarding theatrical form and style, and the changing relationships of audiences and actors, is reflected in most of these new structures. Where a theatre was built to provide *living space* for an already on-going theatrical company, like the Shakespeare Festival Theatre at Stratford, Ontario, solutions to structural problems were easy and the resulting buildings successful. That large (at about 2190 seats) house, opened in 1957, made permanent the production concept developed over the years from 1953, when the festival was established and productions first given. Seats surround a thrust stage on three sides. The fourth side, as designed by Tanya Moiseiwitsch, forms a backdrop in which architectural units of columns, balconies, and steps can be adapted to the needs of different plays. And the exterior of the free-standing building is curiously reminiscent of the circus tent in which performances on the spot first began. By 1963, when the Tyrone Guthrie Theatre opened in Minneapolis, the same designer had modified the regular banks of seats of the Festival Theatre into an interesting asymmetrical design, giving more variety of choice in seating arrangements while maintaining the thrust stage concept.

In theatre structures (the large majority) built without a specific company and/or theatrical concept at hand, it was necessary for the planners to incorporate a variety of theatre spaces in the buildings to take care of whatever contingencies might arise. Philosophically, of course (as well as practically), the rush to brick and stone preceding the building of theatre *companies* is rushing in the wrong direction, and wasteful of both time and money. Structures thus built tend to become monuments rather than living theatres and are often unsuccessful because the structure *imposes* a style rather than growing out of a style. However, Americans particularly seem to be afflicted with an "edifice complex" and many a theatre has

NONREALISTIC DESIGN
Left, one of the scenes in the design by René Allio for Roger Planchon's production of *Tartuffe* in Lyons. All the spaces are variable by means of the movable pieces which form the walls and doorways. Above, design for the Broadway production of *Dylan*, which uses an unlocalized platform construction as a multiple setting. (René Basset; Friedman-Abeles)

been built with no real notion of what it would house.

Theatre planners since World War II have been faced with the basic problem that the realistic, illusionistic theatrical mode is an historical artifact rather than a living practice. Certainly the ornate and deep proscenium arch which was an integral part of earlier theatres is an outmoded fixture. Yet opera, whose repertoire was largely written for the "framed" stage, and many older plays still being performed are meant for this style of theatre. But modern audiences want to be a part of the production, at least to the extent of being in the same room with the performers. So the solution arrived at in theatre construction is to

suppress the proscenium frame—that unwanted line of demarkation between stage and house—and have merely an *opening* which is surrounded simply by the walls of the theatre, with no ornate stage boxes, and with the first row of seats as close to the stage as possible. Often, too, the stage is lowered, so that its floor reaches no higher than the knees of the first row of seated patrons. Thus is the interior of the new Abbey Theatre in Dublin planned.

A second solution is to eliminate the stage opening entirely, so that there is no division of any kind between stage and audience, like the end stage of the Mermaid Theatre in London, opened in 1958, where the six hundred fifty seats rise sharply from

the open area which is the stage, and all lighting fixtures are frankly in view. It is a theatre interior which states that it is, indeed, a theatre, and not a facsimile of reality, and audience and actors share a community of feeling. The thrust is the third solution, and probably the most popular. It is that used at the Vivian Beaumont and the Forum theatres in Lincoln Center, at the Mark Taper Forum in Los Angeles, at Chichester in England, and at many other places. The audience surrounds the acting space on three sides, leaving the fourth—behind the actors—for scenic decoration.

The fourth kind of theatre interior, which has been more and more frequently used, is that where audiences completely surround the performers—the arena stage. It has had a considerable period of development and use. In 1924, Gilmore Brown and Ralph Freund built the Playbox at Pasadena, California, using this idea, although this type of staging had been previously experimented with by Azubah Latham at Teachers College, Columbia University, as early as 1914. In 1932, the Russian director, Okhlopkov, used the same idea in his Realistic Theatre in Moscow, and in 1940, Glenn Hughes opened his Penthouse Theatre at the University of Washington in a building especially designed with an elliptical acting area and auditorium. The idea was taken over by community theatres, Margo Jones opening her theatre-in-the-round in Dallas, Texas, later in the same

EUROPEAN DESIGN
Left, the grandly pictorial setting for *The Girl from the Black Forest* at the Bremen State Theatre in Germany. Above, the semi-transparent steps, lighted from below, which Czech designer Josef Svoboda prepared for a production of *Oedipus* at the Prague National Theatre.

decade; and, in 1950, Arena Stage opened in Washington, D.C., in a converted movie house. The Washington company, in 1961, moved into a specially designed house in the new civic center. As planned by the architect, Harry Weese, the building permits a degree of flexible staging and seating in the seven-hundred-fifty-seat capacity house. It is linked by a passageway-lounge to the working-area building, where offices, workshops, dressingrooms, and lobbies are housed. The auditorium unit contains the rectangular area of the stage itself surrounded by enclosing tiers eight rows deep, behind which is a circulation aisle. Above this aisle is a ring of boxes. The thirty- by forty-foot stage area is trapped, and a lighting grid hung

over it. One tier of seats is arranged for dismounting so that three-sided staging can be accomplished on occasion. Ten years later, Arena Stage added the Kreeger Theatre to its complex—a thrust stage. Arena stages are also being built in England and in France but not, so far, in Germany.

Nevertheless, much of the avant-garde theatre today demands an empty room, a mere open space, where various relationships between audience and actors can be set up for different productions. So theatre plants are beginning to incorporate these, as well. The new Krannert Center at the University of Illinois, for instance, includes under one roof a large concert hall, an opera theatre, a "suppressed proscenium" theatre for drama, a free-form studio theatre equipped with sliding panels and exposed lighting, and a Greek style outdoor amphitheatre. There is no built-in thrust stage, although the studio theatre can be thus arranged. At Lincoln Center the various theatre styles are housed in separate buildings: a large theatre with boxes and galleries for the Metropolitan Opera; an end-stage concert hall—the Philharmonic; a suppressed proscenium "ring"-balconied New York State Theatre for ballet and musical comedy; the Vivian Beaumont with a variable-sized (by means of sliding panels) proscenium stage transforming to a thrust stage by means of an elevator, and semicircular seating; and the Forum with a fixed thrust stage in a one-hundred-ninety-nine-seat house. There is no free-form studio. The John F. Kennedy Center houses a concert hall, an opera house, a theatre for drama, and a studio theatre under one roof, and palatial salons and lobbies. Arts centers, civic theatres, and university structures generally plan generous accommodations for audiences beyond the theatre space itself. Gropius' theatre has never been built, probably because the intricacy and expense of

machine installation and operation is more formidable than building two or three different styles of interiors at the same time. Besides, if there are two houses, two productions can run simultaneously, and thus accommodate more paying customers.

Finally, some new theatre trends would do away with theatres altogether, and play in "found" space which can change from performance to performance. Theatre architecture, by its very nature the most conservative of the elements that make up theatre, might be said to be currently in a state of confusion. What will probably transpire is that multiple use plants or variable houses will continue to be built for some time.

Many different choices available in stage settings

For several years after World War II, American scene design continued to dominate the field. One of the best-known designers in the world is Jo Mielziner, who, beginning in 1924, has designed more than two hundred fifty productions—a roster which reads almost like a history of the best American plays for the last forty-plus years. From 1944 to 1953 he was each year named "best scenic designer" by *Variety*'s Poll of Critics, and consistently won additional awards as well. Two of his most famous designs were done for the same season, 1948–1949. They were for Tennessee Williams' *Summer and Smoke* and Arthur Miller's *Death of a Salesman*, the latter directed by Elia Kazan. He designed these productions (as indeed the majority of all of his productions) for the typical Broadway commercial theatre where the stage is no more than twenty-five to thirty feet in depth with a proscenium opening the same measurement in width and about twenty feet in height. Since both plays demand impressionistic settings rather than realistic ones, he was faced with the problem of creating an illusion of great depth and height in this confined space, as well as providing for rapidly changing scenes. These effects were

A NEW THEATRE FOR SHAKESPEARE
Far left, exterior construction, reminiscent of the tent in which productions began, of the Stratford Shakespearean Festival in Ontario, Canada. Left, interior view of the auditorium, showing the arrangement of the two thousand one hundred ninety seats around three sides of the thrust stage. Above, view toward the stage designed by Tanya Moiseiwitsch. It is a permanent setting, having eight acting levels and a trapdoor in the center. (Stratford Shakespearean Festival)

accomplished by the use of painted scrims (which could show a different scenic background if lighted before or behind), skeletal set pieces, and a most intricate disposition and control of light sources. It was during Mielziner's career in the theatre that the old system of border lights, footlights, and floodlights was displaced by an infinitely variable system of different kinds of spotlights disposed before, behind, and above the settings to "paint with light" as Appia had envisioned. The modern scene designer is, perforce, an expert in lighting and not only puts to use the instruments that have been developed, but (as Mielziner frequently did) aids in the development of new instruments.

It is chiefly in the development of such lighting techniques and instruments that Josef Svoboda, the most renowned of European designers in the present day, has made his great reputation. He was instrumental in setting up in Prague, in 1957, an Institute of Scenography to experiment in scenic techniques. By 1958 he had unveiled his *Lanterna*

Magika, which allowed for moving images of performers to be integrated with the performance of live actors on the stage—a technique which startled visitors to the Montreal World's Fair in the late 1960s. Svoboda designs on the grand scale since his milieu is the Continental theatre which traditionally—and even today—has stage spaces one to one-and-a-half times the size of the auditoriums to which they are connected, with spacious wings and overheads, and working areas integrated with the theatre plants. Svoboda has developed what he calls "kinetic scenography," which is self-changing, three-dimensional, and huge, often using back-lighting for sculptural effects. Just such a design, to which was added a black mirror backdrop, was used in a production of *Hamlet* in 1964; it became famous throughout Europe. Svoboda has been invited to design all over Europe. In 1970 he did the production by England's National Theatre Company of an adaptation (by Simon Gray) of Dostoevsky's *The Idiot*, directed by Anthony Quayle. Even

with the fairly limited stage space of the Old Vic (built in 1818), he contrived a setting with three-dimensional moving pieces which changed in full view of the audience, and a lighting scheme with many sources and variations. The versatility and inventiveness of Czech design is illustrated by the popularity of the Prague Black Light Theatre, a mime troupe which toured the United States in 1971, which uses ultraviolet (black) light to give the impression of props and actors (or parts thereof) floating in space. Such an effect, of course, can only be achieved on a proscenium stage.

Proscenium stages and intricate stage effects have continued to dominate the theatres of Germany where a production in Munich (1969) of Odön von Horvath's *Kasimir and Karoline* had a setting which not only revolved, rose, and sank, but included in the background a revolving wheel twinkling with bulbs, and carnival scenes projected against hanging segments of stylized tent. Most English and American theatres are not equipped to handle such intricate technical productions, and in America especially there is the feeling that the setting should not overwhelm the actors, as such technical virtuosity is likely to do. Projections, however, are often used as part of stage settings, usually against the cloth cyclorama with which most proscenium stages are equipped, and which has replaced the fixed plaster Fortuny skydome of earlier in the century. These days, even the proscenium stage is more likely than not to be treated in non-realistic fashion. For Roger Planchon's 1967 production of Molière's *Tartuffe* in Lyons, René Allio designed a unit set of pipes in forced diminishing perspective, like a cage or huge net, into the interstices of which were set various sized wall-decoration panels, pictures, and doors, with similar units descending from the flies to vary the size of

ANOTHER NEW THEATRE FOR SHAKESPEARE
Above, exterior view of the American Shakespeare Festival Theatre at Stratford, Connecticut. It is octagonal in shape and of wood siding, hence reminiscent of the theatres of Shakespeare's time. Right, interior view of the stage with a scene from *Much Ado About Nothing*. The lattice hangings which form the stage set, designed by Rouben Ter-Arutunian, can be arranged in various ways. There is a generous forestage, set on a rake, and many entrances. (American Shakespeare Festival)

the acting area from scene to scene. It made for an interesting visual statement which reinforced and made active the director's epic theatre concept of the play while at the same time sustaining a feeling of period and place.

The increasing popularity of thrust stages, particularly in England and America, has produced different kinds of problems. Here the surfaces available to the designer are reduced to two: the backwall of the stage and the stage floor itself. He must also contend with the necessity for closing in the top of the acting area, so that the performance does not seem lost in vertical space. The latter is usually accomplished by the use of lights from ceiling coves or other house sources to focus on and illuminate specific volumes of space during performance. If the backwall of the stage is architectural, like that of the Shakespeare Festival Theatre in Stratford, Ontario, then the designer is limited to the use of set pieces, banners, curtains, etc. But if the backwall is simply neutral space, then it can be dressed in a variety of ways. For Milton Katselas' pro-

duction of Williams' *Camino Real* at the Mark Taper Forum in 1968, for instance, designer Peter Wexler used a construction dominated by a huge curving stairway and various arches and elevated segments which (extending as they did in sculptural three-dimensions onto the stage floor) gave many diversified acting areas. And the round form of the walled well, which is integral to the action of the play, gave another three-dimensional element to the stage floor. Where the thrust is backed by proscenium stage space, as at the Vivian Beaumont Theatre in Lincoln Center, the designer and director can choose to leave the stage space out of the design for the production, or it can be incorporated, as Jo Mielziner incorporated it in the production of *Danton's Death* there in 1965, when a wagon stage was pushed forward to the thrust as it was needed, and the perspective afforded by the backing stage was used as a perspective of Paris streets in another scene. The Vivian Beaumont stage also incorporates a "ring revolve" which was used to good purpose in James Hart Stearns' design for *The Caucasian Chalk Circle* in

1966, when it was used not only to change scenic elements, but as a treadmill. Carl Toms, the distinguished English designer, used the thrust stage of the Chichester Festival Theatre in an imaginative way for the 1970 production of Robert Bolt's *Vivat! Vivat Regina!* The backwall of his design centered upon a raised dais with spreading steps, the top of which could be transformed into pulpit, throne room, or bedchamber by the addition of set pieces. This dais was flanked on either side by huge screens with massive swiveling panels, decorated on one side with a Scottish motif and on the other with an Elizabethan. As the action and meaning of the play indicated, these were turned; performers could also make entrances through them. It was a dynamic and interesting design which incorporated the playwright's intention that these two swirling worlds co-existed and affected each other without the two principals ever coming face-to-face. Thrust staging, of course, demands front and side lighting, with only enough back lighting to eliminate shadows, or for especially designed effects. Thus, theatres using thrust

stages are necessarily equipped with multiple possibilities for front and side lighting, and the light control booth is most advantageously placed behind the audience and opposite the stage. Similar problems are posed by the end-stage house, like the Mermaid Theatre in London, where the light sources are also disposed in the house itself. The statement of both the thrust stage and the end stage is that performers and audience are frankly gathered together in one room for an experience which is not life itself, but the art of theatre.

Such a statement is even more apparent in the theatrical form of arena staging, where the audience surrounds the acting space. The designer in this form thinks of the stage as a cube of space, to be decorated and lighted on six sides. So he uses an appropriately designed and painted floor, and set pieces which define the acting area without posing problems of sightlines for the audience. The overhead he defines by controlled lighting, or by suspending fractional pieces, such as beams or frames, to help define the space below. Though in the early days of arena staging—at the Penthouse in Seattle, at the Margo Jones Theatre in Dallas—variable mood lighting was thought impossible to achieve, gradual experimentation developed skills and instruments whereby the resources of modern lighting techniques could be used effectively in arena staging. As early as 1953, Leo Gallenstein and the

MULTIPLE-BUILDING ARTS CENTER
Lincoln Center in New York City has several units in separate structures: the Metropolitan Opera House, the New York State Theatre (chiefly ballet), Philharmonic Hall, an outdoor bandshell, and the Vivian Beaumont Theatre. Far left is an interior view of the Beaumont, showing the thrust stage (which can be lowered for seating) in position. Left is a view of the stage during rehearsal, showing its great depth and width, and the ring revolve which is a part of its equipment. Above, the setting for *Camino Real*, designed by Peter Wexler and used for productions both at the Vivian Beaumont and the Mark Taper Forum. Right, the use of the ring revolve in a production of *The Good Woman of Setzuan*. (Lincoln Center Repertory Company)

author had devised a lighting scheme for Alan Schneider's production of *The Glass Menagerie* at Arena Stage in Washington which allowed for mood lighting, and a light-plot with one hundred twenty-three separate cues. Techniques and instruments have been considerably refined since that time, and lighting possibilities for arena theatres today are as sophisticated as any.

The "empty space" which avant-garde directors were universally demanding by the late 1960s, and which Joan Littlewood had been using for several years before that time, is in itself becoming more complicated and "designed." Begun originally as an exploration of actor-audience relationships in various configurations, depending upon the content of the work in hand (as at New York's Living Theatre since 1951, at Grotowski's Polish Laboratory Theatre since 1959, and America's Open Theatre since 1963), the scope of investigation into the entire theatrical construct was enlarged by the appearance in 1964 of Jan Kott's book *Shakespeare Our Contemporary*. As early as 1965, Puck appeared on stage riding a bicycle in a Théâtre Français production of *A Midsummer Night's Dream*. In 1963, two years after Peter Hall and Peter Brook became directors with the Royal Shakespeare Company, Brook began an experimental theatre unit. In 1967, Jan Kott's ideas strongly influenced the National Theatre's production of *As You Like It*. That same year the Hampstead Theatre Club

was founded and with the abolishing of censorship in 1968, the Open Space, the Arts Laboratory, and the Ambience were opened. Peter Brook published his manifesto, *The Empty Space*, and he and Jean-Louis Barrault planned a "revolutionary" International Center of Theatre Research. By this time, many established theatres in France were opening "experimental studios," and Ariane Mnouchkine had staged *A Midsummer Night's Dream* as a macabre nightmare in a circus. In 1968, also, American director-critic Richard Schechner invented the name "environmental theatre" for productions wherein audience space and acting space are one, with different arrangements (or changing arrangements during the course of performance) for various productions. Many theatrical troupes—professional, semi-professional, and university—are now working in free-form space into which the designer (working in close cooperation with the developing performance) uses various con-structions of platforms, steps, screens, or a variety of sculptural forms which will allow space for unconventional seating of audience as well as space for the performers. The concept is not unlike the cube of space involved in designing for arena productions, except that in so-called environmental theatre the audience space is included into and becomes a part of the design, and the structures therefore must be of substantial materials.

Such schools as Sarah Lawrence College, the California Institute of the Arts, the New York State Universities at Albany and Stony Brook, the City University colleges of Queens and Hunter have either built or are planning to build free-form theatres which, by means of geometric or modular elements, sometimes on hydraulic lifts or series of tracks, can be used in what is hoped to be an infinite variety of ways. Lighting installations in such places are also planned to be infinitely variable, although some proponents

of environmental theatre insist that unvarying direct illumination is the only viable kind of lighting for a theatre presentation designed to break down the barriers between art and life. Thus Peter Brook's *A Midsummer Night's Dream* in 1970 used unvarying white light to illuminate the three-sided white box with several trapezes which comprised the set.

The natural development of the environmental idea, of course, is to dispense with the theatre structure entirely, and to play a performance in the town square, as Luca Ronconi's *Orlando Furioso* was played at Spoleto in 1969 and under a plastic dome in Manhattan's Bryant Park in 1971. A series of variably sized platforms on wheels were acting space for the performers, and these platforms were moved with some rapidity through and among the spectators who stood about in the large, open space. The huge and natural space of the ruins of Persepolis in Iran was put to use by Peter Brook in 1971 for his production of *Orghast,* and, on a smaller scale, street theatre and guerrilla theatre groups everywhere use "found" space. Just as these tendencies would seem to lead to the elimination of theatre structures entirely, so too the set designer would seem to be displaced in favor of a type of engineer-architect, reminiscent of Serlio and Sabbattini in the Renaissance, who planned and built total theatre spaces.

Costume concepts also highly variable

The extremes of the avant-garde theatres eliminate the costume designer as well, for the elimination or blurring of distinctions between audience and performer implies that they shall be similarly dressed, with nothing to mark the performer as "special" or "different" from members of the audience. That is a practice followed by some groups. Another theory is that the essential reality and "honesty" of the performance demands an "honest" approach to the human body; therefore the actors are presented nude or with a simple loincloth. After fifteen hundred years of costumed players, theatre of this kind has eliminated the costume. A third approach of the environmental theatre is that costumes should be constructed of "found" materials as complement to the "found space." Thus André Gregory's *Alice in Wonderland* (1970) was costumed by Eugene and Franne Lee in garments made of second-hand quilts, old rosettes, shawls, and scarves. The use of everyday or "street clothes" for performers is not a revolutionary development per se, since "modern dress" for the classics has been a part of theatre for a very long time indeed. And the reasoning currently given for this choice, while it sounds new in the context of environmental theatre, is exactly the same as it has always been—to involve the audience in the *immediacy* of the statement being made in the performance.

But theatre which is not deliberately experimental or avant-garde has proceeded in the matter of costuming along the lines laid down by the new stagecraft of the early years of the century. The endeavor is the same as that enunciated by Robert Edmond Jones in *The Dramatic Imagination*, referred to earlier. Carl Toms, made a Commander of the Order of the British Empire in 1971 for his services to British theatre, says it again in simpler words:

I begin by delving into the text. I try to find out what attitude one can take, to give the show an original look, but at the same time, which will only build what is already there in the text. Sometimes you have to resist great ideas that don't fit. Basically, one is trying to eliminate the superfluous.

It is not a new credo, but a continuing point of view: design should serve the playwright and the performance.

Costuming a play "in period"—still the most prevalent of choices—has been immeasurably aided by the family of synthetic fabrics (like nylon in all its guises), knit fabrics, and the various plastic materials, including vinyl—to say nothing of spray paints and latex substances. Almost any effect can now be achieved by judicious choice of materials, and at less cost than formerly. When Irene Sharaff designed the costumes for *The King and I* in 1951, they were all made of real silk: costly to acquire and costly to maintain, and offering a real problem because so many of the performers had to wear body makeup. The makeup problem was solved by Eddie Senz, one of the outstanding makeup artists in the world, by the use of water-soluble body makeup. But today synthetic fabrics might also be substituted for the more expensive real silks with no loss of effectiveness. Period costume requires a designer willing to research not only the predominant styles of the period, but also all possible variations thereof, in order that every character in a given play be dressed not only as befits his character, but also as best suits his person. This research encompasses not only dress, but shoes, gloves, hats, and wigs as well. Then all must be fitted to the director's concept of the play and (if the set designer is another person) to the total design concept. Nancy Potts, for instance, in creating the costumes for the APA-Phoenix production of *The Misanthrope* in 1968, produced a varied selection of seventeenth-century clothes which ranged from a very fussy Arsinoé to a comparatively austere Alceste, all within the color palette set by the designer, James Tilton. The effect desired, and beautifully achieved, was that of an aged lithograph. The colors were all shades of brown—from a light cream to a medium dark brown, with some lines in black, and rather than subduing the perfor-

mance, this plan seemed to make the acting
and the dialogue more brilliant. Carl Tom's
period designs for *Vivat! Vivat Regina!* reflected the development of the characters in
the play in that those of Mary became simpler and less adorned, while those of Elizabeth grew heavier and more richly adorned
as the scenes progressed.

The production of *The House of Atreus*,
which Tanya Moiseiwitsch designed for
Tyrone Guthrie at the Minnesota Theatre
Company in 1968, dressed the all-male cast
in heavy robes with full-head masks and
gloves, so that the effect was monumental
and the ancient Greek tragedy played itself
through like a ritual. Masks have been effectively used not only in this performance, but
in a prior one at the Shakespearean Festival
Theatre in Stratford, Ontario. They are
also demanded by such a play as Genet's

The Blacks. Larger than life-size figures were
achieved by the use of masks and papier-
mâché body shells for quite a different
directorial concept in the production of Jean-
Claude van Itallie's *Motel* (a part of *America
Hurrah!*, 1967). Here the effect was awesome
and frightening, as was intended.

Period plays also continue to be costumed
on occasion in dress which is either modern
or of another period from the play itself,
as *Much Ado About Nothing* was done at
Stratford, Connecticut, and again on Broadway in 1972 in a production by Joseph Papp,
or the American Conservatory Theatre's production of *The Misanthrope* in 1969, or most
recently, as *Hamlet* was presented in modern "mod" clothes by Yuri Lyubimov at
Moscow's Taganka Theatre in 1972.

Makeup tends to be more natural these
days, with less and less material used to

achieve effects. Part of this tendency, of course, is attributable to the thrust and arena staging techniques, where proximity to the audience precludes artificiality. A wider variety of cosmetics is now available than ever before, including latex which can be used to "paint'" age over a young face as well as to give a good base for beards. Wigs have also come into popular use, not only for what used to be called "character" parts, but for all kinds of parts, wherever they can be used to create the proper effect.

Though, generally speaking, makeup is applied less heavily today, it is sometimes used deliberately and conspicuously for a mask effect, as in Douglas Turner Ward's *Day of Absence* or for a clown effect as in the National Theatre of the Deaf's *Gianni Schicchi*, or the "little musical," *Godspell*. Many of the new theatre groups, like the Polish Laboratory Theatre, eschew the use of

makeup altogether, saying that (in Grotowski's case at least) the actor should be so well trained that he can, without makeup, force his face and body to any appearance he wishes to create. With other groups, makeup is not used because it seems to them more "honest," a reason which sounds like that given by the great nineteenth-century actress Eleanora Duse.

In the final analysis, it might be said that modern theatre practice in makeup is totally dependent upon the director's concept of the play at hand, and is used to enhance that concept rather than simply to make individual performers more (or less) attractive than they really are.

Many new experiments in acting

The increasing decentralization of theatre since World War II has brought with it great

THEATRE LABORATORIES
The development of plays and performances through long-term ensemble work has been a feature of recent years. Three outstanding groups are pictured here. Far left, a scene from the performance of Brendan Behan's *The Hostage*, developed at the London Theatre Workshop, under the direction of Joan Littlewood. Left, a scene from *Akropolis*, developed by the Polish Laboratory Theatre under the direction of Jerzy Grotowski. Above, a scene from *The Serpent*, developed at the Open Theatre under the direction of Joseph Chaikin and Roberta Sklar. (Friedman-Abeles, Roberta Sklar)

advantages to actors. Not only are more performers able to make a decent, if not lavish, living from the practice of their art, they also are able to develop in that art through the constant practice of it. One might now with some reason say that the entire Western world is more or less in consonance with the idea that the acting profession is one for which individuals can prepare and find reasonable assurance of a lifework. Such a situation has, of course, long been prevalent in Russia and in Germany, where the many state-supported theatres have offered a livelihood to a significant body of professional workers. The growth of the French dramatic centers in the last twenty-five years and the extension of the English repertory theatres in the same period have offered the same benefits to professionals in those countries, while at the same time providing possibilities for training. Thousands of constantly work-

ing actors comprise the profession in both of those countries today, one estimate putting it at five thousand in France and fourteen thousand in England, at least ten thousand in Germany, and many times that number in Russia. Italy alone has fewer than one thousand, perhaps for the reason that Vittorio Gassman (who has continuously tried to increase theatre activity in Italy) has stated: "Everyone is an actor in Italy, preferring to play out the drama in their lives than to pay professionals to do it." But even in Italy, where significant contributions to the development of motion pictures have been an outstanding characteristic in modern times, there are now increasing numbers of permanent theatre companies (*teatro stabile*) and some called *semistabile*, which maintain regular personnel but no permanent home. Anna Proclemer and Giorgio Albertazzi are the leaders of one such troupe, and another is headed by Giorgio de Lulo, Rossella Falk, Romolo Valli, and Elsa Albani. All companies still tour widely, and although each teatro stabile has some state subsidy, there is no national theatre as such, and the possibilities for training are limited. Perhaps the most famous of these companies is Paolo Grazzi's *Piccolo Teatro di Milano.*

In every year since 1966, more professionals have been employed outside New York City than found work within it. There have been a few companies, like the San Francisco Actors Workshop from 1952 to 1965, the APA from 1959, and William Ball's American Conservatory Theatre from 1965, whose original concept was a group of actors working together to make theatre, where the association lasted over a period of years, and (especially in ACT) training is an essential part of the work. But most of these theatres in the United States employ actors on yearly contracts, even though in individual cases they are renewed from year to year. In these theatres the emphasis is, naturally, on performance rather than on training; in the United States training is largely the province of schools and colleges, both private and public. The lack of a national theatre, however, tends to perpetuate a lack of focus in American acting, and graduates of schools and academies do not move so easily into professional positions as is the case in other parts of the Western world. Acting in America is still largely a "free-lance" profession. There are, however, an increasing number of colleges and universities that house professional companies, and the transition from training to profession is gradually easing.

The pattern in Continental Europe is quite different. For instance, students who graduate from the State Theatrical Higher School in Warsaw, Poland (a four-year course with strict requirements) move directly into positions with the many state

TWO COLLEGE PRODUCTIONS
Above, the Hunter College Theatre Workshop production of *The Prodigal.* For this production a large forestage was erected beyond the conventional proscenium arch to cover the orchestra pit; particular attention was given to making all elements work to produce a unified whole. Right, a production at the Baylor University Theatre, where the stage is built with generous side aprons and the seats can swivel to face in different directions. (Baylor University)

theatres of Poland. The same pattern obtains in Russia and in most of the central and eastern European countries. Aside from the Conservatory in Paris, the most important academy in France has been that attached to the Dramatic Center at Strasbourg, where Michel Saint-Denis was long the head. The students work with the professional company, and Saint-Denis expressed the goal as "[to] recreate, by the forcefulness of their acting, their power of human observation, and their perfect mastery of body, a poetical climate arising from the dramatic transposition of reality." When the Juilliard School in New York, moving to the new complex at Lincoln Center, began its drama division in 1967, Saint-Denis joined John Houseman to plan its curriculum and choose its first students. In England, the venerable Royal Academy of Dramatic Art (RADA) and

LAMBDA, as well as the Central School at Albert Hall (where Laurence Olivier had his training) have largely supplied the acting personnel of British theatres, who then typically move (but with nothing like the assurance of the students in Continental state institutions) to provincial companies before essaying the London theatres, or the Royal Shakespeare Company, or the National Theatre.

During the years of the 1950s in New York, the dominant configuration in acting was that of the Actors Studio, which was founded by Lee Strasberg in 1949, and became the shrine of "the Method" in America, as it had been interpreted by the Group Theatre of the previous decade. It was designed as a place for professional actors to extend their skills, and over the years boasted a roster that included such names

as Julie Harris, Marlon Brando, David Wayne, Eli Wallach, Kim Stanley, Paul Newman, Geraldine Page, Shelley Winters, Karl Malden, James Dean, and Anne Bancroft. Many "acting studios" in New York and elsewhere modeled themselves on *the* Studio, although few of them rose to its prestige. By the 1960s, however, there was a sizable group of people who questioned the mystique of self-exploration in minutely psychological terms which had come to be the image of "the Method." A revolutionary Viola Spolin was declaring that "Everyone can act. Everyone can improvise. Anyone who wishes to can play in the theatre and learn to become 'stageworthy,'" and Judith Malina and Julian Beck in New York were forming their Living Theatre (1951) to begin the search for "a style of acting that will produce revelation." In 1963 Joseph Chaikin started his Open Theatre "To

TWO WAYS OF COSTUMING PERIOD PLAYS
Modern designers have frequently departed
from historical accuracy in costuming period
plays, as the two photographs above indicate.
To the left is a scene from *Romeo and Juliet*
at the Stratford (Ontario) Shakespearean
Festival Theatre, and at the right, one from
Tyrone Guthrie's production of *Hamlet* at
the Guthrie Theatre in Minneapolis. On the
other hand, many modern designers adhere
to authenticity, as in the two scenes at right:
left, from the production of *Richard III* at
the Stratford (Ontario) Shakespearean Festival; right, from the APA-Phoenix production
of *The Misanthrope*. (Douglas Spillane; The
Guthrie Theatre; Peter Smith; Van Williams)

redefine the limits of the stage experience . . .
to find ways of reaching each other and the
audience." Those pioneer efforts were followed by the addition of many groups whose
aims were similar; the Firehouse Theatre in
Minneapolis, Center Stage in Los Angeles,
the Compass and the Second City Theatre in
Chicago, the Performance Group, the La-
Mama Experimental Theatre, and the Manhattan Project in New York, and several
others.

In England, the visit of Brecht's Berliner Ensemble to London in 1956 engendered
much discussion and dissatisfaction with current thinking and practice in acting, although
Joan Littlewood (at war with the "establishment" since 1954) had already taken her
troupe to the Paris International Arts Festival and had drawn an Arts Council grant as
a result of the notice she achieved there. In

1963 Peter Brook, influenced by Brecht,
Artaud, and Beckett, began a series of experiments with the younger members of the
Royal Shakespeare Company, of which he was
then a director, and the innovative and startling production of *Marat/Sade* at the Aldwych
in 1964 was the outcome. Subsequently, as
in America, many theatre ensembles came
into existence, more being added each year.

The pattern of Brook in attaching an
experimental unit to an establishment theatre is one that existed in both France and
Russia. The most famous of them all—
Grotowski's Polish Laboratory Theatre in
Wroclaw—has been since 1965 fully supported by the state as a separate institution,
having begun in Opole in 1959 as the Theatre
Laboratory attached to the state theatre
there. Its official title is the Institute for
Research into Acting. Although no such offi-

cially designated "research institution" has been established in Russia thus far, several directors have concluded that, although "everything in the Russian theatre is based on Stanislavski," he was, after all, of his own time and "must be advanced" by further exploration into the possibilities of some sort of combination between the form of Meyerhold and the content of Stanislavski. Valentin Pluchek at the Moscow Theatre of Satire and Yuri Lyubimov at the Taganka Theatre have gone furthest in these explorations.

Needless to say, there are as many processes and points of view as there are dissident voices. The intensity and dedication of Grotowski's researches into "poor theatre" (i.e., stripped of everything but the essentials of actor and audience) fostered many imitations, particularly in America, and particularly after the appearance of his company in

New York in the fall of 1969. In 1971, he felt constrained to return in order to "correct" misapplications of his principles. Many of the new "theatre collectives" are actually (as is Grotowski himself) the direct inheritors of that portion of Stanislavski's teachings which send the actor back into himself for resources. Viola Spolin's "scheme," as she calls it, seems to develop "naturalistic" ability in self-expression, but is not applicable to texts and the demands of playwrights. The same, of course, could be said for much of the Actors Studio work. Chaikin creates his own texts and has never dealt with any other materials. Grotowski, Schechner, and Gregory are true Artaudians in their declaration of "no more masterpieces," for they turn texts to their own use and remake them in their own image. Grotowski over the years has developed a

marvelously competent group of actors, particularly the astonishing Ryszard Ceislak; so far, none of the groups that espouse his principles have matched Grotowski's success.

All the new experimenters insist upon the actor using his full equipment of mind, will, and body—particularly body. Ensembles have developed that insist upon acrobatic and dance facility. These skills can only be good for the acting profession in general. Somewhere along the line since Stanislavski the actor's body was laid to rest and his feelings sublimated. But if the whole new movement

in acting is not to spend itself in self-indulgence (a tendency too often deplorably present), then it must somewhere, somehow ask itself some hard questions about the responsibility of the actor as an interpreter of the playwright's text, the playwright's intention. Perhaps the answer is to be found in the work of the great French actor, Jean-Louis Barrault, who, although devoted to mime and the control thus demanded of the actor, is sufficiently French and sufficiently the inheritor of Copeau to insist that "the actor must work within the play's setting," and "mime and diction are the two sides of

MASKS IN THE MODERN THEATRE
Left, *Oedipus* at the Stratford (Ontario) Shakespearean Festival Theatre; above, a scene from *The Blacks* by Genet. Here are modern examples of the use of masks, one of theatre's oldest devices. They add to the cosmic emphasis of the plays in which they are used. (Theatre Collection, New York Public Library; Martha Swope)

an actor's art, and the visual and auditory sensations must crystallize into a unity for the actor as well as for the audience."

It is undoubtedly true that the minutely realistic acting demanded by cinema and television have necessitated a reaction in which the theatre can define itself as a living experience involving audience as well as actors. Too many of the experimental groups have blurred distinctions between actor and audience and in their zealous insistence that life is art bid fair to destroy the art itself. Perhaps the final word should be that of Laurence Olivier, whom most theatre people in most places and most of the time would nominate the greatest English-speaking actor alive, and perhaps simply the greatest actor alive. He says: "If somebody asked me to put in one sentence what acting was, I should say that acting was the art of persuasion. The actor persuades himself, first, and through himself, the audience."

Summary

In the period since World War II, theatre has exhibited tendencies which reflect the larger movement of the world of which it is a part. It has become more international, with more extensive communication and exchange than has ever before existed. It has also been in turmoil, with experimentation in playwriting, architecture, design, and acting.

Form has been called into question in all these areas. The new playwrights have deliberately called their works "antiplays." Environmental theatre has destroyed the concept of theatre space divided into segments for performance and segments for audience. Design has become nondesign, and acting has begun to insist upon life as the same as art. Everyone can be an actor. Even the distinction between the theatre arts and the visual arts has been amalgamated in "happenings," and dance and theatre have also overlapped. One could question whether or not the death of God will indeed be followed by the death of theatre and finally the death of man himself as an ordering entity. Certainly disorder seems more the rule today than order, with chaos just around the corner. Yet once the eye of the storm is negotiated, calm is sure to follow. A changed world of theatre will undoubtedly emerge, but it is unlikely that theatre will die. It is an art form which, for as long as recorded memory extends, has shown man his own image in the virtual life of the theatre, so that he is led to reflect upon that life and to deepen his perceptions of himself and his world. Theatre is so intrinsic a part of what it means to be human that it will not likely disappear so long as man himself exists.

Play list

Any of the play titles mentioned in the text may profitably be read as basic theatre material for any given period. The list below suggests for easy reference titles of some historical significance. It is strongly recommended that plays be read as the period in which they were first produced are studied. All of those listed here—and a great many more—are easily available nowadays in the many play anthologies which have been published in recent years, particularly in paperback editions.

Primitive and Classic Theatre
(*chapters* 1, 2, 3, 4)

Aeschylus: *Agamemnon*
Aristophanes: *The Birds, The Frogs*
Euripides: *Medea, Electra*
Menander: *The Girl from Samos*
Plautus: *Miles Gloriosus*
Sophocles: *Antigone, Oedipus Rex*
Terence: *Phormio*

The Middle Ages
(*chapter* 5)

The Brome Abraham and Isaac
The Chester Mystery Plays
Everyman
Heywood, John: *Johan, Johan*
Lyndsay, David : *Satire*
of the Three Estates
Master Pierre Pathelin
The Second Shepherds' Play
(Wakefield Cycle)
The York Cycle of Mystery Plays

The Renaissance
(*chapters* 6, 7, 8)

Aretino: one of the dialogues
in *Works*, vol. I
Calderon: *Life Is a Dream*
Dekker, Thomas: *The Shoemakers'*
Holiday
Greene, Robert: *Friar Bacon and*
Friar Bungay
Jonson, Ben: *The Alchemist, Volpone*
Kyd, Thomas: *The Spanish Tragedy*

Lope de Vega: *The Mayor of Zalamea,*
Madrid Steel
Machiavelli, Niccolo: *Mandragola*
Massinger, Philip: *A New Way to Pay*
Old Debts
Shakespeare, William: Any or all
Tasso: *Aminta*

The Seventeenth Century
(*chapters* 9, 10)

Congreve, William: *Love for Love,*
The Way of the World
Corneille, Pierre: *Le Cid*
Dryden, John: *All for Love, or*
The World Well Lost
Etherege, George: *The Man of Mode*
Farquhar, George: *The Beaux Stratagem*
Molière: *The Misanthrope, The Imaginary*
Invalid, Tartuffe
Otway, Thomas: *Venice Preserved*
Racine, Jean: *Athalie, Esther, Phèdre*
Vanbrugh, John: *The Relapse*
Wycherley, William: *The Country Wife*

The Eighteenth Century
(*chapters* 11, 12)

Addison, Joseph: *Cato*
Beaumarchais: *The Barber of Seville,*
The Marriage of Figaro
Cumberland, Richard: *The West Indian*
Goethe, Johann Wolfgang von: *Faust,*
Part 1
Goldoni, Carlo: *The Mistress of the Inn*
Goldsmith, Oliver: *She Stoops to Conquer*
Gozzi, Carlo: *The Three Oranges*
Lessing, G. E.: *Minna von Barnhelm*
Lillo, George: *The London Merchant, or*
The History of George Barnwell
Sheridan, Richard Brinsley: *The School*
for Scandal
Steele, Richard: *The Conscious Lovers*
Voltaire: *Zaïre*

Oriental Theatre
(*chapter* 13)

A Bunraku play
A Kabuki play
A Noh play
Hsiung, H. I.: *Lady Precious Stream*
The Little Clay Cart
Sakuntala

The Nineteenth Century
(*chapters* 14, 15)

Aiken, George L.: *Uncle Tom's Cabin*
Bird, Robert Montgomery: *The Broker of Bogota*
Boker, George Henry: *Francesca da Rimini*
Boucicault, Dion: *The Octoroon, The Poor of New York, London Assurance*
Bulwer-Lytton, Edward: *Richelieu, The Lady of Lyons*
Dumas, Alexandre, *fils*: *The Lady of the Camellias*
Gogol, Nikolai: *The Inspector General*
Hugo, Victor: *Hernani*
Rostand, Edmond: *Cyrano de Bergerac*
Schiller, J. F.: *Maria Stuart*
Turgenev, Ivan: *A Month in the Country*
Wilde, Oscar: *The Importance of Being Earnest, Lady Windermere's Fan*

Modern Theatre
(*chapters* 16, 17, 18)

Beckett, Samuel: *Waiting for Godot*
Behan, Brendan: *The Hostage*
Benavente, Jacinto: *The Bonds of Interest*
Čapek, Karel: *R. U. R.*
Chekhov, Anton: *The Seagull, Uncle Vanya*
Coward, Noel: *Tonight at 8:30*
Fry, Christopher: *The Lady's Not for Burning*
Garcia-Lorca, Federico: *The House of Bernarda Alba, Yerma*
Giraudoux, Jean: *Tiger at the Gates*
Herne, James A.: *Margaret Fleming*
Ibsen, Henrik: *A Doll's House, Hedda Gabler*
Inge, William: *Come Back, Little Sheba*
Ionesco, Eugene: *The Bald Soprano, The Chairs, The Lesson*
Katayev, Valentine: *Squaring the Circle*
Miller, Arthur: *Death of a Salesman, The Crucible*
O'Neill, Eugene: *Marco Millions, Mourning Becomes Electra*
Pinero, Sir Arthur Wing: *The Second Mrs. Tanqueray*
Pinter, Harold: *The Birthday Party, The Caretaker*
Pirandello, Luigi: *Six Characters in Search of an Author*
Rice, Elmer: *The Adding Machine*
Shaw, Bernard: *Pygmalion, Heartbreak House*
Stoppard, Tom: *Rosencrantz and Guildenstern Are Dead*
Weiss, Peter: *Marat/Sade*
Wilder, Thornton: *Our Town, The Skin of Our Teeth*
Williams, Tennessee: *The Glass Menagerie, Summer and Smoke*

Suggested study problems

The following are suggested as types of work problems which may help students to develop familiarity with the milieu of theatre in many times and places. At the same time they may, through such exercises, consolidate and put to use a mass of information which might not otherwise come to life. It is also hoped that the problems may stimulate creative imagination. The individual instructor will no doubt think of many more.

Primitive and Classic Theatre
(*chapters* 1, 2, 3, 4)

1 Write a brief scenario for any one of the American Indian dance-dramas.
2 Pretend that you are I-kher-nefert writing of what you plan to do in your production of the Abydos Passion Play in the year 1868 B.C.
3 Draw up a "character plot" for the play you read, assigning the chief actors to roles, and indicating where supernumeraries appear on stage.
4 For the play you read, draw up a complete prop list for the production as given in its contemporary theatre.
5 Make a stage diagram for the first production of the play you read.
6 Discuss, giving examples, the changing functions of the chorus in three Greek plays.
7 Sketch the wardrobes of the chief actors in *Medea*, including masks.
8 Classify the characters by type in *Miles Gloriosus*, and briefly describe each type.
9 You are present at the first production of a play by Aristophanes. Describe the event.
10 Lay out the playing area for a specific primitive dance-drama, being sure to include audience space, offstage space, entrances, and exits, as well as stage properties.

The Middle Ages
(*chapter* 5)

1 Imagine yourself an eyewitness to the production of an interlude in the Middle Ages. Give an account of it.

2 Describe the stage setting for a fifteenth-century French mystery play.
3 Draw up a descriptive list of costumes for the play you read.
4 Draw a detailed sketch and plan of a pageant wagon for a particular mystery play production. Indicate the production.
5 Imagine yourself a participant in the Feast of Fools. Describe the event.
6 Write a plot outline for a morality, including a list of the characters and a brief description of each character.
7 As a member of a specific English craft guild, write of your assignment in the Corpus Christi Day plays.
8 You are charged with supervising the annual May Day festivities in your village. Write a detailed plan for the event.

The Renaissance
(*chapters* 6, 7, 8)

1 You are a commedia producer. Draw up a scenario for your company as a production for a large fair in a country town.
2 You are present at the opening of the Teatro Olimpico. Describe the event.
3 You are an Italian nobleman planning a pastoral for your garden theatre. Write a letter to the person you have chosen to produce it, explaining what you want.
4 You are a knowledgeable Spanish gentleman who has just seen a Lope de Vega play in a public theatre. Write a critique.
5 You are a contemporary of Calderon and think him superior to Lope de Vega. Write a defense of your point of view.
6 Draw up a seating chart and scale of prices for (a) a private theatre, and (b) a public playhouse, c. 1600 in England.
7 Suppose yourself the casting director for the play you read. Draw up a list of requirements—physical and histrionic— for persons you will audition for each role.
8 For each character in the play you read, draw up a list of costume items and hand props for production in their contemporary theatre.
9 As Ben Jonson, or Sir Philip Sidney, criticize a typical production at an Elizabethan public playhouse.
10 You have just seen a performance of the

play you read; suppose yourself a contemporary and write a letter to a friend in Italy describing your experience.

The Seventeenth Century
(*chapters* 9, 10)

1 As a member of the Académie Française write a paper condemning the performance of *The Cid* you have just seen.
2 As Madame de Maintenon, write a letter to Racine requesting him to compose a play for St. Cyr. Detail exactly what you want.
3 For a court performance of *The Misanthrope*, draw up descriptive program notes, including the spectacular and ballet presentations between the acts.
4 As a contemporary of Dryden, point out his superiority over Shakespeare in his dramatization of the story of Antony and Cleopatra.
5 Draw up a cue sheet for scene shifting in Congreve's *Love for Love* or for *The Way of the World*, giving pieces to be moved and scenes to be set or revealed.
6 You are a member of the court party attending an English Restoration play at the first Drury Lane. Describe your impressions of play and playhouse.
7 Draw up three sample playbills. Include at least one French one.
8 Draw up descriptive costume lists, including hand props, for two plays you read.
9 As Montdory, appeal to Richelieu for permission to perform in Paris outside the jurisdiction of the Hôtel de Bourgogne. Then, as Richelieu, respond to the appeal.
10 Imagine yourself a member of the audience at the opening of Molière's Théâtre Illustré on New Year's Day, 1644. Describe the event.

The Eighteenth Century
(*chapters* 11, 12)

1 Write an imaginary dialogue between Quin and Garrick on the subject of acting.
2 Write a defense of the prevailing method of costuming actresses in the eighteenth century.
3 Write a letter to Garrick, as manager, urging the use of the front curtain and/or act and scene drops.

4 Write a protest to the management of the Comédie Française on the behavior of the audience—of which you are a member.
5 Protest to Goldoni over his attempt to regularize the commedia.
6 As Gottsched, admire Addison's *Cato*.
7 As Voltaire, write an explanation to your cast of your views on acting.
8 You have just seen one of Mme. Favart's "authentic" plays. Write your reaction as a typical viewer.
9 As a member of Hallam's company, write to a theatre friend in England of your first experience of performing in Williamsburg, Virginia, in 1752.
10 As Garrick, write a persuasive presentation to your acting company to convince them that your plan to abolish spectators from the stage is a good one.

Oriental Theatre
(*chapter* 13)

1 Write an imaginary introductory speech for the manager of an acting company in classic India to precede the performance your company is presenting.
2 Draw up an imaginary edict for the establishment of the College of the Pear Garden.
3 Sketch the face makeup for the characters in a Chinese play.
4 Sketch the setting for a Kabuki play, using the revolving stage.
5 Write a description of the presentation of a Noh play in the palace of the emperor.
6 As Chikamatsu, explain to a friend why you prefer writing for the Bunraku theatre.
7 As a Chinese nobleman, invite a friend to accompany you to a "tea-house" theatre. Since he has never attended, detail the experience for him.

The Nineteenth Century
(*chapters* 14, 15)

1 Make up a cue sheet for the claques you hire for a presentation at the Comédie Française.
2 Write a letter to Gogol from Moscow, urging him to return from his self-exile.
3 Congratulate Ibsen on his change to social drama from his earlier styles.

4 As a newspaper correspondent, write a dispatch for an American paper on a French theatre production starring Sarah Bernhardt.
5 As Wagner, write a defense of your design for the Festspielhaus at Bayreuth.
6 Sketch a stage set for a wing-flat and back-shutter presentation of the play you read.
7 As a typical member of the audience, write your reaction to the installation of gas lighting in the Chestnut Street Theatre in Philadelphia in 1816.
8 Write a dispatch to your American newspaper employer on the visit of the Meiningen Company to London in 1881.
9 As a German actor, write a letter to an English colleague, urging his adoption of the new grease-paint makeup.
10 As a participant in the event, write an account of the Astor Place Riot, including what you know of the events which led up to it.

Modern Theatre
(*chapters* 16, 17, 18)

1 As a United States congressman in 1939, write a speech urging the withdrawal of funds from the Federal Theatre Project.
2 Draw up a floor plan and stage plot for a free theatre you are opening in 1900.
3 Write an explanation for your decision to open a theatre specializing in arena staging.
4 As a director, lay out the requirements for a play of your choice, which can function as a working plan for your costume designer.
5 Write an imaginary dialogue between two actors, one of whom is a Method actor, the other not.
6 Conceive a unit setting for a play of your choice. Sketch a floor plan and elevation, and write a rationale for your choice of a unit setting.
7 Make a detailed outline for a modern resident theatre plant to be used by an architect in making plans and renderings.
8 Draw up a prospectus to be used in fund raising for the establishment of an ensemble of performers to do new plays.
9 Cast the play of your choice with the performers of your choice, giving reasons for the casting by an analysis of character traits for the personages of the play, and telling in each case why the particular performer would be right.
10 Write a dialogue between the director and the designer for a play of your choice which is to be staged. The director's choice is for a realistic setting; the designer's is for a nonrealistic one.

Glossary of terms

Act-drop A late eighteenth-century term applied to the painted cloth which closed the proscenium opening between the acts of a play.

Adventurer A term applied in the Restoration to an essentially nontheatrical person buying shares in theatrical companies.

Afterpiece A term which came into use in the eighteenth century to designate that portion of a theatrical entertainment which followed the main presentation; usually a one-act farce.

Agonothetes (*Gr.*) The official who produced the plays presented at the drama festivals.

Alcaldes (*Sp.*) Mayors or magistrates.

Anapesmata (*Gr.*) Traps (*q.v.*).

Angel Modern word for a person who supplies money to finance the production of a play.

Antagonist A word coming from the Greek which designates the character in a play who opposes the protagonist or hero.

Apariencias (*Sp.*) Stage devices which allowed for the sudden appearance of characters.

Aposentos (*Sp.*) The boxes of the corral theatres, the highest priced accommodations.

Apron That part of the stage which extends beyond the proscenium arch and the front curtain; sometimes called the forestage.

Arc light An especially intense and concentrated light source formed by passing an electric current between two rods of carbon; used first at the Paris Opera by M. J. Duboseq in 1846.

Arch border See Border.

Archon (*Gr.*) Public official in ancient Greece who chose the plays and the leading players for the drama festivals.

Artificios (*Sp.*) "Tricks" or stage devices which were intended to surprise the audience.

Atellanae (*Lat.*) Improvised comedy on topical themes.

Aufklärung (*Ger.*) Eighteenth-century German literary movement which upheld French neoclassicism as the model for playwriting.

Author's night Performance of a play from which the author received all the profits; comparable to the actor's benefits.

Autor de comedias (*Sp.*) A company manager in Spain's Golden Age.

Auto sacramental (*Sp.*) A church play; comparable to the French *mystère* and the English saint and cycle play.

Backcloth The flat, painted canvas used generally with a wing-flat (*q.v.*) set to cover the area at the back of the scene; usually hung from the grid (*q.v.*).

Backing flat A canvas-covered frame which is painted and put behind openings in the stage set to conceal the area beyond it.

Backstage All the areas behind the scene set on the stage, including wings, dressingrooms, and so on.

Balcony Applied, particularly in America, to the seating area above the ground floor or orchestra.

Ballad opera A burlesque form, developed in the eighteenth century, characterized by songs written to popular tunes.

Ballet A dramatic presentation in dance and mime to the accompaniment of music.

Barrel system A method of moving scenery from below the stage level.

Batten A pipe or rod suspended from the grid (*q.v.*) upon which can be hung lights or scenery.

Benefit Traditionally, a performance, the profits of which are assigned to a particular performer; in modern American theatre, a performance for which tickets are inflated in price, the profits going to some organization or cause.

Blues A nineteenth-century term for sky borders. See Border.

Boards A term originating from the wooden stage floor; "to tread the boards" is to act, to be "on the boards" is to be an actor.

Bookholder The person in the Elizabethan theatre, who not only "held the book" during the performance, but saw that actors were ready for their entrances and gave them their props (*q.v.*).

Book-keeper The person in the Elizabethan theatre who kept the manuscript copies

514

of the plays as well as the individual parts of the actors.

Booth stage A raised platform with a simple backcloth used for performance by actors.

Border A narrow strip of painted canvas which is fastened at the top edge only to a batten (*q.v.*) to hide the top of the stage as seen from the auditorium; an "arch border" is cut on the lower edge like an arch and painted to blend with side wings which it meets; a "tree border" is cut and painted like a tree; a "sky border" like clouds or sky (sometimes called "blues" or "cloudings").

Box office That portion of the theatre where tickets are sold; probably originating in the slotted box into which Elizabethan theatregoers put their penny for general admission.

Box set A stage arrangement of flats forming three walls, with a ceiling overhead.

Boxiganga (*Sp.*) In the Spanish Golden Age, a traveling company of actors—six or seven men, two women, and a boy.

Brace An extensible wooden stick used in a diagonal position to support flats on stage.

Breeches parts Roles meant to be assigned to men but often played by women.

Bululu (*Sp.*) A lone player traveling on foot.

Bunraku (*Jap.*) The Japanese doll theatre.

Burlesque Originally an exaggeration of word, action, or both, to point out absurdities; now often applied to a type of variety show which lays stress on the female form.

Buskin British word for the Greek kothurnos (*q.v.*).

Cambaleo (*Sp.*) Company of traveling performers, five men and a woman.

Cantores (*Lat.*) The specialized performer who did all the singing required in a specific performance; another performer delivered the spoken words.

Capa y estapa (*Sp.*) "Cloak and sword" play founded upon intrigues, mistaken identities, and so forth.

Carros (*Sp.*) The wagons on which religious plays were given.

Catwalk A narrow bridge suspended from the grid (*q.v.*) to enable stagehands to reach various parts of the scenery and lighting hung in the flies above the stage.

Cavea (*Lat.*) The curved rows of seats for spectators in the Roman theatre.

Cazuela (*Sp.*) Literally "stew-pan"—applied to the section of the theatre assigned to unaccompanied women spectators.

Ceiling A canvas-covered frame usually hinged to fold in half, used to cover the top of a box set.

Cellar The area below the stage area, usually housing machinery employed for changing sets.

Chef d'emploi (*Fr.*) The leading actor in any specified line of parts.

Chiusetti (*Ital.*) Those portions of a commedia performance consisting of lyrical outbursts on the part of the performers.

Choregus (*Gr.*) Citizen of ancient Greece who bore all expenses for festival performances of plays, except for the salary of the leading actor who was paid by the state.

Choreuti (*Gr.*) A member of the classic chorus.

Chorus In ancient Greece, the performers who sang and danced in the orchestra; now more generally applied only to groups who sing, although a group of performers who dance in musical plays is also referred to as a chorus.

Choryphaeus (*Gr.*) The leader of the chorus in classic drama.

Chronicle play Term applied, especially in England, to plays based on historical events; e.g., those of Shakespeare on the English kings.

Circuit Term applied in England to a group of provincial theatres visited at regular intervals by a company of players specifically constituted to do so.

Claque A group of persons hired to applaud at specified times during a performance; originated in the Roman theatre.

Cloudings Borders (*q.v.*) cut and painted to represent clouds.

Cofradias (*Sp.*) Philanthropic organizations which profited from theatrical activity in Spain's Golden Age.

Comedias (*Sp.*) Three-act plays on secular subjects.

Comedias a fantasia (*Sp.*) Full-length plays with romantic subject matter.

Comedias a noticia (*Sp.*) Full-length plays using realistic subject matter.

Comedias de cuerpo (*Sp.*) Full-length plays using historical, mythological, and legendary materials.

Comisario de comedias (*Sp.*) Official charged with the licensing of plays for performance.

Commedia dell'arte (*Ital.*) Comedy which originated in the Italian Renaissance, largely improvised, using stock characters and masks.

Comoedus (*Lat.*) An actor specializing in the performance of comedy.

Compagnies des fous (*Fr.*) Medieval societies generally devoted to the performance of short secular plays.

Compañía (*Sp.*) The largest of the Spanish traveling companies, consisting of from sixteen to thirty persons.

Compañías de parte (*Sp.*) Acting companies organized on the shareholding principle, as distinct from those with a proprietor and fixed salaries.

Confrérie (*Fr.*) Medieval term for an organization formed to produce religious plays.

Constructivism Post-World War I movement in stage design which eschewed realism and concentrated on an arrangement of basic forms in space, with a view to enlarging freedom of movement for the actors.

Copiste (*Fr.*) The prompter, archivist, and copyist of the seventeenth-century French acting company.

Corpus Christi Day Designated by Pope Clement V in 1311 as the Thursday after Trinity Sunday (two months after Easter); became the traditional time for presenting the cycle plays in England.

Corral (*Sp.*) Originally a theatre formed by using the open space within a block of houses; later applied to theatres in general.

Counterweight System of compensating for the weight of flown scenery to expedite its movement on and off the stage.

Curtain Fabric hung in folds in the proscenium opening to hide the stage from the audience; also often used to indicate the end of a performance in phrases such as "at the final curtain."

Curtain raiser Term originating in the nineteenth century to indicate a short play given before the chief offering of the evening.

Cut cloth Variously shaped borders (*q.v.*), particularly in Victorian theatre.

Cycle play A series of Biblical plays as given during the Middle Ages.

Cyclorama A curved canvas drop around the sides and back of the stage which is painted to look like sky, and which allows for the use of flies (*q.v.*).

Dalmatic An ecclesiastical vestment, sometimes used as a costume in the medieval religious plays.

Décorateur (*Fr.*) The seventeenth-century theatre artisan who designed not only the stage sets but the interior of the house as well.

Deus ex machina (*Lat.*) Literally "god from the machine," derived from the practice in classic Greek theatre of having supernatural beings lowered to the stage by the mechane; now applied to any agency that inorganically effects the resolution of a drama.

Dimmer A mechanical device which allows for varying intensities of light to be used on stage.

Director In America, the theatre worker who supervises the preparation of the actors in their parts and is responsible for the unity of the production through consultation with designers and other theatre workers.

Disguising Popular diversion of the Tudor court; generally a masked ball.

Dithyramb In ancient Greece, a chant or choral song detailing the exploits of a god or hero.

Downstage That portion of the stage area closest to the audience.

Dress circle Generally the first tier of boxes in a theatre interior with several tiers.

Drolls Short dramatic pieces, or skits; usually bits from longer plays, given during the Commonwealth and early Restoration.

Drop A piece of scenery, usually of painted canvas, suspended from a batten and having no stiles at the side, but with a rail top and bottom.

Duègnes (*Fr.*) Eighteenth-century term for old comic women characters.

Eccyclema (*Gr.*) Stage device in ancient Greece for revealing scenes purportedly transpiring indoors; a type of wagon (*q.v.*).

Emmelia (*Gr.*) Name of the dance movement used in classic tragedy.

End stage An acting area not marked off from the audience area by a proscenium arch, but with all audience space facing it on one side only.

Entremeses (*Sp.*) Short pieces accompanying longer works.

Environmental theatre That form of production in which both playing space and audience space are fluid and subject to change, either from play to play or even within the same play.

Epilogue A speech, usually in verse, given by one of the actors after the conclusion of a play.

Episkenion (*Gr.*) The second story of the Greek theatre stage house, particularly in Hellenistic times.

Existentialism A modern philosophical movement, particularly popular in French literary circles, which stresses personal decision in the face of a purposeless universe.

Expressionism A movement originating about the time of World War I, which aimed at the artistic expression of emotional reactions rather than the representation of reality.

Fabula palliata (*Lat.*) A form of Roman comedy using Greek materials as subject matter.

Fabula togata (*Lat.*) A form of Roman comedy using Roman materials as subject matter.

Farce A type of comedy in which the emphasis is upon situation rather than upon character; the action of the play is usually broad.

Fastnachtsspiel (*Ger.*) Shrovetide play, mingling religious and popular elements.

Fate tragedy A German nineteenth-century dramatic form in which the plot is concerned with the operation of a curse.

Fescennine verses A type of verse, originating in Etruria, chiefly marriage songs of a rather wanton nature, which remained popular with the Romans to the time of the Empire.

Festaiolo (*Ital.*) Medieval leader of a company of players.

Festoon drape Term applied to a front curtain which is raised by drawing it up at particular spots to different heights so that portions of it remain visible and form a frame for the stage.

Feu (*Fr.*) The sum allotted to actors for lighting and heating their dressingrooms in the seventeenth-century French theatre.

Fiestas de los carros (*Sp.*) Those occasions upon which the autos sacramentales (*q.v.*) were given.

Flat A canvas-covered frame, usually rectangular in shape and painted, used in multiples for setting the scene on stage.

Fleshings A type of leg covering popular in the pastoral dramas of the Italian Renaissance to give better form and color to actors' legs; used occasionally for the same purpose today.

Flies The area above the stage, out of the view of the audience, where scenery may be stored or lifted from the stage area.

Folk play Type of presentation popular in the Middle Ages; subject matter was largely drawn from legendary materials.

Follow spot A concentrated beam light operated so that it will constantly frame a particular performer as he moves about the stage.

Footlights Strips of lights in the floor at the edge of the stage apron, popular from the time of the Restoration but infrequently used in modern theatre.

Forestage Another term for apron (*q.v.*).

Front of house A term applied to all of the areas of a theatre ordinarily assigned to the audience, as distinguished from backstage (*q.v.*).

Frons scaenae (*Lat.*) The elaborately decorated wall of the stage house in the Roman theatre.

Gallery The name usually given to the seating area placed nearest the roof in a theatre and thus farthest from the stage, containing the least expensive seats.

Gangarilla (*Sp.*) Traveling company consisting of three men, and a boy to play the women's parts.

Garnacha (*Sp.*) Type of traveling company consisting of five to six men, one woman, and a boy.

Gas table The device behind the scenes by which a technician controlled the amount and intensity of the stage and house lights during the days when theatres were lit by gas.

Gauze A drop (*q.v.*) of scrim cloth or bobbinet which appears opaque when lit from in front, but practically transparent when lit from behind; it is used for special effects.

Gestes The songs sung by the minstrels of the Middle Ages.

Giggue Sometimes *jig*. An impromptu closing given by one or more of the actors after the play in the days of Shakespeare.

Gleeman The teller of tales and singer of songs in Anglo-Saxon England; usually itinerant.

Gods A term dating from the eighteenth century applied to the occupants of the upper gallery, probably because they were certainly nearest heaven.

Goliard A wandering scholar or clerk of the Middle Ages.

Gracioso (*Sp.*) Literally "farcical actor"; the name given to the comic servant character in the drama of the Golden Age.

Gradas (*Sp.*) The backless benches along the sides of the pit in the corral theatres of Spain.

Green room The social room for performers behind the scenes; probably so called because it was usually hung or painted in green.

Grid The open framework above the stage from which battens (*q.v.*), etc., are suspended.

Grooves The tracks, on the stage floor and overhead, upon which wing flats (*q.v.*) are moved; usually more than one in a given spot.

Ground row A long, low piece of scenery used across the bottom of the stage at the back, usually to hide special lighting equipment.

Guerrilla theatre A planned event of chiefly political orientation arranged to seem real for the purpose of arousing overt reactions from its audience.

Hand props The small, necessary objects carried on or off the stage by the actors in the course of performance.

Hanswurst Popular character on the German stage in the seventeenth and eighteenth centuries; a clown type.

Haupt-und-Staatsaktionen (*Ger.*) A type of seventeenth-century play dealing with events in high places, usually including a Hanswurst as one of the characters.

Heroic drama A term sometimes applied to English neoclassical tragedy of the late seventeenth century.

Heroic feathers Feathers worn on the headdresses of actors and actresses to denote dignity and high station in life; customary for almost a century from Restoration times on.

Hireling An Elizabethan theatre worker who was paid a set fee, and was not a shareholder in the acting company.

Histriones (*Lat.*) Actors.

Housekeeper A person in Elizabethan theatre who, singly or with others, owned and received the income from the theatre buildings themselves, as distinct from the sharers.

Humanism The Renaissance movement which pursued and disseminated the study of Greek and Roman cultures.

Hypokrites (*Gr.*) Actor.

Hyposcenium (*Lat.*) The front wall of the raised stage in the Roman theatre.

Impressionism An early twentieth-century movement in literature which emphasized the immediate effect of actions or objects with little attention to detail; also a movement in painting and in music.

Infami (*Lat.*) A term applied to actors to indicate that they were without civil rights in ancient Rome.

Ingénue The stage role of a young woman, usually naive; the actress who plays such a role.

Inner stage A portion of the area at the back of the stage which can be cut off from the rest by curtains or flats and can be revealed for a change of locale or specialized setting.

Inset A small scene set behind an opening in a larger scene.

Interlude The medieval and early Renaissance English name for a short dramatic sketch.

Intermezzi (Ital.) The fifteenth and sixteenth-century name for interpolations of a light character performed between the acts of serious drama or opera.

Invenciones (Sp.) Contrivances or trick work in stage presentations of the Golden Age.

Jácara (Sp.) A ballad set to music and used as a part of a theatrical entertainment in the seventeenth century.

Jig See Giggue.

Jongleur (Fr.) Medieval word for a traveling juggler or trickster.

Juglares (Sp.) The same performer, in Spain.

Juvenile A stage role for a youthful male; the actor who performs such a part.

Kabuki (Jap.) Popular type of Japanese theatre, usually emphasizing violent action and using more scenery than the classic Noh drama (*q.v.*).

King's box Special seating area for the king and his party, particularly in Restoration theatre, immediately opposite center stage in the first tier of boxes.

Kiva Special hut or house, erected in multiples by the Hopi Indians, for the drama of the Great Serpent.

Kordax (Gr.) The dance form associated with classic comedy.

Kothurnos (Gr.) The thick-soled boot of the actor in classic tragedy.

Kyogen (Jap.) Short sketches given as comic interludes in Noh theatre.

Lazzi (Ital.) Bits of comic business, or action, used by the performers in the commedia dell'arte (*q.v.*).

Liberties In Elizabethan England, the sites of former church holdings, now the property of the Crown, not subject to municipal ordinances.

Libretto (*pl.:* libretti) The words or text of an extended musical composition; the book which contains such text.

Liencos (Sp.) The painted canvas set pieces of the stage in the Golden Age.

Limelight An intense illumination produced by heating a cylinder of lime to incandescence with gas, developed in the nineteenth century; by extension, a position of prominence occupied by a performer, who is said to be "in the limelight."

Lines The words assigned to a particular actor in a given performance.

Loa (Sp.) The prologue, or compliment to the audience, which preceded early Spanish theatrical productions.

Ludi Romani (Lat.) The Roman games, or festivals, which included dramatic performances.

Machiniste (Fr.) Seventeenth-century theatre worker who produced the scenery; now a scene shifter.

Maître des feyntes (Fr.) Medieval term for the artisan who designed and supervised stage effects, chiefly in the religious plays.

Manteaux (Fr.) Eighteenth-century word for the roles of old comic men.

Mask, masque As an object, a face covering as varied and as old as theatre itself; as an entertainment, a presentation stressing spectacle and music.

Mastaba Ancient Egyptian tomb with sloping sides and a flat roof.

Mechane (Gr.) A classic Greek stage device for lowering personages from above the stage.

Melodrama A type of drama stressing a succession of improbable incidents, with chiefly one-dimensional characters.

Method, the An American term for a system of acting, based on the teachings of Stanislavski, stressing inner truth.

Mime Type of theatrical entertainment in Roman times consisting of short dramatic sketches marked by buffoonery and jesting.

Minstrel Traveling singer of gestes (*q.v.*) in medieval times.

Miracle play Medieval plays concerned chiefly with the lives of the saints.

Moralité (Fr.) A didactic play, flourishing in the fourteenth and fifteenth centuries, which used allegorical characters.

Morality play English term for the above.

Mosqueteros (Sp.) Literally, "musketeers"; applied generally to the men in the standing pit of seventeenth-century Spanish theatres.

Multiple setting A type of stage setting where more than one locality is represented on the stage at the same time; sometimes called "simultaneous setting."

Musico (*Sp.*) In the Golden Age, that member of an acting company particularly hired to play a musical instrument.

Mystery play Another name for the cycle plays with Biblical subject matter.

Nachspiel (*Ger.*) Eighteenth-century farce.

Narr (*Ger.*) The medieval fool.

Naturalism A literary movement of the late nineteenth century which stressed the presentation of persons and objects as nearly as possible in their ordinary, everyday forms.

Naumachia (*Lat.*) In Roman times, a simulated sea battle in a flooded colosseum or theatre orchestra; in Renaissance times, a water carnival.

Neoclassic Literary movement, chiefly of the seventeenth century, which stressed adherence to classical forms and materials.

Noh (*Jap.*) Classic Japanese drama dealing with historical or religious materials, played with masks on a particularly constructed stage.

Numberer Theatre official of the Restoration charged with seeing that spectators paid the appropriate admission for whatever portions of the evening's entertainment they witnessed.

Nursery School instituted for the training of actors in the Restoration.

Off stage Toward or beyond the limits of the visible set on stage.

Ombres Chinoises (*Fr.*) A type of shadow show adapted from oriental practice, popular in the eighteenth century.

Onkos (*Gr.*) The raised, dome-shaped top of the actor's mask.

Onnagata (*Jap.*) Female role, played by a male.

On stage The term used to indicate a position in view of the audience.

Open stage See Thrust stage.

Opéra bouffe (*Fr.*) Comic opera of a farcical nature.

Opéra comique (*Fr.*) Comic opera.

Orator Manager of a seventeenth-century French acting company, who made a speech at the end of a performance announcing the next presentation.

Orchestra Originally (*Gr.*), the dancing circle for the chorus in the classic theatre; by extension, the ground floor of present-day theatres.

Ozones Strips of blue cloth hung from battens and used for sky in stage settings.

Pageant In medieval England, the wagon on which the plays of the cycles were presented.

Palais à volonté (*Fr.*) An unlocalized stage setting of palace and temple in eighteenth-century theatre.

Pantomime In Roman times, a type of theatrical presentation in which a chorus sang and actors mimed tragedies and love stories; in later times, a type of stage presentation with elaborate sets and music in which there is no speaking of lines.

Parados (*Gr.*, pl.: *paradoi*) The passageway between the scene house and the rows of seats in the ancient Greek theatre, used by both chorus and audience.

Paraskenia (*Gr.*) Projecting wings at either side of the stage in the ancient Greek theatre.

Paso (*Sp.*) One-act comedy of the seventeenth century.

Pastoral Type of theatrical presentation, originating in the Italian Renaissance, giving an idyllic and artificial representation of country life.

Patent houses Term applied to the theatres of the Restoration which operated by special license from the Crown.

Patio The inner court of a house, open to the sky, early used in the south of Spain for theatrical performances.

Periaktos (*Gr.*, pl.: *periaktoi*) Three-sided set pieces used at either side of the stage in the early Greek theatre; they could be rotated.

Pièces à machines (*Fr.*) Theatrical presentations of the seventeenth century, written and produced primarily to show the wonders of stage machinery.

Pièces rosses (*Fr.*) In the late nineteenth century, plays dealing with unpleasant or ugly aspects of life.

Pinakes (*Gr.*) Painted screens used between

the columns fronting the raised stage of the Hellenistic period.

Pit The ground-floor standing room area of the Elizabethan theatre; now sometimes still used to designate comparable areas in modern theatres.

Platea (Lat.) The unlocalized acting area of the medieval multiple setting.

Platform stage Generally, a stage arrangement whereby the acting area is not behind the proscenium arch, as in the Elizabethan theatre.

Porta regis (Lat.) The great central doorway on the stage of the Roman theatre.

Portae minores (Lat.) The smaller doorways flanking the great central door in the Roman theatre; generally four in number.

Praetextae (Lat.) Plays of the Roman theatre using history as subject matter.

Premier garçon du théâtre (Fr.) Seventeenth-century theatre functionary who performed the duties of stage manager.

Proagon (Gr.) In early Greek times, a presentation by the performers and playwright a few days before a festival performance, designed to arouse interest in the forthcoming production.

Producer In England, generally, the person responsible for the staging of a play; in America, the individual who raises the money for production and oversees all details both artistic and financial.

Prologue An introductory speech, often in verse, given at the beginning of a play, which generally calls attention to the theme of the play.

Prompt To supply an actor with his cue or his line if he has forgotten it.

Prompt box, prompt corner Positions from which prompting is done.

Prompter One who holds the book of the play and prompts.

Property room Storage space for stage props.

Props All objects on stage exclusive of scenery. See also Hand props.

Proscenium Literally, "before the scene"; the frame or arch which encloses the stage area behind which is hung the front curtain.

Protagonist The leading character in a play; first used as a designation in classic Greek theatre.

Pulpitum (Lat.) A raised platform for actors in early Roman times.

Pundoñor (Sp.) "Point of honor"; principal emphasis of the "cape and sword" plays of the Golden Age.

Puys (Fr.) Groups of secular performers in the Middle Ages whose leanings were literary and who presented both farces and religious plays.

Quick-change room Arrangement on stage level for actors requiring a costume change when their time offstage is too short to permit their returning to their dressingrooms.

Rail The piece of wood forming the top or the bottom of a flat.

Rake The slope of the stage floor upward from the audience.

Realism Literary and theatrical movement beginning in the late nineteenth century which attempted to treat subjects with fidelity to nature or to real life.

Régisseur (Fr.) Term applied since the Middle Ages, particularly on the Continent, to the stage director.

Rehearsal The preparation and practice of an acting company for eventual performance before an audience in a given play.

Relieve A set piece in three dimensions; first applied in the Restoration.

Repertorio (Ital.) A set speech of advice or tirade in the commedia dell'arte.

Repertory A type of theatrical organization which has several plays ready to perform, and produces them alternately.

Reveal A false-thickness piece used in the openings of a box set, such as doors or windows, to give the appearance of solidity.

Revolving stage A large turntable in the center of the stage on which varying numbers of sets are placed; it is turned to show a single set to the audience.

Rhetorick In Elizabethan times, the study of voice and gesture in systematized form.

Ritterdramen (Ger.) Nineteenth-century plays of chivalry.

Romancero (Sp.) Early Spanish heroic ballad.

Rührstüke (Ger.) Nineteenth-century sentimental melodrama.

Sacre rappresentazione (Ital.) The "holy drama" or Bible play of the Middle Ages and later.

Satire A type of literary composition which holds up to scorn or ridicule various follies, vices, and abuses, often with the purpose of correcting these excesses.

Satura (Lat.) Literally, "medley"; a kind of variety show popular in early Roman times.

Satyr play Type of classic Greek drama perpetuating the worship of Dionysus, in which the performers were dressed like satyrs; riotous and often lascivious.

Scabilla (Lat.) A kind of wooden tap on the shoes of the dancers in Roman pantomimes.

Scaena ductilis (Lat.) Movable painted screens used between the columns on stages of the early Greek theatre.

Scene The stage setting; also the division of a play or the act of a play; also the locale where the action supposedly takes place.

Scop Traveling entertainer in Anglo-Saxon England.

Segundo galan (Sp.) The second leading man of a theatrical company.

Sequentiae (Lat.) Wordless sequences of notes sung on the last syllable of the "Alleluia" in the Mass of the early medieval church; an early step in the development of the cycle plays.

Set The scenery and properties for an act or scene (n.); also, the act of putting this scenery in place on the stage (v.).

Set piece Any piece of scenery, usually rather small, standing by itself in the scene.

Shadow show Puppets lighted from behind which cast shadows on a screen or cloth hanging between them and the audience.

Sharer Member of an Elizabethan acting company whose income was derived from the division of the profits.

Shares Designated and predetermined portions of the profits of acting companies, particularly in seventeenth-century France and Restoration England; assigned whole or in part to various members.

Shite (Jap.) The leading actor in a Noh company.

Showboat A river packet, fitted out with a theatre, which, in America, traveled from place to place on the great inland rivers, giving performances.

Shutters Two flats which met to close off the scene at the back in the Restoration theatre; they could be drawn off.

Siglo de Oro (Sp.) The Golden Age of Lope de Vega.

Sikinnis (Gr.) Bawdy dance characteristic of the classic satyr play.

Sill irons Term used to describe flat metal pieces used across the bottom of openings in flats to add strength.

Simultaneous setting See Multiple setting.

Skene (Gr.) Name for the scene house in ancient Greek theatres.

Skenography (Gr.) The art of decorating the stage in the classic theatre.

Sky border See Border.

Sky dome Curved plaster dome around the sides and back, and over the top of the stage, for the purpose of creating unusual lighting effects; now generally supplanted by the cyclorama (*q.v.*).

Slips The late eighteenth and early nineteenth century designation for the ends of the upper tiers of seats nearest the stage.

Sociétes joyeuses (Fr.) Groups producing secular plays in the Middle Ages.

Sotie (Fr.) Short, farcical medieval play topical and satirical in nature.

Soubrette The role of a pert young maidservant or lady's maid in a play; the actress playing such a role.

Stage brace See Brace.

Stage door Entrance from the outside to the onstage areas, used by performers and technicians.

Stalls In England, the individual seats in the orchestra between the front of the stage and the pit.

Stiles The wooden strips which form the sides of a flat.

Stock company A more or less permanent company of actors who prepare and present plays in sequence at stated intervals; in America, "summer stock" is applied to such a group functioning through the summer months.

Stock set A standard stage setting of

drawing room, garden, and so forth, used in more than one play.

Sturm und Drang (Ger.) Eighteenth-century literary movement, romantic in nature.

Subplot A secondary line of action in a play.

Super Short for "supernumerary"; a performer who has a small part with no lines to speak.

Surrealism A twentieth-century movement in literature and art, based on the uncontrolled exercise of imagination and, as influenced by psychoanalysis, seeking to suggest the activities of the subconscious mind.

Symbolism The intentional use of objects or persons as symbols in a play in order to invite an audience to find meanings in the imaginative substrata below the level of the logical action.

Tablados (Sp.) Temporary stages of the Golden Age used in conjunction with *carros (q.v.)* in the presentation of elaborate religious plays.

Tableaux vivants (Fr.) Biblical, allegorical, historical, or fanciful scenes, using the still and silent figures of live actors; mounted on platforms or wagons, these scenes were featured in festivities welcoming personages of note during the Renaissance.

Tail The train of the tragedy queen during the Restoration and early eighteenth century.

Tarltonizing The extemporaneous composition of witty verse, from Richard Tarlton, Elizabethan actor who excelled in this pursuit.

Théâtres de la foires (Fr.) Open-air stages and their productions at the great fairs of France and Italy during the late Renaissance and seventeenth century.

Theatrum (Lat.) Amphitheatre-like hall of the early Renaissance, usually small in size.

Theoric money Term used for the sum of money considered the due right of every Athenian citizen to enable him to see the plays at the Great Festival of Dionysus.

Throwline The cord used to tie flats together to form a wall, as in a box set.

Thrust stage Three-sided acting platforms, extending outward from one wall of a theatre interior, with audience seating surrounding three sides.

Thymele (Gr.) The altar set in the center of the orchestra in the ancient Greek theatre.

Thyromata (Gr.) The openings in the stagehouse wall on the second story of the Hellenistic theatre.

Tirade Long, impassioned speech typically written for the leading characters of French neoclassic drama.

Tireman Elizabethan theatre functionary, roughly equivalent to the modern wardrobe master.

Toggle rail The middle rail of a flat.

Tonnelet Short, bell-like skirt formed of wickerwork covered with cloth and decorated with fringe; typically worn as stage costume by early eighteenth-century French heroes.

Tormenter Curtains or flats at the sides of the stage behind the proscenium, forming an inner frame for the stage.

Tragic carpet Green baize covering for the stage floor, put down when a tragedy was to be played, and in use from the late seventeenth to the early nineteenth century.

Tragoedus (Lat.) Roman performer specializing in tragedy.

Tramoyas (Sp.) Devices on the stage allowing for visual illusion and tricks.

Transparencies Term used in the Restoration and after for what the modern theatre knows as a gauze cloth *(q.v.).*

Trap Any opening in the stage floor or walls of the scene which can be closed when and if it is desirable. The grave trap is traditionally center stage in the floor, the corner trap in a corner of the stage; the Corsican trap allowed figures to rise from below stage and seem to glide across the stage while continuously rising; the vamp trap, in the stage floor or the walls of the scenery, allowed actors seemingly to pass through a solid since it consisted of two spring leaves which closed behind him; there are many other variations.

Tree border See Border.

Tribunalia (Lat.) Special boxes, one to either side of the stage, in the Roman theatre.

Trilogy Series of three plays, usually on a single theme or with a single story line.

Tropes Sequentiae (*q.v.*) with words added—one syllable to each note of music.

Upstage In a direction away from the audience.

Vaudeville In the nineteenth century, light topical amusements set to music; more recently a variety show with many differing acts, or "turns."

Velum (*Lat.*) The linen roof sometimes stretched over the spectators in the Roman theatre.

Vestuario (*Sp.*) Name given the dressing-rooms of the actors in theatres of the Golden Age.

Vexillators The medieval standard bearers who gave notice to the public that a cycle play was ready for performance.

Vista Nineteenth-century stage setting featuring a high scene in perspective.

Vomitorii (*Lat.*) The arched exit passage-ways in the Roman theatre.

Wagon stage A number of low platforms mounted on rollers, each carrying a portion of the set, rolled on from the wings to form the complete set.

Well-made play Term applied to the nine-teenth-century dramas of Scribe and Sardou particularly, which were char-acterized by clear-cut plot structures and easily identifiable characters.

Wings Offstage areas to either side of the stage; persons or objects there are said to be "in the wings."

Wing flat A flat at the side of the stage parallel to the footlights or the edge of the stage; matching pairs of these set in perspective formed the standard stage set almost universally fom the Renaissance to the nineteenth century.

Zanni (*Ital.*) Generic term applied to the male servant characters in the commedia dell'arte.

Bibliography

This bibliography is not exhaustive. It lists significant and helpful books in the various periods of theatre, and will serve as a basis for further study and research.

General

Altman, George, and others. *Theatre Pictorial: A History of World Theatre as Recorded in Drawings, Paintings, Engravings, and Photographs.* Berkeley: University of California Press, 1953.

Baker, Blanch M. *Theatre and Allied Arts* (based on *Dramatic Bibliography,* 1933). New York: Blom, 1968.

Baker, Henry Barton. *History of the London Stage, 1576–1903.* 2 vols. London: Routledge & Kegan Paul, 1904.

Bates, Alfred (ed.). *The Drama.* 22 vols. London: Athenian Society, 1903–1909.

Brockett, O. G. *History of the Theatre.* Boston: Allyn & Bacon, 1968.

Brooke, Iris. *Western European Costume and Its Relation to the Theatre.* 2 vols. London: Harrap, 1939–1940.

Cheney, Sheldon. *The Theatre: 3000 Years of Drama, Acting, and Stagecraft.* New York: McKay, 1929. Revised 1952.

Clark, Barrett H. *European Theories of the Drama.* New York: Crown, 1947. Revised 1965.

Cleaver, James. *The Theatre Through the Ages.* London: Harrap, 1946.

Coad, Oral S., and Mims, Edwin, Jr. *The American Stage.* "Pageant of America Series." New Haven, Conn.: Yale University Press, 1929.

Cole, Toby (ed.). *Playwrights on Playwriting: The Meaning and Making of Modern Drama from Ibsen to Ionesco.* New York: Hill & Wang, 1960.

Cole, Toby, and Chinoy, Helen Krich (eds.). *Actors on Acting: The Theories, Techniques, and Practices of the Great Actors of All Times as Told in Their Own Words.* New York: Crown, 1949. Revised 1970.

Cole, Toby, and Chinoy, Helen Krich (eds.). *Directors on Directing: A Sourcebook of Stagecraft.* New York: Bobbs-Merrill, 1963.

Contina, Mila (ed. James Laver). *Fashion: From Ancient Egypt to the Present Day.* New York: Odyssey, 1965.

Fergusson, Francis. *The Idea of a Theatre.* Princeton, N.J.: Princeton University Press, 1949.

Freedley, George, and Reeves, John A. *A History of the Theatre.* New York: Crown, 1941. Revised 1968.

Gassner, John. *Masters of the Drama.* New York: Crown, 1947.

Gassner, John and Allen, Ralph (eds.). *Theatre and Drama in the Making.* 2 vols. Boston: Houghton Mifflin, 1964.

Granville, Wilfred. *Theatre Dictionary: British and American Terms in the Drama, Opera, and Ballet.* New York: Philosophical Library, 1952.

Hartnoll, Phyllis. *The Oxford Companion to the Theatre.* Oxford: Clarendon, 1957. Revised 1967.

Hewitt, Barnard. *Theatre, U.S.A., 1668–1957.* New York: McGraw-Hill, 1959.

Hughes, Glenn. *A History of the American Theatre, 1700–1950.* New York: French, 1951.

Lister, Margot. *Costume: An Illustrated Survey from Ancient Times to the Twentieth Century.* London: Jenkins, 1967.

Macgowan, Kenneth, and Melnitz, William. *The Living Stage.* Englewood Cliffs, N.J.: Prentice-Hall, 1955.

Mantzius, Karl. *A History of Theatrical Art.* 6 vols. Translated by L. von Cassel. London: Duckworth, 1903–1921.

Moses, Montrose J., and Brown, John Mason. *The American Theatre as Seen by Its Critics.* New York: Norton, 1934.

Mullins, Donald. *Development of the Playhouse.* Berkeley: University of California Press, 1970.

Nagler, Alois M. *Sources of Theatrical History.* New York: Theatre Annual, 1952.

Nicoll, Allardyce. *The Development of the Theatre;* 3rd ed., rev. New York: Harcourt Brace Jovanovich, 1948. Revised 1958.

Odell, G. C. D. *Annals of the New York Stage.* 15 vols. New York: Columbia University Press, 1927–1949.

Oenslager, Donald. *Scenery Then and Now.* New York: Norton, 1936.

Quinn, Arthur Hobson. *A History of American Drama from the Beginnings to the Civil War.* New York: Appleton, 1946.

Quinn, Arthur Hobson. *A History of American Drama from the Civil War to the Present Day. New York: Appleton, 1945.

Rigdon, Walter. The Biographical Encyclopedia and Who's Who of the American Theatre. London: Heinemann, 1966.

Sachs, Curt. World History of the Dance. Translated by Bessie Schoenberg. New York: Norton, 1937.

Simonson, Lee. The Stage Is Set. New York: Harcourt Brace Jovanovich, 1932. Third edition, 1960.

Sobel, Bernard. The Theatre Handbook and Digest. New York: Crown, 1959.

Stuart, Donald Clive. The Development of Dramatic Art. New York: Appleton. 1928.

Ward, Alfred Charles. Specimens of English Dramatic Criticism, 17th–20th Centuries. London: Milford, 1945.

Who's Who in the Theatre. London: Pittman, published annually.

Primitive Theatre

Brown, Ivor. First Player: The Origin of Drama. New York: Morrow, 1928.

Budge, E. A. Wallis. Osiris and the Egyptian Resurrection. London: Warner, 1911.

Calverton, V. F. The Making of Man: An Outline of Anthropology. New York: Modern Library, 1931.

Fraser, James George. The Golden Bough: A Study of Magic and Religion. New York: Macmillan, 1922.

Gaster, Theodore H. Thespis: Ritual, Myth, and Drama in the Ancient Near East. New York: Crown, 1950.

Harrison, Jane Ellen. Ancient Art and Ritual. New York: Holt, Rinehart and Winston, 1931.

Havemeyer, Loomis. The Drama of Savage Peoples. New Haven, Conn.: Yale University Press, 1916.

Hunningher, Benjamin. The Origin of the Theatre. New York: Hill & Wang, 1961.

Macgowan, Kenneth, and Rosse, Herman. Masks and Demons. New York: Harcourt Brace Jovanovich, 1923.

Malinowski, Bronislaw. Myth in Primitive Psychology. New York: Norton, 1926.

Ridgeway, William. The Dramas and Dramatic Dances of Non-European Races. London: Cambridge University Press, 1915.

Speck, Frank G., and Broom, Leonard. Cherokee Dance and Drama. In collaboration with Will West Long. Berkeley: University of California Press, 1951.

Greek and Roman Theatre

Allen, James Turney. Stage Antiquities of the Greeks and Romans and Their Influence. New York: McKay, 1927.

Arnott, Peter. An Introduction to the Greek Theatre. New York: Macmillan, 1959.

Beare, W. The Roman Stage: A Short History. London: Methuen, 1950 and 1965.

Bieber, Margarete. The History of Greek and Roman Theatre, rev. ed. Princeton, N.J.: Princeton University Press, 1960.

Cornford, Francis M. The Origin of Attic Comedy. New York: Macmillan, 1934.

Donaldson, John William. The Theatre of the Greeks. London: Bell, 1887.

Flickinger, Roy C. The Greek Theatre and Its Drama, 4th ed. Chicago: University of Chicago Press, 1960.

Fowler, Harold N. History of Roman Literature. New York: Macmillan, 1932.

Haigh, A. E. The Attic Theatre. Oxford: Clarendon, 1907.

Hamilton, Edith. The Greek Way. New York: Norton, 1930.

Harrison, Jane Ellen. Prolegomena to the Study of Greek Religion. London: Cambridge University Press, 1908.

Kitto, H. D. F. Greek Tragedy: A Literary Study, rev. ed. New York: Doubleday, 1950.

Lord, Louis B. Aristophanes: His Plays and Influence. Boston: Marshall Jones, 1925.

Pickard-Cambridge, A. W. The Theatre of Dionysus in Athens. Oxford: Clarendon, 1946.

Pickard-Cambridge, A. W. The Dramatic Festivals of Athens. Oxford: Clarendon, 1953.

Saunders, Catharine. Costume in Roman Comedy. New York: Columbia University Press, 1909.

Vitruvius. Ten Books on Architecture. Translated by Morris Hickey Morgan. Cambridge, Mass.: Harvard University Press, 1914.

Webster, T. B. L. Greek Theatre Production. London: Methuen, 1956.

Medieval Theatre

Chambers, E. K. *The Medieval Stage*. 2 vols. Oxford: Clarendon, 1903.

Cohen, Gustave. *Histoire de la Mise en Scène dans le Théâtre Réligieux du Moyen Age*. Paris: Champion, 1926.

Frank, Grace. *The Medieval French Drama*. Oxford: Clarendon, 1954.

Hardison, O. B., Jr. *Christian Rite and Christian Drama in the Middle Ages*. Baltimore, Md.: Johns Hopkins Press, 1965.

Hussey, Maurice (ed.). *The Chester Mystery Plays*. London: Heinemann, 1957.

Jusserand, J. J. *English Wayfaring Life in the Middle Ages*. Translated by Lucy T. Smith. London: Allen & Unwin, 1897.

Mackenzie, W. Roy. *The English Moralities*. London: Gill, 1914.

Monmerque, L. J. *Théâtre Français au Moyen Age*. Paris: Firmin Didot, 1929. Revised 1963.

Nicoll, Allardyce. *Masks, Mimes, and Miracles*. New York: Harcourt Brace Jovanovich, 1932.

Pollard, Alfred W. *English Miracle Plays, Moralities, and Interludes*. Oxford: Clarendon, 1927.

Purnis, J. O. (ed.). *The York Cycle of Mystery Plays*. New York: Macmillan, 1950.

Rudwin, M. J. *Historical and Bibliographical Survey of the German Religious Drama*. Pittsburgh, Pa.: University of Pittsburgh Press, 1924.

Stratman, Carl J. *Bibliography of Medieval Drama*. Berkeley: University of California Press, 1954.

Stuart, Donald Clive. *Stage Decoration in France in the Middle Ages*. New York: Columbia University Press, 1910.

Young, Karl. *The Drama of the Medieval Church*. 2 vols. Oxford: Clarendon, 1933.

Early Renaissance and Elizabethan Theatre

Adams, John Cranford. *The Globe Playhouse, Its Design and Equipment*. London: Cambridge University Press, 1942.

Adams, Joseph Quincy. *Shakespearean Playhouses*. Boston: Houghton Mifflin, 1917.

Baker, Henry B. *The London Stage, 1576–1888*. London: Hallen, 1889.

Baldwin, Thomas W. *Organization and Personnel of Shakespeare's Company*. Princeton, N.J.: Princeton University Press, 1927.

Beckerman, Bernard. *Shakespeare at the Globe: 1599–1609*. New York: Macmillan, 1962.

Boas, F. S. *An Introduction to Tudor Drama*. Oxford: Clarendon, 1933.

Bradbrook, M. C. *Elizabethan Stage Conditions*. London: Cambridge University Press, 1932.

Brooke, C. F. Tucker. *The Tudor Drama*. Boston: Houghton Mifflin, 1911.

Campbell, Lily B. *Scenes and Machines on the English Stage During the Renaissance*. New York: Macmillan, 1923.

Chambers, E. K. *The Elizabethan Stage*. 4 vols. Oxford: Clarendon, 1923. Revised 1951.

Crawford, J. P. W. *Spanish Drama Before Lope de Vega*. Philadelphia: Lippincott, 1937.

Cunliffe, J. W. *Influence of Seneca on Elizabethan Tragedy*. New York: Steichert, 1925.

Ducharte, Pierre Louis. *The Italian Comedy*. Translated by Randolph T. Weaver. London: Harrap, 1929.

Harbage, Alfred. *Shakespeare's Audience*. New York: Columbia University Press, 1941.

Harbage, Alfred. *Shakespeare and the Rival Traditions*. New York: Macmillan, 1952.

Herrick, Marvin T. *Italian Tragedy in the Renaissance*. Urbana: University of Illinois Press, 1965.

Hewitt, Barnard (ed.). *The Renaissance Stage: Documents of Serlio, Sabbattini, and Furttenbach*. Miami, Fla.: University of Miami Press, 1958.

Hodges, C. Walter. *Shakespeare and the Players*. New York: Coward, McCann & Geoghegan, 1948.

Hodges, C. Walter. *The Globe Restored: A Study of the Elizabethan Theatre*. New York: Coward, McCann & Geoghegan, 1968.

Hotson, Leslie. *Shakespeare's Wooden O*. New York: Macmillan, 1960.

Kennard, James Spencer. *Masks and Marionettes*. New York: Macmillan, 1935.

Kernodle, George R. *From Art to Theatre*. Chicago: University of Chicago Press, 1944.

Knight, G. W. *Principles of Shakespearean Production*. London: Faber & Faber, 1936.

Lawrence, W. J. *Physical Conditions of Elizabethan Public Playhouses*. Cambridge, Mass.: Harvard University Press, 1927.

Lawrence, W. J. *The Elizabethan Playhouse and Other Studies*. 2 vols. London: Russell and Russell, 1963.

Lea, Kathleen M. *The Italian Popular Comedy: A Study in the Commedia dell'Arte*. 2 vols. Oxford: Clarendon, 1934.

Linthicum, M. Channing. *Costume in the Drama of Shakespeare and His Contemporaries*. Oxford: Clarendon, 1936.

Nagler, Alois M. *Shakespeare's Stage*. New Haven, Conn.: Yale University Press, 1959.

Nagler, Alois M. *Theatre Festivals of the Medici, 1539–1637*. New Haven, Conn.: Yale University Press, 1964.

Nungezer, Edwin. *A Dictionary of Actors and Other Persons Associated with the Public Representation of Plays in England Before 1642*. New Haven, Conn.: Yale University Press, 1929.

Poël, William. *Shakespeare in the Theatre*. London: Sidgewick & Jackson, 1913.

Reed, A. W. *Early Tudor Drama*. London: Methuen, 1926.

Rennert, Hugo Albert. *The Spanish Stage in the Time of Lope de Vega*. New York: Hispanic Society, 1909. Dover, 1963.

Reynolds, G. F. *The Staging of Elizabethan Plays at the Red Bull Theatre, 1605–1625*. New York: Modern Language Association, 1940.

Shattuck, C. H. *The Shakespeare Promptbooks: A Descriptive Catalogue*. Urbana: University of Illinois Press, 1965.

Shergold, R. N. *A History of the Spanish Stage from Medieval Times Until the End of the Seventeenth Century*. Oxford: Clarendon, 1967.

Shoemaker, William H. *The Multiple Stage in Spain During the Fifteenth and Sixteenth Centuries*. Princeton, N.J.: Princeton University Press, 1935.

Smith, Irwin. *Shakespeare's Blackfriars Playhouse*. New York: New York University Press, 1964.

Smith, Winifred. *The Commedia dell'Arte*. New York: Columbia University Press, 1912. Revised 1965.

Smith, Winifred. *Italian Actors of the Renaissance*. New York: Coward, McCann & Geoghegan, 1930.

Stopes, Charlotte C. *Burbage and Shakespeare's Stage*. London: Moring, 1918.

Sullivan, Mary. *The Court Masques of James I*. New York: Putnam, 1913.

Thorndike, Ashley H. *Shakespeare's Theatre*. New York: Macmillan, 1916.

Venesky, Alice S. *Pageantry on the Shakespearian Stage*. New York: Crown, 1951.

Welsford, Enid. *The Court Masque*. New York: Macmillan, 1928.

Wickham, Glynne. *Early English Stages*. 2 vols. New York: Columbia University Press, 1959–1963.

Wiley, W. L. *The Early Public Theatre in France*. Cambridge, Mass.: Harvard University Press, 1960.

The Seventeenth Century

Bentley, G. E. *The Seventeenth Century Stage: A Collection of Critical Essays*. Chicago: University of Chicago Press, 1968.

Boswell, Eleanore. *The Restoration Court Stage*. Cambridge, Mass.: Harvard University Press, 1932.

Despois, E. Z. *Le Théâtre Français sous Louis XIV*. Paris: Hachette, 1894.

Elwin, Malcolm. *The Playgoers Handbook to Restoration Drama*. New York: Macmillan, 1928.

Fournel, François Victor. *Les Contemporaines de Molière*. Paris: Firmin Didot, 1863–1875.

Harbage, Alfred. *Thomas Killigrew, Cavalier Dramatist*. Philadelphia: University of Pennsylvania Press, 1930.

Hawkins, Frederick. *Annals of the French Stage from Its Origins to the Death of Racine*. 2 vols. London: Chapman & Hall, 1884.

Hotson, Leslie. *The Commonwealth and Restoration Stage*. Cambridge: Mass.: Harvard University Press, 1928.

Krutch, Joseph Wood. *Comedy and Con-*

science *After the Restoration*. New York: Columbia University Press, 1949.

Lancaster, H. C. *French Dramatic Literature in the Seventeenth Century*. 5 vols. Baltimore, Md.: Johns Hopkins Press, 1929–1936.

Lough, John. *Paris Theatre Audiences in the Seventeenth and Eighteenth Centuries*. Oxford: Oxford University Press, 1957.

Lynch, James J. *Box, Pit, and Gallery: Stage and Society in Johnson's London*. Berkeley: University of California Press, 1953.

McCollum, John I. (ed.). *The Restoration Stage*. Boston: Houghton Mifflin, 1961.

Miles, Dudley. *The Influence of Molière on the Restoration Comedy*. New York: Columbia University Press, 1910.

Nicoll, Allardyce. *History of Restoration Drama*. London: Cambridge University Press, 1923.

Odell, G. C. D. *Shakespeare from Betterton to Irving*. 2 vols. New York: Scribner, 1920.

Ordich, T. F. *Early London Theatres*. London: Stock, 1894.

Rosenfeld, Sybil. *Strolling Players and Drama in the Provinces, 1660–1765*. London: Cambridge University Press, 1935.

Southern, Richard. *Changeable Scenery*. London: Faber & Faber, 1952.

Spencer, Hazelton. *Shakespeare Improved: Restoration Versions*. Cambridge, Mass.: Harvard University Press, 1927.

Summers, Montague. *The Restoration Theatre*. New York: Macmillan, 1934.

Summers, Montague. *The Playhouse of Pepys*. New York: Macmillan, 1935.

Thaler, Alwin. *Shakespeare to Sheridan*. Cambridge, Mass.: Harvard University Press, 1922.

The Eighteenth Century

Aghion, M. *Le Théâtre à Paris au XVIII Siècle*. Paris: Librarie de France, 1926.

Armstrong, Cecil. *The Century of Great Actors*. London: Mills & Bloom, 1912.

Avery, E. L. *Congreve's Plays on the Eighteenth Century Stage*. New York: Modern Language Association, 1951.

Bateson, F. N. W. *English Comic Drama,* *1700–1750*. Oxford: Clarendon, 1929.

Bernbaum, Ernest. *The Drama of Sensibility*. Boston: Ginn, 1915.

Bibiena, Giuseppe Galli Da. *Architectural and Perspective Designs*. New York: Dover, 1964.

Boaden, James. *Memoirs of Mrs. Siddons*. London: Gibbings, 1893.

Bruford, W. H. *Theatre, Drama, and Audience in Goethe's Germany*. London: Routledge & Kegan Paul, 1950.

Carlson, Marvin. *The Theatre of the French Revolution*. Ithaca, N.Y.: Cornell University Press, 1966.

Cibber, Colley. *Apology for His Life*. 2 vols. London: Nimmo, 1888.

Dunlap, William. *History of the American Theatre*. New York: Scott, 1833.

Fitzgerald, P. H. *Life of David Garrick*. London: Simpkin Marshall, 1899.

Fyvie, John. *Comedy Queens of the Georgian Era*. London: Simpkin Marshall, 1899.

Genest, John. *Some Account of the English Stage, 1660–1830*. 10 vols. London: Carrington, 1832.

Goldstein, Malcolm. *Pope and the Augustan Stage*. Stanford, Calif.: Stanford University Press, 1958.

Gray, Charles Harold. *Theatrical Criticism in London to 1795*. New York: Columbia University Press, 1931.

Green, Frederick Charles. *Eighteenth Century France*. New York: Appleton, 1931.

Hawkins, Frederick W. *The French Stage in the Eighteenth Century*. 2 vols. London: Chapman & Hall, 1888.

Hedgecock, Frank. *David Garrick and His French Friends*. London: Stanley Paul, 1911.

Hyde-Smith, Naomi. *A Portrait of Mrs. Siddons*. New York: Viking, 1933.

Jourdain, Eleanor Frances. *Dramatic Theory and Practice in France, 1690–1808*. New York: McKay, 1921.

Knight, Joseph. *David Garrick*. London: Routledge & Kegan Paul, 1894.

Loftus, John. *Steele at Drury Lane*. Berkeley: University of California Press, 1952.

Melville, Lewis. *Stage Favorites of the Eighteenth Century*. London: Hutchinson, 1929.

Molloy, J. Fitzgerald. *Life and Adventures of Peg Woffington*. 2 vols. New York: Dodd, Mead, 1892.

Nettleton, G. H. *English Drama of the Restoration and Eighteenth Century, 1642–1780.* New York: Macmillan, 1914.

Nicoll, Allardyce. *History of Early Eighteenth Century Drama.* London: Cambridge University Press, 1925.

Nicoll, Allardyce. *History of Late Eighteenth Century Drama.* London: Cambridge University Press, 1927.

Paget, Violet. *Studies of the Eighteenth Century in Italy.* New York: McClurg, 1907.

Pedicord, H. W. *Theatrical Public in the Time of Garrick.* New York: Dauber & Pine Bookshops, 1954.

Scholz, Janos. *Baroque and Romantic Stage Design.* New York: Buckhurst, 1949. Dutton, 1962.

Seilhamer, G. O. *History of the American Theatre.* Philadelphia: Globe, 1891.

Sherbo, Arthur. *English Sentimental Drama.* East Lansing: Michigan State University Press, 1957.

Sichel, W. *Sheridan.* 2 vols. Boston: Houghton Mifflin, 1909.

Southern, Richard. *Changeable Scenery.* London: Faber & Faber, 1952.

Stein, Elizabeth. *David Garrick.* New York: Modern Language Association, 1938.

Watson, E. B. *Sheridan to Robertson.* Cambridge, Mass.: Harvard University Press, 1926.

Oriental Theatre

Ando, Tsuruo. *Bunraku: The Puppet Theatre.* London: Walker/Weatherill, 1970.

Arlington, L. C. *Chinese Drama from the Earliest Times to the Present Day.* Shanghai: Kelley and Walsh, 1930.

Arnott, Peter. *The Theatre of Japan.* New York: Macmillan, 1969.

Avand, Muk Raj. *The Indian Theatre.* New York: Roy, 1951.

Bowers, Faubion. *Theatre in the East: A Survey of Asian Dance and Drama.* London: Nelson, 1951.

Buss, Kate. *Studies in the Chinese Drama.* New York: Cape and Smith, 1930.

Chu-Chia-Chien. *Chinese Theatre.* Translated by James A. Graham. London: Bodley Head, 1922.

Edwards, Osman. *Japanese Plays and Playfellows.* London: Heinemann, 1901.

Ernst, Earle. *The Kabuki Theatre.* New York: Oxford University Press, 1957.

Fenollose, E. F., and Pound, Ezra. *Noh, or Accomplishment.* New York: Knopf, 1917.

Gargi, Balwant. *Theatre in India.* New York: Theatre Arts, 1962.

Guhathkurta, P. G. *Bengali Drama.* London: Routledge & Kegan Paul, 1930.

Haas, George C. O. *Dasarupa: A Treatise on Hindu Dramaturgy.* New York: Columbia University Press, 1912.

Hamamura, Yonezo, and others. *Kabuki.* Translated by Fumi Takano. Tokyo: Kenkyusha, 1956.

Horrwitz, E. P. *The Indian Theatre.* London: Blackie, 1912.

Keene, Donald. *Bunraku: Theatre Art and the Japanese Puppet Theatre.* Tokyo: Kodansha International, 1965.

Kincaid, Zoe. *Kabuki: The Popular Stage of Japan.* New York: Macmillan, 1925.

Lombard, Frank Alanson. *An Outline History of the Japanese Drama.* London: Allen & Unwin, 1928.

Scott, A. C. *The Classical Theatre of China.* London: Allen & Unwin, 1957.

Scott, A. C. *The Kabuki Theatre of Japan.* New York: Barnes & Noble, 1964.

Sein, Kenneth, and Withey, Joseph A. *The Great Po Sein: A Chronicle of the Burmese Theatre.* Bloomington: Indiana University Press, 1965.

Waley, Arthur. *The Noh Plays of Japan.* New York: Knopf, 1922.

Wilson, H. H., and others. *The Theatre of the Hindus.* Calcutta: Susil Gupta, 1955.

Yajnik, R. K. *The Indian Theatre.* New York: Dutton, 1934.

Zucker, Adolph Edward. *Chinese Theatre.* Boston: Little, Brown, 1925.

The Nineteenth Century

Appia, Adolphe (ed. Barnard Hewitt). *Work of Living Art and Man Is the Measure of All Things.* Miami, Fla.: University of Miami Press, 1969.

Archer, William. *Eminent Actors.* London: Asperne, 1894.

Arvin, Neil Cole. *Eugène Scribe and the*

French Theatre, 1815–1860. Cambridge, Mass.: Harvard University Press, 1924.

Brereton, Austin. *Life of Henry Irving.* 2 vols. New York: McKay, 1902.

Brown, Thomas Allston. *History of the New York Stage, 1836–1918.* New York: Dodd, Mead, 1923.

Carson, William G. B. *The Theatre on the Frontier: The Early Years of the St. Louis Stage.* Chicago: University of Chicago Press, 1932.

Clarke, A. B. *The Elder and Younger Booth.* New York: Osgood, 1882.

Cole, J. W. *Life and Theatrical Times of Charles Kean.* London: Bentley, 1859.

Cost, March. *I, Rachel.* New York: Vanguard, 1958.

Eaton, Walter Pritchard. *At the New Theatre and Others.* Boston: Small Maynard, 1910.

Filon, P. M. A. *The English Stage.* New York: Dodd, Mead, 1897.

Frohman, Daniel. *Memories of a Manager.* Doubleday, 1911.

Graham, Philip. *Showboats: The History of an American Institution.* Austin: University of Texas Press, 1951.

Grimstead, David. *Melodrama Unveiled: American Theatre and Culture, 1800–1850.* Chicago: University of Chicago Press, 1968.

Grube, Max. *Geschichte du Meiningen.* Berlin: Hesse, 1926.

Hawkins, F. W. *The Life of Edmund Kean.* 2 vols. London: Tinsley, 1869.

Hornblow, Arthur. *History of the Theatre in America.* 2 vols. Philadelphia: Lippincott, 1919.

Hutton, Laurence. *Curiosities of the American Stage.* New York: Harper & Row, 1891.

Kennard, Joseph Spencer. *The Italian Theatre.* 2 vols. New York: Rudge, 1932.

Klenze, Camille von. *From Goethe to Hauptmann.* New York: Viking, 1926.

Lewes, George Henry. *On Actors and the Art of Acting.* New York: Brentano's, 1875.

Mathews, Brander. *The Theatres of Paris.* London: Sampson, Low, Marston, Searle & Rivington, 1880.

Meisel, Martin. *Shaw and the Nineteenth-Century Theatre.* Princeton, N.J.: Princeton University Press, 1963.

Nicoll, Allardyce. *History of Early Nineteenth Century Drama.* London: Cambridge University Press, 1930.

Nicoll, Allardyce. *History of Late Nineteenth Century Drama.* London: Cambridge University Press, 1949.

Pearce, C. E. *Madame Vestris and Her Times.* London: Stanley Paul, 1923.

Rahill, Frank. *The World of Melodrama.* State College: Pennsylvania State University Press, 1967.

Rowell, George. *The Victorian Theatre: A Survey.* London: Oxford University Press, 1956.

Sherson, E. *London's Lost Theatres of the Nineteenth Century.* London: Bodley Head, 1925.

Toynbee, William C. (ed.). *Diaries of William Charles Macready.* New York: Putnam, 1912.

Vardac, A. Nicholas. *Stage to Screen: Theatrical Method from Garrick to Griffith.* Cambridge, Mass.: Harvard University Press, 1949.

Varneke, B. V. *History of the Russian Theatre.* New York: Macmillan, 1951.

Witkowski, George. *German Drama of the Nineteenth Century.* New York: Holt, Rinehart and Winston, 1909.

Wood, William Burke. *Personal Recollections of the Stage.* Philadelphia: Baird, 1854.

The Twentieth Century

Abramson, Doris E. *Negro Playwrights in the American Theatre, 1925–1959.* New York: Columbia University Press, 1969.

Antoine, Andre. *Memories of the Théâtre Libre* (ed. H. D. Albright, translated by Marvin A. Carlson). Miami, Fla.: University of Miami, 1965.

Artaud, Antonin. *Theatre and Its Double.* New York: Grove, 1958.

Bakshy, Alexander. *The Path of the Modern Russian Stage.* Boston: Luce, 1918.

Barrault, Jean-Louis. *The Theatre of Jean-Louis Barrault.* New York: Hill & Wang, 1961.

Blum, Daniel C. *A Pictorial History of the American Theatre, 1900–1956.* New York: Chilton, 1956.

Bowers, Faubion. *Broadway U.S.S.R.: Ballet, Theatre and Entertainment in Russia Today.* New York: Nelson, 1959.

Boyd, Ernest A. *The Contemporary Drama of Ireland*. Boston: Little, Brown, 1928.

Boyle, Walden. *Central and Flexible Staging*. Berkeley: University of California Press, 1955.

Brecht, Bertolt. *Brecht on Theatre*. New York: Hill & Wang, 1964.

Brustein, Robert. *The Theatre of Revolt: An Approach to Modern Drama*. Boston: Atlantic Monthly, 1964.

Brook, Peter. *The Empty Space*. New York: Avon, 1969.

Burris-Meyer, Harold, and Cole, Edward C. *Theatres and Auditoriums*. New York: Reinhold, 1949.

Byrne, Dawson. *The Story of Ireland's National Theatre*. Dublin: Talbot, 1929.

Carter, Huntly. *The New Spirit in the European Theatre, 1914–1924*. Garden City, N.Y.: Doubleday, 1925.

Carter, Huntly. *The Theatre of Max Reinhardt*. London: Palmer, 1914.

Chandler, Frank W. *The Contemporary Drama of France*. Boston: Little, Brown, 1925.

Cheney, Sheldon. *The Art Theatre*. New York: Knopf, 1925.

Cheney, Sheldon. *New Movement in the Theatre*. New York: Kennerley, 1914.

Cheney, Sheldon. *The Open Air Theatre*. New York: Kennerley, 1918.

Cheney, Sheldon. *Stage Decoration*. New York: Day, 1928.

Clark, Barrett H. *The Continental Drama of Today*. New York: Holt, Rinehart and Winston, 1915.

Clark, Barrett H., and Freedley, George. *A History of Modern Drama*. New York: Appleton, 1947.

Clurman, Harold. *The Fervent Years*. New York: Knopf, 1945.

Copeau, Jacques. *Souvenirs du Vieux-Columbier*. Paris: Nouvelles Editions Latines, 1931.

Craig, Gordon. *On the Art of the Theatre*. New York: Dodd, Mead, 1925.

Craig, Gordon. *The Theatre Advancing*. Boston: Little, Brown, 1910.

Craig, Gordon. *Towards a New Theatre*. New York: Dutton, 1913.

Craig, Gordon. *Scene*. New York: Oxford University Press, 1923.

Dickinson, Thomas H. *The Contemporary Drama of England*. Boston: Little, Brown, 1931.

Dickinson, Thomas H. (ed.). *The Theatre in a Changing Europe*. New York: Holt, Rinehart and Winston, 1937.

Driver, Tom. *Romantic Quest and Modern Query: A History of the Modern Theatre*. New York: Delacorte, 1970.

Dukore, Bernard F., and Gerould, Daniel. *Avant-Garde Drama: Major Plays and Documents Post World War I*. New York: Random House, 1970.

Esslin, Martin. *The Theatre of the Absurd*. Garden City, N.Y.: Doubleday, 1961. Revised 1964.

Fay, Gerard. *The Abbey Theatre, Cradle of Genius*. Dublin: Claimore & Reynolds, 1958.

Flanagan, Hallie. *Arena*. New York: Duell, Sloan & Pearce, 1940.

Fuerst, W. L., and Hume, S. J. *Twentieth-Century Stage Decoration*. New York: Knopf, 1928.

Gagey, Edmund H. *Revolution in American Drama*. New York: Columbia University Press, 1947.

Gassner, John. *Directions in Modern Theatre and Drama*. New York: Holt, Rinehart and Winston, 1965.

Gorchakov, Nikolai. *The Theatre in Soviet Russia*. Translated by Edgar Lehrman. New York: Columbia University Press, 1957.

Gorelik, Mordecai. *New Theatres for Old*. New York: French, 1940. Dutton, 1962

Gregor, Joseph and Fülop-Miller, René. *The Russian Theatre*. Philadelphia: Lippincott, 1930.

Gregory, Lady Isabella. *Our Irish Theatre*. New York: Putnam, 1913.

Grossvogel, David I. *The Blasphemers: The Theatre of Brecht, Ionesco, Beckett, Genet*. Ithaca, N.Y.: Cornell University Press, 1965.

Guicharnaud, Jacques. *Modern French Theatre: From Giraudoux to Beckett*. New Haven, Conn.: Yale University Press, 1961.

Guthrie, Tyrone. *A New Theatre*. New York: Knopf, 1965.

Henderson, Archibald (ed.). *Pioneering a People's Theatre*. Chapel Hill: University of North Carolina Press, 1945.

Houghton, Norris. *Advance from Broadway:*

19,000 Miles of American Theatre. New York: Harcourt Brace Jovanovich, 1941.

Houghton, Norris. *Moscow Rehearsal.* New York: Harcourt Brace Jovanovich, 1936.

Jones, Margo. *Theatre-in-the-Round.* New York: Holt, Rinehart and Winston, 1951.

Jones, Robert Edmond. *The Dramatic Imagination: Reflections and Speculations on the Art of the Theatre.* New York: Theatre Arts, 1941.

Jones, Robert Edmond. *Drawings for the Theatre.* New York: Theatre Arts, 1925. Revised 1970.

Joseph, Stephen. *New Theatre Forms.* New York: Theatre Arts, 1968.

Kirby, Michael. *Futurist Theatre.* New York: Dutton, 1971.

Komisarjevsky, Theodore. *The Costume of the Theatre.* London: Bles, 1931.

Kostelanetz, Richard. *The Theatre of Mixed Means: An Introduction to Happenings, Kinetic Environments.* New York: Dial, 1968.

Krutch, Joseph Wood. *The American Drama Since 1918.* New York: Random House, 1939.

Langner, Lawrence. *The Magic Curtain.* New York: Dutton, 1951.

MacClintock, Lander. *The Contemporary Drama of Italy.* Boston: Little, Brown, 1920.

Macgowan, Kenneth. *Footlights Across America.* New York: Harcourt Brace Jovanovich, 1929.

Macgowan, Kenneth, and Jones, Robert Edmond. *Continental Stagecraft.* New York: Harcourt Brace Jovanovich, 1922. Revised 1964.

MacKaye, Percy. *The Civic Theatre.* New York: Kennerley, 1912.

Meyerhold, Vsevolod. *Meyerhold on Theatre.* New York: Hill & Wang, 1969.

Mielziner, Jo. *The Shapes of Our Theatre.* New York: Potter, 1970.

Miller, Anna Irene. *The Independent Theatre in Europe.* New York: Long and Smith, 1927.

Mitchell, Loften. *Black Drama: The Story of the American Negro in the Theatre.* New York: Hawthorn, 1967.

Nemirovitch-Danchenko. *My Life in the Russian Theatre.* Boston: Little, Brown, 1936.

Novick, Julius. *Beyond Broadway: The Quest for Permanent Theatres.* New York: Hill & Wang, 1968.

Phelps, William Lyon. *Twentieth-Century Theatre.* New York: Macmillan, 1918.

Piscator, Maria L. *Piscator Experiment: The Political Theatre.* Carbondale: Southern Illinois University Press, 1970.

Pronko, Leonard Cabell. *The World of Jean Anouilh.* Berkeley: University of California Press, 1961.

Pronko, Leonard Cabell. *Avant-Garde: The Experimental Theatre in France.* Berkeley: University of California Press, 1962.

Samuel, Richard, and Thoms, R. Hinton. *Expressionism in German Life, Literature and the Theatre.* London: Cambridge University Press, 1939.

Schlemmer, Oskar. *The Theatre of the Bauhaus.* Middletown, Conn.: Wesleyan University Press, 1961.

Sayler, Oliver M. *Max Reinhardt and His Theatre.* New York: Brentano's, 1924.

Seltzer, Daniel. *Modern Theatre: Readings and Documents.* Boston: Little, Brown, 1967.

Simonson, Lee. *The Art of Scenic Design: A Pictorial Analysis of Stage Setting and Its Relation to Theatrical Production.* New York: Harper & Row, 1950.

Slonim, Marc. *Russian Theatre: From the Empire to the Soviets.* New York: World Publishing, 1961.

Stanislavski, Constantine, *My Life in Art.* Translated by J. J. Robbins. Boston: Little, Brown, 1938.

Tynan, Kenneth. *Curtains.* New York: Atheneum, 1961.

Van Gyseghem, Andre. *Theatre in Soviet Russia.* London: Faber & Faber, 1935.

Waxman, Samuel M. *Antoine and the Théâtre Libre.* Cambridge, Mass.: Harvard University Press, 1926.

Weiner, Leo. *Contemporary Drama of Russia.* Boston: Little, Brown, 1924.

Wellworth, George. *The Theatre of Protest and Paradox: Developments in the Avant-Garde Drama.* New York: New York University Press. 1964.

Index

Page references in *italic* refer to illustrations.